D1739777

New Directions in Management
and Organization Theory

New Directions in Management and Organization Theory

Edited by

Jeffrey A. Miles

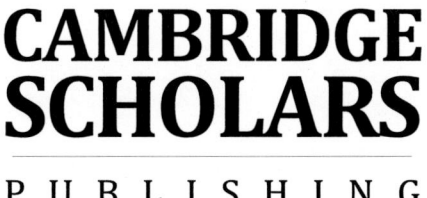

New Directions in Management and Organization Theory,
Edited by Jeffrey A. Miles

This book first published 2014

Cambridge Scholars Publishing

12 Back Chapman Street, Newcastle upon Tyne, NE6 2XX, UK

British Library Cataloguing in Publication Data
A catalogue record for this book is available from the British Library

ISBN (10): 1-4438-5475-1, ISBN (13): 978-1-4438-5475-7

TABLE OF CONTENTS

INTRODUCTION

As I was writing my book, *Management and Organization Theory*, I noticed that the field of management was lamenting the lack of new management and organization theories. For example, I saw that articles in the Academy of Management journals were discussing a serious shortage of new theories, and were contemplating the impact of this shortage on the future of the field of management and organization studies. I pondered what the field could do to help management researchers create new theories. It occurred to me that someone needed to have a conference.

In September of 2012, I went to see Lewis Gale, Dean of the Eberhardt School of Business at the University of the Pacific, where I am a faculty member. I asked him if we could host the world's first management theory conference. The motto of the university has always been "pioneer or perish" and my dean has always worked hard to ensure that the business school is on the cutting edge of innovation in the field of business, so of course he gave me permission to have a conference.

We named the conference the First Management Theory Conference. The purpose of the conference was to help address the shortage of new management and organization theories. The mission of the conference was to facilitate, recognize, and reward the creation of new theories that advance our understanding of management and organizations. We wanted to motivate researchers to create new theories and to provide researchers with a supportive forum where those new theories could be presented, discussed, and published. The conference was held at the University of the Pacific in San Francisco on September 27 and 28, 2013.

Naturally, hosting a conference involves a great deal of time, resources, and sweat equity. Since this was the first conference of its kind in the world, it also involved a certain amount of risk (and stress) as we had no idea if the conference would attract enough interest from management researchers to be successful. Fortunately, management researchers from all over the world responded to the call for papers by submitting ideas for new theories. Additionally, professors were extremely gracious with their time in helping us review submissions.

The conference was also a great success because we had an excellent support team from many individuals at the University of the Pacific. I am very thankful for the help that I received from those in the Eberhardt

School of Business. I extend my thanks to the management faculty for their help reviewing papers and chairing sessions at the conference: Julia Dare, Stefanie Naumann, Chris Sablynski, Dara Szyliowicz, and Dan Wadhwani. I also thank faculty members Tom Brierton and Wenjing Ouyang for their help reviewing papers.

I am especially thankful for the outstanding assistance that I received from the talented support staff at the Eberhardt School of Business. Operations Manager, Rebecca Davis, provided much needed assistance with financial matters, operations, and procedures, for which I am extremely grateful. Administrative Assistant, Sandy Miller, helped with a number of activities for the conference, including awards, catering, and transportation. Multimedia and Design Specialist, Myrna Vick, provided truly outstanding graphics support services, including designing the conference logo, creating the conference website, creating the conference program, and designing the conference lanyards and nametags. Director of Information Services, Mary Nevis, provided IT assistance, including email address, and mass communication and marketing support. Lastly, Faculty Administrative Assistant, Barbara Garcia, provided excellent administrative support, including help with the conference program and nametags. I cannot thank the staff enough for their moral support and encouragement, especially during the many extremely busy and stressful moments before, during, and after, the conference.

I am also extremely thankful for the outstanding assistance that I received from the Arthur A. Dugoni School of Dentistry, University of the Pacific, where the conference was held in San Francisco. First, let me thank the Dean of the Dugoni School, Patrick Ferrillo, for graciously allowing us to host the conference on his campus. We could not have held such a successful conference if it were not for the generosity of Dean Ferrillo. I am also truly thankful for the tremendous support that we received from the staff of the Dugoni School. I cannot express how grateful I am for the amazing help that I received from Administration Coordinator, Karen Yamamoto. Karen provided invaluable help with the facilities at the Dugoni School, including scheduling, parking, catering, signage, coordinating staff and events, and managing equipment and technology in the classrooms. Educational Media Support Technician, Sandra Martino, provided excellent IT support and ensured that all of the technology worked successfully in the classrooms. Building Operations Technician, Robert Pullinger, handled all manner of things in and around the building during the conference, such as managing parking, setting up and tearing down equipment, and maintaining the building environment. Security Corporal, Emilio Fastidio, provided excellent safety and security services for everyone attending the conference. Director of Planning, Roy Bergstrom, also helped ensure that everything flowed smoothly in the facilities. In sum, we thank everyone at the Dugoni school who attended to our needs, and made us feel especially welcome at the conference.

I am extremely grateful to Patrick Lastowski for the tremendous support that he provided to this conference. I cannot thank him enough for the multitude of roles that he played and the number of activities that he performed, including: transporting resources to and from the conference, arranging equipment and signs, greeting faculty, distributing conference programs and nametags, coordinating staff members and their services, guiding faculty and speakers to their destinations, handling problems and issues, cleaning up at the end of the conference, providing much needed moral support, and doing numerous other things that needed to be done during the conference.

I thank Eberhardt School of Business students: Lucas Bach-Hamba, Chennette Carter, Teddy Crepineau, Mario Giannecchini, Hanna Gremp, Diana Hsiao, Junaid Khan, Jesse Kim, Yee Lao, Zhaosong Li, Ashleigh Loew, Beatriz Maya, Danielle Rinck, Sokcon Tim, and Rory Tokunaga. The students did a tremendous job representing the university on a world stage in the field of management. We received tremendous praise for the passion, knowledge, and abilities of our students. I thank them for helping make this conference so successful and so special.

Lastly, I would like to thank and acknowledge University of the Pacific Provost Maria Pallavicini and President Pamela A. Eibeck for their support and encouragement of this conference. The Provost and the President are working tirelessly to help the university fulfill its mission, which is to provide a superior, student-centered learning experience. Additionally, they are working diligently to help the university achieve its vision, which is to create a leading California university that prepares graduates for meaningful lives and successful careers. By supporting and encouraging events such as this conference, the Provost and the President continue to make great progress toward accomplishing the mission and vision of the University of the Pacific.

—Jeffrey A. Miles
December 2013
Stockton, California, USA

OVERVIEW

Theory is the currency of our scholarly realm (Hambrick, 2007). Every top-tier management journal requires a theoretical contribution for a manuscript to be published (Corley & Gioia, 2011). A number of organization and management journal editors, such as the editors of the Academy of Management journals, have commented on the lack of new management and organization theories. A special topic forum in the *Academy of Management Review* noted that most of the theories used by contemporary management researchers were formulated several decades ago, mostly in the 1960s and 1970s, and these theories have persisted, largely intact, since that time (Suddaby, Hardy, & Huy, 2011). This is so despite massive growth and change in the size, prevalence, and influence of organizations in modern society. Unfortunately, management and organization theories have become a "living museum of the 1970s" (Davis, 2010: 691). This situation has become so dire that Amy Hillman, *Academy of Management Review* editor, commented "What is the future of theory?" (Hillman, 2011).

The purpose of the First Management Theory Conference was to help address the shortage of new management and organization theories. The mission of the conference was to facilitate, recognize, and reward the creation of new theories that advance our understanding of management and organizations. We wanted to host a conference that would motivate researchers to create new theories and to provide researchers with a supportive forum where those new theories could be presented, discussed, and published.

This volume is a collection of the best seventeen papers from the First Management Theory Conference based on reviewer ratings and comments. Chapter Seventeen was the winner of the Wiley Outstanding New Management Theory Award, which was presented at the conference. This volume also contains written summaries of the two keynote addresses that were given at the conference by Roy Suddaby (editor of *Academy of Management Review*) and Jeffrey Pfeffer, which comprise Chapters Eighteen and Nineteen.

I would like to note that the seventeen papers were not categorized in any way, such as by their "micro" or "macro" approach. Some researchers believe that there is a great divide or conflict between researchers who primarily explore micro levels of analysis and those who primarily explore macro levels of analysis (Huselid & Becker, 2011). However, some researchers believe that there is less of a divide than is often assumed (Rousseau, 2011). Indeed, many researchers agree that one of the most critical challenges in the field of management and organization research is finding ways to integrate micro- and macro-level research methods and theories (Aguinis, Boyd, Pierce, & Short, 2011).

One of the goals for this conference was to help integrate all of the theories of management and organization. In order to help accomplish this goal, I specifically did not label any of the theories as primarily micro- or macro-level in focus for this volume. All of the theories contained herein are important for all students, researchers, and theorists, and for all kinds and types of research, so I wanted to avoid perpetuating the divide that some of the theories tend to be micro-level theories and some tend to be macro-level theories.

The volume begins with Chapter One by Kannan Srikanth, Sarah Harvey, and Randall S. Peterson. They provide an enhanced theoretical framework for studying performance in diverse groups. They propose that diverse groups' lack of common ground makes them more susceptible to coordination failure, poor performance, and ultimately interpersonal problems (e.g., low trust and poor communication), and that this is a more fundamental reason for low performance in diverse groups than the motivation losses traditionally emphasized in the group diversity literature.

Bin Zhao, Fernando Olivera, and Amy C. Edmondson are the authors of Chapter Two. Building on theories of learning from errors, emotions, self-regulation, motivation, and coping, they propose a model to explain that negative emotions have both stimulating and impairing effects on learning from errors. Their model acknowledges the differential effects of discrete negative emotions on learning from errors.

Chapter Three was written by Jack A. Goncalo and Verena Krause. They focus on a static view of the creative process and review evidence that narcissists can contribute to group creativity. They uncover three critical gaps, suggesting that research: 1) focuses narrowly on one stage of the creative process while neglecting other stages, 2) neglects the fact that events in one stage can impact subsequent stages, and 3) assumes a dynamic process that is not tested empirically. They propose a dynamic model that addresses these gaps and generates a series of novel propositions.

The next paper, Chapter Four, is by Emma Y. Zhao and Karen A. Jehn. They propose that emergent leaders are more likely to cause more conflict compared to assigned leaders due to their difference in power and capability. They present a new framework through which a leader's self-entitlement is likely to affect the relationship between emergent leadership and conflict by exacerbating relationship and process conflict, but ameliorating task conflict. Their model incorporates leader conflict management behaviors (forcing and problem-solving) to moderate the link between conflict and team performance.

Chapter Five was written by Tyler Wry and Jeffrey G. York. Extending work on identity and entrepreneurship, they combine insights from structural and institutional views to develop the concept of the entrepreneurial self. They present a theoretical framework for understanding the role of the entrepreneurial self in the creation of new ventures that provide non-economic benefits.

Rebekah Dibble and Cristina Gibson were the authors of Chapter Six. They examine ways in which emerging forms of collaborative work are critically distinct from traditional forms of organizing. They identify fluidity, impermanence, organizational independence, and environmental volatility as four key features which set collaborative efforts apart from traditional teams. They explore important aspects of collaborative work (internal and external adjustment) that cannot be adequately understood by generalizing from traditional forms.

Chapter Seven was written by Anette Mikes and Robert S. Kaplan. Based on a ten-year field project and over 250 interviews with senior risk officers, they propose a contingency theory of enterprise risk management (ERM) that identifies potential design parameters that can explain observable variation in the "ERM mix" adopted by organizations. They outline a minimum necessary contingency framework enabling empirical researchers to hypothesize about "fit" between contingent variables, such as risk types and the ERM mix, as well as hypothesize about outcomes such as organizational effectiveness.

Yally Avrahampour is the author of Chapter Eight. He introduces an alternative, relational, framing of agency, which is illustrated through an analysis of a particular type of agent, namely, the manager of the defined benefit pension fund. He advocates that the pension manager uses ambiguity to mediate between two principals with conflicting objectives; shareholders and beneficiaries, allocating resources between these two principals and thus facilitating take-up of defined benefit pension provision. In the paper, he proposes that financial sociology is a discipline using a socio-cultural perspective in reformulating agency models.

Chapter Nine was written by Jeffrey Miles. He integrates concepts from the field of medicine with the study of organizations in a new area called Organizational Medicine. The paper argues that some organizations live longer, healthier lives than other organizations because they are better able to overcome organizational illnesses and diseases. He examines twelve organizational diseases and presents two models: 1) a model of organizational population health change, and 2) a model of potential health changes for an individual organization. Lastly, he discusses the need for development and use of organizational quality of well-being (OQWB) scales.

The next chapter was authored by Chester S. Spell and Katerina Bezrukova. Chapter Ten presents a multi-level theory of health management in organizations. They present a model with testable propositions and a research agenda that contributes to understanding of the employer's role in health management, and highlights implications for managers.

Chapter Eleven was authored by Dorota Leszczyńska and Erick Pruchnicki. The paper highlights the link between the transfer of knowledge flows and the location of a multinational company. The authors elaborate a model that provides a better understanding of the impact of embedded knowledge on the efficiency of a localization choice made by a multinational company.

The authors of Chapter Twelve were Tammy L. Madsen, Jennifer L. Woolley, and Kumar Sarangee. They offer theory and propositions regarding how a firm can structure interactions and manage community engagements to facilitate product innovation. They propose methods through which a firm may enhance value creation in the context of product innovation.

Chapter Thirteen was written by Gongming Qian, Lee Li, and Stephen Tallman. This paper proposes that firms use strategic alliances mainly to share resources, costs, and risks, but that this may not be the main rationale for strategic alliances in dynamic environments. This work argues that the possibilities of firms forming strategic alliances are positively correlated with their internal inertia (routinized behavior, organizational structure, age and size).

The next chapter, Chapter Fourteen, was authored by Leigh Anne Liu, Karen D. Loch, and David C. Bruce. They argue that managers need to develop political wisdom, like the mafia's *consiglieri* (an advisor to a mafia boss on political relationships), to effectively navigate the complex maze of government/business relations in emerging markets such as China. They discuss political wisdom in the context of business diplomacy in the global business environments.

Chapter Fifteen was written by Matthew B. Perrigino, who proposes Family Centrality Theory (FCT). The theory explains how the values of a family-central individual translate into action as these individuals navigate the daily challenges of work. He advocates that limiting the amount of time spent working and utilizing flexible work arrangements are the two proposed mechanisms through which these individuals can reduce their amounts of work-family conflict and maximize time spent with family.

Next is Chapter Sixteen, which was authored by Andaç T. Arıkan. He conceptualizes cluster macrocultures as the manifestations of the extent to which identity orientations of the firms inside a cluster are convergent. He offers a conceptual model that outlines the process by which cluster macrocultures emerge and transform. He focuses on the dyadic exchange relationships inside clusters as the nexus of cluster macrocultures, and Arıkan outlines the process by which cluster firms' identity orientations transform as cluster firms collect social proof as to the appropriate ways of approaching negotiation situations during relational practices.

The authors of Chapter Seventeen, Chris P. Long, Sim B. Sitkin, and Laura B. Cardinal, were the winners of the Wiley Outstanding New Management Theory Award, which was presented to them at the conference for this outstanding work. In their paper, they present a theory to explain the drivers of managerial efforts to promote trust, fairness, and control. They theorize how superior-subordinate conflicts stimulate managers' concerns about managerial legitimacy and subordinate dependability in performing tasks. They hypothesize how managers attempt to address these concerns using trustworthiness-promotion, fairness-promotion, and control activities. Lastly, they discuss how their theory refines and extends organizational trust, fairness, and control research.

The last two chapters, Chapter Eighteen and Chapter Nineteen, contain written summaries of the two keynote addresses that were given at the conference. Both of these addresses are excellent examinations of the state of management theory and development. Chapter Eighteen was written by Roy Suddaby, editor of *Academy of Management Review*. He disagrees with the growing consensus that management research has serious ills that could be resolved if we got back to hard empirical data collection and the accumulation of managerial knowledge. He argues that critics of management theory are largely taking issue with fetishistic theory or theory that has become ritualized, mechanical, artificial, and rationalized. He examines three defining elements of fetishistic theory: 1) rationalism, 2) scientism, and 3) self-reflexivity. He advocates that the creation of an indigenous approach to management theory would: 1) balance rationalism and empiricism with a clear mandate toward abduction, 2) be more attentive to the phenomena of management, and 3) create space and legitimacy within our profession for a higher degree of self-reflexivity.

Finally, he notes that we need to develop a more discriminate taste for what constitutes good, and bad, theory.

The final chapter in the volume, Chapter Nineteen, was written by Jeffrey Pfeffer and examines the management theory morass, a sprawling, vast, and sometimes redundant set of ideas. He argues that our obsession with new theory over measurement has led to some predictable consequences: a proliferation of theories, studies of little social importance, a lack of demonstrable progress in knowledge development, the articulation of ideas that may not be testable, a lack of evidence-based management, and various degrees of academic misconduct. He argues that the solutions to the management morass require some fundamental changes in how we evaluate and review colleagues and how we practice science, and may require moving to a more open reviewing process. Lastly, he argues that we need to be more self-reflective and much more aware of the downsides of our preoccupation with management theory.

References

Aguinis, H., Boyd, B. K., Pierce, C. A., & Short, J. C. (2011). Walking new avenues in management research methods and theories: Bridging micro and macro domains. *Journal of Management, 37*, 395-403

Corley, K. G., & Gioia, D. A. (2011). Building theory about theory building: What constitutes a theoretical contribution? *Academy of Management Review, 36*, 12-32.

Davis, G. F. (2010). Do theories of organization progress? *Organizational Research Methods, 13*, 690-709.

Hambrick, D. (2007). The field of management's devotion to theory: Too much of a good thing? *Academy of Management Journal, 50*, 1346-1352.

Hillman, A. (2011). Editor's comments: What is the future of theory? *Academy of Management Review, 36*, 606-608.

Suddaby, R., Hardy, C., & Huy, Q. N. (2011). Introduction to special forum topic: Where are the new theories of organization? *Academy of Management Review, 36*, 236-246.

CHAPTER ONE

COORDINATION FAILURE: A MISSING LINK IN UNDERSTANDING PERFORMANCE IN DIVERSE GROUPS

KANNAN SRIKANTH,
INDIAN SCHOOL OF BUSINESS, INDIA
SARAH HARVEY,
UNIVERSITY COLLEGE LONDON, UK
AND RANDALL S. PETERSON
LONDON BUSINESS SCHOOL, UK

Abstract

This paper provides an enhanced theoretical framework for studying performance in diverse groups. Specifically, we argue that existing work has largely under-appreciated the coordination challenges posed by group diversity. We propose that diverse groups' lack of common ground makes them more susceptible to coordination failure, poor performance, and ultimately interpersonal problems (e.g., low trust and poor communication), and that this is a more fundamental reason for poor performance in diverse groups than the motivation losses traditionally emphasized in the group diversity literature.

Keywords: diversity, coordination, common ground

Introduction

Why do some diverse groups outperform homogenous groups, while others severely underperform? Globalization and increased worker mobility have caused a great urgency in understanding the answers to this question.

This has resulted in an explosion of research on the effects of group diversity of all types (e.g., functional diversity, individual differences, demographic differences, etc.) and has generated significant insight into the paradox of diverse group performance (see Guzzo & Dickson, 1996; van Knippenberg & Schippers, 2007; and Williams & O'Reilly, 1998 for reviews).

Existing research on group diversity has uncovered two opposing forces that influence their performance. Group decision making and creativity both benefit from the variety in the backgrounds, resources, information and skills of group members (e.g., Bantel & Jackson, 1989; Brophy, 1998; Cox & Blake, 1991; and Thompson, 2003). However, diversity is also associated with a lack of cohesion and other interpersonal problems – social divisions between members with salient differences reduce communication and cohesion, increase conflict, and reduce motivation to engage with the team (Lau & Murnighan, 1998; Williams & O'Reilly, 1998). This research stream implies that, by striking a fine balance between the benefits and challenges of diversity, diverse groups can reliably outperform homogeneous groups. Nevertheless, empirical research consistently finds that diversity impairs overall group performance (Williams & O'Reilly, 1998; van Knippenberg and Schippers, 2007). We broaden theory in this area in an attempt to better explain why diverse groups tend to underperform relative to their potential and why some diverse groups perform much better than others.

We specifically propose that the current literature on diverse teams has underestimated the challenges associated with successfully managing diversity. We argue that apart from losses arising from social categorization, diverse groups also suffer from coordination losses. Coordination losses arise from the mis-alignment of group members' actions. We argue here that diverse groups (as opposed to homogeneous groups) have difficulty coordinating their efforts due to a lack of common ground – that is, discrepancies in the knowledge, beliefs and assumptions of group members. We argue that coordination failure is at the heart of the problems faced by diverse teams, but coordination mistakes are often misidentified as arising from interpersonal problems (e.g., low trust, lack of information sharing, etc.) between group members – and this usually creates additional interpersonal problems. We specifically suggest that there are three direct effects of diversity on team performance, rather than the two typically suggested in the literature: 1) the positive effects of informational diversity on decision making and creativity, 2) the negative effects of social category diversity on interpersonal dynamics, and now we would add, 3) the negative effects of lack of common ground on the group's ability to coordinate action.

Interestingly, these three effects are consistent with Steiner's (1972) argument that group performance results from process gains and two types of processes losses – those pertaining to lack of motivation and those that result from poor action alignment or coordination. Research on group diversity has principally concentrated on motivation losses and neglected coordination losses. We believe it is essential to consider both types of losses in order to move the field forward.

The two sources of process losses in diverse groups are highly intertwined and therefore the underlying causes of the "diversity discount" may be difficult to prise apart empirically, but we think the effort is worthwhile in order to facilitate additional ways of improving the performance of diverse groups that are increasingly important in modern work organizations.

The Existing State of Play on Group Diversity –
Information Gains Versus Social Categorization Losses

Diversity has been conceptualized as a double-edged sword (cf. Milliken & Martins, 1996). On one hand, diversity should improve group performance because differences in knowledge and perspectives help groups to develop new and emergent knowledge (Argote, 1999). Group members with different backgrounds and experiences are likely to have access to different information and alternative points of view on the group task. This enables them to develop a more complete understanding of the task, access relevant information, and adopt task appropriate strategies (Bantel & Jackson, 1989; Cox & Blake, 1991; Milliken & Martins, 1996; van Knippenberg, De Dreu, & Homan, 2004).

On the other hand, diversity foments social categorization behaviors that lead to interpersonal problems. Group members tend to categorize one another on the basis of salient characteristics and to identify themselves with a related social category that promotes their self-esteem. Group members then view those not in their category as different from themselves (Hogg & Terry, 2000; Tajfel, 1970; 1981). Social categorization leads to poor group processes such as reduced identification, less information transfer, less participation in decision making, increased conflict and lower cohesiveness (Jehn, Northcraft, & Neale, 1999; Keller, 2001; Pelled, Eisenhardt & Xin, 1999; Pelled, Ledford & Mohrman, 1999; Williams & O'Reilly, 1998).

The causal chain suggested by this literature is that when diverse team members first get together, they tend to identify with others in the group who are similar to themselves. This leads to more interaction within subgroups and little interaction across different sub-groups. The initial lack of communication becomes reinforced over time, resulting in lack of trust and increased conflict between subgroups. Sub-optimal group processes may also lead to a lack of motivation towards the task, as group members feel more committed to their subgroup than the larger team. Ultimately, poor group processes reduce group performance.

The information processing and social categorization perspectives that are applied to diverse teams generally do not show any clear relationship between diversity and performance (see van Knippenberg & Schippers, 2007, for a comprehensive review). Research has therefore turned to identifying variables that modify this relationship. Solutions for improving diverse group performance focus on enabling diverse groups to transcend social categorization, avoiding the consequent interpersonal and group process problems, thereby achieving superior performance. For example, Earley & Mosakowski (2000) suggest that to be effective, diverse teams need to abstract away from individual identities and build a third culture within the team that offers a *common sense of identity* and provides a basis for team interaction. Other remedies include having a cooperative norm (Chatman & Flynn, 2001), a psychologically safe communication environment (Gibson & Gibbs, 2006), or a strong organizational culture that emphasizes what members have in common rather than what makes them unique (Chatman, Polzer, Barsade, & Neale, 1998; Homan, et al., 2008). Van der Vegt & Bunderson (2005) demonstrate directly that identifying with the team improves the performance of diverse groups.

However, there are reasons to look beyond common identity as a normative solution to diverse group performance problems. In their review, van Knippenberg and Schippers (2007, p. 526) suggest "few studies directly assessed social categorization processes and the results are inconsistent enough to raise doubts about the extent to which social categorization is in operation." They suggest that the empirical results observed could also be consistent with simple misunderstanding and disagreement. In the sections below, we fill this gap in the group diversity literature by developing a theory of the antecedents and consequences of coordination failure in groups.

Analyzing Coordination Failure in Groups

In order to perform effectively, groups must minimize two types of potential process losses – those that result from lack of motivation and those that result from lack of coordination (Steiner, 1972; Simon, 1947). Motivation problems result when group members' incentives are not aligned. This may occur because members have private goals or it may be more subtle, occurring because group members lack commitment to the team and shirk team-level responsibilities. The interventions for improving diverse group performance suggested in prior research typically are geared toward addressing this motivation problem, since many scholars believe that motivation problems are more likely in diverse groups than in homogenous groups (e.g., Chatman & Flynn, 2001; Chatman, et al., 1998; and Lovelace, et al., 2001).

Coordination is achieved by the alignment of group members' actions. Coordination involves dividing work between group members, re-integrating work and deciding how to spend the group's time and resources (Hackman, 1987). We define coordination as an outcome in which interacting individuals achieve reciprocal predictability of action[1] (Camerer, 2003; Heath & Staudenmayer, 2000; March & Simon, 1958; Simon, 1947). In contrast to motivational issues, coordination failure results from an inability (rather than an unwillingness) to work together effectively. Simon's memorable example is that a group of highly motivated boat builders will not be successful unless they are all working to the same blueprint (Simon, 1947, p. 8).

Several scholars have suggested that organization theory has significantly underestimated the issue of coordinating, assuming that incentive alignment automatically achieves action alignment or coordination (Grant, 1996; Heath & Staudenmayer, 2000). However, prior studies have shown that even highly motivated groups who want to coordinate with one another suffer lower performance because they neglect group processes that foster coordination (Camerer, 2003; Camerer & Knez, 1996; Heath & Staudenmayer, 2000). Research from across a range of disciplines suggests that coordination problems between group members arise due to lack of common ground or mutual knowledge –

---

[1] Often the term coordination is used both to denote this outcome as well as the process by which this outcome is achieved. Here, we exclusively use the term coordination to refer to the outcome and use the terms "coordinating" or "coordination process" to refer to the process by which a coordinated outcome is achieved.

knowledge that is shared and known to be shared (Camerer, 2003; Schelling, 1960).

Common ground differs from closely related terms such as team mental models and shared mental models in that by definition anything in common ground is shared and *known to be shared*. Clark (1996) argues that common ground arises from two sources of prior knowledge: (1) knowledge of categories, such as those based on nationality, race, gender, culture, profession, residence, hobby, religion etc., called *common ground*, and (2) prior interaction experience, called *personal common ground*.

We believe it is more fruitful to analyze coordination as a function of common ground than as a function of communication, because doing so allows us to understand more precisely when (accidental) mis-coordination occurs, especially when applied to diverse teams. Specifically, there are three sources of coordination problems in groups. First, diverse group members who are unfamiliar with each other are likely to hold differing beliefs about what actions are expected from each other (Camerer, 2003). Second, diverse team members are more likely to have problems communicating with each other (Cronin & Weingart, 2007). Finally, diverse team members tend to have problems re-integrating sub-tasks (Heath & Staudenmayer, 2000).

It is important to note that these three challenges of coordination suggest that common ground improves coordination in groups, and therefore, lack of common ground may be as important a reason for coordination failure in groups as loss of motivation. In addition, coordination failure from these three reasons can arise in groups quite independent of misalignment of goals and incentives. Our primary contention is that *coordination in groups is improved when members share common ground*. We argue that diverse groups are more likely than homogeneous groups to lack common ground and, therefore, viewing diversity through a common ground lens can provide insight into their underperformance.

Viewing Group Diversity through a Common Ground Lens

Coordination is difficult for all groups; for diverse groups, coordination is likely to be even more of a challenge. Diverse groups are likely to have low initial stocks of both communal and personal common ground and are likely to have more difficulty than homogeneous groups generating additional common ground. Therefore, diverse groups face an increased hazard of coordination failure when compared with homogenous groups.

Below we argue that diverse groups have a greater challenge overcoming the three causes for coordination failure discussed above.

1. Diverse Group Members Will Have Differing Beliefs Regarding Expected Actions.

Since group members with diverse affiliations and backgrounds have different perspectives, both their expectations about the beliefs and actions of others will differ greatly. While having different perspectives is a benefit of diversity, it is also one of the costs – the more member motivations differ, the more likely conflict and sub-goal pursuit in groups will emerge (e.g., how many resources are put into surveillance systems).

However, here we wish to concentrate on a more subtle issue – even when group members do *not* actually differ in goals and motivations, but belong to diverse sub-groups, sub-group members are likely to believe their goals and motivations are different (Phillips & Lloyd, 2006; Tajfel, 1970). Diverse group members are likely to have little communal common ground with members of other sub-groups. Therefore, they are more likely to rely on stereotypes to infer the attitudes of socially distinct others than they would when making inferences about in-group members (Ames, 2004; Clement & Krueger, 2002; Krueger & Zeiger, 1993). Since our stereotypes regarding out-group members tend to be less accurate than in-group members (Judd & Park, 1993; Denrell, 2008) diverse group members may misunderstand one another's positions and preferences.

Benefits from informational diversity arise to the extent that diverse group members' beliefs and preferences are articulated, discussed and converged on. If these process differences are unshared or assumed, it may not be possible to understand how each member of the group approaches the joint task, resulting in coordination losses. This principle was recognized by Simon (1947) in his boat building example: the blueprint for the boat serves to standardize decision premises, since everyone believes that each individual builder will make appropriate decisions based on the blueprint.

It is important to note that inability to predict expected actions in this case does not occur due to diversity in goals, but due to diversity in beliefs about goals and the means to achieve those goals. Even if every group member has identical goals (e.g., to build a boat), but each believes that others have different goals, or if group members do not understand how each other's actions contribute to the goal, coordination losses are likely to manifest. As Simon points out:

Even a cooperative pattern may be unstable if each participant is unable to predict what the other is going to do. In these cases, coordination of the behaviors of the two participants is necessary in order that they realize the possibility that they both prefer. *Here conflict of aims is not the question, but imperfect knowledge"* (Simon, 1947; p81; our emphasis).

In addition, because there is more variance in diverse group members' beliefs about motivations and actions and since there is likely to be more variance regarding the possible approaches to attain these goals, members of these groups are also more likely to be wrong in their assumptions of what others in the group will do. Therefore, we propose:

Proposition 1a: Diverse groups are more likely to hold incorrect beliefs about each others' motivations and expected actions than homogenous groups.

Proposition 1b: Diverse groups will have greater difficulty predicting one another's actions than homogeneous groups.

2. Diverse Group Members Will Have Problems in Effective Communication.

Researchers have tended to assume that the lack-of-knowledge-problem identified above is fairly easily resolved through adequate communication. Folk wisdom suggests that teams could always communicate with each other to build common ground thereby achieving coordination. However, communication itself is a coordination game as research in psycholinguistics demonstrates (Clark, 1996). Camerer (2003) observes that the "assumption that communication solves all coordination problems is wrong in practice and wrong in theory."

This folk wisdom is especially deceptive in the diverse team context. Diversity research has generally assumed that the problem for diverse groups is simply an unwillingness to communicate. The real problem is as likely to be that diverse teams have greater difficulty in using communication to generate common ground since they may not have adequate initial stocks of common ground to make communication very effective (cf. Cronin & Weingart, 2007). For example, specialists may occupy different "thought worlds" (Dougherty, 1992), which makes it difficult for them to communicate. Therefore, even after attempts at communication, differences in interpretation remain – which Cronin & Weingart (2007) call "representational gaps."

Communication is difficult in diverse teams for two reasons. Firstly, group members fail to recognize that they lack common ground, and secondly they over-estimate the effectiveness of communication. In the first instance, group members may not communicate sufficiently, not because they lack the motivation, but because they are unaware of the information needs of their colleagues (Camerer, Loewenstein & Weber, 1989; Heath & Staudenmayer, 2000). Second, diverse team members are also likely to overestimate the available stocks of common ground based on any commonly shared characteristic (e.g., membership in the same firm, social community, or functional background) and are likely to discount the differences that other features of diversity create in shared understanding. For example, virtual team members take for granted that individuals in other locations share similar experiences to themselves since they are part of the same project (Cramton, 2001; Kohler and Berry, 2007).

Finally, even when group members recognize lack of common ground, they generally overestimate the efficacy of communication in achieving perfect understanding. As Dougherty (1992) and Bechky (2003) illustrate, members from different thought-worlds have their own schemes of reference, which they use to interpret any communication and inhibits shared understanding from arising even after diligent efforts at communication. This is a difficult problem to solve, since often enough diverse group members do not recognize that gaps in understanding exist, and even when it is recognized, communication is frequently less effective than assumed in bridging these gaps.

Proposition 2a: Diverse groups will have less overlap in their knowledge than homogeneous groups.

Proposition 2b: Diverse groups are more likely to underestimate the amount of coordination required for understanding one another than homogeneous groups.

3. Diverse Groups Are More Likely to Experience Integration Problems.

Finally, diverse groups are likely to have more integration problems than homogenous groups. Heath and Staudenmayer (2000) argue that most groups, especially groups with functional diversity are likely to exhibit partition focus and component focus – where they focus most of their effort on division of labour and improving individual components rather than reintegrating these sub-tasks into the whole. The problems of divergence in expectations and the inadequacy of communication will further exacerbate these problems leading to poor integration of effort across the team members. Therefore, we propose:

> **Proposition 3**: Diverse groups are more likely to have integration problems than homogeneous groups.

In summary, diverse groups are likely to hold a wider variety of beliefs about one another's motivations and actions, leading to an inability to predict one another's actions; to have less common knowledge available for communication, making misunderstandings more likely; and to lack knowledge of how to integrate sub-tasks, making integration problems more likely. In combination, this suggests:

> **Proposition 4**: Coordination failure is more likely in diverse groups than in homogeneous groups.

The Dynamics of Coordination Failure

Coordination failure directly impairs group performance, but it also has indirect effects on the nature of future group interactions. Diverse groups typically do not appreciate the fundamental causes of coordination failure, and are likely attribute these problems to other causes. In particular, group members are likely to mis-attribute coordination problems as motivation problems (Armstrong & Cole, 2002; Crampton, 2001; Heath & Staudenmayer, 2000; Wageman, 2003). Once motivational attributions are made, members behave in ways that exacerbate the underlying coordination failure, for example, by withholding communication, which leads to further process losses[2].

Anecdotal evidence suggests that the misattribution of coordination problems as motivation problems is pervasive (Armstrong & Cole, 2002; Crampton, 2001; Heath & Staudenmayer, 2000; Wageman, 2003). For example, both Cramton (2001) and Armstrong & Cole (2002) find that in virtual teams, small issues escalate suddenly into major conflicts and cause serious group dysfunction. Accidental coordination mishaps, such as

---

[2]The misattribution problem we highlight is different from the conflict that arises from representational gaps that Cronin and Weingart (2007) discuss. They argue that conflict arises because members tend to value their own representations as superior to that of out-group members and may therefore be unwilling to alter their work plans. Here we do not assume motivated lack of cooperation.

forgetting to copy emails to a member of the remote team, are interpreted as purposeful and deliberate attempts to cut others out of an information flow. The "aggrieved" party then retaliates by withholding his or her information. This leads to a vicious cycle in which relationship conflict increases and information transfer decreases (Armstrong & Cole, 2002).

Cramton (2001) provides another example of how small coordination errors can cause major interpersonal issues in teams. In project teams, members from country A initially sent messages to some members of the team in country B, but not others because they had incorrect email addresses. Country B members failed to share this information, and the excluded team members presumed that the country A members "lacked interest" and did not involve them fully in their future discussions. Country A members, on the other hand, only saw an attempt to exclude them. These ill feelings lingered throughout the duration of the project, ultimately causing both poor interpersonal relations and poor performance.

Diverse teams provide a setting in which this type of mis-attribution process is more likely to occur. Because diverse groups lack common ground and also typically lack awareness of this deficiency, small coordination errors may be interpreted as members lacking trust or competence, lacking commitment to the group, or other motivational factors (cf. Simons & Peterson, 2000, on the misattribution of task conflict as relationship conflict). Moreover, the resulting interpersonal problems between group members – lack of trust, decreased communication, and increased conflict – look very much like the interpersonal problems caused by social categorization processes that are often blamed for the poor performance of diverse groups. What we suggest here is that while these interpersonal problems may not be the ultimate cause of performance problems in diverse groups – instead, they may be triggered by coordination failures that result from lack of common ground.

Proposition 5a: In diverse groups, it is more likely that accidental coordination failures result in poor interpersonal relationships than in homogenous groups.

Proposition 5b: In diverse groups, it is more likely that poor interpersonal relationships lead to further deliberate coordination failures than in homogenous groups.

In other words, the causality implied in typical explanations of diverse group performance may actually be reversed. Rather than interpersonal problems leading to decreased coordination, which in turn causes lower performance, coordination failures can also lead to interpersonal problems that further disrupt group process and ultimately reduce performance. Whether this spiral gets initiated or not determines whether the diverse team performance improves or deteriorates with time. We suggest that this explains the large variance in performance empirically observed in diverse teams.

Discussion and Implications

We began our paper by asking the question of why some diverse groups outperform others. Our answer, of course, is that diverse teams in which members develop common ground will outperform those who do not develop common ground. Specifically, teams that do not resolve the coordination failure spiral will experience poor performance. This stands in contrast to the existing literature on diverse teams that largely argues that poor performance results from social categorization processes that cause motivational disengagement and misalignment between group members (cf. Chatman, et al., 1998; see van Knippenberg & Schippers, 2007 for a review). We argue that groups often suffer from coordination neglect – even highly motivated individuals behave in ways that make coordinating more difficult, leading to poor group performance (cf. Heath & Staudenmayer, 2000). Rather ironically, we also suggest that the groups literature as a whole suffers from coordination neglect, largely ignoring an alternative path through which diversity interferes with group performance. We hope that our paper brings coordination questions center-stage in group research and becomes fruitful for understanding group processes and performance in diverse teams. If, as we argue, the problems of diversity can best be understood in terms of coordination failures resulting from a lack of common ground, then there are a number of important theoretical and practical implications that flow from this theoretical perspective.

From a theoretical point of view, there are at least three interrelated implications of our work. Firstly, our model unpacks the process through which diversity exerts its influence on group performance, allowing for the reinterpretation of existing findings on diversity in a way that can reconcile its conflicting results. Secondly, the model suggests the potential for research into a new set of moderators that facilitate performance in diverse groups. Thirdly, our work implies that when common ground does not exist, surface level differences can be an important trigger for ensuring that the benefits of diversity are realized (i.e., contrary to the traditional view in the literature that demographic or surface level diversity is problematic for groups).

Our theory is also consistent with research that identifies moderators that tend to mitigate social categorization problems, typically by increasing the extent to which members identify with the group rather than with a sub-group (Chatman, et al., 1998; Ely & Thomas, 2001; Hobman, Bordia, & Gallois, 2004; Van der Vegt & Bunderson, 2005). We argue that these moderators are also likely to perform a second function in groups – improving common ground and reducing the likelihood of a negative spiral of coordination failure, poor performance and motivation losses. For example, strong organizational cultures improve common ground in the form of shared organizational norms, routines, practices, and history (Chwe, 2001) and have been found to improve the performance of diverse groups (Chatman, et al., 1998). Similarly, time or experience with each other increases personal common ground (Baba, et al., 2004) and has been shown to improve diverse group performance (Chatman & Flynn, 2001; Harrison, Price, & Bell, 1998; Harrison, Price, Gavin, & Florey, 2000). In summary, our perspective provides a unifying theory that can explain contradictory results on the impact of diversity.

In addition to theoretical implications, we see two interrelated practical implications of our work: 1) the importance of focusing groups on improving common ground and preventing misattribution and 2) the more beneficial normative implications of advice to managers based on a coordination theory than a social categorization explanation for diversity.

Our first broad practical implication is the need to focus diverse groups on building common ground, rather than building social cohesion. We have identified a number of possible interventions, many of them derived from the study of virtual and multinational groups, where coordination issues are more obvious. Prior research in cross-functional product development suggests that cross-functional training and job rotation can be excellent avenues for generating shared knowledge amongst team members (Helper et al., 2000; Takeishi, 2002). While such a solution is more clearly applicable to functional diversity, it could be ported to other forms of diversity by encouraging team members to engage in self-inquiry, role-playing, and/or empathetic listening exercises to try to articulate unspoken norms and interpretive schemas.

The advice we offer here for improving diverse group performance differs from traditional interventions aimed at improving social cohesion. In particular, the mechanisms we propose here are aimed at making the differences between group members explicit, rather than building a common group identity in which individual differences are subordinated to the group. By the same token, we suggest that communication is more beneficially aimed at understanding one another than on coordination specifically. The other area in which communication should be focused is at preventing mis-attribution. More specifically, this would involve supporting group norms that encourage members to think about potential misunderstanding and accidental information deficits as causes for mis-coordination and poor performance.

Conclusion

Steiner (1972) observed that teams suffer from two kinds of process losses: motivational and coordination. We do not preclude motivation related losses – they remain in all types of teams and do pose a challenge to a group's ability to reach its performance potential. Our agenda here is to highlight coordination losses. We have argued that coordination is in particular a challenge for diverse teams. While successful groups must be composed of motivated and satisfied members (and social categorization processes may limit these factors), we emphasize that even highly motivated diverse groups can easily suffer performance problems due to coordinating difficulties. Moreover, this coordination loss may be a deeper level cause, in that it also filters back into creating interpersonal and motivational problems in groups. Thus, solving only social categorization and disengagement issues will not resolve interpersonal problems entirely, nor will it do much to improve the performance of diverse groups. Pulling apart these two effects is an important step in furthering research on how to facilitate the performance of the diverse groups that are increasingly important to modern work organizations.

References

Adler, P. S. (1995). Interdepartmental interdependence and coordination. *Organization Science*, *6*,147-167.
Ames, D. (2004). Strategies for social inference: A similar contingency model of projection and stereotyping in attribute prevalence estimates. *Journal of Personality and Social Psychology*, *87*, 573-585.
Argote, L. (1999). *Organizational learning: Creating, retaining and transferring knowledge*. Norwell, MA: Kluwer.
Armstrong, D. J., & Cole, P. (2002). Managing distances and differences in geographically distributed work groups. In P. Hinds & S. Kiesler (Eds.), *Distributed work*. Cambridge, MA: MIT Press.

Bantel, K., & Jackson, S. (1989). Top management and innovations in banking: Does the composition of the team make a difference? *Strategic Management Journal*, *10*, 107-124.

Bechky, B. (2003). Sharing meaning across occupational communities: the transformation of understanding on a production floor. *Organization Science*, *14*(3), 312-330.

—. (2006). Gaffers, gofers and grips: Role based coordination in temporary organizations. *Organization Science*, *17*, 3-21.

Bunderson, J.S., & Sutcliffe, K.M. (2002). Comparing alternative conceptualizations of functional diversity in management teams: Process and performance effects. *Academy of Management Journal*, *45*, 875-893.

Camerer, C. (2003). *Behavioural game theory*. Princeton NJ: Princeton University Press.

Camerer, C., & Knez, M. (1996). Coordination, organizational boundaries, and fads in business practices. *Industrial and Corporate Change*, *5*(1), 89-112.

Camerer, C., Loewenstein, G., & Weber, M. (1989). The curse of knowledge in economic settings: An experimental analysis. *The Journal of Political Economy* , *97*(5): 1232-1254.

Chatman, J. A., Polzer, J. T., Barsad, S. G., & Neale, M. A. (1998). Being different yet feeling similar: The influence of demographic composition and organizational cutlure on work processes and outcomes. *Administrative Science Quarterly*, *43*, 749-781.

Chwe, M. S. (2001). *Rational ritual: Culture, coordination and common knowledge*. Princeton, NJ: Princeton University Press.

Clark, H. (1996). *Using language*. Cambridge, UK: Cambridge University Press.

Clark, K., & Fujimoto, T. (1991). *Product development performance: Strategy, organization, and management in the world auto industry*. Boston, MA: Harvard Business School Press.

Clement, R,. & Krueger, J. (2002). Social categorization moderates social projection. *Journal of Experimental Social Psychology*, *38*, 219-231.

Cooper, R., DeJong, D., Forsythe, B., & Ross, T. (1990). Selection criteria in coordination games: Some experimental results. *American Economic Review*, *80*, 218-33.

Cooper, R., DeJong, D., Forsythe, B., & Ross, T. (1994). Alternative institutions for resolving coordination problems: Experimental evidence on forward induction and pre-play communication. In J. Friedman (Ed.) *Problems of coordination in economic activity*. Dordrecht, The Netherlands: Kluwer.

Cox, T.H., & Blake, S. (1991). Managing cultural diversity: Implications for organizational competitiveness. *Academy of Management Executive, 5,* 45-56.

Crampton, C. (2001). The mutual knowledge problem and its consequences for dispersed collaboration. *Organization Science, 12*(3), 346-371.

Cronin, M. A., & Weingart, L. R. (2007). Representational gaps, information processing, and conflict in functionally diverse teams. *Academy of Management Review, 32*(3), 761-773.

Crowston, K,. & Kammerer, E. (1998). Coordination and collective mind in software requirements development. *IBM Systems Journal, 37(2),* 227–245.

De Dreu, C. K. W., & West, M. A. (2001). Minority dissent and team innovation: The importance of participation in decision making. *Journal of Applied Psychology, 86,* 1191-1201.

Denrell , J. (2008, July). Indirect social influence. *Science, 321,*47-48.

—. (2005). Why most people disapprove of me: Experience sampling in impression formation. *Psychological Review, 112*(4), 951-978.

Dougherty, D. (1992). Interpretive barriers to successful product innovation in large firms. *Organization Science, 3*(2), 179-202.

Earley, C. P., & Mosakowski, E. (2000). Creating hybrid team cultures: An empirical test of transnational team functioning. *Academy of Management Journal, 43*(1), 26-51.

Ely, R., & Thomas, D. (2001). Cultural diversity at work: The effects of diversity perspectives on work group processes and outcomes. *Administrative Science Quarterly, 46,* 229-273.

Ethiraj, S., & Levinthal, D. (2004). Modularity and innovation in complex systems. *Management Science, 50*(2), 159-173.

Ghoshal, S,. & Moran, P. (1996). Bad for practice: A critique of the transaction cost theory. *Academy of Management Review, 21*(1), 13-47.

Grant, R. M. (1996). Toward a knowledge-based theory of the firm. *Strategic Management Journal,* 17, 109-122.

Hackman, J. R. (1987). The design of work teams. In J. W. Lorsch (Ed.), *Handbook of organizational behavior* (pp. 315-342). Englewood Cliffs, NJ: Prentice Hall.

Harrison, D. A., Price, K. H., Gavin, J. H., & Florey, A. T. (2002). Time, teams, and task performance: Changing effects of surface- and deep-level diversity on group functioning. *Academy of Management Journal, 45,*1029-1045.

Heath, C., & Heath, D. (2007). *Made to stick: Why some ideas survive and others die.* New York, NY: Random House.

Heath, C., & Staudenmayer, N. (2000). Coordination neglect: How lay theories of organizing complicate coordination in organizations. In R.I. Sutton & B. Staw (Eds.), *Research in Organization Behaviour*, Vol. 22, (pp.153-193). Greenwich, CT: JAI Press.

Helper, S., MacDuffie, J., & Sabel, C. (2000). Pragmatic collaborations: Advancing knowledge while controlling opportunism. *Industrial and Corporate Change, 9*(3), 443-488.

Hobman, E. V., Bordia, P., & Gallois, C. (2004). Perceived dissimilarity and work group involvement: The moderating effect of group openness to diversity. *Group & Organization Management, 29*(5), 560-587.

Hogg, M. A., & Terry, D. J. (2000). Social identity and self-categorization processes in organizational contexts. *Academy of Management Review, 25*, 121-140.

Hollingshead, A. (1998). Communication, learning and retrieval in transactive memory systems. *Journal of Experimental Social Psychology, 34*, 423-442.

—. (2001). Cognitive interdependence and convergent expectations in transactive memory systems. *Journal of Personality and Social Psychology, 74*, 659-671.

Hollingshead, A. B., & Fraidin, S. N. (2003). Gender stereotypes and assumptions about expertise in transactive memory. *Journal of Experimental Social Psychology, 39*(4), 355-363.

Hornsey, M. J., & Hogg, M. A. (2000). Assimilation and diversity: An integrative model of subgroup relations. *Personality and Social Psychology Review, 4*, 143–156.

Huo, Y. J. (2003). Procedural justice and social regulation across group boundaries: Does subgroup identity undermine relationship-based governance? *Personality and Social Psychology Bulletin, 29*(3), 336-348.

Jehn, K. A., Northcraft, G. B., & Neale, M. A. (1999). Why differences make a difference: A field study of diversity, conflict and performance in workgroups *Administrative Science Quarterly, 44*, 741-764.

Johns, G. (1999). A multi-level theory of self-serving behavior in and by organizations. In R. I. Sutton & B. M. Staw (Eds). *Research in organizational behavior, Vol 2* (pp 1-38). Stamford, CT: JAI Press.

Keller, R. T. (2001). Cross-functional project groups in research and new product development: Diversity, communications, job stress, and outcomes. *Academy of Management Journal, 44* (3), 547-555.

Knez, M., & Camerer, C. (1994). Creating expectational assets in the laboratory: Coordination in 'weakest-link' games. *Strategic Management Journal, 15*, 101-119.

Kogut, B., & Zander, U. (1992). Knowledge of the firm, combinative capabilities, and the replication of technology *Organization Science, 3,* 383-397.

Kohler, T., & Berry, M. (2007). Group coordination and coordination norms in internationally distributed teams. *Working paper, George Mason University.*

Krauss, R. M., & Fussel, S. R. (1991). Perspective taking in communication: Representations of others' knowledge in reference. *Social Cognition, 9,* 2-24.

Krueger, J., & Zeiger, J. S. (1993). Social categorization and the truly false consensus effect. *Journal of Personality and Social Psychology, 65,* 670–680.

Kruglanski, A. W., Webster, D. M., & Klem, A. (1993). Motivated resistance and openness to persuasion in the presence or absence of prior information. *Journal of Personality and Social Psychology, 65,* 861-876.

Kunda, Z., & Spencer, S. J.(2003) When do stereotypes come to mind and when do they color judgment? A goal-based theoretical framework for stereotype activation and application. *Psychological Bulletin, 129,* 522-544.

Lau, D. C., & Murnighan, J. K. (1998). Demographic diversity and faultlines: The compositional dynamics of organizational groups. *Academy of Management Review, 23*(2), 325-340.

Lewis, K., Lange, D., & Gillis, L. (2005). Transactive memory systems, learning, and learning transfer. *Organization Science, 16*(6), 581-598.

Liang, D. W., Moreland, R., & Argote, L. (1995). Group versus individual training and group performance: The mediating role of transactive memory. *Personality and Social Psychology Bulletin, 21,* 384–393.

March, J.G., & Simon, H.A. (1958). *Organizations.* New York: Wiley.

Mehta, J., Starmer, C., & Sugden, R. (1994a). The nature of salience: An experimental investigation of pure coordination games. *American Economic Review, 84,* 658-673.

Mehta, J., Starmer, C., & Sugden, R. (1994b.) Focal points in pure coordination games: An experimental investigation. *Theory and Decision, 36,* 163-185.

Milliken, F. J. & Martins, L. L. (1996). Searching for common threads: Understanding the multiple effects of diversity in organizational groups *Academy of Management Review, 21*(2), 402-434.

Nelson, R. R. & Winter, S. G. (1982). *An evolutionary theory of economic change.* Cambridge, MA: Harvard University Press.

Olson, J. S., Teasley, S., Covi, L., & Olson, G. (2002). The (currently) unique advantages of collocated work. In P. J. Hinds and S. Kiesler (Eds.), *Distributed work* (pp 113-136). Cambridge MIT Press.

Pelled, L. H., Eisenhardt, K. M., & Xin, K. R. (1999). Exploring the black box: An analysis of work group diversity, conflict, and performance. *Administrative Science Quarterly*, *44*(1), 1-28.

Pelled, L. H., Ledford, G. E., & Mohrman, S. A. (1999). Demographic dissimilarity and workplace inclusion. *Journal of Management Studies*, *36*(7), 1013-1031.

Peterson, R. S. & Behfar, K. J. (2003). The dynamic relationship between performance feedback, trust, and conflict in groups: A longitudianl study. *Organizational Behavior and Human Decision Processes*, *92*, 102-112.

Phillips, K. W. (2003). The effect of categorically based expectations on minority influence: The importance of congruence. *Personality and Social Psychology Bulletin*, *29*, 3-13.

Phillips, K. W., & Loyd, D. L. (2006). When surface and deep-level diversity collide: The effects on dissenting group members. *Organizational Behavior and Human Decision Processes*, *99*, 143.

Polzer, J. T., Milton, L. P., & Swann, W. B. J. (2002). Capitalizing on diversity: Interpersonal congruence in small work groups. *Administrative Science Quarterly*, *47*, 296-324.

Puranam, P., Singh, H., & Chaudhuri, S. (2009). Integrating acquired capabilities: When structural integration is (un)necessary. *Organization Science*, *20*(2), 313-328.

Rink, F., & Elmers, N. (2007). The role of expectancies in accepting task-related diversity: Do disappointment and lack of commitment stem from actual differences or violated expectations? *Personality and Social Psychology Bulletin*, *33*, 842-853.

Schelling, T.C. (1960). *The strategy of conflict.* Cambridge, MA: Harvard University Press.

Sedikides, C., Campbell, W. K., Reeder, G. D., & Elliot A. J. (1998). Self-serving bias in relational context. *Journal of Personality and Social Psychology*, *74*(22), 378-386.

Shin, S. J., & Zhou, J. (2007). When is educational specialization heterogeneity related to creativity in research and development teams? Transformational leadership as a moderator. *Journal of Applied Psychology*, *92*(6), 1709-1721.

Simon, H.A. (1947). *Administrative behaviour.* New York, NY: The Free Press.

Simons, T. L., & Peterson, R. S. (2000). Task conflict and relationship conflict in top management teams: The pivotal role of intragroup trust. *Journal of Applied Psychology*, *85*, 102-111.

Srikanth, K. (2007, August). Coordination in business process offshoring. *Academy of Management Annual Meetings Best Paper Proceedings*, Philadelphia, PA.

Stasser, G., Taylor, L. A., & Hanna, C. (1985). Information sampling in structured and unstructured discussions of three- and six-person groups. *Journal of Personality and Social Psychology*, *57*, 67-78.

Stasser, G., & Titus, W. (1985). Pooling of unshared information in group decision making: Biased information sampling during discussion. *Journal of Personality and Social Psychology* , *48*, 1467-1478.

Steiner, I. D. (1972). *Group process and productivity.* New York, NY: Academic Press.

Szulanski, G. (1996). Exploring internal stickiness: Impediments to the transfer of best practice within the firm. *Strategic Management Journal*, *17*, 27-43.

Takeishi, A. (2002). Knowledge partitioning in the inter-firm division of labor: The case of automotive product development. *Organization Science*, *13*(3), 321-338.

Tajfel, H. (1970). Experiments in intergroup discrimination. *Scientific American*, *223*(5), 96-102.

—. (1981). *Human groups and social categories.* Cambridge, UK: Cambridge University Press.

Taylor, D.R., & Doria, J.R. (1981). Self serving and group serving bias in attributions. *Journal of Social Psychology*, *113*(2), 201-212.

Thompson, L. (2003). Improving the creativity of organizational work groups. *Academy of Management Executive*, *17*(1), 96-109.

Tyler, T. R., Lind, E. A., Huo, Y. J. (2000). Cultural values and authority relations: The psychology of conflict resolution across cultures. *Psychology, Public Policy, and Law*, *6*, 1138-1163.

Van der Vegt, G. S., & Bunderson, J. S. (2005). Learning and performance in multidisciplinary teams: The importance of collective team identification. *Academy of Management Journal*, *48*(3), 532-548.

van Knippenberg, D. L., De Dreu, C. K., & Homan, A. C. (2004). Work group diversity and group performance: An integrative model and research agenda. *Journal of Applied Psychology*, *89*, 1008-1022.

van Knippenberg, D. L., & Schippers, M. (2007). Work group diversity. *Annual Review of Psychology*, *58*, 515-541.

Wageman, R. (2003). Virtual processes: Implications for coaching the virtual team. In R. S. Peterson & E. A. Mannix (Eds.), *Leading and managing people in dynamic organizations.* Mahwah, NJ: Lawrence Erlbaum Associates.

Watson, W., Johnson, L., & Merritt, D. (1998). Team orientation, self-orientation and diversity in task groups: their connection to team performance over time. *Group Organization Management, 23,* 161-188.

Weber, R., Camerer, C., Rottenstreich, Y., & Knez, M. (2001). The illusion of leadership: Misattribution of cause in coordination games. *Organization Science, 12*(5), 582-598.

Wegner, D. M., Erber, R., & Raymond, P. (1991). Transactive memory in close relationships. *Journal of Personality and Social Psychology , 61,* 923-929.

Webster, D. M. & Kruglanski, A. W. (1994). Individual Differences in need for cognitive closure. *Journal of Personality and Social Psychology, 67*(6), 1049-1062.

Weisband, S. (2002). Maintaining awareness in distributed team collaborations: Implications for leadership and performance. In P. Hinds & S. Kiesler (Eds.), *Distributed work* (pp 311-334). Cambridge, MA: MIT Press,.

Wheelwright, H., & Clark, K. (1992). *Revolutionizing product development: Quantum leaps in speed, efficiency and quality.* New York, NY: Free Press.

Williams, K., & O'Reilly, C. (1998). Demography and diversity in organizations: A review of 40 years of research. *Research in Organizational Behavior, 20,* 77-140.

CHAPTER TWO

LEARNING FROM ERRORS IN ORGANIZATIONS: THE EFFECTS OF NEGATIVE EMOTIONS ON MOTIVATION AND COGNITION

BIN ZHAO,
SIMON FRASER UNIVERSITY, CANADA
FERNANDO OLIVERA,
THE UNIVERSITY OF WESTERN ONTARIO, CANADA
AND AMY C. EDMONDSON
HARVARD BUSINESS SCHOOL, USA

Abstract

Previous research has suggested that negative emotions have both stimulating and impairing effects on learning from errors. Building on theories of learning from errors, emotions, self-regulation, motivation, and coping, we propose a model to explain this apparent contradiction. We argue that negative emotions may promote or impair learning, depending on their impact on motivation and cognition. The proposed model also acknowledges the differential effects of discrete negative emotions on learning from errors. We discuss additional theoretical considerations and conclude with directions for future research.

Keywords: learning from errors, negative emotions, motivation, cognition

Introduction

The ability to learn from errors has been recognized as a critical determinant of individual, group, and organizational performance (Argote, 1999; Edmondson, 1999; Hofmann & Frese, 2011; March, Sproull, &

Tamuz, 1991; Sitkin, 1992; Weick & Ashford, 2001). For individuals, errors provide valuable opportunities to assess and improve performance, and the ability to learn from errors is thought to be a crucial component of career success (e.g., Boss & Sims, 2008; Keith, 2011; Newton, Khanna, & Thompson, 2008; Ohlsson, 1996; Snell, 1988). For groups and organizations, lessons learned from errors can prevent costly error recurrence and increase productivity (Edmondson, 1996; March et al., 1991; Ramanujam & Goodman, 2011).

Errors provide task feedback from which individuals can draw meaningful lessons. However, learning from errors occurs neither instantaneously nor automatically. Compared to other forms of experiential learning, learning from errors has at least two distinguishing features. First, it typically involves negative emotions. Although errors may not always generate negative emotions, psychological research suggests that individuals' confidence in the level and quality of their performance is challenged when they encounter their own errors, creating strong negative feelings (e.g., Baumeister, Vohs, DeWall, & Zhang, 2007; Lewis, 2000). Research from fields as varied as medicine, training, and entrepreneurship has also found that individuals experience negative emotions upon detecting their own errors (e.g., Bosk, 1979; Boss & Sims, 2008; Edmondson, 1996; Heimbeck, Frese, Sonnentag, & Keith, 2003; Newton et al., 2008; Paget, 1988; Shepherd, 2003). Second, it requires substantial effort to draw lessons from one's own errors. For learning to occur, individuals need to correctly identify the root causes of errors (e.g., Ellis, Mendel, & Nir, 2006; Ohlsson, 1996; Shimizu & Hitt, 2011). Cause-effect associations are sometimes easy to understand, but, more often, it is very difficult to determine the causes of errors because they arise from multiple factors, some of which may not be within the individual's control. This is especially the case in complex organizational settings (Shimizu & Hitt, 2011; Zhao & Olivera, 2006). Thus, learning from errors can be a cognitively demanding activity.

Emotions are momentary, affective feelings that people experience in relation to specific stimuli at specific points in time (e.g., George, 2000; Gross, 1998). We focus on negative emotions triggered by one's own errors because, as suggested by Bandura and Locke (2003), a comprehensive theory of self-regulation (including self-regulated learning through correcting performance errors) must incorporate self-evaluative affective reactions to the quality of one's performance. Emotions directed at others (such as anger) or emotions that are unrelated to the error and irrelevant to current goal pursuit are beyond the scope of our discussion.

Prior work has acknowledged that negative emotions affect learning from errors (e.g., Heimbeck et al., 2003; Kanfer & Ackerman, 1989; Keith & Frese, 2008; Rybowiak, Garst, Frese, & Batinic, 1999); however, there has been little research or theorizing about the underlying mechanisms that link negative emotions and learning from errors. The limited empirical evidence suggests that when people experience negative emotions resulting from errors, their learning is impaired (e.g., Heimbeck et al., 2003; Ilgen & Davis, 2000; Kanfer & Ackerman, 1989; Newton et al., 2008; Rybowiak et al., 1999; Shepherd, 2003). For example, rather than confront errors, individuals may rationalize their errors or ignore the experience altogether, thus curtailing the opportunity to learn (e.g., Newton et al., 2008; Pezzo & Pezzo, 2007; Shepherd, 2003; Weick & Ashford, 2001). These findings are consistent with Seo and colleagues' (Seo, Barrett, & Bartunek, 2004) argument that negative emotions decrease motivation to engage in productive actions and motivate people to adopt an avoidance behavioral orientation. In contrast, there is also research evidence suggesting that negative emotions elicited by errors can actually promote learning in part because they alert people that something is wrong with the current situation that needs to be fixed (e.g., Ellis & Davidi, 2005; Ellis et al., 2006; Snell, 1988). Current frameworks of experiential learning do not explicitly account for these seemingly contradictory effects of negative emotions on learning from errors.

Building on a review of the relevant literature in the interrelated areas-- learning from errors, emotions, self-regulation, motivation, and coping-- we develop an overarching and integrative model in an effort to reconcile conflicting findings and untangle theoretical explanations. Our research extends current theory of the impact of emotion on cognition and motivation in work settings (e.g., Seo et al., 2004) in three ways.

First, we contribute to the burgeoning research on the functional utility of negative emotions in organizational contexts by elaborating both the stimulating and impairing role of negative emotions in learning from errors. In this, we join researchers who challenge the assumption that "negative emotions are always bad" and call for research to explore the functionality of negative emotions (e.g., Parrott, 2002). Similarly, Baumeister and colleagues (2007) argued that a comprehensive theoretical framework about the influence of negative emotions on behavior and decision-making should address their adaptive as well as maladaptive effects.

Second, while Seo and colleagues (2004) discussed the impact of emotion on cognition and motivation in work settings in a general sense, we focus on a specific, common, and important activity at work: learning from errors. We argue that emotions may not affect different kinds of work-related activities in the same way. For example, sadness has been suggested to have little impact on creativity (Baas, De Dreu, and Nijstad, 2008). We do not expect that sadness plays the same role in learning from errors, as in creativity. Instead, we expect that sadness may stimulate or impair learning from errors, depending on the error attribution that an individual makes in a particular error situation.

Third, people experience different kinds of emotions, and if we are to understand how emotions influence decision-making and behavior it is critical to consider the effects of specific emotions, rather than treating emotions along a single valence dimension (i.e., positive vs. negative) (e.g., Roseman, Wiest, & Swartz, 1994; Smith & Ellsworth, 1985; Tangney, Miller, Flicker, & Barlow, 1996; Tangney, Wagner, Fletcher, & Gramzow, 1992). The framework proposed by Seo and colleagues (2004) contributed significantly to our understanding about the impact of positive and negative emotions on motivation and cognition, but did not incorporate discussion of distinct effects of specific emotions. We acknowledge the differential effects of discrete negative emotions on learning from errors in our discussion of the impact of emotion on cognition. A critically important cognitive activity in learning from errors is error attribution, which determines whether individuals can accurately identify the root causes of their errors (e.g., Ohlsson, 1996). Therefore, in addition to the three cognitive elements of expectancy theory discussed by Seo and colleagues (2004), we theorize the influence of negative emotions on error attribution.

In the following sections, we define learning from errors and develop a theoretical model to explain the role of negative emotions on the motivation and cognition involved in learning from errors. To conclude, we discuss additional theoretical considerations and directions for future research.

Learning from Errors Defined

Consistent with Zhao and Olivera (2006), we define errors as "individuals' decisions and behaviors that (a) result in an undesirable gap between an expected and real state; and (b) may lead to actual or potential negative consequences for organizational functioning that could have been avoided" (Zhao & Olivera, 2006: 1013).

Learning from errors in challenging achievement-related situations is an integral part of self-regulation (Bandura & Locke, 2003). Building on prior literature (e.g., Ellis et al., 2006; Ohlsson, 1996; Shepherd, 2003), we conceptualize learning from errors as the process through which individuals: (a) reflect on the nature and causes of the error made (i.e., the wrong action or decision), and (b) make appropriate changes in beliefs, strategies, or actions to correct the error and/or prevent its recurrence. This definition suggests that: (a) this learning process involves component learning activities such as error attribution, and (b) this learning process leads to learning outcomes (i.e., what can be learned from the experience of errors) that help with error management and avoidance. For example, researchers have suggested that reflecting on errors may reveal insights that correct misunderstandings of a situation, and lead to the identification of shortcomings in one's task knowledge that interfere with effective action (Edmondson, 1999; Ellis & Davidi, 2005).

Our focus is on situations where learning from errors is mindful or effortful; that is, when learning requires individuals to purposefully reflect on and analyze an error (e.g., Boss & Sims, 2008; Ohlsson, 1996; Shimizu & Hitt, 2011). Mindful learning demands both motivation and cognitive resources (e.g., Kanfer & Ackerman, 1989; Kluger & DeNisi, 1996; Ohlsson, 1996; Rybowiak et al., 1999). Our theory is not meant to address learning situations that do not require substantial cognitive efforts, such as when "the action performed immediately before error detection was the mistaken one and, consequently, that whatever rule evoked that action is faulty" (Ohlsson, 1996: 249).

This conceptualization of learning from errors is consistent with theories of experiential learning (e.g., Argyris & Schön, 1978; Kolb, 1984; Kolb, Boyatzis, & Mainemelis, 2001). The two key elements of these learning models are: (i) motivation to learn and (ii) cognitive information processing (e.g., reflection) aimed at improving understanding of cause–effect relationships in the work environment.

A Model of Learning from Errors

Although learning from errors has received significant research attention (e.g., Argote, 1999; Argyris & Schön, 1996; Edmondson, 1996, 1999; Hofmann & Frese, 2011; Sitkin, 1992), we lack an integrated theoretical model to explain how negative emotions influence learning from errors and when and why individuals personally learn or fail to learn from their own errors in organizational contexts (cf., Boss & Sims, 2008; Ohlsson, 1996). This paper focuses on the role of negative emotions on learning from errors by investigating the links between negative emotions, motivation, and cognition.

Drawing on research on emotions, we differentiate between two modal responses to emotions elicited by errors: emotion-focused coping and learning from errors. People adopt different coping strategies to deal with negative emotions (Brown, Westbrook, & Challagalla, 2005; Gross, 1998; Lischetzke & Eid, 2003; Lopes, Salovey, Côté, & Beers, 2005). The literature on emotions has identified two main emotion-regulation strategies: emotion-focused and problem-focused (e.g., Lazarus, 1999). Emotion-focused coping is aimed at regulating emotions, while problem-focused coping is about analyzing the situation and taking action to solve the problem that triggered the negative emotions (Lazarus, 1999). In the learning and training literature (e.g., Boekaerts, 2007; Op't Eynde, de Corte, & Verschaffel, 2007), emotion-focused coping refers to task-irrelevant, emotion-regulation activities, such as justifying errors ("This is not really an error because everyone is doing it"). These activities compete with learning from errors for cognitive resources. In contrast, learning from errors is generally viewed as a form of problem-focused coping.

Nonetheless, learning from errors and problem-focused coping are not the same thing; problem-focused coping is a broader concept than learning from errors. Lazarus (1991) defines problem-focused coping as any coping processes that aims at removing or changing the source of stress and distress. An example provided in the book is: "(I)f a neighbor's tree is producing emotional distress because it drops leaves in our yard, we might try to induce the neighbor to cut the tree down or trim it" (Lazarus, 1991: 112).

We integrate insights from the literature on learning from errors, emotions, motivation, and coping, to argue that negative emotions may promote or impair learning, depending on their impact on motivation and cognition, which, in turn, determine whether emotion-focused coping or learning from errors will be initiated. Before moving on to further details, we will first delineate the motivational and cognitional elements considered in the model.

Motivation. Motivation is about the direction and amount of attention allocated to a focal activity (Kanfer & Ackerman, 1989). Emotions are an integral part of the motivational processes underlying the pursuit of goals (Bower, 1992; De Hooge, Zeelenberg, & Breugelmans, 2010a; Izard, 1991; Lazarus, 1991; Zeelenberg, Nelissen, Breugelmans, & Pieters, 2008). Research has suggested that negative emotions elicited by errors and setbacks are characterized by two basic motives: the *approach* motive to examine and fix the problem and the *protect* motive to withdraw from or avoid the problem situation (corresponding to the problem- and emotion-focused coping responses) (e.g., De Hooge et al., 2010a; Lazarus,

1991; Zeelenberg et al., 2008). Accordingly, we argue that, in error situations, negative emotions are associated with two types of motivation: motivation to learn from errors and motivation to protect the self, which we will explain below by referring to the relevant literature.

As noted, we focus on situations where learning requires mindful reflection on, and analysis of, errors. This type of effortful learning cannot occur without a powerful motivational force. In error situations, motivation to learn refers to the extent to which an individual desires to improve task knowledge or skills by analyzing errors. Essentially, motivation to learn reflects a goal of taking assertive action to fix a problem to achieve the desired performance. There is substantial evidence that *motivation to learn* is affected by individual differences (e.g., goal orientation, DeShon & Gillespie, 2005; Dweck & Leggett, 1988; Elliot & McGregor, 1999) and situational factors (e.g., support from a manager or peer, Colquitt, LePine, & Noe, 2000). Our research complements this prior work by considering the influence of negative emotions on motivation to learn from errors. We wish to call attention to the critical role played by emotions in learning because extant research strongly supports the existence of a direct link between emotions and *motivation to learn* (e.g., Baumeister et al., 2007; Briner & Kiefer, 2005; Izard, 1991; Lazarus, 1991).

Establishing and maintaining a positive self-view is a fundamental human motive (DeShon & Gillespie, 2005; Rosenberg, 1979; Schlenker & Leary, 1982). Error-elicited negative emotions provide information about failure to attain a goal and about potential threats to one's perceived competence. Motivation to protect is defined as the extent to which an individual desires to maintain or restore a positive view of the self. Essentially, motivation to protect suggests a goal of defensive ego-protection to restore the threatened self or to prevent further damage to the self-image, without directly addressing the problem.

Cognition. The emotion literature has also acknowledged that emotions directly influence *cognition* (e.g., Elfenbein, 2007; Forgas, 2003; Schwarz, 1990), a link that is supported by research on learning and training (e.g., Bell & Kozlowski, 2008; Bower, 1992; Keith & Frese, 2008; Pekrun et al., 2007; Roese, 1997). Our research contributes to the literature by elaborating on the *how* and *why* mechanisms underlying the associations between negative emotions and cognition involved in learning from errors. Specifically, we focus on those cognitive components that directly influence motivation to learn and learning from errors: error attribution and the three cognitive elements of expectancy theory (i.e., expectancy, instrumentality, and valence beliefs). We summarize all these mechanisms in a model of learning from errors presented in Figure 2-1 and explain the proposed linkages in the following sections.

Negative Emotions and Motivation to Learn

The link between negative emotions and motivation to learn is supported by research on emotions. For example, affect infusion theory and the "affect-as-information" perspective suggest that negative emotion draws attention to the unsatisfactory performance–goal discrepancy and, thereby, motivates people to increase effort to diminish the discrepancy to avoid similar negative emotions in the future (Baumeister et al., 2007; Brown et al., 2005; Elfenbein, 2007; Forgas, 1995; Schwarz & Clore, 1988). Similarly, "emotion as feedback" theory has suggested that emotions function as an instructive feedback system that facilitates learning and control in the course of goal-pursuit (Baumeister et al., 2007; Carver & Scheier, 1990, 1998; Frijda, 1986). Negative emotions are warning signals that a behavior was unsuccessful and that action is required to address the problem.

Prior work on learning also suggests that negative emotions have a motivational role in learning from errors. In a qualitative study of managers' learning patterns in the workplace, participants reported strong negative emotions about errors but also recognized that learning from errors was one of the two most common on-the-job learning activities (Snell, 1988). Drawing from this field research, Snell (1988) argued that negative emotions can promote learning from errors because "… the shock appeared to alert managers to a problem and provide the motivation to devote attention to it" (1988: 328) and "the discomfort appeared to provide the motivation to set something straight or sort something out" (1988: 329).

Negative Emotions and Motivation to Protect

Literature on emotions also supports an association between negative emotions and motivation to protect. Emotion tends to disrupt goal-directed thoughts and behavior, and redirects attention to the emotion itself (e.g., Elfenbein, 2007; Forgas, 2003; Lazarus, 1991; Weiss & Cropanzano, 1996). This type of attention reallocation may impair task-related activities, such as learning from errors, to the extent that individuals reorder their goal priorities and devote their attention to off-task, emotion-management activities. Individuals divert their attention away from the task at hand in such a way that the negative emotions become irrelevant to

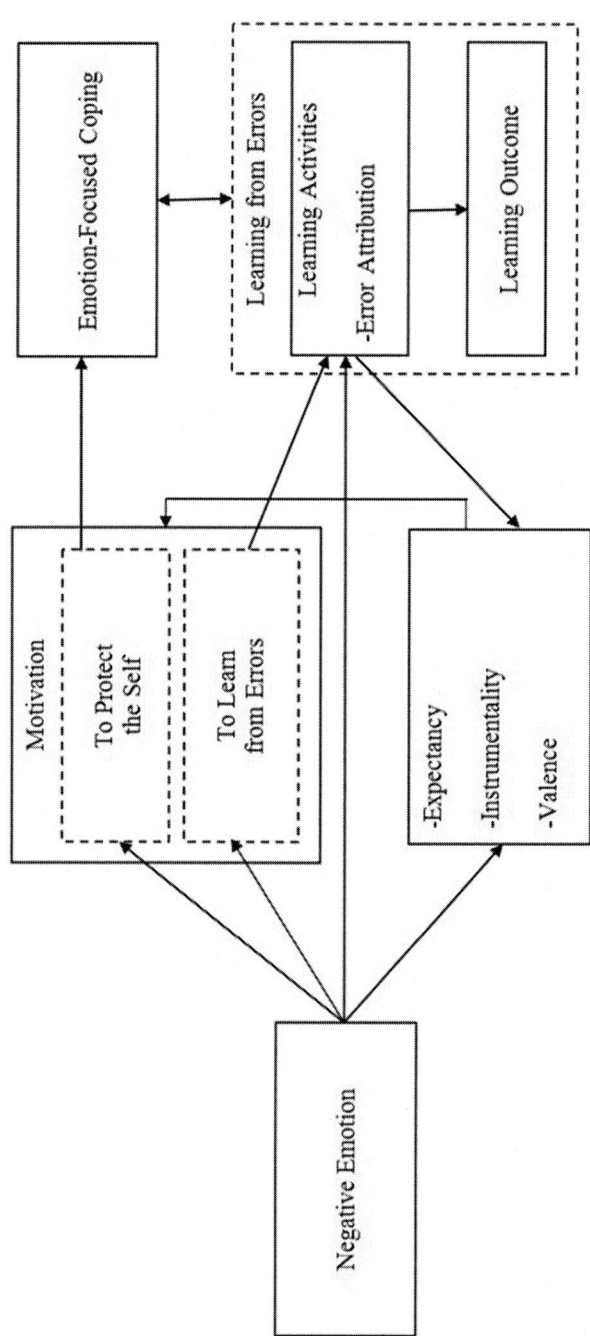

Figure 2-1. A Model of Learning from Errors

the task and stop functioning as task-related signals (Bower, 1992). Errors typically arouse negative emotions concerning the threatened self or threatened well-being (Zhao & Olivera, 2006). Attention to these negative emotions prioritizes self-protection coping responses over task-focused coping and learning activities. Consider a scenario in which an individual tries to alleviate negative self-conscious thoughts and emotions by blaming an error on task difficulty, and then either lowering their performance standard or shifting to a different task. In this scenario, the individual simply concludes that there is no need to reflect on and analyze the root causes of the error; he/she feels no motivation to learn from the error.

Motivation to Learn and Learning Activities

Motivation to learn has been widely studied as a direct antecedent of learning (e.g., Colquitt & Simmering, 1998; Noe & Schmitt, 1986; Noe & Wilk, 1993; LePine, LePine, & Jackson, 2004). In this paper, we specify the role of motivation to learn in situations that involve negative emotions. The learning and training literature has suggested that an essential pre-condition for learning from errors is that, despite negative feedback, individuals still feel motivated to learn so as to direct attention from negative self-conscious thoughts back to task learning (Boekaerts, 2007; Bower, 1992; Kluger & DeNisi, 1996; Op't Eynde et al., 2007). We argue that motivation to learn promotes problem-focused coping in response to the negative emotions elicited by errors and motivates individuals to engage in task-focused, problem-solving activities, such as learning from errors. Here we propose a specific link between motivation to learn and engagement in learning activities (excluding learning outcomes) because simply feeling motivated to learn does not predict whether any valuable lessons will be learned from errors. By definition, motivation to learn is only about directing and allocating cognitive resources to learning activities (e.g., error attribution).

Motivation to Protect and Emotion-Focused Coping

Literature on emotions consistently acknowledges that negative emotions are associated with a desire to avoid or withdraw, which in turn, leads to emotion-focused coping such as inaction or retreat (e.g., Anderson, 2003; Baumeister et al., 2007; Lazarus, 1999). In error situations, emotion-focused coping includes denial and avoidance behaviors (e.g., escaping task-relevant activities) and cognitive and behavioral distraction (e.g., blaming others, pursuing activities that help the individual forget the error and feel good again) (Ilgen & Davis, 2000; Newton et al., 2008; Shepherd, 2003). We argue that motivation to protect is associated with emotion-focused coping and motivates individuals to physically and/or mentally withdraw from the task in an attempt to restore a positive self-image or avoid further damage to their well-being.

Error Attribution and Learning Outcomes

As noted earlier, learning from errors involves a critically important cognitive component activity: error attribution, to determine why a performance discrepancy occurred (e.g., Ellis et al., 2006; Ohlsson, 1996; Shimizu & Hitt, 2011). Error attribution directly influences learning outcomes, that is, whether any valuable lessons will be learned from errors to help minimize or eliminate goal-performance discrepancies. Lessons learned from errors based on incorrect attributions may be irrelevant, invalid, or misleading (Ellis & Davidi, 2005).

Individuals may make *internal* or *external* attributions for their errors. External attributions do not necessarily terminate the learning process if these attributions are in fact a correct assessment of the task environment. The root causes of errors may or may not be intrinsic to the individual. For example, they may result from flaws in organizational systems (Reason, 1990) or the actions or decisions of others (e.g., customers, co-workers, managers). In such situations, individuals may improve their understanding of the external causes and identify ways to prevent them from interfering with future task performance, which constitutes learning (e.g., Ilgen & Davis, 2000; Ohlsson, 1996).

Next, we will discuss how internal attribution affects learning from errors (as summarized in Table 2-1). There are three commonly accepted dimensions of causality in attribution theory: locus (internal vs. external), stability, and controllability (Weiner, 1985). We organize our discussion of the linkage between internal error attribution and learning around the dimension of controllability because whether one believes that he/she can control the cause of an error plays a pivotal role in self-regulated learning (Bandura & Locke, 2003). We do not incorporate stability dimension in our discussion in order to avoid any potential confusion caused by this causal dimension. For example, lack of ability has been used as a typical example of internal stable attribution. However, research by Dweck and colleagues (e.g., Dweck & Leggett, 1988) has suggested that lack of ability can be seen as an unstable attribution, too, because learning-goal oriented people believe that their abilities are malleable and increasable and thus can be improved through learning.

When individuals make internal attributions (i.e., believing that they themselves have caused the error), they may attribute the error to self-related factors at three different levels, which will affect their responses to errors differently. According to motivated action theory (DeShon & Gillespie, 2005), control theory (Carver, 1996; Carver & Scheier, 1998), and feedback intervention theory (Kluger & DeNisi, 1996), an individual's response to perceived performance–goal discrepancies (including errors) is a goal-directed activity that is governed by a hierarchy of goals or standards. Although the hierarchy may vary in complexity depending on the task situation, it always comprises three general levels, in order from highest to lowest: self, task motivation, and task learning. The *self* level contains self concept or identity goals. Goals at the *task motivation* level are about directing and sustaining efforts towards successfully completing the focal task. The *task learning* level comprises goals for specific component activities of the focal task. Individual attention is normally concentrated on the task motivation level, "...but it can be present simultaneously, or with quick alternations, at different levels of hierarchy and across several standards within the hierarchy" (Kluger & DeNisi, 1996: 262).

If an error is perceived as a task-related discrepancy (i.e., negative feedback for task goals), it is simply seen as failure at a particular task. As a result, attention will either remain at the task motivation level or be diverted down to the task learning level (DeShon & Gillespie, 2005; Kluger & DeNisi, 1996). In either case, error attribution will be directed by the goals relevant to the task level (at the task motivation and/or task learning levels). Individuals are likely to attribute errors to specific and controllable factors; thus, they can focus on the actions, decisions, or features of the task environment that led to the errors and engage in bias-free, systematic deep processing of situation-specific information in order to learn for future occasions. For example, when individuals believe that an error has been caused by poor task monitoring, their attention will remain at the task motivation level and they will dedicate additional resources to monitoring the focal task activity. If individuals believe that the error was caused by incorrect task rules, their attention will be directed down to the task learning level and they will try to revise or update their action scripts by checking all the details involved in the focal task. Therefore, we propose that error attribution enhances the likelihood to learn from errors when it occurs at the task motivation or task learning level.

If an error is interpreted as a failure of the self (i.e., negative feedback for goals at the global self level), attention will be directed up to the level of the self, away from the task level(s). Thus, error attribution will be guided by the superordinate goals and standards of the self. In such situations, individuals tend to make global and uncontrollable attributions and engage in task-irrelevant, self-preoccupied cognitions (Abramson, Seligman, & Teasdale, 1978; Mikulincer & Nizan, 1988), which interfere with task-focused performance regulation (Carver, 1996) and learning from errors, in several ways. First, off-task, self-directed thoughts give rise to a desire to defend the ego and maintain global self-related goals, and the resultant ego-defense activities take up resources that could otherwise be used for task-relevant activities, such as learning from errors. Second, individuals tend to focus on "broad personal inadequacy" (perceived to be an uncontrollable cause) as opposed to "inadequacy pertaining to some particular domain of performance" (believed to be a controllable cause) and engage in abstract and self-evaluative information processing that distracts them from the immediate demands of the task situation (Carver, 1996; Vassilopoulos & Watkins, 2009). This type of abstract, self-focused information processing fails to provide individuals with the elaborate and situation-specific details needed to learn from a particular error. This remains true even if the true cause of errors lies at the self-level unless the individual receives intervention and help to learn that the perceived-to-be uncontrollable cause is actually controllable. For example, an individual may attribute an error to her/him being "lazy" as part of her/his character. However, if the individual receives professional help and counseling to learn to better manage her/his time and priorities, s/he may realize that the error can be fixed by doing certain things to change her/his habitual routines.

This argument is reinforced by research showing that concentrating on a flawed global self makes self-regulation of performance difficult. Individuals tend to engage in biased information processing (e.g., Lewis, 2000; Roese, 1997; Tangney, 1990) that protects a positive self-image but makes it hard to correctly locate root causes of errors. For example, hindsight bias may impede learning from errors when people believe that their error was unforeseeable or inevitable, resulting in a premature closure of the sense-making process (Pezzo & Pezzo, 2007). Self-serving biases also may discourage learning when people blame their own errors on other people or situational factors in order to avoid negative feelings and thoughts about themselves (Miller & Ross, 1975; Shimizu & Hitt, 2011; Staw, McKechnie, & Puffer, 1983).

Table 2-1. Error Perception, Focus of Attention, and Error Attribution

Error Perception	Focus of Attention (Hierarchy of Goals)	Error Attribution (Internal)
Self Failure	Self Level (superordinate goals and standards)	Uncontrollable (e.g., lack of aptitude)
Task Failure	Task Motivation Level (direction and sustention of efforts for task completion)	Controllable (e.g., lack of effort)
	Task Learning Level (execution of component task activities)	Controllable (e.g., incorrect task rules)

Learning-Related Cognition and Motivation

In this section, we first explain the association between the three components of expectancy theory and motivation to learn from errors. We then investigate how error attribution indirectly influences motivation through the three dimensions of expectancy theory.

Expectancy theory has been widely used in the learning and training literature. According to expectancy theory (Vroom, 1964), three conditions determine an individual's level of motivation: *valence* (perceived value of certain expected outcomes), *expectancy* (the probability that efforts will lead to performance), and *instrumentality* (the likelihood that performance will result in certain expected outcomes). Drawing on expectancy theory, we argue that individuals are motivated to learn if three conditions hold in error situations. First, they value their original performance goals and thus perceive *valence* in improving their performance by learning from errors; the strength of valence beliefs is positively associated with the perceived relevance of the error to achieving an important performance goal. For example, individuals will be highly motivated to learn if they believe that learning from, and fixing, an error will help them achieve both task-level and self-level goals. Second, individuals will be motivated to learn if they believe in their ability to learn from errors (*expectancy*). *Expectancy* is an individual's assessment of the likelihood that he/she will learn from errors if he/she spends time and effort reflecting on and analyzing errors. Third, individuals will be motivated to learn if they believe learning will help them improve their performance and correct the error situation (*instrumentality*). *Instrumentality* estimates the probability that the insights learned from errors, once put into practice, will help minimize or eliminate future errors and improve performance. The proposed linkages between the three elements of expectancy theory and motivation to learn are supported by motivated action theory (DeShon & Gillespie, 2005), which suggests that expectancies and valence beliefs determine which action will be motivated and selected to reduce the perceived discrepancy on a goal.

Error attribution directly influences expectancy, instrumentality, and valence beliefs, and thus motivation to learn. When individuals make specific attributions at the task motivation level and/or task learning level, their response to an error is guided by their original task goals and they will be likely to value performance improvement through learning from errors (*valence*). Also, individuals who focus on the specific action or decision that caused an error will likely view the situation as controllable. Perceived controllable causality, in turn, encourages individuals to be confident about their ability to successfully initiate and perform learning activities (high *expectancy*) and undo the harm and/or prevent error recurrence (high *instrumentality*). As a result, individuals will feel motivated to engage in learning from errors. Our argument is consistent with theories and findings from the learning and training literature, suggesting that individuals are motivated to learn from errors when they attribute their errors to specific factors that can be controlled and changed (Ellis & Davidi, 2005; Ellis et al., 2006; Ilgen & Davis, 2000; Kanfer, Ackerman, & Heggestad, 1996).

In contrast, if attention moves up to the level of the self, individuals tend to make intrinsic global attributions and focus on the global self. They believe that the whole self (as opposed to a specific feature or action of the self) is uncontrollably flawed and that the situation is out of control. Consequently, individuals prioritize ego-defense over learning from errors (low *valence* attached to learning). They doubt their ability to successfully perform learning activities (low *expectancy*) and perceive the situation to be threatening and hard to fix (low *instrumentality*). As a result, individuals feel motivated to protect the self and engage in ego-defensive coping activities (Boekaerts, 2007; Elliot & Pekrun, 2007; Ilgen & Davis, 2000; Kluger & DeNisi, 1996; Lazarus, 1991). This argument is consistent with the speculation in prior learning and training literature that individuals will not be motivated to learn if they attribute their errors to uncontrollable and unchangeable global attributes (Ilgen & Davis, 2000; Kanfer et al., 1996; Vancouver & Tischner, 2004). However, we acknowledge the possibility that this argument does not hold when self-doubt is temporary. Social cognitive theory has suggested that momentary self-doubt "provides incentives to acquire the knowledge and skills needed to master the challenges" (Bandura & Locke, 2003: 96). We agree and expect that as long as people can switch their focus of attention back to task-level goals after transient scrutiny at the self-level, they may still feel motivated to learn, especially so if their temporary self-doubt actually highlights the valence of learning through error correction (e.g., how learning and performance improvement can contribute to the achievement of a superordinate goal at the self level).

Negative Emotions and Learning-Related Cognition

The link between emotion and cognition is an established finding in the literature on emotion (e.g., Baumeister et al., 2007 Elfenbein, 2007; Schwarz & Clore, 1988). Given our focus on the impact of negative emotions on learning, we draw on research that examines how emotion influences ways in which information is attended to and processed. A good foundation for research in this area is the resource allocation theory proposed by Ellis and Ashbrook (1988, 1989) and Schwarz's (1990) affect-as-information model.

Seo and colleagues (2004) proposed a general theoretical framework that delineates how positive and negative emotions influence motivation in the workplace by affecting cognitive components, such as expectancy beliefs and valence assessment. In this paper, our focus is on learning from errors. As mentioned earlier, error attribution is a critically important cognitive activity because it directly determines whether any valuable lesson will be learned from errors. Therefore we distinguish between attribution-dependent and attribution-independent emotions and explain the influence of these two different types of negative emotions on the three components of expectancy theory. We also discuss the impact of attribution-dependent negative emotions on error attribution.

Weiner (1985) studied the role of causal attributions in generating emotions and proposed that there are attribution-dependent and attribution-independent emotions. Individuals experience outcome-dependent, attribution-independent negative emotions immediately after a negative event occurs. Attribution-independent emotions are "based on the perceived success or failure of the outcome (the 'primary appraisal')," not "the cause of the outcome" (e.g., happy for success and sadness for failure, Weiner, 1985: 560). Seeking causal attributions then generates a different set of emotions: attribution-dependent emotions that are "determined by the perceived cause of the prior outcome" (Weiner, 1985: 560). Examples of attribution-dependent emotions include two typical negative emotions following failure that one feels personally responsible for: guilt (elicited by controllable causes) and shame (based on uncontrollable causes). We expect attribution-dependent and attribution-independent emotions to affect learning-related cognition differently in that attribution-dependent emotions (with their inherent causal ascriptions) directly influence error attribution, whereas attribution-independent emotions (not related to any causal dimension) do not directly influence error attribution.

Next, we use examples of discrete emotions suggested in the error literature to illustrate the differential effects of attribution-dependent and attribution-independent emotions on learning-related cognition. We selected four example emotions—guilt, shame, sadness, and fear—as critical targets because research has consistently identified these emotions as associated with errors and failures relevant to work settings (e.g., Boss & Sims, 2008; Egloff & Krohne, 1996; Heimbeck et al., 2003; Newton et al., 2008; Rybowiak et al., 1999; Shepherd, 2003; Zhao & Olivera, 2006). Furthermore, guilt and shame have been identified as typical attribution-dependent, and fear and sadness as attribution-independent emotions experienced in response to performance setbacks (Weiner, 1985). We acknowledge that "the precise number and identity of discrete emotions are subjects of much debate" in the relatively new literature on discrete emotions (Barsade & Gibson, 2007: 37). Similarly, the proper number and identity of specific negative emotions that should be included in a model of learning from errors presents a source of contention. What follows is our attempt to integrate relevant literature into an informative and useful perspective on the impact of specific emotions on learning from errors, rather than to offer a comprehensive discussion of all potentially relevant emotions.

Attribution-dependent emotions: Guilt and shame. Guilt and shame are two, high arousal, attribution-dependent (related to the causal dimension of controllability), negative emotions typically experienced in error situations (Lewis, 2000; Tangney & Tracy, 2012; Weiner, 1985; Zhao & Olivera, 2006). Guilt is experienced when individuals blame themselves for the specific behavior or decision that caused an error (Lewis, 2000; Tangney et al., 1992; Weiner, 2007). Individuals who feel guilty often report a strong desire to take reparative action and prevent similar negative events from happening again (Baumeister et al., 2007; Lewis, 2000; Tangney et al., 1996). These individuals are highly motivated to learn self-critical lessons so as to prevent the error and its negative consequences from recurring. Therefore, we theorize that guilt increases motivation to learn by enhancing the perceived value of learning and performance improvement (*valence*). Moreover, guilty individuals tend to focus on the specific action or decision that caused the error, which indicates *error attribution* at the task motivation or task learning level. At this level, individuals tend to believe that the situation is controllable. Similarly, Weiner (2007) associates guilt with controllable causality. Individuals who perceive controllable causality are more confident about their ability to work on the root causes of errors and learn (*expectancy*) and to undo the harm done and/or prevent error recurrence (*instrumentality*).

Alternatively, guilt potentially leads to the protect motive "when opportunities for reparation are blocked" or when individuals develop "an exaggerated or distorted sense of responsibility for events beyond their control" (Tangney & Dearing, 2002; Tangney & Tracy, 2012). Individuals tend to engage in emotion-focused coping in these situations because they suffer from chronic self-denial and self-doubt (Nelissen & Zeelenberg, 2009), which indicates error attribution at the self level and low estimates of *expectancy* and *instrumentality*.

Individuals experience shame when they make internal global attributions about errors, believing that the errors reflect negatively on the global self (Lewis, 2000; Tangney et al., 1992; Weiner, 2007). Research by De Hooge and colleagues (e.g., De Hooge, Breugelmans, & Zeelenberg, 2008; De Hooge, Zeelenberg, & Breugelmans, 2007; De Hooge, Zeelenberg, & Breugelmans, 2010b) distinguishes between "chronic or trait-related shame" and "discrete experiences of shame." "Chronic or trait-related shame" implies "a chronically threatened self" that is very difficult, if not impossible, to restore. It is very difficult to alleviate chronic shame because it involves a relatively stable negative evaluation of the global self, as opposed to a specific feature or action of the self (Lewis, 2000; Roese, 1997; Tangney et al., 1996; Tangney et al., 1992). Chronic shame suggests that *error attribution* is occurring at the self level. Individuals who make internal and global attributions tend to engage in task-irrelevant, self-preoccupied cognitions (Abramson et al., 1978; Mikulincer & Nizan, 1988). Consequently, these individuals tend to adopt maladaptive responses to shame, such as hiding or escaping from the situation (Lazarus, 1991; Lewis, 2000; Tangney et al., 1996; Tangney et al., 1992), or making biased, mistaken external attributions in order to redirect blame (Newton et al., 2008; Tangney, 1990; Tangney et al., 1992). We thus expect that chronic or trait-related shame impairs motivation to learn by prioritizing emotion-focused, ego-defensive coping activities over problem-focused learning activities (low *valence* attached to learning). Moreover, concentrating on the global self leads individuals to view the situation as out of control because they believe they are "uncontrollably flawed" as a whole person (Weiner, 2007: 81). As a result, individuals doubt their ability to learn from errors (low *expectancy*) and perceive the situation to be threatening and hard to fix (low *instrumentality*).

We anticipate that discrete experiences of shame may function in the same way as chronic or trait-related shame when individuals believe it is impossible or too risky to restore the self. However, discrete experiences of shame may positively influence learning-related cognition when individuals are able to refocus from the global self level to the task level(s), and concentrate on task-related, situation-specific details. That is, discrete experiences of shame can lead to error attribution at the task-level(s) and thus high estimates of expectancy, instrumentality, and valence when shame is a short-lived emotional state associated with a temporary focus on the global self. Our theory is consistent with the core argument of De Hooge and colleagues (e.g., De Hooge et al., 2008; De Hooge et al., 2007; De Hooge et al., 2010b) that shame reflects a central concern with a threatened self and, thus, when individuals believe they have the ability or opportunity to restore a positive self-image, they will prioritize problem-focused coping over emotion-focused coping.

Attribution-independent emotion: Fear. Prior studies have found that individuals who experience errors often fear punishment, job loss, or damaged reputation (e.g., Bosk, 1979; Edmondson, 1996; Paget, 1988; Sexton, Thomas, & Helmreich, 2000; Uribe, Schweikhart, Pathak, & Marsh, 2002). As an attribution-independent emotion that is unrelated to any dimension of causality, fear does not directly influence *error attribution*. Therefore, our discussion of fear revolves around the impact of this emotion on the three elements of expectancy theory: *expectancy, instrumentality, and valence*.

Fearful people tend to be dominated by a desire to reduce the possibility of harm and to avoid or escape a dangerous situation (Lazarus, 1991; Roseman et al., 1994). As a high arousal, attribution-independent emotion, fear is associated with both adaptive and maladaptive responses (Lazarus, 1991). We theorize that fear may either increase or decrease motivation to learn, depending on its intensity, consistent with the view that intensity is one determinant of the functionality of emotions (Parrott, 2002). Specifically, we theorize that the relationship between the intensity of fear and motivation to learn is best represented by an inverted U-shape where the top of the curve is the optimal level of fear to motivate learning. As the level of fear increases and approaches the top of the curve, fear promotes motivation to learn. When fear becomes too intense, it impairs motivation to learn.

At low levels of intensity, fear is unlikely to be disruptive and does not require immediate regulation. Rather, individuals may simply note that there is a possibility of making the same error and experiencing the same fear in the future. These individuals are likely to be motivated by the long-term benefits of learning and improving (*valence*): eliminating the source of fear by not repeating the errors. Findings from an experimental study by

Ellis and colleagues (2006) suggest that individuals are able to learn from errors in spite of fear, if they know that "the next trial is going to take place soon." They are motivated to learn by the perceived value in immediately improving their performance. Furthermore, when fear is not very intense, competition for limited attentional resources is low because individuals perceive little need to engage in emotion-focused coping. Consequently, it is likely that individuals will believe that they have enough resources to handle the situation and learn from the error (*expectancy*), and that they will be able to fix the problem and improve the situation (*instrumentality*). Increasing fear motivates individuals to learn by increasing the severity of the "warning;" it reminds individuals of the need to learn and prompts them to eliminate the threat by seeking out the root causes of errors and avoiding error recurrence. At the optimal level of intensity, fear is a potent warning signal but is not disruptive enough to stimulate emotion-focused coping.

However, once the level of fear rises above the optimal point of intensity, individuals are likely to feel a strong need for immediate mood repair. In such situations, it is more salient to undertake ego-defense activities than long-term performance improvement (i.e., low *valence* attached to learning). At this point, individuals may, consciously or unconsciously, prioritize emotion-focused coping. In order to alleviate the distressing emotion of fear, they may engage in task-irrelevant coping activities such as justifying errors, covering-up errors, or avoiding the task altogether (e.g., Baumeister et al., 2007; Boekaerts, 2007; Ilgen & Davis, 2000) in order to physically or mentally "escape" the error situation. Such emotion-focused coping demands most, if not all, of an individual's cognitive capacity, and "...the resulting depletion of regulatory resources would leave them unable to regulate their behavior in other ways that would be more beneficial and constructive in the long run" (Tice, Bratslavsky, & Baumeister, 2001: 55). In other words, individuals may be overwhelmed with the pressing need to improve their affective states and dedicate their attention to emotion-focused coping activities. They will perceive that they lack the necessary cognitive resources for learning and doubt that they can successfully engage in full-scale, in-depth reflection and analysis of errors (low *expectancy*). They will not be optimistic about the likelihood of improving their performance (low *instrumentality*). Supporting our theory, Rich and Woolever (1988) found that people who are fearful of taking a test suffer from poor performance when their expectancies are unfavorable, whereas people whose expectancies are manipulated to be favorable are able to improve their performance. Similar findings can be found in research on *state test anxiety* in prior work on student achievement in the classroom (e.g., Elliot & McGregor, 1999).

Note that our theory of the impact of fear is different from the Yerkes–Dodson law of cognitive psychology (Y-D law, Yerkes & Dodson, 1908; Easterbrook, 1959) in at least three important ways. First, our theory elaborates on the linkage between the intensity of fear and motivation to learn, whereas the Y-D law theorizes the linkage between the arousal of emotions (negative as well as positive) and cognitive performance. The basic tenet of the Y-D law proposes an inverted-U impact of arousal on cognitive performance: increasing arousal narrows attention and decreases the amount of task-relevant information that can be processed by the cognitive system. The Y-D law can be used to explain the direct linkage between fear and learning from errors, but not the association between fear and motivation to learn.

Second, while the Y-D law focuses on the *arousal* dimension of emotion, our theory is based on the dimension of *intensity*. Arousal refers to activation, drive, mobilization, or energy (e.g., Yerkes & Dodson, 1908; Baas et al., 2008), a physiological state mobilized by emotions. Intensity is defined as the extent to which individuals experience emotions (Catino & Patriotta, 2013; Lazarus, 1991), and the intensity of emotions is determined by the perceived magnitude and significance (implications for goal pursuit and well-being) of the performance-goal discrepancies (Higgins, 1987, 1999; Lazarus, 1991).

Third, our theory builds on the literature on fear as a discrete emotion and describes the complex dynamics involved in the role of fear on learning from errors. Although the Y-D law has been extensively used to explain the effects of arousal on cognitive performance, researchers have called for further work on the multi-dimensional aspects of the Y-D law (e.g., Hancock & Ganey, 2003; Hanoch & Vitouch, 2004; Reinecke & Trepte, 2008). In particular, the general uni-dimensional conceptualization of arousal has been criticized for being simplistic and failing to distinguish the arousal associated with each discrete emotion (e.g., Hanoch & Vitouch, 2004; Lazarus, 1991; Reinecke & Trepte, 2008; Thayer, 1989). The specificity of emotions is an important dimension to consider in conceptualizing arousal, because each specific emotion "involves a specific attitude, conflict, and perhaps a specific pattern of physiological change" (Lazarus, 1991: 76; similar observation and empirical evidence has been reported in Ekman, Levenson, & Friesen, 1983; Levenson, Ekman, & Friesen, 1990).

Attribution-dependent and attribution-independent emotion: Sadness. The error literature also suggests that sadness impacts learning from errors (Boss & Sims, 2008; Newton et al., 2008; Shepherd, 2003; Zhao, 2011). Individuals experience sadness when they feel displeased about an undesirable event, such as failure to achieve an important goal (e.g., Izard, 1991; Lazarus, 1991; Ortony, Clore, & Collins, 1988). Although most prior work has categorized sadness, like fear, as an outcome-dependent and attribution-independent emotion, we examine the influence of sadness in this separate section for two reasons. First, the literature on emotions theorizes fear as an emotion of high arousal and sadness as an emotion of low arousal (e.g., Russell, Weiss, & Mendelsohn, 1989; Weiner, 1985). Therefore, unlike fear, sadness has been associated with the absence of a clear action tendency (e.g., Lazarus, 1991).

Second, a close examination of prior work reveals two different conceptualizations of sadness. The first view conceptualizes sadness as an attribution-dependent emotion, an emotional experience that is based on individuals' attributions of misfortunes to impersonal circumstances beyond anyone's control (Keltner, Ellsworth, & Edwards, 1993). The second view simply defines sadness as an outcome-dependent, attribution-independent feeling that arises from loss and helplessness (e.g., Izard, 1991), without specifying the perceived controllability of the causality of misfortunes. This difference is evident in Izard's statement that "if the sadness is due to some disappointment or failure that could have been prevented, sadness could motivate you to solve the problem" (Izard, 1991: 191).

Not surprisingly, the literature also contains two conflicting views about the role of sadness in motivation. Some research describes sadness as a passive emotion that does not motivate restorative actions (e.g., Ellsworth & Smith, 1988; Lazarus, 1991; Smith & Kirby, 2001; Smith & Lazarus, 1990). Other work presents sadness as a constructive emotion that motivates individuals to solve problems and learn from errors (e.g., Baumeister et al., 2007; Izard, 1991; Johnson-Laird & Oatley, 2000).

Considering these two perspectives, we propose that sadness may either enhance or impair motivation to learn, depending on the *error attribution* that individuals make in a particular error situation. When an individual attributes errors to situational factors beyond his/her control, sadness decreases motivation to learn. The individual is likely to withdraw from the distressing situation in the belief that nothing can be done to prevent error recurrence because errors will occur anyway, no matter what (low *expectancy* and *instrumentality*). He/she will focus on mood repair and prioritize task-irrelevant, emotion-focused coping (low *valence* attached to learning). Thus, individuals will not be motivated to examine and learn from the errors they believe are caused by uncontrollable contextual factors. Supporting our argument, research suggests that sadness based on perceptions of a "hopeless" situation is associated with withdrawal behavior that interferes with learning from errors (Izard, 1977; Shepherd, 2003; Smith & Kirby, 2001; Smith & Lazarus, 1990). Moreover, the intensity of sadness likely increases as the perception of uncontrollability intensifies (Pekrun et al., 2007). This argument explains why intense sadness, such as depression and grief, interferes with learning from errors (Boss & Sims, 2008; Newton et al., 2008; Shepherd, 2003).

Sadness promotes motivation to learn when individuals believe that errors could have been avoided. Perceived controllability of causation indicates that the individual is highly likely to evaluate the error situation as manageable and controllable, to believe he/she has enough resources to work on the "controllable" causes and learn from errors (*expectancy*), and ultimately fix the situation (*instrumentality*). Perceived controllability of causation also motivates the individual to engage in learning from errors upon recognizing the value of learning and the benefits of long-term performance improvement; namely, avoiding recurrence of the error and its negative consequences (*valence*). For example, researchers have suggested that sadness activates functional counterfactual thinking, which helps individuals learn from negative events so as to avoid repeating the misfortune in the future (e.g., Baumeister et al., 2007; Johnson-Laird & Oatley, 2000).

Emotion- and Problem-Focused Coping

It is worth noting that problem- and emotion-focused coping "are seldom, if ever, separated. Both are essential parts of the total coping effort, and ideally, each facilitates the other … coping functions and strategies should never be thought of in either-or terms, but as a complex of interconnected thoughts and actions aimed at improving the troubled relationship with the environment." (Lazarus, 1999: 124). In other words, emotion-focused and problem-focused coping are not mutually exclusive, although at any given point one or the other is likely to dominate. Either coping approach may serve more than one function. For example, when individuals adopt problem-focused coping, they first engage in unpleasant self-conscious error reflection, which does not mean that they do not care about improving their emotional states; rather, they recognize that learning from errors promises relief from negative feelings further down the road (Baumeister et al., 2007; Roese, 1997). Empirical evidence suggests that individuals who pursue a learning-oriented coping approach experience fewer negative emotions and adjust better than those who engage in emotion-focused coping (e.g., Op't Eynde et al., 2007; Segerstrom, Stanton, Alden, & Shortridge, 2003).

If individuals engage in emotion-focused coping activities, they may not be able to learn from errors for two reasons. First, they lack the cognitive resources needed for learning because emotion-focused coping demands most, if not all, of an individual's cognitive capacity. According to resource allocation theory (Ellis & Ashbrook, 1988, 1989), cognitive resources are limited and scarce, and negative emotions interfere with learning by withdrawing the cognitive effort needed for reflecting on and analyzing errors (Ilgen & Davis, 2000; Kanfer & Ackerman, 1989; Kluger & DeNisi, 1996; Kuhl, 1984).

Second, in addition to competing for limited cognitive resources, emotion-focused coping introduces biases into cognitive processing and error attribution, which inhibits systematic, in-depth processing of error-related information for learning. Ego-defensive coping activities often involve off-task cognitions or activities that help individuals accept the error and improve how they feel about the situation. For example, individuals who engage in emotion-focused coping may attribute errors to situational factors (e.g., task too difficult, unreasonable schedule, unsupportive coworkers, unfriendly customers), or to forgivable circumstances ("I was feeling sick," "I was too tired"). This type of external attribution may immediately alleviate self-conscious negative feelings, but inhibit learning from errors if it is misattribution that leads to illusionary conclusions about causality. In situations where off-task cognitions or activities are not involved, ego-defensive emotion coping may impair learning through selective information processing: Individuals may simply choose to block out or ignore all the information relevant to errors (Dweck, Mangels, & Good, 2004).

However, emotion-focused coping may facilitate learning for those who are able to effectively resolve their internal turmoil (e.g., Bell & Kozlowski, 2008; Carver & Scheier, 1990; Keith & Frese, 2005; Roese, 1997; Snell, 1988). In other words, individuals who engage in emotion-focused coping may still be able to learn from errors if they can switch back to task-focused thinking once they have recovered from the negative emotions, especially if emotion-focused coping does not involve biased information processing. However, failed emotion-focused coping results in the greatest cognitive interference---ruminative thoughts about errors and failures, which undermine learning and often leads to depression (Carver, 1996; Tangney & Tracy, 2012). Supporting our argument, prior research has suggested that if individuals are good at regulating emotions, they tend to be efficient and effective at reducing or eliminating negative self-focused thoughts and are capable of redirecting attention away from defending their ego to improving their performance (Boekaerts, 2007; Vancouver & Tischner, 2004). Consequently, their learning activities are less likely to be impaired by negative emotions than those of individuals who are not so adept at emotion control. Similarly, some have argued that negative emotions trigger different types of counterfactual or retrospective thinking (e.g., Lischetzke & Eid, 2003; Mor & Winquist, 2002; Roese, 1997). People who are good at emotion regulation tend to *reflect*, whereas people who cannot recognize and manage emotions well tend to *ruminate*. Ruminative responses are characterized by recurring, past-oriented, negative thoughts about the self; *ruminators* find it difficult to switch their attention from negative self-aspects to positive ones. On the other hand, reflective thoughts are a functional, problem-solving-oriented form of private self-consciousness; *reflectors* are adept at recovering from negative experience and directing attention back to work (Bower, 1992; Lischetzke & Eid, 2003; Roese, 1997). In sum, rumination interferes with, whereas reflection aids, cognitive information processing that helps people learn from, and adapt to, negative events such as errors.

Discussion

This paper addresses the topic of when and why individuals learn — or do not learn — from the errors they make at work. When individuals face an opportunity to learn from their own errors, they confront a crucial tension between the desire for accurate information about an error's causes and the desire to defend the ego. How these competing pressures are resolved will determine an individual's level of learning and ability to adapt to the work environment (Weick & Ashford, 2001). We have presented a theory about the role of negative emotions in learning from errors to help explain the conditions under which the tension is resolved in favor of learning. We proposed both inhibiting and stimulating roles of negative emotions by focusing on the mechanisms through which negative emotions affect both motivation to learn and learning-related cognition. Next, we will discuss some remaining issues before we move on to directions for future research.

Dimensions of Emotion

Our theory has addressed two dimensions of emotions: *intensity* and *specificity* which, along with the valence dimension (positive or negative), have been suggested to be meaningfully related to learning from errors (e.g., Catino & Patriotta, 2013; Zhao, 2011). Other dimensions of emotion, regulatory focus (promotion- or prevention-focused) and arousal, are not part of our core argument for the following reasons. By definition, negative emotions related to a promotion-focus arise from unsuccessful attainment of desired results, whereas those with a prevention-focus are associated with unsuccessful avoidance of undesired end states (e.g., Baas et al., 2008). In error situations, regulatory focus is not a distinguishing dimension for negative emotions elicited by errors because errors include both "unsuccessful attainment of desired results" and "unsuccessful avoidance of undesired end states" (and therefore an error-related negative emotion can be framed as promotion- as well as prevention-focused).

We did not theorize about the arousal dimension because we believe it is premature to develop propositions about the effects of this dimension on learning from errors. Although the Y-D law has been extensively used to explain the effects of arousal on cognitive performance, researchers have called for further work on the multi-dimensional aspects of the Y-D law (e.g., Hancock & Ganey, 2003; Hanoch & Vitouch, 2004; Reinecke & Trepte, 2008). In particular, the general uni-dimensional conceptualization of arousal has been criticized for being simplistic and failing to distinguish (a) between the arousal of negative and positive emotions; and (b) the arousal associated with each discrete emotion (e.g., Hanoch & Vitouch, 2004; Lazarus, 1991; Reinecke & Trepte, 2008; Thayer, 1989). The specificity of emotions is an important dimension to consider in conceptualizing arousal because each specific emotion "involves a specific attitude, conflict, and perhaps a specific pattern of physiological change" (Lazarus, 1991: 76; similar observation and empirical evidence has been reported in Ekman, Levenson, & Friesen, 1983; Levenson, Ekman, & Friesen, 1990). For example, the literature on emotions theorizes fear as an emotion of high arousal and sadness as an emotion of low arousal (e.g., Baumeister et al., 2007; Russell, Weiss, & Mendelsohn, 1989). Instead of arguing that fear always interferes with learning and sadness always stimulates learning, our paper has described the more complex dynamics involved in the role of these two specific negative emotions on learning from errors. We have argued that fear and sadness can be either functional or dysfunctional for learning purposes.In the following section we discuss future research directions for learning from errors, concentrating on factors of *contextual* and individual *difference*.

Future Directions

We have conceptualized learning from errors as an effortful activity that is often laden with emotions (e.g., Boss & Sims, 2008; Newton et al., 2008; Shepherd, 2003; Snell, 1988). A variety of situational and individual factors may explain when and why learning from errors occurs (or does not occur).

One contextual factor with prior associations with learning from errors is psychological safety. Edmondson (1999) found that individuals in environments high in psychological safety may be better able to take advantage of the learning opportunities that errors provide. We speculate that psychological safety helps promote learning from errors by alleviating negative emotions and reducing the perceived need for emotion-focused coping. Individuals who perceive errors as challenges (as opposed to threats) and prioritize problem-focused coping will engage in learning. Furthermore, psychological safety alleviates image concerns and dampens perceptions of errors as threats, which, in turn, reduces the intensity of fear associated with errors. We argue that psychological safety, as a perceptual appraisal of the work environment, serves as a *cognitive reappraisal* that encourages framing an error situation as a challenge, instead of a threat to the self. Cognitive coping (a form of emotion-focused coping) can influence emotions through situation reappraisal (Elfenbein, 2007; Jordan, Ashkanasy, & Härtel, 2002; Lazarus, 1991); we change the way we feel about a negative situation by constructing a different relational meaning of the situation without changing the actual person-environment relationship (Lazarus, 1991). Therefore, situation reappraisal can influence both emotion elicitation and regulation by changing our attentional focus and our perception of the immediate demands of the situation (Elfenbein, 2007; Lewis, 2000).

Another important area for research is the role that individual differences play in the process of learning from errors. For instance, there is evidence that people differ in their ability to handle negative emotions (e.g., Gross & John, 2003). Individuals who can contain their negative emotions well may engage in the learning process without much interference from negative emotions (Boekaerts, 2007; Herold, Davis, Fedor, & Parsons, 2002; LePine et al., 2004; Linnenbrink, 2007; Lopes et al., 2005; Roese, 1997). Emotionally stable individuals are less prone to respond to an error with counterproductive coping activities because they are less likely to interpret the situation as threatening and thus less likely to suffer from distressing negative emotions (e.g., Martinko & Zellars, 1998; Matthews & Deary, 1998; Roese, 1997). These people may also be so adept at managing negative emotions that their emotion regulation activities do not put the same demand on attentional resources as those with poor emotion regulation abilities. As a result, individuals who are skilled at emotion control are more adept at directing cognitive resources back to task-learning activities. For example, research has suggested that, compared with people who are less able to regulate emotions, people who are good at emotion regulation are better able to learn from errors because they are better at inhibiting dysfunctional counterfactual thinking (e.g., unhealthy ruminations) and are thus less likely to suffer from long-term emotional dysfunctions, such as depression or stress disorder (e.g., Op't Eynde et al., 2007; Roese, 1997; Vancouver & Tischner, 2004).

Individual difference factors, such as self-efficacy and goal orientations, are also worth research attention. Prior work has suggested that self-efficacy (e.g., Ilgen & Davids, 2000; Kluger & DeNisi, 1996) and goal orientations (e.g., DeShon & Gillespie, 2005; Dweck et al., 2004; Elliot & Church, 1997; Nussbaum & Dweck, 2008) affect learning from errors. The theory proposed in this paper helps further research in this area by elaborating on the underlying mechanisms of the impact of these two individual difference factors on learning from errors. People with high self-efficacy or learning goal-orientation tend to believe in their own ability to fix the problem and learn. Therefore, we expect that self-efficacy and learning goal-orientation enhance motivation to learn by maintaining high *expectancy* and *instrumentality* beliefs in error situations. Moreover, self-efficacy and learning goal-orientation may also promote learning from errors by shifting focus away from the self. People with high self-efficacy or learning goal-orientation have been found to continue to value the original high performance standard when facing errors (high *valence*). They are predisposed to appraise an error situation as a challenging learning opportunity, rather than a threat to the self (e.g., Boekaerts, 2007; DeShon & Gillespie, 2005; Dweck et al., 2004; Ilgen & Davids, 2000; Nussbaum & Dweck, 2008). They are less likely to be obsessed with negative thoughts about the self and thus more adept at switching attention from the self back to the task (e.g., Dweck et al., 2004; Kanfer et al., 1996; Kluger & DeNisi, 1996; Linnenbrink, 2007; Turner & Waugh, 2007). It would be worthwhile to examine the joint effects of self-efficacy and learning goal-orientation in future research, because these two personality traits have been theorized to play similar roles in challenging learning situations (e.g., Boekaerts, 2007; Ilgen & Davids, 2000; Linnenbrink, 2007).

Conclusion

Errors can be distressing or valuable, depending on whether or not we learn from them. Managers and trainers who understand the variations and consequences of individual responses can help turn errors into positive events. We argue that negative emotions can play either functional or dysfunctional roles when individuals struggle to resolve error-related, internal tensions between problem-solving and ego-defense.

Research on learning from errors has important theoretical and practical implications. From a theoretical perspective, we know little about how individuals, groups, and organizations learn from negative events such as errors and failures. In practical terms, organizations stand to benefit from new knowledge about how individuals respond to and learn from errors, inasmuch as this knowledge can contribute to managing and preventing errors and improving productivity. For the purpose of employee development and training, understanding the role of negative emotions in learning from errors may serve to remind managers and trainers that negative emotions are not always a bad thing. More importantly, organizations can help employees learn from errors by: (a) providing a safe, learning-oriented environment, (b) responding to errors with direct and task-specific feedback that discourages individuals from taking errors personally, and (c) offering assistance so that individuals' expectancy and instrumentality beliefs will not be impaired, which, in turn, helps enhance motivation to learn.

References

Abramson, L. Y., Seligman, M. E. P., & Teasdale, J. (1978). Learned helplessness in humans: Critique and reformulation. *Journal of Abnormal Psychology, 87*, 49–74.

Anderson, C. J. (2003). The psychology of doing nothing: Forms of decision avoidance result from reason and emotion. *Psychological Bulletin, 129*, 139–167.

Argote, L. (1999). *Organizational learning: Creating, retaining and transferring knowledge*. Boston: Kluwer Academic Publishers.

Argyris, C., & Schön, D. A. (1978). *Organizational Learning: A theory of action perspective*. Reading, MA: Addison-Wesley.

Argyris, C., & Schön, D. A. (1996). *Organizational Learning II: Theory, method, and practice*. Reading, MA: Addison-Wesley.

Baas, M., De Dreu, C. K. W., & Nijstad, B. A. (2008). A meta-analysis of 25 years of mood-creativity research: Hedonic tone, activation, or regulatory focus? *Psychological Bulletin*, 134, 779-806.

Bandura, A., & Locke, E. A. (2003). Negative self-efficacy and goal effects revisited. *Journal of Applied Psychology*, 88(1), 87-99.

Barsade, S. G., & Gibson, D. E. (2007). Why does affect matter in organizations? *Academy of Management Perspectives*, 21, 36–59.

Baumeister, R. F., Vohs, K. D., DeWall, C. N., & Zhang, L. (2007). How emotion shapes behavior: Feedback, anticipation, and reflection, rather than direct causation. *Personality and Social Psychology Review*, 11, 167–203.

Bell, B. S., & Kozlowski, S. W. J. (2008). Active learning: Effects of core training design elements on self-regulatory processes, learning, and adaptability. *Journal of Applied Psychology*, 93, 296–316.

Boekaerts, M. (2007). Understanding students' affective processes in the classroom. In P. A. Schutz & R. Pekrun (Eds.), *Emotion in education* (pp. 37–56). Boston, MA: Academic Press.

Bosk, C. L. (1979). *Forgive and remember: Managing medical failure.* Chicago, IL: University of Chicago Press.

Boss, A. D., & Sims, H. P., Jr. (2008). Everyone fails! Using emotion regulation and self-leadership for recovery. *Journal of Managerial Psychology*, 23, 135–150.

Bower, G. H. (1992). How might emotions affect learning? In S. A. Christianson (Ed.), *The handbook of emotion and memory: Research and theory* (pp. 3–32). Hillsdale, NJ: Lawrence Erlbaum.

Briner, R. B., & Kiefer, T. (2005). Psychological research into the experience of emotion at work: Definitely older, but are we any wiser? In N. M. Ashkanasy, C. E. J. Härtel, & W. J. Zerbe (Eds.), *The effect of affect in organizational settings* (Vol. 1, pp. 289–315). Oxford, UK: Elsevier.

Brown, S. P., Westbrook, R. A., & Challagalla, G. (2005). Good cope, bad cope: Adaptive and maladaptive coping strategies following a critical negative work event. *Journal of Applied Psychology*, 90, 792–798.

Carver, C. S. (1996). Cognitive interference and the structure of behaviour. In G. Sarason, G. R. Pierce, & B. R. Sarason (Eds.), *Cognitive interference: Theories, methods, and findings* (pp. 25–45). Mahwah, NJ: Erlbaum.

Carver, C. S., & Scheier, M. F. (1990). Origins and functions of positive and negative affect: A control–process view. *Psychological Review*, 97, 19–35.

Carver, C. S., & Scheier, M. F. (1998). *On the self-regulation of behavior.* New York, NY: Cambridge University Press.

Catino, M., & Patriotta, G. (2013). Learning from errors: Cognition, emotions and safety culture at the Italian Air Force, *Organization Studies*, 34(4), 437-467.

Colquitt, J. A., LePine, J. A., & Noe, R. A. (2000). Toward an integrative theory of training motivation: A meta-analytic path analysis of 20 years of research. *Journal of Applied Psychology*, *85*, 678–707.

Colquitt, J. A., & Simmering, M. J. (1998). Conscientiousness, goal orientation, and motivation to learn during the learning process: A longitudinal study. *Journal of Applied Psychology*, *83*, 654–665.

De Hooge, I. E., Breugelmans, S. M., & Zeelenberg, M. (2008). Not so ugly after all: When shame acts as a commitment device. *Journal of Personality & Social Psychology*, *95*, 933–943.

De Hooge, I. E., Zeelenberg, M., & Breugelmans, S. M. (2007). Moral sentiments and cooperation: Differential influences of shame and guilt. *Cognition and Emotion*, *21*, 1025–1042.

De Hooge, I. E., Zeelenberg, M., & Breugelmans, S. M. (2010a). Self-conscious emotions and social functioning. In I. Nyklicek, A. J. J. M. Vingerhoets, & M. Zeelenberg (Eds.), *Emotion regulation: Conceptual and clinical issues* (pp. 197–210). New York, NY: Springer, 197–210.

De Hooge, I. E., Zeelenberg, M., & Breugelmans, S. M. (2010b). Restore and protect motivations following shame. *Cognition and Emotion*, *24*, 111–127.

DeShon, R. P., & Gillespie, J. Z. (2005). A motivated action theory account of goal orientation. *Journal of Applied Psychology*, *90*, 1096–1127.

Dweck, C. S., Mangels, J., & Good, C. (2004). Motivational effects on attention, cognition, and performance. In D.Y. Dai & R. J. Sternberg (Eds.), *Motivation, emotion, and cognition: Integrated perspectives on intellectual functioning* (pp. 41–55). Mahwah, NJ: Erlbaum.

Dweck, C. S., & Leggett, E. L. (1988). A social-cognitive approach to motivation and personality. *Psychological Review*, *95*, 256–273.

Edmondson, A. C. (1996). Learning from mistakes is easier said than done: Group and organizational influences on the detection and correction of human error. *Journal of Applied Behavioral Science*, *32*, 5–32.

—. (1999). Psychological safety and learning behavior in work teams. *Administrative Science Quarterly*, *44*, 350–383.

Egloff, B., & Krohne, H. W. (1996). Repressive emotional discreteness after failure. *Journal of Personality & Social Psychology, 70*, 1318–1326.

Ekman, P., Levenson, R. W., & Friesen, W. V. (1983). Autonomic nervous system activity distinguishes among emotions. *Science, 221*, 1208-1210.

Elfenbein, H. A. (2007). Emotion in organizations: A review and theoretical integration. *The Academy of Management Annals, 1*, 315–386.

Elliot, A. J., & Church, M. A. (1997). A hierarchical model of approach and avoidance achievement motivation. *Journal of Personality & Social Psychology, 72*, 218–232.

Elliot, A. J., & McGregor, H. A. (1999). Test anxiety and the hierarchical model of approach and avoidance achievement motivation. *Journal of Personality & Social Psychology, 76*, 628–644.

Elliot, A. J., & Pekrun, R. (2007). Emotion in the hierarchical model of approach–avoidance achievement motivation. In P. A. Schutz & R. Pekrun (Eds.), *Emotion in education* (pp. 57–73). Boston, MA: Academic Press.

Ellis, H. C., & Ashbrook, P. W. (1998). Resource allocation model of the effects of depressed mood states on memory. In K. Fiedler & J. Forgas (Eds.), *Affect, cognition and social behavior* (pp. 3–32). Toronto, CA: Hogrefe.

Ellis, H. C., & Ashbrook, P. W. (1999). The "state" of mood and memory research: A selective review. *Journal of Social Behavior and Personality, 4*(2), 1–21.

Ellis, S., & Davidi, I. (2005). After-event reviews: Drawing lessons from successful and failed experience. *Journal of Applied Psychology, 90*, 857–871.

Ellis, S., Mendel, R., & Nir, M. (2006). Learning from successful and failed experience: The moderating role of kind of after-event review. *Journal of Applied Psychology, 91*, 669–680.

Ellsworth, P. C., & Smith, C. (1988). From appraisal to emotion: Differences among unpleasant feelings. *Motivation and Emotion, 12*, 271–302.

Forgas, J. P. (1995). Mood and judgment: The affect infusion model (AIM). *Psychological Bulletin, 117*, 39–66.

—. (2003). Affective influences on attitudes and judgments. In R. Davidson, K. Scherer, & H. Goldsmith (Eds.), *Handbook of affective sciences* (pp. 596–618). New York: Oxford University Press.

Frijda, N. H. (1986). *The emotions.* Cambridge, UK: Cambridge University Press.

George, J. M. (2000). Emotions and leadership: The role of emotional intelligence. *Human Relations, 53,* 1027–1055.

Gross, J. J. (1998). The emerging field of emotion regulation: An integrative review. *Review of General Psychology, 2,* 271–299.

Gross, J. J., & John, O. P. (2003). Individual differences in two emotion regulation processes: Implications for affect, relationships, and well-being. *Journal of Personality & Social Psychology, 85,* 348–362.

Hancock, P. A., & Ganey, H. C. N. (2003). From the inverted-U to the extended-U: The evolution of a law of psychology. *Human Performance in Extreme Environments, 7,* 5-14.

Hanoch, Y., & Vitouch, O. (2004). When less is more: Information, emotional arousal and the ecological reframing of the Yerkes-Dodson Law. *Theory and Psychology, 14,* 427- 452.

Heimbeck, D., Frese, M., Sonnentag, S., & Keith, N. (2003). Integrating errors into the training process: The function of error management instructions and the role of goal orientation. *Personnel Psychology, 56*(2), 333–361.

Herold, D. M., Davis, W., Fedor, D. B., & Parsons, C. K. (2002). Dispositional influences on transfer of learning in multistage training programs. *Personnel Psychology, 55,* 851–869.

Hofmann, D. A., & Frese, M. (2011). Errors, error taxonomies, error prevention, and error management: Laying the groundwork for discussing errors in organizations. In D. A. Hofmann & M. Frese (Eds.), *Errors in organizations* (pp. 1–43). New York, NY: Routledge.

Ilgen, D. R., & Davis, C. A. (2000). Bearing bad news: Reactions to negative performance feedback. *Applied Psychology: An International Review, 49,* 550–565.

Izard, C. E. (1977). *Human emotions.* New York, NY: Plenum Press.

—. (1991). *The psychology of emotions.* New York, NY: Plenum Press.

Johnson-Laird, P. N., & Oatley, K. (2000). The cognitive and social construction of emotions. In M. Lewis & J. M. Haviland-Jones (Eds.), *Handbook of emotions* (2nd ed., pp. 458–475). New York, NY: Guilford Press.

Jordan, P. J., Ashkanasy, N. M., & Härtel, C. E. J. (2002). Emotional intelligence as a moderator of emotional and behavioral reactions to job insecurity. *Academy of Management Review, 27,* 361–372.

Kanfer, R., & Ackerman, P. L. (1989). Motivation and cognitive abilities: An integrative/aptitude-treatment interaction approach to skill acquisition. *Journal of Applied Psychology, 74,* 657–690.

Kanfer, R., Ackerman, P. L., & Heggestad, E. D. (1996). Motivational skills and self-regulation for learning: A trait perspective. *Learning and Individual Differences, 8*, 185–209.

Keith, N. (2011). Learning through errors in training. In D. A. Hofmann & M. Frese (Eds.), *Errors in organizations* (pp. 45–65). New York, NY: Routledge.

Keith, N., & Frese, M. (2005). Self-regulation in error management training: Emotion control and metacognition as mediators of performance effects. *Journal of Applied Psychology, 90*, 677–691.

Keith, N., & Frese, M. (2008). Effectiveness of error management training: A meta-analysis. *Journal of Applied Psychology, 93*, 59–69.

Keltner, D., Ellsworth, P. C., & Edwards, K. (1993). Beyond simple pessimism: Effects of sadness and anger on social perception. *Journal of Personality & Social Psychology, 64*, 740–752.

Kluger, A. N., & DeNisi, A. (1996). The effects of feedback interventions on performance: A historical review, a meta-analysis, and a preliminary feedback intervention theory. *Psychological Bulletin, 119*, 254–284.

Kolb, D. A. (1984). *Experiential learning: Experience as the source of learning and development*. Englewood Cliffs, NJ: Prentice Hall.

Kolb, D. A., Boyatzis, R.E., & Mainemelis, C. (2001). Experiential learning theory: Previous research and new directions. In R. J. Sternberg & L. F. Zhang (Eds.), *Perspectives on cognitive, learning, and thinking styles* (pp. 227–247). Mahwah, NJ: Lawrence Erlbaum.

Kuhl, J. (1984). Volitional aspects of achievement motivation and learned helplessness: Toward a comprehensive theory of action control. In B. A. Maher & W. B. Maher (Eds.), *Progress in experimental personality research: Normal personality processes* (Vol. 13, pp. 99–170). New York, NY: Academic Press.

Lazarus, R. S. (1991). *Emotion and adaptation*. New York, NY: Oxford University Press.

—. (1999). *Stress and emotion: A new synthesis*. New York, NY: Springer.

LePine, J. A., LePine, M. A., & Jackson, C. L. (2004). Challenge and hindrance stress: Relationships with exhaustion, motivation to learn, and learning performance. *Journal of Applied Psychology, 89*, 883–891.

Levenson, R. W., Ekman, P., & Friesen, W. V. (1990). Voluntary facial action generates emotion-specific autonomic nervous system activity. *Psychophysiology, 27*, 363-384.

Lewis, M. (2000). Self-conscious emotions: Embarrassment, pride, shame, and guilt. In M. Lewis & J. M. Haviland-Jones (Eds.), *Handbook of emotions* (2nd ed., pp. 623–636). New York, NY: Guilford Press.

Linnenbrink, E. A. (2007). The role of affect in student learning: A multi-dimensional approach to considering the interaction of affect, motivation, and engagement. In P. A. Schutz & R. Pekrun (Eds.), *Emotion in education,* (pp. 107–124). Boston, MA: Academic Press.

Lischetzke, T., & Eid, M. (2003). Is attention to feelings beneficial or detrimental to affective well-being? Mood regulation as a moderator variable. *Emotion, 3,* 361–377.

Lopes, P. N., Salovey, P., Côté, S., & Beers, M. (2005). Emotion regulation abilities and the quality of social interaction. *Emotion, 5,* 113–118.

March, J. G., Sproull, L. S., & Tamuz, M. (1991). Learning from samples of one or fewer. *Organization Science, 2,* 1–13.

Martinko, M. J., & Zellars, K. (1998). Toward a theory of workplace violence and aggression: A cognitive appraisal perspective. In R. W. Griffin, A. O'Leary-Kelly, & J. M. Collins (Eds.), *Dysfunctional behavior in organizations: Violent and deviant behavior* (pp. 1–42). Stamford, CA: JAI Press.

Matthews, G., & Deary, I. J. (1998). *Personality traits.* Cambridge, UK: Cambridge University Press.

Mikulincer, M., & Nizan, B. (1988). Causal attribution, cognitive interference, and the generalization of learned helplessness. *Journal of Personality & Social Psychology, 55,* 470– 478.

Miller, D. T., & Ross, M. (1975). Self-serving biases in the attribution of causality: Fact or fiction? *Psychological Bulletin, 82,* 213–225.

Mor, N., & Winquist, J. (2002). Self-focused attention and negative affect: A meta-analysis. *Psychological Bulletin, 128,* 638–662.

Nelissen, R. M. A., & Zeelenberg, M. (2009). Moral emotions as determinants of third-party punishment: Anger, guilt, and the functions of altruistic sanctions. *Judgment and Decision Making, 4*(7), 543–553.

Newton, N. A., Khanna, C., & Thompson, J. (2008). Workplace failure: Mastering the last taboo. *Consulting Psychology Journal: Practice and Research, 60,* 227–245.

Noe, R. A., & Schmitt, N. (1986). The influence of trainee attitudes on training effectiveness: Test of a model. *Personnel Psychology, 39,* 497–523.

Noe, R. A., & Wilk, S. L. (1993). Investigation of the factors that influence employees' participation in development activities. *Journal of Applied Psychology, 78,* 291–302.

Nussbaum, A. D., & Dweck, C. S. (2008). Defensiveness vs. remediation: Self-theories and modes of self-esteem maintenance. *Personality and Social Psychology Bulletin, 34*(5), 127–134.

Ohlsson, S. (1996). Learning from performance errors. *Psychological Review, 103*, 241–262.

Op't Eynde, P., de Corte, E., & Verschaffel, L. (2007). Students' emotions: A key component of self-regulated learning? In P. A. Schutz & R. Pekrun (Eds.), *Emotion in education* (pp. 185–204). Boston, MA: Academic Press.

Ortony, A., Clore, G. L., & Collins, A. (1988). *The cognitive structure of emotions*. New York, NY: Cambridge University Press.

Paget, M. A. (1988). *The unity of mistakes*. Philadelphia, PA: Temple University Press.

Parrott, W. G. (2002). The functional utility of negative emotions. In L. F. Barrett & P. Salovey (Eds.), *Wisdom in feeling: Psychological processes in emotional intelligence* (pp. 341–359). New York, NY: Guilford Press.

Pekrun, R., Frenzel, A. C., Göetz, T., & Perry, R. P. (2007). The control-value theory of achievement emotions: An integrative approach to emotions in education. In P. A. Schutz & R. Pekrun (Eds.), *Emotion in education* (pp. 13–36). Boston, MA: Academic Press.

Pezzo, M. V., & Pezzo, S. P. (2007). Making sense of failure: A motivated model of hindsight bias. *Social Cognition, 25*, 147–164.

Ramanujam, R., & Goodman, P. S. (2011). The link between organizational errors and adverse consequences: The role of error-correcting and error-amplifying feedback processes. In D. A. Hofmann & M. Frese (Eds.), *Errors in organizations* (pp. 245–272). New York, NY: Routledge.

Reason, J. T. (1990). *Human error*. New York, NY: Cambridge University Press.

Reinecke, L., & Trepte, S. (2008). In a working mood? The effects of mood management processes on subsequent cognitive performance. *Journal of Media Psychology: Theories, Methods, and Applications, 20*, 3-14.

Rich, A. R., & Woolever, D. K. (1988). Expectancy and self-focused attention: Experimental support for the self-regulation model of test anxiety: *Journal of Social & Clinical Psychology, 7*, 246–259.

Roese, N. J. (1997). Counterfactual thinking. *Psychological Bulletin, 121*, 133–148.

Roseman, I. J., Wiest, C., & Swartz, T. S. (1994). Phenomenology, behaviors, and goals differentiate discrete emotions. *Journal of Personality & Social Psychology*, *67*, 206–221.

Rosenberg, M. (1979). *Conceiving the self.* New York, NY: Basic Books.

Russell, J. A., Weiss, A., & Mendelsohn, G. A. (1989). Affect Grid: A single-item scale of pleasure and arousal. *Journal of Personality and Social Psychology*, 57, 493-502.

Rybowiak, V., Garst, H., Frese, M., & Batinic, B. (1999). Error orientation questionnaire (EOQ): Reliability, validity, and different language equivalence. *Journal of Organizational Behavior*, *20*, 527–547.

Schlenker, B. R., & Leary, M. R. (1982). Social anxiety and self-presentation: A conceptualization and model. *Psychological Bulletin*, *92*, 641–669.

Schwarz, N. (1990). Feelings as information: Informational and motivational functions of affective states. In E. T. Higgins & R. M. Sorrentino (Eds.), *Handbook of motivation and cognition: Foundations of social behavior* (Vol. 2, pp. 527–561). New York, NY: Guilford.

Schwarz, N., & Clore, G. L. (1988). How do I feel about it? The informative function of affective states. In K. Fiedler & J. Forgas (Eds.), *Affect, cognition, and social behavior* (pp. 44–62). Toronto, CA: C.J. Hogrefe.

Segerstrom, S. C., Stanton, A. L., Alden, L. E., & Shortridge, B. E. (2003). A multidimensional structure for repetitive thought: What's on your mind, and how, and how much? *Journal of Personality & Social Psychology*, *85*, 909–921.

Seo, M., Barrett, L. F., & Bartunek, J. M. (2004). The role of affective experience in work motivation. *Academy of Management Review*, *29*, 423–439.

Sexton, J. B., Thomas, E. J., & Helmreich, R. L. (2000). Error, stress, and teamwork in medicine and aviation: Cross sectional surveys. *British Medical Journal*, *320*, 745–749.

Shepherd, D. A. (2003). Learning from business failure: Propositions of grief recovery for the self-employed. *Academy of Management Review*, *28*, 318–328.

Shimizu, K., & Hitt, M. A. (2011). Errors at the top of the hierarchy. In D. A. Hofmann & M. Frese (Eds.), *Errors in organizations* (pp. 199–224). New York, NY: Routledge.

Sitkin, S. B. (1992). Learning through failure: The strategy of small losses. In B. M. Staw & L. L. Cummings (Eds.), *Research in Organizational Behavior* (Vol. 14, pp. 231–266). Greenwich, CT: JAI Press.

Smith, C. A., & Ellsworth, P. C. (1985). Patterns of cognitive appraisal in emotion. *Journal of Personality & Social Psychology, 48*, 813–838.

Smith, C. A., & Kirby, L. D. (2001). Toward delivering on the promise of appraisal theory. In K. R. Scherer, R. Klaus, A. Schorr, & T. Johnstone (Eds.), *Appraisal processes in emotion: Theory, methods, research* (pp. 121–138). New York, NY: Oxford University Press.

Smith, C. A., & Lazarus, R. S. (1990). Emotion and adaptation. In L. A. Pervin (Ed.), *Handbook of personality theory and research* (pp. 609–637). New York, NY: Guilford.

Snell, R. S. (1988). The emotional cost of managerial learning at work. *Management Education and Development, 19*(4), 322–340.

Staw, B., McKechnie, P. & Puffer, S. (1983). The justification of organizational performance. *Administrative Science Quarterly, 28*, 582–600.

Tangney, J. P. (1990). Assessing individual differences in proneness to shame and guilt: Development of the self-conscious affect and attribution inventory. *Journal of Personality & Social Psychology, 59*, 102–111.

Tangney, J. P., & Dearing, R. (2002). *Shame and guilt.* New York, NY: Guilford.

Tangney, J. P., Miller, R. S., Flicker, L., & Barlow, D. H. (1996). Are shame, guilt, and embarrassment distinct emotions? *Journal of Personality & Social Psychology, 70*, 1256–1269.

Tangney, J. P., & Tracy, J. L. (2012). Self-conscious emotions. In M. Leary & J. P. Tangney (Eds.), *Handbook of self and identity* (2nd ed., pp. 446–478). New York, NY: Guilford.

Tangney, J. P., Wagner, P., Fletcher, C., & Gramzow, R. (1992). Shamed into anger? The relation of shame and guilt to anger and self-reported aggression. *Journal of Personality & Social Psychology, 62*, 669–675.

Thayer, R. E. (1989). *The biopsychology of mood and arousal.* New York: Oxford University Press.

Tice, D. M., Bratslavsky, E., & Baumeister, R. F. (2001). Emotional distress regulation takes precedence over impulse control: If you feel bad, do it! *Journal of Personality & Social Psychology, 80*, 53–67.

Tucker, A., & Edmondson, A. (2003). Why hospitals don't learn from failures: Organizational and psychological dynamics that inhibit system change. *California Management Review, 45*(2), 1–18.

Turner, J. E., & Waugh, R. M. (2007). A dynamical systems perspective regarding students' learning processes: Shame reactions and emergent self-organizations. In P. A. Schutz & R. Pekrun (Eds.), *Emotion in education* (pp. 125–146). Boston, MA: Academic Press.

Uribe, C. L., Schweikhart, S. B., Pathak, D. S., & Marsh, G. B. (2002). Perceived barriers to medical-error reporting: An exploratory investigation. *Journal of Healthcare Management, 47*(4), 264–279.

Vancouver, J. B., & Tischner, E. C. (2004). The effect of feedback sign on task performance depends on self-concept discrepancies. *Journal of Applied Psychology, 89,* 1092–1098.

Vassilopoulos, S. P., & Watkins, E. R. (2009). Adaptive and maladaptive self-focus: A pilot extension study with individuals high and low in fear of negative evaluation. *Behavior Therapy, 40,* 181–189.

Vroom, V. H. (1964). *Work and motivation.* New York, NY: Wiley.

Weick, K. E., & Ashford, S. J. (2001). Learning in organizations. In F. M. Jablin & L. L. Putnam (Eds.), *The new handbook of organizational communication* (pp. 704–731). Thousand Oaks, CA: Sage.

Weiner, B. (2007). Examining emotional diversity in the classroom: An attribution theorist considers the moral emotions. In P. A. Schutz & R. Pekrun (Eds.), *Emotion in education* (pp. 75–88). Boston, MA: Academic Press.

—. (1985). An attributional theory of achievement motivation and emotion. *Psychological Review, 92,* 548–573.

Weiss, H. M., & Cropanzano, R. (1996). Affective events theory: A theoretical discussion of the structure, causes and consequences of affective experiences at work. *Research in Organizational Behavior, 18,* 1–74.

Zeelenberg, M., Nelissen, R. M. A., Breugelmans, S. M., & Pieters, R. (2008). On emotion specificity in decision making: Why feeling is for doing. *Judgment and Decision Making, 3*(1), 18–27.

Zhao, B. (2011). Learning from errors: The role of context, emotion, and personality. *Journal of Organizational Behavior, 32,* 435–463.

Zhao, B., & Olivera, F. (2006). Error reporting in organizations. *Academy of Management Review, 31,* 1012–1030.

CHAPTER THREE

NARCISSISM AND CREATIVITY OVER TIME: TOWARD A DYNAMIC MODEL OF GROUP CREATIVITY

JACK A. GONCALO AND VERENA KRAUSE
CORNELL UNIVERSITY, USA

Abstract

The literature on group creativity is representative of most research on groups: Rather than incorporate a dynamic view of the creative process it has largely viewed creativity from a static point of view (Cronin, Weingart, & Todorova, 2011). Here, we focus on an example of this static approach: Research linking narcissism to group creativity (Goncalo, Flynn & Kim, 2010). First, we review the evidence that narcissists can contribute to group creativity. We uncover three critical gaps: The research focuses narrowly on one stage of the creative process while neglecting other stages, it neglects the fact that events in one stage can impact subsequent stages, and it assumes a dynamic process that is not tested empirically. Second, we propose a dynamic model that addresses these gaps and thus generates a series of novel propositions. Finally, we suggest an empirical approach that might be useful for studying group creativity over time.

Keywords: narcissism, creativity, groups, time

Introduction

A creative idea is one that diverges from existing solutions in an appropriate or feasible way (Amabile, 1983). In organizations such ideas may relate to a wide variety of domains such as organizational products, practices, services or procedures (Shalley & Gilson, 2004). As the organizational environment becomes increasingly competitive (Barnett & Hansen, 1996), creative ideas are viewed as an important advantage because they may lead firms in a profitable new direction (Amabile, 1996).

In order to meet the demand for creative solutions, organizations have employed a variety of strategies, including the formation of teams (Paulus & Yang, 2000) to promote idea generation. In her comprehensive review of the literature on creativity, George (2007) noted that most of the research on group creativity has been conducted in the laboratory with groups that have no history of interaction nor any expectation that they will interact again. This stream of laboratory research has yielded many important insights that are useful for managing short term interactions between people who meet for the first time to generate a wide range of ideas; a brainstorming process that is foundational to creativity in organizations (Paulus & Yang, 2000).

Yet, there has been wide agreement for many decades that the creative process unfolds in stages that may extend over a longer period of time (West, 2002; Lubart, 2001). In other words, teams must not only generate new ideas but they must also decide which ideas to implement and then undertake the process of bringing their favored idea to fruition (West, 2002). Moreover, merely generating a wide range of solutions does not guarantee that those ideas will be identified as creative nor that they will be implemented (Nijstad & De Dreu, 2002; West, 2002; Rietzschel, Nijstad & Stroebe, 2006). Indeed, many organizations claim to want creative solutions, but fail to pursue them when they have the opportunity to do so (Mueller, Goncalo & Kamdar, 2011; Mueller, Melwani & Goncalo, 2012).

Unfortunately, the literature on group creativity is therefore typical of most research on groups and teams: Rather than incorporate a dynamic view of the creative process over time it has largely viewed creativity as a static process (George, 2007; Cronin, Weingart, & Todorova, 2011). In this paper, we focus on a particular example of this static approach: Recent research linking narcissism to group creativity (Goncalo, Flynn & Kim, 2010). We intend to use this concrete example to illustrate how time can be fruitfully incorporated into our models of group creativity and to highlight the potential insights that may emerge from a more dynamic perspective. First, we review the evidence that narcissists can contribute to group creativity (Goncalo et al., 2010). Our critique uncovers three critical gaps in this research: It focuses narrowly on one stage of the creative process while neglecting other stages; it neglects the fact that events in one stage can impact subsequent stages, and it assumes a dynamic process that is not actually tested empirically. Second, we propose a dynamic model that, at least in part, addressed these gaps and in doing so generates novel propositions that can be tested in future research. Finally, we conclude by suggesting an empirical approach for studying group creativity over time.

Narcissism and group creativity

The personality trait narcissism refers to a set of egocentric traits including self-admiration, self-centeredness, and high self-regard (Sedikides, Rudich, Gregg, Kumashiro, & Rusbult, 2004). Individuals scoring high in narcissism have an exaggerated sense of entitlement, a constant need for attention and a strong desire to be admired by others (Bogart, Benotsch, & Pavlovic, 2004). Narcissists frequently use singular personal pronouns (e.g., I, me) in speech (Raskin & Shaw, 1998) and may often ignore others in conversation (Kernis & Sun, 1994). They report a lesser need for intimacy (Carroll, 1987) and have little empathy for their peers, even those in need (Watson, Grisham, Trotter, & Biderman, 1984). Given these seemingly anti-social characteristics, it is somewhat surprising that narcissists tend to emerge as leaders (Brunell, Gentry, Campbell, Hoffman, Kuhnert, & Demaree, 2008), even at the highest levels of organizations (Chatterjee & Hambrick, 2007). The initially positive impression individuals have of their narcissistic colleagues may fade over time, however, as they realize that narcissists are in fact less agreeable, less well adjusted, less warm, and more hostile and arrogant than others (Paulhus, 1998). Paradoxically, there is some evidence that the presence of narcissists is not inevitably destructive. In the next section we review recent evidence that narcissists, even though they themselves are not necessarily creative, may in fact contribute to the creativity of the groups to which they belong.

Existing theory linking narcissism to group creativity

The personality composition of a group may shape group processes and performance (Moreland & Levine, 1991). Recent research has shown that creativity may also be facilitated by the right mix of personalities in a group (Miron-Spektor, Erez, & Naveh, 2011; Schilpzand, Herold, & Shalley, 2011). For example, groups are more creative when some of their members are open to new experience (Schilpzand, et al., 2011; Baer, Oldham, Jacobsohn & Hollingshead, 2008) and when they have a mix of creative individuals as well as members who are more conforming and attentive to detail as they hold the group together and ensure that ideas are implemented (Miron-Spektor, et al., 2011).

While most research regards narcissism as largely negative, Goncalo, Flynn and Kim (2010) theorized that narcissism may actually have a positive impact on group creativity. Group creativity depends heavily on the open expression of ideas because people may extend, combine, and improve upon the contributions made by others (Nijstad, Stroebe, & Lodewijkx, 2002). This process of idea expression and recombination allows groups to realize more creative solutions than any one individual could have reached alone (Simonton, 1999). However, considerable research on group brainstorming has found that many good ideas remain unexpressed, leading groups to underperform compared with nominal groups of individuals who work alone (Diehl & Stroebe, 1987). There is strong evidence that social influence processes can mitigate or even reverse some of the problems inherent to face-to-face brainstorming and thereby promote group creativity (Paulus & Dzindolet, 1993). For example, competition can facilitate idea expression because the desire to assert one's value and acquire status (Pettit & Lount, 2010) may motivate people to express ideas they might otherwise withhold from the group discussion (Dugosh & Paulus, 2005; Munkes & Diehl, 2003; Beersma & De Dreu, 2005; Goncalo & Kim, 2010).

There are two separate streams of research that provide evidence consistent with this perspective. First, research on social motives has shown that groups of people with a pro-self orientation (i.e., the goal is to maximize one's own outcomes relative to others) are more creative than groups of people with a pro-social orientation (i.e., the goal is to cooperate to maximize outcomes for both oneself and others) (Beersma & De Dreu, 2005). Second, research adopting a cultural values frame has shown that groups of people primed to be individualistic generate more novel ideas than groups of people primed to be collectivistic (Goncalo & Staw, 2006; Goncalo & Duguid, 2012). Taken together, these streams of research suggest that the creative potential of groups may be realized when the competitive drive to be superior compels each group member to attempt to propose the most novel ideas (Beersma & De Dreu, 2005; Dugosh & Paulus, 2005; Munkes & Diehl, 2003).

Narcissists crave attention and recognition for their valued attributes and contributions (e.g., John & Robbins, 1994) and so they may be more willing to compete with their fellow team mates to suggest more novel solutions. The competition between narcissistic group members may lead the group to uncover new sources of information and new perspectives that can then be recombined to generate novel ideas (De Dreu, Nijstad &

van Knippenberg, 2008). For example, narcissists may contribute to a more efficient exchange of ideas by reducing production blocking (Diehl & Stroebe, 1987). Production blocking is a conversational bottleneck that occurs when group members wait for their turn to speak; individuals may forget some of their ideas or even run out of time to express their ideas while listening to others (Nijstad, et al., 2002). Highly narcissistic individuals may be less patient with such turn-taking and tend to "break into" the other person's turn, or not listen as attentively to the other person's ideas and thereby be less likely to forget their own ideas. A somewhat counterintuitive prediction is that this self-focus and aggressive conversational style, while impolite, could reduce production blocking and thereby increase the group's creative output. Indeed, there is recent evidence that people in competitive groups are more likely to interrupt their teammates to express their own ideas and that doing so actually increases the total number of ideas expressed (Goncalo & Kim, 2010).

Recently, a growing number of scholars are calling for organizational scholars to re-examine the common implicit assumption of linear relationships between variables (Le, Oh, Robbins, Ilies, Holland & Westrick, 2011; Pierce & Aguinis, 2013). They argue that even beneficial inputs can be detrimental to outcomes at excessive levels and conversely, even seemingly harmful inputs might be beneficial at lower or more manageable levels. According to Pierce and Aguinis (2013), researchers would rather posit linear associations because they are easier to explain. Indeed, the relationship between narcissism and group creativity may not be as straightforward as a simple positive and linear association. Goncalo and colleagues (2010) also predicted that as more narcissists join the group, competition can escalate to the point of obstructing the group's ability to reach closure, synthesize new ideas, and complete tasks on time (Jehn & Mannix, 2001). Groups with lower levels of competition may be more efficient and more capable of coordinating their efforts, which would be an advantage when the group moves beyond the idea generation stage to actually select an idea and bring it to fruition (Rietzschel, Nijstad & Stroebe, 2006). Given these tradeoffs, they predicted a curvilinear, inverted U-shaped relationship: the more narcissists there are in the group, the more creative the group's performance will be up to an inflection point when additional narcissists begin to have a negative effect on group creativity.

Empirical test

Goncalo et al. (2010) tested their curvilinear hypothesis in a study of student project teams from an introductory course in organizational behavior. Each team of four was asked to analyze a real organization making use of the concepts and methods highlighted in the course. Part of the assignment required the group to propose a solution to the problem they identified. In this part of the assignment, groups were instructed to generate novel plans that the organization could implement to improve their problems and build on their strengths. The solutions were not intended to be wild or unrealistic. In fact, they were explicitly instructed to come up with feasible action items—things the organization could do given its constraints. These solutions were then coded for creativity.

In addition, surveys designed to assess the creative process were handed out at the mid-point of the group project, halfway between the assignment to groups, and the final deadline. The mid-point was chosen because previous research has shown that the mid-point is when high performing groups experience a concentrated burst of activity at which time they debate competing task-related perspectives (Gersick, 1988). Therefore, it is at this particular stage of a group's development when the authors reasoned that the creative process might be most relevant and important to observe.

The results showed a significant curvilinear effect of narcissism on group creativity such that the more narcissists there were in the group, the more creative the group was to an inflection point, where the effect of narcissism on group creativity became negative. The results suggest that narcissism influenced group creativity by changing the group process, particularly given that narcissists failed to outperform less narcissistic individuals on several tests of individual creative problem solving.

A theoretical and methodological critique

The finding that narcissists can contribute to creative outcomes in groups is intriguing but the theory and empirical test fall short in at least three important respects that are quite common in the literature on group creativity (George, 2007). Here we critique the Goncalo et al. (2010) study with two goals in mind: To demonstrate the shortcomings of that particular piece and also to use this critique as a starting point for the introduction of more dynamic models to the literature on group creativity.

(1) The theory focuses on one stage of the creative process while neglecting other stages

Goncalo et al. (2010) reasoned that a few narcissists in a group may contribute to idea generation but too many narcissists may prevent the group from choosing an idea and actually implementing it. Their theorizing implies that group creativity unfolds in stages. Yet, rather than specifying a separate prediction at each stage of the creative process, they predicted a curvilinear effect of narcissism on group creativity as though it is a unitary construct that can be observed only at one point in time (the end of the project). In fact, narcissists may be more useful in terms of inspiring a competitive norm at the idea generation stage that motivates idea expression than they might be at the implementation stage at which point the desire for attention may impede the group's progress towards the deadline. This logic would suggest two separate predictions (one at each stage). Moreover, the form of the relationship would also differ at each stage; the relationship between narcissism and creative idea generation would be linear and positive while the relationship between narcissism and implementation would be linear and negative. Interestingly, neither prediction is curvilinear. In sum, a more dynamic view of the creative process (one that we outline in the next section) would suggest that creativity may occur at multiple stages and that narcissism may have a different impact on each stage of the process.

(2) The theory assumes a dynamic process that is not actually tested.

In the Goncalo et al. (2010) study, creativity was measured in two ways, (as a self-reported process) and as an outcome that was coded from each group's final report of their suggested solution to an organizational problem. The group's creative process was measured in a survey administered at the mid-point of the group's interaction on the assumption that the mid-point might be particularly critical because it is at this time that a flurry of activity related to the project might occur (e.g., Gersick, 1988). This empirical approach is problematic for at least three reasons. First, the dynamics that play out before and in between these time points are not explored. For example, the same measure of systematic thinking could have been taken at the beginning and at the conclusion of the project as well as the mid-point, in order to verify whether the effect of narcissism persists over time, attenuates at certain stages or perhaps even changes form at different points in time.

Second, survey items asking participants whether they debated different perspectives and explored alternative solutions may tap their experience at the midpoint, at an earlier stage or a mixture of their recollections from both stages. It would be useful to know whether narcissism influenced the systematic processing of ideas throughout the group project or whether this effect was restricted to the midpoint or earlier. Given that the assignment required groups to propose a single solution, we can assume they had to select one idea from among more than one option. But the really difficult decision of which idea to implement was not necessarily made at the midpoint. If the decision did not take place at the point at which the survey was administered, there is a chance that the decision was overturned during the second half of the group project and another idea was implemented instead. It is also possible that idea selection took place at different times for different groups. In fact, Goncalo et al. (2010) predicted that narcissists should slow the process such that idea selection and implementation might be delayed making it even more crucial to measure the process more than once.

Finally, the fact that narcissism was measured at the beginning, systematic thinking at the midpoint, and the creativity of the proposed solution at the end might suggest a meditational process in which the level of narcissism of the group influences systematic thinking, which, in turn, influences creativity. However, they found that systematic thinking and creativity were uncorrelated. Multiple measures of the creative process over time might help specify the point at which systematic thinking might actually influence the final outcome.

(3) The theory neglects the fact that events in one stage can impact subsequent stages.

An advantage of specifying the effect of narcissism at each stage of the creative process is that we can begin to theorize about how creativity at one stage can impact subsequent stages. For example, narcissists may contribute to a competitive norm that promotes idea generation but that norm may carry-over to subsequent stages and impede the group's ability to implement their ideas. Alternatively, the number and quality of ideas generated may have no direct impact on the quality of the idea selected (Rietzschel et al., 2006) thus neutralizing a positive effect that narcissists may have on the creative process and potentially making their presence a liability for other group performance outcomes.

In sum, the three critical shortcomings we identified in the existing research on narcissistic personality composition and group creativity arose because the critical role of time was not seriously considered. These gaps in our understanding of what is most likely a dynamic process provide a starting point for generating new theoretical propositions.

A dynamic model of narcissism and group creativity over time

In order to develop a dynamic model of group creativity over time, it is important to first specify what distinguishes "early" from "late" in a group's interaction (Jehn & Mannix, 2001). The most straightforward way to delineate the early from the late stage is simply by the midpoint of the allotted time: The early stage occurs prior to the midpoint and the late stage occurs after the midpoint. Indeed, groups undergo a critical transition at the midpoint during which time they may stop work, notice that the deadline is near and complete tasks at a more urgent pace (Gersick, 1988; 1989). In other words, although the dynamic passage of time is a continuous experience, there are certain events that may distinguish an "early" from a "late" phase (McGrath, Arrow, & Berdahl, 2000).

According to Tuckman's (1965) model, groups go through an initial forming stage in which they get to know each other, test inter-personal boundaries and orient themselves to the task. During the early phase, effective teams may also reach explicit agreements about how the group will work together to complete tasks in a timely manner (Mathieu & Rapp, 2009). The development of these agreements may prompt the group to clarify important issues such as group members' roles and responsibilities as well as their task related abilities and work styles (Mathieu & Rapp, 2009). In other words, during the early stages groups may be concerned primarily with planning for the future while in the later stage they may focus more intently on task execution as the deadline nears (Okhuysen & Waller, 2002).

The creative process in our model has three critical time periods that are tied to the stages identified by Gersick (1988). Each of the three time periods map onto a different stage of the creative process. During the *early stage*, group members generate a wide range of ideas while not necessarily evaluating them (Diehl & Stroebe, 1987). During the *middle stage*, group members start to narrow down the number of ideas and eventually select one final idea (Reitzschel et al., 2006). During the *late phase*, group members implement the selected idea (West, 2002). We propose that narcissism has different effects at each of these three stages.

Though narcissism is a continuous variable, we make two important simplifying assumptions for clarity of exposition. First, we assume that groups can vary such that narcissists are either (a) the only narcissist in the group (b) in the minority or (c) in the majority which at the extreme would mean that the entire group is composed of narcissistic individuals. These distinctions map on to the proportions that are typically important in relating group composition to group processes and group performance (Chatman, Boisnier, Spataro, Anderson & Berdahl, 2008) and they allow us to talk about narcissistic group composition as it is likely to be meaningfully perceived in groups (individuals are viewed as narcissistic or they are not). Second, we assume that social perceivers can distinguish the narcissists from the non-narcissists in their group. We base this assumption on research showing that observers can obtain highly reliable ratings of subjects' narcissism after fairly short interactions (John & Robins, 1994) and that peer ratings of narcissism are far more accurate than ratings of other personality traits (Clifton, Turkheimer & Oltmanns, 2009).

Narcissism and creativity at time 1 (early stage)

In the early, idea generation stage narcissists may dominate the conversation by contributing a large number of ideas because they are extraverted (Miller & Campbell, 2008) and it is important to them to be at the center of attention (Sedikides et al., 2004). Narcissists believe that they are better than others (Campbell, Rudich, & Sedikides, 2002) and feel the need to demonstrate this (Nevicka, De Hoogh, Van Vianen, Beersma, & McIlwain, 2011).

Because each narcissist is self-absorbed and wants to be at the center of attention, competition among narcissists easily ensues (Goncalo et al., 2010). Each narcissist wants to contribute a better idea than the others. During the discussion of ideas, the narcissists thus establish a competitive norm that may, in turn, influence non-narcissists either by making the norm salient (Cialdini, Reno & Kallgren, 1990) or through a more implicit process of social contagion (Barsade, 2002). This competitive norm stimulates the generation of unique, creative ideas because every group member wants to outperform the others (Rijsman, 1974). Furthermore, the competitive norm forces group members to think their ideas through and argue well in order to convince others that their idea is the best. The emergence of a competitive norm is generally beneficial for creative idea generation because a larger number of unique ideas are generated than when this norm is absent (Cummings & Oldham, 1997; Shalley & Oldham, 1997; Munkes & Diehl, 2003). This leads to our first proposition:

Proposition 1: Narcissism is positively correlated with the emergence of a competitive norm at the early stage of the group project and a competitive norm, in turn, stimulates the expression of creative ideas.

Narcissism and creativity at time 2 (middle stage)

At the middle stage of a group project the focus may turn from idea generation to idea selection, particularly if the group perceives that at the mid-point time is becoming limited (Gersick, 1988). When there is only one highly narcissistic individual, it is likely that their idea will be selected with minimal conflict. Narcissists enjoy having an audience who admires them (Campbell et al., 2002), so they attempt to appear charming and confident to others. This initial "act" works in their favor, at least at the outset, because non-narcissists perceive them as popular, and likable (Back, Schmukle & Egloff, 2010). Furthermore, each narcissist is convinced of his or her ideas and thus confidently presents and defends them if necessary, which convinces others that the ideas suggested by narcissistic individuals are more creative than they really are (Goncalo et al., 2010).

Narcissists may not be objectively creative, but their high levels of self-confidence may nevertheless influence the way others evaluate their ideas. Although researchers have numerous tools at their disposal for measuring creativity, there are many contexts in which creativity is judged by observers who lack rigorous criteria (Amabile, 1982; Taylor & Barron, 1963) and are subject to attributional biases (Kasof, 1995). For example, in a qualitative study of Hollywood "pitches," Elsbach and Kramer (2003) found that judgments of creativity were influenced by perceptions of the "pitcher" and the extent to which they matched the prototypical traits of a highly creative person, such as "charismatic" and "witty."

This research suggests that perceptions of creative ability may be separate from whether a product is objectively creative (Mueller et al., 2011). It also suggests that certain behaviors of the person who expresses creative ideas, especially their energy, enthusiasm, and conviction, can prompt evaluators to judge their ideas to be more creative than they actually are. This second point is supported by the classical research on social influence in which behaviors that signal confidence, such as taking the head seat prior to a group discussion, can make one's ideas seem more plausible and convincing (Nemeth & Wachtler, 1974). More recent research also suggests that dominant individuals are more likely to attain social status in groups because others inaccurately perceive them as more competent (Anderson & Kilduff, 2009).

Goncalo et al. (2010) found that narcissists are at a significant advantage in these evaluations because they will be both highly confident that they are more creative than others and more inclined to publicly share these flattering self-views with people who are in a position to evaluate their ideas. In the absence of any objective information about an idea's creative quality or criteria on which to base such an evaluation, narcissists' self-aggrandizing behaviors may be persuasive, particularly because they match evaluators' prototypes of how highly creative people tend to behave (Elsbach & Kramer, 2003). This social influence process, more than the objective creativity of the idea itself, could help explain why narcissists appear creative to others (Deutschman, 2005: 44). Non-narcissists might thus readily accept the narcissist's ideas as the best ones and might be willing to implement the narcissist's favorite idea without much discussion. Thus, our first proposition is as follows:

> **Proposition 2:** Non-narcissists perceive narcissists as creative at the middle stage even if their ideas are not more creative than the ideas suggested by others.

As the number of narcissists in the group increases (while remaining in the minority), the effect of narcissism on idea selection may initially be positive because conflict between narcissistic group members may slow the group and prevent them from reaching premature closure when discussing which idea should be selected. Relationship conflict is always deleterious (De Dreu & Weingart, 2003), but moderate levels of task conflict may be beneficial at the idea selection stage. For example, dissent at this stage may prompt the group to consider a wider range of potential solutions, to scrutinize the solutions more carefully and in a less biased way (Nemeth & Rogers, 1996).

Once the number of narcissists in the group has reached a majority, however, potentially beneficial task conflict may be more likely to transform into relationship conflict (Greer, Jehn & Mannix, 2008). Individuals may freely suggest a wide range of potential solutions at the idea generation stage without criticism, but at some point the list of ideas will need to be scrutinized as the group converges on the one solution they want to select and pursue to fruition.

The process of idea selection may pose a threat to narcissists because all of them want one of their own ideas to be selected for implementation (while perhaps secretly insecure that their ideas are not worthy of selection). Narcissists may seem to have high self-esteem because they are so extroverted and overtly confident, but they are, in fact, generally riddled with self-doubt and score below average on implicit self-esteem measures

(Zeigler-Hill, 2005). Thus, a narcissist's self-esteem hinges on his or her idea being praised, selected and implemented by the group. Therefore, the more narcissists belong to the group the more conflict is likely to ensue. At this point less narcissistic group members may realize that the narcissists in their midst are not as charming and creative as they seemed initially. Instead, the level of relationship conflict in the group may highlight the fact that narcissists are self-centered to the point of being willing to allow the project to fail if their ideas are criticized or overlooked. Thus, groups with a majority of narcissists might come to an impasse.

Furthermore, with a majority of narcissists in the group the likelihood that conflict will entail personal attacks is higher. Narcissists have a grandiose sense of self (Stuke & Sporer, 2002), are disagreeable (Miller & Campbell, 2008; Paulhus & Williams, 2002), and very extroverted (Miller & Campbell, 2008), which translates into people who are verbose, interrupt others, and try to manipulate them (Raskin & Hall, 1981). Narcissists may even react with verbal aggression when their ego is threatened (Stucke & Sporer, 2002), which might occur when others criticize their ideas during the idea selection stage. With a majority of narcissists in the group the likelihood increases that there will be an upward spiral of destructive personal attacks in which narcissists prod each other to higher and higher levels of relationship conflict. Such relationship conflict over interpersonal style, values, and taste has consistently been shown to be detrimental to team performance (De Dreu & Weingart, 2003). This leads to the following propositions:

Proposition 3: Narcissism will impact both the type of conflict and the level of conflict at the middle stage of idea selection. There will be a low level of conflict when there is only a single narcissistic individual in the group. With narcissists in the minority task conflict will initially increase to a point at which narcissists become the majority which will trigger increasing levels of relationship conflict.

Proposition 4a-b: The relationship between narcissism and the creativity of the group's selected idea will be an inverted U-shape. (4a) The least creative ideas will be selected when there is only a single narcissistic individual (because there will be no conflict to spur thoughtful decision making) and when there are only narcissists in the group (because the level of relationship conflict will be high). (4b) The most creative ideas will be selected by groups when the narcissists in the group comprise the minority.

Narcissism and creativity at time 3 (late stage)

The implementation stage of the creative process may not demand creativity as much as efficiency and coordination so that the group can turn their idea into a final product or proposal. It is this stage of the process that is most likely to be affected by events that have already occurred in earlier stages. During the implementation stage, groups with one narcissist will quickly implement an uncreative idea selected in the previous stage without much reflection. Moreover, ideas are likely to be selected not because they are objectively creative, but because the lone narcissist in the group sold the idea with confidence and charisma. At this point, the group is unlikely to be aware that their idea is ordinary or even of low quality and will move to the implementation stage without a very objective evaluation of their idea. Groups with a minority of narcissists will generate task related conflicts that can help generate and identify more creative solutions, but will not necessarily cause long lasting conflict that might interfere with idea implementation. Finally, the high levels of relationship conflict that the groups with a majority of narcissists generated during the idea selection stage will likely carry over to the implementation stage. Narcissistic group members whose ideas were not chosen may try to sabotage the implementation of other peoples' ideas, withhold effort and generally impede the progress of the group as retribution for perceived slights. The most narcissistic groups are therefore more likely to be late in delivering a final product or worse they may fail to deliver one at all. Thus, we predict the following:

> **Proposition 5**: There will be an inverted U-shaped relationship between the number of narcissists in the group and the effectiveness of idea implementation.

Once the groups have finished their project and implemented their new product or process, they are likely to receive external feedback. The groups in which a lone narcissist convinced the rest of their group to pursue his/her idea may have helped the group to quickly move on to the idea implementation stage. However, the narcissist's confidence may belie the fact that their ideas are not particularly good or creative and once the group receives more accurate and likely negative feedback from external evaluators, the experience of failure may cause the group to disband. Conversely, groups with a majority of narcissists may also dissolve, not because they lacked the necessary level of conflict that would prevent them from reaching premature closure but because they are riddled with so much destructive relationship conflict that future collaborations would be strained. The group process that we posit may be characteristic of groups in which the narcissists are in the minority (e.g., task as opposed to relationship conflict) may make such groups more likely to succeed and also because of this positive feedback, to choose to collaborate again (Lawler, 2001). Therefore, we predict the following:

Proposition 6: Groups in which the narcissists are in the minority are more likely to experience success on a project which will, in turn, cause them to choose to collaborate again on a subsequent project.

Unfortunately, past success and repeat collaboration may also have a downside. The problem with repeat collaboration is that during the first project, team members have obtained mental models of how to structure their work and their relationships with one another. These enduring, cognitive structures tend to carry over into new projects, effectively reducing aberration from procedures and modes of thinking (Skilton & Dooley, 2010). In addition, the shared experience of past success may lead to further collaboration but it may also increase confidence in past solutions and thereby limit the exploration of new ideas (Audia & Goncalo, 2007). This process might increase the speed with which the project is completed the second time around because everyone has their set roles, but excessive confidence in the status quo can ultimately reduce creative output. Having a minority of narcissists in the group might counteract this problem. The narcissists will likely continue to compete and cause conflict in the group because they are unwilling to settle or compromise. They are less likely to adhere to procedures that worked for the past project if they were not leading them. Thus, we predict the following:

Proposition 7: The number of narcissists in the group will moderate the consequences of past success on subsequent creativity such that the more narcissists in the group, the less likely past success will constrain exploration (so long as narcissists are not in the majority).

The Moderating Role of Audience Attention

Given that narcissists crave attention, they are the most competitive and motivated when they have an audience because there is an opportunity to achieve glory (Campbell et al., 2002). In fact, an evaluative audience that holds narcissists accountable for their actions - as is the case in most organizational work teams - fuels narcissists' desire to self-enhance to a larger degree than without an audience or when they are not accountable

(Collins & Stukas, 2008). We thus propose that audience scrutiny will exacerbate all of the effects of narcissism we have discussed up to this point. An audience will spur narcissists to compete and get into conflict to a larger degree than groups who are not evaluated by an audience or where the audience is less salient. Furthermore, narcissists are known to engage in self-defeating behaviors such as aggression (Miller, Campbell, Young, Lakey, Reidy, Zeichner, & Goodie, 2009), and an audience might exaggerate those behaviors further. The following proposition emerges:

> **Proposition 8:** Audience scrutiny is going to strengthen the effects of narcissism on the group process over time (e.g., competition and conflict).

Narcissism and the Pace of Creative Work

An important feature of our dynamic model of group creativity is that the progression from one stage to another is not necessarily uniform. We know from prior research (Gersick, 1988) that there is often a critical mid-point transition during which groups may pick up the pace of their work. However, different groups may spend a different amount of time in each stage and may even return to an earlier stage before moving forward. Thus, our dynamic model incorporates the possibility that groups may spend more time in certain stages than others. For example, groups with a majority of narcissists are likely to spend considerably more time in each stage than groups with a minority of narcissists or a single narcissist. For instance, in the idea selection stage the level of relationship conflict will be high in groups with a majority of narcissists and thus hold up the selection of a single idea. In contrast, groups with a lone narcissist might move through the idea selection stage rather quickly because the narcissist will be able to convince the other group members of the superiority of his or her idea without stimulating much debate. One obvious consequence, of course, is that the higher the number of narcissists in the group the more time is needed to complete a project. However, though they may take longer to complete a project, the product is not necessarily of higher quality due to the destructive conflict that may arise. Nevertheless, it is likely that narcissists will influence the pace at which creative work is completed.

> **Proposition 9a-b:** As the number of narcissists in the group increases, (a) the longer the group will spend at each stage of the creative process and (b) the less likely the group will be able to complete projects on time.

Additionally, our dynamic model also incorporates the potential for the group to return to an earlier stage. For example, during the implementation stage, groups who were taken in by the charm of the lone narcissist might discover at a later stage that the idea they were persuaded to select might be of poor quality or inappropriate to solving the problem. A dilemma like this one might necessitate the return to a former stage. It might be necessary to select another idea that is more feasible from the list of generated ideas. Or it might even be necessary to return to the idea generation stage in order to incorporate knowledge gained during the implementation stage into the process of generating new ideas. Another intriguing possibility is that more narcissistic group members might try to persuade the group to return to the idea generation stage in order to get another opportunity at getting their idea selected. Feedback loops of this kind not only add realism to the model but they also present an exciting and largely untapped opportunity for future research. In sum, we predict the following:

Proposition 10: The more narcissists there are in a group, the more likely the group will return to an earlier stage of the creative process after having progressed to a later stage.

Toward A More Dynamic Model Of Group Creativity

We focused specifically on narcissism because it was a useful vehicle for thinking about how a group's creative process might unfold over time. In doing so, we uncovered several more general principles that might be useful as researchers of group creativity begin to incorporate time into their models.

(1) Creativity-relevant traits can cause the emergence of creativity-relevant norms

The characteristics of individual group members (e.g., personality traits) may give rise to the emergence of group level phenomena like shared norms that, over time, cannot be reduced to the individual level. This process has been documented in groups research (Kozlowski, Gully, Nason, & Smith, 1999; Cronin et al., 2011) but has not been connected to creative outcomes at the group level. For example, there is emerging evidence that certain types of traits are conducive to a group's creativity (e.g., Baer et al., 2008; Miron-Spektor et al., 2012). This process may occur at the individual level as certain traits, such as openness to new experience, which are known to stimulate creative thought (Silvia,

Nusbaum, Berg, Martin & O'Connor, 2009). Creativity relevant traits may also influence group creativity via shared norms as, for example, the willingness of those who are open to new experience may inspire the rest of the group to engage in more exploratory behavior which, over time, could give rise to a strong norm for exploration that survives and impacts creativity even as the individuals who are high on that trait may have left the group. We suspect that this process may also explain how narcissists can impact group creativity even though, as individuals, there is no evidence that they are particularly creative. It is possible that their behavior may be contributing to a norm like competition that might make the group as a whole more productive.

(2) Events in one stage of the creative process can influence
   subsequent stages

It seems logical that the creative process in groups may unfold through a series of stages that may each require a different set of norms. For example, the early stage of idea generation may require that we withhold criticism to ensure that a wide range of ideas are freely expressed (Diehl & Stroebe, 1987). However, at the idea selection stage, criticism must be allowed in order for groups to converge on the best solution. Interesting, however, the events in one stage of the creative process may carry over and become problematic at subsequent stages. For example, a strong norm to avoid criticism during the idea generation stage may increase the number of ideas generated but that norm would become problematic at the idea selection stage if individuals are uncomfortable pointing out the flaws in the ideas suggested by others. The avoidance of criticism could cause the group to select the least controversial idea but such ideas are not likely to be particularly creative.

It is also possible that criticism during the idea selection stage could extend beyond the task and transform into more destructive relationship conflict (Greer et al., 2010). Such conflicts could carry over into the implementation stage and cause group members to withhold effort out of resentment (why did the group not choose my idea?). In other words, groups might not easily shift their norms to suit each stage nor might they readily forget the events of earlier stages.

(3) Groups can return to an earlier stage of the creative process

The idea generation, selection and implementation stages, while conceptually discrete, may become intertwined as the group progresses.

For example, the group may modify ideas generated in the early stage if they realize during the implementation stage that the idea they selected is not feasible. The process may in fact be iterative as groups continue to generate new ideas at later stages, combine different ideas during the selection stage to arrive at a novel solution or modify ideas during the implementation stage to make the selected idea more practical. In other words, feedback loops are likely to be important to any dynamic model of the creative process. The most creative groups may not progress through each stage in a linear way.

(4) The pace may differ and the pace itself may have implications for creativity

It would be interesting to investigate how creative groups choose to allot their time and whether the speed at which groups progress through each stage might have performance implications. The more creative a group is during the idea generation stage, the more time they might need during the selection stage to consider a wide range of ideas that may cross very different categories. Groups may face a critical tradeoff between speed on the one hand and creativity on the other. Highly creative groups may also find themselves under intense time pressure during the implementation stage if they spend a long time generating ideas and deliberating over which idea to select.

Methodological Considerations for Future Research

Testing our propositions will require a methodological approach that differs from the approach used by Goncalo et al. (2010) and indeed most studies of group creativity. In this section, we suggest some methodological considerations that might be useful for testing a dynamic model of group creativity.

The experimental method is limited in its ability to capture the creative process over time as most experiments are necessarily quite short and focused on testing propositions relevant to a single stage rather than multiple stages. Alternatively, a field study in an organization using ongoing groups would be ideal for capturing the process as it occurs in a real world setting. However, it would be difficult to control what kinds of tasks the groups are working on, how the groups were formed and for what purpose. Such an endeavor would undoubtedly be worthwhile but may be daunting; it is not surprising that this kind of work is extremely rare (e.g., Amabile, Barsade, Mueller, & Staw, 2005 as an excellent example). We think it may be possible to test some initial hypotheses about group creativity over time using classroom project teams. An advantage of this approach is that there is substantial control over the parameters of the task, the formation of groups and the criteria that researchers may apply in judging creative output. In addition, it may be easier to observe such groups at every stage of the process from idea generation to implementation in a fixed period of time. Unlike the laboratory, such groups are working together on a task with real consequences for them and they are working over the course of several weeks rather than one hour. Given the relative dearth of longitudinal research on group creativity, on balance, it may be better for researchers to begin with a more doable method rather than ignore group dynamics entirely in favor of the increasingly common scenario method in which participants imagine "hypothetical" groups with no interaction (Moreland, Hogg & Hains, 1994). Here we offer some specific suggestions for how such a study might be conducted.

Task: Each team project may involve choosing a topic within organizational behavior (e.g., job satisfaction, employee motivation, leadership) and then examining that topic within the context of an actual organization. The task should involve multiple steps, including the selection of an organization to study, establishing a contact person, selecting a particular issue to study, gathering relevant information about the organization, analyzing the problem and suggesting a solution in a final group term paper. Groups should only be required to hand in their final project and they should not receive any feedback, nor should they submit any preliminary assignments before the final project deadline. Ideally, the team project would be worth a substantial portion of their final grade so the students have a reason to take their project seriously. In addition, the fact that the assignment asks them to contact a real organization may mean that such contact could lead to summer internships or job offers at the organizations they chose to study, thus making the project even more consequential.

Timing: Given that the primary goal is to observe how the creative process unfolds, the question of how to time data collection is critical. Assuming a typical 15-week semester, students should be randomly assigned to project teams by the course instructor in week 7 of the semester at the latest to give ample time for teams to interact and form a meaningful working relationship. In order to obtain a comprehensive view of the process, survey data should be collected at five different points in time. Several weeks prior to the assignment of teams (to reduce demand effects), participants should complete a questionnaire containing basic demographic information (time 0) including a measure of narcissism if that trait is the independent variable. Two weeks after groups are formed, participants should complete measures of their group process such as intra-group conflict and group norms such as competition-cooperation (time 1). Subsequent surveys should be identical and should be completed at approximately one week intervals with the last survey completed at the end of the semester during the week the final project is submitted (times 2-5). It would also be valuable to include items that would capture which stage of the process groups are actually in so that it would be possible to trace when groups transition from one stage to the next, the factors that might lead to that transition, whether some groups progress through these stages at the same pace (or skip some stages entirely) and how the overall pattern might impact the final product. The groups should not receive any feedback about their project prior to turning in the final paper so as to prevent knowledge of their performance shaping their perception of the group process (Staw, 1975). At each survey collection, participants should complete the questionnaire independently and return it directly to the researchers.

Additionally, the students could keep anonymous diaries on the events at group meetings and other interactions between group members. Such personal diary entries often entail rich information about conflicts, emotions, and Eureka moments, which might provide unexpected as well as confirm expected insights into the group process (Amabile et al., 2005).

Conclusion

In sum, we proposed a dynamic group model that incorporates and connects the three stages of the creative process. It consists of an early, idea generation stage, a middle, idea selection stage and a late, idea implementation stage. Several novel propositions emerged from our theory including the idea that narcissists can (a) have different consequences at different stages of the project, (b) that they can set in motion events like conflict that can impact subsequent stages of the process and (c) that they can compel groups to speed through certain stages or return to earlier stages. By focusing on the role of narcissism, we were able to give a concrete illustration of how a dynamic model of group creativity might play out. But more importantly, we intend our model to be a general template for theorizing about the creative process over time. We encourage other researchers to use our model as a starting point to gain new insights into the group processes that occur over time to either stifle or stimulate creative performance.

References

Amabile, T. M. (1982). Social psychology of creativity: A consensual assessment technique. *Journal of Personality and Social Psychology*, *43*, 997-1013.

—. (1983). The social psychology of creativity: A componential conceptualization. *Journal of Personality and Social Psychology, 45*, 357-376.

—. (1996). *Creativity in context.* Boulder, CO: Westview Press. Anderson, C. A., & Kilduff, G. J. (2009). Why do dominant personalities attain influence in face-to-face groups? The competence signaling effects of trait dominance. *Journal of Personality and Social Psychology, 96,* 491-503.

Amabile, T. M., Barsade, S. G., Mueller, J. S., & Staw, B. M. (2005). Affect and creativity at work. *Administrative Science Quarterly, 50,* 367-403.

Audia, P.G., & Goncalo, J.A. (2007). Success and creativity over time: A study of inventors in the hard-disk drive industry. *Management Science*, 53, 1-15.

Back, M. D., Schmukle, S. C., & Egloff, B. (2010). Why are narcissists so charming at first sight? Decoding the narcissism-popularity link at zero acquaintance. *Journal of Personality and Social Psychology, 98,* 132-145.

Baer, M., Oldham, G. R., Jacobsohn, G. C., & Hollingshead, A. B. (2008). The personality composition of teams and creativity: The moderating role of team creative confidence. *The Journal of Creative Behavior, 42,* 255-282.

Barnett, W. P., & Hansen, M. T. (1996). The red queen in organizational evolution. *Strategic Management Journal, 17,* 139-157.

Barsade, S. G. (2002). The ripple effect: Emotional contagion and its influence on group behavior. *Administrative Science Quarterly, 47,* 644-675.

Beersma, B., & De Dreu, C. K. W. (2005). Conflict's consequences: The effects of social motives on post-negotiation creative and convergent group functioning and performance. *Journal of Personality and Social Psychology*, *89*, 345-357.

Bogart, L. M., Benotsch, E. G., & Pavlovic, J. D. (2004). Feeling superior but threatened: The relation of narcissism to social comparison. *Basic and Applied Social Psychology, 26,* 35-44.

Brunell, A. B., Gentry, W. A., Campbell, W. K., Hoffman, B. J., Kuhnert, K. W., & DeMarree, K. G. (2008). Leader emergence: The case of the narcissistic leader. *Personality and Social Psychology Bulletin, 34,* 1663-1676.

Campbell, W. K., Rudich, E. A., & Sedikides, C. (2002). Narcissism, self-esteem, and the positivity of self-views: Two portraits of self-love. *Personality and Social Psychology Bulletin, 28,* 358-368.

Carroll, L. (1987). A study of narcissism, affiliation and power motives among students in business administration. *Psychological Reports, 61,* 355-358.

Chatman, J. A., Boisnier, A. D., Spataro, S. E., Anderson, C., & Berdahl, J. L. (2008). Being distinctive versus being conspicuous: The effects of numeric status and sex-stereotyped tasks on individual performance in groups. *Organizational Behavior and Human Decision Processes, 107,* 141-160.

Chatterjee, A., & Hambrick, D. C. (2007). It's all about me: Narcissistic chief executive officers and their effects on company strategy and performance. *Administrative Science Quarterly, 52,* 351-386.

Cialdini, R. B., Reno, R. R., & Kallgren, C. A. (1990). A focus theory of normative conduct: recycling the concept of norms to reduce littering in public places. *Journal of Personality and Social Psychology, 58,* 1015-1026.

Clifton, A., Turkheimer, E., & Oltmanns, T. F. (2009). Personality disorder in social networks: Network position as a marker of interpersonal dysfunction. *Social Networks, 31,* 26-32.

Collins, D. R., & Stukas, A. A. (2008). Narcissism and self-presentation: The moderating effects of accountability and contingencies of self-worth. *Journal of Research in Personality, 42,* 1629-1634.

Cronin, M. A., Weingart, L. R., & Todorova, G. (2011). Dynamics in groups: Are we there yet? *Academy of Management Annals, 5,* 571-612.

Cummings, A. & Oldham, G. R. (1997). Enhancing creativity: managing work contexts for the high potential employee. *California Management Review, 40,* 22-38.

De Dreu, C. K. W., Nijstad, B. A., & van Knippenberg, D. (2008). Motivated information processing in group judgment and decision making. *Personality and Social Psychology Review, 12,* 22-49.

De Dreu, C. K. W., & Weingart, L. R. (2003). Task versus relationship conflict, team performance, and team member satisfaction: A meta-analysis. *Journal of Applied Psychology, 88,* 741-449.

Deutschman, A. (2005). Is your boss a psychopath? *Fast Company, 96,* 44-52.

Diehl, M., & Stroebe, W. (1987). Productivity loss in brainstorming groups: Toward the solution of a riddle. *Journal of Personality and Social Psychology, 53*, 497-509.

Dugosh, K. L., & Paulus, P. B. (2005). Cognitive and social comparison processes in brainstorming. *Journal of Experimental Social Psychology, 41*, 313-320.

Elsbach, K. D., & Kramer, R. M. (2003). Assessing creativity in Hollywood pitch meetings: Evidence for a dual process model of creativity. *Academy of Management Journal, 46*, 283-301.

George, J. M. (2007). Creativity in Organizations. *The Academy of Management Annals, 1*, 439-477.

Gersick, C. (1988). Time and transition in work teams: Toward a new model of group development. *Academy of Management Journal, 32*, 274-309.

Gersick, C. J. G. (1989). Marking time: Predictable transitions in task groups. *The Academy of Management Journal, 32*, 274-309.

Goncalo, J.A., & Duguid, M.M. (2012). Follow the crowd in a new direction: When conformity pressure facilitates group creativity (and when it does not). *Organizational Behavior and Human Decision Processes, 18*, 14-23.

Goncalo, J. A., Flynn, F. J., & Kim, S. H. (2010). Are two narcissists better than one? The link between narcissism, perceived creativity, and creative performance. *Personality and Social Psychology Bulletin, 36*, 1484-1495.

Goncalo, J. A., & Kim, S. H. (2010). Distributive justice beliefs and group idea generation: Does a belief in equity facilitate productivity? *Journal of Experimental Social Psychology, 46*, 836-840.

Goncalo, J. A., & Staw, B. M. (2006). Individualism-collectivism and group creativity. *Organizational Behavior and Human Decision Processes, 100*, 96-109.

Greer, L. L., Jehn, K. A., & Mannix, E. A. (2008). Conflict transformation - A longitudinal investigation of the relationships between different types of intragroup conflict and the moderating role of conflict resolution. *Small Group Research, 39*, 278-302.

Jehn, K. A., & Mannix, E. A. (2001). The dynamic nature of conflict: A longitudinal study of intra-group conflict and group performance. *Academy of Management Journal, 44*, 238-251.

John, O. P., & Robbins, R. W. (1994). Accuracy and bias in self-perception: Individual differences in self enhancement and the role of narcissism. *Journal of Personality and Social Psychology, 66*, 206-219.

Kasof, J. (1995). Explaining creativity: The attributional perspective. *Creativity Research Journal, 8*, 311-356.

Kernis, M. H., & Sun, C. R. (1994). Narcissism and reactions to interpersonal feedback. *Journal of Research in Personality, 28*, 4-13.

Kozlowski, S. W. J., Gully, S. M., Nason, E. R., & Smith, E. M. (1999). Developing adaptive teams: A theory of comilation and performance across levels and time. In D. R. Ilgen & E. D Pulakos (Eds.), *The changing nature of performance: Implications for staffing, motivation, and development* (pp. 240-292). San Francisco: Jossey-Bass.

Lawler, E. J. (2001). An affect theory of social exchange [Electronic version]. *American Journal of Sociology 107*, 321-352.

Le, H., Oh, I.-S., R. S. B., Illies, R., Holland, E., & Westrick, P. (2011). Too much of a good thing: Curvilinear relationships between personality traits and job performance. Journal of Applied Psychology, 96, 113-133.

Lubart, T. I. (2001). Models of the creative process: Past, present and future. *Creativity Research Journal, 13,* 295-308.

Mathieu, J. E., & Rapp, T. L. (2009). Laying the foundation for successful team performance trajectories: The roles of team charters and performance strategies. *Journal of Applied Psychology, 94,* 90-103.

Miller, J. D., & Campbell, W. K. (2008). Comparing clinical and social-personality conceptualizations of narcissism. *Journal of Personality, 76,* 449-476.

Miller, J. D., Campbell, W. K., Young, D. L., Lakey, C. E., Reidy, D. E., Zeichner, A., & Goodie, A. S. (2009). Examining the relations among narcissism, impulsivity, and self-defeating behaviors. *Journal of Personality, 77,* 761-794.

Miron-Spektor, E., Erez, M., & Naveh, E. (2011). The effect of conformist and attentive-to-detail members on team innovation: reconciling the innovation paradox. *Academy of Management Journal, 54,* 740-760.

Moreland, R. L., & Levine, J. M. (2001). Socialization in organizations and work groups. *Groups at work: Theory and research.* Turner, M. E. (Ed.). 69-112.

Moreland, R. L., Hogg, M. A., & Hains, S. C. (1994). Back to the future: Social psychological research on groups. *Journal of Experimental Social Psychology, 30,* 527-555

Mueller, J. S., Goncalo, J. A., & Kamdar, D. (2011). Recognizing creative leadership: Can creative idea expression negatively relate to perceptions of leadership potential?, *Journal of Experimental Social Psychology, 47,* 494-498.

Mueller, J. S., Melwani, S., & Goncalo, J. A. (2012). The bias against creativity: Why people desire but reject creative ideas. *Psychological Science, 23,* 13-17.

Munkes, J., & Diehl, M. (2003). Matching or competition? Performance comparison processes in an idea generation task. *Group Processes and Intergroup Relations, 6,* 305-320.

Nemeth, C. J., Connell, J. B., Rogers, J. D., & Brown, K. S. (2001). Improving decision making by means of dissent. *Journal of Applied Social Psychology, 31,* 48-58.

Nemeth, C., & Rogers, J. (1996). Dissent and the search for information. *British Journal of Social Psychology, 35,* 67-76.

Nemeth, C., & Wachtler, J. (1974). Creating the perceptions of consistency and confidence: A necessary condition for minority influence. *Sociometry, 37,* 529-540.

Nevicka, B., De Hoogh, A. H. B., Van Vianen, A. E. M., Beersma, B., & McIlwain, D. (2011). All I need is a stage to shine: Narcissists' leader emergence and performance. The Leadership Quarterly, 22, 910-925.

Nijstad, B. A., & De Dreu, C. K. W. (2002). Creativity and group innovation. *Applied Psychology: An International Review, 51,* 400-406.

Nijstad, B. A., Stroebe, W., & Lodewijkx, H. F. M. (2002). Cognitive stimulation and interference in groups: Exposure effects in an idea generation task. *Journal of Experimental Social Psychology, 38,* 535-544.

Okhuysen, G. A., & Waller, M. J. (2002). Focusing on midpoint transitions: An analysis of boundary conditions. *Academy of Management Journal, 45,* 1056-1065.

Paulus, P. B., & Yang, H. C. (2000). Idea generation in groups: A basis for creativity in organizations. *Organizational Behavior and Human Decision Processes, 82,* 76-87.

Paulus, P.B., & Dzindolet, M. T. (1993). Social influence processes in group brainstorming. *Journal of Personality and Social Psychology, 64,* 575-586.

Paulhus, D. L. (1998). Interpersonal and intrapsychic adaptiveness of trait self-enhancement: A mixed blessing? *Journal of Personality and Social Psychology, 74,* 1197-1208.

Paulhus, D. L., & Williams, K. M. (2002). The dark triad of personality: Narcissism, Machiavellianism and psychopathy. *Journal of Research in Personality, 36,* 556-563.

Pettit, N. C., & Lount, R. B. (2010). Looking down and ramping up: The impact of status differences on effort in intergroup contexts. *Journal of Experimental Social Psychology, 46*, 9-20.

Pierce, J. R., & Aguinis, H. (2013). The too-much-of-a-good-thing effect in management. *Journal of Management, 39*, 313-338.

Raskin, R., & Hall, C. S. (1981). The narcissistic personality inventory: Alternate form reliability and further evidence of construct validity. *Journal of Personality Assessment, 45*, 159-162.

Raskin, R. N., & Shaw, R. (1988). Narcissism and the use of personal pronouns. *Journal of Personality, 56*, 393-404.

Rietzschel, E., Nijstad, B., & Stroebe, W. (2006). Productivity is not enough: A comparison of interactive and nominal brain-storming groups on idea generation and selection. *Journal of Experimental Social Psychology, 42*, 244-251.

Rijsman, J. B. (1974). Factors in social comparison of performance influencing actual performance. *European Journal of Social Psychology,* 4(3), 279–311.

Schilpzand, M. C., Herold, D. M., & Shalley, C. E. (2011). Members' openness to experience and teams' creative performance. *Small Group Research, 42*, 55-76.

Sedikides, C., Rudich, E. A., Gregg, A. P., Kumashiro, M., & Rusbult, C. (2004). Are normal narcissists psychologically healthy?: Self-esteem matters. *Journal of Personality and Social Psychology, 87*, 400-416.

Shalley, C. E., & Gilson, L. L. (2004). What leaders need to know: A review of social and contextual factors that can foster or hinder creativity. *Leadership Quarterly, 15*, 33-53.

Shalley, C. E., & Oldham, G. R. (1997). Competition and creative performance: effects of competitor presence and visibility. *Creativity Research Journal, 10*, 337-345.

Silvia, P. J., Nusbaum, E. C., Berg, C., Martin, C., & O'Connor, A. (2009). Openness to experience, plasticity, and creativity: Exploring lower order, higher-order, and interactive effects. *Journal of Research in Personality*, 43, 1087–1090.

Simonton, D. K. (1999). Creativity as blind variation and selective retention: Is the creative process Darwinian? *Psychological Inquiry, 10*, 309-328.

Stucke, T. S., & Sporer, S. L. (2002). When a grandiose self-image is threatened: narcissism and self-concept clarity as predictors of negative emotions and aggression following ego-threat. *Journal of Personality, 70*, 509-532.

Taylor, C. W., & Barron, F. (1963). *Scientific creativity*. New York, NY: Wiley.

Tuckman, B. 1965. Developmental sequence in small groups. *Psychological Bulletin, 63,* 384–99

Watson, P. J., Grisham, S. O., Trotter, M. V., & Biderman, M. D. (1984). Narcissism and empathy: Validity evidence for the narcissistic personality inventory. *Journal of Personality Assessment, 48,* 301-306.

West, M. A. (2002). Sparkling fountains or stagnant ponds: An integrative model of creativity and innovation implementation in work groups. *Applied Psychology: An International Review, 51,* 355-424.

Zeigler-Hill, V. (2005). Discrepancies between implicit and explicit self-esteem: Implications for narcissism and self-esteem instability. *Journal of Personality, 74,* 119-144.

CHAPTER FOUR

A THEORY OF EMERGENT LEADERS, CONFLICT AND PERFORMANCE

EMMA Y. ZHAO AND KAREN A. JEHN
UNIVERSITY OF MELBOURNE, AUSTRALIA

Abstract

Leaders can cause conflict and influence the relationship between conflict and team outcomes. First, we propose that emergent leaders are more likely to cause more conflict compared to assigned leaders (leaders appointed by the organization or governing body) due to their difference in power and capability. Second, we have developed a new framework through which a leader's self-entitlement is likely to affect the relationship between emergent leadership and conflict by exacerbating relationship and process conflict, but ameliorating task conflict. Furthermore, our model incorporates leader conflict management behaviors (forcing and problem-solving) to moderate the link between conflict and team performance. We suggest that forcing behavior is likely to decrease team performance, whereas leaders that employ problem-solving behaviors to solve conflict will contribute to comparatively better team performance. Practical contributions of the model and future research directions are also discussed.

Keywords: emergent leaders; conflict; performance; teams.

Introduction

Conflict often occurs in situations where individuals interact with each other (cf. Jehn & Bendersky, 2003). Conflict can therefore be prevalent in work teams and there is often a need to identify the cause of conflict and also how to address the conflict. Leaders have a special role in teams and contribute to various team processes such as effectiveness and team performance (e.g., Dionne, Yammarino, Atwater & Spangler, 2004; Hiller, Day, & Vance, 2005; Morgeson, DeRue, & Karam, 2010). We propose that in context of lower competency and ineffectiveness in managing their power bases, emergent leaders can contribute to conflict (over and above assigned leaders), that entitlement moderates this relationship, and finally conflict management style of the emergent leader moderates the relationship between conflict and team performance. Recent surveys by consulting firms like Deloitt (Kwan, Schwartz, & Liakopoulos, 2010) show that the top concern for global firms in their talent strategies are competing for talent and developing leaders/succession planning. Thus, firms actively promote leader emergence throughout their organization and in response 'leader hopefuls' seek out leadership opportunities wherever possible. In our model, we would like to highlight the potential downside to advocating everyone to be leaders and instead focus on how emergent leaders could be detrimental to team processes.

The answer to how emergent leaders may cause conflict could lie in certain personality factors. Certainly, not all leaders cause conflict; however, in the case of emergent leaders we suggest that in the context of lower competency and ineffectiveness in managing their power bases, they are more likely to contribute to conflict. In terms of personality factors, our current model (see Figure 4-1) explores leader self-entitlement as the moderating factor in emergent leadership and conflict. Emergent leaders are not given a leadership position in the traditional sense (i.e., dictated or designated by the organization), but rather they emerge as a product of team processes (Yoo & Alavi, 2003) often in self-managed teams. There is also evidence advocating that certain types of leaders and leader behaviors may cause havoc on their subordinates and teams (Jensen & Raver, 2012; Kets de Vries & Miller, 1985; Rispens, Giebels & Jehn, 2010; Tepper, 2000). For example, research has identified that leaders with narcissistic personalities tend to cause extreme/volatile company performance (i.e., excellent performance or very poor performance, no middle ground; Chatterjee & Hambrick, 2007), lowered work performance (Judge, LePine, & Rich, 2006), resource destruction (Campbell, Bush, Brunell, & Shelton, 2005) and reduction of likeability by peers as time passes (Paulhus, 1998). Similarly, studies on abusive supervisors have found that employees experience psychological distress, aggression, decreased family well-being, deviant organizational behaviors (cf. Tepper, 2007) and even supervisor directed deviance (Mitchell & Ambrose, 2007). Previous research on entitlement shows that highly entitled individuals have an irrational belief that they deserve more than others (Jehn & Bezrukova,

2010) and have a reduced sense of empathy for others (Watson, Grisham, Trotter, & Biderman, 1984). Thus we propose that entitlement moderates the relationship between emergent leadership and conflict in that when entitlement in leaders is high the relationship between emergent leader to conflict will be stronger (direction vary depending on types of conflict). This framework allows us to explore how different roles within the team may cause conflict through variations in entitlement.

Figure 4-1. Effect Of Leader On Conflict And Team Performance

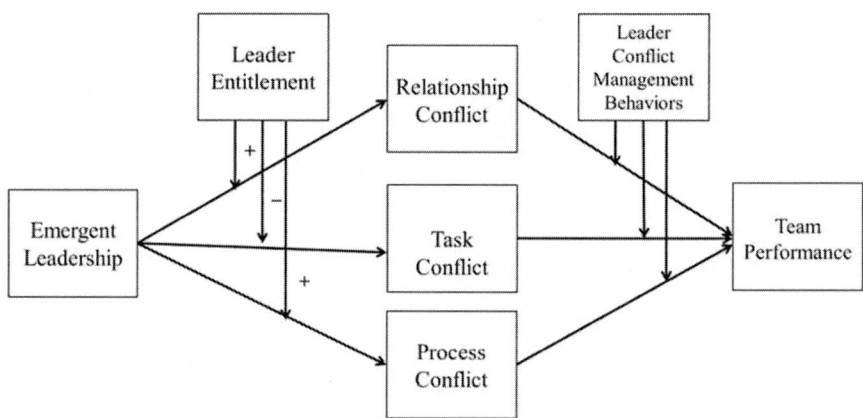

Additionally, we theorize that leader conflict management behaviors are an important moderator in the conflict-performance relationship (see Figure 4-1). Jehn and Mannix (2001) suggested that leaders are crucial in setting norms and promoting constructive behaviors to increase chances of success for the team. Thus we suggest that certain leader conflict management behaviors are likely to influence the relationship between conflict and team performance.

We will produce a variety of unique propositions on the relationship between leadership, conflict and team outcomes. The first part of the chapter will explore the relationship between conflict, and leadership, in which we will also define conflict and explore the reasons as to why we discuss separate types of conflict (relationship, task and process conflict) rather than conflict as a general concept. Following on from this, we will discuss the moderating role of entitlement on the emergent leadership and conflict relationship. Lastly, we will examine the moderating role of leader conflict management behavior on the link between conflict and team performance.

Leadership and Conflict

Conflict is defined as a perceived difference, discrepancy, or incompatibility in desires, interests, beliefs, or values between individuals or groups (Boulding, 1963; Wall & Callister, 1995). Conflict is categorized into three different types; relationship, task, and process conflicts (Jehn, 1995, 1997; Jehn & Mannix, 2001; Jehn, Northcraft & Neale, 1999). Relationship conflict refers to conflict that arises due to a disagreement or incompatibility on a personal level. Relationship conflict tends to be charged with negative emotions between conflicting parties. Task conflict is a disagreement on the group task itself; either on the outcomes or the content of the task that is being performed. Process conflict is a disagreement on *how* a task should be accomplished, specifically, it relates to the delegation of duties and resources. As we are interested in emergent leaders' contribution to conflict, to better understand the unique position of the emergent leader, in section only we will seek to compare emergent leaders with traditional type leaders; that is assigned (or formal) leaders.

Emergent Leadership and Conflict

We propose that leadership can contribute to conflict in two different ways, 1) as the cause of conflict and 2) that leader conflict management behaviors in response to existing conflict may act as the exacebater in the conflict-outcome relationship (see Figure 4-1). Most of the current literature on leadership and conflict focus on how leaders effectively manage conflict in order to reduce aggravation. However, scholars and practitioners often forget that leaders can also be the cause of conflict. For instance, they may hoard glory and resources so that team members are unable to complete their tasks in a satisfactory manner (e.g., Sims & Brinkmann, 2002; Sparrow & Liden, 1997); hence the leader causes dissatisfaction and conflict in the team. In teams with emergent leaders, these contributors to conflict are likely to be greater compared to assigned leaders as there may be conflict between individuals if more than one person wants to be the leader. In another scenario, the emerged leader can be talented in managing group goals and tasks, but may not have the ability to effectively manage conflict (especially if they have no prior experiences in managing teams); hence they may exacerbate the conflict situation.

From the social identity perspective of leadership, leaders emerge as a product of the team prototype (the ideal team member that represents the group's identity) (see Hogg, 2001). Over time, leaders are considered more distinct from the group due to differences in their structural role (Hogg & Reid, 2001). Hence leaders become the 'other' in their own group, thus giving them a distinct role. As a leader's role may involve defining goals, delegating tasks, and managing team relationships (cf. Zaccaro, Rittman & Marks, 2001); these are all distinctively related to conflict. In our current model, we aim to explore the causal relationship between emergent leadership and conflict as well as touching on the role of leadership conflict management behaviors in the link between conflict and team performance (see Figure 4-1).

Emergent Leadership in Context of Power and Conflict

Leadership implies the ability for one person to influence others to achieve a common goal (Yukl, 2006). Influence over others can be gained if an individual has power. Thus power is one of the bases for influence. There are multiple types of power. Five types of power were initially noted by French and Raven (1959) which included reward power, coercive power, legitimate power, referent power, and expert power. Later, Hersey, Blanchard and Natemeyer (1979) expanded the five sources of power to seven sources with the inclusion of informational and connection power. The five original types of power can be conceptualized into two broad categories; position (legitimate, coercive, and reward powers) and personal power (referent and expert power) (Bass, 1960; Conger & Kanungo, 1987). Position power is power that is given to an individual due to their formal title in the organization, in other words they are assigned leaders. Whereas personal power is derived from the individual and/or from the relationship between the individual and their team.

It is possible to argue that emergent leaders might be at a slight disadvantage compared to assigned leaders. Emergent leaders are not able to draw on position power, but instead need to obtain personal power through other means. Assigned leaders can lead without seeking further power (if they wish to), and rely on position power. Using an extreme example, monarchs, like Prince Charles, are born with a title and position in society; whether they have personal power does not influence the authority they hold. Robin Hood is the Prince of Thieves, which is a title given to him due to his personal power and has little to do with his birth or position in society. In organizations, position power is less absolute, hence can be gained or lost considerably easier and quicker. For example, CEOs and leaders often resign or are removed from office due to an inability to perform, which is frequently measured by fiscal means such as a reduction in profit and share prices. Furthermore, following on from the discussion above, we note that assigned leaders may lose their position due to lack of effectiveness; equally, emergent leaders may need to continually prove their competence to remain in power. This can cause *relationship* conflict between leader and other contenders for leadership (cf. Jehn & Bendersky, 2003). Bendersky and Hays (2012) coined a new type of conflict called 'status conflict' and defined this as conflict over their status within their group's social hierarchy. It was found that status conflict has detrimental effects on group performance (Bendersky & Hays, 2012). Therefore multiple individuals with high power can also cause conflict. Conflict is higher in teams with high power (teams that are higher in hierarchy) as compared with those in low power (Greer, Caruso, & Jehn, 2011). This may be due to the continued tension between the members in the high powered team trying to gain more resources. Lack of leadership clarity and conflict over leadership has negative consequences for the team including lower support for innovation and lower participation levels within the team (West, Borrill, Dawson, Brodbeck, Shapiro, & Haward, 2003). Therefore it is possible that emergent leadership, or contention to be the emergent leader, can be the cause of conflict (see Figure 4-1) more so than among assigned leaders.

Leader Competency and Conflict

How competent a leader is can influence group conflict. For example, process conflict can occur between a leader and a group member if a leader distributes rewards based on favoritism rather than contribution (as the leader is unaware of how to manage relationships in a competent manner). It may even affect the cohesion of the group as team members might start forming alliances due to the perceived changes in social status of one individual over the other and members can divide into opposing sides (cf. Bendersky & Hays, 2012). Emergent leaders may be more prone to cause conflict than assigned leaders as they may not be aware of the best way to manage their team, due to lack of training or experience. Hence competency also plays a part in causing conflict. Taking the example from above of playing favorites, it may be that the emergent leader consciously plays favoritism due to their misplaced belief that in doing so they are securing the support of certain members of the team (thereby believing they are increasing personal power), but is completely unaware of the dire consequences this simple act may provoke.

Competency or capability of leaders can also be defined by two categories: task and interpersonal (Bass & Bass, 2008). We propose that task competence is likely to be related to task conflict and interpersonal competence is likely to be related to relationship conflict. Emergent leaders may cause more *task* conflict than assigned leaders. This is because they may not be capable or skilled enough to clearly define the task that the team needs to achieve or they may lack the ability to identify specific requirements that need to be met in order to successfully perform tasks. Others within the group who do have these skills and knowledge may disagree with the emergent leader's ideas on how to complete the task, therefore creating process conflict.

It is also possible that emergent leaders contribute more to relationship conflict compared to assigned leaders. Emergent leaders may lack the ability to deal effectively with relationship issues within the team (interpersonal competence). If leaders are able to understand, care for, or consider others, they are more likely than other team members to decrease conflict (e.g., Baron, 1989). Leadership (e.g., transformational leaders) and (e.g., change) management research all stress the importance of understanding, considering, and effectively communicating ideas to meet the needs of their followers (e.g., Bass, 1990; Kotter, 1995). If emergent leaders are unaware of these areas (perhaps no prior training or experience as leaders compared to assigned leaders), then they are likely to cause relationship conflict and potentially lose their role as emergent leaders in a team.

Therefore we propose emergent leaders may cause more conflict within teams than traditional assigned leaders in conditions where they are not competent and are unable to effectively manage personal power.

Proposition 1: Emergent leaders are more likely to cause relationship, task and process conflicts compared to assigned leaders.

Entitlement as a Moderator

High self-entitlement is a belief that one deserves more than others regardless of one's effort (Jehn & Bezrukova, 2010). Individuals with high self-entitlement are often characterized by a lack of empathy for others (Watson et. al., 1984). Both psychological entitlement and the entitlement dimension in the Narcissistic Personality Inventory (NPI; it is proposed that the dimension in the NPI is a more pathological variant of psychological entitlement) are correlated with higher disagreeableness such as deceitfulness, higher tendency to be non-compliant, and immodesty (Pryor, Miller, & Gaughan, 2008). Consequences of high psychological entitlement include deservingness of higher pay compared to others (Campbell, Bonacci, Shelton, Exline, & Bushman, 2004), aggression following ego threat (Campbell et. al., 2004), higher self-serving bias (Harvey & Martinko, 2009), and highly entitled individuals are likely to have chronic relationship conflict and hostility (through chronic self-image goals; Moeller, Crocker, & Bushman, 2009). These are all factors that may exacerbate conflict within groups (Please see Figure 4-1).

Entitlement is expected to affect each type of conflict differently. We propose that higher entitlement in emergent leaders is likely to produce higher relationship conflict. This is because it is possible that due to their high self-regard and enhancement (Paulhus, 1998), they are initially liked by their peers, but their extreme arrogance will cause their likability to decrease over time. They also have a tendency to be incredibly warm initially and then drastically cold towards others later, which will affect their relationships with subordinates. For example, imagine working with someone who experiences that is warm and caring one second and then suddenly cold and hostile the next. It becomes very hard to predict their attitudes and actions, hence creating relationship conflict within the team.

Proposition 2a: Entitlement will moderate the relationship between emergent leadership and relationship conflict such that the relationship between emergent leadership and relationship conflict is more positive when entitlement is high.

Entitlement is likely to contribute to a stronger and negative relationship between emergent leaders and process conflict. Entitlement has been found to be related to a decrease of allocation of resources to others (Campbell et. al., 2004). Hence we believe it is highly probable that entitled leaders are more likely to keep 'good' resources and delegate better duties for themselves. As teams begin to notice these actions and deeds, they are more likely to become disgruntled and hence process conflict will transpire. Their tendency to lie and be non-compliant suggests that they may act in discordance to others in the team in order to complete the assigned work. Thereby causing conflict in the team on how things should be done.

Proposition 2b: Entitlement will moderate the relationship between emergent leadership and process conflict such that the relationship between emergent leadership and process conflict is more positive when entitlement is high.

In contrast to both relationship and process conflicts, we propose that the relationship between emergent leadership and task conflict may not be exacerbated by entitlement in conditions where there is low correlation between task and relationship conflict within the team. Entitled individuals can seem confident and can make quick decisions (see Jones & Paulhus, 2011; Campbell, Goodie, & Foster, 2004), therefore team members are more likely to draw confidence from the leader and make quick decisions on tasks. Higher self-entitlement is also related to lower empathy for others (Watson et. al., 1984), therefore they potentially are able to make hard decisions that benefit task completion over and above consideration for others. Thus, entitlement may actually assist in ameliorating the relationship between emergent leaders and conflict. However, drawing on findings from de Wit and colleagues (2012), we believe that the proposition only holds true when the correlation between task conflict and relationship conflict is low.

In line with the rationale, we propose that:

Proposition 2c: Entitlement will moderate the relationship between emergent leadership and task conflict such that the relationship between emergent leadership and task conflict is negative when entitlement is high, when the correlation between task and relationship conflict is low.

Effect of Conflict on Performance

The three types of conflict evoke different interactions among team members. Several studies have noted the different effects of the types of conflict on performance (de Wit, Greer & Jehn, 2012). Notably, a moderate amount of task conflict may be beneficial to teams in certain situations and depend upon team member beliefs (e.g., task conflict with no negative emotional attachments to the conflict and a belief that the conflict is resolvable) (Jehn, 1994; 1997). However, relationship conflict and process conflict have few potential benefits to performance regardless of degree of conflict that is present in the team. In a recent meta-analysis, de Wit, Greer and Jehn (2012) developed further insight into the different conflict types and their effects on team outcomes. Various moderators were also examined. They found that collectively, all conflict types were more negatively correlated with proximal group outcomes (outcomes that are an immediate response to the conflict, e.g., affective states) than distal group outcomes (outcomes that are temporally further than proximal outcomes, e.g., group performance). In the distinction between conflict types, task conflict is negatively related to proximal outcomes but to a lesser degree than process and relationship conflict. The relationship between task conflict and outcomes was also moderated by co-occurrence of conflict types (a combination of conflict types) and organizational level (top management teams vs. lower hierarchy teams). Task conflict and group performance had a more positive relationship 1) if the correlation between task and relationship conflict is weak, 2) in top management teams as compared to non-top management teams, and 3) in situations where performance were either measured through financial gains and decision quality rather than overall performance. Thus the relationship between conflict types and team outcomes is not straightforward, but rather moderated by various factors. In our model, we will examine team performance as the outcome and propose that leader conflict management behavior moderates the relationship. We also wish to develop our theory in terms of different conflict types. It is more intuitive and informative to study conflict this way as conflict types vary in their effects on team outcomes.

In the current model, conflict is exacerbated by the entitled leader (see Figure 4-1), but once the conflict is in existence, leaders can attempt to resolve the conflict through appropriate conflict management behaviors. At present, limited research has been published examining the leader's ability to manage conflict (Goldman, Cropanzano, Stein, & Benson, 2008). Very few researchers have looked at the moderating effects of leader conflict management behaviors on the relationship between conflict and team level performance. A recent study on the moderating effects of leader conflict management behaviors on the conflict-stress relationship (Romer, Rispens, Giebels, & Euwema, 2012) has shown that forcing (leader imposes the solution they prefer to end the dispute) and avoiding behaviors (leader chooses not to involve themselves into the conflict) elevate stress, whereas problem solving behaviors (leader finds a solution that addresses everyone's concerns) buffer the relationship between conflict and stress outcomes. In our model, we believe that forcing and problem solving behaviors are more closely related to team performance (negatively and positively). Forcing behaviors are more likely to contribute to a decrease in performance, and problem solving behaviors are more likely to reduce conflict within teams and therefore teams are likely to perform better. This is because forcing behaviors imply that the leader is unable to or chooses not to be empathetic to the disputing parties. Third party autocratic behavior (forcing one's own ideas on to disputing parties) has also been shown to have a negative correlation with perceived third party fairness (Karambayya, Brett, & Lytle, 1992). Perceptions of injustice in turn can have a negative effect on individual and team performance (e.g., Cohen-Charash & Spector, 2001; Colquitt, Noe, &

Jackson, 2002; Simons & Roberson, 2003). Additionally, problem solving behaviors are more likely to enhance performance as the underlying issues are addressed and participants are likely to feel that the proceedings were fair and solutions acceptable for them. In one study, problem solving (or collaborating behaviors as referred to in the study) was the only conflict management style that existed in teams that were both high on performance and satisfaction (Behfar, Peterson, Mannix & Trochim, 2008). Additionally forcing conflict management behaviors were predominately utilized by teams that were both low on performance and satisfaction (Behfar, et. al., 2008). This study, however, did not look at the third party conflict management behaviors of leaders, but instead at the general conflict management behaviors of the team.

Leaders are generally the first point of call to resolve conflict. If the leaders are capable of managing or resolving the conflict, then teams can continue to perform effectively. If they are unable to settle the conflict, it is possible that the matter may escalate and lead to members threatening and deceiving each other (Jehn, 1997), and this can result in other negative behaviors such as bullying (Einarsen, 2000). Thus the conflict management behaviors of leaders can exacerbate or ameliorate the relationship between conflict inception and team outcomes.

We believe that forcing conflict management behaviors of emergent leaders will lead to lower team performance for all conflict types, whereas problem-solving behaviors are more likely to lead to increased performance:

Proposition 3a: An emergent leader's forcing conflict management behaviors will lead to lower performance when acting as a moderator between all conflict types and team performance.

Proposition 3b: An emergent leader's problem-solving conflict management behaviors will lead to increase in performance when acting as a moderator between all conflict types and team performance.

Discussion

At some point in an individual's working life, they will encounter conflict either as a bystander or as a participant. However, research on the relationship between leaders and conflict is still, oddly, in its inception. In this chapter we propose a novel framework incorporating entitlement as a moderator in the link between emergent leadership and conflict. We also explored the importance of how leader conflict management behaviors can moderate the relationship between conflict and team performance.

Theoretical Contributions

Our framework proposes that entitlement exacerbates the relationship between emergent leaders and relationship and process conflicts. However, entitlement may ameliorate the relationship between emergent leaders and task conflict. In our model, we are interested in theorizing how emergent leaders can cause more conflict than assigned leaders due to two reasons; power and competency. In terms of power, emergent leaders need to gain personal power (as position power is not accessible by emergent leaders), through various means. If more than one individual wants to be the emergent leader, contention for power could cause conflict. Another way in which emergent leaders can cause conflict is through competency. If they are not capable (e.g., they may not have led a team before), then there may be unrest in the team as they are unable to effectively define tasks, manage team processes, or build quality relationships.

Entitlement is able to moderate the relationship between emergent leadership and conflict due to various characteristics of entitlement that are tied to ameliorating or exacerbating conflict. For example they lack empathy (thereby possibly causing relationship conflict with others), believe they deserve more than others (could hoard good resources and distribute others to subordinates, thereby process conflict), but they are quick decision makers and have higher perceived confidence (quick to decide on tasks and seem confident about decisions, thus ameliorate task conflict when correlation between task and relationship conflict is low). By proposing this model, we contribute to current conflict literature through the theory that roles within teams and personality attributes of the people in those roles are important factors in affecting conflict within teams.

Leader conflict management behaviors can alter the effects of conflict on team performance. At the team level, the leader is believed to be the person most responsible for resolving conflicts (Epitropaki & Martin, 2004). Our analysis suggests that leader conflict management behavior is able to critically affect the conflict to performance relationship. Leader problem-solving behaviors during the conflict management process can lead to better team outcomes as the leader is able to find a solution that addresses the concerns of each party. On the other hand, leader forcing behaviors during conflict management are likely to aggravate the conflicting parties and contribute to lowered performance as forcing behaviors are likely to induce feelings of being unjustly treated and lower the satisfaction of employees (e.g., Behfar, et. al., 2008; Cohen-Charash & Spector, 2001). Forcing behaviors may seem like a quick resolution, but we know from the negotiations and mediation literature that forcing the mediator's solution on the dispute is not always constructive to resolving conflict (cf. Fisher et. al., 1991). This is because each party (including the leader) has different underlying interests (Fisher et. al., 1991). Thus our model builds on current research in conflict management in terms of the importance of the leader's role and behavior in handling conflicts and its influence on team performance.

Overall, we hope our model is able to contribute to the existing literature on leadership as a team process (e.g., shared leadership; Carson, Tesluk, & Marrone, 2007, distributed leadership; Gronn, 2002). Specifically, emergent leaders are a product of team processes (competence and power depending on the needs of the team) and that differences between individuals (entitlement and conflict management style) are likely to affect the quality of the relationships within the team as well as other processes such as conflict and performance.

Practical Contributions

Through studying entitlement, researchers will be able to inform teams with emergent leaders how to identify and manage behaviors of entitled leaders. Therefore, team training and development could incorporate certain activities to alleviate tension that is caused by entitlement before it develops into conflict. Leadership training could also include teachings on entitlement. This will enable leaders to recognize damaging entitlement behaviors (in themselves or others) and attempt to limit these behaviors from occurring in the team. It could also assist organizations in constructing teams. For example, organizations may want to purposely place an entitled individual in a team that requires a quick decision maker and have systems in place to manage the dynamics.

Although conflict is best resolved as quickly as possible, organizations need to understand that not all conflict management behaviors lead to positive outcomes; some may cause a decrease in performance. To avoid a loss in performance, organizational training on conflict management should emphasize the importance of adopting problem-solving behaviors during conflict management. Leaders could also be taught to seek advice or ultimately suggest an alternate third party if they believe that they are unable to successfully resolve the conflict, rather than forcing their solution on to the conflicting parties. Leaders are then able to exhibit effective conflict management behaviors as they understand that the quality of resolution is more important than the speed of resolution.

Future Research Directions

Temporal component of teams. Past research has shown that the amount of time members have spent in a team affects team processes such as performance (e.g., Harrison, Mohammed, McGrath, Florey, & Vanderstoep, 2006), thus it is likely that the time aspect of teams could be a focus for future studies. Research could compare the conflict management behaviors of emergent leaders in terms of time constraints. The first potential comparison angle may concern the frequency of the adopted conflict management behavior. For example, teams may be formed for a relatively short period in order to complete certain tasks (e.g., project teams); leaders may be more likely to adopt a forcing behavior so that the matter can be quickly solved. Whereas in a team that has been established for a long time and will continue to exist in the foreseeable future, it is possible that leaders will adopt a problem solving approach. The second comparison angle would be on the effect of the conflict management behavior on performance. If the relationship is expected to be short, team members may not invest into the conflict as compared to those in established teams. It could mean that performance may be influenced to a lesser extent in temporary teams when forcing conflict management behaviors are used by leaders as compared to established teams. Additionally, problem solving behaviors may have less of a positive effect on performance in temporary teams compared to established teams as problem solving takes time and may actually distract members from the task at hand and thus affect conflict.

Difference in effort expended between emergent and assigned leaders. It takes effort to manage conflict. As described in our definition of problem-solving conflict management behaviors, we know that in order to resolve the issue, the leader needs to expend effort to understand the different points of view. In the case of emergent leaders, perhaps they are not as willing to exert time into managing conflict if they themselves do not have an invested interest in the outcome (i.e., the outcome will affect them directly in some way). They may not see their role as including aspects such as managing team conflict. However it could also be argued that emergent leaders may exert more effort to managing conflict as it is not normally their place to do so. Through managing conflict, they could see it as an investment into their position as the emergent leader as they are a product of team processes. They may relish the opportunity to flaunt their conflict management skills. Furthermore, it is likely that emergent leaders may want to improve upon their formal leadership prospects, thus allocating a greater amount of effort to ensure the team functions to the best of its ability. Thus this area could benefit from further analysis and exploration.

Conflict management style of leaders. Future research could test the existence of a fourth conflict management behavior; oblivion. In research on conflict asymmetry, team members often have different perceptions of conflict and this leads to different outcomes for the team and themselves (Jehn, Rispens & Thatcher, 2010). Oblivion is the condition whereby individuals within the team may not see or sense conflict in their team. For example, team members may intentionally hide their conflict with others in the team; therefore those uninvolved (in this case the leader) might not be aware of conflict within the team. Or it could simply be that the leader is not perceptive enough to identify conflict. If the leader is oblivious to the conflict, then they cannot and do not attempt to resolve the issue. Research could also examine whether oblivion will affect team outcomes differently to similar conflict management behaviors (e.g., avoiding).

Conclusion

We developed a framework to address the shortage of literature on the relationship between emergent leadership, and its effects on conflict and performance. In this chapter, we have incorporated prior research to encapsulate a series of conditions and processes where we sought to explain the possible connections between why emergent leaders may influence conflict when they are less competent and unable to effectively manage personal power. In addition, we present arguments on how differences in leaders (i.e. entitlement) may exacerbate the relationship between leadership and conflict. Furthermore, our model highlights the importance of leader conflict management styles on the relationship between conflict and team performance.

Our model will hopefully assist scholars in understanding leaders as a part of an ongoing team process. The more we understand how members within a team interact and take on different roles, the more we can explain the variations in how they influence conflict and the performance of the team. We hope our framework is able to assist organizations in recognizing leader attributes that may exacerbate conflict and in identifying conflict management behaviors that are best able to assist with increasing team performance.

References

Baron, R. A. (1989). Personality and organizational conflict: Effects of the type a behavior pattern and self-monitoring. *Organizational Behavior and Human Decision Processes, 44*(2), 281-296.

Bass, B. M. (1960). *Leadership, psychology, and organizational behavior.* New York: Harper.

—. (1990). From Transactional to Transformational Leadership: Learning to Share the Vision. *Organizational Dynamics, 18*(3), 19-31.

Bass, B. M., & Bass, R. (2008). *The Bass Handbook of Leadership: Theory, Research, and Managerial Applications* (4 ed.). New York: Free Press.

Behfar, K. J., Peterson, R. S., Mannix, E. A., & Trochim, W. M. K. (2008). 'The critical role of conflict resolution in teams: A close look at the links between conflict type, conflict management strategies, and team outcomes': Correction. *Journal of Applied Psychology, 93*(2), 462-462.

Bendersky, C., & Hays, N. A. (2012). Status Conflict in Groups. *Organization Science*(2), 323.

Boulding, K. (1963). *Conflict and defense.* New York: Harper and Row.

Campbell, W. K., Bonacci, A. M., Shelton, J., Exline, J. J., & Bushman, B. J. (2004). Psychological Entitlement: Interpersonal Consequences and Validation of a Self-Report Measure. *Journal of personality assessment, 83*(1), 29-45.

Campbell, W. K., Bush, C. P., Brunell, A. B., & Shelton, J. (2005). Understanding the Social Costs of Narcissism: The Case of the Tragedy of the Commons. *Personality and Social Psychology Bulletin, 31*(10), 1358-1368.

Campbell, W. K., Goodie, A. S., & Foster, J. D. (2004). Narcissism, confidence, and risk attitude. *Journal of Behavioral Decision Making, 17*(4), 297-311.

Carson, J. B., Tesluk,P. E., & Marrone, J. A. (2007). Shared leadership in teams: An investigation of antecedent conditions and performance. *Academy of Management Journal, 50(5),* 1217-1234.

Chatterjee, A., & Hambrick, D. C. (2007). It's All about Me: Narcissistic Chief Executive Officers and Their Effects on Company Strategy and Performance. *Administrative Science Quarterly, 52*(3), 351-386.

Cohen-Charash, Y., & Spector, P. E. (2001). The Role of Justice in Organizations: A Meta-Analysis. *Organizational Behavior and Human Decision Processes, 86*(2), 278-321.

Colquitt, J. A., Noe, R. A., & Jackson, C. L. (2002). Justice in Teams:

A Theory of Emergent Leaders, Conflict and Performance   107

Antecedents and consequences of procedural justice climate. *Personnel Psychology, 55*(1), 83-109.

Conger, J. A., & Kanungo, R. N. (1987). Toward a Behavioral Theory of Charismatic Leadership in Organizational Settings. *Academy of Management Review, 12*(4), 637-647.

de Wit, F. R. C., Greer, L. L., & Jehn, K. A. (2012). The paradox of intragroup conflict: A meta-analysis. *Journal of applied psychology, 97*(2), 360.

Dionne, S. D., Yammarino, F. J., Atwater, L. E., & Spangler, W. D. (2004). Transformational leadership and team performance. *Journal of Organizational Change Management, 17*(2), 177-193.

Einarsen, S. (2000). Bullying and harassment at work: a review of the Scandinavian approach. *Aggression and Violent Behavior*, 5, 379-401.

Epitropaki, O., & Martin, R. (2004). Implicit Leadership Theories in Applied Settings: Factor Structure, Generalizability, and Stability Over Time. *Journal of Applied Psychology, 89*(2), 293-310.

Fisher, R., Ury, W., & Patton, B. (1991). *Getting to Yes: Negotiating Agreement Without Giving In* (2 ed.). New York: Penguin Books.

French, J. R. P., & Raven, B. (1959). The bases of social power. In D. Cartwright & A. Zander (Eds.), *Group dynamics*. New York: Harper & Row.

Goldman, B. M., Cropanzano, R., Stein, J., & Benson, L. III. (2008). The role of third parties/mediation in managing conflict in organizations. In M. J. G. Carsten K. W. De Dreu (Ed.), *The Psychology of Conflict and Conflict Management in Organizations* (pp. 291-320). New York: Lawrence Erlbaum.

Greer, L. L., Caruso, H. M., & Jehn, K. A. (2011). The bigger they are, the harder they fall: Linking team power, team conflict, and performance. *Organizational Behavior and Human Decision Processes, 116*(1), 116-128.

Gronn, P. (2002). Distributed leadership as a unit of analysis. *The Leadership Quarterly, 13(4),* 423-451.

Harrison, D. A., Mohammed, S., McGrath, J. E., Florey, A. T., & Vanderstoep, S. W. (2003). Time matters in team performance: Effects of member familiarity, entrainment, and task discontinuity on speed and quality. *Personnel Psychology, 56*(3), 633-669.

Harvey, P., & Martinko, M. J. (2009). An empirical examination of the role of attributions in psychological entitlement and its outcomes. *Journal of Organizational Behavior, 30*(4), 459-476.

Hersey, P., Blachard, K. H., & Natemeyer, W. E. (1979). Situational Leadership, Perception, and the Impact of Power. *Group &*

108   Chapter Four

Organization Studies, 4(4), 418-428.

Hiller, N. J., Day, D. V., & Vance, R. J. (2006). Collective enactment of leadership roles and team effectiveness: A field study. *The Leadership Quarterly, 17*(4), 387-397.

Hogg, M. A. (2001). Social Categorization, Depersonalization, and Group Behavior. In M. A. Hogg & R. S. Tindale (Eds.), *Blackwell Handbook of Social Psychology: Group Processes*. Oxford: Blackwell.

Hogg, M. A., & Reid, S. A. (2001). Social Identity, Leadership, and Power. In A. Y. Lee-Chai & J. A. Bargh (Eds.), *The Use and Abuse of Power: Multiple Perspectives on the Causes of Corruption*. Philadelphia: Psychology Press.

Jehn, K. A. (1994). Enhancing effectiveness: An investigation of advantages and disadvantages of value-based intragroup conflict. *The International journal of conflict management, 5*(3), 223.

—. (1995). A Multimethod Examination of the Benefits and Detriments of Intragroup Conflict. *Administrative Science Quarterly, 40*(2), 256-282.

—. (1997). A Qualitative Analysis of Conflict Types and Dimensions in Organizational Groups. *Administrative Science Quarterly, 42*(3), 530-557.

Jehn, K., & Bendersky, C. (2003). Intragroup Conflict in Organizations: A Contingency Perspective on the Conflict-Outcome Relationship *Intragroup Conflict in Organizations: A Contingency Perspective on the Conflict-Outcome Relationship B2 - Intragroup Conflict in Organizations: A Contingency Perspective on the Conflict-Outcome Relationship* (pp. 189-244). Oxford, UK: Elsevier.

Jehn, K. A., & Bezrukova, K. (2010). The faultline activation process and the effects of activated faultlines on coalition formation, conflict, and group outcomes. *Organizational Behavior & Human Decision Processes, 112*(1), 24-42.

Jehn, K. A., & Mannix, E. A. (2001). The Dynamic Nature of Conflict: A Longitudinal Study of Intragroup Conflict and Group Performance. *Academy of Management Journal, 44*(2), 238.

Jehn, K. A., Northcraft, G. B., & Neale, M. A. (1999). Why Differences Make a Difference: A Field Study of Diversity, Conflict, and Performance in Workgroups. *Administrative Science Quarterly, 44*(4), 741-763.

Jehn, K. A., Rispens, S., & Thatcher, S. M. B. (2010). The Effects of Conflict Asymmetry on Work Group and Individual Outcomes. *Academy of Management Journal, 53*(3), 596-616.

Jensen, J. M., & Raver, J. L. (2012). When Self-Management and Surveillance Collide Consequences for Employees' Organizational

Citizenship and Counterproductive Work Behaviors. *Group & Organization Management, 37*(3), 308.

Jones, D. N., & Paulhus, D. L. (2011). The role of impulsivity in the Dark Triad of personality. *Personality & Individual Differences, 51*(5), 679-682.

Judge, T. A., LePine, J. A., & Rich, B. L. (2006). Loving Yourself Abundantly: Relationship of the Narcissistic Personality to Self- and Other Perceptions of Workplace Deviance, Leadership, and Task and Contextual Performance. *Journal of applied psychology, 91*(4), 762-776.

Karambayya, R., Brett, J. M., & Lytle, A. (1992). Effects of formal authority and experience on third-party roles, outcomes, and perceptions of fairness *Academy of Management Journal, 35*(2), 426.

Kets de Vries, M. F. R., & Miller, D. (1985). Narcissism and Leadership: An Object Relations Perspective. *Human Relations, 38*(6), 583-601.

Kotter, J. P. (1995). Leading Change - Why Transformation Efforts Fail. *Harvard Business Review, 73*(2), 59-67.

Kwan, A., Schwartz, J., & Liakopoulos, A. (2010). *Talent Edge 2020: Blueprints for the new normal.* Retrieved on October 26, 2013, from http://dupress.com/articles/talent-edge-2020-blueprints-for-the-new-normal/?id=us%3Ael%3Adc%3Aredirect.

Mitchell, M. S., & Ambrose, M. L. (2007). Abusive supervision and workplace deviance and the moderating effects of negative reciprocity beliefs. *Journal of applied psychology, 92*(4), 1159-1168.

Moeller, S. J., Crocker, J., & Bushman, B. J. (2009). Creating hostility and conflict: Effects of entitlement and self-image goals. *Journal of Experimental Social Psychology, 45*(2), 448-452.

Morgeson, F. P., DeRue, D. S., & Karam, E. P. (2010). Leadership in Teams: A Functional Approach to Understanding Leadership Structures and Processes. *Journal of Management, 36*(1), 5-39.

Paulhus, D. L. (1998). Interpersonal and intrapsychic adaptiveness of trait self-enhancement: A mixed blessing? *Journal of personality and social psychology, 74*(5), 1197.

Pryor, L. R., Miller, J. D., & Gaughan, E. T. (2008). A Comparison of the Psychological Entitlement Scale and the Narcissistic Personality Inventory's Entitlement Scale: Relations With General Personality Traits and Personality Disorders. *Journal of personality assessment, 90*(5), 517-520.

Rispens, S., Giebels, E. & Jehn, K.A. (2010). Explaining hostile actions: integrating theories of abusive supervision and conflict assymetry. In B. Schyns, & Hansbrough, T. (Ed.), *When leadership goes wrong:*

destructive leadership, mistakes and ethical failures (pp. 203-222). Charlotte: Information Age Publishing.

Romer, M., Rispens, S., Giebels, E., & Euwema, M. C. (2012). A Helping Hand? The Moderating Role of Leaders' Conflict Management Behavior on the Conflict-Stress Relationship of Employees. *Negotiation Journal, 28*(3), 253-277.

Simons, T., & Roberson, Q. (2003). Why Managers Should Care About Fairness: The Effects of Aggregate Justice Perceptions on Organizational Outcomes. [Article]. *Journal of Applied Psychology, 88*(3), 432-443.

Sims, R. R., & Brinkmann, J. (2002). Leaders as Moral Role Models: The Case of John Gutfreund at Salomon Brothers. *Journal of business ethics, 35*(4), 327-339.

Sparrow, R. T., & Liden, R. C. (1997). Process and Structure in Leader-Member Exchange. *Academy of Management Review, 22*(2), 522-552.

Tepper, B. J. (2000). Consequences of Abusive Supervision. *Academy of Management Journal, 43*(2), 178-190.

—. (2007). Abusive Supervision in Work Organizations: Review, Synthesis, and Research Agenda. *Journal of Management, 33*(3), 261-289.

Wall Jr, J. A., & Callister, R. R. (1995). Conflict and its Management. *Journal of Management, 21*(3), 515.

Watson, P. J., Grisham, S. O., Trotter, M. V., & Biderman, M. D. (1984). Narcissism and Empathy: Validity Evidence for the Narcissistic Personality Inventory. *Journal of personality assessment, 48*(3), 301.

West, M. A., Borrill, C. S., Dawson, J. F., Brodbeck, F., Shapiro, D. A., & Haward, B. Leadership clarity and team innovation in health care. *The Leadership Quarterly, 14*, 393-410.

Yoo, Y., & Alavi, M. (2004). Emergent leadership in virtual teams: what do emergent leaders do? *Information and Organization, 14*(1), 27-58.

Yukl, G. (2006). *Leadership in organizations* (6th ed.). Upper Saddle River: Prentice Hall.

Zaccaro, S. J., Rittman, A. L., & Marks, M. A. (2001). Team leadership. *The Leadership Quarterly, 12*(4), 451.

CHAPTER FIVE

MONEY, LOVE, AND CHANGE: THE ENTREPRENEURIAL SELF AND THE CREATION OF NEW VENTURES

TYLER WRY[1]
WHARTON SCHOOL, UNIVERSITY OF PENNSYLVANIA, USA
AND JEFFREY G. YORK
UNIVERSITY OF COLORADO BOULDER, USA

Abstract

The creation of social and environmental benefits by entrepreneurs has emerged as an area of scholarly interest, yet we have little understanding of why some entrepreneurs pursue these goals. Extending work on identity and entrepreneurship, we combine insights from structural and institutional views to develop the concept of the entrepreneurial self. We develop a theoretical framework for understanding the role of the entrepreneurial self in the creation of new ventures that provide non-economic benefits.

Keywords: identity, entrepreneurship, entrepreneurial self, new ventures

Introduction

Some live their days,
hidden from themselves,
afraid of money love and change.
—Trey Anastasio

---

[1] Authors contributed equally and are listed alphabetically.

In his seminal work, Venkataraman (1997: 120) argues that entrepreneurship as a scholarly field seeks to understand how opportunities are discovered, created, and exploited, by whom, and with what economic, psychological and social consequences. While this definition theoretically encompasses the creation of caring and compassionate organizations, research in entrepreneurship has focused almost exclusively on economic motivations and consequences (see Aldrich & Ruef, 2006; Shane, 2003; Thornton, 1999 for reviews). The extant literature reflects a strong assumption that entrepreneurship is dominated by market logic, under which actors seek to identify and exploit opportunities for economic gain (Thornton, 2004).[2] While the financial aspects of entrepreneurship are undoubtedly important, a focus on these aspects alone gives an incomplete account of the entrepreneurial process.

There is considerable evidence that entrepreneurship is not always driven by the prospect of personal gain alone. New ventures can be infused with a variety of values (Selznick, 1957), potentially manifesting in a deep commitment to social and environmental issues within an existing organizational form (Choi & Gray, 2008; Whetten & Mackey, 2010) or the creation of new organizations that address these issues directly (Cohen & Winn, 2007; Sine & Lee, 2009; Weber, Heinze, & DeSoucey, 2008; York & Venkataraman, 2010). The potential of these firms to create positive social and environmental value—non-excludable public goods which benefit stakeholders beyond owners and investors (Olson, 1971; Ostrom, 2000)— makes understanding the conditions of their emergence a matter of both practical and theoretical importance (Cohen & Winn, 2007; Margolis & Walsh, 2003; Meek, Pacheco, & York, 2010; Orlitzky, Schmidt, & Rynes, 2003).

The creation of public goods through entrepreneurial action has recently emerged as a topic of considerable scholarly attention (for reviews see Hall, Daneke, & Lenox, 2010; Short, Moss & Lumpkin, 2009). To date, however, there has been little theoretical development related to the question of why entrepreneurs engage in such pursuits. Some have suggested that public goods can be transformed into economic opportunities, assumedly giving rise to financial incentives (Cohen & Winn, 2007; Pacheco, Dean, & Payne, 2010). However, this perspective overlooks the potential influence of non-economic factors (Margolis &

---

[2] We recognize that entrepreneurship is not limited to business creation – actors can create a variety of different types of organizations in the non-profit domain as well. However, for the purposes of this paper, we follow the main strands of extant entrepreneurship literature and focus on for-profit business creation (Aldrich & Ruef, 2006).

Walsh, 2003; Wry, 2009). Many entrepreneurs value environmental and social objectives intrinsically and pursue them vigorously even when it is not financially expedient (Choi & Gray, 2008; Sine & Lee, 2009; Weber et al., 2008). Thus, there is an unresolved theoretical question: Why do some entrepreneurs explicitly pursue the creation of public goods in their ventures, while others do not? In this paper, we seek to address this question by combining insights from structural (Stryker, 1980; Stryker, 1989) and institutional approaches to identity (Glynn, 2008; Navis & Glynn, 2010; Rindova, Dalpiaz, & Ravasi, 2010; Thornton & Ocasio, 1999, 2008; Wry, Lounsbury, & Glynn, 2010).

We seek to make several contributions: 1) a deeper understanding of entrepreneurial processes as they relate to the creation of public goods, 2) expanded treatment of the relationship between logics and individual identities, showing how this largely overlooked level of institutional analysis (Schneiberg & Clemens, 2006; Thornton & Ocasio, 2008) can offer insight into entrepreneurial action, and 3) greater specification of the relationship between identity and entrepreneurship, which is currently under theorized (Cardon et al., 2009), especially as it relates to higher-order institutional factors (Navis & Glynn, 2010).

We begin with a theoretical synthesis of the literature on logics, plural identities, and self and use this as the basis for defining the concept of "entrepreneurial self." We then develop propositions about the influence of the entrepreneurial self in shaping the types of firms that an entrepreneur founds, including arguments about why certain entrepreneurs are more likely to pursue the creation of public goods in their ventures. Throughout the paper we utilize illustrative quotes from entrepreneurs to help bring our theory to life; we do not intend these quotes to provide evidence, but simply examples of our arguments. We conclude with a discussion of the implications of our theorizing for the literatures on identity, institutions, and entrepreneurship as well as for the practice of social entrepreneurship.

Identity in Entrepreneurship: The Entrepreneurial Self

The process of entrepreneurship focuses on sequential actions that bring "future" goods and services into existence (Venkataraman, 1997). While the role of the entrepreneur in society is open to a wide range of interpretations and definitions, entrepreneurship as a field of study has coalesced around understanding the process through which actors: a) discover and create opportunities; b) choose to exploit those opportunities; and c) create strategies to pursue these opportunities (Shane, 3003). While Venkatarman canonically states that the field is also concerned with the "… connection between the pursuit of a future market and the creation of social wealth" (Venkataraman, 1997: 135), entrepreneurship scholars have primarily focused on these processes as they relate to private wealth creation (Aldrich & Ruef, 2006; Schoonhoven & Romanelli, 2001; Shane, 2003).

This tendency to focus on the profit-motive stems largely from the economic roots of entrepreneurship as a field. Early definitions of the entrepreneur range from the Kirznerian "alert" arbitrageur who seizes opportunities and pushes markets towards equilibrium (Kirzner, 1979) to the Schumpterian innovator who creates disequilibrium through creative destruction (Schumpeter, 1934). Regardless of the defined role of the entrepreneur, he/she seeks to discover "mutually profitable" (Kirzner, 1979:150) opportunities: entrepreneurs are conceived of as economic agents (Venkataraman, 1997; Hayek, 1945). Building on these foundations, the majority of current conceptions assume that entrepreneurial endeavors are driven by a financial calculus (see Aldrich & Ruef, 2006; Shane, 2003). While there is a general recognition of social benefits – such as job creation and economic growth – that can result from the entrepreneurial pursuit of private wealth, studies examining the simultaneous creation of private *and* public value are far less common (see Cohen & Winn, 2007; Dean & McMullen, 2007; York & Venkataraman, 2010 for exceptions). To date, the role of identity in such ventures has not been considered.

In this paper, we draw on social psychology research that argues identity plays an important role in shaping behavior and motivating action. Structural identity theory (Mead, 1934; Stryker, 1980; Stryker, 1989) posits a concept of 'self' composed of multiple identities, each achieving primacy, or saliency, at different times and decision points in one's life. From this perspective, individuals make choices and behave in ways that conform to internalized and valued sets of meanings that comprise their definition of "who I am" (Cast, 2004; Stryker, 1989). Individuals are motivated to act in concert with the precepts of their highly valued and salient identities because this verifies their sense of self, leads to positive affect, and is a source of self-esteem (Burke, 2004; Stets, 2004; Seo, Barrett, & Bartunek, 2004).

Given these motivational qualities, we anticipate that entrepreneurs will pursue ventures that accord with their highly salient identities (Cardon et al., 2009). However, reflecting the market orientation of entrepreneurship research, extant approaches reflect a strong assumption that the entrepreneur identity is linked to a market logic that motivates the pursuit of private wealth creation (Hoang & Gimeno, 2010; Murnieks & Mosakowski, 2007). While there is some recognition that this can manifest differently based on an actor's commitment to his/her role as an inventor, founder, or developer (Cardon et al., 2009), little consideration is given to how identity may relate to non-economic motivations. This is a significant limitation because the relationship between creating public and private value is tenuous in for-profit firms (Choi & Gray, 2008; Margolis & Walsh, 2003; Orlitzky et al., 2003; Wry, 2009) and many entrepreneurs value environmental and social objectives intrinsically (Dacin, Dacin, & Matear, 2010; Choi & Gray, 2008). For example, John Mackey, founder of Whole Foods Market notes that:

> It is the function of company leadership to develop solutions that continually work for the common good... At Whole Foods, we measure our success by how much value we can create for all six of our most important stakeholders: customers, employees, investors, vendors, communities, and the environment... I believe such programs would be completely justifiable even if they produced no profits and no [public relations benefits] (Reason, 2005).

Current conceptions of the entrepreneur identity provide a partial explanation for such examples, but are unable to account for the apparent non-economic motives. And, while contextual factors such as a supportive funding environment, broad social approval, and a well-developed market infrastructure are undoubtedly important as well (Hoffman, 1999; Lounsbury, Ventresca, & Hirsch, 2003; Pacheco et al., 2010; Sine & Lee, 2009; Weber et al., 2008), we suggest an that identity-based approach which attends to economic *and* non-economic motivations has significant potential to enrich our understanding of why some entrepreneurs work to create simultaneous public and private value in their ventures.

Institutional Logics and the Entrepreneurial Self

Following extant literature, we believe that identity is a strong motivational force, importantly shaping entrepreneurial action (Cardon et al., 2009; Glynn, 2008; Hoang & Gimeno, 2010; Murnieks & Mosakowski, 2007; Navis & Glynn, 2010; Rao et al., 2003). However, there is a need to extend beyond the economic aspects of the entrepreneur identity. Structural identity theory provides this extension as it accounts for the multiple and potentially contradictory identities that an individual holds (Mead, 1934; Stryker, 1980; Stryker & Serpe, 1994). The central argument is that identities flow from participation in social groups and, because individuals are members of multiple groups, they have manifold identities which comprise their overall conception of 'self' (Mead, 1934; Stryker,

1980; Stryker & Burke, 2000). Each identity carries a set of socially sanctioned expectations for appropriate action. For example, the professor identity is accompanied by expectations to conduct research, teach, and provide service to the academic community. While identities are linked to a specific context, they are also generalizable and transsituational, even when contradictory (Sewell, 1992; Stryker & Serpe, 1994). We expect that entrepreneurs have multifaceted selves and that non-market identities may spillover and affect how they answer the question, "What does an entrepreneur like me do in a situation like this?"

One criticism of structural identity theory is that it does not provide a strong link between identities and broader, high-level, systems of beliefs, values, and practices (see Gecas, 2000; Gecas & Mortimer, 1987). The literature linking identities to institutional logics provides a useful conceptual bridge. As with structural identity theory, a logics approach holds that individual identities are rooted in social collectives that comprise categories of individuals and organizations (see Thornton & Ocasio, 2008). Identifying as a group member is equivalent to identifying with the group's logic and this provides a strong link between logics and individual action (Thornton & Ocasio, 2008: 111). While the logics incumbent to real world collectives are group-specific, they reflect to a considerable degree the logics associated with six primary sectors of Western society – markets, corporations, states, professions, families, and religions (Thornton, 2004). Each of these logics is distinct and specifies the legitimacy of different beliefs, values, and practices. While there is some variation – for example, different professions, families, and religions may have different logics – at a broad level of abstraction, market and corporation logics are oriented toward private wealth creation, while professional, familial, and religious logics value professional norms, family and community welfare, and divine salvation, respectively (Friedland & Alford, 1991; Thornton, 2004).

In providing the rationale for their preferred values and practices, non-market logics can motivate action that would be considered irrational from an economic perspective. For example, studies have shown that organizations and practices designed to create public goods face strong barriers when market logic is dominant (Hoffman, 1999; Pacheco et al., 2010). However, their emergence is facilitated by the rise of alternate logics that stress their value and appropriateness– even when their financial viability is questionable (see Hoffman, 1999; Lounsbury et al., 2003; Sine & Lee, 2009; Weber et al., 2008). For example, the history of grass-fed ranches can be traced back to the efforts of social movement activists who criticized commercial ranching as harmful to the environment and advocated for the value of grass-fed products as an environmentally sustainable alternative (Weber et al., 2008). Similarly, Sine and Lee (2009) showed that the founding of wind energy firms was enabled by groups like the Sierra Club who promoted the desirability of wind-power generation, laying the foundation for broader acceptance of this new organizational form based on non-market rationale.

As the above examples indicate, studies of non-market logics and entrepreneurial activity typically focus on institutional entrepreneurs whose identities are linked to a specific logic that they work to integrate into a field (see Schneiberg & Lounsbury, 2008 for a review). This approach is symptomatic of studies in institutional theory, more generally, where the assumption is that multiple logics co-exist uneasily because of their divergent and often conflicting beliefs, values, and practices (Hargrave & Van de Ven, 2006; Thronton & Ocasio, 2008). Accordingly, specific groups of actors are generally viewed as carriers of *one* specific logic (Lounsbury, 2007; Reay & Hinings, 2005; Scott et al., 2000). Recently, however, studies have begun to recognize that organizations can have institutionally plural identities that bridge multiple logics and integrate practices associated with each (Battilana & Dorado, 2010; Glynn, 2002; Kraatz & Block, 2008; Pache & Santos, 2010a, 2010b). While the locus of identity in this work is the organization, individuals also "live across institutions" – they have varied work histories and professional affiliations and may actively participate in families, religions, and other social groups – and thus may hold multiple identities, each associated with a different logic (Friedland & Alford, 1991: 248; Sewell, 1992).

Synthesizing the structural (Stryker, 1980; Stryker & Serpe, 1994) and institutional logics (Glynn, 2008; Thornton, 2004; Thornton & Ocasio, 2008) approaches to identity, we define the "entrepreneurial self" as the institutionally plural identities held by an entrepreneur, by virtue of his/her work history and professional training, as well as familial, religious, and other social affiliations, which rationalize different values and practices and potentially influence his/her behavior as an entrepreneur. Because entrepreneurship is a fundamentally economic endeavor, our baseline hypothesis is that identities based on a market logic will be relevant for most entrepreneurs (Cardon et al., 2009; Hoang & Gimeno, 2010). However, by highlighting the potential for the entrepreneurial self to bridge multiple logics, we suggest that actors may carry a broader set of institutionally derived identities with them as they engage in entrepreneurial pursuits. As Thornton and Ocasio (2008: 105) note:

Theories which 'retreat from society' – emphasizing market mechanisms to aggregate individual utilities and preferences... – begin to fail. Instead, institutional sectors, for example families, professions, states, and religions locate the origins of values and utilities – and these values and utilities cannot be traded off as simple economic alternatives.

Table 5-1 provides an overview of the relationships between market versus non-market logics, identities, values, and desired outcomes as they relate to entrepreneurship.[3] It is important to note, however, that individual identities may emphasize particular aspects of a logic and thus motivate different types of action. For example, a familial logic may result in nepotism and the pursuit of private wealth for family members (Morck & Yeung, 2004), a commitment to employee welfare (James, 2006), and/or a commitment to making the world a better place for one's children (Dyer & Whetten, 2006), depending on how broadly "family" is construed.

With this caveat in mind, we note that there is considerable evidence – outlined in Table 5-1 and presented in detail throughout the paper – showing that identities associated with familial, professional, and religious logics can motivate entrepreneurs to pursue the creation of public goods through their ventures (see Choi & Gray, 2008; Powell & Sandholtz, 2010; York & Venkataraman, 2010). As such, we propose:

> **Proposition 1**: Entrepreneurs whose entrepreneurial self includes identities linked to multiple institutional logics are more likely to engage in the pursuit of simultaneous public and private value creation through a new venture.

Identity Relevance and the Expression of Self through Entrepreneurship

Given that the entrepreneurial self is potentially comprised of institutionally plural identities – each rationalizing distinct values, practices, and material outcomes – we expect that its relationship with action is contingent and complex (Stryker & Serpe, 1994). The presence of an identity linked to a professional, familial, or religious logic is no guarantee it will be relevant to the entrepreneur as he/she works to launch a new venture. Because logics and their associated identities are tied to specific social groups, they have the strongest influence on action in the context where they were

---

[3] We exclude the corporation and state logics. The former because it relates primarily to the internal workings of extant firms with respect to internal hierarchy, diversification, etc.; the latter because it focuses primarily of the workings of nation states, rather than the firms which operate within them (see Thornton, 2004: 44-45).

formed (Stryker, 1980; Stryker & Serpe, 1994; Thornton & Ocasio, 1999, 2008). For example, a mastery of quantitative research methods is likely to arouse very different responses from one's professional colleagues than it would from one's family. At the same time, the identities comprising the self are arrayed hierarchically according to their salience (Stryker & Serpe, 1994). Highly salient identities are strongly motivational: acting in accordance with their beliefs, values, and practices verifies important self-conceptions, leading to positive affect and self-esteem (Dutton, Roberts, & Bednar, 2010); discrepant actions are associated with negative emotions (Burke, 2004; Stets, 2004). Others who share in an identity are also likely to react positively to identity-consistent behavior while greeting identity-contravention with derision (Lounsbury et al., 2003; Stryker & Serpe, 1994; Thornton, 2004). For these reasons, highly salient identities tend to be trans-situational, spilling over across multiple domains and affecting action in each (Friedland & Alford, 1991; Sewell, 1992; Stryker, 1980; Stryker & Serpe, 1994).

When multiple identities are highly salient, they compete for expression, pointing to courses of action that may be complementary or conflicting. In either case, it necessitates that their holder consider the consequences of an action for multiple identities and the potential tradeoffs associated with balancing manifold interests. As noted, we expect that identities based on a market logic will be salient for most entrepreneurs (Aldrich & Ruef, 2006). However, when identities associated with familial, religious, or professional logics are also salient they may provide strong and concurrent motivations, increasing the likelihood that an entrepreneur will pursue public and private objectives through his/her venture.

Identities are likely to become more salient when they are 1) performed regularly, 2) complementary, and, 3) associated with meaningful relationships (Deaux, 1996; Stryker & Serpe, 1994). With regard to performance, evidence suggests that the relationship between identity and action is bi-directional and mutually reinforcing: identities guide action, and identity-consistent action reinforces the salience of an identity (Burke, 2004; Stryker, 2000). Behavioral expressions of an identity affirm that an individual is a particular kind of person, both to him/herself and to others, providing positive affect and reinforcing the salience of the identity. For example, the salience of a religious identity was reinforced for John Mackey, founder of Whole Foods Market, through the active study of religion at the University of Texas Austin, subsequently spilling over into the "do-no-harm" practices embodied in his organization (Arlidge, 2006; Reason, 2005).

Table 5-1. Market Versus Non-Market Logics: Identities, Values, and Outcomes

	Market Logic	Non-Market Logics		
		Families	Religions	Professions
Sources of Identity	Role in creating economic wealth For-profit business employment Previous venturing	Role as a family member Role as community member (social groups as family)	Religious affiliation Church participation	Professional training and affiliation Role in professional association
Basis of Values	Self-interest	Family/community welfare	Moral principles linked to divine salvation	Altruistic professional norms
Typically Valued Outcomes	Private wealth creation Aldrich & Ruef, 2006 Kirzner, 1979 Schumpeter, 1934 Shane, 2003 Venkataraman, 1997	Employee welfare Greenwood et al., 2010 James, 2006 Family economic security Morck & Yeung, 2004 Steier, 2003 Clean environment for future generations Choi & Gray, 2008 Dyer & Whetten, 2006 York & Venkataraman, 2010	Employee welfare Culliton, 1949 James, 2006 Public service Audebrand & Pauchant, 2009 Schwartz, 2006 Caring for environment as 'god's' creation Choi & Gray, 2008 Polyface, 2010 Weber et al., 2008	Service to the profession Abbott, 1988 Greenwood et al., 2002 Integration of professional norms into a firm Battilana & Dorado, 2010 Lounsbury, 2007 Lounsbury et al., 2003 Powell & Sandholtz, 2010
Illustrative Quotations	"The social responsibility of business is to increase its profits" (Friedman, 1970) "entrepreneurial opportunities... are situations that entail the discovery of new means-ends relationships... could really generate economic value" (Company's & McMullen, 2007)	"We love [our children]. We want a better world for them. You know, you can make enough money to make a happy family doing just about anything. But this business and what we're doing here... taking human nature and turning it into energy... could really challenge all other means of electrical generation." (Interv.)	"Sure, I want to make money, but not at any cost. I'm a religious guy; my church and my family and friends are important to me. What would they think if I was getting rich on the backs of people who had trouble paying their rent and groceries?" (Interview)	"Smalley's accomplishments as [a scientist and entrepreneur] were formidable... his contribution to society is best measured by his passion that science can and will deliver a better world. 'Be a scientist, save the world' was his mantra." (Rice, 2006)

Identities may also become more salient when they are mutually reinforcing. As Stryker notes, "[the] self must be seen as multifaceted, composed of parts sometimes highly interdependent and sometimes not, some conflicting and some reinforcing, a self variously organized" (2000: 27). Given their roots in different logics, familial, religious, and professional identities may have elements that are convergent or divergent in various proportions (Thornton, 2004; Thornton & Ocasio, 1999, 2008). For example, an entrepreneur may have a strong familial identity that emphasizes creating wealth and security for immediate family members, a professional identity as an accountant, and a religious identity that stresses the importance of public service. In such a situation, the salience of the religious identity may be reduced vis-à-vis others because of the complementarities between accounting practices, profit maximization, and creating family wealth.

Conversely, an entrepreneur's non-economic identities may be well aligned and mutually reinforcing. For example, scientist/entrepreneur Richard Smalley's entrepreneurial self was comprised of identities that stressed the public service of scientists (professional logic), divinity and the need to care for God's creations (religious logic), and the importance of security and prosperity for the human community (familial logic):

> The burden of proof is on those who don't believe that genesis was right, and there was a creation, and that the Creator is still involved. We are the only species that can destroy the Earth or take care of it and nurture all that live on this very special planet... working on this planet is an absolute moral code... let's go out and do what we were put on Earth to do (Richard Smalley as quoted in Tuskegee, 2004).

> Dr. Smalley's accomplishments as [a scientist and entrepreneur] were formidable... his contribution to society is best measured by his passion that science can and will deliver a better world. 'Be a scientist, save the world' was his mantra. (Rice, 2006).

Reflecting the salience of these mutually reinforcing identities, Smalley created Carbon Nanotechnologies Inc. to commercialize his scientific discoveries and help to pursue his vision of providing clean, cheap, and universally available energy so as to address the "top ten problems of humanity for the next 50 years" (Smalley, 1995).

Particular aspects of the self may also become more salient when they are associated with meaningful relationships (Deaux, 1996). This can take two forms: 1) the number and frequency of relationships associated with an identity, and 2) the affective depth of these relationships (Stryker & Serpe, 1994). The argument is analogous to that of "embeddedness" in institutional theory, which holds that logics exert the strongest influence on those who are most deeply embedded in the groups where they prevail (Battilana, 2006; Greenwood & Suddaby, 2006). In both cases, the central insight is that, in addition to internalizing an identity, actors receive feedback about their behavior from others who partake in it. Identity-consistent action is associated with positive responses, and fosters feelings of belonging and association with the group. Discordant action is greeted with negative reactions, regardless of the context where it takes place (Croidieu & Monin, 2009; Lounsbury et al., 2003; Thornton & Ocasio, 2008). For example, Powell and Sandholtz (2010) found that biotechnology firms founded by academic scientists (professional logic) actively published their research findings – despite the fact that this compromised their competitive position – because founders retained numerous and strong ties to colleagues who praised their conformance to scientific norms (Mody, 2009).

More generally, a particular aspect of the entrepreneurial self may become more salient when the relationships associated with an entrepreneur's various identities overlap (Uzzi, 1997). For example, Bill Marriott, Marriott Hotels founder, is very active in the Mormon Church and seeks partnerships with businesses founded by other Mormon entrepreneurs (Rosenwald, 2007). The following quote taken from an interview conducted by the first author with the founder of a Canadian dry-cleaning chain illustrates the link between relationships and the salience of an entrepreneur's non-economic identities:

> Sure, I want to make money, but not at any cost. I'm a religious guy; my church and my family and friends are important to me. What would they think if I was getting rich on the backs of people who had trouble paying their rent and groceries? I pay my people more than my competitors because it's the right thing to do... I would hate to run into someone down the road who was walking with a cane because of conditions in my shop.

As such, we propose:

> **Proposition 2**: The entrepreneurial self is most likely to motivate the production of public goods when an entrepreneur has highly salient identities associated with familial, religious, or professional logics.

The concept of the entrepreneurial self has implications for multiples steps of the venturing process, and thus for understanding the emergence of public goods through entrepreneurship. In particular, opportunity recognition, creation, and exploitation are fundamental to entrepreneurship (Shane & Venkataraman, 2000: 218). In this context, opportunities are defined as situations that entail the discovery of new means-ends relationships in which new goods, services, raw materials, and organizing methods are introduced (Casson, 2003; Eckhardt & Shane, 2003; Shane & Venkataraman, 2000). For some scholars, opportunities are objective phenomenon waiting to be discovered by astute actors (Kirzner, 1979); for others, opportunities are created through idiosyncratic processes of interpretation and enactment (Eisenhardt & Schoonhoven, 2001; Shane, 2000; Weick, 1979). Without wading into this debate, we suggest that the entrepreneurial self shapes opportunity recognition because salient identities 1) value different outcomes and thus affect how opportunities are defined, 2) affect the issues that an actor attends to and how these are interpreted, and 3) provide cognitive resources for creating novel lines of action that cross identities and logics.

The Entrepreneurial Self and Opportunity

Regardless of how opportunities are conceptualized ontologically, there is a general consensus that they relate to "the creation of economic wealth" (Alvarez & Barney, 2010: 559; Companys & McMullen, 2006: 301). While we expect that this is an important aspect of how entrepreneurs understand opportunities, the literature makes clear that identities associated with different logics value different outcomes (Stryker, 1980; Thornton, 2004; Thornton & Ocasio, 2008). The value of an opportunity is not neutral or natural; it is assessed according to the tenets of a particular logic (Friedland & Alford, 1991; Dutton et al., 2010; Glynn, 2002; Lounsbury, 2007; Rao et al., 2003; Thornton, 2004). While opportunities are closely associated with wealth creation under a market logic, this is not necessarily so for religious, professional, and familial logics (Thornton, 2004). As such, the concept of entrepreneurial self suggests that assessments about the value of an opportunity will vary among individual entrepreneurs and cannot necessarily be reduced to a simple economic calculus.

When the self is dominated by an identity linked to a market logic, an entrepreneur will likely be attuned to arbitrage opportunities in line with the classical entrepreneurship literature (Kirzner, 1979; Hayek, 1945). However, a broader set of evaluation criteria become relevant when the entrepreneurial self is comprised of concurrently salient market and non-market identities. Thus, while starting a wind farm or grass-fed ranch, or paying higher prices to support local suppliers may not be rational according to a pure market logic (Choi & Gray, 2008: 347; Sine & Lee, 2009: 150; Weber et al., 543), entrepreneurs may see them as valuable opportunities to enact their salient professional, familial, or religious identities. Indeed, in a study of fifty socially responsible entrepreneurs, Choi and Gray (2008) found that:

> Making an environmental or social difference was a key motivation for these entrepreneurs ... [they] perceived the business enterprise as a vehicle for not only achieving their personal financial goals, but also for accommodating their strong social and environmental values (Choi & Gray, 2008: 343).

Elaborating this type of multifaceted opportunity recognition, Weber and colleagues (2008) noted that a number of entrepreneurs who founded sustainable, grass-fed, ranches also had expertise relevant to starting traditional feedlot operations, potentially a much more lucrative financial venture. Despite the economic attractiveness of the potential feedlot opportunity, these entrepreneurs demurred, viewing it as a business model that exploited land and animals in ways that were inconsistent with their identities as environmentalists (professional logic), church members (religious logic), and family members who wanted a clean environment for their children (familial logic). One rancher, clearly articulating his religious identity, said that in grass-fed ranching he was "working for God" (Weber et al., 2008: 544). Put succinctly, the authors note that:

> Financial motivations certainly mattered, because producers had to make a living from farming. Nevertheless, the decision to enter and persist... benefited from a broader vocabulary of motives... they obtained emotional energy from connecting their work to a sense of self... creating the experience of a unified personal identity across private and occupational domains (Weber et al., 2008: 543).

Similarly, wind-power entrepreneurship was extremely risky from a financial perspective – especially in the early days of its emergence (Sine & Lee, 2009). At the same time, its focus on the generation of clean and sustainable energy resonated with many nascent entrepreneurs who were willing to take on considerable financial risks in exchange for creating public goods in line with their salient identities (Sine & Lee, 2009: 126). For example, in an interview conducted by the second author, a company founder described how his salient familial identity led him to perceive a valuable opportunity in launching this type of firm:

The mission ... is making the world a better place. I'm a father. I've had a heart attack, as I've explained to you. My vision of life is a lot different than a lot of people's. [my partners], who are brothers, they've faced their own adversities in life... We love [our children]. We want a better world for them... this business and what we're doing here... taking human nature and turning it into energy... could really challenge all other means of electrical generation.

As such, we propose:

Proposition 3: When the entrepreneurial self includes salient identities linked to religious, familial, or professional logics, a nascent entrepreneur is more likely to value the potential of an opportunity to produce public goods.

Attention, Interpretation and Opportunity Recognition

The information flowing to a nascent entrepreneur and his/her interpretation of it have been shown to be important factors in opportunity recognition (Sarasvathy, 2001; Sarasvathy et al. 2005; Shane, 2000). In particular, changing environmental conditions related to technological advances, regulatory changes, and shifting consumer preferences can be important catalysts for opportunity recognition that allows actors to leverage their existing knowledge stocks to create new types of businesses (Schumpeter, 1934; Shane, 2000). However, environmental shifts are meaningless to the entrepreneurial process if a nascent entrepreneur doesn't have knowledge of them. For example, Shane's (2000) classic study of opportunity recognition found that nascent entrepreneurs recognized different opportunities associated with a single MIT invention. Yet, none of these actors were actively searching for business opportunities; they learned about the invention through their existing information channels that, in turn, spurred entrepreneurial responses related to their specific expertise.

We expect that the entrepreneurial self will affect the information that a nascent entrepreneur attends to as well as their response to it. Actors cannot attend to every aspect of their environment (March & Olson, 1976, 1989). Given this cognitive limitation, individuals rely on heuristics, such as their identities, to focus attention on specific aspects of the world around them (Ocasio, 1997; Stryker, 1980; Thornton, 2004). When an individual has salient identities associated with non-economic logics, their attention will likely focus in these areas. For example, a nascent entrepreneur with a salient identity linked to environmental sustainability is likely to seek out and attend to information they consider relevant to this issue (Ocasio, 1997; Thornton, 2004). Renewable energy entrepreneurship and grass-fed ranching provide good examples. With regards to the former, many nascent entrepreneurs had salient professional identities as non-profit executives or engineers and others had salient religious or familial identities that valued a clean environment (York & Venkataraman, 2010). These identities made their holders attentive to stories about "dirty energy" as well as the activities of groups like the Sierra Club who promoted the adoption of clean energy technologies (Sine & Lee, 2009). Likewise, in grass-fed ranching, salient religious and familial identities focused the attention of would-be entrepreneurs on stories that criticized the feedlot system and connected grass-fed production to larger moral issues (Weber et al., 2008: 535). Thus we propose:

> **Proposition 4**: When the entrepreneurial self includes salient identities linked to religious, familial, or professional logics, a nascent entrepreneur is more likely to attend to issues and information associated with these identities, increasing the likelihood that they will recognize opportunities to create public goods.

In addition to focusing attention on issues and information that go beyond market considerations, we expect that a multifaceted entrepreneurial self will affect how such information is interpreted. The types of opportunities that an individual recognizes are highly correlated with their knowledge because actors interpret information according to their own unique frames of reference (Shane, 2000). One way that this can play out is through the process of effectuation (Sarasvathy, 2001; 2008) where entrepreneurs respond to stimuli based on "who I know, what I know, and *who I am.*" Following this view, opportunities are "social constructions that do not exist independent of the beliefs of entrepreneurs" (Alvarez & Barnery, 2010: 565). As such, we anticipate that a nascent entrepreneur's salient identities will affect opportunity recognition because, as Thornton notes, "the assumptions, values, beliefs, and rules that constitute institutional logics determine what answers and solutions are available and appropriate in… organizations and markets" (2004: 13). For example, there were many ways that information about electrical deregulation in the Eastern United States might have been interpreted as an entrepreneurial opportunity. However, for a renewable energy entrepreneur interviewed by the second author, a salient professional identity as a non-profit executive and a familial identity which placed value on financial security led him to see it an opportunity for a financially viable business that was consistent with the values of his professional and familial identities:

> I'd spent 10 years doing non-profit environmental work. So, I was a passionate believer in clean energy…wanted to leave the world a better place than when I found it, or not worse… [also] my second child was born and I had no way to retire or put her through school… I had 10 years running the energy work for a non-profit, uh, trying to promote clean energy in six western states… I took that experience and tried to, move it back east to a competitive electric market where customers were switching away from their electric supplier, and turn it into a viable business.

Similarly, in 1961, William and Lucille Salatin moved their young family to Virginia's Shenandoah Valley, purchasing "the most worn-out, eroded, abused farm in the area" (Polyface, 2010). While this barren piece of land might have been interpreted in a variety of ways, potentially as a traditional farm or industrial development site, the Salatin's interpreted it as an opportunity to transpose their salient religious and familial identities into the food production industry so as to create a novel, non-industrial producer. Their farm provided a vehicle to pursue both economic profits and enact their salient non-market identities:

> Believing that the Creator's design is still the best pattern for the biological world, [our] family invites like-minded folks to join in the farm's mission: to develop emotionally, economically, environmentally enhancing agricultural enterprises… that now support three generations [of our family]… it makes me very hopeful for my son's generation that perhaps Polyface's dreams may carry over and downward (Polyface, 2010).

As such, we propose:

Proposition 5: When the entrepreneurial self includes salient identities linked to religious, familial, or professional logics, a nascent entrepreneur is more likely to interpret environmental stimuli as a new venture opportunity to create public goods.

Recognizing Opportunities to Create Public Good within the Nascent Firm

While the preceding discussion has focused on how the entrepreneurial self might lend itself to opportunity recognition related to creating new types of organizations oriented toward creating public goods, opportunity recognition can also relate to the ongoing pursuit of value creation. While this is typically conceptualized as identifying and pursuing opportunities for innovative goods, services, or processes that lead to wealth creation (Gaglio, 2004; Hitt et al., 2001), it may also pertain to the creation of public goods. For instance, an entrepreneur may identify a valuable economic opportunity associated with a traditional type of organization, such as our earlier example of the Canadian dry-cleaning chain, but view it as a forum where potential opportunities exist to create public goods in line with their broader set of salient identities.

Salient identities, and their associated logics, may provide interpretive frameworks that sensitize an entrepreneur to opportunities for creating diverse types of value through the policies and strategies that they implement in a nascent firm (Ocasio, 1997; Stryker, 1980; Thornton, 2004). In this way, the entrepreneurial self can function as a tool-kit (Swidler, 1986) when identities associated with market and non-market logics are concurrently salient, enabling the creative transposition of non-market logics into decisions related to everyday decisions such as employee remuneration and resource acquisition (Boxenbaum & Battilana, 2005; Dutton, Worline, Frost, & Lilius, 2006). Indeed, in their study of fifty responsible entrepreneurs, Choi and Gray found that "these... companies often made deliberate and carefully considered decisions that would potentially reduce profits" (Choi & Gray, 2008: 347). For example, Tom Chappell, founder of Tom's of Maine, was a devout Episcopalian (religious logic) with strong personal beliefs in the value of people and nature. This identity led Chappell to make decisions such as using recyclable aluminum tubes for his company's toothpaste instead of less expense, but non-recyclable, plastic laminates like other manufacturers (Chappell, 1993).

Such decisions about pursuing opportunities to create public goods through business operations are by no means limited to traditional types of firms. For example, one biodiesel entrepreneur interviewed by the second author talked about how his identities as a father (familial logic) and environmentalist (professional logic) pushed him to make considerations along each step of the value chain, beyond the environmental impact of his final product:

> We wanted to design the business to be operated as sustainably as we could, using waste products as a feedstock as much as we could, and have our operations be as green as we could make them... We spent a lot of time looking into... how are we going to operate a plant? What fuels are we going to use? Can we incorporate solar? How are we going to treat our waste? Can we use a bio-digester? And some of these things just don't

necessarily make economic sense... because we're focused on a sustainable approach... And so that does limit some of the things you do.

As such, we propose:

Proposition 6: When the entrepreneurial self includes salient identities linked to religious, familial, or professional logics, a nascent entrepreneur is more likely to identify opportunities to create public goods through the operation of his/her venture.

Discussion and Conclusion

We began by observing that while the provision of public goods through entrepreneurship has begun to emerge as a prominent area of scholarly attention (Hall et al., 2010; Short et al., 2009), we have little insight into the question of why some, but not all, entrepreneurs pursue such ventures. To help address this gap, we advocated for the expanded consideration of the relationship between identity and entrepreneurship. At a micro level, entrepreneurship scholars have begun to draw on the concept of identity to explain entrepreneurial motivations and passion (Cardon et al., 2009; Hoang & Gimeno, 2010; Murnieks & Mosakowski, 2007). However, this work is limited in its focus on the economic contexts of entrepreneurship. Going beyond economic contexts, organizational theorists have identified the role of social movements in promulgating sets of understandings that are supportive to the emergence of firms that pursue environmental and social objectives (Lounsbury et al., 2003; Sine & Lee, 2009; Weber et al., 2008). Yet, the motivations of the entrepreneurs who actually launch these ventures are largely overlooked. Integrating structural (Stryker, 1980; Stryker & Serpe, 1994) and institutional logics perspectives on identity (Glynn, 2008; Navis & Glynn, 2010; Thornton & Ocasio, 1999, 2008; Wry et al., 2010), we developed the concept of the entrepreneurial self, arguing that it has considerable potential to illuminate the genesis of public goods by entrepreneurs.

In particular, we built on evidence suggesting that individuals can have plural identities that bridge multiple logics (Friedland & Alford, 1991; Kraatz & Block, 2008; Pache & Santos, 2010a, b) to argue that the entrepreneurial self is potentially comprised of identities that accord with divergent values, beliefs, and practices. When entrepreneurs have salient identities linked with non-market professional, familial, or religious logics in tandem with a market-logic identity, we suggest they will be more likely to pursue the creation of public goods through their ventures.

Drawing on diverse examples, we argued that salient non-market identities shape the opportunities recognized by a nascent entrepreneur and how these are evaluated.

We make several contributions to the literatures on institutions, identity, and entrepreneurship. With regards to institutions, we focus attention on the relationship between logics and individuals. While theorists have long noted the potential for logics to guide action at the individual level (Friedland & Alford, 1991; Thornton, 2004; Thornton & Ocasio, 1999, 2008), this role has been largely overlooked in the institutional analysis of fields and markets where studies focus primarily on organizations (Schneiberg & Clemens, 2006). When individuals are invoked, it is typically as "hyper-muscular" institutional entrepreneurs who work to radically affect extant institutional arrangements (see Hardy & McGuire, 2008). While the identity position of an actor can affect such processes (Battilana, 2006; Maguire, Lawrence, & Hardy, 2004), we show the importance of considering how these identities are themselves institutionally shaped. We also suggest that identities affect how individuals act within a field beyond participating in change projects.

Moreover, in explicating the potentially plural nature of individual identities, we extend the consideration of institutional logics beyond approaches that assume that actors are the carriers of *one* logic as they act within a field (Hargrave & Van de Ven, 2006). While it has long been noted that logics exist in both "conflict and cooperation" (Friedland & Alford, 1991; Thornton & Ocasio, 1999) studies have focused much more on the former (see Hargrave & Van de Ven, 2006). As such, investigating the entrepreneurial self has potential to spur insight into the coexistence of divergent logics and how these are negotiated and managed, thus contributing to a more well rounded "relational" approach to institutional logics (Jones & Livne-Tarandach, 2008).

By highlighting an entrepreneur's logic-bridging identities, we also build on emergent insights about institutionally plural identification (Kraatz & Block, 2008; Pache & Santos, 2010a, b). However, while studies to date have argued that conflicting institutional demands are exogenously imposed, we suggest they can be endogenous to an organization. By focalizing the entrepreneurial self, we note that individuals, as well as organizations, can be institutionally plural, and that this can create a strong intrinsic motivation to act in concert with the tenets of multiple logics concurrently. In this way, we reach back, creating a bridge to early institutional approaches which highlight the potential for multiple sources of rationality to be infused into an organization, but through the imprint of a founder's identities (Stinchombe, 1965), rather than the interests of multiple constituencies present at founding (see Selznick, 1957). As such, we offer an opportunity to reclaim and extend seminal lines of institutional thought.

One particularly germane line of inquiry would be to investigate the role of entrepreneurs with multiple salient identities in creating new categories, fields, and markets. Studies have shown the importance of extra-field actors in field and market creation (e.g., Lounsbury et al., 2003; Hiatt et al., 2009; Sine & Lee, 2009; Weber et al., 2008), but the contribution of entrepreneurs who are active in these emergent domains has been largely overlooked: we believe that they may play an important role. For one, the entrepreneurial self is likely a source of variation within an existing organization population; the enactment of multiple identities giving rise to novel practices and organizational structures (Navis & Glynn, 2010). As such, the entrepreneurial self suggests an additional avenue around the "paradox of embeddedness" (Battilana, 2006) and highlights the potential for logic-bridging identities to catalyze innovative action. In this way, our approach may contribute to emergent understandings about the potential for entrepreneurs to introduce innovations that reshape fields and markets without actively trying to do so (Tracey, Phillips, & Jarvis, 2010). In addition, multiple salient identities may give rise to new types of organizations focused on the provision of public goods (Cohen & Winn, 2007). To this end, future research should investigate the temporal ordering of entrepreneurial action and social movement advocacy (Sine & Lee, 2009; Weber et al., 2009) in the process of market formation, as well as the potentially symbiotic (as opposed to uni-directional) relationship that may inhere between the meanings and practices pursued by these different classes of actors.

Finally, we provide for an expanded treatment of identity in the entrepreneurship literature (Cardon et al., 2009; Hoang & Gimeno, 2010; Murnieks & Mosakowski, 2007). While extant approaches are ill at ease to account for non-economic motives in the venturing process, our concept of the entrepreneurial self illuminates the multiple identities and forms of rationality that can be relevant. As entrepreneurs often think of ventures as very personal, clearly the role of identity is crucial for understanding the types of venture an entrepreneur engages in. While the exploration of traits which determine who will become an entrepreneur has largely been a dead-end, discovering why certain individuals become a specific *type* of entrepreneur has large implications for the societal outcomes of entrepreneurship (Venkataraman, 2002). In this regard, we see the potential for future work that integrates insights about the entrepreneurial self with existing dimensions of the "entrepreneur identity" (Cardon et al.,

2009). For example, what are the implications of salient non-market identities for entrepreneurs who are passionate about inventing, founding, or developing new organizations?

Through offering testable propositions on the role of identity, we also contribute to the emergent literature on social entrepreneurship (Dacin et al., 2010; Short, et al., 2009). We agree with Dacin and colleagues, that rather than focusing on social entrepreneurship as a distinct type of entrepreneurial action, or a separate field of research, research should focus on the social consequences of entrepreneurship (Venkataraman, 1997). By understanding how simultaneous benefits are produced for the entrepreneur and for society, we can address important questions about how and why some individuals pursue opportunities related to public goods production (Shane, 2003). In providing a lens to understand the diverse motivations for entrepreneurship, the concept of entrepreneurial self provides a foundation to guide future studies in this milieu.

Indeed, by highlighting the non-economic motivations for entrepreneurship, our approach has implications for all aspects of the entrepreneurial process. In addition to shaping opportunity recognition, persistence, and resource acquisition in the ways we have suggested, consideration of the entrepreneurial self opens up a multitude of avenues for further research. We envision particularly fertile ground studying the relationship between non-economic motivations and new venture finance. While we have suggested that not fitting into existing organizational frameworks can make it more difficult to access resources, this may change over time (Thornton & Ocasio, 1999, 2008), potentially resulting in ventures with institutionally plural identities accessing multiple funding sources (Zuckerman et al., 2003). For example, as the density of grass-fed ranches and wind power ventures increased, so did funding sources targeting these organizations (Sine & Lee, 2009; Weber et al., 2009). Indeed, one can imagine a scenario where salient identities linked to environmental protection (familial or religious logic), wealth creation (market logic) and a scientific profession (professional logic) could come together in a venture using nanotechnology for clean energy production. Such an organization might potentially access grants for nanotech and cleantech (Berube, 2006) as well as the venture capital market.

Further research might also investigate shifts in the composition of the entrepreneurial self through the venturing process. Enacting a non-market identity can increase its salience to an entrepreneur, but so too can enacting a market identity (Stryker, 1980; Stryker & Serpe, 1994). While these may exist in a productive balance, one or the other may become prominent. In some cases, this may result in well-intentioned entrepreneurs abandoning public goods creation in the pursuit of private wealth creation. Understanding the conditions under which such shifts are likely to occur is an important task for future research.

In developing the concept of entrepreneurial self, we theorized across multiple levels of analysis to offer unique insight into the genesis of such public goods through entrepreneurial action. When entrepreneurs have salient identities that bridge institutional logics, it can motivate them to not only create private wealth, but also work for the betterment of society in the process. As Philosopher William James (1892) said, "properly speaking, a man has as many social selves as there are individuals who recognize him." When entrepreneurs hold these multiple selves as salient, not only new businesses, but public goods, are created.

References

Aldrich, H., & Ruef, M. (2006). *Organizations evolving* (2nd Edition). Sage, London, UK.

Albert, S., & Whetten, D. (1985). Organizational identity. *Research in Organizational Behavior, 7*, 263-295.

Aldrich, H. E., & Fiol, C. (1994). Fools rush in? The institutional context of industry creation. *Academy of Management Review, 19*, 645-671.

Alvarez, S., & Barney, J. (2010). Entrepreneurship and epistemology: The philosophical underpinnings of the study of entrepreneurial opportunities. *The Academy of Management Annals, 4*(1), 557-583.

Arlidge, J. (2006). Peace, love and profits: Meet the world's richest organic grocer. The Observer. Accessed from http://www.guardian.co.uk/lifeandstyle/2006/jan/29/foodanddrink.organics, October, 2010.

Audebrand, L. K., & Pauchant, T. C. (2009). Can the fair trade movement enrich traditional business ethics? An historical study of its founders in Mexico. *Journal of Business Ethics, 87*, 343-353.

Baron, RA. (2008). The role of affect in the entrepreneurial process. *Academy of Management Review, 33*, 328-340.

Battilana, J. (2006). Agency and institutions: The enabling role of individuals' social position. *Organization, 13*, 653-676.

Battilana, J., & Dorado, S. (2010). Building sustainable hybrid organizations: The case of commercial microfinance organizations. *Academy of Management Journal*, forthcoming.

Boxenbaum, E., & Battilana, J. (2005). Importation as innovation: Transposing managerial practices across fields. *Strategic Organization, 4*, 355-383.

Burke, P. J. (2004). Identities, events, and moods. In J. H.Turner (Ed.). *Theory and research on human emotions* (Vol. 21) (pp. 25-49). New York, NY: Elsevier.

Busenitz, L,. & Barney, J. B. (1997). Differences between entrepreneurs and managers in large organizations: Biases and heuristics in strategic decision –making. *Journal of Business Venturing, 12*, 9-30.

Cardon, M. S., Wincent, J., Singh, J., & Drnovsek, M. (2009). The Nature and Experience of Entrepreneurial Passion. *Academy of Management Review, 34*(3), 511-532.

Carroll, A. (1999). Corporate social responsibility: Evolution of a definitional construct. *Business & Society, 38*, 268-295.

Casson, M. (2003). *The entrepreneur: An economic theory*. Northampton, MA: Elgar.

Cast, A. D. (2004). Well-being and the transition to parenthood: An identity theory approach. *Sociological Perspectives, 47*(1), 55-78.

Chappell, T. (1993). *The soul of a business: Managing for profit and the common good*. New York, NY: Bantam Books.

Choi, D. Y., & Gray, E. R. (2008). Socially responsible entrepreneurs: What do they do to create and build their companies? *Business Horizons, 51*, 341-352.

Cohen, B. D., & Winn, M. I. (2007). Market imperfections: Opportunity and sustainable entrepreneurship. *Journal of Business Venturing, 22*, 29-49.

Companys, Y., & McMullen, J. S. (2006). Strategic entrepreneurs at work: The nature, discovery, and exploitation of entrepreneurial opportunities. *Small Business Economics, 28*(4): 301-322.

Corley, K. & Gioia, D. (2004). Identity ambiguity and change in the wake of a corporate spin-off. *Administrative Science Quarterly, 49*, 173-208.

Croidieu, G., & Monin, P. (2009). Why successful innovations don't diffuse: Identity based interpretations of appropriateness in the Saint Emilion, Languedoc, Piedmont, and Golan Heights wine regions. Working paper, Lyon: EM Lyon.

Culliton, J. W. (1949). Business and religion. *Harvard Business Review, 27*, 265-271.

Dacin, T. M., Dacin, P. A., & Matear, M. (2010). Social entrepreneurship: Why we don't need a new theory and how we move forward from here. *Academy of Management Perspectives, 24*, 37-57.

Dean, T. J., & McMullen, J. S. (2007). Toward a theory of sustainable entrepreneurship: Reducing environmental degradation through entrepreneurial action. *Journal of Business Venturing, 22*, 50-67.

Deaux, K. (1996). Social identification. In ET. Higgins & AW. Kruglanski (Eds.). Social psychology: Handbook of basic principles. New York, NY: Guilford.

Dyer, W. G., & Whetten, D. (2006). Family firms and social responsibility: Evidence from the S&P 500. *Entrepreneurship Theory and Practice, 30*, 785-802.

Dutton, J. E., Worline, M. C., Frost, P. J., & Lilius, J. (2006). Explaining Compassion Organizing. *Administrative Science Quarterly, 51*, 59-96.

Dutton, J. E., Roberts, L. M., & Bednar, J. (2010). Pathways for positive identity construction at work: Four types of positive identity and the building of social resources. *Academy of Management Review, 35*(2), 265-293.

Eckhardt, J. T., & Shane, S. (2003). Opportunities and entrepreneurship. *Journal of Management, 29*, 333-349.

Eisenhardt, K. M. & Schoonhoven, C. B. (1990). Organizational growth: Linking founding team, strategy, environment, and growth among U.S. semiconductor ventures, 1978–1988. *Administrative Science Quarterly, 35*, 504–529.

Friedland, R., & Alford, R. (1991). Bringing society back in: Symbols, practices, and institutional contradictions. In W. Powell & P. DiMaggio (Eds.), The new institutionalism in organizational analysis. Chicago, IL: University of Chicago Press.

Friedman, M. (1970). The only social responsibility of business is to make a profit. New York Times, September, 13.

Gaglio, C. M. (2004). The role of mental simulations and counterfactual thinking in the opportunity identification process. *Entrepreneurship Theory and Practice, 28*, 533-552

Gecas, V. (2000). Value identities, self-motives, and social movements. In S. Stryker, TJ. Owens, & RW. White (Eds.), Self, identity, and social movements. University of Minnesota Press: Minneapolis, MN.

Gecas, V., & Mortimer, J. (1987). Stability and change in the self-concept from adolescence to adulthood. In T. M. Honess, & K. M. Yardley (Eds.), *Self and identity*. London, UK: Routledge & Kegan Paul.

Glynn, M. A. (2002). Chord and discord: Organizational crisis, institutional shifts, and the musical canon of the symphony. *Poetics, 30*(1-2), 63-85

—. (2008). Beyond constraint: How institutions enable identities. In R. Greenwood, C. Oliver, K. Sahlin, & R. Suddaby, (Eds.), *The Sage handbook of organizational institutionalism*. Thousand Oaks, CA: Sage.

Glynn, M. A., & Lounsbury, M. (2005). From the critics' corner: Logic blending, discursive change and authenticity in a cultural production system. *Journal of Management Studies, 42*, 1031-1055.

Greenwood, R., & Suddaby, R. (2006). Institutional entrepreneurship in mature fields: The big five accounting firms. *Academy of Management Journal, 49*, 27-48.

Greenwood, R., Diaz. M. A., Li, S. X., & Lorente, J. C. (2010). The multiplicity of institutional logics and the heterogeneity of organizational responses. Organization Science, forthcoming.

Hall, J. K., Daneke, G. A. & Lenox, M . J. (2010). Sustainable development and entrepreneurship: Past contributions and future directions. *Journal of Business Venturing, 25*(5), 439-449.

Hardy, C., & McGuire, S. (2008). Institutional entrepreneurship. In R. Greenwood, et al., (Eds.), *The Sage handbook of organizational institutionalism*. Thousand Oaks, CA: Sage.

Hargrave, T., & Van de Ven, A. (2006). A collective action model of institutional innovation. *Academy of Management Review, 31*, 864-888.

Hayek, F. A. (1945). The use of knowledge in society. *The American Economic Review, 35*(4), 519-530.

Hiatt, S., Sine, W., & Tolbert, P. (2009). From Pabst to Pepsi: The deinstitutionalization of social practices and the creation of entrepreneurial opportunities. *Administrative Science Quarterly, 54*, 635-667.

Hitt, R. D., Ireland, R. D., Camp, S. M., & Sexton, D. L. (2001). *Strategic entrepreneurship: Creating a new mindset*. Oxford, UK: Blackwell Publishing.

Hoang, H., & Gimeno, J. (2010). Becoming a founder: How founder role identity affects entrepreneurial transitions and persistence in founding. *Journal of Business Venturing, 25*, 41-53.

Hoffman, A. (1999). Institutional evolution and change: Environmentalism and the US chemical industry. *Academy of Management Journal, 42*, 351-371.

Hsu, G., & Hannan, M. T. (2005). Identities genres and organizational forms. *Organization Science, 16*, 474-490.

James, H. (2006). *Family capitalism, Wendels, Haniels, Falks, and the continental European model*. Cambridge, MA: Belnap Press of Harvard University Press.

James, W. (1892). *Psychology*. New York, NY: Henry Holt & Company.

Jones, C., & Livine-Tarandach, R. (2008). Designing a frame: Rhetorical strategies of architects. *Journal of Organizational Behavior, 29*, 1075-1099.

Kirzner, I. (1979). *Perception, opportunity, and profit.* Chicago, IL: University of Chicago Press.

Kraatz, M. S., & Block, E. S. (2008). Organizational implications of institutional pluralism. In R. Greenwood, et al., (Eds.), *The Sage handbook of organizational institutionalism.* Thousand Oaks, CA: Sage.

Lenox, M. J., & Eesley, C. E. (2009). Private environmental activism and the selection and response of firm targets. *Journal of Economics & Management Strategy, 18*(1), 45-73.

Lounsbury, M. (2007). A tale of two cities: Competing logics and practice variation in the professionalizing of mutual funds. *Academy of Management Journal, 50*, 289-307.

Lounsbury, M., & Glynn, M. A. (2001). Cultural entrepreneurship: stories, legitimacy, and the acquisition of resources. *Strategic Management Journal, 22*, 545-564.

Lounsbury, M., Wry, T., & Jennings, P. D. (2010). Into the void: Institutional sources of de novo organizational identities in nanotechnology exploration. Working paper, Edmonton: University of Alberta.

Lounsbury, M., Ventresca, M., & Hirsch, P. (2003). Social movements, field frames and industry emergence: A cultural-political perspective on U.S. recycling. *Socio-Economic Review, 1*, 71-104.

Maguire, S., Lawrence, T., & Hardy, C. (2004). Institutional entrepreneurship in an emerging field: HIV/AIDS treatment advocacy in Canada. *Academy of Management Journal, 47*, 657-679.

March, J. G., & Olsen, J. P. (1976). *Ambiguity and choice in organizations.* Bergen, NW: Universitetsforlaget.

March, J. G., & Olsen, J. P. (1989). *Rediscovering institutions: The organizational basis of politics.* New York, NY: The Free Press.

Margolis, J., & Walsh, J. (2003). Misery loves companies: Rethinking social initiatives by business. *Administrative Science Quarterly, 48*, 268-305.

Mead, G. H. (1934). *Mind, self & society from the standpoint of a behaviorist.* University of Chicago Press: Chicago, IL.

Meek, W., Pacheco, D. F., & York, J. G. (2010). The impact of social norms on entrepreneurial action: Evidence from the environmental entrepreneurship context. *Journal of Business Venturing, 25*, 493-509.

Mody, C. (2009). Garden of nanotech: A role for the social sciences and humanities in nanotechnology. *Chemical Heritage Magazine, 27*, 1-5.

Morck, R., & Yeung, B. (2004). Family control and the rent-seeking society. *Entrepreneurship Theory and Practice, 28*, 391–409.

Murnieks, C., & Mosakowski, E. (2007). Who am I? Looking inside the entrepreneurial identity. *Frontiers of Entrepreneurship Research, 27*, 1-14.

Navis, C., & Glynn, M. A. (2010). The entrepreneurial identity: How legitimate distinctiveness affects investors' judgments of new venture plausibility. *Academy of Management Review*. forthcoming.

Ocasio, W. (1997). Towards an attention-based view of the firm. *Strategic Management Journal, 18*, 187-206

Olson, M. (1971). *The logic of collective action: Public goods and the theory of groups*. Cambridge, MA: Harvard University Press.

Orlitzy, M., Schmidt, F. L., & Rynes, S. L. (2003). Corporate social and financial performance: A meta-analysis. *Organization Studies, 24*(3), 403-441.

Ostrom, E. (2000). Collective action and the evolution of social norms. *Journal of Economic Perspectives, 14*, 137-158.

Pache, A. C., & Santos, F. M. (2010a). when worlds collide: The internal dynamics of organizational responses to conflicting institutional demands. *Academy of Management Review*, forthcoming

Pache, A. C., & Santos, F. M. (2010b). inside the hybrid organization: An organizational level view of responses to conflicting institutional demands. *Administrative Science Quarterly*, forthcoming.

Pacheco, D. F., Dean, T. J., & Payne, D. S. (2010). Escaping the green prison: Entrepreneurship and the creation of opportunities for sustainable development. *Journal of Business Venturing, 25*(5), 464-480.

Polyface. (2010, October). Our story. Accessed from http://www.polyfacefarms.com/story.aspx.

Powell, W. W., & Sandholtz, K. (2010). Chance, cécessité, et caïveté: Ingredients to create a new organizational form. In J. Padgett and W. W. Powell (Eds), *The emergence of organizations and markets*. Princeton, NJ: Princeton University Press, forthcoming.

Pratt, M. G., Foreman, P. (2000). Classifying managerial responses to multiple organizational identities. *Academy of Management Review, 25*, 18-42.

Rao, H., Monin, P., & Durand, R. (2003). Institutional change in Toque Ville: Nouvelle cuisine as an identity movement in French gastronomy. *American Journal of Sociology, 108*, 795-843.

Reason. (2005). Rethinking the social responsibilities of business: A Reason debate featuring Milton Friedman, Whole Foods' John Mackey and Cyprus Semiconductors' TJ Rodgers. Accessed from http://www.wholefoodsmarket.com/blog/category/6861/social%20resp onsibility, October, 2010.

Reay, T., & Hinings, C. R. (2005). The recomposition of an organizational field: Healthcare in Alberta. *Organization Studies, 26*, 351-384.

Rice. (2006). Nanotech pioneer, Nobel laureate Richard Smalley dead at 62. Accessed from http://media.rice.edu/media/NewsBot.asp?MODE=VIEW&ID=7890, June, 2009.

Rindova, V., Dalpiaz, E. & Ravasi, D. (2010). A cultural quest: A study of organizational use of new cultural resources in strategy formation. *Organization Science*, forthcoming.

Rosenwald, M. (2007, October). Rootbeer roots. The Washington Post. Accessed from http://www.washingtonpost.com/wp-dyn/content/article /2007/06/26/AR2007062601413.html.

Sarasvathy, S. (2001). Causation and effectuation: Toward a theoretical shift from economic inevitability to entrepreneurial contingency. *The Academy of Management Review, 26*, 243-263.

—. (2008). *Effectuation: Elements of entrepreneurial expertise.* Cheltenham, UK: Edward Elgar.

Sarasvathy, S., Dew, N., Velamuri, S., & Venkataraman, S. (2005). Three views of entrepreneurial opportunity. In Z. Acs & D. Audretsch (Eds.), *Handbook of entrepreneurship research: An interdisciplinary survey and introduction.* New York, NY: Springer.

Schneiberg, M., & Clemens, E. (2006). Typical tools for the job: Research strategies in institutional analysis. *Sociological Theory, 24*, 195-227.

Schneiberg, M., & Lounsbury, M. (2008). Social movements and institutional analysis. In R. Greenwood, et al. (eds.), *The Sage handbook of organizational institutionalism.* Thousand Oaks, CA: Sage.

Schoonhoven, C. B. & Romanelli, E. (2001). *The entrepreneurship dynamic: origins of entrepreneurship and the evolution of industries.* Stanford, CA: Stanford University Press.

Schumpeter, J. A. (1934). *The theory of the economic development.* Oxford, UK: Oxford University Press.

Schwartz, M. S. (2006). God as a managerial stakeholder. *Journal of Business Ethics, 2*, 291-306.

Scott, W. R., Ruef, M., Mendel, P. J., & Caronna, C. J. (2000). *Institutional change and healthcare organizations: From professional dominance to managed care*. Chicago, IL: University of Chicago Press.

Selznick, P. (1957). *Leadership and administration*. Evanston, IL: Row Peterson.

Seo, M., Barrett, L. F., & Bartunek, J. M. (2004). The role of affective experience in work motivation. *Academy of Management Review, 29*(3): 423-439.

Sewell, W. F. (1992). A theory of structure: Duality, agency, and transformation. *American Journal of Sociology, 98*, 1-29.

Shane, S. (2000). Prior Knowledge and the Discovery of Entrepreneurial Opportunities. *Organization Science, 11*, 448-469.

—. (2003). *A general theory of entrepreneurship: The individual-opportunity nexus*. Cheltenham, US: Elgar.

Shane, S., & Venkataraman, S. (2000). The promise of entrepreneurship as a field of research. *Academy of Management Review, 25*, 217-226.

Short, J. C., Moss, T. M. & Lumpkin, T. (2009). Research in social entrepreneurship; Past contributions and future opportunities. *Strategic Entrepreneurship Journal, 3*(2), 161-194.

Simon, M. Houghton, S. M., & Aquino, K. (2000). Cognitive biases, risk perception and venture formation: How individuals decide to start companies. *Journal of Business Venturing, 15*,113-134.

Sine, W., & Lee, B. (2009). Tilting at windmills? The environmental movement and the emergence of the US wind energy sector. *Administrative Science Quarterly, 54*, 123-155.

Smalley, R. (1995). Nanotechnology and the next 50 years. Accessed from http://smalley.rice. edu, March, 2008.

—. (2005). Letter sent to the Hope College Alumni Banquet. Holland, MI: Hope College Office of Public Relations.

Steier, L. (2003). Variants of agency contracts in family financed ventures: The multiple roles of family. *Journal of Business Venturing, 18*, 597-618

Stets, J. E. (2004). Emotions in identity theory: The effect of status. In J. H. Turner (Ed.), *Theory and research on human emotions*. New York, NY: Elsevier.

Stinchcombe, A. L. (1965). Social structure and organizations. In J.G. March (Ed.), *Handbook of organization*. Chicago, IL: Rand McNally & Company.

Stryker, S. (1980). *Symbolic interactionism: A social structural version*. Menlo Park, CA: Benjamin Cummings.

—. (1989). Further developments in identity theory: Singularity versus multiplicity of self. In J. Berger, M. Zelditch, & B. Anderson (Eds.), *Sociological theories in progress*. London, UK: Sage.

—. (2000). Identity competition: Key to differential social movement participation? In S. Stryker, T. J. Owens, & R. White (Eds.), *Self, identity, and social movements*. Minneapolis, MN: University of Minnesota Press.

Stryker, S., & Burke, P. J. (2000). The past, present, and future of an identity theory. *Social Psychology Quarterly, 63*, 284-297.

Stryker, S., & Serpe, R. T. (1994). Identity salience and psychological centrality: Equivalent, overlapping, or complementary concepts? *Social Psychology Quarterly, 57*, 16-35.

Swidler, A. (1986). Culture in action: Symbols and strategies. *American Sociological Review, 51*, 273-286.

Thornton, P. (1999). The sociology of entrepreneurship. *Annual Review of Sociology, 25*, 19-46.

—. (2004). *Markets from culture: Institutional logics and organizational decisions in higher education publishing*. Stanford, CA: Stanford University Press.

Thornton, P. H., & Ocasio, W. (1999). Institutional logics and the historical contingency of power in organizations: Executive succession in the higher education publishing industry, 1958-1990. *American Journal of Sociology, 105*, 801-843.

Thornton, P. H., & Ocasio, W. (2008). Institutional logics. In R. Greenwood, et al. (Eds.), *The Sage handbook of organizational institutionalism*. Thousand Oaks, CA: Sage.

Tracey, P., Phillips, N., & Jarvis, O. (2010). Bridging institutional entrepreneurship and the creation of new organizational forms: A multi-level model. *Organization Science*, forthcoming.

Tuskegee. (2004). Scholarship convocation speaker challenges scholars to serve the greater good. Accessed from http://www.tuskegee.edu/Global/story.asp?S=2382961, August, 2010.

Uzzi, B. (1997). Social structure and competition in interfirm networks: The paradox of embeddedness. *Administrative Science Quarterly, 42*, 35-67.

Venkataraman, S. (1997). The distinctive domain of entrepreneurship research: An editor's perspective. In J. Katz & R. Brockhaus (Eds.), *Advances in entrepreneurship, firm emergence, and growth* (pp. 119-138). Greenwich, CT: JAI Press.

Waddock, S., & Graves, S. (1997). The corporate social performance – financial performance link. *Strategic Management Journal, 18*, 303-319.

Weber, K., Heinz, K., & DeSoucey, M. (2008). Forage for thought: Mobilizing codes for grass-fed meat and dairy products. *Administrative Science Quarterly, 53*, 529-567.

Weick, K. E. (1979). *The social psychology of organizing*. Reading, MA: Addison Wesley.

Whetten, D., & Mackey, A. (2010). Investigating the adoption and persistence of distinctive organizational practices: An organizational identity perspective. Working paper, Brigham Young University.

Wry, T. (2009). Does Business and society scholarship matter to society: Pursuing a normative agenda with critical realism and neoinstitutional theory. *Journal of Business Ethics, 89*, 151-171.

Wry, T., Lounsbury, M., & Glynn, M. A. (2010). Legitimating nascent collective identities: Coordinating cultural entrepreneurship. *Organization Science*, forthcoming.

York, J. G., & Venkataraman, S. (2010). The entrepreneur-environment nexus: Uncertainty, innovation, and allocation. *Journal of Business Venturing, 25*, 449-463.

Zuckerman, E. W. (1999). The categorical imperative: Securities analysts and the illegitimacy discount. *American Journal of Sociology, 104*, 1398-1438.

Zuckerman, E. W., Kim, T. Y., Ukanwa, K., & von Rittman, J. (2003). Robust identities or non-identities? Typecasting in the feature firm labor market. *American Journal of Sociology, 108*, 1018-1074.

Chapter Six

The Collaboration Conundrum: A New Theory for an Emerging Organizational Form

Rebekah Dibble
University of San Francisco, USA
and Cristina Gibson
University of Western Australia, Australia

Abstract

We draw attention to the ways in which emerging forms of collaborative work, organized to pool expertise, resources, or social networks for the creation of a specific product or service, are critically distinct from more traditional forms of organizing. We identify fluidity, impermanence, organizational independence, and environmental volatility as four key features which set collaborative efforts apart from traditional teams. Given these distinctions, there are important aspects of collaborative work today that cannot be adequately understood by generalizing from more traditional forms. We focus here on two such aspects—internal and external adjustment—and examine the implications of adjustment for performance in collaborative endeavors.

Keywords: collaboration, fluidity, impermanence, organizational independence, and environmental volatility, teams

Introduction

Teams have traditionally been defined as individuals working interdependently with clear boundaries, stable membership, and clearly defined authority (Hackman, 2002). Through our ever increasing understanding of these traditional forms of organizing, we have become more effective, more efficient, and more adept at improving vital inputs, processes and outputs. In recent years, with increasing globalization and the use of technology, much of the work that was conducted previously in traditional teams is now conducted in new ways, with a high degree of fluidity (participants come and go at different points during their work together); impermanence (participants disband with the completion of their objective); organizational independence (membership often spans organizational boundaries or members may not be embedded in any organization); and environmental volatility (severe time constraints, rapidly changing environmental conditions, or a constantly changing group of external constituents). A critical task for organizational scholars of the twenty-first century is to begin to address the abundance of collaborating that takes place under these conditions, outside the realm of traditional teams.

As examples of this, consider the combination of medical personnel, law enforcement officers, government officials, transportation specialists, technology experts, humanitarian volunteers, and representatives of non-profit relief organizations to relieve victims of a natural disaster, or the integration of the skills and ideas of researchers, engineers, operations managers, and marketing executives to design a new product. As this type of organizing has the potential to unite the best talent without the cumbersome financial commitment of permanent hiring arrangements for each required skill set, it is reasonable to assume that the trend toward fluid, temporary, organizationally independent, dynamic work structures will continue to become even more popular, particularly in times of economic uncertainty. However, many of our established theories developed to address typical teamwork challenges and scenarios are insufficient to deal with those faced in new forms of collaborative work (Mortensen, 2012). There is much that we need to understand about how collaborative endeavors today differ from more traditional organizational forms and how to optimize them given these differences. By shifting or at least broadening our focus to include such important new forms of organizing, acknowledging and probing their nuances and idiosyncrasies, and striving to learn how to make them more effective, we will advance theory in profitable ways. For example, learning how participants in new collaborative endeavors cope with internal challenges as well as challenges related to interaction with the external environment are important questions that we have only begun to examine. We argue that these issues are critical to address both theoretically and empirically in the context of collaborative endeavors.

We first elaborate on the most salient features of collaborative endeavors that differentiate them from more traditional forms. We argue that an understanding of where a collaboration lies on each of four key features—fluidity, impermanence, organizational independence, and environmental volatility—provides clues as to the types of challenges participants are likely to experience. Hence, we illustrate the vital role of these characteristics for organizational action by examining how they relate to unique challenges. In turn, we argue that identifying the nature of the challenges is critical to determining the appropriate response to the challenges. Thus, we next examine two particularly critical processes that participants in non-traditional collaborative endeavors can implement in response to challenges —internal and external adjustment. We explore how adjustment occurs, why one particular adjustment method may be prevalent over another, and what the implications of different types and levels of adjustment may be for performance. Finally, we conclude by highlighting three essential issues for future research to extend our theory which have come to our attention through our observation of a variety of collaborative endeavors. The road map for our theory is presented in Figure 6-1.

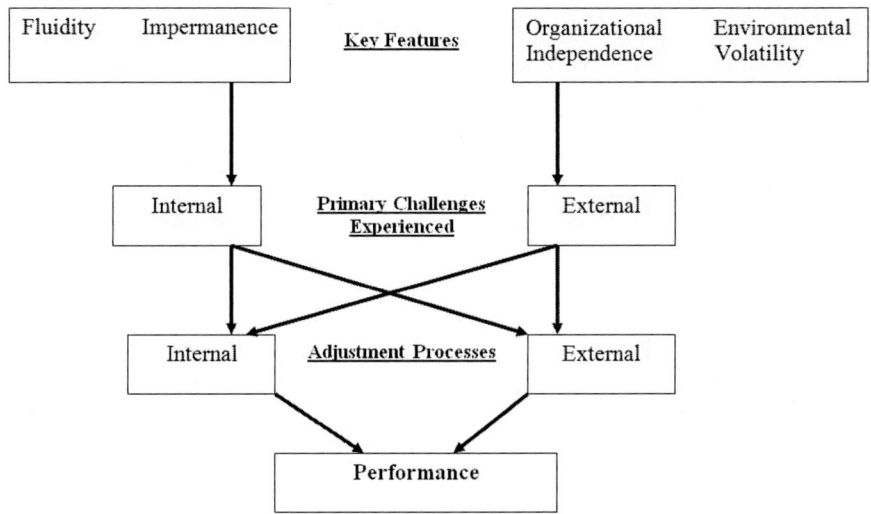

Figure 6-1. Overview of Framework for Organizational Action in Collaborative Endeavors

Distinguishing Features of Collaborative Endeavors

We suggest that collaborative forms of organizing can be characterized based on their degree of fluidity, permanence, organizational independence, and environmental volatility (see Table 6-1). Each of these dimensions represents a continuum and collective work efforts can be described by the degree to which each dimension characterizes the work that occurs within them, with traditional teams at the low end of each of these key features of collaborating. What has yet to be addressed is collaborative work on the opposite end of the continuum. This is our focus in this section.

Fluidity

Unlike in traditional teams, collaborative endeavors increasingly consist of participants who come and go at various points in time (Mortensen, 2012). Some collaborators may remain with the work effort from inception to completion while others engage and disengage throughout the process as needed. For example, in a film making team, while certain participants (e.g., producers and directors) may remain fully engaged from the beginning to the end of the film making process, others (e.g., editors, actors, sound mixers) may join the team just as their skills are required, leaving to work on other collaborations as their work concludes (Blair, Grey & Randle, 2001). Such fluidity enables a team to bring on critical skill sets as needed without unnecessarily tying up participants' schedules and allowing them to participate simultaneously in multiple collaborative efforts. As such, highly fluid collaborative endeavors don't incur the cost of keeping these individuals "on staff." Fluidity also presents a variety of challenges, including the need to bring newcomers on board as efficiently as possible with rapid transfer of information, despite potentiallyamorphous roles (Bechky, 2006) and a less established transactive memory system in which there may be substantial ambiguity in terms of who knows what and who will do what (Sydow, Lindkvist, & DeFillippi, 2004). The transfer of critical skills and information often must take place quickly and informally.

Impermanence

The second key dimension which distinguishes work in non-traditional collaborative endeavors is their lack of permanence. While traditional teams and the organizations within which they exist are ongoing in nature,

Table 6-1. A Continuum of Collaborative Work Forms

Entity Type	Definition	Fluidity	Lack of Permanence	Organizational Independence	Environmental Volatility
Temporary Team-based Collaborations	Temporary, multi-party, non-organizationally-embedded entities organized for the purpose of pooling expertise, resources, information or social networks to create a specific product or service (Gibson & Dibble, 2013)	High	High	High	High
Temporary Teams	Groups of individuals that engage temporarily to accomplish a concrete and finite goal (Saunders & Ahuja, 2006)	High	High	High or Low	High
Extreme Action Teams	Teams whose members come together to perform urgent and critical tasks while dealing with frequent changes in team member composition and training new members (Klein et al., 2006)	High	High	Low	High
Networks	Temporary combination of individuals from a variety of firms (or with no organizational affiliation) for a particular project (Jones, 1996)	High	Moderate	High or Low	High
X-Teams	Teams designed to be externally oriented (i.e., manage across boundaries) and highly adaptive (Ancona, Bresman, & Kaeufer, 2002)	High	Unspecified	Moderate	High
Projects	Temporary entities that produce one-time outputs within a particular time frame (Mankin, Cohen, & Bikson, 1996; Cohen & Bailey, 1997)	High	High	Low	Low
Committees	Generally sub-components of an organization to oversee a project or decision-making process impractical for the organization to perform (Lumsden, 2004)	High or Low	High or Low	Low	Low
Cross Organizational Teams	Groups of individuals based within a host organization; may include members external to the host organization (Schopler, 1987)	Moderate	High or Low	Low	Low
Ad Hoc Teams	Teams where members are recruited from different existing departments within an organization to solve a particular customer request (Hefke & Stojanovic, 2004)	Low	High	Low	Low
Self-Managing Teams	Groups of employees (usually <20 people) that are responsible for delivering a product or service to an internal or external customer (Alper et al., 1998)	Low	High or Low	Low	Low
Traditional Teams	Individuals working interdependently with clear boundaries, stable membership, and clearly defined authority (Hackman, 2002)	Low	Low	Low	Low

increasingly, collaborative efforts are temporary. They bring participants together for the purpose of achieving a particular, one-time objective, after which these individuals may not ever work together again. Impermanence enables the existence of unique, small-scale projects with timely impact. Consider the instance of a humanitarian project to provide housing for needy families. The temporary nature of this type of collaborative effort permits dozens of individuals from different cultural, organizational, and functional backgrounds to unite for a short span of time to not only create a valuable product (homes for disadvantaged families) but to create a rich cultural exchange and community building opportunity. Such an urgent, rich, experience of working with highly diverse individuals is less likely to occur within a more permanent structure, where momentum and homophily work against such spontaneous and varied efforts (Kelly & Amburgey, 1991; Schippers, Den Hartog, Koopman, & Wienk, 2003). However, when participants come together only temporarily, many of these individuals may not have worked together before. As such, there are no problem-solving routines in place such as those which are typical in long standing teams and organizations (Feldman & Pentland, 2003). This presents a variety of interesting challenges related to the ways in which participants learn, work together, resolve conflicts, and interact with external constituents unfamiliar with the collaborative effort due to its short existence.

Organizational Independence

Traditional teams are typically composed of individuals brought together from within the boundaries of a common organization which provides the team with critical resources (Raven, 2003). Alternatively, emerging forms of collaborative work may be composed of individuals with a variety of organizational affiliations, or no organizational affiliations, as is the case when independent contractors join together to complete a work effort. Organizational independence results in a lack of embeddedness. Coinciding with this organizational boundary spanning, there may be other boundaries spanned, such as functional or disciplinary groups, or regional or national cultural affiliations. For example, a collaborative effort formed to prosecute an organization in a corporate lawsuit might consist of individuals from a variety of functional backgrounds and organizations (e.g., document specialists, economic scholars, lawyers, business executives, and government officials) and cultural backgrounds. Such diversity can produce benefits for the participants in the form of access to diverse networks and inclusion of the best talent without incurring the investment costs required in more permanent arrangements (Larson, 1992). Nevertheless, similar to the distributed teams discussed by Hinds and Bailey (2003), collaborative efforts in which members originate in a variety of cultural, organizational, and functional settings may also lack a shared context, creating challenges related to the potential for conflict, a lack of shared understanding, and divergent goals and expectations. Further, without being embedded in a single, shared organizational context, the boundary between the collaborative effort and the external environment is more permeable, making the work effort more susceptible to changes that occur in the environment, which are likely to be complex, as described below.

Environmental Volatility

Volatility is the degree of diverse and unpredictable environmental features that must be addressed by the participants in the collaborative endeavor (Dess & Beard, 1984; Scott, 1998; Mathieu, Marks, & Zaccaro, 2001), and affects the extent to which it is possible to forecast challenges in advance (Waller, 1999; Sutcliffe, 1994). While traditional organizations operate in conjunction with a fairly established and stable set of external constituents (e.g., clients, suppliers, community stakeholders, etc.), participants in emerging forms of collaborative work may face a new set of external constituents for each new collaborative objective (e.g., each home building endeavor, each film project, each new product development enterprise). Additionally, such work frequently occurs in the midst of (and at times in response to) environmental dynamism and uncertainty. Similar to the network partnerships that Powell (1990) described, temporary collaborative efforts may be formed as a more nimble means of rapidly responding to changing market conditions. Further, these collaborative efforts may be formed in order to deal with an urgent crisis (as in the case of the emergency response teams formed to respond to the devastation that followed Hurricane Katrina). This urgency and dynamism means that strategies for meeting constituent (customer, client and stakeholder) needs may be in flux or even unknown, necessitating ongoing scanning and diagnosing and continuous shifts in interactions with the environment as a result (Miller & Friesen, 1983).

Fundamental Challenges in Collaborative Endeavors

Many of the challenges experienced in collaborative efforts today are inherent in the nature of collaborative work, and are not fully addressed by traditional organization theory (Mortensen, 2012). We argue that to be able to respond to such challenges, an important first step is to identify the locus

—that is whether the challenge originates from inside the collaborative endeavor or outside of it. Like the literature on teams (e.g., Cohen & Bailey, 1997), we use a relatively subjective and psychological approach to understanding what is "internal" and what is "external." That is, we consider all those participants (and their associated resources) who would identify themselves as a member of the collaborative endeavor to be internal to it, and those that would not so self-identify to be external to it. Internal members may include leaders, founders, independent contributors, operators, or technicians who contribute knowledge, skills or resources directly to the collaborative effort and identify themselves as a member of it, even if only temporarily, at some point in its duration.[1] Examples of those external to the collaborative effort may include clients, customers, members of funding or regulatory agencies or government officials, who may receive or evaluate the knowledge, products, or services that the internal members create, but who do not consider themselves to be members of the collaborative effort. We recognize that the internal-external boundary is somewhat permeable, and indeed suggest that this permeability is likely greater when participants do not share or have organizational affiliations. Yet, as a starting point, we find this internal-external distinction to be useful in order to highlight how collaborative efforts differ from more traditional forms of organizing, as well as how they differ from each other.[2]

In the sections that follow, we develop propositions regarding the relationship between the four key features of collaborative work and internal and external challenges, suggesting that the relative proportion of internal versus external challenges is based on the extent to which the collaborative effort demonstrates fluidity, impermanence, organizational independence, and environmental volatility. Identifying the locus of challenges is important, because as we will elaborate later, optimal adjustment responses are likely to depend on whether the locus is internal or external.

Internal Challenges

Internal challenges are related to the way the participants work together with each other (Dibble & Gibson, 2013) and may include sudden or drastic

---

[1] Similar to Ancona, Bresman, & Kaeufer's (2002) work on layers of team membership, we acknowledge that some members may be more "core" while others may be more "peripheral," but for our purposes here, we consider both core and peripheral members to be "internal."
[2] We also acknowledge that in highly fluid collaborations, there may be shifts between internal versus external membership. We take up this issue again in our discussion section, as a key avenue for future research.

changes in membership (e.g., the need to incorporate new members or the need to compensate for the loss of others), conflicts between collaboration members, the need to reconfigure roles, or challenges associated with structural modifications within the work effort. An example of an internal challenge that a collaborative effort might face is a discrepancy between two key members of a product development team regarding the scope of the project to be undertaken. In this type of situation, the requirements established by external constituents may be vague and open to discussion and interpretation among those who are internal to the collaborative effort. Disagreement about direction or fundamental processes may represent a significant internal challenge.

The organizational behavior literature has focused on concepts that bear some similarity to our concept of internal challenges. Examples of this include research on group conflict, cultural differences, and role coordination. For example, the literature on group conflict has examined antecedents to conflict such as autonomy (Langfred, 2007), diversity (Pelled, Eisenhardt & Xin, 1999; Phillips & Thomas-Hunt, 2007), and personality (Peterson, Davidson, & Moynihan, 2007), along with debates about the implications of conflict for group and organizational performance (De Dreu & Weingart, 2003; Behfar & Thompson, 2007). However, this research has assumed fairly stable role structures and a permanent organizational "home." The lack of shared history inherent in the temporary nature of much of collaborative work today may create the opportunity for internal conflict related to uncertainty about norms, processes and expectations in participants' work together. Additionally, the fluid nature of work (with participants coming and going at various points in time) may enhance the likelihood for misunderstandings and conflict related to role reconfiguration and shifts in values and priorities.

Similarly, organizational scholars have examined the ways in which differences in national culture among team members create challenges in the way individuals work together. For example, this research has examined the cross-cultural challenges experienced by global virtual teams (Zakaria, Amelinckx, & Wilemon, 2004), the impact of cultural diversity on task group performance (Watson, Kumar, & Michaelsen, 1993), and the relationship between cultural gaps and role ambiguity in international joint ventures (Shenkar & Zeira, 1992). However, cultural differences may be even more salient when members do not have any established history which would allow them to understand the commonly held values of a participant's culture. Additionally, participants may come and go before these differences can be fully appreciated and accommodated.

Unlike other organizational scholars who have addressed various types of internal challenges in the context of more stable teams and organizations, Bechky (2006) addressed a particular type of internal challenge—role coordination—in the context of temporary organizations, which she defined as "flexible, discontinuous, and ephemeral" entities governed through network relationships (rather than traditional lines of authority) which bring together unfamiliar individuals required to work interdependently on complex tasks (Bechky, 2006). While Bechky addresses the challenge of role coordination in temporary organizations, the professionals she examined were accustomed to working repeatedly in similar configurations with individuals engaging in standard, union derived roles and reporting structures that remained stable from project to project. Her research does not address how role coordination might take place in less developed genres which may involve participants without formal or professional training or who are not in the practice of engaging in pre-specified roles (e.g., humanitarian work, ad hoc consulting teams, medical projects involving specialists for one-time procedures).

We argue that across the four key features of collaborative work, the two dimensions which present the greatest internal challenges are fluidity and impermanence. Prior research indicates that stable institutionalized roles enable participants to organize work and maintain continuity (Bechky, 2006; Baker & Faulkner, 1991) and that transactive memory associated with these roles is positively related to performance, because it allows teams to develop specialized knowledge and more effectively use it, thereby facilitating joint recall of a greater amount task-relevant information (Lewis, 2003; Austin, 2003). However, when role definition and role incumbents are in flux, this creates ambiguity that can cause internal challenges (Callero, 1994; Eys & Carron, 2001). Impermanence is also likely to create internal challenges in that it hinders the development of routines. It has been suggested that routines promote a collective ability to enact recognizable patterns of action (Nelson & Winter, 1982; Pentland & Rueter, 1994). Recent research also demonstrates that routines serve as a valuable means of adaptation, where elements from past experiences with a particular routine are combined to deal with current challenges, thus influencing future interpretations of a routine (Feldman & Pentland, 2003). In the absence of these routines, every new development in the collaborative effort necessitates reformulation of information processing (Gibson, 2001; Gibson & Earley, 2007), and coordinative behaviors (Shenhar, 2001; Bechky, 2006).

High levels of organizational independence and environmental volatility may also result in internal challenges, but on balance the challenges associated

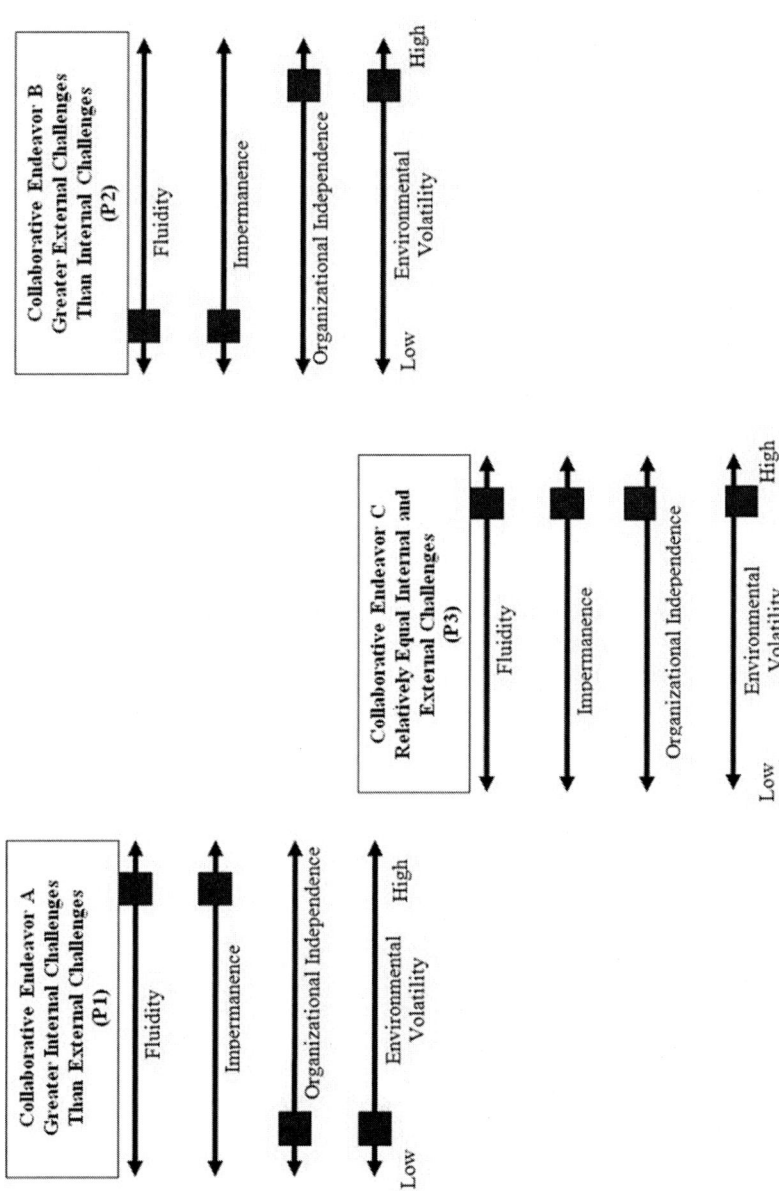

Figure 6-2. The Relationship Between Features of Collaborative Work and Locus of Challenges

associated with these features are more likely to be external (as addressed in our next section). That is, when the four features are experienced to some extent, there is the potential for both internal and external challenges. However, in order to pave a path forward toward understanding adjustment to the challenges, we propose that it is useful to think about the *proportion* of internal to external challenges being experienced. And particularly when fluidity and impermanence are high, a greater proportion of the challenges experienced are likely to be internal rather than external. This feature of our framework is illustrated in "Collaborative Endeavor A" in Figure 6-2 and summarized in our first proposition.

> **Proposition 1**: The greater the degree of fluidity and impermanence, the higher the proportion of internal challenges to external challenges experienced by a collaborative work effort (i.e., across all challenges experienced, a greater number will be internal than external).

External Challenges

External challenges experienced by a collaborative endeavor include challenges originating outside the immediate collaborative context and may include challenges related to the physical setting in which the participants work; challenges related to the political, regulatory, economic or cultural context in which they are situated (Dibble & Gibson, 2013); challenges originating in key organizations with which the collaborative endeavor interacts (e.g., unions, customers, key constituents); and challenges related to the environmental context created by various member affiliations (e.g., unions, guilds, professional associations). Challenges that occur as a result of changes in the external environment, creating the need to adjust, may occur as a result of moving from one location to another or as a result of changes within a particular environmental context.

Examples of external challenges that a collaborative endeavor might face include the delay of critical processes by external regulatory agencies, failure of external suppliers to meet delivery deadlines, or economic crises that result in loss of funding or the ability to pay by external constituents. In a research collaboration, the timetable for the project may be delayed as members wait for approval from government, university, or funding entities, creating an external challenge as other concurrent and subsequent tasks must be rescheduled, work to be performed by both internal members and external contractors must be delayed, and the ability to reach key deadlines in a timely manner becomes uncertain.

The organizational literature has addressed topics similar to external challenges, including the impact of hostile government on organizations, challenges associated with differences between various national cultures, and environmental shocks. However, this research has largely been conducted at the organizational level of analysis (including research on joint ventures between two organizations) and at the individual level of analysis (e.g., literature on expatriation and repatriation). Our study of external challenges addresses external challenges among smaller, often organizationally independent entities.

Government and political challenges represent one type of external challenge with which participants in collaborative endeavors contend. Research in the domain of political science, sociology, and organization and management that has examined the challenges created by government for organizations bears some similarity to the phenomenon of external challenges addressed here. For example, research has examined the impact of government ideology (e.g., governments that are inherently hostile to independent organization, e.g., Pearce, 2001), government capability (e.g., the extent to which governments are capable of effectively enacting and enforcing rule of law, e.g., Wang, 2006), and government corruption on organization and management (e.g., Rose-Ackerman, 1997; Henisz & Zelner, 2001; see Pearce, Dibble, & Klein, 2009, for a review). However, non-traditional collaborative endeavors often function without the financial resources and institutional legitimacy of traditional organizations, and their organizational independence may make them particularly susceptible to the types of external challenges presented by government hostility and corruption, creating a unique way of experiencing this type of external challenge.

Research on national cultural distance has examined the challenges inherent in working amid cultural unfamiliarity. Differences between home and host national cultures may provide a novel or challenging external contextual feature for newly expatriated employees (Hofstede, 2001; Mendenhall & Oddou, 1985) and foreign divisions of multinational organizations (Lawrence & Lorsch, 1967; Rosenzweig & Singh, 1991). Additionally, national culture may manifest itself as a type of external challenge when the external constituents with whom collaborators interact originate from dissimilar cultures (e.g., Jarvenpaa & Leidner, 1999). However, when collaborative work is organizationally independent, cultural differences may represent an even more severe external challenge than in the context of a traditional organization or for a single expatriate, because there may be no infrastructure or organizational resources (i.e., an HR staff) that can be tapped in the process of adjusting to such challenges.

Additionally, many collaborative endeavors take place in response to environmental volatility, and cultural differences experienced may be coupled with other types of external complexity, requiring even greater need for adjustment.

Similarly the literature on shocks has examined unanticipated, disruptive, exogenous events which occur in an organization's external environment (Rottner, 2007). For example, Meyer, Gaba, & Colwell (2005) identified three distinct forms of organizational shocks: jolts (transient shocks that temporarily impact organizations and organizational fields); step functions (changes that move through organizational fields leaving a permanent mark on their features); and oscillations (recurring cycles of shocks). Examples of external shocks cited in Meyer et al's (2005) study include strikes, changes in government regulations, and fluctuations in the availability of venture capital. Again, these shocks are assumed to target organizations; when collaborative efforts occur independent of organizations, these shocks are likely magnified or intertwined with other environmental complexities.

In contrast to internal challenges, we argue that the two dimensions which present the greatest external challenges for non-traditional collaborative endeavors are organizational independence and environmental volatility. Organizational independence (i.e. lack of a single uniting organizational affiliation) is likely to increase challenges related to securing resources for connecting and coordinating across contexts. That is, members are likely to represent very different contexts, and the difficulties in sharing and combining "situated" knowledge across diverse contexts have been well documented in the literature on dispersed teams (Cramton, 2001; Sole & Edmondson, 2000). Organizational independence also suggests greater permeability of the boundary between the collaborative effort and its environment, meaning there are fewer organizational systems and structures that can "buffer" the work effort from the environment than in traditional organizations (Thompson, 1967; Lynn, 2005). Environmental volatility suggests a diversity of elements that are constantly changing, which prohibits proactive forecasting, such that networks and contracts (even informal or implicit contracts) with external constituents must be constantly re-negotiated (Zajac et al., 2000).

Thinking again in terms of the proportion of external to internal challenges, we argue that particularly when organizational independence and environmental volatility are high, a greater proportion of the challenges experienced will be external rather than internal. This feature of our framework is illustrated in "Collaborative Endeavor B" in Figure 6-2 and summarized in our second proposition. We do acknowledge that high levels of fluidity and impermanence may also result in external challenges; however, on balance we suggest that the challenges associated with these defining characteristics are more likely to be internal.

> **Proposition 2**: The greater the degree of organizational independence and environmental volatility, the higher the proportion of external challenges to internal challenges experienced by a collaborative work effort (i.e., across all challenges experienced, a greater number will be external than internal).

At the extreme, some collaborative efforts may experience high levels of all four key features. An example of a collaborative effort with simultaneously high fluidity, impermanence, organizational independence and environmental volatility is a documentary film making team in which only the director (who also serves as a producer) remains working on the film throughout the duration of its production, while screenwriters, actors, camera operators and editors are only periodically involved. Further the entire project takes place over a matter of two months, before and after which no member will work together again. The participants are all non-union independent contractors, none is embedded in a production company or has other organizational affiliations. The environment is composed of multiple conceptual, filming and editing locations, each of which is very different from each other in terms of cultural, legal, and economic conditions, and particularly the filming location is in chaotic flux as political conditions are quickly changing over the course of the 2 month project. In this collaborative effort, we anticipate a relatively equal number of internal and external challenges, as illustrated in "Collaborative Endeavor C" in Figure 6-2 and in our third proposition below.

> **Proposition 3:** Collaborative work efforts with a high level of fluidity, impermanence, organizational independence, and environmental volatility will experience a relatively equal proportion of internal and external challenges.

Essential Collaborative Processes

To be sure, there are many important processes that occur in collaborative efforts today, many of which will look and feel different from those in traditional organizational forms, and numerous of which will have varied implications for effectiveness. Coinciding with the unique challenges, we focus here on two aspects of collaborative action — the processes of internal and external adjustment. That is, aside from the locus of the challenge which stimulates change, adjustment processes may occur inside the collaborative work effort in response to either internal or external challenges; or, a collaborative endeavor may adjust the way it interacts with outside constituents in response to internal or external challenges (Dibble & Gibson, 2013). In this section, we define internal and external adjustment and explain how each is similar to, yet critically distinct from, related concepts. Next we examine the issue of selecting an adjustment method and make some conjectures as to how a collaborative effort might choose one means of adjustment more frequently than another.

Internal Adjustment

We define internal adjustment as participants' ability to spontaneously adjust interaction among members in response to imminent and unanticipated challenges arising in both the internal and external environments. Internal adjustment likely exists on a continuum ranging from minor adjustments to major adjustments (Dibble & Gibson, 2013). Moderate forms of internal adjustment might include strategies such as problem resolution or role reconfiguration (Dibble & Gibson, 2013). Processes similar to internal adjustment in collaborations have been investigated in literature on teams and projects, under the rubrics of reflexivity, improvisation, and bricolage. Below, we review this literature and show that these concepts bear some similarity to internal adjustment, yet are critically distinct, demonstrating the value-added of the collaboration-focus of our theory. These comparisons are summarized in Table 6-2.

An internal adjustment such as role reconfiguration may be implemented in response to loss of collaboration members as a result of internal or external forces. Arrow and McGrath (1993) conducted a longitudinal study of 22 student teams and observed the impact of group member change on performance. They found that groups that experienced membership changes (either experimentally imposed additions or spontaneous losses such as absences) performed better on a group internal process task than those groups that had stable membership. They proposed that "even the reshuffling of duties required when a member was missing may all have helped group members reflect on how and what they were doing as groups" (Arrow & McGrath, 1993: 359). In this instance internal reshuffling of roles constituted the internal adjustment to an internally or externally imposed challenge. This research is suggestive of the ways in which internal adjustment (e.g., reconfiguring the roles of group members)

Table 6-2. Constructs Similar to Internal and External Adjustment in Collaborative Entities

Concept	Author	Locus of Change	Challenge That Stimulated Change	Technique	Outcome
Role-Based Coordination	Bechky, 2006	Internal	Coordination of tasks under extreme time pressure	Learning and negotiation of role structures	Sustained coordination of behavior and understanding of roles across projects
Contextualization	Katz & Te'eni, 2007	Internal	Misunderstandings in computer-mediated communication	Contextualization of computer-mediated messages	Effective adaptation when collaborators represent different perspectives
Bricolage	Baker & Nelson (2005)	Internal	Dealing with a challenging community resident (Chao, 1999); engineering and design challenges (Lanzara, 1999)	Bricolage: "making do by applying combinations of the resources at hand to new problems and opportunities" (Baker & Nelson, 2005: 333)	Evidence of positive, neutral and negative outcomes resulting from adjusting via bricolage
Improvisation	Cunha et al., 1999	Internal	External complexity (e.g., Barret, 1998); flaws in mental models (e.g., Crossan et al. 1996)	Improvisation: "the conception of action as it unfolds, drawing on available material, cognitive, affective, and social resources." (Cunha et al., 1999: 302)	Evidence of positive and negative outcomes resulting from organizational improvisation
Dispersed Expertise	Boh et al., 2007	Internal	Needs for expertise residing in a remote location on projects in dispersed organizations	Balancing the need to bring in off-site expertise against coordination costs for a project	A curvilinear relationship between dispersion (for expertise) and returns: when project dispersion reaches 30-50% of members, coordination costs of dispersion may exceed returns
Conflict Management/ Task Reflexivity	Tjosvold et al., 2003	Internal	Team conflict	Cooperative conflict management and task reflexivity	Higher team performance
Mutual Adjustment	Zimmermann & Sparrow (2007)	Internal	Adaptation to expatriate setting	Mutual adjustment	Improved relational and work outcomes
Individual/Group Reflexivity	Gurtner et al., 2007	Internal	Information asymmetry and the need to combine diverse information to assess the threat level of airplanes in a military simulation	Individual or group reflexivity (reflection and adaptation either in the form of a group discussion or individually)	Performance in the "individual" and "group" reflexivity conditions were not significantly different and patterns indicated better performance in the individual than the group reflexivity condition.
Team Adaptation	Marks et al. (2000)	Internal	The need to confront novel elements in the team environment	The derivation and use of new strategies and techniques for confronting novelty in the team environment	Team-interaction training and enhanced leader briefings allowed teams to more accurately adjust their mental models when confronted with new environments than teams that did not receive these manipulations.

Table 6-2 (continued). Constructs Similar to Internal and External Adjustment in Collaborative Entities

Concept	Author	Locus of Change	Challenge That Stimulated Change	Technique	Outcome
Informing, Parading, and Probing	Ancona, 1990	Internal/ External	Interaction with external constituents and managing internal team dynamics	Informing (focus on internal team processes), parading (emphasis on team building and visibility among external constituents), and probing (extensive interaction with external constituents)	Probing teams (those teams focused on interaction with external constituents) perform better than teams focused exclusively on internal team dynamics when teams are externally dependent.
External Knowledge Acquisition	Zellmer-Bruhn (2003)	External	Interruptive events	Seeking and integrating external (outside the team) knowledge and adapting team routines	Interruptions serve as a trigger for knowledge transfer effort which in turn increases the acquisition of new team routines. Interruptions impact knowledge acquisition directly and indirectly through the increase of knowledge transfer effort.
Entrainment	Ancona & Chong (1996)	External	Unsynchronized cycles or paces of a related internal or external activity	Entrainment: "the adjustment of the pace or cycle of an activity to match or synchronize with that of another [internal or external] activity" (Ancona & Chong, 1996: 253)	Not an empirical piece, but they argue that entities that are more open to their environment are more likely to entrain to the rhythms, paces or cycles of their environments than those having impermeable boundaries
Strategic Technology Networks	Dittrich & Duysters, 2007	External	Changing technological environment	Establishment of strategic technology networks	Networks assist in the ability to adjust to changing market conditions.
Proactive and Competitive-Aggressive Adaptation	Lumpkin & Dess, 2001	External	Environmental opportunities and threats	Proactive and competitive-aggressive adaptations	Proactiveness will be related to performance in dynamic environments and growth industries and competitive-aggressiveness will be related to performance in hostile environments and mature industries
X-Teams	Ancona, Bresman and Kaeufer, 2002	External	Dynamic characteristics of work, technology and customer demands	Implementation of X-Teams (teams that manage across boundaries)	Evidence that X-teams lead to successful outcomes. However, the authors recommend their use when organizational structures are flat and with multiple alliances, when teams are dependent on complex, dispersed, rapidly changing information, and when tasks are intertwined with external tasks
Boundary Spanning	Ancona & Caldwell (2000)	External	Complex work conditions; high interdependence w/ other organizational units	Boundary spanning and the development of external relationships	Evidence of a positive relationship between boundary spanning and performance when tasks are uncertain

may allow a collaboration to enhance its performance in the face of internal and external challenges.

Extending Arrow and McGrath's research on membership fluidity and role reconfiguration, Kane, Argote and Levine (2005) examined internal adjustment (incorporating new knowledge into an existing routine) to internal challenges (removal and integration of a fluid, rotating group member and the need to improve production routines) in temporary, fluid student groups, and examined the impact of membership in a superordinate group as a factor in these groups' ability to successfully adjust. They found that adjustment (integration of knowledge possessed by a rotating group member) occurred more successfully when all group members had a shared identity as members of a superordinate group. This finding highlights a potential challenge for collaborative efforts today above and beyond those experienced by more traditional teams embedded within an overarching organization: the need to internally adjust among collaborators who do not share a pre-existing superordinate identity. Hence there is a need to examine the impact of internal adjustment to internal and external challenges in the context of organizationally independent collaborations.

Bechky (2006) examined the ways in which role structures are learned and negotiated in temporary organizations (e.g., film projects in the commercial film industry). This research provides us with valuable insights into how collaborators are able to quickly adapt to the challenge of beginning a new collaborative endeavor. However, the temporary organizations that Bechky (2006) examined may look more traditional than the collaborative forms we address here, in the sense that they may exist as a subset of a larger, more stable organization such as a film studio, while many collaborative efforts today are characterized by organizational independence.

Reflexivity has been defined as "the extent to which group members overtly reflect upon the group's objectives, strategies, and processes and adapt them to current or anticipated endogenous or environmental circumstances (Carter & West, 1998; West, 1996: 559). Reflexivity has been related to outcomes such as team effectiveness (Carter & West, 1998), team innovation (Tjosvold, Tang, & West, 2004), and the reduction of preventable adverse events in surgical teams (Vashdi, Bamberger, Erez, and Weiss-Meilik, 2007); as well as antecedents such as team composition (Schippers, Den Hartog, Koopman, & Wienk, 2003) and cooperative goals (Tjosvold et al., 2004). However, while reflexivity focuses on a group's ability to systematically reflect on past performance, anticipate potential challenges and revise its strategy to appropriately adapt, internal adjustment focuses on a more spontaneous capability to respond to challenges that arise in terms of work structures and processes by changing the way members work with one another. While reflexivity requires overt reflection and adaptation, internal adjustment is more informal and may be an unstructured reaction to an imminent challenge.

Improvisation has been conceptualized in a variety of ways including shifting away from an agreed plan in order to speed up implementation (Leyborne & Sadler-Smith, 2006), the unfolding of creative actions in the face of uncertainty and unprecedented events (Vera & Rodriguez-Lopez, 2007), simultaneous creation and execution of plans (Moorman & Miner, 1998; Samra, Lynn & Reilly, 2008), and radical innovative activity from prior behavior (Weick, 1993). Internal adjustment bears some similarity to the concept of improvisation in the sense that it is a spontaneous reaction or adaptation. For example, internal adjustment may entail an improvisational response that may take the form of an actor in a film team improvising lines as a means of adjusting to an internal challenge created by another actor forgetting his lines. While improvisation may occur as a result of a need to respond to an unplanned event, the opportunity for improvisation may be created by design. For example, a new product development team may incorporate opportunities for improvisation (opportunity for action outside standard plans and routines) into their work processes. Conversely, internal adjustment usually occurs as a response to an unanticipated (and often undesirable) challenge occurring in the internal or external environment.

Internal adjustment also bears some resemblance to the concept of bricolage, which has been defined as the act of drawing upon or making do with resources that are readily at hand, and creating new forms from tools and materials already in a group's possession, applying combinations of the resources at hand to new problems and opportunities (Baker & Nelson, 2005; Baker, Miner, & Eesley, 2003; Levi-Strauss, 1966). Similar to bricolage, internal adjustment may involve spontaneous adaptation by making creative use of existing resources or bringing together existing resources in creative ways. Additionally, internal adjustment may entail members of a collaboration working together to devise ways of adapting materials or tools they have on-hand to meet their resource needs. However, internal adjustment is distinct from bricolage in the sense that it involves more than just adapting resources in their possession to meet current needs. Internal adjustment may also entail adjustments such as interpersonal conflict resolution and revising plans in order to spontaneously adapt to challenges or opportunities arising in the internal or external environment.

External Adjustment

External adjustment may occur alongside internal adjustment, but entails different behavioral responses. Specifically, external adjustment encompasses changes vís a vís interaction with external constituents (Gibson & Dibble, 2008; Gibson & Dibble, 2013; Dibble & Gibson, 2013). Strategies for external adjustment may range along a continuum from minor modification to more substantial modification and include processes such as negotiating with key constituents in the external environment, repositioning a product or service for new markets or constituents, reframing the mission or purpose, and changing behavior in interactions with the external environment. When relatively minor challenges are experienced in the internal context or external environment, negotiation with external constituents may be one means of externally adjusting. In the case of a film making project, the challenge of securing access to a particular filming location or the challenge of scheduling a more favorable timeline with a skilled laborer may be examples where negotiation is an appropriate form of adjustment. Changing the way in which collaborators behave in their interactions with external constituents constitutes a more effortful means of externally adjusting. This might entail expanding a contract with an external firm to include more or fewer individuals or responsibilities vís a vís the collaborative effort than were previously involved.

Processes similar to external adjustment have been investigated in literature on teams and organizations, ranging from boundary spanning to adaptation. Below (and in Table 6-2), we review this literature and show that although these concepts bear some resemblance to external adjustment, they are critically distinct.

Ancona (1990) studied a sample of five teams charged with consulting school districts in the New England area. She examined three specific strategies regarding the interaction of these teams with their external environments (in this case, the "external environment" referred to the clients that were being served) including informing (a strategy which focused largely on internal team building and informing its external constituents of its strategy), parading (a strategy that focused simultaneously on internal team building but with an emphasis on making the team more visible to its external constituents), and probing (a strategy which focused on "a high level of interaction with the environment to revise teams' knowledge of their regions and meet customer demands" (Ancona, 1990: 348)). She proposed and found that in teams that are dependent on their external environment, a "probing" strategy—a strategy focused on interaction with external constituents (in this case the commissioner and the school districts teams were assigned to serve)—would lead to higher performance.

Subsequent work by Ancona and Caldwell (1992) consisted of a qualitative examination of specific *types* of external activities that product development teams engaged in including ambassadorial activities (communicating with upper management in order to lobby for support or resources or to buffer the team from excessive outside pressure), task coordinator activities (coordinating task-related activities with outside entities), scout activities (activities related to scanning the environment for information related to competition or technology), and guard activities (protecting the team from unintentional information leakage). They found a positive relationship between ambassadorial activity and team performance and a negative relationship between prolonged scouting activities and team performance.

Ancona and her colleagues addressed "external" activities that were outside a given team but still within a single organization within which the teams were embedded. Our framework addresses whether *changing* the type or extent of interaction with external constituents outside any particular organizational affiliation results in better performance. This distinction is important as external adjustment may be even more challenging and more critical when participants each belong to different organizations, or do not have an organizational affiliation, and so have different perspectives and expectations, and fewer formal interfaces (Dibble & Gibson, 2013).

The literature on alliances and networks has also addressed topics similar to external adjustment. For example Ariño et al. (2008) examined the question of whether small firms were more likely to adjust to challenges regarding governance misalignment through renegotiating contracts vís a vís their alliance partners. They found that while small firms do not appear to adjust their contracts with alliance partners in general any more or less than other types of firms, they were less likely to make contractual adjustments in response to governance misalignments than larger firms. Additionally, they found that alliances were more likely to renegotiate their contracts when the contracts were less complex. While this research examined some of the key contextual conditions related to whether or not firms adjust to external challenges, it did not examine the impact that this type of adjustment has on performance, and did not address the type of temporary collaborative endeavors examined here. Without organizational embeddedness, such work efforts may be less likely to have the resources necessary to engage in certain types of adjustment (such as renegotiating a contract to remedy governance misalignment). On the other hand, the organizationally independent nature of collaborative endeavors (which may necessitate that they operate with fewer financial resources) may make them more likely to engage in other types of adjustments (e.g., negotiating for better rates with suppliers).

Additionally, Dittrich and Duysters (2007) drew upon interviews with experts on Nokia's alliance strategy and analysis of two alliance databases to examine the ways that networks have been used to adjust to challenges associated with changes in technological environments experienced by research and development alliances. Through a combination of qualitative and quantitative methods, they found evidence for the importance of strategic networks, which offer flexibility, innovation, speed, and the ability to make smooth adjustments in the presence of a dynamic technological environment. While the establishment of external networks is an important method for adjusting to external challenges, this is only one of many ways in which collaborative endeavors may externally adjust. Further, the authors focused solely on R&D alliances which are special because they typically involve large firms, with significant financial and technological resources that help equip them to deal with the types of challenges examined here. Additionally, membership in a large overarching firm may insulate R&D teams from many of the challenges to which organizationally independent collaborations would remain exposed (e.g., lack of funding, loss of a critical skill, or the need to access a particular type of equipment or facility).

To summarize our approach thus far, extant literature that deals with adjustment in collaborative efforts contributes some valuable insights that further our understanding of the types of adjustments participants make both internally and externally. However, no framework that we are aware of has incorporated a simultaneous examination of internal adjustment and external adjustment as we have defined these concepts here. Further, prior research on concepts related to adjustment at other levels of analysis cannot be generalized to address these issues in the context of non-traditional collaborative endeavors, because they fail to address the co-occurrence of key features of collaborative work such as fluidity, impermanence, organizational independence, and environmental volatility.

Adjustment and Performance

Perhaps the most important issue associated with the concept of adjustment is whether or not it makes a positive difference for performance. Prior research that has investigated the relationship between concepts similar to internal adjustment and performance, as well as the relationship between concepts similar to external adjustment and performance, has produced equivocal results (see Table 6-2). This suggests that the answer to this question may depend on the nature of the challenges. We develop propositions in this regard in this final section.

Internal Adjustment and Performance

Recent literature has isolated specific forms of internal adjustment and its implications for traditional teams and organizations. In addition to the work by Bechky (2006), Tjosvold, Hui, and Yu (2003) examined work teams in 100 firms located in Shanghai with an interest in the ways that teams' responses to conflict impact performance. They found that cooperative forms of conflict management promoted task reflexivity (defined as the extent to which teams collectively reflect upon objectives, strategies and processes and adapt as needed) which was positively related to performance (captured by manager survey responses). Task reflexivity is similar to internal adjustment in the sense that it involves changing the way that teams work together in order to adjust to challenges arising in their internal context, yet it involves monitoring and overt reflection in advance of a challenge occurring while internal adjustment may be a much more spontaneous type of adaptation. Likewise, Zimmermann and Sparrow (2007: 69) conducted a one-year longitudinal study of eleven teams (consisting of four combinations of nationalities: German/English, German/Indian, German/Japanese, and German/Austrian) in two German companies and found that mutual adjustment (which they defined as "the process by which members of different nationalities achieve a fit and reduced conflict between each other with regard to their differences in work practices and interaction styles") was positively related to improved work outcomes.

While these studies provide evidence for a positive relationship between internal adjustment-like processes and performance, other studies have suggested that the relationship may not be a simple, positive, linear relationship. For example, Boh, Ren, Kiesler, and Bussjaeger (2007) examined challenges related to lack of a critical skill set on the dispersed project sites of a professional service organization. The adjustments they observed entailed matching individuals with specific skill sets to needs for these skills across geographically dispersed project sites. Dispersion of organizational expertise is an example of internal adjustment in the sense that it involves adjusting (or reconfiguring) the way geographically dispersed members of an organization work together, in response to a challenge or need at a particular location. These scholars found that organizations' responses to a need for expertise on a particular project (i.e., by matching experts to projects across locations) had a positive effect on project returns, but only up to a point. Their results showed that when dispersion reached 30-50% of project members, coordination costs of dispersion exceed the returns, and net earnings became negative.

Taken together, these results suggest the need for a more precise specification of the relationship between internal adjustment and performance.

We suggest that the nature of the challenges being experienced (the stimuli to which the collaborative endeavor is adjusting) matters a great deal. Or stated another way, the relationship between internal adjustment and performance will be moderated by the type of challenge. More specifically, we anticipate the more that the participants face internal challenges in contrast to external challenges, the greater the effect that internal adjustment will have on performance. Such an approach acknowledges that, as stated in our propositions above, internal adjustment can be a functional response to both internal and external challenges. Yet if internal challenges dominate, then an over reliance on external adjustment (i.e., extremely low internal adjustment and extremely high external adjustment) is likely to be dysfunctional. The follow proposition captures this:

> **Proposition 4**: The greater the proportion of internal challenges to external challenges, the stronger the relationship between internal adjustment and collaborative performance.

External Adjustment and Performance

As with internal adjustment, prior literature has identified a variety of ways in which collaborative endeavors respond to changes in their external environment and the outcomes associated with these adjustments. For example, Ancona, Bresman, and Kaeufer (2002) conducted an empirical study that provided evidence that adaptive teams with an external orientation are useful in overcoming the challenges associated with dynamic work conditions, technology and customer demands. They concluded that the use of these teams may be related to higher performance, especially when organizational structures are flat with multiple alliances; when teams are dependent on complex, dispersed, and rapidly changing information; and when organizational tasks are intertwined with external tasks. While Ancona et al. (2002) described the relationship between the externally-oriented, adaptive characteristics of teams and team performance, these teams existed within an organization and they did not address adjustment vís a vís external constituents outside the organization.

Other research on external adjustment-like processes has suggested that the relationship with performance may not be positive and linear, and instead may be moderated by context. For example, Lumpkin and Dess (2001) queried executives from 94 firms to understand how firms adapt to the challenges of environmental opportunities and threats. Findings suggested that firm adaptations in the form of proactiveness (an opportunity-seeking strategy that seeks to anticipate future demand) are more likely to result in high performance when firms operate in dynamic environments and growth industries, and that adaptations in the form of competitive-aggressiveness (defined as the effort by a firm to outperform rivals by assuming a combative posture) are more likely to be associated with high performance for firms operating in hostile environments. They concluded that not all dimensions of adaptations to environmental conditions will be positively related to performance under all conditions.

Here, we anticipate that the efficaciousness of external adjustment is dependent on the nature of the challenges being experienced (the stimuli to which the collaborative endeavor is externally adjusting), such that the relationship between external adjustment and performance will be moderated by the type of challenge. More specifically, we anticipate the more that the collaborative effort faces external challenges in contrast to internal challenges, the greater the effect that external adjustment will have on performance. Again, such an approach acknowledges that, as stated in our propositions above, external adjustment can be a functional response to both internal and external challenges. Yet if external challenges dominate, then an over reliance on internal adjustment (i.e., extremely low external adjustment and extremely high internal adjustment) is likely to be dysfunctional. The follow proposition captures this:

> **Proposition 5**: The greater the proportion of external challenges to internal challenges, the stronger the relationship between external adjustment and collaborative performance.

Discussion

Our aim in this paper has been to draw attention to the ways in which work in non-traditional collaborative endeavors differs from more traditional forms of organizing. We argue that various forms of collaborative organizing range along a continuum based on their degree of fluidity, permanence, organizational independence, and environmental volatility. We suggest that the features that distinguish non-traditional collaborative endeavors from other forms of organizing also necessitate different forms of adjustment. For example, a collaborative effort which is high in fluidity and lack of permanence, yet low in organizational independence and environmental volatility may require a different type of adjustment strategy than one characterized by low fluidity and lack of permanence and high organizational independence and environmental volatility. Additionally, we have identified internal adjustment and external adjustment as two critical processes in collaborative endeavors, noting that generalizing from more traditional organizational forms in order to understand adjustment processes in the non-traditional forms would be unwise.

Theoretical Contributions

This research makes several valuable contributions to theory. First, we develop a theoretical framework for collaborative adjustment that increases our understanding of the ways in which participants most effectively adjust to the inherent challenges that occur when individuals come together to work in dynamic and temporary collaborative structures. In doing so we integrate theory examining group attributes and processes with research centered in open systems theory that examines collaborative interaction with and response to the vibrant and often volatile environmental contexts to which such collaborative efforts belong.

Specifically, we extend Thompson's (1967) notions of organizational responses to the environment. Thompson (1967) identified three possible strategies for anticipating environmental fluctuation including buffering, smoothing, and forecasting. However, as is the tradition in organizational theory, he focused on large, stable organizations. Temporary collaborative work efforts are inherently smaller and more fluid, and may operate independently of over-arching organizations and in very dynamic settings. As such, due to limitations in resources or experience, they may be unable to close themselves off from challenges occurring in their external environments (e.g., through anticipation of challenges or through the ability to fulfill all of its own needs without looking to external resources). The "closed system of logic" that Thompson (1967: 22) suggested may be employed to buffer organizations when "environmental fluctuations can be anticipated" must be replaced by the ability to expediently adjust. Our theory begins to address how this type of adjustment takes place.

Additionally, we propose that theories of organizational effectiveness look different when examined in the context of fluid, temporary collaborative endeavors. For example, Gladstein's (1984) model of task group effectiveness proposes that group processes are related to group effectiveness, moderated by the nature and context of the task (e.g., task complexity, environmental uncertainty, and interdependence). While much of this theory is still relevant for non-traditional collaborative endeavors, we argue that the antecedents to group processes that Gladstein proposed will look very different in the context of such work efforts. For example, group composition traits that she proposed as antecedents to group process include adequate skills and organizational tenure. In the context of temporary work efforts, participants may have to learn to make do with a shortage of critical skills and participants will most likely belong to various organizations or they may not have any organizational affiliation. In a model of effectiveness for these work efforts, critical elements of composition might include commitment, efficacy, or other antecedents that serve to provide a source of energy and motivation as well as the necessary resources to adjust.

Finally, we extend theory on organizational learning and adaptation. It has been suggested that "change, learning, and adaptation have all been used to refer to the process by which organizations adjust to their environment" (Fiol & Lyles, 1985: 805). However, organizational learning, as it has traditionally been discussed in the literature differs from the concept of adjustment we focus on here in at least two critical ways. Levitt and March (1988) argued that organizational learning is routine-based and history-dependent. It is routine-based in the sense that organizational action involves matching processes to situations rather than devising choices. They noted that "routines are based on interpretations of the past more than anticipations of the future" (Levitt & March, 1988). Additionally, Levitt and March (1988) viewed organizational learning as history-dependent. They noted that lessons from the history of the organization are captured in the routines that the organization enacts. While these ideas about organizational learning are applicable for more traditional teams and organizations, they will most likely look different when the short-term nature of members' work together does not permit the accumulation of history or routines. Hence, this research suggests that theories of organizational learning need to be adapted for many collaborative endeavors today, in order to identify ways in which learning, change, and adaptation take place in the context of a short-term work arrangement, fluid member participation, organizational independence, and a dynamic external environment.

Future Research

We extend prior models of team effectiveness by highlight the increasing primacy of adjusting to challenges related to a finite reservoir of skills, the loss and addition of participants, and the lack of participation in an overarching organization that may otherwise serve to buffer, protect, or supply the collaborative endeavor with critical resources. Our framework suggests several significant avenues for future research, including issues related to identifying internal versus external participants and conceptualizing effectiveness.

Internal vs. external participants. While who's "in" and who's "out" may be a fairly simple issue in teams and traditional organizations, the line between "internal" and "external" participants may be much harder to define in non-traditional collaborative endeavors. We developed our framework with a preliminary idea of how to define the "internal" and "external" players. However, this distinction is likely to evolve. That is, individuals who begin their association as "external" contributors may over time, begin to see themselves increasingly as "internal" members. This issue of fuzzy boundaries may have interesting implications for collaborative identity, motivation, structure and design. Understanding how identities form and change, and how being "central" or "peripheral" impacts the roles participants engage in, are important topics of future research. For example, external contractors may, after repeated interactions with members, shift from seeing themselves as detached external resources to viewing themselves as core contributors to the collaborative vision (i.e., "internal" members). This type of identity shift may have implications for the extent to which contractors are willing to make special accommodations and invest additional time and effort. Additionally, the extent to which such contractors come to be viewed as more "internal" by other participants may impact the extent to which their expertise is viewed as credible, with the status afforded to specialists diluted over time. Understanding how and to what extent collaborative identity shifts take place is an important empirical question.

Conceptualizing effectiveness. Another interesting implication of the eclectic nature of collaborative endeavors is that individuals from various cultural, organizational and functional backgrounds bring together a diversity of values and priorities, which may result in a proliferation of goals and objectives. For example, in a humanitarian home building project, the goal for some participants may be to complete the home on time, within budget, and according to the engineering specifications required by inspectors. For others, a more critical objective may be building a sense of community and providing an experience for volunteers such that they are motivated to continue to support humanitarian work. Understanding how best to motivate and reward workers with different and evolving objectives is likely to be very challenging. The existence of varied goals and objectives may also create a challenge for measuring performance or may result in a variety of confounding performance objectives. As such, it will be important to examine the relationship between collaboration adjustment and a variety of performance measures, as adjustment may be positively related to some and negatively related to others.

Conclusion

In summary, being able to identify features of work that distinguish collaborative efforts today from their more traditional precursors is a critical first step in developing new theory for new ways of working collectively. In doing so, we have highlighted the critical processes of internal adjustment and external adjustment. We hope that beginning to address the most common ways that collaborative efforts adjust and the implications of adjustment for performance will motivate further interest in filling the remaining gaps in our understanding of collaborative processes, encourage the extension of our framework, and allow us to be more precise in future studies of collaborative work.

References

Alper, S., Tjosvold, D., & Law, K. S. (1998). Interdependence and controversy in group decision making: Antecedents to effective self-managing teams. *Organizational Behavior and Human Decision Processes*, 74(1), 33.

Ancona, D.G. (1990). Outward bound: Strategies for team survival in an organization, *Academy of Management Journal,* 33(2), 334-365.

Ancona, D., Bresman, H., & Kaeufer, K. (2002, Spring). The comparative advantage of X-teams. *MIT Sloan Management Review*, *43*(3), 33-39.

Ancona, D. G., & Caldwell, D. F. (1992). Bridging the boundary: External activity and performance in organizational teams. *Administrative Science Quarterly,* 37, 634-665.

Ancona, D. G,. & Caldwell, D. F. (2000). Compose teams to assure successful boundary activity. In Locke, E. A. (ed.), *Handbook of principles of organizational behavior* (pp. 199-210). Oxford, UK: Blackwell Publishers.

Ancona, D., & Chong, C. (1996). Entrainment: Pace, cycle, and rhythm in organizational behavior. *Research in Organizational Behavior, 18,* 251-284.

Ariño, A., Ragozzino, R., & Reuer, J. J. (2008). Alliance dynamics for entrepreneurial firms. *Journal of Management Studies*, 45, 147-168.

Arrow, H., & McGrath, J. E. (1993). Membership matters: How member change and continuity affect small group structure, process, and performance. *Small Group Research*, *24*(3), 334-361.

Austin, J. R. (2003). Transactive memory in organizational groups: The effects of content, consensus, specialization, and accuracy on group performance. *Journal of Applied Psychology*, *88*(5), 866-878.

Baker, W. E. & Faulkner, R. R. (1991). Role as resource in the Hollywood film industry. *American Journal of Sociology, 97*(2), 279-309.

Baker, T., Miner, A. S., & Eesley, D. T. (2003). Improvising firms: Bricolage, account giving and improvisational competencies in the founding process. *Research Policy, 32*, 255-276.

Baker, T. & Nelson, R. E. (2005). Creating something from nothing: Resource construction through entrepreneurial bricolage. *Administrative Science Quarterly, 50*, 329-366.

Bechky, B. A. (2006). Gaffers, gofers, and grips: Role-based coordination in temporary organizations. *Organization Science, 17*(1), 3-21.

Behfar, K. J,. & Thompson, L. L. (2007). Conflict within and between organizational groups: Functional, dysfunctional, and quasifunctional perspectives. In K. J. Behfar & L. L. Thompson (Eds.), *Conflict in Organizational Groups: New Directions in Theory and Practice* (pp. 3-35). Evanston, IL: Northwestern University Press.

Blair, H., Grey, S., & Randle, K. (2001). Working in film—Employment in a project based industry. *Personnel Review, 30*(2), 170-185.

Boh, W. F., Ren, Y., Kiesler, S., & Bussjaeger, R. (2007). Expertise and collaboration in the geographically dispersed organization. *Organization Science, 18*(4), 595-612.

Callero, P. L. 1994. From role-playing to role-using: Understanding role as resource. *Social Psychology Quarterly, 57*(3): 228-243.

Carter, S. M. & West, M. A. (1998). Reflexivity, effectiveness, and mental health in BBC-TV production teams. *Small Group Research, 29*, 583-601.

Chao, E. (1999). The Maoist shaman and the madman: Ritual bricolage, failed ritual, and failed ritual theory. *Cultural Anthropology, 14*, 505-534.

Cohen, S. G,. & Bailey, D. E. (1997). What makes teams work: Group effectiveness research from the shop floor to the executive suite. *Journal of Management, 23*, 239-290.

Cramton, C. D. (2001). The mutual knowledge problem and its consequences for dispersed collaboration. *Organization Science, 12*, 346-371.

Crossan, M. M., White, R. E., Lane, H. W., & Klus, L. (1996). The improvising organization: Where planning meets opportunity. *Organizational Dynamics, 24*(4), 20-35.

Cunha, M., Cunha, J. V., & Kamoche, K. (1999). Organizational improvisation: What, when, how and why. *International Journal of Management Reviews, 1*(3), 299-341.

De Dreu, C. K. W. & Weingart, L. R.(2003). Task versus relationship conflict, team performance, and team member satisfaction: A meta-analysis. *Journal of Applied Psychology, 88*(4), 741-749.

Dess, G. G., & Beard, D. W. 1984. Dimensions of organizational task environment. *Administrative Science Quarterly,* 28: 274-291.

Dibble, R., & Gibson, C. B. (2013). Collaboration for the common good: An examination of challenges and adjustment processes in multicultural collaborations. *Journal of Organizational Behavior, 34*(6), 764-790.

Dittrich, K., & Duysters, G. (2007). Networking as a means to strategy change: The case of open innovation in mobile telephony. *Journal of Product Innovation Management, 24,* 510-521.

Eys, M. A. & Carron, A. V. 2001. Role ambiguity, task cohesion, and task self-efficacy. *Small Group Research,* 32: 356-373.

Feldman, M. S., & Pentland, B. T. (2003). Reconceptualizing organizational routines as a source of flexibility and change. *Administrative Science Quarterly, 48*(1), 94-118.

Fiol, C. M., & Lyles, M. A. (1985). Organizational learning. *Academy of Management Review, 10*(4), 803-813.

Gibson, C. B. 2001. From knowledge accumulation to accommodation: Cycles of collective cognition in work groups. *Journal of Organizational Behavior,* 22(2): 121-134.

Gibson, C.B., & Dibble, R. (2013). Excess may do harm: Investigating the effect of team external environment on external activities in teams. *Organization Science, 24*(3), 697-715.

Gibson, C. B,. & Dibble, R. (2008). Culture inside and out: Developing a collaboration's capacity to externally adjust. In S. Ang & L. Van Dyne (Eds.), *Handbook on cultural intelligence* (pp. 221-240). New York: M. E. Sharpe.

Gibson, C. B,. & Earley, P. C.(2007). Collective cognition in action: Accumulation, interaction, examination, and accommodation in the development and operation of group efficacy beliefs in the workplace. *Academy of Management Review, 32*(2), 438-458.

Gladstein, D. L. (1984). Groups in context: A model of task group effectiveness. *Administrative Science Quarterly, 29*(4), 499-517.

Gurtner, A., Tschan, F., Semmer, N. K., & Nagele, C. (2007). Getting groups to develop good strategies: Effects of reflexivity interventions on team process, team performance, and shared mental models. *Organizational Behavior and Human Decision Processes, 102,* 127-142.

Hackman, J. R. (2002). *Leading teams: Setting the stage for great performances*. Boston, MA: Harvard Business School Press.

Hefke, M., & Stojanovic, L. (2004). An ontology-based approach for competence bundling and composition of ad-hoc teams in an organization. *Proceedings of I-KNOW '04, Gratz, Austria, 2004*, 126-134.

Henisz, W. J., & Zelner, B. A. (2001). The institutional environment for telecommunications investment. *Journal of Economic Management Strategies, 10*, 123-147.

Hinds, P. J., & Bailey, D. E. (003). Out of sight, out of sync: Understanding conflict in distributed teams. *Organization Science, 14*(6), 615-632.

Hofstede, G. 2001. *Culture's consequences*. Thousand Oaks, CA: Sage Publications.

Jarvenpaa, S. L., & Leidner, D. E. (1999). Communication and trust in global virtual teams. *Organization Science, 10*(6), 791-815.

Jones, C. (1996). Careers in project networks: The case of the film industry. In M. B. Arthur & D. Rousseau (Eds.), *The boundaryless career: A new employment principle for a new organizational era (pp. 58-75)*. New York: Oxford University Press.

Kane, A. A., Argote, L., & Levine, J. M. (2005). Knowledge transfer between groups via personnel rotation: Effects of social identity and knowledge quality. *Organizational Behavior and Human Decision Processes, 96*, 56-71.

Katz, A. & Te'eni, D. 2007. The contingent impact of contextualization on computer-mediated collaboration. *Organization Science*, 18(2): 261-279.

Kelly, D., & Amburgey, T. L. (1991). Organizational inertia and momentum: A dynamic model of strategic change. *Academy of Management Journal, 34*(3), 591-612.

Klein, K. J., Ziegert, J. C., Knight, A. P., & Xiao, Y. (2006). Dynamic delegation: Shared, hierarchical, and deindividualized leadership in extreme action teams. *Administrative Science Quarterly, 51*, 590-621.

Langfred, C. (2007). Conflict and autonomy in teams: Integration and new directions for research. In K. J. Behfar & L. L. Thompson (Eds.), *Conflict in organizational groups: New directions in theory and practice* (pp. 181-204). Evanston, IL: Northwestern University Press.

Lanzara, G. F. (1999). Between transient constructs and persistent structures: Designing systems in action. *Journal of Strategic Information Systems, 8*, 331-349.

Larson, A. 1992. Network dyads in entrepreneurial settings: A study of the governance of exchange relationships. *Administrative Science Quarterly*, 37(1): 76-104.

Lawrence, P. R., & Lorsch, J. W. (1967). *Organization and environment.* Boston: Harvard University Press.

Levi-Strauss, C. (1966). *The savage mind.* Chicago, IL: University of Chicago Press.

Levitt, B., & March, J. G. (1988). Organizational learning. Annual Review of Sociology, *14*, 319-340.

Lewis, K. (2003). Measuring transactive memory systems in the field: Scale development and validation. *Journal of Applied Psychology*, *88*(4), 587-604.

Lumpkin, G. T., & Dess, G. G. (2001). Linking two dimensions of entrepreneurial orientation to firm performance: The moderating role of environment and industry life cycle. *Journal of Business Venturing*, *16*, 429-451.

Lumsden, A. J. (2004). The role and responsibilities of directors on board sub-committees. Available at SSRN: http://ssrn.com/abstract=990201.

Lynn, M. L. (2005). Organizational buffering: Managing boundaries and cores. *Organization Studies*, *26*(1), 37-61.

Mankin, D., Cohen, S. G., Bikson, T. K. (1996). *Teams and technology: Fulfilling the promise of the new organization.* Boston, MA: Harvard Business School Press.

Marks, M. A., Zaccaro, S. J., & Mathieu, J. E. (2000). Performance implications of leader briefings and team-interaction training for team adaptation to novel environments. *Journal of Applied Psychology*, *85*(6), 971-986.

Mathieu, J.E., Marks, M.S., & Zaccaro, S.J. (2001). Multi-team systems. In N. Anderson, D. Ones, H. K. Sinangil, & C. Viswesvaran, (Eds), *International handbook of work and organizational psychology* (pp. 289-313). London: Sage.

Mendenhall, M. & Oddou, G. (1985). The dimensions of expatriate acculturation: A review. *Academy of Management Review*, *10*(1), 39-47.

Meyer, A. D., Gaba, V., & Colwell, K. A. (2005). Organizing far from equilibrium: Nonlinear change in organizational fields. *Organization Science*, *16*(5), 456-473.

Miller, D., & Friesen, P. H. (1983). Strategy-making and environment: The third link. *Strategic Management Journal*, *4*(3), 221-235.

Moorman, C., & Miner, A. S. (1998). The convergence of planning and execution: Improvisation in new product development. *Journal of Marketing*, *62*, 1-20.

Mortensen, M. 2012. From teams to recombinant collaboration: Understanding the evolution of organizational work. *INSEAD Working Papers Collection*, 2: 1-31.

Nelson, S. G,. & Winter, R. R. (1982). *An evolutionary theory of economic change.* Cambridge, MA: Harvard University Press.

Pearce, J. L. (2001). *Organization and management in the embrace of government.* Mahwah, NJ: Lawrence Erlbaum Associates.

Pearce, J. L., Dibble, R., & Klein, K. (2009). The effects of governments on management and organizations. *Academy of Management Annals*, *3*, 503-541.

Pelled, L. H., Eisenhardt, K. M., & Xin, K. R. (1999). Exploring the black box: An analysis of work group diversity, conflict, and performance. *Administrative Science Quarterly*, *44*(1), 1-28.

Pentland, B. T. & Rueter, H. H. 1994. Organizational routines as grammars of action. *Administrative Science Quarterly*, 39: 484-510.

Peterson, R. S., Davidson, J., & Moynihan, L. M. (2007). Does one rotten apple spoil the barrel? Using a configuration approach to assess the conflict-inducing effects of a high-neuroticism team member. In K. J. Behfar & L. L. Thompson (Eds.), *Conflict in Organizational Groups: New Directions in Theory and Practice* (pp. 93-112). Evanston, IL: Northwestern University Press.

Phillips, K. W. & Thomas-Hunt, M. C. (2007). Garnering the benefits of conflict: The role of diversity and status distance in groups. In K. J. Behfar & L. L. Thompson (Eds.), *Conflict in Organizational Groups: New Directions in Theory and Practice* (pp. 37-55). Evanston, IL: Northwestern University Press.

Powell, W. W. (1990). Neither market nor hierarchy: Network forms of organization. In B. M. Staw and L. L. Cummings (Eds.), *Research in Organizational Behavior*, *12*, 295-336. Greenwich, CT: JAI Press.

Raven, A. (2003). Team or community of practice: Aligning tasks, structures, and technologies. In Gibson, C. B. & Cohen, S. G. (Eds.), *Virtual teams that work* (pp. 292-306). SF, CA: Jossey-Bass.

Rose-Ackerman, S. (1997). The political economy of corruption. In Elliott, K. A.(Ed.), *Corruption and the global economy* (Vol. 14)(pp. 31-60). Washington, D. C.: Institute for International Economics.

Rosenzweig, P. M,. & Singh, J. V. (1991). Organizational environments and the multinational enterprise. *Academy of Management Review*, *16*(2), 340-361.

Rottner, R. (2007). *Growth rings: Resource emergence and evolution and the organizational resilience of R&D ventures.* Working paper, University of California, Irvine.

Samra, Y. M., Lynn, G. S., & Reilly, R. R. (2008). Effect of improvisation on product cycle time and product success: A study of new product development (NPD) teams in the United States. *International Journal of Management, 25*(1), 175-185.

Saunders, C. S., & Ahuja, M. K. (2006). Are all distributed teams the same? Differentiating between temporary and ongoing distributed teams. *Small Group Research, 37,* 662-700.

Schippers, M. C., Den Hartog, D. N., Koopman, P. L., & Wienk, J. A. (2003). Diversity and team outcomes: The moderating effects of outcome interdependence and group longevity and the mediating effect of reflexivity. *Journal of Organizational Behavior, 24,* 779-802.

Schopler, J. H. (1987). Interorganizational groups: Origins, structure, and outcomes. *Academy of Management Review, 12*(4), 702-713.

Scott, W. R. (1998). *Organizations: Rational, natural, and open systems.* Saddle River, NJ: Prentice Hall.

Shenhar, A. J. (2001). Contingent management in temporary, dynamic organizations: The comparative analysis of projects. *Journal of High Tech Management Research, 12,* 239-271.

Shenkar, O., & Zeira, Y. (1992). Role conflict and role ambiguity of chief executive officers in international joint ventures. *Journal of International Business Studies, 23*(1), 55-75.

Sole, D., & Edmondson, A. (2000). *Knowledge sharing in virtual teams.* Harvard Business School Working Paper.

Sutcliffe, K. M. (1994). What executives notice: Accurate perceptions in top management teams. *Academy of Management Journal, 37,* 1360-1378.

Sydow, J., Lindkvist, L., & DeFillippi, R. (2004). Project-based organizations, embeddedness and repositories of knowledge: Editorial. Organization Studies, *25*(9), 1475-1489.

Thompson, J. D. (1967). *Organizations in action.* New York: McGraw-Hill.

Tjosvold, D., Hui, C., & Yu, Z. (2003). Conflict management and task reflexivity for team in-role and extra-role performance in China. *International Journal of Conflict Management, 14*(2), 141-163.

Tjosvold, D., Tang, M. M. L., West, M. (2004). Reflexivity for team innovation in China: The contribution of goal interdependence. *Group & Organizational Management, 29*(5), 540-559.

Vashdi, D. R., Bamberger, P. A., Erez, M., & Weiss-Meilik, A. (2007). Briefing-debriefing: Using a reflexive organizational learning model from the military to enhance the performance of surgical teams. *Human Resource Management, 46*(1), 115-142.

Vera, D., & Rodriguez-Lopez, A. (2007). Leading improvisation: Lessons from the American Revolution. *Organizational Dynamics, 36*(3), 303-319.

Waller, M. J. (1999). The timing of adaptive responses to non-routine events. *Academy of Management Journal, 42*, 127-137.

Wang, Y. (2006). In marketplace and boardroom: What do we know and not know about China's nonstate enterprises? In A. S. Tsui, Y. Bian, & L. Cheng (Eds.), *China's domestic private firms* (pp. 196-205). Armonk, NY & London, England: M. E. Sharpe.

Watson, W. E., Kumar, K., & Michaelsen, L. K. (1993). Cultural diversity's impact on interaction process and performance: Comparing homogeneous and diverse task groups. *Academy of Management Journal, 36*(3), 590-602.

Weick, K. E. (1993). The collapse of sensemaking in organizations: The Mann Gulch disaster. *Administrative Science Quarterly, 38*, 628-653.

West, M. A. (1996). Reflexivity and work group effectiveness: A conceptual integration. In M. A. West (Ed.), *Handbook of work group psychology* (pp. 555-579). Chichester, UK: Wiley.

Zajac, E. J., Kraatz, M. S., & Bresser, R. K. F. (2000). Modeling the dynamics of strategic fit: A normative approach to strategic change. *Strategic Management Journal, 21*, 429-453.

Zakaria, N., Amelinckx, A., & Wilemon, D. (2004). Working together apart? Building a knowledge-sharing culture for global virtual teams. *Creativity and Innovation Management, 13*(1), 15-29.

Zellmer-Bruhn, M. E. (2003). Interruptive events and team knowledge acquisition. *Management Science, 49*(4), 514-528.

Zimmermann, A. & Sparrow, P. (2007). Mutual adjustment processes in international teams: Lessons for the study of expatriation. *International Studies of Management & Organization, 37*(3), 65-88.

CHAPTER SEVEN

WHEN ONE SIZE DOESN'T FIT ALL: EVOLVING DIRECTIONS IN THE RESEARCH AND PRACTICE OF ENTERPRISE RISK MANAGEMENT

ANETTE MIKES AND ROBERT S. KAPLAN
HARVARD BUSINESS SCHOOL, USA

Abstract

Academics are increasingly examining the adoption and impact of ERM, but the studies are inconsistent and inconclusive, due, we believe, to an inadequate specification of how ERM is used in practice. Based on a ten-year field project and over 250 interviews with senior risk officers, we put forward a contingency theory of ERM, identifying potential design parameters that can explain observable variation in the "ERM mix" adopted by organizations. We also add a new contingent variable: the type of risk that a specific ERM practice addresses. We outline a "minimum necessary contingency framework" (Otley, 1980) that is sufficiently nuanced, while still empirically observable, that empirical researchers may, in due course, hypothesize about "fit" between contingent variables, such as risk types and the ERM mix, as well as about outcomes such as organizational effectiveness.

Keywords: enterprise risk management, contingency framework, organizational effectiveness

Introduction

Enterprise risk management (ERM) has become a crucial component of contemporary corporate governance reforms, with an abundance of principles, guidelines, and standards. While advocates argue that efficient risk management practices are the solution to the problem of how to avoid corporate disasters and failures (National Commission on the BP Deepwater Horizon Oil Spill and Offshore Drilling, 2011), some skeptics see ERM as part of the problem itself (Power, 2004; Power, 2009). We have ample regulations and prescriptive frameworks for "enlightened" risk management, including the risk disclosure recommendations in the UK Turnbull report; the COSO Enterprise Risk Management Framework; and the International Standards Organisation's *ISO 31000:2009, Risk Management—Principles and Guidelines on Implementation*. The Toronto Stock Exchange requires the establishment and disclosure of a company's risk management function, and the Dodd–Frank Wall Street Reform and Consumer Protection Act requires large publicly traded financial firms to have a separate board risk committee composed of independent directors. Credit-rating agencies now evaluate how firms manage risks, with Moody's and Standard & Poor's (S&P) having an explicit focus on ERM in the energy, financial services, and insurance industries (Moody's Analytics, 2010; S&P, 2013).

With such an abundance of principles, guidelines, and standards, scholars might conclude that risk management is a mature discipline with proven unambiguous concepts and tools that need only regulations and compliance to be put into widespread practice. We disagree. We believe that risk management approaches are largely unproven and still emerging. Apparently, so do the many practitioners who have expressed dissatisfaction with the proposed normative and regulatory ERM frameworks (CFO Research Services and Towers Perrin, 2008; Beasley, Branson, & Hancock, 2010), and academic researchers, who scrutinize the determinants and consequences of risk management.

Academics have proposed multiple contingency theories of ERM. By adopting a contingency approach to ERM research, researchers avoid recommending a universal risk management system that should be applied in all circumstances. Instead, they search for the specific circumstances that would guide the selection of an appropriate risk management system for an individual enterprise. But the empirical studies that set out to document the prevalence and effectiveness of ERM have so far produced few significant results, largely, we believe, because their contingency perspectives use inadequate and incomplete specifications of how ERM is implemented in practice. We propose—based on a ten-year field project, involving over 250 interviews with chief risk officers—a more comprehensive specification of ERM and identify the parameters that could serve as a solid foundation for a contingency theory of ERM design and implementation.

Past Research on ERM Adoption and Performance

Risk management's plethora of guidelines, frameworks, and tools has provided a tempting subject for academic research. Academic studies of ERM, following the long-standing approach of contingency theory in organizational and management control research (Chenhall, 2003; Chenhall, 2005), have explored the dependence of ERM performance outcomes on organizational context. We have classified this literature into three categories, corresponding to three common contingency approaches: selection studies, congruence studies, and longitudinal field studies.

In the first stream, the researchers attempt to use firm-specific contextual variables to explain the presence (or lack) of ERM. Based on the normative literature (COSO, 2004; International Standards Organisation, 2009), some studies verified the influence of boards and executive teams in securing ERM adoption (Beasley, Clune, & Hermanson, 2005; Desender, 2007), while others found the presence of an internal risk specialist to be associated with ERM adoption (Kleffner, Lee, & McGannon, 2003; Beasley et al., 2005; Paape & Speklé, 2012).

Another common observation is that firms carrying higher risk of financial distress (as measured by leverage or volatility of operating cash flows) are more likely than less-risky ones to adopt ERM (Liebenberg &Hoyt, 2003; Pagach &Warr, 2011). But empirical findings about some of the less-than-obvious contingency variables are mixed and even contradictory.

Implicitly embracing the "survival of the fittest" principle, selection studies assume that only firms with effective combinations of context and ERM are observed, as those with an inappropriate combination will not survive. However, this form of Darwinism would apply only if ERM were indeed a mature discipline or if researchers could verify the continuing existence of the associations initially found in cross-sectional studies. Given the evolving nature of ERM, selection studies have identified few significant and design-relevant ERM variables and have so far ignored the process whereby organizations, over time, attempt to match their ERM to firm-specific contingencies. Nevertheless, these initial inquiries spurred the second stream of large-sample studies that tried to assess whether ERM practices, on average, have contributed to better firm performance.

Studies examining the performance implications of ERM implementations include Pagach and Warr, 2010; Pagach and Warr, 2011; Beasley, Pagach, and Warr, 2008; Hoyt and Liebenberg, 2011; Ellul and

Yerramilli, 2012; Baxter, Bedard, Hoitash, and Yezegel, 2012. Like other management control studies undertaken from a congruence perspective (Chenhall, 2005), these papers aim to correlate firm performance with firm-specific contextual variables and ERM implementation, attempting to find which combinations of context and ERM are more effective than others.

The researchers initially performed stock exchange studies to observe whether financial markets attribute value to ERM implementation, but with mixed results. The financial crisis of 2007-2008 offered a new testing ground for examining the effect of ERM on the performance of financial services firms. The results, again, were mixed and inconclusive. Why? Large-sample cross-sectional studies focus on the adoption of a particular risk management framework (for example, COSO's ERM) but ignore how the framework was implemented by the organization's leadership and employees. The effectiveness of risk management ultimately depends less on the guiding framework than on the people who set up, coordinate, and contribute to risk management processes. For example, all Wall Street financial firms had risk management functions and CROs during the expansionary period of 2002-2006. But some of these firms failed in the subsequent crisis while others survived quite well. The existence of a risk management department and an individual with the title of chief risk officer explains very little about the quality, depth, breadth, and impact of a firm's risk management processes.

The third and emerging stream of empirical work on ERM uses small-sample or field studies to understand risk management *in situ*, as an organizational and social practice, and has compiled sufficient evidence to suggest that risk management practices vary considerably across firms, even within an industry (Tufano, 1996; Mikes, 2009; Mikes, 2011).

In the remainder of this chapter, we propose contingency variables that explain some of the variation we have observed in companies' risk management processes. A useful contingency theory, however, must be more powerful than "it depends." The emerging theory should have an hypothesis about the specific linkages between organization-specific factors and the design of its ERM structure and systems, as well as a performance hypothesis about how improving the fit between an organization's specific factors and its ERM system design will improve its performance along specific, measurable dimensions.

We propose the following practice-based definition of ERM:

Enterprise risk management consists of active and intrusive processes that:
(1) are capable of challenging existing assumptions about the world within

and outside the organization; (2) communicate risk information with the use of distinct tools (such as risk maps, stress tests, and scenarios); (3) collectively address gaps in the control of risks that other control functions (such as internal audit and other boundary controls) leave unaddressed; and, in doing so, (4) complement—but do not displace—existing management control practices.

Unpacking the "ERM Mix"

Our field studies (and others') illustrate different approaches and roles for the risk management function (Mikes, 2009; Mikes, Hall, & Millo, 2013; Power, Ashby, & Palermo, 2013). Some act as the *independent overseer* role, with an exclusive focus on compliance and internal controls. Others have moved beyond this to a *business partner* role. For example, risk management in some firms is embedded within the formal planning and resource allocation process and also influences key strategic decisions, such as approval or veto of new projects or products. In the *independent facilitator* role, risk management does not influence formal decision making but does acquire agenda-setting power and information with which to facilitate risk communication across the organization and the discussion of key strategic uncertainties. In the *dual or hybrid* role, the risk function balances compliance with business orientation by deploying separate groups of independent and embedded risk managers.

The variety of ERM implementation suggests that any observed "ERM mix" can and should be unpacked into a set of fundamental risk management components. These components (and their determinants) include:

Processes for identifying, assessing, and prioritizing risks. Risk identification can take place face-to-face or through self-assessments prompted remotely by a centralized database or risk register. Face-to-face meetings can be intensive, interactive meetings between the risk expert and the line managers, or open discussions among employees from different functions, specialist groups, and hierarchical levels. Risk discussions can be confined to senior line managers and staff or can be decentralized by engaging front-line, support, and administrative staff as well.

Linkages from risk management to other important control processes: Many of the companies we observed linked their risk assessment process to major resource allocation processes. Other firms aspire to link risk assessments with performance measurement, such as embedding it within the enterprise's balanced scorecard (Woods, 2009) or by single risk-adjusted measures (Mikes, 2009) – thereby realizing the ideal of risk-based performance management.

Further research is required to explicate contextual factors that may influence the shape of risk identification process and its linkages to other controls: but based on contingency research on management control systems (Simons, 2005), a number of organizational design parameters (span of control; span of accountability; span of influence and span of support) are likely to be relevant.

Frequency of risk meetings. While some firms carry out formal updates on risks at annual or biannual risk review meetings, others hold risk workshops throughout the year. In banks where risks can change hourly, and even from one trade to the next, we have observed continuous risk monitoring and assessment by embedded risk managers. We conclude from this variety that the frequency of risk identification and assessment processes must match the velocity of risk evolution, a bit of common sense that nevertheless tends to be lost in a "one size fits all," rules-based compliance framework.

Risk tools. Most companies use multidimensional visualizations, such as risk maps, to quantify risks along likelihood, impact, and controllability dimensions (Jordan et al., 2013). Companies with extensive historical data on asset pricing, covariance, and risk events go beyond simple risk map summaries by introducing data- and analysis-intensive statistical assessments, such as value-at-risk calculations and stress tests. We conclude from this variety that the choice of risk tools, ranging from qualitative descriptions and scenarios to the measurement of expected and unexpected loss, will be conditioned by: (1) the availability of data and knowledge about a particular risk (loss), and (2) how relevant and reliable the available risk tools are in the eyes of risk experts and everyone else using the tools. Field research in financial services, where the raw data for risk analysis tends to be plentiful, suggests that the selection of particular risk tools tends to be associated with the firm's calculative culture—the measurable attitudes that senior decision makers display towards the use of sophisticated risk models (Mikes, 2008; Mikes, 2009; Mikes, 2011). While some risk functions have a culture of *quantitative enthusiasm,* focusing on extensive risk measurement and risk-based performance management, others have a culture of *quantitative skepticism*, focusing instead on qualitative discourse and the mobilization of expert opinions about emerging risk issues.

How Risk Types Also Matter

Beyond dimensions related to the organizational context for risk management, Kaplan and Mikes (2012) introduced a taxonomy for classifying different types of risks events. Each of the taxonomy's three risk categories—preventable, strategy, and external—has a different source, a different degree of controllability, and a different approach for identification, mitigation, and management.

Preventable (Category I) risks arise from routine operational breakdowns or from employees' unauthorized, illegal, unethical, incorrect, or inappropriate actions. Companies gain nothing by tolerating such risks; they are inherently undesirable. Depending on the firm's tolerance for failure and on the existence of cost-effective controls, management should strive to reduce the incidence of preventable risks to zero.

In contrast, organizations voluntarily take on *strategy execution (Category II) risks* in order to generate superior returns. For example, some companies operate in inherently hazardous industries, such as mining, chemicals, and oil and gas exploration. Others, such as high-technology, pharmaceutical, medical device, and aerospace companies must engage in high-risk research projects to develop new products. Managers can identify and influence both the likelihood and the impact of their strategy execution risks, but some residual strategy risk will always remain.

External (Category III) risks arise from events that the company cannot influence. Some of these risks are closely entwined with the firm's strategic choices and are therefore related to strategy execution risk. Managers are often unaware of external risks and, even when made aware, are unable to plausibly assess their likelihood. But that should not be the control objective for this category of risk. As external risks are, by definition, unavoidable and impossible to predict, the concern should be with the organization's resilience, should they occur. The assessment (and enhancement) of organizational resilience requires that the company introduce a process of risk envisionment—using experience, intuition, and imagination—to suggest plausible future disaster scenarios. Once a particular risk has been envisioned, managers can contemplate how the organization can respond—is their current resilience adequate to cope in the future, or does it need to be increased?

While some risk management frameworks suggest that risk managers should focus mainly on preventable risks (as an enhancement of the internal audit process), others suggest that the ERM mix should focus mainly on strategy execution risks (COSO, 2004; International Standards

Organisation, 2009). We propose that risk management will be most effective when it matches *the inherent nature and controllability of the different types of risk* the organization faces. Our conclusion is that effective risk management "depends;" it is contingent on the organization's context and circumstances. We can offer preliminary ideas about what risk management likely depends *on*.

Although the measurement of organizational effectiveness will ultimately be the test of a contingency theory of ERM, the complexity of forces affecting organizational performance may initially call for the use of intervening variables as dependent variables in research studies. Initially, user satisfaction surveys and managerial perceptions of the ERM function are potential indicators of ERM effectiveness (Otley, 1980), as is the very tenure and maturity of the risk management function, as we found in our cases.

Given the evolving nature of risk control, it is unclear which of the tools and practices now in use will ultimately make up a "common body of knowledge" that can define the profession of enterprise risk management. We encourage future research to refine our practice-based definition of risk management and to complete and operationalize the contingency variables involved. In-depth, small sample, or longitudinal field studies should elicit a fascinating and revealing variety of context-specific practices and should, in due course, help us understand the causes and value of such variety. Over time, deductive and empirical researchers can hypothesize about and test the fit between ERM practices and different contexts. At that point, we can start codifying and standardizing a set of appropriate and *contingent* risk management practices.

References

Baxter, R., Bedard, J. C., Hoitash, R., & Yezegel, A. (2012). Enterprise risk management program quality: Determinants, value relevance, and the financial crisis. *Contemporary Accounting Research*, Forthcoming.

Beasley, M. S., Clune, R., & Hermanson, D. R. (2005). Enterprise risk management: An empirical analysis of factors associated with the extent of implementation. *Journal of Accounting and Public Policy, 24*, 521–531.

Beasley, M., Pagach, D., & Warr, R. (2008). Information conveyed in hiring announcements of senior executives overseeing enterprise-wide risk management processes. *Journal of Accounting, Auditing and Finance, 28*, 311–332.

Beasley, M. S, Branson, B. C., & Hancock, B. V. (2010). Are you identifying your most significant risks? *Strategic Finance, 92*, 29–35.

CFO Research Services, and Towers Perrin. (2008). *Senior finance executives on the current financial turmoil.* Boston, MA: CFO Publishing Corp.

Chenhall, R. H. (2003). Management control systems design within its organizational context: Findings from contingency-based research and directions for the future. *Accounting, Organizations and Society, 28*, 127–168.

—. (2005). The contingent design of performance measures. In A. Bhimani (Ed.), *Contemporary Issues in Management Accounting* (pp. 92–116). New York, NY: Oxford University Press, USA.

Committee of Sponsoring Organizations of the Treadway Commission (COSO). (2004). *Enterprise risk management framework.* New York, NY: American Institute of Certified Public Accountants.

Desender, K. (2007). On the determinants of enterprise risk management implementation. Available at: http://papers.ssrn.com/sol3/papers.cfm?abstract_id=1025982.

Ellul, A., & Yerramilli, V. (2012). Stronger risk controls, lower risk: Evidence from U.S. bank holding companies. *Journal of Finance. 68*, 1757–1803.

Hoyt, R. E., & Liebenberg, A. P. (2011). The value of enterprise risk management. *The Journal of Risk and Insurance, 78*, 795–822.

International Standards Organisation (ISO). (2009). *ISO 31000:2009, Risk management—Principles and guidelines.* Geneva: International Standards Organisation.

Jordan, S., Jørgensen, L., & Mitterhofer, H. (2013). Performing risk and the project: Risk maps as mediating instruments. *Management Accounting Research, 24*, 156–174.

Kaplan, R. S., & Mikes, A. (2012). Managing risks: A new framework. *Harvard Business Review, 90*, 48-60.

Kleffner, A. E., Lee, R. B., & McGannon, B. (2003). The effect of corporate governance on the use of enterprise risk management: Evidence from Canada. *Risk Management and Insurance Review, 6*, 53–73.

Liebenberg, A. P., & Hoyt, R. E. (2003). The determinants of enterprise risk management: Evidence from the appointment of chief risk officers. *Risk Management and Insurance Review, 6*, 37–52.

Mikes, A. (2008). Chief risk officers at crunch time: Compliance champions or business partners? *Journal of Risk Management in Financial Institutions, 2*, 7–25.

—. (2009). Risk management and calculative cultures. *Management Accounting Research, 20*, 18–40.

—. (2011). From counting risk to making risk count: Boundary-work in risk management. *Accounting, Organizations and Society, 36*, 226–245.

Mikes, A., Hall, M., & Millo, Y. (2013). How experts gain influence. *Harvard Business Review 91*, 70–74.

Moody's Analytics, Inc. (2010). Enterprise Risk Management. Available at: https://www.google.com/url?sa=t&rct=j&q=&esrc=s&source=web &cd=1&ved=0CEgQFjAA&url=http%3A%2F%2Fwww.moodysanaly tics.com%2F~%2Fmedia%2FBrochures%2FAOE_Overview_Brochur es%2FEnterprise-Risk-Solutions-Brochure.ashx&ei=90lUUvfNMIe14 AOxsoDYCQ&usg=AFQjCNGmoXRIFOnbKl5CT5bOSfpVAXGIaA &sig2=_usdgQVbAzCOIneNXYtR1A&bvm=bv.53537100,d.dmg

National Commission on the BP Deepwater Horizon Oil Spill and Offshore Drilling (National Commission). (2011). *Deep Water: The Gulf Oil Disaster and the Future of Offshore Drilling*. Report to the President. Available at: http://www.oilspillcommission.gov/final-report, accessed January 2013.

Otley, D. T. (1980). The contingency theory of management accounting: Achievement and prognosis. *Accounting, Organizations and Society, 5*, 413–428.

Paape, L., & Speklé, R. F. (2012). The adoption and design of enterprise risk management practices: An empirical study. *European Accounting Review, 21*, 533–564.

Pagach, D., & Warr, R. (2010). The effects of enterprise risk management on firm performance. Available at: http://papers.ssrn.com/sol3/papers.cfm?abstract_id=1155218.

Pagach, D., & Warr, R. (2011). The characteristics of firms that hire chief risk officers. *The Journal of Risk and Insurance, 78*, 185–211.

Power, M. (2004). *The risk management of everything: Rethinking the politics of uncertainty*. London, UK: Demos.

—. (2009). The risk management of nothing. *Accounting, Organizations and Society, 34*, 849–855.

Power, M., Ashby, S., & Palermo, T. (2013). *Risk Culture in financial organisations*. London, UK: Research Report for London School of Economics, Centre for the Analysis of Risk and Regulation.

Simons, R. (2005). *Levers of Organization Design*. Boston, MA: Harvard Business Review Press.

Standard & Poor's Financial Services LLC. (2013). Ratings Direct: Criteria, insurance, general: Enterprise risk management. New York, NY: McGraw-Hill. Available at:
https://www.google.com/url?sa=t&rct=j&q=&esrc=s&source=web&cd=2&ved=0CE8QFjAB&url=http%3A%2F%2Fwww.standardandpoors.com%2Fspf%2Fupload%2FRatings_US%2FEnterprise_Risk_Management_5_7_13.pdf&ei=gkhUUuWPKrbK4AOs5IHQCQ&usg=AFQjCNGZDFgzHS6rapcAkCCqA_cPu0g-Mw&sig2=DUiif0dOed12MLMBfktvhA&bvm=bv.53537100,d.dmg

Tufano, P. (1996). Who manages risk? An empirical examination of risk management practices in the gold mining industry. *Journal of Finance, 51*, 1097–1137.

Woods, M. (2009). A contingency theory perspective on the risk management control system within Birmingham City Council. *Management Accounting Research, 20*, 68–91.

CHAPTER EIGHT

THE PRINCIPAL'S SOLUTION: A PERSPECTIVE ON MANAGERIAL AGENCY FROM FINANCIAL SOCIOLOGY

YALLY AVRAHAMPOUR
LONDON SCHOOL OF ECONOMICS & POLITICAL SCIENCE, UK

Abstract

Financial economics characterizes the relationship between principals and agents as consisting in information asymmetry. This paper introduces an alternative, relational, framing of agency which is illustrated through an analysis of a particular type of agent, namely, the manager of the defined benefit pension fund. The pension manager uses ambiguity to mediate between two principals with conflicting objectives; shareholders and beneficiaries, allocating resources between these two principals and thus facilitating take-up of defined benefit pension provision. Ambiguity is here defined as opaque pension fund financial accounting standards and discretionary actuarial practice. Financial sociology is proposed as, in part, a discipline using a socio-cultural perspective in reformulating agency models.

Keywords: financial sociology, models of agency, management, accounting, pension funds

Introduction

The financial economic literature treats information asymmetry as the key characteristic of the relationship between principals and agents. An agent, such as a manager, possessing information that is unavailable to a principal, such as an equity investor, may use that information to act in ways that are in the agent's interests but not the principal's (Jensen & Meckling, 1976; Ross, 1973). In this conception a condition of the separation of ownership and control within firms (Berle & Means, [1932] 2006) is that principals can adequately monitor agents through such mechanisms as transparent financial accounting, an active market for corporate control and well-designed corporate governance systems. A consequence of this theoretical framing is that accounts of the historical trend towards increased separation of ownership and control in firms present this as the consequence of continual improvement in governance practices (Cheffins, 2008; Kiser & Cai, 2003). Thus, an account examining the emergence of organizations characterized by separation of ownership and control that seeks to challenge agency theory's thesis that this was the consequence of improved standards of governance must demonstrate that principals and agents are willing to participate in such organizations when standards are increasingly permissive. This implies the need to reconsider the relationship between governance and organization, for example by providing an alternative account of the relationship between principals and agents.

This paper engages in this task by developing an alternative model of agency to that provided by agency theory, drawing on socio-cultural themes informing relational theory (Long Lingo & O'Mahony, 2010; Obstfeld, 2005) and the social constructivist argument that accounting and financial practices are cultural frames that do not merely describe a pre-existing social reality but also construct a shared understanding of that reality (Burchell, Clubb, Hopwood, & Hughes, 1980; Mackenzie, 2006, Schumpeter, [1918] 1953). The particular organizations characterized by separation of ownership and control to which the model is applied in this paper are defined benefit pension funds, where principals, namely, shareholders and beneficiaries, have little say over the management of the pension fund (Davis, 2009). There was a rapid take-up of defined benefit pension provision in the mid-twentieth century and equally rapid closure of these funds over the past decade. These shifts were concurrent with decentralization and centralization, respectively, of pension fund management to the pension manager.

Background: Defined Benefit Pension Provision, Actuarial and Accounting Practices

In occupational pension provision beneficiaries' pension is safeguarded through the creation of a pension fund, usually in the form of a trust, with a separate legal identity from that of the firm sponsoring the pension fund.

Contributions are paid to the pension fund by the sponsor and, frequently, also the beneficiaries. These contributions constitute the pension fund's assets, which are used to pay beneficiaries' income in retirement. In sponsoring a pension fund, a firm selects between two types of benefit design; defined contribution and defined benefit. In defined contribution pension provision no guarantees are given to beneficiaries regarding their level of retirement income. The pension received reflects the contributions made and the returns achieved in investing these monies. In defined benefit pension provision the sponsoring employer guarantees beneficiaries a level of retirement income, typically a function of the number of years the beneficiary was employed in the firm and the beneficiary's salary. These guarantees constitute the pension fund's liabilities.

The sponsor's contributions to the pension fund are determined by the actuarial valuation, which has statistical and financial elements. The first consists in the selection of statistical assumptions relating to mortality, withdrawal rates, retirement rates, proportions married, rates of new entrants and salary increases to estimate the magnitude of future retirement payments to the beneficiaries (Blake, 2003; Crabbe & Poyser, 1953). The second consists primarily in the use of discounted income or 'compound interest' techniques to assign a present value to these statistically determined magnitudes and to assign a value to the assets. It is discretion in the second, financial, element of the actuarial valuation that is considered key here. A pension fund is solvent, broadly speaking, if the value of assets calculated on a market basis equals or exceeds the value of liabilities when the discount rate used to value these liabilities is the risk free rate. When a pension fund is solvent on such an actuarial basis it may be transferred from the sponsor to an insurance company without the need for further sponsor contributions. Such a valuation reflects the 'market value' of the pension fund. Alternatively, the actuary may use discretion in the selection of techniques used to assign values to these assets and liabilities. Under such a circumstance different interpretations of the financial health of the pension fund emerge, introducing ambiguity and opacity. For example, in such a case the pension fund may be said to be fully funded but not solvent.

Briefly stated, pension fund accounting practice is concerned primarily with the disclosure of the cost of pension provision to the sponsoring firm and of any deficit or surplus that may emerge as a consequence of a difference between the values of pension fund assets and liabilities. Pension fund financial accounting either utilizes the actuarial techniques used to determine the contributions or employs a distinct actuarial calculation within the accounting standard. Either way, if the cost of pension provision and the values of assets and liabilities are calculated on a solvency basis and reported using this basis, these disclosures may be said to be transparent. Otherwise, they may be said to be, to differing degrees, opaque.

A Relational Model of Managerial Agency Applied to Pension Provision and Pension Fund Management

There are two principals in defined benefit pension provision. The shareholders of the sponsoring firm contribute resources to the pension fund. Beneficiaries of the pension fund defer income to retirement by participating in defined benefit pension provision. Shareholders and beneficiaries have conflicting objectives. Shareholders wish to reduce the contributions made to the pension fund since such contributions decrease profits and dividends. Beneficiaries seek greater contributions to the pension fund since this improves the security of their benefits. The agent of shareholders is the Chief Financial Officer (CFO). The agent of beneficiaries is the board of trustees. The pension manager reports to the CFO and simultaneously advises the board of trustees on the setting of investment policy. The pension manager is thus the agent of two principals with conflicting objectives. The pension manager utilizes ambiguity; that is, discretionary actuarial practices and opacity in pension fund financial accounting, to suspend the reality of conflict between these two principals. The pension manager at one time satisfies shareholders' goal of increased profits by reducing contributions and thus sacrificing the goal of beneficiaries for security and at other times satisfies beneficiaries' goal of increased security by increasing contributions and sacrificing the goal of shareholders.

This relational account presents changes in the rate at which sponsoring firms' either establish pension funds or close them as the consequence of changes in the actuarial practices used to calculate sponsor contributions and accounting standards used to report these values to external parties. When disclosures are opaque mediation by the pension manager takes place, conflict between shareholders and beneficiaries is reduced and defined benefit pension provision takes off. Conversely, increased transparency constrains mediation by the pension manager and leads to decline in defined benefit pension provision. Changing standards relating to the actuarial assessment of contributions and accounting disclosures determine whether pension fund management is centralized or decentralized and thereby determine the rise and decline of occupational pension provision. Such socio-cultural arrangements are robust over extended periods, empirically spanning decades, but in principle indefinitely until change in standards occurs.

Financial Sociology

By integrating a conception of cognition as socially constructed with a model of the relationship between principals and agents within firms, this paper proposes a financially oriented extension of economic sociology. Economic sociology has, over the past thirty years, applied the sociological lens to empirical phenomena previously considered the exclusive domain of economics (Smelser & Swedberg, 1994). Financial sociology proposes a further theoretically oriented encroachment into the domain of economics by arguing that sociology should provide models of agency and governance, such as the relational model outlined here, as alternatives for the models provided by financial economics. This approach seeks to improve the quality of the dialogue between sociological and economic theory by providing a parallel set of explanations to those provided by financial economics regarding a broad range of questions relating to the relationship between governance, firms and markets. Further, such a theoretical framing can be used to explain a wide range of phenomena, including those only tangentially related to financial markets.

Thus, for example, applied to the analysis of pension fund management, financial sociology argues that the optimal outcome for shareholders and beneficiaries is achieved when a not insignificant degree of ambiguity exists about the pension manager's actions in managing the pension fund. In contrast, the financial economic literature presents agents such as the pension manager, CFO, trustee board and advisors more generally as potentially utilizing an informational advantage relative to principals to maximize their own wealth rather than that of principals (Gold, 2005; Coronado & Sharpe, 2003; Exley, Mehta, & Smith, 1997). In this perspective, the rise of defined benefit pension provision was the consequence of inadequate monitoring by shareholders of managers. Financial economics and financial sociology differ in their account of the history and in their assessment of how much governance is right, but the accounts provided by the two perspectives are comparable and debate can focus on the underlying assumptions and framing. In this respect and at this time a relational, financial sociological approach has much to offer our understanding of management.

References

Berle, A. & Means, G. (2006 [1932]). *The modern corporation and private property* (8th ed.). New Brunswick, New Jersey: Transaction Publishers.

Blake, D. (2003). *Pension schemes and pension funds in the United Kingdom*. Oxford: Oxford University Press.

Burchell, S., Clubb, C., Hopwood, A, & Hughes, J. (1980). The roles of accounting in organizations and society. *Accounting Organizations & Society, 5*, 5-27.

Cheffins, B. (2008). *Corporate ownership and control*. Oxford: Oxford University Press.

Coronado, J., & Sharpe, S. (2003). Did pension fund accounting contribute to a stock market bubble? *Brookings Papers on Economic Activity 1*, 323-359.

Crabbe, R., & Poyser, C. (1953). *Pension and widows' and orphans' funds*. Cambridge: Cambridge University Press.

Davis, G. (2009). *Managed by the markets: How finance reshaped America*. Oxford: Oxford University Press.

Exley, J, Mehta, S., & Smith, A. (1997). The financial theory of defined benefit pension schemes. *British Actuarial Journal, 3*, 835-966.

Gold, J. (2005). Accounting/actuarial bias enables equity investment by Defined benefits pension plans. *North American Actuarial Journal, 9*, 1-21.

Jensen, M., & Meckling, W. (1976). Theory of the firm: Managerial behaviour, agency costs and ownership structure. *Journal of Financial Economics, 3*, 305-360.

Long Lingo, E., & O'Mahony, S. (2010). Nexus work: Brokerage on creative projects. *Administrative Science Quarterly, 55*, 47-81.

Mackenzie, D. (2006). *A machine not a camera: How financial models shape markets*. Cambridge, MA: MIT Press.

Obstfeld, D. (2005). Social networks, the tertius iungens orientation and involvement in innovation. *Administrative Science Quarterly, 50*, 100-130.

Ross, S. (1973). The economic theory of agency: The principal's problem. *American Economic Review, 63*, 134-139

Schumpeter, J. (1953 [1918]). Crisis of the tax state. In Stolper Wolfgang and Richard Musgrave (Trans.) *International economic papers* (Vol. 4, pp. 1 – 71). London: Macmillan.

Smelser, N., & Swedberg, R. eds. (1994). *Handbook of economic sociology* (1st ed.) Princeton, New York: Princeton University Press.

Chapter Nine

Organizational Medicine: Why Do Some Organizations Live Longer, Healthier Lives Than Other Organizations?

Jeffrey A. Miles
University of the Pacific, USA

Abstract

This work integrates concepts from the field of medicine with the study of organizations in a new area called Organizational Medicine. The primary focus is on the organization as patient. Organizational medicine follows a preventive approach with a goal to protect, promote, and maintain the health and well-being of organizations and to prevent and overcome disease, disability, and death of organizations. Two models are presented: 1) a model of organizational population health change, and 2) a model of potential health changes for an individual organization. Twelve types of organizational disease are discussed that influence an organization's morbidity (level of health) and mortality (longevity). Organizational summary measures of population health (SMPH) that incorporate both morbidity and mortality, are discussed. The use of SMPHs for creating the life path of an organization's changing health-related quality of life (HRQL) and for creating survivorship functions for a population of organizations are also discussed. Lastly, the need for organizational quality of well-being scales (OQWB scales), and the methods for creating such scales, are examined.

Keywords: organizational medicine, disease, health, morbidity, mortality, health-related quality of life

Introduction

Organization scholars have defined and described organizations in numerous ways (Morgan, 2006). One of the most fruitful has been to treat organizations as biological organisms (Chapman & Ashton, 1914; Marshall, 1920; Boulding, 1950; Penrose, 1952; Stauffer, 1949). Every biological organism goes through a series of stages in their life called "life cycle" or "life history" (Adizes, 1979, 1989; Lodahl & Mitchell, 1980). Life history can be defined as the entire sequence of behavioral, physiological, and morphological changes that an organism passes through during its natural development from conception to death (Shea, 1990). The organizational life cycle describes the various stages of development and growth during an organization's life and focuses on the natural, metamorphic processes associated with an organization's birth, maturation, decline and death (Whetten, 1987a).

A life cycle approach to organizations is appealing in that organizations follow a predetermined, predictable pattern of developmental stages that flows from birth to death (Adizes, 1979; Downs, 1967; Greiner, 1972; Lavoie & Culbert, 1978; Lester, Parnell, & Carraher, 2003; Lyden, 1975; Miles, 1980; Torbert, 1974). In the life cycle, the pattern of growth can be labeled according to stages: 1) conception, 2) birth, 3) infant, 4) child, 5) adolescent, 6) adult, 7) senior adult, 8) death, and 9) post-mortem (Bogin, 1988; Bogin & Smith, 1996).

Many reasons have been examined in organization studies regarding the death of organizations, such as: age, size, strategy, relational density, ties or linkages, etc. The purpose of this paper is to examine how an organization's longevity is determined by its level of health, or morbidity. My aim in this paper is to move toward an integration of modern medical and health care theory, principles, and practices and the study of organizations. The main focus is to treat the organization as a medical patient, with the central question, "Why do some organizations live longer, healthier lives than other organizations?" I will also explore the answer to that question, which is "because they are better able to prevent and overcome organizational diseases and illnesses that negatively influence their health and well-being than are other organizations."

Organizational Medicine

The field of medicine is concerned with the prevention, diagnosis, and treatment of disease in organisms. If this approach is applied to organizations, then organizational medicine would be defined as: "the sum total of the knowledge, skills, and practices based on the theories, beliefs, and experiences in the maintenance of organizational health and fitness, as well as in the prevention, diagnosis, alleviation, improvement, and treatment of organizational disease or illness" (adapted from Murray, Salomon, Mathers, & Lopez, 1984: WHO). Following the lead of distinguished researchers in the field of medicine, I suggest that organizational medicine seeks to understand the health and longevity distributions of organizations, and more generally seeks to answer the question "Why do some organizations live longer, healthier lives than other organizations?"

Organization as Patient

The focal unit in organization studies has been of particular concern for a great deal of time (Freeman, 1980). The focal unit refers to the entities about which the researcher wishes to make generalizations (Mathieu & Chen, 2011). In the field of medicine, the "patient" is the primary focal unit. A patient can be defined as one who receives organizational medical attention, care, or treatment.

In organizational medicine, the organization is treated as the patient. Borrowing from the field of medicine, organizational medicine follows a multilevel approach (Rousseau, 1985). Research attention can be focused on a part of the organization, such as a single employee, a workgroup, a section, or a division, and research attention can be focused on the entire organization, a community of organizations, and even on a population of organizations.

Additionally, the field of medicine has taken on the perspective that care and treatment should be patient-centered (Cliff, 2012; Frampton & Charmel, 2009). Patient-centered care can be defined as providing care that is respectful of and responsive to individual patient preferences, needs, and values, and ensuring that these guide all clinical decisions. Organizational medicine should follow this same approach and be respectful and responsive to the organizational patient's unique concerns, needs, and values during all treatments and intervention decisions.

Organizational Disease, Illness, and Sickness

Organizational researchers have wondered for decades why some organizations live longer than others. For example, Sheppard (1994) asked the question, "What are the differences between failing firms and healthy ones?" Organizational medicine follows the view in the medical field that some organizations live longer and have healthier lives than other organizations because they prevent and overcome organizational disease.

The concepts of disease, illness, and sickness are paramount in the field of medicine. As such, it is important to define these terms precisely and make note of the similarities and differences among them. Many researchers have tried to define these terms, but there is no universal agreement on their meaning and usage. Disease (or "dis-ease" from old French and thereby from Latin) literally means the absence of ease ("des" means "a reversal," and "aise" means "ease"). In other words, a disease is an impediment to free movement.

Nowadays the term disease is spelled without a hyphen and has come to be defined as a disorder of structure, function, or process in an organism of such a degree as to produce or threaten to produce a detectable disorder (adapted from Boyd, 2000). Disease involves objectivity in that a medical doctor is able to see, touch, or measure when a disease is present in a patient.

Illness can be defined as a feeling of unhealthiness that is completely personal and interior to the person of the patient. Often illness accompanies disease, but the disease may be undetectable or undeclared, as often occurs in the early stages of a disease. For the most part, physicians are not partial to illnesses in the absence of disease.

Sickness can be defined as the external and public mode of unhealth, or lack of health. Sickness is exterior to the person of the patient. Being "sick" is a social role, a social status, or a negotiated position in society. Sickness is viewed more positively when disease is present and viewed less positively when disease is absent and only illness is present. However, even the presence of disease in sickness does not guarantee a favorable societal view. Individuals with an acute, or short-term disease, from which they recover quickly are often viewed more favorably in society than those with chronic, or long-term diseases which last a long time and/or from which a patient may never recover.

Adapting from the field of medicine, organizational disease is defined as: an impairment, interruption, disorder, or cessation of the processes, systems, functions, and/or structures of an entire organization or its parts, or across multiple organizations. Disease is typically manifested by distinguishing signs and symptoms, and is a response: to environmental factors, to specific infective agents, to inherent defects in the organization, or to combinations of these factors.

Organizational illness can be defined as a feeling of unhealthiness that is completely personal and interior to the organization. Often organizational illness accompanies disease, but the disease may be undetectable or undeclared, as often occurs in the early stages of a disease.

Organizational sickness can be defined as the external and public mode of unhealth, or lack of health for an organization, part of an organization, or across multiple organizations. Sickness is exterior to the organization. An organization that is "sick" plays a social role, has a social status, or has a negotiated position in society.

A Healthy Organization

The concept of "health" is vital in the field of medicine. Researchers have defined health from two different perspectives. Some define health as the possession of something. For example, health can refer to an ideal condition, such as having "a state of complete physical, mental, and social wellbeing." Conversely, some medical researchers have defined health as the absence of something, such as the absence of disease, illness, or sickness. However, this approach is not without problems. Organisms can have a disease without feeling ill, and organisms can have unwanted symptoms when no disease seems to be present.

The World Health Organization (WHO) recommends that health be defined in the affirmative. Adapting from the World Health Organization's definition of health, organizational health is defined as: "the extent to which an organization is able to realize aspirations, satisfy needs, and to effectively change or cope with the environment." More specifically, an organization can be healthy when it demonstrates progress toward accomplishing its vision, mission, strategies, and goals, when it satisfies the needs of its shareholders and stakeholders, and when it successfully copes with changing demands in its environment, including its industry and marketplace.

All of these concepts can be applied to organizations with a focus on keeping organizations healthy. Indeed, some authors have argued that the only thing that matters is whether or not an organization stays healthy Lencioni (2012).

Preventive Medicine

Organizational medicine follows a preventive approach. Preventive medicine is the specialty of medical practice that focuses on the health of individuals, communities, and defined populations. Its goal is to protect, promote, and maintain health and well-being and to prevent disease, disability, and death. Borrowing from the medical field, organizational medicine focuses on protecting, promoting, and maintaining the health of individual organizations, the health of communities of organizations, the health of populations of organizations, and health across populations of organizations. A key focus is on preventing and overcoming disease in organizations.

A Population of Organizations

Organizational medicine is concerned both with the aggregate health of organizations and with the health of one specific organization. The concepts of organizational medicine can be applied to one organization, to a community of organizations, or to a population of organizations. A community of organizations refers to a local group of organizations in a given area that share common characteristics. A population of organizations refers to the total number of organizations in a given place or region with a shared affinity, who unite around a specific issue, purpose, or goal (adapted from Labonte, 1988). This can be defined in a number of ways, such as geographically or politically, although with the use of modern communication and information technology, physical boundaries are becoming less and less necessary when analyzing populations of organizations (adapted from Young, 1998).

Primary prevention efforts at the population level focus on addressing the broad social, behavioral, economic, cultural, and environmental factors that can positively or negatively influence the health of a population of organizations (adapted from Lawson & Bauman, 2001). This approach follows the view that the most efficient way to prevent health problems in an individual organization is to reduce the whole population's level of risk, and requires health strategies that target an entire population of organizations.

A Model Of Organizational Population Health Change

Medical researchers have made significant strides in defining dimensions of health and in clarifying the process of population health change. A conceptual outline of the dimensions of organizational population health change is shown in Figure 9-1 (adapted from Verbrugge & Jette, 1994). There are four dimensions of organizational population health change: 1) organizational diseases, 2) loss of functioning, 3) disability, and 4) death. Each of these dimensions will be discussed separately.

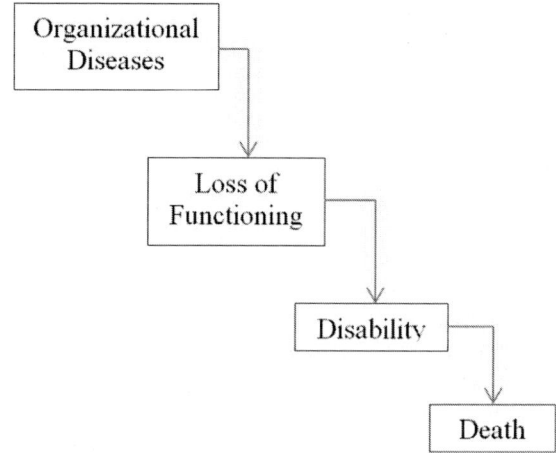

Figure 9-1. A Model of Organizational Population Health Change

Dimension One: Organizational Diseases

Organizations have essentially the same internal systems and processes as living organisms. All organizations adjust system and process variables to changing internal and environmental conditions and circumstance. Pathology occurs in any biological organism when system and process variables remain outside of desirable homeostatic ranges (Miller & Miller, 1991).

Pathology is the science that examines the causes and effects of disease in an organism. Pathology is the foundation of every aspect of medicine, from diagnostic testing and monitoring of chronic diseases to cutting-edge research and innovative technologies. Pathology plays a vital role across all facets of medicine throughout the life of an organism, from pre-conception to post mortem. Indeed, medicine is pathology.

Borrowing from the medical definition, pathology is the essence of organizational medicine, and can be defined as: "the scientific study of the nature of organizational disease and its causes, processes, development, and consequences." In organizations, a pathology includes any abnormal, unhealthy, maladjusted, or inefficient state that occurs within an organization's systems, subsystems, processes, procedures, policies, and methods, especially those that force an organization's variables outside of their normal, steady-state range (Miller & Miller, 1991). Many parallels can be drawn between individual and organizational pathologies (Kets de Vries & Miller, 1984).

Types of Organizational Disease

Diseases can be acute, episodic, or chronic. Acute diseases are those that last a short period of time, typically three months or less, then go away, either on their own or through planned actions taken by the organization. Episodic diseases are those that occur then go away repeatedly over a specific period of time, such as every year or every season. Chronic diseases are those that last for a long period of time before receding, or they last indefinitely, such as for the rest of the organization's life.

Disease involves objectivity in that a medical doctor is able to see, touch, or measure when a disease is present in a patient. In organizations, there can be many types of diseases that lead to organizational impairment and dysfunction (Samuel, 2012). Following this view, twelve types of disease were adapted from the medical field and applied to organizations: 1) breakdowns, 2) blockages, 3) injuries, 4) imbalances, 5) misalignments, 6) shortages, 7) surpluses, 8) toxins, 9) addictions, 10) contagions, 11) tumors, and 12) parasites. Each of these types of organizational disease will be discussed separately.

Breakdowns. The first type of disease is an organic breakdown or deterioration. In the human body, examples of breakdowns include tooth decay, heart failure, and senility of the brain. In an organization, breakdowns refer to the deterioration of equipment, components, and other mechanical items. In addition, organization breakdowns refer to the deterioration of systems, processes, and functions that no longer work the way they once did. For example, an historically effective online ordering process may fail when too many customers try to access an antiquated system at the same time. Additionally, organizations must import and utilize resources from their environment in order to survive (Katz & Kahn, 1966). An organization can experience a strain when resources become scarce and the organization has to work much harder than normal to secure those resources, which can lead to a system breakdown (Staw & Szwajkowski, 1980).

Blockages. Another type of organic disease is a blockage that occurs in some sort of flow, such as in the nervous system, circulatory system, or respiratory system. Examples of blockages in the human body include: kidney stones, blood clots, and embolisms in the arteries. In organizations, blockages are anything that can stop flows, such as information flows, communication flows, resource flows, etc. For example, the flow of information in a report may be blocked by an old requirement that it be hand-checked and approved before being disseminated to the entire organization, rather than transmit that information in real time.

Injuries. In the medical field, injuries can be defined as harm or damage that is done to part or all of an organism. In organizations, injuries happen when part or all of an organization is damaged in some way. Examples of organizational injuries include: fire, theft, earthquakes, vandalism, sabotage, accidents, and weather-related damage.

Imbalances. Homeostasis is a key concept in biological organisms, and comes from the Greek words for "standing still." An organism is in a state of equilibrium, or homeostasis, when the internal conditions of the living organism remain stable regardless of what happens in the external environment. In homeostasis, the organism tries to maintain constant internal conditions, such as body temperature, pH level, glucose level, and hormone levels (Canon, 1929; 1932) Organizations also try to maintain homeostasis, but imbalances can happen which throw an organization out of equilibrium. For example, if an organization devotes too much time, attention, and resources to one part of the organization at the expense of others, then an imbalance has occurred.

Misalignments. In the medical field, alignment is defined as the relationship of the individual body segments to each other. It is the most basic position of the body before movement begins. Proper alignment places a minimum amount of strain on the muscles and ligaments. Deviations from proper alignment will cause muscle fatigue and a greater risk of injury. For organizations, alignment is defined as the relationships of the vision, mission, strategies, organizational goals, process goals, system goals, and job goals. When all of these organizational segments support and properly assist each other, then an organization is in proper alignment and will function well. Lack of alignment can put strain on the organization and can cause a greater risk of injury and breakdown, and can lead to loss of functioning. For example, an organization really wanted to produce a new type of product, but its mission statement specifically forbade it (Miller & Miller, 1991).

Shortages. Many resources are important for vital functioning in the human body. For example, a shortage of vitamins, minerals, fiber, water, and oxygen can all lead to system and process damage. Organizations also need adequate supplies of vital resources in order to maintain proper health and functioning of important processes and systems (Ashby, 1956). Organisms tend to stay healthy when they have required amounts of resources within a stable range. However, disease can occur when required resources fall below acceptable levels (Tracy, 1993). For example, serious problems could result for an iron smelting plant that used wood for fuel if the organization cut down all of the nearby forests and ran out of trees. Additionally, an example of a resource shortage would be when the materials needed for an important project were unavailable, back-ordered, or too costly for the organization (Miller & Miller, 1991).

Surpluses. A human being who has a surplus of fat is more likely to develop health problems, such as: heart disease, stroke, diabetes, certain types of cancer, gout, and gallbladder disease, compared to a lean individual. Organizations can suffer similar effects on their processes and systems when they have surpluses, or excesses, of resources that impede proper organizational functioning (Miller & Miller, 1991; Tracy, 1993).

When an organism faces a shortage of food, it tends to slow its metabolism and to increase storage of fat so that it requires less food and maintains the reserves that it does possess. Organisms act this way in order to increase their chances of survival during times of food shortages (Merkt & Taylor, 1994). When organizations are threatened, they can act in the same way as other organisms by hoarding resources in order to protect themselves during bad times (Latham & Brown, 2009). Although hoarding resources can help an organization survive in the short-term, doing so can limit or damage other important ways in which the organization should perform in the mid- and long-term.

A great deal of research in operations management has examined the approach that lean organizations will be more effective than non-lean ones (George, 2002). A lean organization creates more value for customers with fewer resources. In addition, an organization can be "overweight" such as by having an abundance of free-riders or rent-seekers, or what Numagami, Karube, & Kato (2010) called "deadweight" that can impede proper organizational functioning.

Toxins. A toxin is any poisonous substance that can cause serious debilitating injury or death. Some of the most common toxins for humans include: pain medicines, cleaning substances, animal bites, cosmetics, and plants. There is a plethora of popular-press business books examining the problems of toxins in the workplace: toxic leaders, toxic managers, toxic employees, and toxic workplaces, etc. For example, in toxic organizations people don't smile, they don't laugh, and there is no positive energy (Goldman, 2009; Pfeffer, 1998).

Addictions. In the human body, an addiction is a persistent, compulsive dependence on a behavior or way of thinking that provides a pleasant reward for that individual. People can be addicted to substances like drugs or alcohol, or they can be addicted to behaviors, such as gambling and sex (Alavi, Ferdosi, Jannatifard, Eslami, Alaghemandan, & Setare, 2011). Organizations can suffer from addictions as well. For example, organizations can be addicted to ways of thinking and ways of doing things that provide internal rewards, but no longer work for the external world.

For example, an organization can be addicted to meeting with customers by flying to locations and staying in expensive hotels with costly meals. However, the better choice for a cash-strapped organization might be for employees to use internet video-conferencing from their own offices to meet with distant customers instead.

Contagions. A contagion refers to something that is transmitted either from place to place inside an organism or from one organism to another. There are various types of contagions such as emotional, social, behavioral, and financial. The study of contagions across industries has received considerable research attention in the field of finance (Kuusk, Paas, & Viikmaa, 2011). An example of a contagion effect would be a "run on the bank" when word spreads quickly that a bank is failing and customers rush to the bank to withdraw their money before the bank collapses (Garrat & Keister, 2009).

Tumors. In the human body, a tumor can be defined as an abnormal, uncontrolled growth that possess no useful function for the organism. A tumor may get to the point that it causes harm or loss of functioning for the organism. The same can be said of tumors in organizations. A tumor in an organization refers to any abnormal, uncontrolled growth of people, equipment, finances, or other resources that serves no useful function for the organization, but consumes resources that could be used elsewhere. For example, a leader might start a new division, but then retire, and no one even remembers why the division was created, but the division continues to survive and consume resources in the organization.

Parasites. A parasite is an organism that grows, feeds, and survives on or in another organism, but does not contribute anything in return. Parasites can also cause harm when an organism has to use energy to create an immune response to fight a parasite (Robar, Murray, & Burness, 2011). In an organizational setting, a neighboring organization could steal office supplies, electrical power, or other resources from an organization and contribute nothing to assist the health of the host organization.

These twelve types of organizational disease can all be physically observed by an organizational researcher. In addition, there are a great many possible organizational pathologies, including psychological and psychiatric disorders. For example, Kets de Vries and Miller (1984) borrowed from the American Psychiatric Association's (1984) *Diagnostic and Statistical Manual of Mental Disorders* and created five types of organizational pathology:1) paranoid, 2) compulsive, 3) dramatic, 4) depressive, and 5) schizoid. Additionally, Samuel (2012) described dozens of organizational maladies, disorders, and deficiencies all drawn from human pathologies.

Dimension Two: Loss of Functioning

The first dimension in the model of organizational population health change (shown in Figure 9-1) is organizational diseases. The second dimension is loss of functioning. Functioning refers to the ability of an organism to perform certain necessary or desired tasks and actions. Functioning includes the tasks and actions that the organism "can do" whether or not the organism chooses to do them (Verbrugge & Jette, 1994). Borrowing from this medical perspective, organizational functioning includes those tasks and actions that the organization can or could perform, its capabilities, whether or not the organization actually accomplishes those tasks and actions in the present.

Loss of functioning means that an organism can no longer perform desired or necessary tasks and actions (Verbrugge & Jette, 1994). Typically, organisms lose functioning due to some sort of disease (CDC, 2010). The same can be said for organizations. Organizational loss of functioning refers to an organization's inability to perform the tasks and actions that it was once able to perform. Organizational diseases are typically a major reason why organizations lose functional abilities and capabilities.

Dimension Three: Disability

In the medical field, when an individual experiences chronic and acute conditions that affect the functioning of specific systems and processes and affect that person's abilities to act in necessary, usual, and expected ways, then that person has what is called a "disability." A disability can be thought of as an "inability" or "incapacity" in what the individual does. The term "disablement" applies generally to all types of pathology and refers to the trend of: 1) functional consequences, and 2) all factors that influence the direction, pace, and patterns of functional change over time (Verbrugge & Jette, 1994). The disablement process is particularly important as most people live with chronic conditions rather than die from them (Rothenberg & Koplan, 1990).

One of the most significant changes in the focus on human population health has been a move toward the concept of living with and dying with (rather than "dying from") disease. Additionally researchers and policymakers have moved toward a focus on the toll of suffering and the burden of dysfunction attributable to chronic conditions. Researchers are now focusing on the disease burden facing individuals and its impact on loss of functioning and disability (Rothenberg & Koplan, 1990).

Loss of functioning can lead to disability in organisms, but that is not always the case. Sometimes an individual might lose function, such as when a person injures their writing hand, but that may not lead to permanent disability if that person is then able to learn to write effectively with their other hand. In other words, loss of functioning describes what an organism "can do" but disability describes what a person "does do."

The concept of disability or disablement can be examined in two ways. First, loss of functioning can lead to a decline in an organism's ability to do what it once was able to do. Second, disease can lead to loss of functioning, which can lead to an organism not being able to do what it should be able to do in its life stage. Both of these definitions reflect a difference in current versus ideal states of functioning for the organism.

In this context, disability refers to the situation in which an individual's abilities or limitations are determined by its interaction with its environment. That individual's disability, or limitation, is dependent on how well that individual's environment accommodates the loss of functioning (CDC, 2010). Some environments might accommodate a great deal of loss of functioning, thereby lessening the impact of the disability, whereas other environments might not accommodate any loss of functioning, thereby increasing the severity of the disability for the individual, and increasing the disease burden on that individual. For example, a highly competitive and rapidly changing environment might not accommodate any level of disability. However, a non-competitive, static environment might accommodate a great deal of disability with limited consequences for an individual.

The American Society of Anesthesiologists (ASA) classifies disability according to seven categories. They use the word "individual" to refer to a specific human patient. However, the word "individual" was replaced with the word "organization" in order to apply these categories to an organization as the individual patient under examination:

0. A healthy organization with no disease
1. An at-risk organization with potential to develop disease
2. An organization with mild disease
3. An organization with severe disease
4. An organization with severe disease that is a constant threat to organizational life
5. A near-death organization that is not expected to survive without a major intervention.
6. A dead organization whose resources are being sold off to other organizations.

These seven categories of disability apply well to organizations.

A great deal has been written about the decline of an organization's ability to function since the late 1970s (Cameron, Whetten, & Kim, 1987; Miles, 1980; Whetten, 1980a, 1980b, 1987a, 1987b). Many researchers have focused on the deterioration aspects of an organization's functioning in their definition of decline (Lamberg & Pajunen, 2005). Cameron, Whetten, & Kim (1987) discuss twelve organizational dysfunctions of decline.

Weitzel & Jonsson (1989) incorporated a number of earlier definitions of organizational decline into a definition that is similar to the medical definition of disability used here. They define decline as occurring when organizations "fail to anticipate, recognize, avoid, neutralize, or adapt to external or internal pressures that threaten the organization's long-term survival" (p. 94). Furthermore, "decline begins when an organization fails to anticipate or recognize and effectively respond to any deterioration of organizational performance that threatens long-term survival" (p. 94). They argue that if decline is to be avoided, then a proactive, preventive approach must be taken to recognize early indicators of decline and to address problems early and swiftly. Mone, McKinley, and Barker (1998) note that organizational decline represents the gap between an organization's performance and its aspirations. That definition of decline is very similar to the way that organizational disability is defined here, namely, as the gap between an organization's current health level and its aspirational level.

Researchers have been particularly interested in managerial response and adaptation to organizations experiencing performance deterioration (e.g., Filatotchev, Buck, & Zhukov, 2000; Staw, Sandelands, & Dutton, 1981). All of those studies focus on managerial reactions to decline, the search for ways to turn organizations around, and the risks involved in various turnaround methods. Those approaches to organizational decline fit nicely alongside the medical perspective of organizational disability. In sum, the decline or disability stage in an organization's life cycle can signal the imminent death of that organization (Lester, Parnell, & Carraher, 2003).

Dimension Four: Death

The fourth dimension in the model of organizational population health change (shown in Figure 9-1) is death. Much has been written about why organization die, but much less has been written about how the process of organizational death unfolds (Sutton, 1987). Whetten (1987a) noted that organizational death has been the least studied of all of the organizational life cycle stages.

Following from the medical perspective, the organizational health change process starts with organizational diseases and illnesses. Organizational diseases and illnesses must occur before there are losses in functioning or losses in the organization's ability to perform certain desired tasks and actions. Next, loss of functioning can then result in an organization being unable to perform expected tasks, roles, and activities, both internal and external to the organization. Organizational disability is a precursor for an organization's death (Verbrugge & Jette, 1994). Lastly, death is the end of the process. Over time, just as for humans, change can occur in some or all of these four organizational dimensions, including getting or living with disease, experiencing loss of functioning, developing a disability, and finally dying (Crimmins, Hayward, & Saito, 1996).

Organizational death is defined as the final cessation of the organization's activities and functions. Sheppard (1994) noted that organizational death occurs when an organization stops performing those functions that we expect from it. Sutton (1987) noted that when organizations die the former members agree that the organization is defunct, and the activities conducted by the organization are no longer accomplished intact.

Organizational researchers have bemoaned the lack of large-scale studies of multiple organizations experiencing decline (e.g., Carmeli & Sheaffer, 2009). The model presented in Figure 1 provides an approach and framework that could be used for large-scale comparison and tracking of organizational community or of organizational population health and well-being over time. All of the dimensions could be assessed using summary health measures (described below).

A Model of Potential Health Changes for an Individual Organization

The model of organizational population health change shown in Figure 9-1 is only appropriate for organizational population health change and not appropriate for individual organizational life cycle change. The complexity of change at the individual organization level is shown in Figure 9-2. Each arrow in the figure represents a potential health change for an individual organization.

The sum of the health changes across individual organizations is what produces organizational population health changes. An individual organization can skip life stages, and might not even experience any life stages other than conception, birth, and death. Individual organizations can experience health changes multi-directionally. For example, an individual organization may decline, but then regain functioning, only to decline again. However, for the population of organizations, typically health risk factors lead to disease, then to loss of ability, then to disability, then to death.

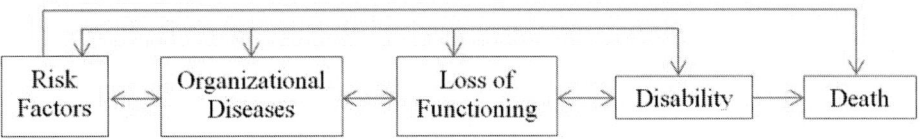

Figure 9-2. Potential health changes for an individual organization

The model of potential health changes for an individual organization presented here was adapted from the Centers for Disease Control (CDC)'s (2010) and is composed of five life stages: risk factors, organizational diseases, loss of functioning, disability, and death.

Risk Factors

In medicine, health risk factors are chemical, psychological, physiological, environmental or genetic conditions that make it more likely someone will develop a disease. According to the Centers for Disease Control (CDC), typical common risk factors for disease include: family history of disease, alcohol consumption, tobacco use, bad diet, elevated cholesterol, high blood pressure, illicit drug use, inappropriate sexual activity, substance abuse, physical inactivity, and being overweight.

The health of organizations can be similarly influenced by health risk factors. Typical organizational health risk factors fall into four categories: 1) ignorable risks, 2) nuisance risks, 3) insurable risks, and 4) serious risks. Ignorable risks are those with relatively minor consequences and relatively low likelihood of occurrence. For example, having a flat tire or not finding an empty parking space on the way to an important client pitch meeting. Nuisance risks are little things that can frequently go wrong, but their impact can be minimized with easy changes in behavior. For example, ordering enough supplies to keep the office running smoothly so that no one runs out of paper or toner. Insurable risks have major consequences even though their chances of occurrence are not very likely, but their impact can be minimized through insurance coverage. For example, insurable risk includes protecting against loss of valuable knowledge, skills, and abilities of key employees by having life insurance that covers those employees. Serious risks are those with a relatively high likelihood of occurrence that also have major potential consequences for the organization should they occur. There are seven typical serious health risks for organizations: 1) market risks, 2) competitive risks, 3) technology and operational risks, 4) financial risks, 5) human resource risks, 6) legal and regulatory risks, and 7) systemic industry risks (Cayenne Consulting, 2010).

Family history is one of the most important human health risks. The same can be said for organizations. Research on the founding of organizations has shown that genealogical connections to prior entities can influence the composition and performance of new organizations (Klepper & Sleeper, 2005; Phillips, 2002, 2005). Additionally, the shape that a new organization eventually takes relies heavily on resources available to its parent founders through their previous organizations (Agarwal, Echambadi, Franco, & Sarkar, 2004; Helfat & Lieberman, 2002; Klepper & Sleeper, 2005).

Measuring Organizational Health

Organizational health is the extent to which an organization is able to realize aspirations, to satisfy its needs, and to change and/or cope with the environment. A population refers to a group of organizations. Therefore, organizational population health is a conceptual framework for thinking about why some populations of organizations are healthier and live longer than other organizations, and includes policy development, research agendas, and resources allocations that follow from it (adapted from Young, 1998). Organizational population health policy has a goal of improving the health of organizations and organizational populations by investing in the determinants of organizational health through policies, treatments, and interventions that affect these determinants (Kindig, 2007). The best way to improve the health of one organization is by improving the health of the population of organizations. Figure 9-3 shows the points of treatment and intervention opportunities in the health change process.

Organizational population health is measured by health status indicators and is influenced by social, economic, and physical environments, by personal organizational health practices, individual capacity and coping skills, early organizational development experiences, and internal and external interventions (adapted from Aday, 2005; Dunn & Hayes, 1999). The health state or health status of an organization or an organizational population refers to an organization's health at any point in time usually measured as morbidity or some indicator of a health-related quality of life (Last, 2001). When a measure of organizational life expectancy, or mortality, is added to the health status measure, then it produces a more expansive concept of population health outcome (Kindig, 2007).

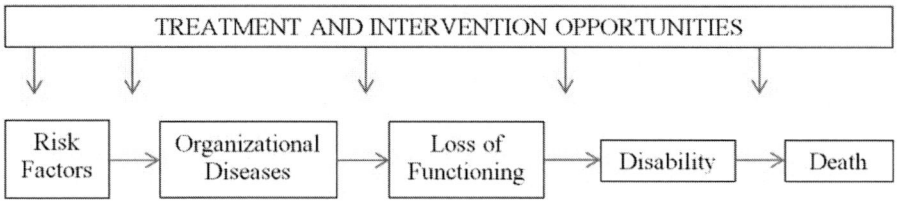

Figure 9-3. Organizational health treatment and intervention opportunities

The goal of organizational medicine follows a preventive approach with a goal to protect, promote, and maintain the health and well-being of organizations, and to prevent and overcome disease, inability, and death of organizations. To make progress toward that goal, researchers will need to compare and evaluate programs that address different benefits for different diseases in different populations. Additionally, researchers will need to document levels and changes in an organizational patient's health status over time.

Health status can be measured in many ways (Murray, Salomon, & Mathers, 2000). However, mortality is the most common measure of an individual's health. A researcher reports whether or not a patient is alive or dead. To be meaningful, mortality must be expressed in the form of a mortality rate, which is the proportion of deaths from a specific cause during some defined time period, such as over one year. For human patients, mortality rates are usually adjusted for age. A case mortality, or fatality, rate can be determined by dividing the number of people who died during a specific time period by the number of people living with the same disease.

Human health has primarily been measured by mortality-based indicators. Death rates and life expectancies have typically been disaggregated and presented by researchers regarding sociodemographics and other descriptors to evaluate population health and to monitor the impact of health interventions. Organizational mortality rate refers to the number of deaths in a population of organizations within a prescribed time period, expressed as crude death rates or death rates specific to diseases, age, and other attributes (Turnock, 2004).

The reporting of mortality rates has both advantages and disadvantages. Mortality rates are helpful because they are hard data that are easy to comprehend by almost anyone. However, mortality rates ignore the number of people living with a disease. This is an important omission because many health care services that can improve an individual's health and well-being do not influence mortality rates.

However, health status can also be assessed by measuring an individual's health outcomes, such as symptoms, function, and mortality, as those more directly influence the quality of an individual's life. The measure of health status that has been shown to best meet the needs of researchers, decision makers, and policy makers are preference- or utility-based measures of generic health-related quality of life (HRQOL) that provide a comprehensive description of health and overall well-being.

Morbidity is the most common measure of an individual's health status, and is reported in terms of a person's function or role performance. An individual's score for health-related quality of life (HRQL) provides a comprehensive description of their health and overall well-being. HRQL measures can provide information solely about a specific disease or more generically about the overall health of an individual.

Organizational morbidity rate refers to any departure from a state of physiological or psychological well-being and is synonymous with illness or sickness (Last, 2001). Unfortunately, mortality-based rates are not very useful because they don't provide much information for making even basic judgments about the health of a population, or about the comparative impact of an intervention or other types of treatment. They also do not record the influences of chronic disease and disability on population health. Additionally, people tend to live with chronic conditions rather than simply die from them (Verbrugge & Jette, 1994).

To combat this problem, summary measures of population health have been created (Gold, Stevenson, & Fryback, 2002; Murray, Salomon, & Mathers, 2000). Summary measure of population health (SMPH) is a measure of organizational population health that includes the combined impact of organizational death and morbidity to be considered simultaneously (Gold, Stevenson, & Fryback, 2002). The concept of combining health status data with mortality data in a life table to generate life estimates of expected years of life for individuals in various health states has been around since the 1960s (Sanders, 1964; Sullivan, 1971).

Survivorship Function for a Population of Organizations

Organizational health expectancies and health gaps can be displayed together on a survivorship curve. Figure 9-4 shows a simple survivorship curve S(x) for a hypothetical population of organizations. For each age along the x-axis, the curve shows the proportion of an initial birth cohort of organizations that will be alive at that age. The area in space A shows time lived at each age in full health. The area under space B shows time lived at each age in less than full health. As such, the life expectancy for an organization at birth is equal to A+B (the total area under the survivorship curve) (Mathers, Salomon, Murray, & Lopez, 2003; Murray, Salomon, & Mathers, 2000).

More formally expressed: health expectancy = A + f(B) where f(.) is a function that weights time spent in area B by the severity of the health states that B represents.

Health gaps quantify the difference between the actual health of a population and some health norm or health goal for that population. Health gaps account for time lived in less than perfect health. The organizational health goal expressed in Figure 4 would be for every organization to live in a state of ideal health until the age marked by the vertical line on the right side of the figure, which encloses area C. In this example, the target goal would be for every organization in the population to live in full health until the of age 100 years.

The health gap for an organization is a function of areas B and C. More formally expressed: health gap = C + g(B) where g(.) is a function that weighs time spent in B. Full health is expressed as a value of 1.0 for a health expectancy. However, when expressing a health gap, death is expressed a 1.0. This is because health gaps measure the undesirable difference between current health and some norm for population health.

In Figure 9-4, area C is the area between the survivorship function and the target survivorship function. These are years of life lost measures, which are measures of mortality gap. These measure the gap in years between age at death and some arbitrary age, such as age 100.

Quality of Well-Being Scale

The health-related quality of life for a patient can be evaluated in hundreds of different ways that are either specific to a certain disease or generic referring to overall health. Some researchers report that measures that examine the overall general health of the patient are more desirable than those that examine health relative to a specific disease (Kaplan, 1988).

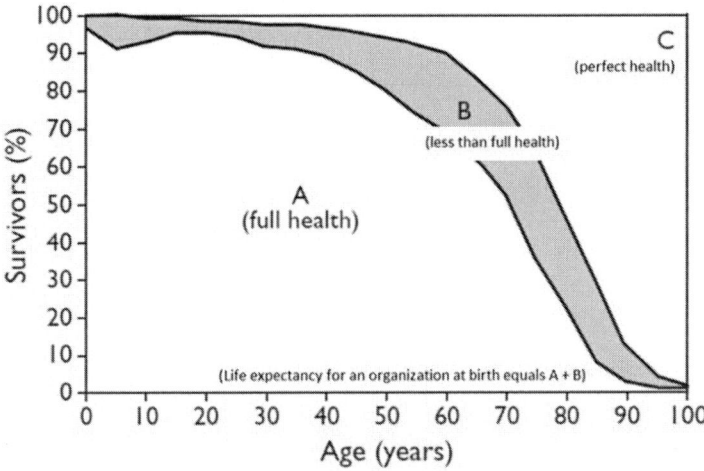

Figure 9-4. Survivorship function for a population of organizations

The Quality of Well-Being (QWB) scale is a generic, preference-based measure of HRQOL, and one of the most commonly used general HRQOL instruments (Coons, Rao, Keininger, & Hays, 2000). The QWB scale is comprised of a list of general symptoms or functions. Individuals are asked to report whether or not they experienced those symptoms in the last three days. For example, "Did you have a headache?" Each of the symptoms and functions are weighted, which results in a QWB score for the patient ranging from 0 (death) to 1.0 (perfect health.

After a mean QWB score has been calculated for the level of morbidity or wellness in a sample of organizations, the mean score can be multiplied by the amount of time at that level of wellness to calculate a QALY score. A QALY is the equivalent of one completely well year of life, or a year with optimal functioning with no health problems or symptoms. Quality-adjusted life years (QALYs) are a measure of health expectancy, which is something good to be maximized. A QALY score represents an organization's health at one given point in time. A valuation of 1.0 represents full health on the QALY scale and a valuation of 0.0 represents full death on the QALY scale. A QALY scale has internal properties, meaning that changes of equal amount anywhere on a scale of 0.0 to 1.0 can be interpreted as equivalent to one another.

For example, a person could catch the flu and be rated by experts (or self-assessed) to have a set of symptoms and a loss of functioning rated as a .5 on a scale of 1.0 (completely healthy) to 0.0 (dead). If that person remained in that health state for 10 days, then their QALY score would be calculated as (10 days/365 days in a year * .5) = .01 QALY. Then, if in that community of individuals, 1,000 people caught the flu for the same amount of time, the well years lost would be calculated as 1,000 * .01 QALY which is equal to ten years of perfect health for one person lost due to the flu. The QALY is useful and multipurpose because it can be used generically to compare small health consequences for a large number of people, and can be used to compare large health consequences for a small number of people.

Organizational Quality of Well-Being Scale (OQWB Scale)

Organizational researchers have commented that the development of a system of diagnostic tools for the early identification of conditions leading to organizational decline would be highly desirable (Weitzel & Jonsson, 1989). The health-related quality of life for an organization could be established following these same procedures either for each specific organizational disease or illness, or for the overall, general health of an organization. An Organizational Quality of Well-Being (OQWB) scale would be a generic, preference-based measure of HRQOL. The OQWB scale would be comprised of a list of general symptoms or functions. Individuals in organizations, such as CEOs, higher-ranking officials, or even typical employees, or subject matter experts outside of the organization, would be asked to report whether or not an organization experienced those symptoms in the last three days. For example, "Have you had a shortage of resources?" Each of the symptoms and functions would be weighted, which results in an OQWB score for the patient ranging from 0.0 (death) to 1.0 (perfect health).

After a mean OQWB score has been calculated for the level of morbidity or wellness in a sample of organizations, the mean score could be multiplied by the amount of time at that level of wellness to calculate a QALY score. For example, an organization could have an employee strike and be rated by experts (or self-assessed) to have a set of symptoms and a loss of functioning rated as a .5 on a scale of 1.0 (completely healthy) to 0.0 (dead). If that organization remained in that health state for 10 days, then their QALY score would be calculated as (10 days/365 days in a year * .5) = .01 QALY. Then, if in that community of organizations, 100 other organizations had employees go out on strike for the same amount of time, the well years lost would be calculated as 100 * .01 QALY which is equal to one year of perfect health for one organization lost due to the strike. The QALY is useful and multipurpose because it can be used generically to compare small health consequences for a large number of organizations, and can be used to compare large health consequences for a small number of organizations.

OQWB scales could be created for the overall health of an organization and a population of organizations, and separate scales could be created for each specific organizational disease (Coons, Rao, Keininger, & Hays, 2000). For example, an OQWB scale could be created to assess to what extent an organization had any sort of misalignment. In the medical field, alignment is defined as the relationship of the individual body segments to each other. It is the most basic position of the body before movement begins. Proper alignment places a minimum amount of strain on the muscles and ligaments. Deviations from proper alignment will cause muscle fatigue and a greater risk of injury. For organizations, alignment is defined as the relationships of the vision, mission, strategies, organizational goals, process goals, system goals, and job goals. When all of these organizational segments support and properly assist each other, then an organization is in proper alignment and will function well. Lack of alignment can put strain on the organization and can cause a greater risk of injury and breakdown, and can lead to loss of functioning. An OQWB scale could be created to assess the extent of alignment of an organization's vision, mission, strategies, organizational goals, process goals, and job-level goals. The scale would measure the existence of strain on the organization due to any misalignment.

Some work has already been done to create such measures. Taormina (1991) developed a diagnostic tool and procedure for resolving organizational problems called Qualitative Living Systems Analysis (QLSA). The procedure was likened to the medical examination procedure used by a physician, but was applied to organizations. The procedure involves four steps: 1) obtain a case history, 2) analyze the organization's subsystems and identify pathologies, 3) make a diagnosis, and 4) prescribe solutions.

However, if the greatest benefits of applying methods used in the field of medicine are to be successfully applied to the study of organizations, then a great deal of work will need to be done to create effective OQWB scales. Following the specifications of Kaplan (1988) for human patients, OQWB scales could be created by doing the following: 1) create a set of mutually exclusive and collectively exhaustive levels of organizational functioning, 2) generate an exhaustive set of organizational symptoms and functional problems, 3) establish weights for each of the organizational symptoms and functional problems, and 4) use the weights to create a scale of optional functioning with 1.0 for perfect organizational "health" and 0.0 for organizational "death." For example, one type of organizational blockage might be a full employee strike. The weight given to such a loss of functioning might be a .5.

Creating OQWB scales might take considerable effort from organizational researchers. However, based on the results obtained in the field of medicine and population health, then those efforts would be highly rewarded through: 1) greater understanding of why some organizations live longer and healthier lives than other organizations, and 2) greater knowledge of what organizational researchers could do to better improve the health and well-being of individual and populations of organizations.

Discussion

My aim in this paper has been to move toward an integration of modern medical and health care theory, principles, and practices and the study of organizations. The main focus has been to treat the organization as a medical patient, with the central question, "Why do some organizations live longer, healthier lives than other organizations?" This question allows for a variety of models to be created in the analysis of variations of organizational health and longevity.

Many reasons have been examined in organization studies regarding the mortality level of organizations, such as: age, size, strategy, relational density, and ties or linkages, etc. I have examined another factor that determines an organizational longevity, namely its level of health or morbidity level. This may be a more important factor than the others as organizations can live a long time, but in poor health. Humans are living longer and longer, so their mortality levels are tending to decrease. However, humans are living longer in poorer and poorer health, so their morbidity levels are actually increasing. This phenomenon has resulted in humans having a longer, but lower, quality of life (Crimmins, Hayward, & Saito, 1994). This same phenomenon may be occurring for organizations. Organizations may be living longer, but having lower quality of life, which has great implications for the field of organization studies. Further research will need to examine such trends for organizations.

Applying from the field of medicine, I created a basic definition of organizational medicine, which is the sum total of the knowledge, skills, and practices based on the theories, beliefs, and experiences in the maintenance of organizational health and fitness, as well as in the prevention, diagnosis, alleviation, improvement, and treatment of organizational disease or illness. Organizational medicine seeks to understand and improve the health and longevity of a single organization, and also the health and longevity of a community or a population of organizations.

Borrowing from a population health perspective, a model of organizational population health change was examined. The approach taken was that the best way to improve the health of one organization is by improving the health of a community or of a population of organizations. At the population level, organizations tend to develop organizational diseases, then to experience loss of function, then disability, and then death. This model provides researchers with the ability to examine the morbidity levels of a population of organizations in each stage of the organizational population health change. This information can then be used to compare and contrast the health changes of organizations over time, and can be used to apply treatments and interventions expeditiously to help improve the health and longevity of organizations, which would greatly benefit the field of organization studies.

Also borrowing from a population health perspective, a model of potential health change for individual organizations was presented. The model shows that health or morbidity level of a single organization can range from perfect health (with no disease) to near death (with terminal disease), and finally to death. Unlike for a population of organizations, the health of individual organizations can move multi-directionally from healthy to unhealthy and back to healthy again in an endless cycle. Some organizations may only experience risk factors but never develop any ability-interfering disease, while other organizations may develop a plethora of life-threatening diseases that no interventions can help save from demise. Borrowing from a population health perspective enables the individual health of an organization to be methodically determined and tracked in a life path diagram that charts the changing HRQL of an organization over time. This is a very useful and practical approach to examining the health of organizations that would also greatly benefit the field of organization studies.

Another very useful method that can be borrowed from the medical field and applied to the study of organizations is: 1) the use of health assessment methods to uncover information about the health and well-being of an organization, and 2) the use of summary health measures that document the combined morbidity and mortality level of an organization. Dozens of summary health measures can be borrowed from the medical field, applied to organizations, and then tracked over time. These summary measures would greatly improve the ability of organizational researchers to track and compare the health of individual organizations and the health of communities or populations of organizations from conception to death, and even to post-mortem.

However, the greatest challenges or opportunities for organizational researchers lie in the development and the creation of OQWBs (organizational quality of well-being scales). Hundreds of different QWB (quality of well-being) scales have been created that examine either general human health or disease-specific human health. Similar scales will need to be created to assess specific diseases in organizations and to assess overall, general organizational health.

Much work will need to be done to create OQWB scales with the power of current human QWB scales. For that to happen, organizational researchers will need to create scale items that assess specific organizational health symptoms and disabilities. For instance, the United States Federal Reserve expects large, complex bank holding companies to hold sufficient capital in order to maintain access to funding, to continue to serve as credit intermediaries, to meet their obligations to creditors and counterparties, and to continue operations, even under adverse economic conditions. The Federal Reserve administered "stress tests" in order to assess the health of bank holding companies. Similar measures will need to be determined for specific organizational diseases, such as for "misalignment" of an organization's vision, mission, strategy, organization-level goals, process-level goals, and job-level goals. Scale items will need to assess symptoms and disabilities associated with each specific organizational pathology. Additionally, OQWB scales will need to be standardized and normalized so that they can apply to all organizations and be used to compare and contrast the health of organizations in a community or in a population of organizations over time.

The use of standardized OQWB measures will enable the use of organizational survivorship function curves for a population of organizations. This type of information will be extremely useful for organizational researchers, practicing managers, and organizations in general. Standardized health assessment scales will enable researchers to make predictions about the expected health and mortality rates of individual organizations at any time in an organization's life span from conception to death, and will provide information such as the estimated life expectancy for an entire population of organizations. This kind of information will have many benefits for those in and out of the field of organization studies.

Organizational survivorship function curve information will also be of great benefit to those researchers and consultants who aim to improve organizational health and longevity through treatment and intervention methods. Summary health measures and survivorship function curves can help pinpoint where organizations are particularly susceptible to organizational disease and where best to devote research time and energies to development treatments and interventions that can help organizations recover from organizational disease, or can help prevent organizational disease from developing in the first place.

In summary, the integration of the field of medicine with the study of organizations offers a plethora of benefits for a great many audiences interested in the longevity of fully-functioning organizations. Why do some organizations live longer, healthier lives than other organizations? Because those organizations are better able to prevent and overcome organizational diseases and illnesses that negatively influence their health and well-being than are other organizations.

References

Aday, L. A. (Ed.) (2005). *Reinventing public health: Policies and practices for a health nation*. San Francisco, CA: Jossey-Bass.

Adizes, I. (1979). Organizational passages: Diagnosing and treating life cycle problems in organizations. *Organizational Dynamics, 8*(1), 3-24.

Adizes, L. (1989). Corporate life cycles: How and why corporations grow and die and what to do about it. Englewood-Cliffs, NJ: Prentice Hall.

Agarwal, R., Echambadi, R., Franco, A. M., & Sarkar, M. (2004). Knowledge transfer through inheritance: Spin-out generation, development, and survival. *Academy of Management Journal, 47*, 501-522.

Alavi, S. S., Ferdosi, M., Jannatifard, F., Eslami, M., Alaghemandan, H., & Setare, M. (2011). Behavioral addiction versus substance addiction: Correspondence of psychiatric and psychological views. *International Journal of Preventive Medicine, 3*(4), 290-294.

American Psychiatric Association (APA) (1984). *Diagnostic and statistical manual of mental disorder*. Washington, DC: American Psychiatric Association.

Ashby, W. R. (1956). *An introduction to cybernetics*. London: Methuen.

Bogin, B. (1988). *Patterns of human growth*. New York: Cambridge University Press.

Boin, A., Kuipers, S., Steenbergen, M. (2010, July). The life and death of public organizations: A question of institutional design. *Governance: An International Journal of Policy, Administration, and Institutions, 23*, 385-410.

Boulding, K. E. (1950). *A reconstruction of economics*. New York: Wiley.

Boyd, K. M. (2000). Disease, illness, sickness, health, healing and wholeness: Exploring some elusive concepts. *Journal of Medical Ethics: Medical Humanities, 26*, 9-17.

Cameron, K. S., Whetten, D. A., & Kim, M. U. (1987). Organizational dysfunctions of decline. *Academy of Management Journal, 30*, 126-138.

Cannon, W. B. (1929). Organization for physiological homeostasis. *Physiological Review, 9*, 399-431.

Cannon, W. B. (1932). *The wisdom of the body*. New York: W. W. Norton & Company, Inc.

Carmeli, A., & Sheaffer, Z. (2009). How leadership characteristics affect organizational decline and downsizing. *Journal of Business Ethics, 86*, 363-378.

Chapman, S. J., & Ashton, T. S. (1914). The sizes of businesses, mainly in the textile industries. *Journal of the Royal Statistical Society, 77*, 469-555.

Cliff, B. (2012, November/December). Patient-centered care: The role of healthcare leadership. *Journal of Healthcare Management, 57*(6), 381-383.

Coons, S. J., Rao, S., Keininger, D. L., & Hays, R. D. (2000, January). A comparative review of generic quality-of-life instruments. *Pharmacoeconomics, 17*(1), 13-35.

Crimmins, E., & Hayward, M. D., & Saito, Y. (1996). Differentials in active life expectancy in the older population of the United States. *Journals of Gerontology Series B: Psychological Sciences and Social Sciences, 51*(B3), S111-S120.

Downs, A. (1967). The life cycle of bureaus. In Downs, A. (Ed.), *Inside bureaucracy*. San Francisco, CA: Little, Brown, & Company.

Dunn, J. R., & Hayes, M. V. (1999, November/December). Toward a lexicon of population health. *Canadian Journal of Public Health Supplement*, S7-10.

Filatotchev, I., Buck, T., & Zhukov, V. (2000). Downsizing in privatized firms in Russia, Ukraine and Belarus. *Academy of Management Journal, 43*(3), 286-304.

Frampton, S., & Charmel, P. (Eds.). (2009). *Putting patients first: Best practices in patient centered care* (2nd Ed.). San Francisco: Jossey-Bass.

Freeman, J. H. (1980). The unit problem in organizational research. In W. M. (Ed.), *Frontiers in organization and management* (pp. 59-68). New York: Praeger.

Garrat, R., & Keister, T. (2009, August). Bank runs as coordination failures: An experimental study. *Journal of Economic Behavior & Organization,71*(2), 300-317.

George, M. (2002). *Lean six sigma : Combining six sigma quality with lean production speed.* New York: McGraw-Hill.

Gold, M. R., Stevenson, D., & Fryback, D. G. (2002). HALYs, and QALYs, and DALYs, oh my: Similarities and differences in summary measures of population health. *Annual Review of Public Health, 23,* 115-134.

Goldman, A. (2009) *Transforming toxic leaders.* Stanford, CA: Stanford University Press.

Greiner, L. (1972). Evolution and revolution as organizations grow. *Harvard Business Review, 49,* 37-46.

Helfat, C. E., & Lieberman, M. B. (2002). The birth of capabilities: Market entry and the importance of prehistory. *Industrial and Corporate Change, 11,* 725-760.

Kaplan, R. M. (1988). New health promotion indicators: the general health policy model. *Health Promotion, 3*(1), 35-49.

Kets de Vries, M. F. R., & Miller, D. (1984). *The neurotic organization: Diagnosing and changing counterproductive styles of management.* San Francisco, CA: Jossey-Bass.

Kindig, D. A. (2007). Understanding population health terminology. *Milbank Quarterly, 85,* 139-161.

Klepper, S., & Sleeper, S. (2005, August). Entry by spinoffs. *Management Science, 51*(8), 1291-1306.

Kuusk, A., Paas, T., & Viikmaa, K. (2011). Financial contagion of the 2008 crisis: Is there any evidence of financial contagion from the US to Baltic states. *Eastern Journal of European Studies, 2*(2), 61-76.

Labonte, R, (Ed.) (1988). *Heart health inequalities: Second report.* Health and Welfare Canada, Ottawa.

Lamberg, J.-A., & Pajunen, K. (2005). Beyond the metaphor: The morphology of organizational decline and turnaround. *Human Relations, 58,* 947-980.

Last, J. M. (2001). *A dictionary of epidemiology* (4th ed.). New York. NY: Oxford University Press.

Latham, S. F., & Brown, M. (2009). Managerial risk, innovation, and organizational decline. *Journal of Management, 35*(2), 258-281.

Lavoie, D., & Culbert, S. A. (1978). Stages in organization and development. *Human Relations, 31,* 417-438.

Lawson, J. S., & Bauman, A. E. (2001). *Public health Australia: An introduction.* Roseville, New South Wales: McGraw Hill.

Lencioni, P. (2012). *The advantage: Why organizational health trumps everything else in business.* San Francisco, CA: Jossey-Bass.

Lodahl, T., & Mitchell, S. (1980). Drift if the development of innovative organizations. In J. Kimberly, & R. Miles, R. (Eds.), *The Organizational life cycle* (pp. 184-207). San Francisco, CA: Jossey-Bass.

Lyden, F. J. (1975). Using Parsons's functional analysis in the study of public organizations. *Administrative Science Quarterly, 20,* 59-70.

Marshall, A. (1920). *Principles of economics* (8th ed.). London, UK: Macmillan.

Mathers, C. D., Salomon, J. A., Murray, C. J. L., & Lopez, A. (2003). Alternative summary measures of average population. In C. J. L. Murrey, & D. B. Evans (Eds.), *Health systems performance assessment: Debates, methods and empiricism* (Chapter 27, pp. 319-334). Geneva: World Health Organization.

Mathieu, J. E., & Chen, G. (2011). The etiology of the multilevel paradigm in management research. *Journal of Management, 37,* 610-641.

McKinley, W. (1993). Organizational decline and adaptation: Theoretical controversies. *Organization Science, 4,* 1-9

Merkt, J. R., & Taylor, C. R. (1994, December). "Metabolic switch" for desert survival. *Proceedings of the National Academy of Science, 91,* 12313-12316.

Miles, R. H. (1980). The role of organizational learning in the early creation and development of organizations. In J. R. Kimberly, & R. H. Miles, (Eds,). *The organizational life cycle.* San Francisco, CA: Jossey-Bass.

Miller, J. G., & Miller, J. L. (1991, October). A living systems analysis of organizational pathology. *Behavioral Science, 36,* 239-252.

Mone, M. A., McKinley, W., & Barker, III, V. L. (1998). Organizational decline and innovation: A contingency framework. *Academy of Management Review, 23,* 115-132.

Morgan, G. (2006). *Images of organization.* Thousand Oaks, CA: Sage.

Murray, C. J. L., Salomon, J. A., & Mathers, C. (2000). A critical examination of summary measures of population health. *Bulletin of the World Health Organization, 78*(8), 981-994.

Murray, C. J. L., Salomon, J. A., Mathers, C. D., & Lopez, A. D.(1984). *Summary measures of population health concepts, ethics, measurement and applications.* Geneva, Switzerland: World Health Organization.

Numagami, T., Karube, M., & Kato, T. (2010, November). Organizational deadweight: Learning from Japan. *Academy of Management Perspectives*, *24*(4), 25-37.

Penrose, E. T. (1952). Biological analogies in the theory of the firm. *American Economic Review*, *4*, 804-819.

Pfeffer, J. (1998). *The human equation: Building profits by putting people first*. Cambridge, MA: Harvard Business Review Press.

Phillips, D. J. (2002). A genealogical approach to organizational life chances: The parent-progeny transfer among Silicon Valley law firms, 1946-1996. *Administrative Science Quarterly*, *47*, 474-506.

Robar, N., Murray, D. L., & Burness, G. (2011). Effects of parasites on host energy expenditure: The resting metabolic rate stalemate. *Canadian Journal of Zoology*, *89*, 1146-1155.

Rothenberg, R. G., & Koplan, J. P. (1990). Chronic disease in the 1990s. In L. Breslow, J. E. Fielding, & L. B. Lave, (Eds.), *Annual Review of Public Health* (Vol. 11). Palo Alto, CA: Annual Reviews, Inc.

Rousseau, D. M. (1985). Issues of level in organizational research: Multi-level and cross-level perspectives. *Research in Organizational Behavior*, *7*, 1-37.

Samuel, Y. (2012). *Organizational pathology: Life and death of organizations*. Piscataway, NJ: Transaction Publishers.

Sanders, B. S. (1964). Measuring community health levels. *American Journal of Public Health*, *54*, 1063-1070.

Sheppard, J. P. (1994). Strategy and bankruptcy: An exploration into organizational death. *Journal of Management*, *20*(4), 795-833.

Stauffer, R. C. (Ed.) (1949). *Science and civilization*. Madison, WI: University of Wisconsin Press.

Staw, B. M., Sandelands, L. E., & Dutton, J. E. (1981). Threat-rigidity effects in organizational behavior: A multilevel analysis. *Administrative Science Quarterly*, *26*(4), 501-524

Staw, B. M., & Szwajkowski, E. (1980). The scarcity-munificence component of organizational environment and the commission of illegal acts. In D. Katz, R. L. Kahn, & J. S. Adams, (Eds.), *The study of organizations*. San Francisco, CA: Jossey-Bass.

Sullivan, D. F. (1971). A single index of mortality and morbidity. *HSMHA Health Reports*, *86*, 347-354.

Sutton, R. I. (1987). The process of organizational death: Disbanding and reconnecting. *Administrative Science Quarterly*, *32*, 542-569.

Taormina, R. J. (1991, July). Organizational analysis of information processing using living systems theory. *Behavioral Science*, *36*, 196-223.

Torbert, W. R. (1974). Pre-bureaucratic and post-bureaucratic stages of organization development. *Interpersonal Development, 5*, 1-25.

Tracy, L. (1993, July). Living systems applications: Applications of living system theory to the study of management and organizational behavior. *Behavioral Science, 38*(3), 218-230.

Turnock, B. J. (2004). *Public health: What it is and how it* works (3rd Ed.). Sudbury, MA: Jones & Bartlett Publishers.

Verbrugge, L. M., & Jette, A. M. (1994). The disablement process. *Social Science & Medicine, 38*(1), 1-14.

Weitzel, W., & Jonsson, E. (1989). Decline in organizations: A literature integration and extension. *Administrative Science Quarterly, 34*, 91-109.

Whetten, D. A. (1987a). Organizational growth and decline processes. *Annual Review of Sociology, 13*, 335-358.

—. (1987b). Organization growth and decline processes. In W. R. Scott, & J. F. Short (Eds.), *Annual review of sociology*, Vol. 13 (pp. 335-358). Palo Alto, CA: Annual Review.

—. (1980a). Organizational decline: A neglected topic in organizational science. *Academy of Management Review, 5*, 577-588.

—. (1980b). Sources, responses, and effects of organizational decline. In J. R. Kimberly, R. H. Miles, and Associates (Eds.), *The organizational life cycle* (pp. 342-374). San Francisco, CA: Jossey-Bass.

Young, R. C. (1988). Is population ecology a useful paradigm for the study of organizations? *American Journal of Sociology, 94*, 1-24.

CHAPTER TEN

A THEORY OF PREVENTIVE HEALTH IN ORGANIZATIONS[1]

CHESTER S. SPELL
RUTGERS UNIVERSITY, USA,
SAN JOSE STATE UNIVERSITY, USA
AND KATERINA BEZRUKOVA
SANTA CLARA UNIVERSITY, USA

Abstract

Employers of all stripes have become increasingly and intimately involved in the health of their employees, and encouraging behaviors related to good health. Yet, there is a great deal of unexplained variability in employer approaches to managing employee health and very little effort has been made by organizational scholars to explain these differences. We explore this question by first focusing on different health-related interests of employers using the human resource management strategy literature. Then, the role of demographic characteristics of employees relevant to health management is considered derived from psychological research. Finally, sociological literature focusing on extra-organizational factors is reviewed for institutional-based perspectives on health management. The result of this integration is a multi-level theory of health management in organizations. It is hoped that our model, testable propositions, and research agenda contribute to understanding of the employer's role in health management and point out implications for managers, one of the most critical business issues as reported by present day managers.

Keywords: Employer health management, Strategic HRM, employee health-related behaviors

[1] This research was supported by Santa Clara University Faculty Grant.

Introduction

Morgan Spurlock's 2004 film *Super Size Me* is about a man eating exclusively at McDonald's for a month (at the end of which he was twenty-four pounds heavier, with associated increases in cholesterol level (230), mood swings, and the like. Made to bring attention to what the Surgeon General termed an epidemic, *Super Size Me* is ultimately about the tangible outcomes of specific health-related behaviors. While these behaviors (which can also include smoking, excessive alcohol use, etc.) are individual choices, employers have taken an intense interest in these behaviors of their employees. As a primary payer of health insurance premiums, many businesses have a real financial stake in the health care expenses associated with health behaviors, and thus have a keen interest in shaping and managing these behaviors. For instance, some organizations offer a variety of health initiatives—about a third of organizations have obesity reduction programs (Pronk, 2005), 85 percent of large employers have at least one program promoting health (Marshall & Heffes, 2004), and one fourth track or screen employee health (Hall, 2008).

Yet, while the attention organizations devote to the issue of employee health intensifies, management scholars have failed to systematically address the issue of employer health management, defined as employer sponsored fitness programs, weight loss, smoking cessation, stress management, substance abuse prevention, hypertension, and health education (Wolfe, Ulrich, & Parker, 1987). A search of the literature reveals only Wolfe et al's (1987) review which provided the definition of employee health management we adopt, along with DeGroot and Kiker's (2003) review of health management strategy with virtually no research specifically on health management published since 1987. This level of attention to such a fundamental business concern is no doubt partly because the issue itself is made of multiple facets. With the multitude of ways employers try to encourage healthy behaviors, there are many potential drivers of health management programs and their effects. Yet, as Brief, Butcher, George, and Link (1993) accurately pointed out, much of the research on well-being has been atheoretical, and there has been little attention, since their study, to develop theory on how some of drivers, such as workplace practices, work relationships, and other aspects of organizational life are related to health outcomes.

To address this complex problem, our paper brings together literatures from multiple disciplines that complement each other in adding to our understanding of why, and to what extent, employers try to manage employee health. While, as noted, the attention to health management itself has been sparse, research on the implications of working conditions and stress for individual health is a useful place to start and certainly establishes the importance of health management in workplace settings. In fact, previous research on specific employee health programs has examined types of individual health initiatives found in organizations (e.g., Gebhard & Crump, 1990; Harrison & Liska, 1994; Kossek & Block, 1993), program outcomes and their fairness (e.g., Falkenberg, 1987; Spell & Bezrukova, in press), and associated costs (Erfurt, Foote, & Heirich, 1992), this research has typically focused on only one aspect of health programs and has not considered the scope of different ways an employer can be involved in employee health related behaviors. Yet, as has been observed in recent NSF workshops on multi-disciplinary research (Paletz, Smith-Doerr, & Vardi, 2010), studies conducted in idiosyncratic styles limited to a single discipline are of value but hard to compare to other research. Our goal is therefore to integrate the literature on this topic into a coherent and useful whole to provide a comprehensive understanding of how and why organizations manage employee health.

First, we draw on the human resource management literature that focuses upon employer interests regarding employee health behavior. The simple answer to why employers try to manage employee health would be to save money. For instance, employers may engage in these practices to drive certain attitudinal and behavioral changes from their employees. This idea can be illustrated by a quote from Eric Schiermeyer, co-founder of Zynga, who hired acupuncturists to help his staff stay healthy and be more emotionally balanced, claiming: "If you treat your employee like an Olympic athlete, they will provide extraordinary value." Secondly, we use psychology work that provides insights into how people define themselves including decisions they made with respect to health management. This perspective may explain how employers respond to increasing health care costs based on the context and demographics of their workforce. Third, we build on sociology work to explain how employer interests regarding health behavior are shaped by entities outside the organization, such as legal compliance and being 'up to date' with management practices across organizations or industries. We draw on institutional theory to predict these organizational responses to government action on health reform, media attention to health care and preventive health, and associated normative pressure on firms to promote healthy behaviors.

The obvious practical implications and need for theory development in the area of employee health management reflects on Corley and Goia's (2011) assertion that real theoretical contributions rest on both originality but also practical and scientific utility. There has been plentiful research showing that health care costs are related to lifestyle and health related behaviors (Aldana, 2001; Bly, Jones, & Richardson, 1986; Phillips, 2009), yet, a comprehensive theory to explain such management decisions associated with employee health behaviors is still missing. We thus review these three areas of literature and what they have to say about employee health management. While our theoretical contribution is an integration of these disciplines to help understand the multi-faceted issues of employee health behaviors, we also recognize other implications of this study and how it might be applied. Recent legislation in the United States (the Affordable Care Act of 2010) has made this a 'white-hot' issue in America, yet the widely assumed connection between healthy employees and productivity (DeGroot & Kiker, 2003; Falkenberg, 1987; Liu, Wang, Zhan, & Shi, 2009; Manning, et al., 1989) makes this is an international issue as well. Employers all over the world have an interest in developing a more informed response to the increasing burden of ill employees and preventive health measures that can be executed in the workplace setting. By connecting organizational characteristics, employer interests and workforce factors with health management, we hope to contribute to a systematic approach that can be applied across many work contexts.

Employee Health Management

Organizational Trends over Time

Since at least the 1920s employers have attempted to shape employee health. Those efforts were typically driven by the belief that employees would perform better when they are healthier. For instance, one of the ways employers have long been involved in employee health through attempting to influence employee drinking behavior. Employers' initiatives to address employee drinking habits was often integrated with Alcoholics Anonymous (AA), which from its beginnings in the 1930's held that alcoholism was permanent and fatal disease if not treated. Beginning with DuPont in the late 1930's and later in a few other companies, AA members were involved in helping supervisors to recognize that alcoholism was a disease and to refer employees with signs of alcohol abuse to medical care (Weiss, 2005). Some employers investigated employee paychecks to see if they had been cashed at bars and if found drinking, were sent directly to physicians for treatment; this procedure was called 'constructive coercion' (Weiss, 2005).

Steele and Trice (1995) as well as Roman and Blum (1992) have described how job-based alcoholism programs and Employee Assistance

Programs grew in popularity in US workplaces as an alternative to AA. These programs were much less likely to rely on recovering alcoholics to operate them like in AA, and relied more on self-referrals and formally trained and credentialed staff. In addition to EAPs, drug testing programs, especially in larger companies, expanded greatly in the 1980's and early 1990's. At the same time, the federal government put pressure via the Drug Free Workplace Act and other very public efforts to foster a "War on Drugs." EAPs expanded in number and scope as well, supposedly to support rehabilitation of drug using employees and to complement drug testing efforts. Organizations may have embraced drug testing for several reasons, including perceived productivity problems due to drug use or workplace safety issues. However, it has been found that institutional factors, including normative pressure from the government and industry groups, as well as media attention to employee drug use, were among the most significant predictors of adoption of drug testing and treatment initiatives in this period (Spell & Blum, 2005).

During the 1960's, organizations began to expand their wellness and health programs to areas outside of alcoholism. Smoking cessation programs became increasingly popular when harmful effects of tobacco became widely known (Manning, Osland, & Osland, 1989). A 1978-79 survey reported that almost 50 percent of all U.S. businesses had policies that restricted or prohibited smoking (National Interagency Council on Smoking and Health, 1980). Organizations also became interested in their employees' personal problems, specifically issues related to mental health (DeGroot et al., 2003) and physical fitness (Harrison et al., 1994). Following these trends, EAPs increasingly included mental health services and psychological counseling (Forrest, 1983). Complementing these efforts in many companies included wellness initiatives, weight-loss programs, employer sponsored "fun-runs' and a myriad of other programs and incentives (see Table 10-1 for some examples of employer HRB initiatives and their prevalence in the U.S. workplace over the past few decades). Corporations such as North American Rockwell Corp., Goodyear Rubber Co., Xerox, and PepsiCo, were early examples of health promotion, "corporate fitness," and weight control programs (Conrad, 1987). Like the earlier wellness programs, the fitness-related programs were conducted by company employees to emphasize healthy behaviors within and outside of the workplace in the hopes that this will reduce future employee health-related issues (DeGroot et al., 2003; Gebhardt et al., 1990).

Table 10-1. Percentage Of All Companies With Selected Health Promotion And Health Screening/Tracking Programs By Year Surveyed.

Program	1986	1992	1999	2004
Blood pressure screening	16	32	29	36
Cholesterol screening	--	20	22	29
Cancer screening	--	12	9	22
Diabetes screening	--	--	--	27
Health Risk screening	29	14	18	24
Fitness Program	22	--	25	16
Nutrition classes/education	--	--	23	23
Weight Control	--	15	14	21
Smoking Cessation classes	35	--	13	19
Stress Management	27	--	26	25
Alcohol and Drug education	--	--	28	36
Back injury prevention	28	--	53	45
Prenatal education	--	--	12	--
Work-family balance	--	--	18	--
AIDs/HIV education	--	--	25	15
Violence prevention	--	--	36	--

-- data not available for that year

Sources: Association for Worksite Health Promotion, National Worksite Health Promotion Survey, 2000; Linnan, L.,Bowling, M., Chiidress, J., Lindsay, G., Blakey, C., Pronk, S., Wieker, S., and Royall, P. (2008), Results of the 2004 National Worksite Health Promotion Survey. *American Journal of Public Health, 98,* 1503-1509; Fielding, J., & Piserchia, P. (1989) Frequency of Worksite Health Promotion Activities. *American Journal of Public Health, 79,* 16-20.

More recently, employers have increasingly focused on screening job applicants and current employees for HRBs or/and health conditions (Conlin, 2007). For instance, some employers screen for behaviors such as smoking tobacco and use of legal prescription drugs through drug tests that have previously been focused on detecting presence of illegal drugs.

Employees found to be legally using prescription drugs can be discharged if the employer judges use of pain-killers or other drugs as a threat to workplace safety (Zezima & Goodnough, 2010). Other employers test employees for pre-existing conditions such as high cholesterol, hypertension, and diabetes. Such interventions are often driven not only by the cost-cutting rationale but also by incentives provided by organizations such as the American Heart Association. This association recognizes organizations through "Worksite Innovation Awards" that promote individual organizational efforts to encourage healthy behaviors (American Heart Association, 2010). One example is the voluntary screening program of the supermarket chain Safeway, where employees (and spouses) who meet weight, cholesterol and other measures are within certain ranges are rewarded with reduced premiums for health care (Frederick, 2010).

These more recent organizational trends demonstrate that the ways in which employers have gotten involved in managing employee health-related behaviors are becoming much more intense and multifaceted. However, apart from a few accounts claiming success in controlling overall health care expenses (Frederick, 2010), the choices organizations make do not seem to be guided in any systematic way or by evidence - based research. In response to this issue, management researchers have been increasingly interested in understanding the effects of these important organizational developments, yet as we show below, comprehensive understanding of the rationale behind employer involvement, and why there is so much variability in the extent to which the issue of health behavior is addressed, remains elusive.

The Occupational Health Literature

While Armstrong (2009) has traced the origins of the term 'health-related behaviors' to the middle of the last century, where it was first associated with healthcare interventions, only more recently have specific interventions associated with managing employee health and wellness been examined in a systematic fashion. Reviews of research on employer efforts to influence health-related behavior have primarily focused on understanding the effectiveness of different initiatives on individual employees as well as organizational outcomes (e.g., productivity, health insurance costs). For instance, Danna and Griffin's (1999) review of organizational health literature examined a number of studies indicating the benefits (e.g., mental, physiological) of health promotion and assessment in enhancing employee health. Yet, they pointed out that the overall efficacy of employer efforts to affect employee health has not been universally determined. Phillips (2009), in a multi-organizational study, also concluded that the effect of wellness and screening programs to control costs "cannot be statistically verified." Others have considered the implications of health insurance premiums and insurance availability on preventive health behaviors (Sudano &Baker, 2003). While this research has made tremendous efforts in understanding the consequences of programs for individuals and the decisions behind employer sponsored insurance offerings, in general, it did not explain why there are so many differences in adopting health initiatives among organizations. Yet, this question is more fundamental than considering effectiveness or insurance availability, since if the health initiatives are effective, many employees of companies with little investments in health behaviors are disadvantaged. However, to the extent the programs are not effective, some employers are making inefficient investments in their human resources.

We approach this complex problem by drawing on past work found in the occupational health literature, and the substantial if indirect evidence that employee individual behaviors at work lead to significant physiological and emotional outcomes (e.g., mental health). Also, leadership style has been related to health and happiness at work (Quick & Quick, 2004); and mood has been related to better immune system functioning (Stone, Neale, Cox, & Napoli, 1994). Most of these studies have approached the topic of employer involvement in health from the micro-level perspective, concerned mostly with the individual employee behaviors. Recently, there has been important research that has also taken into consideration organizational and other macro-level factors (e.g., organizational practices, culture) to explain employee health behaviors (e.g., Macik-Frey, Quick, & Nelson, 2007). Also, Brief et al. (1993) established the theoretical connection between life circumstances, subjective well-being and health; they found that personality (negative affectivity) and objective health were both related to subjective assessments of well-being. Building on this important work, we integrate research from both levels (micro and macro) to propose a *multi-level* framework on management action associated with employee health.

While a comprehensive theory tying organizational and individual concepts together is not to be found, research has examined health behaviors and employer efforts to shape them from a number of theories. For example, research on stress management interventions and its effect on behavior has applied organizational learning theory (Mikkelson, Saksvik, & Landsbergis, 2000), risk management theory (Cox, Karanika, Griffths, & Houdmont, 2007), or a combination of rational (focusing on the effect of formal structures) or humanistic theory (focus on informal structures) (Nielsen, Fredslund, Christensen, & Albertsen, 2006). In a qualitative study, Randall, Cox, and Griffiths (2007) used cognitive appraisal theory and considered the role of context in stress management interventions and employee well-being. Turning to initiatives directed at specific behaviors, Manning and colleagues (1989) used an information processing model to study the effect of smoking cessation programs on eating habits (the programs made eating habits poorer) and mental health (programs reduced psychological well-being). Using a goal setting approach, Harrison and Liska (1994) studied fitness programs and found that employees with high risks of health problems perceived more barriers to participating in the fitness programs. All this body of work suggests that while a wide variety of theoretical lenses have been applied, none of them have answered the overarching question of why some organizations have embraced the role of actively managing employee health behavior whereas others have shunned it. We try to fill this gap by taking on a *multi-theoretic* approach to explain what drives employers to get involved in employee health related behaviors.

Review, Theory, and Propositions

Strategic HRM part of the theory

Wolfe and colleagues' (1987) review of employer health management suggested that concern about health care costs should lead to strategic selection of health management programs that would affect individual outcomes like productivity and employee stability (lower turnover) among others. DeGroot and Kiker (2003) reiterated the argument that health management should be strategically designed to see any real impact. Yet very little of these ideas have been explicitly theorized about or tested since these reviews, and we still know next to nothing about the real reasons behind management adoption of health initiatives. What can shed more light on these reasons is the strategic HRM literature as it relates to employer health management. Although research on HRM does not directly explore the relationship between the extent employer resources are devoted to rewards and development and employer health management, this body of work has extensively addressed the direct barter relationship, or essentially a social exchange that occurs (as it relates to productivity or turnover) between employee and employers. We thus consider this literature to identify factors and specify relationships that may affect the link between commitment of resources and employer health management. Derived from what we do know about resources, employee characteristics, and organizational context, we depict our proposed model of these relationships in Figure 10-1 and Table 10-2.

First, we focus on the level of resources organizations commit to their employees (e.g., firm-specific training, high compensation, or recognition for achievement, Shaw, Dineen, Fang, & Vellella, 2009) and their relationship to ways employers get involved in affecting healthy behaviors or employer health management (our independent and dependent variables, respectively, see Figure 10-1). We do this because there is a long and substantial body of research in this literature suggesting that the level of employer resources devoted to rewarding and developing/training employees influences employee attitudes, productivity, and turnover (Becker & Huselid, 2006; Huselid, 1995; Lepak, Taylor, Tekleab, Marrone, & Cohen, 2007; Subramony, Krause, Norton, & Burns, 2008; A.S. Tsui, Pierce, Porter, & Tripoli, 1997; Tsui & Wu, 2005; Zhang, Tsui, Song, Li, & Jia, 2008). In the context of organizations and from the social exchange perspective, employers offer employees rewards (e.g., incentive pay programs, training) that can be seen as valuable by employees in return for efforts to achieve organizational objectives that benefit employers (Gould, 1979; Shaw, Dineen, Fang, & Vellella, 2009). Batt and Colvin (2011) recently showed how long-term investments are related to lower voluntary and involuntary turnover rates. Some of this literature investigates the employee-organization relationship and how it affects investments by employees as well as employers (Tsui & Wu, 2005; Zhang, et al., 2008), while other literature focuses on the benefits of employee investments (Lepak, et al., 2007; Tsui, et al., 1997). We build on this relevant work and further theorize about the implications of differences in HRM practices for employer health management.

Theoretically, Maertz and Griffeth (2004) show that investments in employees through high pay and training are a way to reduce uncertainty associated with low productivity and high turnover where the employer must continually have to attract, select and otherwise manage new employees that bring with them many unknowns with respect to ability, motivation, etc. Having a workforce of mostly long-term "known quantity" employees reduces these uncertainties. Consider Wal-Mart, which has been criticized in the past for providing little support in terms of

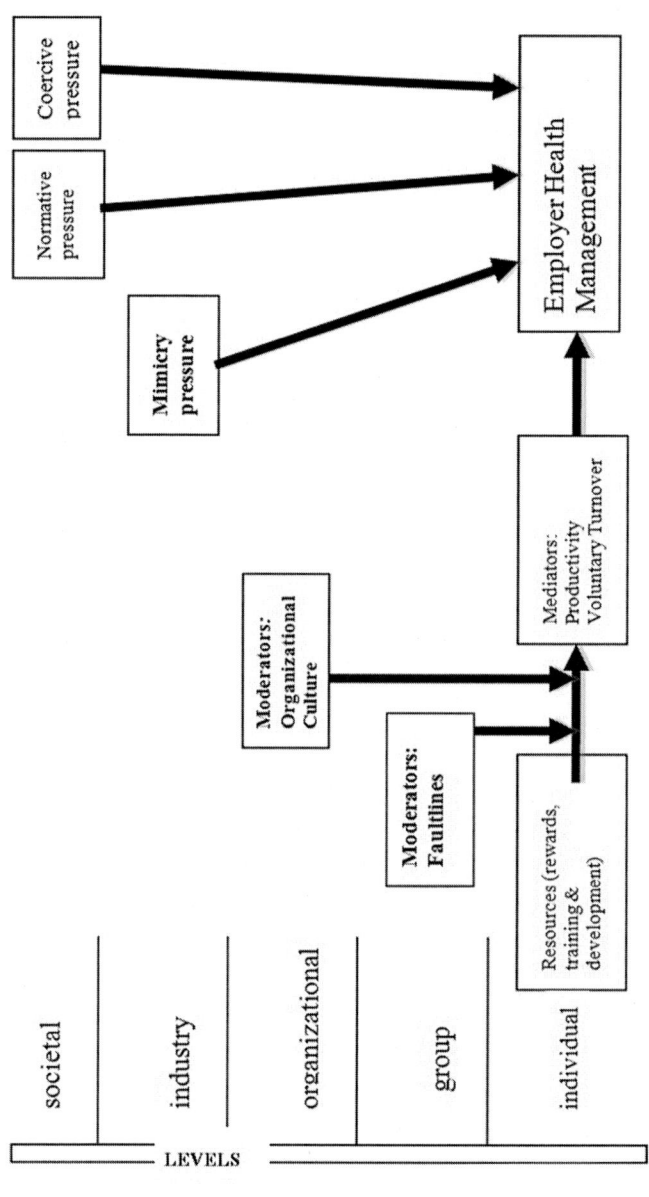

Figure 10-1. Relationships Depicted In The Framework On Employer Health Management. *Note.* Each variable box is placed at the respective analysis level. Individual level variables are based on strategic HRM literature. Group and organizational level variables are based on social psychological literature. Pressure variables are based on the institutional perspective.

Table 10-2: Relevant literatures and associated research questions/variables.

Literature	Research Question-Variable		Analysis Level
strategic HRM	IV: Resources		Individual
strategic HRM	Mediators:	Productivity	Individual
strategic HRM		Turnover	Individual
Organizational Psychology	Moderators:	Organizational culture	Organization
Organizational Psychology		Faultlines	Group
Sociology	External Factors:	Coercive pressures	Societal
		Mimicry pressures	Industry
Sociology		Normative pressures	Societal
	DV:	Employer management of HRBs	

health care or health promotion for employees (and in fact, encouraging them to seek government-sponsored health care, Zellner, 2005). This lack of involvement (at least at the time) is perhaps not surprising from a social exchange view given that their workforce is one of high turnover (44 percent annually) with relatively little training for most of their non-management employees. Contrast this with Costco, which is known for its low turnover (6 percent after the first year), relatively high pay compared to Wal-Mart, and extensive health benefits (Cascio, 2006). So, we expect that the more resources an employer puts into employees, especially rewarding and developing them (for instance, Google gives their employees credit points for being healthy), the more likely the employer will expect a longer term relationship with the employee (Shaw, et al., 2009) and consequently will be more interested in employees' personal health. Based on this, we propose:

> **Proposition 1** (P1): Organizations that put more resources to rewarding and developing employees will be more likely to get involved in health management.

Next, we turn our attention to prior research on organizational factors that may intervene in the connection between resources for rewards/development and employer health management. Prior research by Bernaki and Baun (1984) and Fielding (1982) as well as Wolfe et al. (1987) suggest that employer health management initiatives may be related to employee productivity. Thus, we investigate productivity in our model, defined as total outputs of employees (e.g., revenue, sales) divided by labor inputs (e.g., number of hours worked) (Samuelson & Nordhaus, 1989; Whitman, Van Rooy, & Viswesvaran, 2010). In a recent meta-analysis, Whitman and colleagues (2010) view productivity at the unit (e.g., establishment) level as a function of collective productivity of individual employees, and argue that unit level productivity is influenced by norms that originate in members of the workforce (e.g., we all work really hard to be productive), which translates into organizational productivity. Their analysis of over 5,000 work units from 60 studies established the relationships between collective job satisfaction, withdrawal behaviors, and other attitudes with productivity, yet the connection with employer health management has not been explored.

We extend this by proposing that reciprocation of employees for rewards and other valued resources from the employer will be related to enhanced productivity; in turn this will increase the likelihood the employer will try to influence employee HRBs. This is because employees who perceive that the ratio of organizational resources devoted to them (e.g., pay, training/development) to their own contributions is appropriate and fair will be more likely to commit to the organization (Hrebeniak & Alutto, 1972) and also be more productive (Arthur, 1994; Guthrie, Spell, & Nyamori, 2002; Huselid, 1995). Further, based on the widely held belief that healthier employees are more committed and productive (DeGroot & Kiker, 2003; Falkenberg, 1987; Liu, Wang, Zhan, & Shi, 2009; Manning, et al., 1989), making the effort to encourage healthy behaviors by employees would seem a key way to maintain and preserve productivity. Organizations with high levels of resources devoted to getting productive employees in the first place would be likewise interested in maintaining productivity through health management. So, based on this literature, we expect a relationship between the level of resources employers devote in rewarding and developing employees and employee productivity, which then leads to more involvement in health management of employees.

> **Proposition 2** (P2): Employee productivity will mediate the positive relationship between employer resources put into rewarding and developing employees and employer health management, such that the more resources committed, the higher the productivity, which will increase the likelihood to get involved in health management.

We next consider turnover since employer initiatives to influence health behaviors have been also been seen as a way to reduce turnover and absenteeism through attracting more health conscious employees and as a motivation for retention and attendance (Wolfe et al., 1987).

A wealth of research suggests that increased investment in employees through rewards and development is related to lower turnover (Arthur, 1994; Batt, 2002; Huselid, 1995; Osterman, 1987; Shaw, Delery, Jenkins, & Gupta, 1998; Trevor & Nyberg, 2008). Much of this research has investigated antecedents of turnover such as organizational politics (Chang, Rosen, & Levy, 2009), organizational change (Fugate, Kinicki, & Prussia, 2008; Trevor & Nyberg, 2008), employee personality traits (Zimmerman, 2008), and HR practices (Batt, 2002; Guthrie, 2001; Shaw & Gupta, 2007; Sun, Aryee, & Law, 2007). Yet, little research has explored organizational outcomes as a result of turnover outside of organizational performance (Kacmar, Andrews, Van Rooy, & Steilberg, 2006; Shaw, Duffy, Johnson, & Lockhart, 2005; Shaw, Gupta, & Delery, 2005) and even less considered how turnover might be related to employer involvement in health management. We thus, add to the literature by considering turnover's mediating role between employer resources and health management. Trevor and Nyberg (2008) suggested that turnover itself is a result of mismatch between what employees put in to the organization and what they get in return. We focus on voluntary turnover (the average annual percentage of employees leaving the organization on their volition, Guthrie, 2001; Huselid, 1995) because reduced voluntary turnover reflects feelings of commitment, and the urge to reciprocate arising from the exchange relationship between an organization and an employee.

We predict that organizations devoting a lot of resources to rewarding and developing/training employees demonstrate commitment to them; they would expect the employees to feel increased obligations to the employer, which would result in lower voluntary turnover. We further argue that organizations with low turnover will be more likely to engage in health management since more attention will be drawn to the issues of employee health. High turnover has been shown to cause organizations to neglect and draw resources away from concerns like maintenance and safety (Shaw, Duffy, et al., 2005; Shaw, Gupta, et al., 2005); it seems likely that dealing with high turnover also draws attention away from employee health issues, whereas low turnover organizations will direct more attention to health management. Further, employees in low turnover organizations are, on average, at the organization long enough for initiatives related to health management to have an impact and also be seen as cost beneficial for the company. For example, for an organization to sponsor a weight loss program, employees need to stay on after completing a program for a substantial period of time for a program to pay off (e.g., in reduced health care costs).

Proposition 3 (P3): Voluntary turnover will mediate the positive relationship between employer resources put into rewarding and developing employees and employer health management, such that the more resources committed, the less turnover, which will increase the likelihood to get involved in health management.

Psychology-based part of the theory

Research in organizational psychology provides insights into other potential drivers of health management programs. One of such drivers is organizational diversity and demographics such as age and gender makeup within an organization that can be related to collective health of employees (Wegge et al., 2008). For instance, membership in some social groups has been often linked to stereotypes about health (e.g., substance abuse problems among Russian males). While organizations are recognizing the importance of managing demographic diversity in many areas, including its implications for health (Bezrukova, Spell, & Perry, 2010), researchers have approached the topic of diversity with a wide array of theoretical interests, conceptualizations, and measurements both across and within various disciplines (e.g., Bezrukova, Jehn, Zanutto, & Thatcher, 2009; Bezrukova, Thatcher, & Jehn, 2007; Blau, 1977; Harrison & Klein, 2007; Joshi & Roh, 2009; Kanter, 1977; Pfeffer, 1983; Reskin, McBrier, & Kmec, 1999; Williams & O'Reilly, 1998). We do not attempt to resolve controversies around the numerous conceptualizations and operationalizations of diversity, but rather build on this prior work to offer one of the ways (among many others) to understand diversity's role in employer health management. Recognizing that many different demographic characteristics may potentially be at play in affecting employer involvement in health (e.g., gender, age of workforce, Spell & Bezrukova, 2010), we use the faultline perspective that considers multiple demographic characteristics (e.g., gender, race, age, socio-economic status, etc.) simultaneously (c.f., Bezrukova, Thatcher, & Jehn, 2007).

Drawing on social identity and social categorization theories (Tajfel, 1982; Tajfel & Turner, 1979) we argue that faultlines will be instrumental in understanding the decisions behind employers health management. Research suggests that, in fact, homogeneous subgroups resulting from faultlines can serve as a trigger for social categorization processes (Joshi & Roh, 2009) making stereotypes about people more salient. Such research suggests that consistent with this argument, stereotypes about health behaviors of certain subgroups may be triggered for managers of workforces that have faultlines, shaping the ways the organization gets involved in health of their employees. Such stereotypes may lead managers of say, a high-tech company in Silicon Valley that employs young Russian-descent male employees among others, to devote less effort to health promotion/assessment with respect to drinking behaviors. This is because they may feel the program may face too many challenges and a significant portion of employees will be unlikely to respond with desired behaviors given that some forms of substance use can be culturally required in some groups (Oetting, Donnermeyer, Trimble, & Beauvais, 1998). In contrast, a company with a very diverse workforce (no strong faultlines) would not trigger these stereotypes and managers would be more likely to believe their efforts at managing health will be fruitful.

Proposition 4 (P4): Faultlines will moderate the relationship between employer resources put into rewarding and developing employees and employee health management, such that the positive relationship will remain when the workforce has no faultlines and be weaker when the workforce has strong faultlines.

An important assumption in psychological research is that situational or contextual features have a powerful impact on people. One aspect of the contextual environment that can shape employee behavior in organizations is organizationally-based cultures. For example, Neely (2012) has noted the significance of a culture of health as part of business strategy and a correlate to effectively implementing health promotion programs. Culture refers to a set of norms and values that are widely shared and strongly held by a group of people (Chatman & Barsade, 1995; O'Reilly & Chatman, 1996). In conceptualizing organization-based cultures it is important to consider the content of a culture (Chatman & Jehn, 1994; O'Reilly, Chatman, & Caldwell, 1991). For instance, organization-based cultures may reflect preferred ways to perform group tasks such as being innovative, career-oriented, people-oriented, or outcome-oriented (e.g., Jehn, 1994; Jehn & Bezrukova, 2004; O'Reilly, et al., 1991). Of particular interest for our study is a culture with a health orientation that emphasizes the extent to which employee health is valued in an organization (Abbott, 2008).

Although a culture emphasizing healthy employees has been examined as a strategy for higher revenues and enhanced earnings (Abbott, 2008), no research to our knowledge has looked at how a culture of health can shape the connection between organizational resources and employer health management. However, connections between work context and employer health management have been established. For example, organizational level work family support was related to work-family support from supervisors, which could include health-related aspects (Kossek, Pichler, Bodner, & Hammer, in press). Frone and Brown (2010) showed that workplace social norms on drinking and drug use predicted actual substance use and impairment both before and during work. More directly related to health promotion interventions, Sorensen (2009) found that work environment was related to individual smoking behavior and participation in health promotion programs. We extend this research on work context to include more specific cultural perspectives relevant to health. As an illustration of how a culture of health may be recognized, consider two universities of roughly the same size, both research-oriented. At one, we observed the frequency of mass emails to staff sent (multiple times a week) about availability of organic foods to staff for pick up on the campus, regular stress-reduction and wellness seminars, and other fitness related programs. At the other university, over a span of an entire semester we observed no similar wellness or health related messages (nor were printed materials distributed to staff).

Based on social identity and social categorization theories (Tajfel,

1982; Tajfel & Turner, 1979), researchers posit that organizational culture can serve as a common frame of reference (Boisnier & Chatman, 2003) providing common, shared, and aligned goals and expectations with respect to employee health. When organizational culture emphasizes healthy behaviors, organizations that put resources into their employees will pay more attention to health-related issues and will act in ways consistent with the respective cultural values. By reinforcing positive views of health and rewarding health-related behaviors (O'Reilly & Chatman, 1996), organizations with a culture emphasizing health will be even more likely to allocate efforts directed towards employees' health if employer resources are already put into rewarding and developing employees. In contrast, when organizational culture has a little emphasis on health, goals and expectations are not dedicated to health, there is little impetus for organizations to leverage their resources and align any effort towards health-related initiatives or get involved in health management.

Proposition 5 (P5): Organizational culture will moderate the relationship between resources put into rewarding and developing employees and employer health management, such that as the positive relationship will be stronger when organizational culture has a strong emphasis on health and this relationship will be weaker when organizational culture has a weak emphasis on health.

Sociology-based part of the theory

Finally, we consider employer interests regarding health behavior as they relate to interests of entities outside the organization. Wolfe et al. (1987) have observed that societal norms and institutional pressure is a major trigger for the adoption of employer initiatives to manage employees' health behaviors, yet, this relationship has never been developed in subsequent research since Wolfe et al's model. So, we turn our attention to sociology literature grounded in institutional theory. While there is not a wealth of literature adopting institutional perspectives on employer health management specifically, research has examined various aspects of workplace health from an institutional framework, including management's response to factors outside the organization that has implications for employee health. For example, in their conceptual framework, Sorensen et al. (2011) noted that the interface between communities and an organizational (in addition to work an family connections) was a critical component of advancing employee health. Pomeranz (2011) describes how public agencies, especially local health departments, have institutional power to influence both regulations (e.g., menu requirements on food) and other legislation to reduce obesity among the population. In a contrasting perspective on institutional power, Anarci, Escaleras, and Register (2009) found that corruption in public institutions was related (negatively) to and access to drinking water and sanitation in an Indian context. Other institutional work has investigated managed health care and how employer goals are communicated in this context (Castel & Fredberg, 2010; Barbour & Lammers, 2007). Yet no research has attempted to explain the adoption of employer initiatives to manage employees' health using institutional perspectives. .

In their development of institutional theory, DiMaggio and Powell (1983) proposed that organizations often act in response to pressures associated with societal norms, government, and professional groups–all of which have become intensely involved in the issue of employee health in recent years. To build on this literature and apply the institutional view to employer health initiatives and management, we further focus on types of pressures that are major tenets of institutional theory and are critical to our model (e.g., coercive, mimicry, normative) and their influence on employer health management.

Coercive pressures are forces exerted on organizations by other organizations upon which they are dependent (DiMaggio & Powell, 1983). As such, coercive pressure is based on the perceived ability to punish an influence target for failing to comply with the focal actor's interests, which in this case would be compliance with some directive (Raven, Schwartzwald, & Koslowsky, 1998). Coercive pressure may thus result from laws, regulations or other directives exerted on organizations. In other words, organizations strive to align their own activities with legal directives from significant stakeholders (e.g., regulatory agencies). Edleman and Suchman (1997) note that under coercive pressure, organizations act because the law commands them to do so and imposes sanctions for noncompliance. Past research has shown that coercive pressures have been at play in influencing organizations to adopt financial electronic data exchange technology (Teo, Wei, & Benhasat, 2003), force change in company strategy (Westphal & Bednar, 2008), and legitimize employee claims to fair treatment (Edelman, 1990; Edelman & Suchman, 1997).

Similarly, turning to our construct of employer health management, while there are many regulations on organizations concerning the administration of health insurance depending on the national system of health care followed, up to this point little direct pressure has been put on business to get engaged in health management of employees. However, as an example, some of the recently approved regulations in the U.S. with respect to national health care reform may require many employers to provide health insurance, impose new regulations in the form of insurance plans such as reduced co-payments for preventive health screenings or require coverage for preventive health and, importantly, create a regulatory environment that legitimizes employer efforts at contributing to a healthy workforce. For example, new provisions there require employers with over 50 employees to provide time for new mothers to express, or pump, breast milk since breastfed babies are thought to have less risk for many diseases (Pear, 2010b). These changes likely increase pressure on organizations to align their management action with these directives and become more involved in the health of their employees. While the such federal laws have gotten the most attention recently, many states have their own separate regulations or may even chose to enforce these regulations differentially. Generally, this means that differences in state or national regulations, and how regulations might apply to different industries, may differentially exert coercive pressure on individual organizations. Overall, we consider coercive pressures as an important predictor of organizational management of employee health.

> **Proposition 6** (P6): Organizations will be more likely to engage in health management when coercive pressures with respect to employee health are high.

Mimetic pressures are defined as forces that cause an organization to change over time to become more like other organizations in its environment (DiMaggio & Powell, 1983). Mimetic pressure can result when uncertainty about valued outcomes (e.g., organizational productivity, employee turnover) causes organizations to imitate other firms (DiMaggio & Powell, 1983), producing a bandwagon effect (Tolbert & Zucker, 1983). Here, modeling the organization's practices or programs with others like them is a way to reduce this uncertainty. For example, Goodstein (1994) suggested that organizations are more likely to adopt childcare services when they are the established norm within their industry and, in a separate study, found employers closely connected with other organizations who had eldercare programs were more likely to adopt similar programs (Goodstein, 1995).

Other research has shown that organizations may adopt practices like EAPs and drug testing when the proportion of organizations within their industry or labor market that have already adopted the practices is high (Spell & Blum, 2005). All of these findings are consistent with a key assertion of institutional theory that claims concern over legitimacy leads organizations to align their practices with other organizations to which they compare themselves. Thus, if enough organizations in the same industry or labor market adopt practices that try to encourage healthy employee behavior, organizations without them may feel pressure to align their efforts with those of others by likewise adopting the programs or practices. This means organizations are more likely to engage in health management if there are firms in their local labor market that have already done so, or if many in their industry have adopted practices connected to health-related behaviors.

Proposition 7 (P7): Organizations will be more likely to engage in health management when mimicry pressures with respect to employee health are high.

Finally, normative pressures are defined as powerful influences through media or other stakeholders (e.g., professional organizations, trade associations) on organizations to act in concert with accepted business practices (DiMaggio & Powell, 1991). DiMaggio and Powell (1991) suggested that organizations adopt new practices consistent and aligned with the norms and values of other organizations and key stakeholders. Such pressures are also connected with efforts to appear legitimate and progressive. Building on these ideas, we are interested in understanding whether normative pressures such as media discourse play a part in the likelihood of employer health management. Prior work on normative pressures related to HRM practices has established connections between this pressure and internal labor markets (e.g., Dobbin, Sutton, Meyer, & Scott, 1993), however its connection with organizational involvement in employee HRBs has been largely overlooked.

We build and extend this work by theorizing about how normative pressures at the societal level through, for example, discourse in industry trade publications can influence employer action regarding employee HRBs. Based on the neo-institutional view, media and other sources place normative pressures on managers to align their practices with societal expectations (Abrahamson, 1996; Abrahamson & Fairchild, 1999). Further, to appear legitimate and progressive, organizations can respond to increased normative pressure by acting on those pressures and engage in health management. For instance, Spell & Blum (2005) found that media discourse on workplace substance abuse was related to future likelihood of employer adoption of drug testing and EAPs in a U.S. sample. As an illustration, subsequent to extensive media coverage of their business practices with respect to health benefits, Wal-Mart engaged in a public relations campaign to revamp its reputation as an employer by touting how many of its employees have health insurance and other employee health benefits among other efforts to improve its public standing (Zimmerman,

2009). This case illustrates the importance of considering the role of normative pressures from the environment in explaining the variability in employer health management.

> **Proposition 8** (P8): Organizations will be more likely to engage in health management when normative pressures with respect to employee health are high.

Discussion and Implications

Health care costs are rapidly increasing globally. Among OECD countries, health care spending is rising faster than overall economic growth, taking a bigger percentage of gross domestic product (GDP) over time (OECD, 2011). Yet, while organizations attempt to respond to this important economic issue by offering a variety of health initiatives, organizational scientists are way behind in their understanding of employer health management. A major gap in current organizational science is a lack of knowledge about what drives employers to sponsor initiatives that are not directly work-related, often costly, or have no apparent evidence of success. This is a complex problem that has received attention from multiple disciplines. Yet, as has been observed in National Science Foundation workshops on multi-disciplinary research (Paletz, Smith-Doerr, & Vardi, 2010), studies that are restricted to one perspective or unit of analysis do not lend themselves to comparison with research outside that perspective. We thus approach this problem by integrating the literature from strategic human resource management (HRM), organizational psychology, and sociology to develop a novel framework on management action associated with employee health.

Theoretical Contributions

First, from the micro-level perspective, the association of employee rewards and development-related practices to employer health management is made through a *social exchange* framework. We argued that productivity and turnover will explain the employee-organizational exchange relationship as it relates to health. The exchange relationship as driven by employer investments in human resources has been supported by a wealth of previous research (e.g., Guthrie, 2001; Huselid, 1995) in showing how the employer resources are related to productivity and turnover. But our model extends these findings to show how employers who have a committed workforce as an outcome of the exchange relationship would in turn be more likely to proactively try to affect employee health behavior. In this sense, micro-level theory on social exchange contributes to our understanding of management action with respect to employee health and can lead to specific, testable hypotheses.

Second, from the macro-level perspective, we built on the institutional perspective to model how external political and industry level forces further shape individual employer responses. We pointed out additional implications of the *institutional* predictions, especially those that deal with the role of media discourse and dissemination of information about health management. This perspective suggests it is not just the act of an organization encouraging healthy behaviors or providing health screenings that is important, but also how it is portrayed in the media. For instance, our rationale behind tone of discourse suggests that whether health screening is portrayed as benefit valued by employees , or an invasion of privacy (Conlin, 2007), the tone of such discourse would be critical in terms of pressure on other firms to try to shape employee health. We argued that positive anecdotes or other attention in the media would be a key driver of further adoption of such practices. These macro-level processes contribute to our understanding of how stakeholders and forces external to the organization can shape management's decisions on how, and to what extent, an organization gets involved in health management

Third, integrating theoretical perspectives at both levels, we use social identity and categorization perspectives to show how diverse constructs (e.g., demographic faultlines and organizational culture focused on health) at the group and establishment levels can serve as boundary conditions to the resources-health management link. For example, we argued that the relationship between organizational resources and health management would be moderated by demographic faultlines and the organizational culture of health. This means that exchange relationships that have proven so powerful in predicting turnover and productivity, do not act alone, but interact to explain what actually happens within and across organizations with respect to influencing employee health behavior. There has been some research that focused on resource dependence and institutional perspectives in explaining organizational response to work-family issues and other employee benefits (e.g., Goodstein, 1994; Ingram & Simons, 1995). We extend this work by specifying the processes by which the variability in involvement across organizations can be explained with respect to employee health management.

Thus, this research identifies key factors that can predict what drives a largely overlooked but transformative construct – employer management of employee behaviors related to personal health that is at the crux of very salient economic and social problems. In doing so, we point out where we can begin to understand the motivations behind efforts to shape health behaviors. As an example, to the extent in which external forces like media push organizations to shape employee health in a positive direction, this indicates an attempt to appear as a 'good place to work' to potential and current employees. The workforce characteristics predict whether and how an employer attempts to influence health behaviors (demographics) may indicate that organizations are driven by simple exchange relationships in preserving their economic investment in their labor. A well-designed empirical test of the relationships proposed here would likely move us closer to understanding the forces driving employer involvement.

Empirical Considerations

There are several directions that empirical research could take to move forward our understanding of employer health management. Perhaps the most relevant at this point is the development of a valid scale of the extent employers are engaged in health management. One approach is to conduct a study based on archival file data collection based on organizational websites and interviews with organizational representatives (e.g., benefits managers, line managers, and employees). Through this data collection, one could develop a comprehensive list of up-to-date health-related organizational initiatives. A valid and reliable measurement approach to operationalizing employer health management based on recent developments in latent class cluster analysis (LCCA) (see DiStefano & Kamphaus, 2006) could be further considered and compared with previous approaches to assess employer involvement such as summary measures that count number of initiatives (Goodstein, 1995). Using this measurement approach, one could include multiple methodologies and multiple data sources to develop a valid measurement system to test our full model (see Figure 10-1 and Table 10-2). Using different formats (i.e., interviews, surveys, content analysis of annual reports and websites), one could ensure that no valuable data are lost and, following recommendations in the psychometric literature (e.g., Ghiselli, Campbell, & Zedeck, 1981; Hinkin, 1998), one would be able to develop more accurate and complete measures that capture the full domain of the conceptual definitions, operationalized constructs, and levels of analysis.

In addition to defining constructs, in any empirical study there would be relevant sampling considerations and boundary conditions. For instance, it would be important to distinguish self-insured companies from those that do not self-insure. Companies that self-insure have much stronger incentives to try to affect employee health than ones not self-insuring and may be a significant factor in the decision to offer programs like wellness initiatives.

Another consideration for empirical testing is the temporal nature of employer health management itself. Clearly, as we have pointed out in Table 10-1, employer approaches to health management have changed over time. Thus, any empirical efforts at testing the model should consider a longitudinal approach; perhaps through event history analysis of the adoption of particular employer initiatives. Another reason we urge longitudinal efforts in any empirical testing is the dynamic nature of most of the study variables we have presented as well as work characteristics. For example, technological changes in the contemporary workplace may be influencing the psychological health of employees in ways that are not well understood. Despite the growing prevalence of virtual teams and telecommuting resulting in less face-to face social interaction, there is little research on the prevalence and impact of isolation on virtual employees. While the negative psychological outcomes of isolation associated with virtual work have been noted (Anderson & Anderson, 2003), others claim that virtual work may enhance social support and development of relationships (Walther, 1995). Thus, while the effect of these changes, especially on employee psychological health, is not known, this may have relevance for how involved an employer wants to be in managing employee health.

A Research Agenda

We have focused in this paper on the reasons why employers try to encourage individuals to adopt and maintain behaviors related to reduced risk for many diseases. From reviewing the research, the model we propose to explain employer actions has, however, wider implications for the overall issue of employee health management. We have already established how some employers might offer a wide range of services designed to get employees to modify health behaviors (e.g., health promotion, health assessment, education) other employers do not. But while some employees would potentially use such programs in their workplace if offered, (and among individuals is a subset of whose experience actually prevents some diseases) other people find they are not available in their workplace and can not therefore benefit. For these people, their organization might have chosen to not adopt such programs or otherwise try to influence health behavior due to lack of evidence-based return on their investment, lack of use/interest by employees in prior efforts, or lack of resources.

Synthesizing the above observations, there is a subset of employees that would benefit (through reduced risk of disease) that actually would embrace efforts by employers to get them to improve health behaviors. There is, at the same time, a subset of employers willing to invest in such efforts and pursue efforts to influence employees to engage in behaviors that reduce health related risks. While there is very little empirical evidence about the extent these subsets overlap, it seems clear there is a mismatch between the interests of individual employees (e.g., the extent they, individually desire and are motivated to enhance/maintain health) and interests of employees (e.g., desire to control health costs through preventive measures, and/or convey to stakeholders they are proactive in promoting healthy behavior). To the extent that these interests are not aligned, there is inefficiency in organizational health promotion and health management efforts. Future research should continue, as we have in this paper, to focus on the employer decision to try to influence and manage health behaviors (since that decision must first happen in order to gauge the efficacy of such employer efforts). But at the same time, more attention should also be given to how organizational needs and goals compare to the motivation and goals of individual employees to participate (or, if the programs are mandatory, how they would react to such initiatives). An integration of theories on individual and organizational level will need to be done to understand the employer's role and further develop our framework of employer health management.

There are many other open questions related to understanding the employer's role in influencing health-behaviors, and how that role aligns with employee interests. Here we outline some topics that the present state of knowledge would be fruitful for exploration.

Changes over time. Much of the research on employer rationale for promoting healthy behavior treats it as a static phenomena. In reality, it seems almost certain that as a firm's makeup of the workforce, context or working environment, or human resource strategy changes, its focus on health behaviors of employees will change too. Since a great deal of research shows that these factors are in fact dynamic, including those related to health behaviors (Nielsen et al., 2006), it would suggest that those interested in studying employer health management treat the perspective we have developed here (or whatever perspective they use) as a dynamic one and adopt temporal models to apply to the health behavior issue.

Employee interests in health behaviors. One of the authors knows an executive in the trucking industry who related how he tried to get truckers to adopt healthier eating habits. This executive became known as the 'fruit guy' by the truckers since he arranged for fresh fruits to be on hand at morning meetings instead of the traditional doughnuts. He noted the cultural expectations and how difficult they were to overcome in altering health behaviors of his employees. Yet, similar stories may be told of other industries and firms- the relationship between employer and employee interests we have explored in our model may to a great extent depend on how motivated individual employee are to embrace particular health behaviors. The vast literature on change and inertia (Ford, Ford, & D'Amelio, 2008) may be very relevant in how it applies to understanding the employee incentives to do what their firm encourages them to do with respect to personal behaviors and are not explicitly part of tasks and jobs.

Interventions. Employer interventions in the realm of health assessment and promotion can mean anything from informally encouraging good eating habits (fresh fruit in a employee lounge) to incentives for healthy behavior, stress management classes, to wide-scale health monitoring programs and on-site exercise facilities. One of the outstanding issues with respect to how certain organizational interventions might impact both business and individual outcomes is the range of interventions making up health management almost certainly means a range of outcomes and effects. Small (in cost) interventions may or may not) yield affects very different from those involving large capital outlays such as exercise gyms, comprehensive health monitoring of all employees, and similar initiatives. In fact, it has been found that simple prompts for individuals to engage in some activity (e.g., take some relaxation time, go get a flu shot) may be the most effective strategy of all in changing health behavior (Lanesh, Dey, Srivastava, & Figler, 2011; Research shows, 2011). In a recent review, (Nielsen, Randall, Holten, & Gonzalez, 2010) describe employee health and well-being interventions through job and work redesign. While approaches such as Risk Management, Management Standards, Health Circles, Work Positive and Prevenlab have common elements they have to date not been validated. We have barely begun to tease out these effects and get a sense of what types of interventions get the biggest "bang for the buck" in terms of health care cots, long term employee health and stress reduction, and other beneficial effects.

Industry level and cultural influences. Prior research has demonstrated the influence media exerts on organizational adoption of initiatives related to work process (Abrahamson & Fairchild, 1999) and in fact, aspects of behavioral health (e.g.., substance abuse treatment, Spell & Blum, 2005).

Yet, much more remains to be learned about not only media influence on organizational efforts related to health management but industry level effects in the form of mimicry pressures (Dimaggio & Powell, 1991) on firms to copy what competitors are doing, and pressure to align with normative standards in their industry (Goodstein, 1994). Also, while employers are not legally mandated to directly influence health behaviors of employees, the government's role in encouraging and healthy behaviors should not be overlooked, no matter which nation hosts the employer. Employers who perceive that the government holds health behaviors as a priority might be likely to demonstrate compliance with this priority (among others) to gain favor from the state in matters regarding employment regulations and other issues (Edelman, 1990). One agenda item along these lines could be to consider the interaction of media influence with governmental action regarding health behaviors, since rarely have these two potential drivers of management action been considered together in the same study. Also, the role of industry changes and technological innovation on involvement in health behaviors has been almost untouched by researchers. The rapid expansion of drug testing of employees and applicants (as well as rehabilitation programs for drug users) expanded in the 1980's in the United States may have been aided by the availability of cheap technologies and laboratories for collecting and testing the samples, even as the accuracy of those technologies were called into question (Spell & Blum, 2005). Similarly, the recent availability of personal devices that monitor health and vital indicators (blood pressure and heart rate) among other information makes assessment and tracking of such data feasible by employers and employees and may continue to grow in popularity as the makers of these devices market them to business (Panel Discussion, 2011).

Conclusion

We have several hopes for the lines of research reviewed here. We hope that this body of research, and empirical tests that arise from it, will help the public sector in the development of health policy as many policy implications involve preventive health and employer roles connected to health behavior (details depending on the national context and other factors). We also hope this will inspire more innovative study on the implications of employer health management, an assessment of evidence-based interventions on long-term employee health and ultimately, the implications for health care costs. So, hopefully the ideas expressed in this paper and potential empirical results arising from it will ultimately lead to a more informed response to the increasing burden of health care costs. Recent developments in the public and political sector in the U.S. connected to health care, as well as increasing health costs across most developed countries, mean that the employer's role in health expenses of working adults is likely to continue to develop, and this has intensified attention to individual behavior as a way to control long-term health care costs. As a result, the employers' role in promoting and regulating employee health-related behaviors may expand (or at least be a salient issue within many organizations). This makes studying how employers respond a potentially very fruitful area for management research. This paper is therefore a plea for management scholars to build on the research presented here, and consider focusing more attention upon employer health management and efforts to influence health-related behaviors.

References

Abbott, R. K. (2008). Creating a culture of health: A value-driven strategy for organizational success. *Journal of Compensation & Benefits, 24,* 28-33.

Abrahamson, E. (1996). Management Fashion. *Academy of Management Review,* 21, 254-285.

Abrahamson, E., & Fairchild, G. (1999). Management fashions: Lifecycles, triggers, and collective learning processes. *Administrative Science Quarterly,* 44, 708-740.

Aldana, S. (2001, May-June). Financial impact of health promotion programs: A comprehensive review of the literature. *American Journal of Health Promotion, 15*(5), 296-320.

Anbarci,N. Escaleras, M., & Register. C. (2009). The 111 Effects of Public Sector Corruption in the Water and Sanitation Sector. *Land Economics,* 85, 363-377

Armstrong, D. (2009). Origins of the problems of health-related behaviors: A genealogical study. *Social Studies of Science,* 39, 909-926.

Arthur, J. (1994). Effects of human resource systems on manufacturing performance and turnover. *Academy of Management Journal,* 37, 670-687.

Barbour, J., & Lammers, J. (2007). Health Care Institutions, Communication, and Physicians' Experience of Managed Care. *Management Communication Quarterly, 21,*201-231.

Batt, R. (2002). Managing customer services: Human resource practices, quit rates, and sales growth. *Academy of Management Journal,* 45, 587-597.

Becker, B., & Huselid, M. (2006). Strategic human resources management: Where do we go from here? *Journal of Management, 32,* 898-925.

Bernacki, E.J., & Baun. W.B.1984. The relationship of job performance o exercise adherence in a corporate fitness program. *Journal of Occupational Medicine, 26.,* 529-531.

Bezrukova, K., Jehn, K. A., Zanutto, E., & Thatcher, S. M. B. (2009). Do workgroup faultlines help or hurt? A moderated model of faultlines, team identification, and group performance. *Organization Science,* 20(1), 35-50.

Bezrukova, K., Spell, C. S., & Perry, J. (2010). Coping with injustice: Faultlines and mental health in diverse workgroups. *Personnel Psychology, 63,* 727-759.

Bezrukova, K., Thatcher, S. M. B., & Jehn, K. A. (2007). Group heterogeneity and faultlines: Comparing alignment and dispersion theories of group composition. In K. J. Behfar & L. L. Thompson (Eds.), *Conflict in Organizational Groups: New Directions in Theory and Practice* (pp. 57-92). Evanston, IL: The Northwestern University Press.

Blau, P. (1977). *Inequality and composition: A primitive theory of social structure.* New York, NY: Free Press.

Bly J, Jones, R.C., and Richardson, J.E., (1986). Impact of Worksite Health Promotion on Health Care Costs and Utilization: Evaluation of Johnson & Johnson's Live for Life Program. *Journal of the American Medical Association,* 256: 3235–3240.

Boisnier, A., & Chatman, J. A. (2003). The role of subcultures in agile organizations. In R. Peterson & E. A. Mannix (Eds.), *Leading and managing people in dynamic organizations* (pp. 87-112). Mahwah, NJ: Earlbaum.

Brief, A.P., Butcher, A.H., George, J.M., & Link, K.E. 1993. Integrating bottom-up and top-down theories of subjective well-being: The case of health. *Personality and Social Psychology, 64,* 646-653.

Butler, M. & Teagarden, M. 1993. Strategic management of worker health, safety, and environmental issues in Mexico's *Maquiladora* industry. *Human Resource Management, 32,* 479-503.

Cascio, W. F. (2006). Decency means more than "Always low prices": A comparison of Costco to Walmart's Sam's Club. *Academy of Management Perspectives,* 20(3), 26-37.

Castel, P., & Friedberg, E. (2010). Institutional Change as an Interactive Process: The Case of the Modernization of the French Cancer Centers. *Organization Science,* 21, 311–330.

Chang, C. H., Rosen, C. C., & Levy, P. E. (2009). The relationship between perceptions of organizational politics and employee attitudes, strain and behavior: A meta-analytic examination. *Academy of Management Journal, 52*(4), 779-801.

Chatman, J. A., & Barsade, S. G. (1995). Personality, organizational culture and cooperation: Evidence from a business simulation. *Administrative Science Quarterly, 40,* 423-443.

Chatman, J. A., & Jehn, K. A. (1994). Assessing the relationship between industry characteristics and organizational culture: How different can you be? *Academy of Management Journal, 37*(3), 522-553.

Cox, T., Karanika, M., Griffths, A., & Houdmont, J. (2007). Evaluating organization-level work stress interventions: Beyond traditional methods. *Work & Stress, 21,* 348-362.

Danna, K., & Griffin, R. (1999). Health and Well-being in the workplace: A review and synthesis of the literature. *Journal of Management, 25,* 357-384.

DeGroot, T., & Kiker, S. (2003). A meta- analysis of the non-monetary effects of employee health management programs. *Human Resource Management, 42,* 53-69.

DiMaggio, P., & Powell, W. (1983). The iron cage revisited: Institutional isomorphism and collective rationality in organizational fields. *American Sociological Review, 48,* 147-160.

DiMaggio, P., & Powell, W. (1991). *The new institutionalism in organizational analysis.* Chicago, IL: University of Chicago Press.

Dobbin, F., Sutton, J. R., Meyer, J. W., & Scott, W. R. (1993). Equal opportunity law and the construction of internal labor markets. *American Journal of Sociology, 99,* 396-427.

Edelman, L. B. (1990). Legal environments and organizational governance: The expansion of due process in the American workplace. *American Journal of Sociology, 95,* 1401-1440.

Edelman, L. B., & Suchman, M. C. (1997). The legal environment of organizations. *Annual Review of Sociology, 23,* 479-515.

Erfurt, J. C., Foote, A., & Heirich, M. A. (1992). The cost-effectiveness of worksite wellness programs for hypertension, control, weight loss, smoking cessation, and exercise. *Personnel Psychology, 45,* 5-27.

Falkenberg, L. E. (1987). Employee fitness programs: Their impact on the employee and the organization. *Academy of Management Review, 12,* 511-522.

Fielding, J. 1982. Effectiveness of health improvement programs. *Journal of Occupational Medicine, 24,* 907-916.

Ford, J. D.; Ford, L. W. & D'Amelio, A. (2008). Resistance to change: The rest of the story..*Academy of Management Review*, 33, 362-377

Fugate, M., Kinicki, A. J., & Prussia, G. P. (2008). Employee coping with organizational change: An examination of alternative theoretical perspectives and models. *Personnel Psychology*, 61, 1-36.

Gebhard, D. L., & Crump, C. E. (1990). Employee fitness and wellness programs in the workplace. *American Psychologist*, 45, 262-272.

Ghiselli, E. E., Campbell, J. P., & Zedeck, S. (1981). *Measurement theory for the behavioral sciences*. San Francisco, CA: W.H.Freeman.

Gibson, C. B., & Zellmer-Bruhn, M. E. (2001). Metaphors and meaning: An intercultural analysis of the concept of teamwork. *Administrative Science Quarterly*, 46, 274-303.

Goodstein, J. (1994). Institutional pressures and strategic responsiveness: Employer involvement in work-family issues. *Academy of Management Journal*, 37, 350-382.

—. (1995). Employer involvement in eldercare: an organizational adaptation perspective. *Academy of Management Journal*, 38, 1657-1167.

Gould, S. (1979). An equity-exchange model of organizational involvement. *Academy of Management Review*, 4, 53-62.

Gurt, J., Schwennen, C., & Elke, G., (2011). Health-specific leadership: Is there an association between leader consideration for the health of employees and their strain and well-being? *Work & Stress*, 25, 108-127.

Guthrie, J. (2001). High-involvement work practices, turnover, and productivity: Evidence from New Zealand. *Academy of Management Journal*, 44, 180-190.

Guthrie, J., Spell, C., & Nyamori, O. (2002). Correlates and consequences of high involvement work practices: the role of competitive strategy. *International Journal of Human Resource Management*, 13, 183-197.

Hall, B. (2008). Health Incentives: The science and art of motivating healthy behaviors. *Benefits Quarterly*, 21(2), 12-22.

Harrison, D. A., & Klein, K. J. (2007). What's the difference? Diversity constructs as separation, variety, or disparity in organizations. *Academy of Management Review*, 32(4), 1199-1228.

Harrison, D. A., & Liska, L. Z. (1994). Promoting regular exercise in organizational fitness programs: Health-related differences in motivational building blocks. *Personnel Psychology*, 47, 47-71.

Hinkin, T. R. (1998). A brief tutorial on the development of measures for use in questionnaires. *Organizational Research Methods*, 1, 104-121.

Hrebeniak, L. G., & Alutto, J. A. (1972). Personal and role-related factors in the development of organizational commitment. *Administrative Science Quarterly,* 17, 555-573.

Huselid, M. (1995). The impact of human resource management practices on turnover, productivity, and corporate financial performance. *Academy of Management Journal,* 38, 635-672.

Jehn, K. A. (1994). Enhancing effectiveness: An investigation of advantages and disadvantages of value-based intragroup conflict. *International Journal of Conflict Management,* 5(3), 223-238.

Jehn, K. A., & Bezrukova, K. (2004). A field study of group diversity, group context, and performance. *Journal of Organizational Behavior,* 25(6), 703-729.

Joshi, A., & Roh, H. (2009). The role of context in work team diversity research: A meta-analytic review. *Academy of Management Journal,* 52(3), 599-627.

Kacmar, K. M., Andrews, M. C., Van Rooy, D. L., & Steilberg, R. C. (2006). Sure everyone can be replaced ... but at what cost? Turnover as a predictor of unit-level performance. *Academy of Management Journal,* 49(1), 133–144.

Kanter, R. (1977). *Men and Women of the Corporation.* New York, NY: Basic Books.

Kossek, E., & Block, R. (1993). The employer as social arbiter: Considerations in limiting involvement in off-the-job behavior. *Employee Responsibilities and Rights Journal,* 6, 139-155.

Lanese, B.S., Dey, D., Srivastava, P., & Figler, R. (2011). Introducing the Health Coach at Primary Care Practice: Impact on Quality and Cost (Part 1). Hospital Topics, 89(1):16–22.

Lepak, D. P., Taylor, M. S., Tekleab, A. G., Marrone, J. A., & Cohen, D. J. (2007). An examination of the use of high-investment human resource systems for core and support employees. *Human Resource Management,* 46, 223-246.

Liu, S., Wang, M., Zhan, Y., & Shi, J. (2009). Daily work stress and alcohol use: Testing the cross-level moderation effects of neuroticism and job involvement. *Personnel Psychology,* 62, 575-597.

Macik-Frey, M., Quick, J. C., & Nelson, D. (2007). Advances in occupational health: From a stressful beginning to a positive future. *Journal of Management,* 33, 809-840.

Maertz, C. P., & Griffeth, R. W. (2004). Eight motivational forces and voluntary turnover: A theoretical synthesis with implications for research. *Journal of Management,* 30, 667-683.

Manning, M. R., Osland, J. S., & Osland, A. (1989). Work-related consequences of smoking cessation. *Academy of Management Journal,* 32, 606-621.

Marchington, M., Rubery, J., & Grimshaw, D. (2011). Alignment, integration, and consistency in HRM across multi-employer networks. *Human Resource Management, 50,* 313–339

Marshall, J., & Heffes, E. (2004). Health and Productivity Programs More Common. *Financial Executive,* 20(7), 11-12.

Mikkelson, A., Saksvik, P. O., & Landsbergis, P. (2000). The impact of participatory organizational intervention on job stress in community health institutions. *Work & Stress,* 14, 156-170.

Neely, M. (2012). Wellness Strategies for Smaller Businesses. *Benefits Quarterly, 28(3),* 16-19.

Nielsen, K., Fredslund, H., Christensen, K. B., & Albertsen, K. (2006). Success or failure? Interpreting and understanding the impact of interventions in four similar worksites. *Work & Stress,* 20, 272-287.

Oetting, E., Donnermeyer, J. F., Trimble, J. E., & Beauvais, F. (1998). Primary socialization theory: Culture, ethnicity, and cultural identification. The links between culture and substance use. *Substance Use & Misuse,* 33(10), 2075-2107.

O'Reilly, C. A., & Chatman, J. A. (1996). Culture as social control: Corporations, culture, and commitment. In B. M. Staw & L. L. Cummings (Eds.), *Research in organizational behavior* (pp. 157-200). Greenwich, CT: JAI Press.

O'Reilly, C. A., Chatman, J. A., & Caldwell, D. F. (1991). People and organizational culture: A profile comparison approach to assessing person-organization fit. *Academy of Management Journal,* 34(3), 487-516.

Organisation for Economic Co-operation and Development (2010), OECD Health Data, *OECD Health Statistics* (database), updated February 14, 2011. downloaded from http://www.oecd.org/health/healthdata.

Osterman, P. (1987). Turnover, employment security, and the performance of the firm. In M. M. Kliener, R. N. Block, M. Roomkin & S. W. Salsberg (Eds.), *Human resources and the performance of the firm* (pp. 275-317). Washington, DC: BNA Press.

Paletz, S., Smith-Doerr, L., & Vardi, I. (2010). *Interdisciplinary Collaboration in Innovative Science and Engineering Fields*: National Science Foundation Workshop Report.

Panel Discussion of Venture Captial Opportunities (2011). Tech Crunch Conference, Mountain View, CA.

Pear, R. (2010b, July 14, 2010). Health Plans Must Provide Some Tests at No Cost. *New York Times.*

Pfeffer, J. (1983). Organizational demography. *Research in Organizational Behavior,* 5, 299-357.

Phillips, J. F. (2009). Using an Ounce of Prevention: Does It Reduce Health Care Expenditures and Reap Pounds of Profits? A Study of the Financial Impact of Wellness and Health Risk Screening Programs. *Journal of Health Care Finance,* 36(2), 1–12.

Pomeranz, J. (2011). The Unique Authority of State and Local Health Departments to Address Obesity, *American Journal of Public Health,* 101, 1192-1197.

Pronk, S. (2005). Population Health Improvement. *Benefits Quarterly,* 21(3), 12-16.

Quick, J. C., & Quick, J. D. (2004). Healthy, happy, productive work: A leadership challenege. *Organizational Dynamics,* 33, 329-337.

Randall, R., Cox, T., & Griffiths, A. (2007). Participants' acounts of a stress management intervention. *Human Relations,* 60, 1181-1209.

Raven, B. H., Schwartzwald, J., & Koslowshy, M. (1998). Conceptualizing and measuring a power/interaction model of interpersonal influence. *Journal of Applied Social Psychology,* 28, 307-332.

Research shows carefully worded nudge may be just what employers need to promote prevention in the workplace. (2011, July 15). *Managed Care Outlook,* p. 7-8.

Reskin, B. F., McBrier, D. B., & Kmec, J. A. (1999). The determinants and consequences of workplace sex and race composition. *Annual Review of Sociology,* 25, 335-361.

Samuelson, P., & Nordhaus, P. (1989). *Economics.* New York, NY: McGraw-Hill.

Shaw, J. D., Delery, J. E., Jenkins, G. D., & Gupta, N. (1998). An organizational-level analysis of voluntary and involuntary turnover. *Academy of Management Journal,* 41, 511-525.

Shaw, J. D., Dineen, B., Fang, R., & Vellella, R. (2009). Employee-organization exchange relationships, HRM practices, and quit rates of good and poor performers. *Academy of Management Journal,* 52, 1016-1033.

Shaw, J. D., Duffy, M. K., Johnson, J. J., & Lockhart, D. (2005). Turnover, social capital losses, and performance. *Academy of Management Journal,* 48, 594-606.

Shaw, J. D., & Gupta, N. (2007). Pay system characteristics and quit patterns of good, average, and poor performers. *Personnel Psychology,* 60, 903-928.

Shaw, J. D., Gupta, N., & Delery, J. E. (2005). Alternative conceptualizations of the relationship between voluntary turnover and organizational performance. *Academy of Management Journal, 48*, 50-68.

Sonpar, K. Handelman, J.M., & Dastmalchian, A. (2009). Implementing New Institutional Logics in Pioneering Organizations: The Burden of Justifying Ethical Appropriateness□and Trustworthiness. *Journal of Business Ethics, 90,* 345–359.

Sonpar K., Pazzaglia, F., & Kornijenko, J. (2010). The Paradox and Constraints of Legitimacy *Journal of Business Ethics, 95,* 1–21.

Sorensen, G, Landsbergis, P, Hammer, L, Amick B.C., Linnan, L.,□ Yancey, A., Welch, L.S., Goetzel, R.Z., Flannery, K.M., Pratt,C. (2011). Preventing Chronic Disease in the Workplace: A Workshop Report and Recommendations. *American Journal of Public Health |* Supplement 1, 101, No. S1

Spell, C., & Bezrukova, K. (2010). A Question of balance? Women, men and high performance organizations. *French review of social sciences "Travail, Genre et Société,"* 23, 193-201.

Spell, C., & Bezrukova, K. (in press). Perceptions of justice in employee benefits. In M. J. Sirgy & N. P. Reilly (Eds.), *Handbook of Quality-of-Life Programs: Enhancing Ethics and Improving Quality of Life at Work*: Springer Publishing Company.

Spell, C., & Blum, T. (2005). The adoption of workplace substance abuse programs: Strategic choice and institutional perspectives. *Academy of Management Journal, 48*, 1125-1142.

Stone, A. A., Neale, J. M., Cox, D. S., & Napoil, A. (1994). Daily events are associated with a secretory immune response to an oral antigen in men. *Health Psychology,* 13, 400-418.

Subramony, M., Krause, N., Norton, J., & Burns, G. (2008). The Relationship Between Human Resource Investments and Organizational Performance: A Firm-Level Examination of Equilibrium Theory. *Journal of Applied Psychology, 93,* 778 -788.

Sun, L. Y., Aryee, S., & Law, K. S. (2007). High performance human resources practices, citizenship behavior and organizational performance: A relational perspective. *Academy of Management Journal, 50*, 558-577.

Tajfel, H. (1982). Social psychology of intergroup relations. *Annual Review of Psychology,* 33, 1-39.

Tajfel, H., & Turner, J. C. (1979). An integrative theory of intergroup conflict. In W. G. Austin & S. Worchel (Eds.), *The social psychology of intergroup relations* (pp. 33-47). Monterey, CA: Brooks/Cole.

Teo, H. H., Wei, K. K., & Benhasat, I. (2003). Predicting intention to adopt interorganizational linkages: An institutional perspective. *MIS Quarterly,* 27, 19-49.

Tetrick, L., Perrewe, P., & Griffin, M. (2010). Employee Work-Related Health, Stress, and Safety. In J. Farr & N. Tippins (Eds.), *Handbook of Employee Selection.* London, UK: Taylor&Francis Group.

Tolbert, P. S., & Zucker, L. (1983). Institutional Sources of Change in the Formal Structure of Organizations: The Diffusion of Civil Service Reform, 1880-1935. *Administrative Science Quarterly,* 28, 22-39.

Towers-Perrin. (2009). *2009 Health care cost survey--The health dividend: Capturing the value of employee health,* from http://www.wellnessindiana.org/2009_Healthcare_Cost_Survey.pdf

Trevor, C. O., & Nyberg, A. J. (2008). Keeping your headcount when all about you are losing theirs: Downsizing, voluntary turnover rates, and the moderating role of HR practices. *Academy of Management Journal,* 51, 259-276.

Tsui, A. S., Pierce, J. L., Porter, L. W., & Tripoli, A. M. (1997). Alternative approaches to the employee-organization relationship: Does investment in employees pay off? *Academy of Management Journal,* 40, 1089-1121.

Tsui, A. S., & Wu, J. B. (2005). The new employment relationship versus the mutual investment approach: Implications for human resource management. *Human Resource Management,* 44, 115-121.

Wegge, J., Roth, C., Kanfer, R., Neubach, B., Schmidt, K..(2008). Age and Gender Diversity as Determinants of Performance and Health in a Public Organization: The Role of Task Complexity and Group Size. *Journal of Applied Psychology. 93,* 1301-1313.

Westphal, J. D., & Bednar, M. K. (2008). The pacification of institutional investors. *Administrative Science Quarterly,* 53, 29-72.

Whitman, D. S., Van Rooy, D. L., & Viswesvaran, C. (2010). Satisfaction, Citizenship behaviors, and performance in work units: A meta-analysis of collective construct relations. *Personnel Psychology,* 63, 41-81.

Williams, K., & O'Reilly, C. A. (1998). Demography and diversity: A review of 40 years of research. In B. M. Staw & L. L. Cummings (Eds.), *Research in Organizational Behavior* (pp. 77-140). Greenwich, CT: JAI Press.

Wolfe, R. Ulrich, D. & Parker, D.F. 1987. Employer health management programs: A review, crtiqu, and research agenda. *Journal of Management, 13,* 603-615.

Zellmer-Bruhn, M., & Gibson, C. (2006). Multinational organization context: Implications for team learning and performance. *Academy of Management Journal,* 49(3), 501-518.

Zellner, W. (2005, 02/10/2005). Wal-Mart's clean bill of health? *BusinessWeek Online.*

Zhang, A., Tsui, A., Song, L., Li, C., & Jia, L. (2008). How do I trust thee? The Employee-organization relationship, supervisory support, and middle manager trust in the organization. *Human Resource Management,* 47, 111-132.

Zimmerman, A. (2009, 07/16/2009). Wal-Mart's image moves from demon to darling. *Wall Street Journal-Eastern Edition, 254,* B1-B4.

Zimmerman, R. D. (2008). Understanding the impact of personality traits on individuals' turnover decisions: A meta-analytic path model. *Personnel Psychology,* 61(2), 309-348.

CHAPTER ELEVEN

THEORY AND MATHEMATICAL MODEL OF THE INFLUENCE OF KNOWLEDGE TRANSFER ON THE LOCATION OF A MULTINATIONAL

DOROTA LESZCZYŃSKA
IPAG BUSINESS SCHOOL, FRANCE
AND ERICK PRUCHNICKI
ECOLE POLYTECHNIQUE UNIVERSITAIRE DE LILLE, FRANCE

Abstract

Research has not yet shed much light on the performance of the location choice of multinational companies. The aim of this work is to highlight the link between the transfer of knowledge flows and the location of a multinational company. We put forward a conceptual approach that formulates the equations of a mathematical modelization of consequential location performance. Our research has led us to highlight some types of managerial behaviors that will ensure location performance within a cluster.

Keywords: cluster, knowledge flows, location, mathematical equations, performance

Introduction

The trend of research concerning organizational approach based on knowledge (Eisenhardt & Santos, 2002) has gradually emerged as the main perspective aiming at explaining the movements of multinational companies. The most recent publications (Yang et al., 2011) underscore that the idea of bringing together learning on the one hand and the cluster's prospects on the other hand opens up a fruitful and promising way of studying the competitiveness of multinational companies. For instance, Gupta and Govindarajan (1991) conceptualize multinational firms as being networks for transactions, functioning via knowledge flows. Davenport and Prusak (1998) define a knowledge flow as being a fluid combination of experiments, a running exchange of essential values, of contextual information, and of shrewd expert evaluations.

Research work concerning organizational approach based on knowledge has focused on the study of contexts in which knowledge flows are highlighted. In this perspective, a good deal of research work has been undertaken in order to elaborate the theory of clusters, based on knowledge. (Maskell, 2001; Mehrizi & Bontis, 2009). A cluster has therefore been conceptualized as a site in which the creation of embedded knowledge is stimulated, as a consequence of the geographic and organizational closeness of local companies. (Rallet & Torre, 2005, p. 50). This research work has shown the assets of clusters, which influence the choice of multinational companies as far as their location is concerned. (Rugman, 2005). However, the significant indicators in order to predict the long-term efficiency of a new location contemplated by a multinational company are still unknown (Goerzen & Asmussen, 2007). Originating from this statement, the question which has prompted our reflection can be expressed in the following words: how to predict the location performance of a multinational within a cluster?

This research aims at showing the influence of knowledge flows transfer on the efficiency of the location choice. Then we shall formulate the equations of a mathematical modelization. The mathematical model actually shows that, when the multinational company is not capable of integrating such knowledge into its structure, the local business relationship breaks off. We shall then be able to submit our views to a discussion, and to underline the fact that there is indeed a link between the transfer of knowledge flow and the success of the location of a multinational company within a cluster.

Location of a Multinational Company and The Transfer of Knowledge: An Ingenious Link?

For a long time, it has been generally assumed that this was a one-way transfer, from multinational companies towards local businesses. (Lin, 2005). Nowadays, as competition between multinational companies has become harder and harder, their location choice has become a major strategic issue (Gimeno et al., 2005), and local actors' knowledge may very well have an influence on its success. Referring to Spicer's new terminology (2006), we shall therefore consider knowledge transfer of a convergent type, that is to say, from local to international level.

As they look for new sources of external knowledge flows, multinational companies select some specific geographical sites for their implantation. Porter (1994, p. 37) underlines the fact that competitive advantage is determined by an appropriately located innovation process, and underscores the crucial importance of the location choice made by the multinational company. Most costs and risks are consequently linked to obstacles raised by distance and her immediate result on the effective transmission of explicit and tacit knowledge (Ambos & Ambos, 2009). Finally, the links between location strategies of multinationals and the degree of tacitness of local knowledge are pointed out (Biggiero, 2000, p. 111).

Organizational Knowledge

The usual distinction between tacit and explicit knowledge derives from the articulate or implicit nature of the considered knowledge. Tacit knowledge is inarticulate, it is essentially personal by nature; such a knowledge is difficult to transfer (Dhanaraj et al., 2004). On the contrary, explicit knowledge can be codified and transmitted much more easily (Inkpen &Wang, 2006).

However, the distinction between tacit and explicit knowledge should not be considered as a dichotomy but rather as a spectrum with both types of knowledge – tacit and explicit – at the extremes. (Inkpen & Dinur, 1998). The consideration of transfer speed in an organization as far as knowledge flows are is undoubtedly useful in order to evaluate how long these transfers will take, and how much they will cost. In their research work, Inkpen and Wang (2006) have observed that tacit knowledge is difficult to assess, and, consequently, that a company in a phase of learning often keeps on concentrating on its explicit knowledge which is easier to transmit (and which is less valuable). Embeddedness is another significant feature of knowledge which has an influence on learning capacity. Its transmission requires face-to-face interactions (Nielsen, 2005; Leszczyńska, 2013).

Companies should transfer their knowledge according to difficulty, starting with the easiest category: explicit knowledge, then tacit knowledge, then embedded knowledge. The estimation of transfer duration and costs in each category is obviously dependent on increasing difficulty, therefore on the order in which this transfer is made. Consequently, embedded knowledge transfer, which does exist in some branches of industry, is the final learning stage. Distance hardly ever influences the duration and costs of a transfer of explicit knowledge, whereas distance is important when the duration and costs of a transfer of tacit and embedded knowledge have to be estimated.

The Context of an Industrial Cluster

For instance, Knickerbocker (1973) underscores the direct movements of investments made by American multinational companies towards clusters. Porter (2000, p. 254) gives the following definition of a cluster: "a geographically close compact group of inter-related companies with common institutions of their own." Knowledge is embedded within a cluster, that is to say within small innovative companies each of them part of a cooperative, regional, industrial ruling system.

This knowledge is essentially accessible to the actors at work within the limits of the cluster. At the same time, recent studies demonstrate the geographic concentration of innovation, and show that knowledge developments are directly dependent on the networks formed by companies which are embedded in the same region (Bell et al., 2009). The major specific feature of innovation, revealed in research work about clusters, corresponds to the necessity of transferring tacit knowledge flows through organisational frontiers. The geographic nearness of partners reduces the importance of issues linked to tacit knowledge transfer because it allows as higher frequency of face-to-face interactions (Ambos & Ambos, 2009, p. 11). On the contrary, explicit knowledge can be easily codified and transferred in a formalized language. Therefore, geographic nearness is not crucial as far as the transfer of explicit knowledge flows is concerned.

Mathematical Model

The aim of our model is to propose a mathematical tool to determine the long-term financial results for a multinational which is looking for a new location. This is a problem of complex complementarity mentioned by Buckley and Carter (2004, p 381). The objective for our model proposed is to enable the group to choose the best location for a future site.

A feature of locating a multinational in a cluster is the transfer of knowledge between the companies in the cluster and the multinational. Transferring knowledge from the cluster towards the multinational leads to interactions between this new knowledge and the knowledge already present in the multinational. This results in innovation, gains in productivity and so financial gains. For the multinational, the performance which results from this location is equal to the difference between the financial gains and the costs produced by the knowledge transfer.

However, the gain in performance for the multinational company may result in an increased competition between the multinational company and the cluster, and the effect of this may be a drop in the financial results and a loss of performance for the companies of the cluster.

The knowledge to be transferred is selected so as to maximize the global performance, that is to say the total amount of performance achieved by both the multinational companies and the companies in the cluster, deriving from all the transfers which were carried out as the new implantation was under way. In order to ensure the stability of the new location, the performance of the multinational company and of each company in the cluster must be positive, which means that the knowledge transfers should globally by profitable to all partners. Obviously the necessity of stability lessens the performance of the implantation under way, but it also avoids a rupture of the local partnership. It ensures a long-term knowledge transfer until the ultimate stage of embedded knowledge is reached, generating more and more performance.

The evaluation of gains and drops of the financial results linked to knowledge transfer can only be made from a thorough examination of the structure of the companies in the cluster, and of the structure of the multinational company. The cost of a knowledge transfer can be calculated from the general structure of the knowledge (K) involved which is partitioned into a "n" number of groups – K_j with "j" ranging from 1 to n. This partitioning is established so that K_1 only contains explicit knowledge whereas K_n only contains embedded knowledge. Each group of intermediate knowledge (K_j with j ranging from 2 to n-1) contains both tacit and explicit knowledge which are not independent, and the proportion of tacit knowledge gradually increases with "j" (in reference to Inkpen and Dinur's knowledge spectrum, 1998). The transfer of the knowledge group K_j from the cluster to the multinational company takes place in T_j days and has a financial cost of F_j. As distance has a greater influence on the transfer of tacit and embedded knowledge than on the transfer of explicit knowledge, T_j and F_j are functions related to j. Therefore, the complete knowledge transfer takes a time $T=T_1+...T_j+...T_n$ for a total cost of $F=F_1+...F_j+...F_n$. In the transfer costs we can certainly include the costs related to geographical distance.

We suppose that the knowledge transferred from the cluster to the multinational during the time period i, defined as:

$[Tt_i, Tt_{i+1}[$ for T_k $i=0$, n with $Tt_j = \Sigma_{k=1,j} T_k$

for $j=0$, n and choosing $Tt_{n+1} \gg Tt_n$

are only operational – and intervene effectively in the calculation of performance- after the total transfer of each of the packets of knowledge (K_j for $j=1$, n); so the total operational knowledge transferred during the time period i after implantation of the new site is:

$Ct_i = \Sigma_{j=1,n} K_j$ for $i=0$, n

Generally, the total knowledge acquired by a firm is broken down at a moment of time t into three parts according to its end use (Ghiglino, 2012, Milgrom and Roberts, 1995):

$$Ca_\alpha(t) = Ca_\alpha^1(t) + Ca_\alpha^2(t) + Ca_\alpha^3(t)$$

From this, the Greek lower index (here) α has a value of 1 for the multinational and 2 for the cluster company. As for the upper index, it relates to the type of knowledge:

if $i=1$, it represents knowledge leading to improvements is production processes,

if $i=2$, it represents knowledge associated to product innovations,

if $i=3$, it represents knowledge with no direct incidence on production.

To take account of the speed with which the knowledge is created at the moment t, represented mathematically by the total derivative of the function Ca_α^i corresponding to the rate of fresh knowledge generated at time t and denoted traditionally as $d\ Ca_\alpha^i(t)\ /\ dt$, we use a Cobb-Douglas type function (Jones, 2005; de Dominicis et al., 2013):

$$\frac{d\,C_\alpha^i(t)}{dt} = \lambda_\alpha^i H_\alpha(t)^{\gamma_\alpha^i} Ca_\alpha^i(t)^{\Phi_\alpha^i} X_\alpha^{\theta_\alpha^i} \qquad (1)$$

with $\lambda_\alpha^i > 0, \quad \gamma_\alpha^i > 0, \quad \Phi_\alpha^i > 0, \quad \theta_\alpha^i > 0,$

in this function $H_\alpha(t)$ and $Ca_\alpha^i(t)$ represent respectively research activity and the total knowledge acquired at the moment t; $X_\alpha(t)$ is a local variable which influences innovation positively, for example the share capital or the structure of the local economy at moment t.

The performance of the multinational ($\alpha=1$) or of the cluster company ($\alpha=2$) over the period of time i (i=0, n), resulting only from the benefit of the acquired knowledge, can be written using the concept of complementarity which mathematically leads to the use of the supermodular class of functions (Milgrom and Roberts 1990, 1995):

$$\prod_{\alpha i}(A_{\alpha\,i}) = \pi_{\alpha i}\,(q_{\alpha i}, i_{\alpha i}, r_{\alpha i}) - R_{\alpha i}\,(r_{\alpha i}, e_{\alpha i}, f_{\alpha i}, m_{\alpha i}) - I_{\alpha i}\,(i_{\alpha i}, f_{\alpha i}, a_{\alpha i}, h_{\alpha i}), \quad (2)$$

In the equation below, $A_{\alpha i} = (q_{\alpha i}, i_{\alpha i}, r_{\alpha i}\ a_{\alpha i}, e_{\alpha i}, f_{\alpha i}, h_{\alpha i}, m_{\alpha i})$, $q_{\alpha i}$ represents the quantities produced over the period of time i (i=0, n), $i_{\alpha i}$ represents the average frequency of knowledge linked to an improvement in production processes over the period of time 0:

$$i_{\alpha 0} = \frac{Ca_{\alpha 0}^1}{T_{\alpha 0}}$$

For subsequent periods of time (i=1, n):

$$i_{\alpha i} = \frac{Ca_\alpha^1(Tt_i)}{(T_{\alpha 0} + Tt_i)}$$

where $Ca_{\alpha 0}^i$ and $T_{0\alpha}$ represent respectively the total knowledge leading to an improvement of production processes, and the age of company α at the moment of the purchase.

$r_{\alpha i}$ represents the average frequency of knowledge leading to product innovation over the period of time 0:

$$r_{\alpha 0} = \frac{Ca_{\alpha 0}^2}{T_{\alpha 0}}$$

For subsequent periods of time (i=1, n):

$$r_{\alpha i} = \frac{Ca_{\alpha}^2(Tt_i)}{(T_{\alpha 0} + Tt_i)}$$

where $Ca_{\alpha 0}^2$ represents all the knowledge leading to product innovation in company α at the time of the purchase. Moreover $\pi_{\alpha i}(q_{\alpha i}, i_{\alpha i}, r_{\alpha i})$ represents the operating profit and is a supermodular function of its three variables $q_{\alpha i}, i_{\alpha i}, r_{\alpha i}$.

$I_{\alpha i}$ ($i_{\alpha i}, f_{\alpha i}, a_{\alpha i}, h_{\alpha i}$) represents the costs resulting from innovations in production processes. Moreover $(-I_{\alpha})$ is a supermodular function of its four variables $i_{\alpha i}, f_{\alpha i}, a_{\alpha i}, h_{\alpha i}$: $f_{\alpha i}$ represents the level of training of the workforce, $a_{\alpha i}$ represents the level of autonomy of the workforce given their knowledge of production processes, $h_{\alpha i}$ the level of horizontal communication.

$R_{\alpha i}$ ($r_{\alpha i}, e_{\alpha i}, f_{\alpha i}, m_{\alpha i}$) represents the costs resulting from product innovation, moreover $(-R_{\alpha i})$ is a supemodular function of its four variables $r_{\alpha i}, e_{\alpha i}, f_{\alpha i}$ and $m_{\alpha i}$: $e_{\alpha i}$ represents the efficiency of the design process, $m_{\alpha i}$ represents the manufacturing flexibility.

So, the mathematical problem consists in finding the location which optimises the performance of the local structure at the moment Tt_{n+1} (which is seen as well downstream of the time Tt_n of transfer of all the knowledge), which means, using the performance of company α given by equation (2) looking for:

$$\sum_{i=0}^{n} \sum_{\alpha=1}^{2} \Pi_{\alpha i}(A_{\alpha i}) - F_i ,$$

with the constraints or conditions for stability expressing that the performance of the cluster company (α=2) must remain positive at the moment Tt_j (j =1, n+1):

$$\sum_{i=0}^{j-1}\sum_{\alpha=1}^{2}\Pi_{2i}\left(A_{2i}\right)+\beta_i F_i > 0 , \qquad (3)$$

$\beta_i \in \,]0, 1[$ being a coefficient making it possible to pay back to the cluster company the cost of knowledge transfer for the period i.

The non-respect of one of these conditions for a time Tt_j can result in the breaking off of the local alliance, as mentioned later in the discussion.

We obtain $Ca_{\alpha}^{k}(Tt_i)$ (for k=1, 2 and i=1, n) ; by integrating the differential equation (1) over the period i($\varphi_{\alpha}^{i} \neq 1$) we see that the change in quantity of knowledge in company α is given by the following recurrence relation, for i=1, n:

$$Ca_{\alpha}^{k}\left(Tt_i\right)^{-\Phi_{\alpha}^{i}+1} = \lambda_{\alpha}^{i}\left(-\Phi_{\alpha}^{i}+1\right)\int H_{\alpha}(t)^{\gamma_{\alpha}^{i}} X_{\alpha}(t)^{\theta_{\alpha}^{i}}$$

$$+ Ca_{\alpha}^{k}\left(Tt_{i-1}\right)^{-\Phi_{\alpha}^{i}+1} + \left(2 - \alpha\right)C_{i}^{k} , \qquad (4)$$

with the initial condition at the moment of implantation:

$$Ca_{\alpha}^{k}(0) = Ca_{\alpha 0}^{k}$$

The last term of the second member of the equation (4) (($2-\alpha$) C_i^{k})corresponds to the quantity of operational knowledge transferred from the cluster company to the multinational (we obtain C_i^{k} for 1=α); of course it vanishes for 2=α(cluster).

For example, the knowledge transfer might be associated to production of an identical product by the multinational and by the cluster company. If, after the knowledge transfer, the production cost per unit is lower for the multinational than for the cluster company (these costs can be quantified using the supermodular functions depending on $A_{\alpha i}$), production of this product should be halted in the cluster company. Thus, the corresponding knowledge will no longer be included in the calculation of the frequencies $i_{\alpha i}$ or $r_{\alpha i}$ mentioned above, which will result in a reduction in the overall performance of the cluster company.However, if these production costs remain more or less identical for the cluster company and for the multinational, production can be maintained. Using data available on the multinational and the cluster company, the parameters used for equations (1) and (2) can be evaluated over each period of time. The supermodular profit functions (equation (2)) can be assumed to be quadratic (Miravete & Pernias, 2006).

Discussion

In this publication, we have tried to clarify the complex issues brought up by the location of a multinational company within a cluster, raising all along the following crucial question: what is the efficiency of such a location? Indeed, the decision to enter a regional cluster is usually taken whereas performance results are considered uncertain. Our whole reflection work has demonstrated that it is significant to take the transfer of knowledge flow into consideration in order to answer this question. Our mathematical model shows that the multinational company chooses its new implantation with a view to reach an optimal level of performance.

In order to make this mathematical model operational, it is necessary to evaluate all the issues and distances involved: geographical, administrative (institutional), economic and linguistic, and their subsequent costs as the transfer are being actived (Rallet & Torre, 2005). Research works (Porter, 2000, p. 32) highlight the fact that interactions between the companies of a cluster result in a larger volume of innovations (and of their subsequent competitive advantages) than the one which would have been generated in the companies of the cluster had operated separately. This dynamics develops even more as knowledge flows are being transferred between the multinational company and the whole cluster. Therefore, the localization will be effectively optimized if the multinational company really participates in the local processes of knowledge transfers within the cluster (Jacquier-Roux & Paraponaris, 2011). The question may actually be raised in the following words: considering the volume of innovations generated separately by the multinational company and the cluster, what volume of innovations can be expected in the event of their collaboration?

Other investigations would certainly be welcome to improve by a quantitative study that would make the link between the proposed mathematical model and the efficiency of the location of a multinational in a cluster. In order to illustrate the impact of knowledge flows on the performance of multinational companies after a new implantation, we could study an industrial cluster. For example, the French perfume industrial cluster (in Grasse) has attracted multinational agribusiness, cosmetic and pharmaceutical industries. These multinational companies have attempted to transfer the knowledge flows originating from the producers of aromas and perfume compositions, and from perfume creators. This knowledge remains tacit, private and personal, and cannot be transferred unless a direct contact is established.

Keeping this idea in mind, we have constructed our study with the first objective to elaborate a model in order to have a better understanding of the impact of embedded knowledge on the efficiency of a localization choice made by a multinational company. While the importance of knowledge flows is a major issue in the process of wealth creation, the purpose of multinational companies is to take advantage of this asset when choosing a new localization. Therefore, a cluster's knowledge is considered valuable only as a complement to fundamental specific capacities of multinational companies. We propose that the influence of the transfer of knowledge flows in the localization choice made by a multinational company may be apprehended through a mathematical model allowing to take some knowledge specific features and indicators into consideration.

References

Ambos, T. C., & Ambos, B. (2009). The impact of distance on knowledge transfer effectiveness in multinational corporations. *Journal of International Management Fox School of Business*, *15*, 1-14.

Bell, S. J., Tracey, P., & Heide, J. B. (2009). The organization of regional clusters. *Academy of Management Review*, *34*(4), 623-642.

Biggiero, L. (2000). The location of multinationals in industrial districts: knowledge transfer in biomedicals. *Journal of Technology Transfer*, 27, 111-122.

Buckley, P.J., & Carter M.J. (2004). A formal analysis of knowledge combination in multinational enterprises. *Journal of International Business Studies*, *35*, 371-384.

Davenport, T.H., & Prusak, L. (1998). *Working knowledge*. Boston: Harvard Business School Press.

De Dominicis, L., Florax, R. J. G. M., & De Groot, H. L. F. (2013). Regional clusters of innovative activity in Europe: are social capital and geographical proximity key determinants? *Applied Economics*, *45*, 2325-2355.

Dhanaraj, C., Lyles, M. A., Steensma, H. K., & Tihanyi, L. (2004). Managing tacit and explicit knowledge transfer in IJVs: The role of *relational embeddedness and the impact on performance. Journal of International Business Studies*, *35*, 428-442.

Eisenhardt, K. M., & Santos, F. M. (2002). Knowledge-based view. A new theory of strategy. In A. Pettigrew, H. Thomas, & R. Whittington (Eds). *Handbook of strategy and management* (pp. 139-164). Thousand Oaks, CA: Sage.

Ghiglino, C. (2012). Random walk to innovation: Why productivity follows a power law. *Journal of Economic Theory*, *147*, 713-737.

Gimeno, J., Hoskisson, R. E., Beal, B. B., & Wan, W. P. (2005). Explaining the clustering of international expansion moves: A critical test in the u.s. telecommunications industry. *Academy of Management Journal*, *48*(2), 297-319.

Goerzen, A., & Asmussen, C. G. (2007). The geographic orientation of multinational enterprises and its implications for performance. *Research in Global Strategic Management*, Iss. 13, 65-83.

Gupta, A.K., & Govindarajan, V. (1991). Knowledge flows and the structure of control within multinational corporations. *Academy of Management Review*, *16*, 768-792.

Inkpen, A.C., & Dinur, A. (1998). Knowledge management processes and international joint ventures. *Organization Science*, *9*, 454-468.

Inkpen, A.C., & Wang, P. (2006). The China-Singapore Suzhou Industrial Park: A knowledge transfer network. *Journal of Management Studies*, *43*, 779-811.

Jacquier-Roux, V., & Paraponaris, C. (2011). L'objectif de l'internationalisation de la R&D des firmes: de la circulation au partage des connaissances tacite situées. *Management International*,*16*(1), 75-83. Publié par HEC Montréal et Université Paris Dauphine.

Jones, Ch.I. (2005). Growth and ideas. In P. Aghion and S. Durlauf (Eds.), *Handbook of economic growth* (Elsevier),ume 1B, 1063-1111.

Knickerbocker, F. T. (1973). Oligopolistic reaction and the multinational enterprise. Cambridge, MA: Harvard University Press.

Leszczyńska, D. (2013). Historical Trajectory and Knowledge Embeddedness: A Case Study in the French Perfume Cluster. *Management & Organizational History*, *8*(3), 290-305.

Lin, X. (2005). Local partner acquisition of managerial knowledge in international joint ventures: Focusing on foreign management control, *Management International Review*, *45*, 219-237.

Mehrizi, M.H.R., & Bontis, N. (2009) A cluster analysis of the KM field, *Management Decision*, *47*(5),792 – 805.

Milgrom, P., & Roberts, J. (1990). The economics of modern manufacturing: Technology, strategy and organization. *American Economic Review, 80*(3), 511-528.

Milgrom, P., & Roberts, J. (1995). Complementarities and fit strategy, structure, and organizational change in manufacturing. *Journal of Accounting & Economics, 19*, 179-208.

Min, H., & Melachrinoudis, E. (1996). Dynamic location and entry mode selection of mutinational manufacturing facilities under uncertainty: A chance-constrained goal programming approach. *International Transactions in Operational Research, 3*(1), 65-76.

Miravete, E. J., & Pernias, J. C. (2006). Innovation complementarity and scale of production. *The Journal of Industrial Economics,* LIV(1),1-29.

Nielsen, B. B. (2005). The role of knowledge embeddedness in the creation of synergies in strategic alliances. *Journal of Business Research, 58*(9), 1194.

Porter, M. E. (1994). The role of location in competition. *Journal of the Economics of Business, 1*(1), 35-39.

—. (2000). Location, clusters and economic strategy. In G. L. Clark, M. Feldman, & M. Gertler (Eds.), *The Oxford handbook of Economic geography* (pp. 253-274). Oxford: Oxford University Press.

Provan, K. G., Fish, A., & Sydow, J. (2007). Interorganizational networks at the network level: a review of the empirical literature on whole networks. *Journal of Management, 33*(3), 479-516.

Rallet, A., & Torre, A. (2005). Proximity and location. *Regional Studies, 39*(1), 47-59.

Rugman, A. M. (2005). *The regional multinationals.* Cambridge University Press, Cambridge.

Spicer, A. (2006). Beyond the convergence-divergence debate: The role of spatial scales in transforming organizational logic. *Organization Studies, 27*(10), 1467-1483.

Yang, H., Lin, Z., & Peng, M. W. (2011). Behind acquisitions of alliance partners: exploratory learning and network embeddedness. *Academy of Management Journal, 54*(5), 1069-1080.

Chapter Twelve

Using Internet-Based Collaboration Technologies for Innovation: Crowdsourcing vs. Expertsourcing

Tammy L. Madsen, Jennifer L. Woolley, and Kumar Sarangee
Santa Clara University, USA

Abstract

Internet-based collaboration technologies provide organizations new and valuable tools to engage online communities in innovation. We argue that effectively leveraging internet-based collaboration technologies and online communities for product innovation requires careful consideration of a community's composition and the organizational processes and mechanisms for engaging the community in joint development or co-innovation. We focus on community engagements that generate private goods for a host firm and consider two types of communities: crowd-based and expert-based. Building on literature on user innovation, open innovation, and demand side value creation, we offer theory and propositions regarding how a firm can structure interactions and manage community engagements to facilitate product innovation. More specifically, we propose that, in the context of product innovation, a firm may enhance value creation from online communities when it: 1) employs expertsourcing vs. crowdsourcing, 2) uses internet-based collaboration technologies to facilitate iterative content development among community members and between community members and the host firm; 3) allows for task or problem evolution during a community engagement; 4) strategically involves community members in content management; and 5) time-bounds the duration of a community's work on a task or problem. Interviews with executives in firms using collaboration technologies for innovation also inform our theory development. By specifying the above, we are able to be clearer than prior work about the conditions for creating value when engaging online communities in co-innovation.

Keywords: crowdsourcing, expertsourcing, innovation, online communities

Introduction

Firms are increasingly leveraging internet-based collaboration technologies (CT) to involve a wide range of participants in joint product innovation or co-innovation (e.g., Fuller, 2010; Dahlander & Frederiksen, 2011; Jeppesen & Frederiksen, 2006; Nambisan & Baron, 2010; Prahalad and Ramaswamy, 2004; Prandelli, Verona, and Raccagni, 2006; Sawhney, Verona, and Prandelli, 2005). [1] Broadly defined, internet-based CT are software tools and applications that initiate and leverage social activity within an online platform to facilitate interaction and collaboration among members of an online community and between members of a community and a firm (Kaplan & Haenlein, 2010; Kleeman, Vob, and Rieder, 2008: 11).[2] Online communities are formally defined as aggregations of dispersed actors, typically lacking a common affiliation, "but united by a shared instrumental goal – in this case, creating, adapting, adopting or disseminating" information goods (e.g., Faraj et al., 2011; Glaser, 2001; Sproull & Arriaga, 2007; West & Lakhani, 2008: 2). Collaboration technologies enable organizations to engage the creativity and problem solving skills of firm-hosted online communities of users, employees, and other experts in the creation, development and refinement of products or services (e.g., Fuller, 2010; Sawhney et al., 2005). As a result, their use may yield innovations that strongly fit user preferences while also accelerating the pace and lowering the cost of product innovation.

Organizational scholars are beginning to explore CT-based innovation activities from different but complementary angles. Work from a community member viewpoint investigates how heterogeneity in members' characteristics and motivations affect their participation (e.g., Faraj et al., 2011; von Hippel & von Krough, 2003) and, in turn, a firm's product

---

[1] Such as Dell, Netflix, Cisco, IBM, Dupont, HP, Solidworks, Amway, AT&T, Starbucks, Kraft, Del Monte Foods, Salesforce, Facebook, P&G, NetApp, etc..
[2] These technologies include a wide range of internet-based tools such as discussion forums, virtual community platforms, electronic bulletin boards, virtual product design toolkits, virtualization software for product scenarios and testing, and collaboration platforms etc., (e.g., Kaplan & Haenlein, 2010; Miller, Fabian & Lin, 2009).

innovation efforts (e.g., Fuller, 2010; Jeppesen & Frederiksen, 2006; Nambisan, 2002, 2010; Nambisan & Baron, 2010). Studies examining online communities from a firm perspective offer guidance regarding community design and development (e.g., Nambisan, 2002; Sawhney & Prandelli, 2000) and how communities might be used to affect product demand (e.g., Miller et al., 2009). A third line of inquiry describes how online communities might be leveraged in different stages of the product innovation process and describes the potential outcomes of CT-based innovation (e.g., Fuller, 2010; Prandelli et. al., 2006; Sawhney et. al., 2005). Finally, related work highlights the roles of different types of external actors, such as crowds, in innovation (see Afuah & Tucci, 2012; Lakhani, 2011). Despite the growing, albeit fragmented, literature in this area and the rampant adoption of CT-based innovation initiatives by firms, our understanding of the conditions under which different approaches to CT-based innovation will create value for a firm's product innovation activities remains limited. We seek to contribute to the extant literature by specifying a set of conditions and mechansims that facilitate value creation in CT-based innovation activities focused on developing private goods for a firm.

At least two general forms of CT-based innovation have emerged – *open and semi-open*.[3] Open collaborative innovation includes crowdsourcing as well as traditional open source models. In crowdsourcing, a firm broadcasts a problem (via an open call) to an undefined group of solvers that are external to the firm (Howe, 2006, 2008; Afuah & Tucci, 2012). In this form, the outcome is primarily a private good owned by the focal firm, but a firm also might provide an award and/or royalties to a crowd member. A common example of crowdsourcing is Netflix's open call for an algorithm to improve its movie suggestions to customers. Though community membership is open to the public in both crowdsourcing and open source models, a critical difference between the two is that in open

---

[3] In a third form, closed collaborative innovation, firms use internet-based collaboration technologies to facilitate the development of new ideas internally among employees or a subset of employees. As such, the communities are closed to the public. The outcomes of the collaborative innovation are also private to the firm. For example, in 2001, IBM launched IBM Jams, time bounded conferences held online to unite employees around a specific topic (Bjelland & Wood, 2008). Jams are intended to assist IBM in identifying new market opportunities and novel solutions and are not simply forums for basic idea generation. In the first 10 years, IBM's internal Jams involved over 300,000 employees around the world and assisted the company in capturing a mix of ideas that did not appear on the firm's technology roadmaps via traditional channels. IBM has also has provided the Jam model as a service to other organizations.

source models (such as Linux or Mozilla's Firefox) community generated content is predominately a public good though, not purely public (von Hippel, 2002; von Hippel & von Krogh, 2003).

An alternative form that has gained prominence during the last ten years is a *semi-open collaborative innovation* model. In this form, members of a private online community, comprised of members of a host firm and invited experts from outside the firm's boundaries, generate content that is a private good owned by the host firm.[4] In this *expertsourcing* approach, the host firm ultimately plans to commercialize products based on this private good. For example, Kraft, the creator of powerhouse brands in the food industry, worked with a closed online community of consumers or users, health care professionals, and fitness trainers to develop new set of products. Kraft and the community co-created 48 South Beach Diet branded entrees, snacks and frozen food within six months, a time to market record for Kraft. In addition, the new products generated over $100 million in sales. Similarly, Del Monte Foods' Pet Products Division found that despite using traditional market research techniques, they lacked the depth of user understanding necessary for successful product development. To facilitate the interactive exploration of user needs and preferences, the Pet Products Division created a closed online community called, "I love my dog, dogs are people too." In collaboration with this community, Del Monte developed a new dog snack, Snausages Breakfast Bites, in six weeks. Shifting to the B2B domain, in 2006, Salesforce.com launched a website, Idea-Exchange, to solicit business users' feedback on a new product's features. The content generated informed Salesforce.com's product offerings and in turn, accelerated rollout and reduced time to market.

Common to expertsourcing and crowdsourcing is the sharing of information goods across a firm's boundaries. Critical distinctions however lie with the community composition (open and public versus semi-open (closed) and private), the locus of innovation (the community versus the community and the firm), and the degree and structure of

---

[4] Baldwin and von Hippel (2011) define "closed collaborative innovation" based on the outcome of the engagement ("closed" indicates the outcome is private to the focal firm and not a public good). Building on their work, we refer to semi-open collaborative innovation forms as those where community membership is by invitation only (e.g., closed to the general public but includes members from outside a firm's boundaries) and when collaborative innovation generates private goods for a firm. Thus, in our discussion, the terminology of closed or open refers to the attributes of a community *and* the outcome generated from the community engagement (see Table 12-1 for examples of each form).

interactivity and collaboration among community members and with the host firm. These differences raise intriguing questions regarding the conditions under which the use of online communities and internet-based collaboration technologies will yield benefits for a host firm's product innovation processes and their outcomes. For instance, which type of community, expert versus crowd, might be more fruitful for product innovation? How might firms structure the interactions in expert-based communities to facilitate productive innovation? How can firms effectively organize and manage community engagements to enhance the innovation process?

We explore these questions by drawing on work on user innovation (e.g., von Hippel, 1988, 2005; see also Bogers, Afuah & Bastian, 2010, for a review), open innovation (e.g., Chesbrough, 2003; West, Vanhaverbeke, & Chesbrough, 2006), and demand side value creation which calls for more explicit attention to the role of customers in value creation (e.g., Adner & Zemsky, 2006; Bowman & Ambrosini, 2000; Priem, 2007). We begin with an overview of key concepts and background theory. The subsequent sections present theory and propositions to advance our understanding of how organizations may create value via CT-based innovation. Our work also is informed by fieldwork and interviews with over 30 firms employing internet-based collaboration technologies for product innovation. Multiple key informants at each firm were interviewed for 1 to 1.5 hours using a semi-structured interview protocol document. Interview data was augmented by private company documents, including white papers, case studies, and presentations, and by content on websites specific to a firm's CT-based innovation processes and activities.[5]

Background Theory and Key Concepts

The following discussion provides a brief overview of relevant theory on value creation, open innovation and different types of online communities. Importantly, while anecdotal evidence suggests that CT-based innovation (non-open source) creates value for a firm, systematic empirical evidence using explicit measures of value creation, is sparse. In addition, the term value creation is often used loosely and with different perceived interpretations. Hence, we begin with the definition of value creation relative to customers where we identify how the demand-side view of value creation maps to the concept of open innovation. Our intent is to

---

[5] Most firms in our study agreed to allow their names to be used. In cases where firms requested anonymity, a pseudonym replaces a firm's name (e.g., Sunflower, Nasturtium, Carnation).

clarify concepts that underscore firms' motivations for using CT for innovation and also, to identify important links in extant theory that inform our theoretical development and propositions.

It is widely recognized that a firm's innovation activities benefit from interactions with external actors such as users, field experts and other stakeholders (Chesbrough, 2003; Chesbrough, West, & Vanhaverbeke, 2006; Mansfield, 1986; von Hippel, 1998; 2005). While devoting attention to consumers or users seems an obvious necessity in strategic positioning, empirical work in strategy and organization theory tends to focus primarily on supply side (or firm-specific) activities associated with value creation (such as building barriers to imitation or barriers to entry, engineering a firm's value chain, developing generic strategies, etc..) rather than the consumer or demand-side (for a review, see Priem, 2007). Yet, consumers "validate the value of a products and services" (Priem, 2007: 219; von Hippel, 1998, 2005) based on their perceptions of how well a product's quality aligns with their needs, experiences, beliefs and expectations. A consumer's perceived benefits in the consumption of a product or service are referred to as use value (Bowman and Ambrosini, 2000; Priem, 2007). Work shows that enhancing consumer use value increases a consumer's willingness to pay for a product or service (Adner and Zemsky, 2006). Further, a consumer's surplus is defined as the difference between use value and the price of a product or service (Hoopes, Madsen and Walker, 2003). Value creation relative to customers thus involves innovations that increase the gap between a product's perceived use value and its price. Such value creation also increases the opportunities for a firm to capture value.[6] Thus, activities that enhance a firm's ability to aid consumers in maximizing use value serve as one critical precondition for value capture (Hoopes et al., 2003; Priem, 2007). It follows that collaborating with consumers (users) and other field experts in CT-based innovation activities can enhance a firm's understanding of the perceived use value of a potential product or innovation and, in turn, increase the likelihood of its adoption by consumers.

This notion of marrying the creativity, knowledge and information goods of external sources with a firm's internal development efforts aligns with the concept of open innovation, formally defined as '. . . the use of purposive inflows and outflows of knowledge to accelerate internal

---

[6] Since a detailed review of the concepts of value creation and capture are beyond the scope of this paper, our discussion highlights some of the core ideas that are relevant to our paper's focus. For a detailed dialogue of these concepts, please see Bowman and Ambrosini (2000), Hoopes, Madsen and Walker (2003) and Priem (2007).

innovation, and expand the markets for external use of innovation, respectively' (Chesbrough, 2006b: 1). That is, open innovation includes interacting and cooperating with actors external to a firm's boundaries in the development of innovations. While initial work on open innovation focused on formal contractual relationships that cross a firm's boundaries, recent work and practice suggests that the traditional concept spans beyond the boundary of formal contractual agreements and includes informal, non-contractual forms of collaborative value creation involving communities of actors (Gassman, Enkel and Chesbrough, 2010; West and Lakhani, 2008). This presents an opportunity for intersecting work on open innovation and value creation with work on communities for innovation (West and Lakhani, 2008). Some scholars refer to this alternative form of open innovation as customer co-creation (Piller, Ihl and Vossen, 2011; Prahalad and Ramaswamy, 2004). However, innovation-oriented online communities are not solely limited to customers or users of a firm's goods or services (West and Lakhani, 2008; von Hippel, 2005). Instead, firms' innovation activities also may benefit from the input of other types of external actors such as field experts in adjacent or complementary fields whose expertise is built on experience, or non-obvious problem solvers operating in distant knowledge domains (Afuah and Tucci, 2012; Lakhani, 2011). In addition, these activities involve at least two modes of open innovation, 'outside-in' where external sources serve as a static source of input to a firm (providing primarily solution-based content), and 'externally coupled' where external sources operate more as a dynamic resource by engaging in collaboration with a firm on ideation and problem solving (Enkel et al., 2009). These two modes of open innovation (outside-in and externally coupled) align with two types of online communities used for innovation: open, crowd-based and semi-open, expert-based, respectively. The following (and Table 12-1) further summarizes some of the distinctive features of these two types of communities.

Crowdsourcing. As noted previously, crowdsourcing is a distributed problem solving model where a task or problem is outsourced to an undefined group of participants external to an organization (a crowd) via an open call or general solicitation (Howe, 2006). The crowd typically forms an online community (Howe, 2006). Community members usually are not evaluated or pre-qualified for membership; however, in some cases, members of a crowd might be asked to demonstrate a baseline level of knowledge or expertise when submitting a solution or idea in response to an open call. One perceived benefit of crowdsourcing is that firms are able to engage non-obvious problem solvers and innovators in identifying

Table 12-1. Forms Of Community And Internet-Based Collaboration For Innovation

	Open Collaborative Innovation		Semi-Open Collaborative Innovation	Closed Collaborative Innovation
Type of Community	*Crowdsourcing:* Open to Public	*Crowd:* Open to public; may be partially vetted	*Expertsourcing:* Invitation only	*Expertsourcing:* Closed to the public
Sourcing Type: Outside-in (External) vs. Coupling (Internal and External)	External: Outside- in	External: Outside-in	External & Internal Coupling	Internal Coupling
Purpose	Solution Seeking	Iterative building on a product or service; General idea generation	Task Specific Relative to the Product Innovation Process (1 or more stages)	Task Specific
Host	Focal Firm	Focal Firm, User Community, or non-Focal Firm	Focal Firm	Focal Firm
Community Composition	Members have no relation to the focal firm	Typically, users of the firm's product (service); may also include non-user experts, hobbyists	Users of the firm's product (service), members of the host firm, &/or field experts	Members of the host firm or a subset of the host firm's members (dept., group, etc.)
Locus of Innovation	Crowd	Community	Partnership: Community & Firm	Partnership: Community & Firm
Degree of Firm X Community Collaboration	Low	Low to Moderate	High	High
Source of Value Creation	Crowd	Community Members & Community Members' Interactions	Community Members, Community Members' Interactions, and Community Members' Interactions with the Firm	Community Members, Community Members' Interactions, and Community Members' Interactions with the Firm
Outcome: Public or Private Good?	Private	Public & Private	Private	Private
Who Primarily Captures Value?	Firm	Firm and/or Members	Firm	Firm
Examples	Netflix, Cisco iPrize	Linux, Firefox, Apache	Yp.com (AT&T); Del Monte Foods; Solidworks; Salesforce; NetApp; Kraft; IBM	SAP's InnoJams; IBM Jams

a solution to a problem or task and, in turn, reduce the costs of distant search (Afuah and Tucci, 2012). A common example of crowdsourcing is Netflix's 2006-2009 open competition for an algorithm to better predict user ratings for a movie based on their previous ratings of other movies. Netflix opened a subset of their own rating data for the community to use.

Several attributes of crowdsourcing are notable. Typically, individuals or groups in a crowd act autonomously to develop a solution rather than elaborating on the ideas of the others (Howe, 2006; Jeppesen and Lakhani, 2010; Lakhani, 2011). In addition, an award may be offered by the firm seeking a solution, but is not a prerequisite for crowdsourcing. For example, Netflix awarded $50,000 to community members who provided an algorithm that improved upon their own by at least one percent, and $1,000,000 to the first inventor that improved the performance by at least ten percent. In general, the firm posting the call also rarely interacts with members of the crowd developing a solution. Thus, collaboration among members of the crowd and between the crowd and the focal firm is typically low.[7] As a result, the locus of innovation lies in the crowd itself, with solution-based content flowing from the crowd to the firm. In this tournament approach, the winning solution is selected by the firm that broadcast the problem and the winning "solver" may receive an award. For example, Cisco created Cisco iPrize, where entrepreneurs submit ideas and proposals in hopes of being Cisco's next billion dollar business. The 2010 competition involved 2900 participants and 824 ideas; 32 finalists were culled from this set and the winning submission received a $250,000 award for Cisco to license their idea.[8] Given these conditions, crowdsourcing is often considered a form of outsourcing where a focal firm is sourcing a solution from a crowd (Howe, 2006; Afuah and Tucci, 2012).

Expertsourcing. While examples of crowdsourcing frequent the popular press (e.g., Netflix, Cisco iPrize; My Starbucks Idea, Innovate with Kraft, Proctor and Gamble's VocalPoint), expertsourcing has emerged as a common approach for the use of CT-based innovation. In this approach, a host organization defines who qualifies for membership in an online community that is created to support a specific innovation project or task. Thus, community membership is by invitation only (closed to the general public), rather than unrestricted (open to the general public). Members of expert communities typically include end users of a firm's products or services, but a host organization also might invite individuals from complementary areas of business or users of competitors' products to participate. As noted in the Kraft example, the firm involved an online community of consumers, healthcare professionals and fitness trainers to co-develop a new set of South Beach Diet products. The intuition is that collectively, the expert members hold relevant knowledge or skills based on their experience with a firm's product, have a shared understanding of the firm's product, and have an interest in the product's development and efficacy.[9] As a result, the community's expertise allows a firm to exploit complementarities in learning (Demsetz, 1986). Collectively, these attributes

---

[7] A variant of this approach involves teams of crowd members collaborating to develop a solution. For example, InnoCentive, a firm that works to connect solution seekers with a crowd of solvers, allows members of a crowd to work in small teams on a solution to a specified problem (www.innocentive.com).

[8] For additional details, see:
http://www.cisco.com/web/solutions/iprize/index.html.

[9] Experts are defined as individuals who have knowledge or skills based on their experience or training (http://www.merriam-webster.com/dictionary/expert).

promote interaction among community members and in turn, support the iterative development of ideas (e.g., Dahlander and Frederiksen, 2011; Nambisan and Baron, 2010). Additionally, members of the host organization actively participate in the community. Here, community members are viewed as partners in the innovation process and not simply submitters of content or solutions. Recent work shows that creating a sense of partnership with a firm enhances a community member's contributions to a firm's innovation activities (Nambisan and Baron, 2010). It follows that value creation lies with collaboration among members *and* with collaboration between members and the firm. In this context, communities can contribute needs-based content as well as participate in developing solution-based content. Thus, the locus of innovation lies in the joint engagement of the community and the focal firm rather than primarily within the community (such as in crowdsourcing).[10]

Theory and propositions

As noted above, although work is emerging in this area (e.g., Fuller, 2010; Nambisan, 2002; Nambisan & Baron, 2010; Prandelli et al., 2006; Sawhney et al., 2005), the conditions under which CT-based community engagements will enhance a firm's product innovation processes and its outcomes require further exploration. Prior work argues that success in leveraging online communities for innovation relies on the composition of a community and the organizational practices or mechanisms put in place to support collaborative knowledge creation and evolution (Nambisan, 2002; West & Lakhani, 2008). Building on the above, we first explore which type of community, expert versus crowd, might be more fruitful for product innovation. Next, we examine a subset of factors related to

---

[10]. While our focus is not on open-source forms of CT-based innovation, open-source models might be considered a hybrid from of crowdsourcing and expertsourcing (see column 2 in Table 12-1). In this variant, members of an online community hold knowledge and capabilities related to a particular product or service. The firm that developed the product or service may, or may not, host the community, and community membership is unrestricted. These types of communities often experience the continuous entry and exit of members, making it difficult to determine the composition of the community at any point in time. Members engage in collective action by iterating on content generated by each other to develop or evolve a product or service. Thus, the locus of innovation lies with the community. The collective action nature of this approach thus distinguishes it from general crowdsourcing and shifts it closer on a continuum to an expertsourcing model. In addition, both the firm and community members may gain private benefits from their involvement in the community.

organizing and managing community engagements in support of product innovation – the roles of iterative content development, content management, and time management.

Community Composition

Many organizations are embracing crowdsourcing as a path to enhancing innovation or problem solving. The underlying assumption is that any member of a crowd has the capacity to be a problem solver or innovator. Yet, expertise and problem solving capabilities are heterogeneously distributed among members of a given 'crowd' or community (e.g., Hayek, 1945). As a result, some members of a crowd may hold knowledge relevant to the focal task or problem whereas others may not. For instance, individuals that have self-selected to solve a problem but are unqualified to do so may offer sub-optimal or non-useful solutions. As a consequence, any given crowd may generate a wide gamut of solutions that the focal firm must spend time and resources evaluating. Under these conditions, the firm's cost and duration of search may increase (Fleming, 2001). In other words, the efficacy of using a crowd for innovation and/or problem solving is, in part, dependent on the composition of the crowd.

In the context of product innovation, expert-based communities provide at least three types of benefits relative to crowd-based communities. First, one group of experts includes experienced users or consumers of a firm's products or services that are vetted by the firm before being invited to participate in the community. Consequently, each member of a community has well developed knowledge and cognitive frames that shape and refine their approach to problem solving (Felin et al., 2012; Kaplan and Tripsas, 2008; Walsh, 1995). Given their experience, these members are likely to hold knowledge that is more relevant to a firm's products or services than non-users. Indeed, product experience strengthens a community member's degree of innovativeness (Dahlander and Frederiksen, 2011). As a result, these community members are likely to contribute content that is specific to a firm's trajectory for its product or service innovations (Bogers, Afuah and Bastian, 2010; Franke and Shah, 2003; Franke, von Hippel, and Schreier, 2006). Moreover, in a study examining the results of an online idea sourcing contest, the users of a firm's products, on average, generated ideas that were more novel and beneficial for customers than those generated by the firm's product development professionals (Poetz & Scheier, *forthcoming*).

Second, a portion of a user's expertise may be situated in how a product is used and in the user's relationship with the product (Tyre & von

Hippel, 1997). The latter often involves sticky or difficult to transfer knowledge that is critical to problem solving and product innovation (von Hippel, 1994, 1998). Work suggests that a user's sticky knowledge, along with a user's perceived benefits of an innovation, increases the likelihood that the user will develop distinctive innovations that align with a firm's needs or objectives (von Hippel, 1988; 2005). As a result, users may contribute content to a community that has, on average, a stronger fit with the host firm's products or services and with the firm's objectives than non-users.

Third, to the extent that some portion of this sticky knowledge is common among members of a community, it might be expressed in a common language. A common language eases the communication of knowledge and information (Grant, 1996; Kogut and Zander, 1992). This commonality among community members also facilitates the sharing and integration of knowledge that is not common among them (e.g., Hoopes and Postrel, 1999). In the context of product development, a shared or common understanding also enables the coordination of activities and reduces the likelihood of costly mistakes (Hoopes & Postrel, 1999). Taken together, these conditions support the iterative development of ideas in a community and in turn, increase the efficiency of knowledge aggregation (Grant, 1996). As a result, expertsourcing may be more effective for CT-based innovation activities compared to crowdsourcing.

In contrast, some work suggests that a firm's innovation sourcing may benefit more from the use of crowds versus experts. One argument is that experts hold specialized knowledge and, consequently, only search locally for new knowledge (Schilling, 2005).[11] To the extent that local search bounds the scope of knowledge creation or development, innovation-oriented content developed by expert communities may be more competence-enhancing and/or incremental compared to competence-destroying and/or radical (Katila and Ahuja, 2002; Katila, 2002; Rosenkopf and Nerkar, 2001). In contrast, sourcing from a crowd provides access to distant, knowledge that spans the boundaries of experts and the focal firm. Such distant search or exploration increases the possibility of novel content or solution generation (e.g., Fleming, 2001; Levinthal and March, 1981) and in turn, radical innovation (Rosenkopf and Nerkar, 2001).

However, distant search is more applicable for complex and highly uncertain problems that are easy to articulate and will benefit from knowledge beyond an organization's core expertise (Afuah & Tucci, 2012; Jeppesen and Lakhani, 2010). In contrast, when a problem or task is part

---

[13.] In addition, a core group of experts may become too myopic or inwardly focused and in turn, ignore potentially novel ideas (Schilling, 2005).

of a predefined product roadmap or established innovation process, local knowledge may be more beneficial to the focal firm's innovation efforts than non-local knowledge. Under these conditions, experts' experiences, and the tacit insights associated with them, will be directly related to the firm's products or services (Dahlander & Frederiksen, 2010; Poetz & Scheier, forthcoming). This familiarity increases the likelihood that community members will succeed in developing and contributing content useful to the focal firm's product innovation activities (Poetz & Scheier, *forthcoming*). Second, crowds are typically commissioned solely for solution-based content related to a particular problem call (e.g., Afuah & Tucci, 2012; Jeppesen & Lakhani, 2010); whereas, expert communities may be commissioned for different types of content including needs-based and solution-based content. Since content reflecting users' needs and use preferences is critical to creating value from product innovation, expert communities may be more effective in the context of product innovation than crowds.

Several organizations we observed leveraged expert communities for innovation. AT&T Interactive, a unit of AT&T, engaged an expert community for the development of a new version of their yellow pages website, yp.com. A core group of experts was defined based on their backgrounds and their degrees of active engagement on yp.com. A subset of this group, identified as top tier experts, was further engaged for feedback as the development effort progressed. In combination, this hierarchy of expert communities accelerated the time to market with a new version of yp.com. More importantly, the communities identified product features that were not part of AT&T's roadmap, but were valued by the community. As a result, the final project provided a tighter fit with user needs and preferences – in other words, needs- and use- based content. Conversely, Dell's IdeaStorm is an open community that allows anyone to register as a member. All members may post ideas and rate ideas posted by others. Dell monitors the contributions and culls ideas from the vast number of postings. While this approach might contribute to a large volume and range of ideas for product innovations, many suggestions are not meaningful to the firm and are not adopted (see Bayus, 2010).[12] The large volume of ideas generated also increases the amount of time required for idea evaluation, thereby increasing the cycle time of the innovation process. Based on the preceding arguments and observations, our baseline proposition is:

---

[12] For instance, ideas such as a bamboo laptop case (submitted to Dell's IdeaStorm) may appeal to some users but may have limited impact in terms of increasing the amount of value a firm captures.

Proposition 1: The use of internet-based collaboration technologies for product innovation is more effective when a firm uses an expert-based community as compared to a crowd.

Community Interaction: The Role of Iterative Development

Variation exists in how firms use internet-based collaboration technologies to facilitate communication and interaction with online communities and among community members. Prior work devotes less attention to these differences and how they may affect the efficacy of innovation activities in non-open source contexts (exceptions include Faraj et al., 2011). To elucidate our point, hypothetically a firm might broadcast a problem to a crowd (one-to-many)[13] or members of a community might post content on a host's site (many-to-one), but no interaction among members or between members and the host is intended. Conversely, a firm might use technologies to facilitate the iterative creation and refinement of content. In this case, the technologies employed provide for real time collaboration among community members and between community members and the host firm. This collective engagement forms the basis of a connection among a community's members (Brown and Duguid, 1991; Knorr-Cetina, 1999). Although one-way communication allows the amassing of ideas, engaging community members as joint innovators -- creators, testers, and developers of new products -- requires reciprocal interaction, or cross-talk, among community members and between community members and the host firm. Our premise is that the efficacy of co-innovation depends on members of the community and the firm operating in a feedback loop. This exchange process allows members to to share, refine, and disseminate content and, in turn, facilitates learning and problem solving among community members (Brown & Duguid, 1991).

This reciprocal interaction is central to supporting iterative content development and problem solving, and consequently, the innovation process (Birkinshaw, Hamel & Mol, 2008; Leonard-Barton, 1994). A distinctive benefit of iterative development stems from the opportunity for community members *and* a firm to engage in a dialogue and build on one another's ideas over time. As a starting point, a community member may contribute a baseline idea to the community's online domain hosted by a focal firm. Other community members may comment on the idea, adding to or refining its content. As members interact with each other iteratively,

---

[13] As previously mentioned, familiar examples include Netflix crowdsourcing an algorithm innovation and Cisco's iPrize approach. Firms such as InnoCentive provide a service that broadcasts a firm's problem to a crowd (see Lakhani, 2011).

the base idea evolves (Kane et al., 2009). The host firm also may contribute to an idea's evolution or offer content that addresses members' questions during the iterative development process such as insights into the feasibility of an idea generated in the community. This process provides an opportunity for the integration, adaptation and recombination of information and knowledge that was previously separate or disconnected.

Iterative development also provides other modes of value creation in CT-based product innovation activities. First, when information on the needs of a host firm and users are sticky, iterative idea development may reduce the costs of information or knowledge transfer. The explanation is that the intermediate outputs generated at each stage of the iteration process typically are less sticky than the entire bundle of knowledge or information needed to produce a collective output (Tyre & von Hippel, 1993; von Hippel, 1994). Consequently, the iterative process may reduce the time and costs associated with knowledge transfer or sharing. Further, the use of CT for innovation may yield an additional cost benefit by providing a firm the ability to access information, knowledge, or problem solving skills distributed across a wide range of community members *and* to do so concurrently.

Other benefits arise from leveraging iterative content development. For instance, using internet-based CT to support iterative content development in a community also centralizes the intermediate outputs of the iterative development processes in one location online. As a result, a firm and its community members are exposed to, and interact with, the same content simultaneously.[14] In contrast, traditional, non-internet based marketing techniques in support of product innovation typically lack the opportunity for rapid, ongoing, and concurrent bilateral interaction among a wide array of users and between the users and a focal firm. Given these differences, the use of internet-based CT may accelerate the iterative development process and in turn, reduce the costs associated with a firm's innovation process. Last, the use of internet-based CT that only provide for unidirectional flow of content from a user to a firm disengages a user from understanding the impact of a given suggestion or idea. As a consequence, a user may discount their perceived role in a firm's innovation activities and reduce their commitment to a project (e.g., Fuller, 2010; Nambisan & Baron, 2010).

The iterative development approach described above not only allows for content evolution during a community engagement, but also for

---

[14] For example, a firm in our study, Sunflower, informs their community members that they are part of a community feedback loop.

problem or task evolution. As individuals work on a problem or task, they may uncover the "real" problem that differs from the original problem or they may uncover information that requires re-specifying or redefining the focal problem or task. To the extent that solving the wrong problem or specified task is costly, understanding the "real" problem associated with a particular innovation activity is vital to the efficacy and timing of a firm's product innovation process and its outcomes. The evolution of a problem space also assists firms in overcoming core-rigidities that often constrain generative development (Leonard-Barton, 1994). In contrast, in traditional crowdsourcing, members of the crowd are tasked with developing a solution to a "fixed" problem. As such, the problem may not evolve during the problem solving process (solution developing process), even if a more accurate articulation of the problem emerges during the process (Lakhani, 2011). For example, InnoCentive, an intermediary that connects solution seekers with solvers, broadcasts a firm's problem to a crowd of solvers. However, without iterative communication, the problem may not evolve while the crowd is developing solutions. Under these conditions, the solutions generated by a crowd may not address the "real" problem or true need facing the focal firm. This lack of transparency compromises and dilutes the value of the solutions produced and, in turn, the value captured by the focal firm. Thus, the firm may need to repeat a particular task or the solution development process, which might unnecessarily increase the costs, and duration, of the product innovation process.

Based on the above, we argue that in expertsourcing, efficacious CT-based product innovation requires that a firm design and manage the community engagement to enable iterative development among community members and the host firm. We also suggest that a firm may benefit more if it allows for task and/or problem evolution during on online community engagement. Such iterative development is critical to engaging community members as co-innovators or problem solvers and to facilitating the accretion of community learning in a way that strengthens the quality of the product innovation process.

> **Proposition 2**: In CT-based product innovation, the greater the extent to which a host firm leverages internet-based collaboration technologies to support iterative content development among community members and between community members and the firm, the higher the likelihood that the firm will create value from the community engagement.

> **Proposition 3**: In CT-based product innovation, the greater the opportunity for task or problem evolution during a community

engagement, the higher the likelihood that a host firm will create value from the community engagement.

Content Management

Firms leveraging CT to support innovation often are faced with processing large amounts of content generated by a community's members. However, not all community-generated content has equal value to a firm and too much input increases the complexity of the innovation process. In addition, the bounded rationality of managers limits their capacity to acquire, store and process knowledge (Simon, 1945, 1991). As a result, to fully utilize a community's contributions, firms must develop methods for content management, the evaluation and selection of material generated by the community.

The methods for managing community-generated content in the context of product innovation vary on at least two dimensions: how content is sorted and aggregated (e.g., evaluated) and how solutions are selected. Regarding sorting and aggregation, a community voting or ranking system may be used to cull the top ideas or solutions from the pool of content generated by a community. Alternatively, a host firm may use a panel of experts from the firm to sort content and identify the best ideas or solutions. In sum, the choice is whether the community or firm identifies the best content from the content pool. Once the best content is identified, different actors may be involved in selecting an idea/solutions (or set of ideas/solutions) for implementation or for use in the next phase of the innovation process. Similar to the sorting and aggregation approach, the firm may make the final selection or use a community vote for the final selection. For example, in My Starbucks Idea online community members can vote or rank each idea submitted; however a team of employees reviews all ideas and determines which are presented to management for potential implementation.

In the context of product innovation efforts, several organizational benefits arise when a community is involved in content management. First, shifting the content evaluation and selection activities to a community reduces the time and manpower a host firm must devote to these activities. As a result, involving the community in content management activities may lower the costs of, and time required to, identify optimal solutions for a given stage of the product innovation process. Second, involving a community in selecting content for implementation further legitimizes the community's voice and in turn, may strengthen the community's commitment to a host firm (e.g., Nambisan and Baron, 2010; Wiertz & de

Ruyter, 2007). However, the implications of engaging a community in content management vary based on the composition of the community – that is, whether the community is expert or crowd based – and the purpose of the engagement – whether the community members are viewed as partners in co-innovation (as a dynamic resource) or only as a static resource (as input providers).

In expert-based communities, where one set of community members are users of a firm's goods or services, members may be more likely to adopt a product that includes attributes that were evaluated and/or selected based on community contributions as compared to situations where community input was not solicited and utilized. In this way, community involvement in content management may enhance customer retention and subsequently, the adoption rate for a host firm's products or services that result from the co-innovation effort. Further, as emphasized above, in expert-based communities, a community member views himself as a partner in the innovation process. As a result, omitting community members from evaluation and selection activities associated with the innovation process while benefiting from their content generation efforts may reduce their commitment to the partnership. Members may perceive that the host firm does not value their input and, in turn, be reluctant to contribute to the community in the future. This effect may be more detrimental to a host firm's innovation efforts when a community is engaged to support the entire product innovation process, from ideation to product launch, as compared to when a community is engaged on a one-time basis for bounded problem or task. In the case of the former, loss of community members at any stage of the innovation process may compromise the accretion of learning and in turn, the value created in CT-based innovation.

In contrast, members of a crowd are more loosely coupled to a host firm relative to members of expert communities. Further, individuals in a "crowd" may not perceive themselves as partnering with a host firm but instead, as providing an input (solution) to the firm. As such, a crowd's members may value involvement in content aggregating via polling or rating systems but, as compared to expert communities, have lower expectations regarding their involvement in selecting the ultimate solution from a pool of solutions submitted via a broadcast call. In addition, using community members for content management is detrimental when they lack sufficient knowledge about a firm's innovation trajectory. Specifically, since the members of a crowd may be less knowledgeable regarding a host firm's products and innovation process than experts who are deliberately outsourced by the firm due to their competence, the evaluation of online content by a crowd's members might yield weak insights for the host firm.

Observations from the field underscore the need for firms to consider how they will manage content in CT-based innovation activities. For instance, an executive at Carnation warned, "Be wary of the fact that you should have a proper process in place to absorb the information coming in…. A lot of haphazard random information is stored and you need to be a good at managing it/sorting it." Some firms we observed relied primarily on software based content management (such as polling systems); whereas others complemented these software tools with community monitors or moderators that were members of the host firm. In addition, firms leverage community polling or rating systems in different ways. One firm in our study, Hibiscus, uses content management software to solicit experts and evaluate ideas contributed by the expert community. The software distributes (online) evaluation forms to community members and organizes responses; this process reduced the managerial time required for sorting and aggregating content. An executive at Hibiscus found that by using the software content, management managers "get to see the quick view of the idea and decisions can be made rapidly…when doing this purely collaboratively it was taking too long." Hibiscus also uses community monitors and moderators to manage feedback from community members. This involvement ensures the timely interaction with community members and is critical to winnowing beneficial content from the entire pool of content.

Content management also takes other forms. Another firm in our study, Nasturtium, prefers to use members of the host firm instead of software to manage and cull content. Nasturtium integrates the use of CT for innovation into their marketing teams; team members monitor an online community and ensure that a Nasturtium employee responds to community members' posts within three to four days. When a user post is not addressed in a timely manner, Nasturtium's product managers and active users are directly charged to respond. Executives at Nasturtium found that timely interaction with community members improved member retention. However, Nasturtium managers complained that content management by employees took too much time away from other projects and that other priorities suffered.

We also observed that firms lacking content management mechanisms often struggle with achieving benefits from the use of CT for innovation. For example, the firm Sunflower lacked a method or dedicated support for content management. While content flowed from the community to the firm, the firm's interactions with the community were infrequent. Over time, Sunflower found that the quality and level of participation of the community members eroded, largely because members perceived that the firm did not value their voice.

Building on the above, we propose that community involvement in content management enhances CT-based innovation efforts. However, we also suggest that in CT-based product innovation, involving members of expert-based communities in content management will yield greater benefits for a host firm as compared to involving members of a crowd.

> **Proposition 4:** Involving community members in content management will enhance the value created via CT-based innovation activities.

> **Proposition 5:** In CT-based product innovation, involving expert-based communities in content management will yield greater benefits for a host firm than as compared to involving a crowd in content management.

The Role of Time in Community Engagements

Obtaining benefits from collaborative innovation activities does not occur instantly upon inception, but requires engagement from participants over time. The amount of time a community member spends contributing to a community has both positive and negative effects for CT-based innovation (Faraj et al., 2011). Since community engagement can be designed to limit the amount of time provided for member interaction, understanding the implications of time is important. In particular, time-bounding, or restricting the duration of a community's engagement on a task, problem or activity, is critical to the efficacy of CT-based innovation.

In this context, time-bounding community engagement may yield benefits at two levels – for the focal task and for the organization's innovation activities as a whole. At the task level, time-bounding an engagement may ensure the active and focused participation of a community. When firms explicitly impose a deadline for contributions, community members most interested in participating may contribute more readily instead of postponing their contributions. Work also suggests that limiting the amount of time for a particular task tends to induce more focused effort from a community's members and reduces the likelihood that the focus dissipates (e.g., Faraj et al., 2011). Such focused or concentrated efforts may strengthen a member's task orientation (Nambisan, 2002) and in turn, the quality of his contribution. Indeed, work suggests that community members respond to time-bounding by prioritizing their contributions (see Faraj et al., 2011). To the extent that time bounding raises the average quality of content generated in a community engagement, a firm might also be able to devote less time to evaluating and filtering non-pertinent content. In sum, time-bounding a community's engagement on a particular task may enhance the efficacy of contributions and, in part, lower the costs associated with content management.

At the organizational level, time-bounding may enhance the efficiency of a specific innovation task and the product innovation process as a whole. First, the online nature of collaboration technologies enables communities and firms to engage in rapid exchange. Thus, firms may benefit from a faster rate of iterative content development than innovation efforts not using CT. The rapid pace of engagement also might assist firms in identifying and rectifying flaws early in the development process. Likewise, when a firm involves a community for multiple stages of the firm's product innovation process, time-bounding each activity may reduce the total cycle time required for the innovation process. To the extent that time-bounding enhances the efficiency of a CT-based innovation related tasks and given the lower relative costs of CT-based innovation efforts, time-bounding provides firms the opportunity to perform a given task multiple times. Such replication may assist a firm in tailoring a product or service to user preferences and improve market acceptance accordingly. Taken together, the above arguments suggest that time- bounding may promote community participation and efficient collaborative innovation thereby enhancing the outcomes of a specific innovation task and a firm's overall innovation process.

However, time-bounding may limit the range, quantity and/or scope of a community's contributions. First, time-bounding a community's engagement on a task or problem limits the amount of time that a community may work in iterative development and in turn, the amount of content that might be generated. Similarly, "the more time people spend evolving others' contributed ideas and responding to others' comments on those ideas, the more the ideas can evolve" (Faraj, 2011). Conversely, since not all content has equal value, more content might not necessarily equate to "better" content. A community therefore must have sufficient time to meaningfully contribute to the innovation process, but not so much time as to lose focus.

Several firms employ time-bounding mechanisms in their innovation focused community engagements. Firms such as BrightIdea and Spigit implement time-specific innovation campaigns to allow their clients to quickly capture ideation and feedback in support of a specific innovation objective. As discussed, IBM's Jams are time-bounded (limited to 72 hours) to accelerate the development of innovative ideas. SAP employs a similar time-bounded model in their InnoJams, which typically last 48 hours. In an InnoJam, members of an expert community actively iterate on each other's ideas throughout the session and senior managers monitor the content real-time. At the conclusion, SAP screens the ideas and identifies the top ideas for future development. A recent InnoJam resulted in 12 ideas receiving recognition and attention for development and implementation; 48 additional ideas were publicized to the entire SAP organization and are being considered for further exploration.[15]

Proposition 6: Time-bounding a community's activities will increase the value created via CT-based product innovation.

Time may play an additional role when a firm engages a community for the entire product innovation process as compared to only one task in the whole process. First, individual members' commitments to a co-innovation effort may be strengthened when they anticipate an ongoing or long-term interaction with a focal firm. More specifically, with the expectation of being involved in repeated, ongoing interactions as compared to a one-shot engagement, members may invest more time and effort in understanding the firm's objectives and in understanding other members' "social cues" (Nambisan, 2002: 400). These types of relational investments may increase a member's perceived switching costs (Burnham, Frels & Mahajan, 2003; Hagel & Armstrong, 1997; Shapiro and Varian, 1999) and thus, increase the prospects of retaining a community member for the entire duration of a firm's product innovation process. Such retention is critical to maintaining continuity in a product co-innovation effort. Indeed, if community membership erodes as the product innovation process evolves, knowledge developed in different stages of the process may be disconnected and/or dissipated. For example, glitches in the flow of tacit knowledge and information between stages may disrupt the process and negatively affect its results (Hoopes & Postrel, 1999). In addition, the stability of community membership may allow a firm to avoid incomplete convergence in the evolution of content developed in a community (Faraj et al., 2011) and, in turn, in the outcomes of CT-based innovation. This is important to firms since incomplete convergence can potentially compromise the reciprocal feedback

---

[15] For additional SAP InnoJam examples, see
www.sdn.sap.com/irj/scn/weblogs?blog=/pub/wlg/24873 and
www.sdn.sap.com/irj/sdn/sapinnojam.

necessary for ongoing collaboration (Faraj et al., 2011: 7). The lack of feedback on content submitted by a member also may reduce the member's willingness to contribute to the community in the future.

Given the above, we suggest that time-bounding may have a larger positive effect on the efficacy of a CT-based innovation effort when a community is used for ongoing or repeated engagement (such as the entire product innovation process) as compared to when a community is tapped for a one-time, or non-repeated, engagement (such as a for a one time task).

Proposition 7: Time-bounding a community's activities will have a larger positive effect on the efficacy of CT-based product innovation when a community is used for repeated engagement as compared to non-repeated (one-time) engagement.

Discussion and Future Research Directions

Overall, the use of internet-based CT is rapidly growing with immense ramifications for both theory and practice. However, not all online communities are created equal. Extant work recognizes differences in online communities, but thus far, says little about the implications for value creation in co-innovation. In this paper, we argued that differences in community composition are critical to creating value from firm-hosted communities commissioned for co-innovation. In particular, we introduced expertsourcing as a new form of firm-community collaboration and illustrated how it varies from crowdsourcing and traditional open source models. We then explored factors related to organizing and managing online community collaborations for product innovation – the roles of iterative content development (including problem or task evolution), content management, and time-bounding. We conclude that, in the context of product innovation, a firm may enhance value creation from online communities when it: 1) employs expertsourcing versus crowdsourcing; 2) uses internet-based collaboration technologies to facilitate iterative development among community members *and* between community members and the host firm; 3) allows for task or problem evolution during a community engagement; 4) involves community members in content management; and 5) time-bounds the duration of a community's work on a task or problem. By specifying the above, we clarify the conditions under which engaging online communities using internet-based collaboration technologies might benefit a firm's innovation activities.

Taken together, the above allows us to contribute to theory on open innovation and the use of online communities for co-innovation. The involvement of users in new product innovation has witnessed a broad array of research from multiple viewpoints. For one, work initially framed the concept of open innovation with an emphasis on formal contractual relationships that cross firm boundaries (e.g., Chesbrough, 2003). Our theory emphasizes that open innovation extends to informal, non-contractual, boundary crossing relationships as well. Specifically, we examine one category of informal relationships, online communities engaged in co-innovation with a firm. By collaborating with a range of experts in building knowledge and solving problems, firms may broaden their understanding of unserved needs and gain insights into novel approaches to problem solving. The lack of a formal contractual structure between online communities and a firm however, suggests that firms need to carefully consider how to organize and manage online communities in order to create and appropriate value in CT-based innovation activities. As such, we specified five conditions (see above) to optimize co-innovation with expert-based communities. These conditions may substitute, in part, for an organization's lack of formal control and contractual relationship with an online community.

Involving online communities as co-innovators also has potential theoretical implications for organizational design and development. In particular, who in an organization is responsible for organizing, managing and monitoring an online expert community engaged for a particular innovation task? Should community management be the responsibility of product developers, marketing managers or a firm's information technology staff, or should organizations establish a new, autonomous role? Further, to the extent that treating customers as partners increases the efficacy of their contributions (e.g., Mills & Morris, 1986; Nambisan and Baron, 2010), organizational actors involved in co-innovation may need to develop new relational and knowledge integration capabilities. At the same time, the importance of these capabilities may vary with the purpose and duration of a community's engagement (for example, they may be more important when the engagement spans multiples stages of a product innovation process as compared to a single stage). Value creation from community co-innovation initiatives requires understanding and optimizing these resource allocation differences.

This study raises another question: how might firms garner organizational support for community-based innovation initiatives? In our interviews with over 35 firms, we consistently observed that product developers and marketing managers were reluctant to collaborate with online communities in support of product innovation. In many cases, even when additional organizational resources and support were provided, product and project teams were unwilling to leverage technologies to support development. More often than not such initiatives were championed by a manager that was passionate about understanding how social media and internet based technologies could be used to support innovation. However, these individuals typically had to push online communities to product developers, marketing staff and/or to business units and assertively encourage their use. In one firm we studied, this situation slowly reversed over time as product developers began to recognize the value of an online community's engagement. Importantly, the source and engagement of support may influence how firm interacts with an online community and if that interaction is useful.

To manage the scope of the paper, we left out other choices and details related to employing online communities for co-innovation. First, several extant studies explicitly focus on the nature of a firm's problem or task as an important starting point in this context (Afuah and Tucci, 2012; Foss et al., 2011; Fuller, 2010; Lakhani, 2011; Nambisan, 2002). Consistent with this work, a focus on product innovation, in part, guides our theory. However, further work is needed to understand how the conditions proposed here influence other types of innovation such as process innovation or different types of products. Second, while our level of analysis is the community-firm engagement, other work takes a micro view, directing attention to community members' identity, motivations for participation, and contributions (Nambisan, 2002, 2010; Nambisan and Baron, 2010). Third, recent work on open source models emphasizes the importance of establishing a participation architecture for online communities (for instance, see West and O'Mahony, 2007). While expertsourcing and crowdsourcing are distinct from open source models (see Table 12-1), a subset of our propositions focus on organizing and managing community participation for co-innovation. Last, recent theoretical and empirical work examines different aspects of crowdsourcing (e.g., Afuah and Tucci, 2012; Jeppesen and Lakhani, 2010; Dahlander and Frederiksen, 2011); whereas we introduce a new sourcing form, expertsourcing. Our intent is to address a gap in the extant literature by fine tuning emerging theory on the role of crowdsourcing and expertsourcing for co-innovation. Nonetheless, as the above suggests, multiple factors and theoretical lenses play a role in unraveling these phenomena.

Other areas of inquiry also warrant exploration. For instance, few firms consider the role of intellectual property rights when engaging crowds or experts in innovation. One exception is the intermediary firm InnoCentive which instituted a formal multi-country system to account for IP created by problem solvers operating around the world. In contrast, other early adopters of crowdsourcing and expertsourcing for problem solving or innovation have ignored IP issues entirely. In most cases, the focal firm assumes ownership of content developed in an engagement. Further work is warranted to understand the conditions under which such behavior is appropriate. For instance, how might a firm manage IP issues when community members are located in countries with very different IP laws? Theoretical and empirical work that unbundles the challenges in managing both foreground and background IP in these contexts is warranted.

In addition, popular press examples suggest that crowds can be used for any activities, including those that do not involve problem solving or collaboration, such as brand marketing, advertising, and information distribution. Such efforts often rely on one-way communication between community members and a firm. Shifting traditional marketing practices from offline to online, such as surveying customers for feedback, may enhance reach and reduce costs (assuming effective content management mechanisms are in place), but such efforts typically do not engage community members in joint development or problem solving. This is a critical distinction. Future work might tease out these differences in more depth to understand the various modes of crowdsourcing and expertsourcing. For instance, online communities may serve as a static resource or a dynamic resource. These different roles have significant implications for implementation.

Firms are rapidly adopting a variety of approaches for leveraging online communities in product innovation. Yet, many struggle with understanding the organizational processes and mechanisms needed to ensure these efforts create value for a firm. Against this backdrop, we view this study as an important first step in exposing, and understanding, some of the critical "who, what, when, why and how" questions associated with CT-based co-innovation. Indeed, each area we examined may merit a separate research paper to fully develop the micro-conditions and macro-conditions that shape their efficacy. For instance, 'who' should a firm invite to participate in an expert-based community? 'How' do these types of communities differ from other types of firm-sponsored communities? 'What' other organizing conditions might affect 'how' an online community collaborates with a firm on innovation activities? And, 'when' should a firm engage different types of online communities in co-innovation? Clearly, the phenomenon is quite complex. Nonetheless, this study makes traction by improving our theoretical understanding of the organizing factors critical to creating and capturing value from expertsourcing for co-innovation.

References

Adner, R., Zemsky, P. (2006). A demand-based perspective on sustainable competitive advantage. *Strategic Management Journal, 27*, 215-239.

Afuah A, & Tucci C. (2012). Crowdsourcing as a solution to distant search. *Academy of Management Review*, forthcoming.

Baldwin, C., & von Hippel, E. (2011). Modeling a paradigm shift: from producer innovation to user and open collaborative innovation. *Organization Science, 22*, 1399-1417.

Bayus, B. L. (2010). Crowdsourcing and Individual Creativity Over Time: The Detrimental Effects of Past Success. Working paper (available at SSRN), Kenan-Flagler Business School, UNC.

Bjelland, O.M., Wood, R. C. (2008). An inside view of IBM's innovation jam. *Sloan Management Review, 50*, 31-40.

Birkinshaw, J,. & Hamel, G., Mol, M. J.(2008). Management innovation. *Academy of Management Review, 33*, 825-845.

Bogers, M., Afuah, A., & Bastian, B. (2010). Users as innovators: a review, critique, and future directions. *Journal of Management, 36*, 857-875.

Bowman, C., Ambrosini, V. (2000). Value creation versus value capture: towards a coherent definition of value in strategy. *British Journal of Management, 11*, 1-15.

Brown, J. S, & Duguid, P. (1991). Organizational learning and communities-of- practice: toward a unified view of working, learning, and innovation. *Organization Science, 2*, 40-57.

Burnham, T.A., Frels, J. K, & Mahajan, V. (2003). Consumer switching costs: A typology, antecedents, and consequences. *Journal of the Academy of Marketing Science, 31*, 109-126.

Chesbrough, H.W. (2003). *Open innovation: the new imperative for creating and profiting from technology*. Cambridge, MA: Harvard Business School Publishing.

Chesbrough, H. (2006a). Open innovation: A new paradigm for understanding industrial innovation. In H. Chesbrough; W. Vanhaverbeke; J. West (Eds.), *Open Innovation: Researching a New Paradigm*: 1-12. Oxford: Oxford University Press.

Chesbrough, H. W. (2006b). *Open business models: how to thrive in the new innovation landscape*. Cambridge, MA: Harvard Business School Publishing.

Chesbrough, H. W., Vanhaverbeke, W., West, J. (2006). *Open innovation: researching a new paradigm.* Oxford: Oxford University Press.

Dahlander, L., Frederiksen, L.(2011). The core and cosmopolitans: a relational view of innovation in user communities. *Organization Science,* forthcoming.

Dahlander, L., Frederiksen, L., &Rullani, F. (2008). Online communities and open innovation: governance and symbolic value creation. *Industry and Innovation, 15,* 115-123.

de Jong, J., von Hippel, E. (2009). Transfers of user process innovations to process equipment producers: A study of Dutch high-tech firms. *Research Policy, 38,* 1181-1191.

Enkel, E., Gassmann, O., Chesbrough, H. (2009). Open R&D and open innovation: Exploring the phenomenon. *R&D Management, 39,* 311-316.

Faraj, S., Jarvenpaa, S. L., Majchrzak, A. (2011). Knowledge collaboration in online communities. *Organization Science, 22,* 1224-1239.

Felin, T., Foss, N., Heimeriks, K., &Madsen, T. L. (2012). Microfoundations of routines and capabilities: individuals, process, and structure. *Journal of Management Studies,* forthcoming.

Fleming, L. (2001). Recombinant uncertainty in technological search. *Management Science, 47,* 117-132.

Fos, N.J., Laursen, K., Pedersen, T. (2010). Linking customer interaction and innovation: the mediating role of new organizational practices. *Organization Science, 22, 980-999.*

Franke, N., Shah, S. (2003). How communities support innovative activities: An exploration of assistance and sharing among endusers. *Research Policy, 32,* 157-178.

Franke, N., von Hippel, E., & Schreier, M. (2006). Finding commercially attractive user innovations: a test of lead-user theory. *The Journal of Product Innovation Management, 23,* 301-314.

Fuller, J. (2010). Refining virtual co-creation from a consumer perspective. *California Management Review, 52,* 98-122.

Fuller, J., Bartl, M., Ernst, H., & Muhlbacher, H. (2006). Community based innovation: How to integrate members of virtual communities into new product development. *Electronic Commerce Research, 6,* 57-73.

Gassman, O., Enkel, E., Chesbrough, H. (2010). the future of open innovation. *R&D Management, 40,* 213-221.

Gläser, J. (2001). 'Producing Communities' as a Theoretical Challenge. *Proceedings of TheAustralian Sociological Association* (TASA), Pp. 1-11.

Grant, R. M. (1996). Towards a knowledge-based theory of the firm. *Strategic Management Journal, 17*, 109-122.

Grönlund, J., Sjödin, D., Frishammar, J. (2010). Open innovation and the stage-gate process: a revised model for new product development. *California Management Review, 52*(3), 106-131

Hagel, J., & Armstrong, A. G. (1997). *Expanding markets through virtual communities.* MA: Harvard Business Press.

Hayek, F. A. (1945). The use of knowledge in society. *American Economic Review*, 35, 519-532.

Hoopes, D., Madsen, T. L, Walker, G. (2003). Why is there a resource-based view? Toward a theory of competitive heterogeneity. *Strategic Management Journal, 24*, 889-902.

Hoopes, D. G., & Postrel, S. (1999). Shared knowledge, glitches, and product development in a scientific software company. *Strategic Management Journal, 20*, 837–865.

Howe, J. (2006). The Rise of Crowdsourcing. *Wired.* www.wired.com/wired/archive/14.06/crowds.html viewed May, 2009.

—. (2008). *Crowdsourcing: Why the power of the crowd is driving the future of business.* NY: Crown Business.

Huston, L., Nabil, S. (2006). Connect and Develop – Inside P&Gs new model for innovation, *Harvard Business Review, 84*, 58-66.

Jeppesen, L. B, & Lakhani, K. R. (2010). Marginality and problem solving effectiveness in broadcast search. *Organization Science, 21*, 1016-1033.

Jeppesen, L. B., Frederiksen, L. (2006). Why do users contribute to firm-hosted user communities? the case of computer controlled music instruments, *Organization Science, 17*, 45-63.

Kane, G. C., Majchrzak, A., Johnson, J., Chen, G. (2009). A longitudinal model of perspective making and perspective taking within fluid online collectives. Proc. International Conference on Information Systems, Phoenix, AZ. AIS Electronic Library, paper 10.

Kaplan, A. M., Haenlein, M. (2010). Users of the world, unite! The challenges and opportunities of Social Media, *Business Horizons, 53*, 59-68.

Kaplan, S., & Tripsas, M. (2008). Thinking about Technology: Applying a cognitive lens to technical change. *Research Policy, 37*, 790-805.

Katila, R. (2002). New product search over time: Past ideas in their prime? *Academy of Management Journal, 45*, 995-1010.

Katila, R., Ahuja, G. (2002). Something old, something new: A longitudinal study of search behavior and new product introduction. *Academy of Management Journal, 45*, 1183-1194.

Kleeman, F., Vob, G. G., Rieder, K. (2008). Un(der)paid Innovators: The commercial utilization of consumer work through crowdsourcing. *Science, Technology and Innovation Studies*, *4*, 5-26.

Knorr-Cetina, K. (1999). *Epistemic cultures: How the sciences make knowledge*. Harvard University Press, Cambridge, MA.

Kogut, B., & Zander, U. (1992). Knowledge of the firm, combinative capabilities, and the replication of technology. *Organization Science*, 3: 383-397.

Lakhani, K. R. (2011). InnoCentive.com (A) Case. HBS No. 608-170, Harvard Business School Publishing.

Leonard-Barton, D. (1992). Core capabilities and core rigidities: A paradox in managing new product development. *Strategic Management Journal*, *13*, 111-125.

Levinthal, D. A., & March, J. G. (1981). A model of adaptive organizational search. *Journal of Economic Behavior and Organization*, *2*, 307-333.

Miller, K. D., Fabian, F., & Lin, S. (2009). Strategies for online Communities. *Strategic Management Journal*, *30*, 305-322.

Murray, F., & O'Mahoney, S. O. (2007). Exploring the foundations of cumulative innovation: implications for organization science. *Organization Science*, *18*, 1006-1021.

Nambisan, S. (2010). Different roles, different strokes: Organizing virtual customer environments to promote two types of customer contributions. *Organization Science*, *21*, 554-572.

—. (2002). Designing virtual customer environments for new product development: toward a theory. *Academy of Management Review, 27*, 392-413.

Nambisan, S., Baron, R. A. (2010). Different roles, different strokes: organizing virtual customer environments to promote two types of customer contributions. *Organization Science*, *21*, 554-572.

Nuvolari, A. (2004). Collective invention during the British Industrial Revolution: the case of the Cornish pumping engine. *Cambridge Journal of Economics*, *28*, 347-363.

Poetz, M. K., & Scheier, M. F. (2012). The value of crowdsourcing: Can users really compete with professionals in generating new product ideas? *Journal of Product Innovation Management*, forthcoming.

Prahalad, C. K., & Ramaswamy, V. (2004). Co-Creation Experiences: The Next Practice in Value Creation. *Journal of Interactive Marketing*, *18*, 5-14.

Prandelli, E., Verona, G., & Raccagni, D. (2006). Diffusion of web-based product innovation. *California Management Review*. *48*, 109-135.

Piller, F., Ihl, C., & Vossen, A. (2011). A typology of customer co-creation in the innovation process. In H. Hanekop & V. Wittke (Eds.), *New forms of collaborative production and innovation: Economic, social, legal and technical characteristics and conditions.* Göttingen, Germany: University of Göttingen.

Priem, R. (2007). A consumer perspective on value creation. *Academy of Management Review, 32,* 219-235.

Rosenkopf, L., & Neerkar, A. (2001). Beyond local search: Boundary-spanning, exploration, and impact in the optical disk industry. *Strategic Management Journal, 22,* 287-306.

Sawhney, M., Prandelli, E. (2000). Communities of creation: managing distributed innovation in turbulent markets. *California Management Review,* 42(4), 24-54

Sawhney, M., Verona, G., & Prandelli, E. (2005). Collaborating to create: The internet as a platform for customer engagement in product innovation. *Journal of Interactive Marketing, 19*(4), 4-17.

Schilling, M. A. (2005). *Strategic management of technological innovation.* McGraw-Hill/Irwin.

Shapiro ,C., & Varian, H. R. (1999). *Information rules: A strategic guide to the network economy.* MA: Harvard Business School Press.

Simon, H. A. (1991). Bounded rationality and organizational learning. *Organization Science, 2,* 125-134.

—. (1976 /1945). *Administrative behavior: A study of decision-making processes in administrative organization* (3rd ed.). New York: Free Press.

Sproull, L., Arriaga, M. (2007). Online communities. In H. Bidgoli (Ed.), *Handbook of computer networks* (Vol. 3). New York: John Wiley.

Teece, D. J. (1987). Profiting from Technological Innovation: Implications for Integration, Collaboration, Licensing, and Public Policy. In D. J. Teece (Ed.), *The competitive challenge: strategies for industrial innovation and renewal,* 185-221. Cambridge, MA: Ballinger.

Tyre, M. J., von Hippel, E. (1997). The situated nature of adaptive learning in organizations. *Organization Science, 8,* 71-83.

Von Hippel, E. (1988). *The sources of innovation.* Oxford: New York University Press.

—. (1994). 'Sticky information' and the locus of problem solving: Implications for innovation. *Management Science, 40*(4), 429-439.

—. (1998). Economics of product development by users: The impact of 'sticky' local information. *Management Science, 44*(5), 629-644.

—. (2002). Horizontal innovation networks – by and for users. *Industrial and Corporate Change, 16,* 293-315.

—. (2005). *Democratizing innovation*. Cambridge, MA: The MIT Press.

Von Hippel, E., & Finkelstein, S. N. (1979). Analysis of innovation in automated clinical chemistry analyzers. *Science & Public Policy, 6,* 24-37.

Von Hippel, E., & von Krogh, G. (2003). Open source software and the "private-collective" innovation model: Issues for organization science. *Organization Science, 14*(2), 209-223.

Walsh, J. P. (1995). Managerial and organizational cognition: notes from a trip down memory lane. *Organization Science, 6,* 280-321.

West, J., & Lakhani, K. R. (2008). Getting clear about communities in open innovation. *Industry and Innovation, 15,* 223-231.

West, J., Vanhaverbeke, W., & Chesbrough, H. (2006). Open innovation: a research agenda. In H. Chesbrough, W. Vanhaverbeke, & J. West (Eds.), *Open innovation: researching a new paradigm* (pp. 285-307). Oxford: Oxford University Press.

CHAPTER THIRTEEN

THE ROLES OF STRATEGIC ALLIANCES IN DYNAMIC ENVIRONMENTS: AN ORGANIZATIONAL INERTIA PERSPECTIVE

GONGMING QIAN,
THE CHINESE UNIVERSITY OF HONG KONG, HONG KONG, PRC
LEE LI
YORK UNIVERSITY, CANADA
AND STEPHEN TALLMAN
UNIVERSITY OF RICHMOND, USA

Abstract

The traditional strategic management literature posits that firms use strategic alliances mainly to share resources, costs, and risks. This paper proposes that such sharing may not be the main rationale for strategic alliances in dynamic environments. Environmental dynamism incurs high transaction costs and disrupts the resource complementarity between partners, and thus destroys the basis for sharing. This study argues that strategic alliances in dynamic environments are used mainly to protect the partners' core structures. Firms need inflexibility and stability of their core structures for survival. As such, the possibilities of firms forming strategic alliances are positively correlated with firms' internal inertia. That is, the possibilities are related to firms' routinized behavior, organizational structure, age and size.

Keywords: alliances, organizational inertia, organizational evolution, routines

Introduction

Why do firms resort to strategic alliances in dynamic environments? The traditional management literature provides a straightforward answer for the use of alliances; that is, the main function of strategic alliances is for partners to share resources, costs and risks for a particular transaction (Sampson, 2007). The answer is manifested in the traditional definition of strategic alliances as voluntary agreements between firms involving exchange, sharing or codevelopment of products, technologies, or services (e.g., Gulati, 1998). Sharing resources, costs and risks reduces investments and the possible losses that can accrue to whole ownership while increasing flexibility. It also provides a greater degree of monitoring and control of the transaction than do arms' length market transactions. Existing studies indicate that sharing resources, costs and risks between partners leads to a variety of benefits, which include access to complementary assets, joint competitive advantages, external legitimacy, and strategic networks (e.g., Baum, Calabrese & Silverman, 2000; Harrison, Hoskisson, Hitt & Ireland, 2001; King, Covin & Hegarty, 2003; Park & Ungson, 1997). Many of these benefits are most likely to occur in relatively stable environments, where transaction-specific investment and interpersonal and interorganizational familiarity are most effectively employed. As such, the assumption that strategic alliances mainly work in stable environments seems justified.

However, empirical studies show that the use of alliances or joint ventures increases for transactions in volatile settings (Brouthers, 2002; Contractor & Lorange, 1988; Harrigan, 1988; Luo, 2007). These empirical findings are interesting because alliances incur high costs in dynamic environments. Existing studies show that strategic alliances incur high transaction costs, such as increased risk of partner opportunism or costs of monitoring, preventing, or punishing that opportunism, and that these transaction costs are positively correlated with environmental dynamism (Williamson, 1975). Empirical studies have confirmed the existence of transaction costs in strategic alliances and their possibly devastating consequences (e.g., Luo, 2007). For example, Joshi & Nerkar (2011) found that strategic alliances inhibit rather than promote innovation in dynamic settings. Lin et al. (2009) found that partners' resources may not be complementary continuously in dynamic environments. Based on such evidence, some studies conclude that strategic alliances may not last for long in dynamic environments (e.g., Cui, Calantone & Griffith, 2011). Dynamic environments raise the level of exogenous uncertainty – that is, firms have less assurance that transaction-specific investments will pay off when the environment is changeable. At the same time, partners are more likely to find that adherence to contractual terms will not be beneficial. Thus, alliances are likely to have fewer benefits from resource complementarity and greater costs from governance issues, particularly relating to failure to perform, in more uncertain, more dynamic environments. This begs the question of why strategic alliances have value in dynamic environments, given that these high transaction costs and low levels of resource complementarity eliminate the benefits typically assessed for alliances, and risks can be avoided by simply avoiding the transaction completely. Thus, it seems reasonable to assume that strategic alliances are used in such environments for purposes other than transaction-related resource, cost, and risk sharing.

One view that predicts a higher value for alliance strategies under conditions of greater uncertainty is a real options perspective (Kogut 1991; Folta 1998). Real options theory suggests that alliances provide an option to defer commitment while maintaining a growth option on markets, and that this 'option value' is particularly high under conditions of greater uncertainty, particularly exogenous uncertainty (Adner & Levinthal, 2004). To some extent, increased option value may offset the increasingly uncertain value of 'resources in place' under conditions of increased uncertainty or dynamism (McGrath, Ferrier & Mendelow, 2004). While widely used to explain the use of alliances under conditions of uncertainty, real options models do appear to assume that the focal firm can decide to defer or exercise options at its own pleasure. They focus on the ability to defer capital investment until uncertainties resolve, but generally fail to recognize that the potential for opportunism that reduces the value of resources in place for the alliance may also limit growth option value by putting alliances at risk of collapse due to partner shirking or holdup.

This study offers an additional rationale for the use of strategic alliances in dynamic environments, although one that is complementary to the real options approach. We propose that when external environments are dynamic, the value of sharing resources, costs, and risks in the case of a specific transaction may be fleeting and not very substantial. Therefore, modeling strategic alliances as ways to exploit the firm's core capabilities in the external market more efficiently fails to incorporate the benefits provided in a stable environment. Building on the organizational inertia perspective, this study proposes a new rationale for strategic alliances in a dynamic environment; that is, firms in dynamic environments resort to strategic alliances mainly to protect their existing core capabilities by outsourcing new routines, functions, and processes as a means of surviving dramatic and disruptive environmental change. This perspective indicates that firms cannot adapt rationally to continuous disruptive environmental change because established procedures, roles, and structures make them inert relative to the environment (Barnett & Carroll, 1995).

Although this ecological perspective does not directly discuss the issue of strategic alliances, the argument that firms cannot adjust internally fast enough to keep up with shifting environmental conditions is a good place to start to explore the nature of strategic alliances in dynamic environments. As internal adaptation and restructuring are difficult to maintain in dynamic environments, firms must resort to strategic alliances to access new organizational functions and processes from external sources to pursue innovative and adaptive architectural solutions. Strategic alliances thus allow firms to retain existing resources and capabilities and simultaneously create, perform, and evaluate new functions and processes to cope with disruptive environmental change at reduced organizational and financial costs. This approach suggests that alliances can simultaneously protect the firm's assets in place and still provide the possibility of future benefits as the environment stabilizes. Indeed, even in the absence of conditions that emphasize either immediate asset complementarity or growth option value, protecting core asset value provides a strong incentive to seek alliances.

The arguments proposed in this study have important theoretical implications. Strategic alliance studies have been dominated by the resource-based view and transaction cost frameworks. Organizational ecology is a very different approach from the resource-based view and transaction cost economics. Organizational ecology assumes that organizations cannot adapt rationally to environmental changes. Rather, organization structure evolves as a function of environmental selection. Internal adaptation to environmental changes for individual firms, as opposed to populations, is difficult, if not impossible, in a dynamic setting because the necessary directions and size of any changes are ambiguous and unpredictable and because internal change tends to lag external change (Dierickx & Cool, 1989). Therefore, environmental selection is more descriptive of a dynamic environment than is adaptation by partners. Mutual adaptation can be even more difficult between partners in such settings because they face different internal and external problems. In relating strategic alliances to the solution for firm inertia, this study uses firm ecology models to explain why firms, even large and old firms, may resort to strategic alliances in dynamic environments, even though they do not suffer resource shortages.

Theoretical Foundation

We define strategic alliances as structured agreements through which cooperative relationships are established between firms. Strategic alliances can take various forms, to include joint ventures, cooperative marketing arrangements, and joint R&D projects, all of which aim to govern joint decision-making by partners (Phene & Tallman, 2012). Such a broad definition does not restrict the partner relationships to exchange and sharing of resources, costs and risks but includes all motives for cooperation between partners. Based on previous studies (e.g., Davis, Eisenhardt & Bingham, 2009), environmental dynamism is defined in this study as unstability and unpredictability on the part of environments characterized by high levels of dramatic and disruptive changes and that are beyond the control of the firm. Changes in industry structure, emergence of revolutionary innovations, the instability of market demand, and the possibility of environmental shocks are key sources of environmental or exogenous uncertainty (Zahra, Neubaum, & Huse, 1997). Environmental dynamism also produces deficits in the information needed to identify and understand cause-and-effect relationships (Sirmon, Hitt & Ireland 2007). Survival in such harsh, even overwhelming, settings is often viewed as a major accomplishment for independent firms (Zahra et al., 1997).

The organizational inertia perspective argues that firms cannot adapt rationally to rapidly changing environments because individual firms tend toward inertia and cannot change easily or quickly (e.g., Peli, Bruggeman, Masuch, & Nuallain, 1994). As such, environments select and determine organizational structures. In other words, when environmental conditions change rapidly and continuously, new firms or new forms of organization emerge and mal-adapted firms die and are replaced.

The organizational inertia perspective is derived from biology, in which it is argued that genes determine the action repertoire of organisms. A firm's 'genes' are its core structures, which consist of four elements: stated goals, authority structures, core technologies, and marketing strategies (Hannan & Freeman, 1984). Because of their genes, dogs cannot become monkeys. Similarly, a restaurant cannot turn into a TV manufacturer. Firms with similar genes make up a population.

A firm's genes, i.e., its core structures, capabilities, and assets, result in inertia, inhibiting its flexibility and adaptability (Peli et al., 1994). These core structures lead to sunk costs, political coalitions, and the hazard of losing legitimacy when a firm's goals change. These factors in combination restrict the possibility of the firm's rational adaptation to environmental changes. A firm's operating systems, decision-making processes, norms, and routines are based on these fundamental core elements (Haveman, 1993). Externally, firms are embedded in the institutional and technical structures of their environment (Amburgey, Kelly & Barnett, 1993). Internally, established roles and formal organizational rules are difficult to alter quickly (Nelson & Winter, 1982). Certain organizational members are inclined to resist change, as their political and economic interests are associated with existing orders or structures (Hannan, Polos, & Carrroll, 2003). Moreover, learning is time dependent, as it involves feedback over time (Hannan et al., 2003). Individual and organizational inertia are much more relevant to the firm when environments become turbulent (Hannan & Freeman, 1989), as the effects of change are less predictable and the time available to consider the effects of potential change is shortened.

Structural Inertia and Dynamic Environments

The hazards of core structural change are manifested in three ways. First, core structural changes ruin a firm's reliability and accountability (Hannan & Freeman 1984). The firm exists because it is able to perform reliably and to account rationally for its actions. Firms need particular capabilities to produce collective products of a given quality repeatedly, and must be able to document the sequence and outcome of their organizational decisions, rules, and actions. Reliability and accountability are high when a firm's goals are institutionalized and its patterns of activity are routinized. In a world of uncertainty, external entities such as investors and customers value a firm's reliability and accountability more than its efficiency (Hannan & Freeman, 1989). Reorganization alters such institutionalization and routinization, and thus resets the firm's reputation for reliability and accountability (Hannan & Freeman, 1984).

Second, a firm's core structure produces and reproduces the routines that define its knowledge and competence (Amburgey et al., 1993). Routines refer to repetitive patterns of activities by firm members, both as individuals and as groups. Routines are the source of continuity in the behavioral patterns of firms (Nelson & Winter, 1982). If a firm attempts to reorganize its core structures, it destroys routine reproducibility and continuity, which may ultimately lead to the failure of the firm (Hannan & Freeman 1984). Moreover, many routines involve extensive indirect interaction with the external environment (Nelson & Winter, 1982). A change in such routines will involve disruptive modifications to ties or linkages between the firm and its environment. Even a change in routines that do not involve direct interaction with the environment can have a disruptive effect on a firm's links with external actors through spillover effects (Amburgey et al., 1993).

Third, reorganization involves a large number of resources and means that organizational learning must start anew higher up the learning curve (Peli et al., 1994). Even if a firm survives a major reorganization, its environment may change in unexpected ways, and the reorganization may have been in vain. Thus, due to these internal and external factors, core structural changes are precarious, and lead to a higher probability of firm failure (Barnett & Carroll, 1995; Hannan & Freeman, 1984). This is why, when dramatic and disruptive changes occur in the external environment, some existing firms fail and new firms appear (Barnett & Carroll, 1995).

In addition to core structural impacts, other factors at the individual, organizational, and interorganizational levels contribute to organizational inertia (Oliver, 1997). At the individual level, managers' norms, habits, and unconscious conformity to traditions constrain their ability to change. At the firm level, firm culture, shared belief systems, and political processes support given ways of managing existing structures and behavior. At the interorganizational level, pressure from governments and investors forces firms to continue to use approved behavior. Organizational inertia also results from the psychological behavior of managers. Managers tend to avoid changes when they perceive unexpected environmental threats. Existing studies show that managers tend to contract authority, reduce experimentation, and focus on existing resources when they perceive environmental threats (Gilbert, 2005). These three types of behavior all increase organizational inertia.

Inertia associated with a firm's core structures has important implications. Due to such inertia, any attempt to reorganize a firm's core structure to fit environmental change can be risky and even fatal (Barnett & Carroll, 1995; Peli et al., 1994). Organizations can adapt their operations to a certain degree. However, if such adaptation involves changes in core structures, the changes can be dangerous. The adaptation involves a large amount of resources and may ruin the firm's reliability and accountability. Moreover, the firm's learning must start anew higher up on the new curve. Such adaptation is ever more dangerous in a dynamic environment because such adaptation is more likely to be in vain when environmental changes are unpredictable and frequent. As such, the organizational inertia perspective concludes that inert organizations - those that resist the temptation to adapt - may be less at risk than flexible organizations (Peli et al., 1994).

Strategic Alliances and Structural Inertia

The inertia suffered by firms imposes a challenge for firms in dynamic environments. On the one hand, they must change their activities in the marketplace in order to adapt to frequent environmental changes; on the other, they must try to preserve as much as possible their core structures in order to survive. Strategic alliances provide an optimal solution for firms to manage the challenge. Through cooperative relationships between firms, strategic alliances minimally disrupt a firm's existing core structures but provide new routines, new functions, new structures and new processes that allow a company to survive external turbulence. Through strategic alliances, a firm can outsource new routines, new functions, new structures and new processes without disrupting existing ones. As new routines, functions, structures and processes are implemented by partners, the focal firm's existing routines, functions, structures and processes may remain essentially intact as may its reputation for reliability and accountability.

Environmental dynamism is an important concern driving the search for a new strategic alliance rationale because this dynamism undermines sharing of resources, costs and risks between partners, usually described in existing literature. Environmental dynamism frequently leads to dramatic market jolts, which means that the value of resource complementarity between partners is at best temporary (Goerzen, 2007). Moreover, exogenous uncertainty makes the value of complementarities between partner core assets difficult to predict (Madhok & Tallman, 1998). As such, firms do not know what opportunities or threats will arise in their environments and are therefore unable to predict, even probabilistically, what technologies, markets, products, etc. can be combined for success at generating value in the marketplace.

Further, environmental dynamism makes it difficult for partners to specify and enforce each other's responsibilities and obligations in sharing resources, costs and risks. Due to the ambiguity and unpredictability of environmental dynamism, strategic alliances in a dynamic setting are based on inherently incomplete contracts in which each partner's responsibilities and benefits can only be poorly defined (Williamson, 1985). Information deficits and ambiguous cause-and-effect relationships associated with environmental dynamism make it extremely difficult for partners to specify, monitor, and control contract contingencies and are more likely to provide incentives for partners to break contractual commitments (Luo, 2007). The return on partner specific investments (Madhok & Tallman 1998) and the development of inter-partner trust (Gulati, 1995) will be limited by the frequent disruptions implicit in a dynamic environment. Consequently, firms bear the relational risks to collaborators of the opportunistic exploitation by their partners (Williamson, 1985). Relational uncertainties may be tied more to holdup or shirking, in which partners fail to perform as specified in the contract, as environmental conditions shift, than to misappropriation of proprietary knowledge, which has uncertain value in any case.

If firms use strategic alliances to stabilize their core structure, rather than share resources, costs and risks, the significance of their resource complementarity and the importance to specify and monitor their mutual responsibilities and obligations is reduced. Partners are relatively independent because their existing core structure is well preserved and consequently, their organization borders remain relatively well defined. Sharing resources, costs and risks may occur between partners but such sharing is not the major intention. Partners in these strategic alliances are more flexible and less committed than those who use partnerships mainly to share resources, costs, and risks.

The use of strategic alliances to protect a firm's core structure is manifested in four areas. First, such alliances protect a firm's existing goals that do not match the new environment. Strategic alliances offer firms an opportunity to outsource various production, R&D, distribution, or marketing tasks to their partners, which allows the firm to address new market opportunities. This means that the firm can retain its existing goals while adding new products, new competencies, or new assets to exploit new opportunities.

Second, strategic alliances protect a firm's existing core technologies that may be out-of-date. Strategic alliances enable a firm to shift quickly and effectively to applying new technologies but do not, at least in the short term, affect the firm's original core technologies. A firm can draw on the new skills and competencies of its partners to engage in innovation and technology development. As these new skills and competencies are outsourced, this is not a strongly path-dependent process, and more importantly, the new skills or competencies will not initially impact the firm's existing core technologies, as they are located outside of the firm's boundaries. Furthermore, as the partners implement the main acquisition, production, R&D, and output tasks related to the new technologies, the firm's routines, roles, and rules are largely preserved. This gives the firm time to modify and gradually adapt its internal structure to the new technological environment.

Third, strategic alliances enable a firm to reorganize the means of accomplishing its goals while keeping its existing authority structure intact. To fit the new environment, some new activities must be implemented and these new activities will affect the firm's authority structure. Strategic alliances allow a firm to outsource these new activities to partners and retain its existing authority structure. A firm can, for example, take a minority ownership position in a joint venture to produce new products and leave the management of the joint venture to its partner. In this way the firm will not have to alter its existing authority structure on entering a new market segment created by innovation, and although a certain degree of coordination or adaptation will be necessary, the existing core productive routines of the firm will not be disrupted.

Finally, strategic alliances make it possible for a firm to subdue the dynamism of marketing strategies when faced with unexpected environmental change. Through strategic alliances, firms can retain their existing marketing strategies by taking a downstream partner to implement changes in products, prices, distribution, or promotion. A firm can, for example, develop new products but engage a partner to distribute or promote those products. Dramatic price changes can also be implemented by an intermediary partner. More importantly, strategic alliances allow a firm to retain its market positioning. In a rapidly changing environment, short product and technology life cycles require frequent repositioning, which may confuse customers, and, on many occasions, lead to positioning failure (Porter, 1985). Through strategic alliances, however, a firm can maintain its existing position by specializing in a particular range of products (e.g., high-end products) and leaving other ranges (e.g., low-end products) to its partners.

We noted that this ecological approach is compatible with a real options approach to the use of strategic alliances in dynamic environments. If the focal firm engages in a variety of alliances in response to its need to function effectively in the environment while protecting its core competences and structures, it can observe the relative success levels of the alliances and at whatever time the environment stabilizes, the focal firm will be in a strong position to increase its investment in or acquire successful alliances while terminating less effective partnerships. We note that this perspective allows the firm to engage in a real options-compatible enacted strategy without necessarily using conscious real option reasoning in developing its strategic intentions and planning.

Take Microsoft's recent partnerships with cellphone partners as an example. In 1999, Ericsson and Microsoft announced a joint venture to develop products that provide fast access to the Internet from any device. Business analysts could argue that the joint venture aimed to pool different but complementary technical resources for innovations. However, in 2011 when Microsoft had already become an expert on phone business, it signed an alliance agreement with Nokia that Nokia would make Microsoft's Windows Phone 7 its primary OS platform. The Nokia-Microsoft agreement was not to share resources. Through this agreement, both partners keep their core structures to survive the market turmoil stirred up by Apple iPhone. Nokia keeps its goals, authority structure and marketing strategies, such as positioning and distribution strategies. Microsoft keeps its core technologies, authority structure, and marketing strategies intact when it expands into Nokia's territories.

Although strategic alliances do not alter a firm's core structures, as time goes by the firm may realize that some part of its core structures may not fit the alliance arrangements, and may gradually modify them accordingly, or it may internalize certain of the alliances by 'exercising its call options' on them. Strategic alliances therefore may provide a firm with time to adapt to environmental changes, and buffer them from their disruptive effects.

Strategic Alliances In Dynamic Environments

Routinized Behavior and Strategic Alliances

Organizational inertia perspective suggests that routinized behavior is a major source of organizational inertia. Routine is a repetitive pattern of activity by organizational members, both individuals and group, in response to a defined stimulus (Amburgey et al., 1993; Pentland & Rueter, 1994). Routinized behavior is a fixed set of activities by these people or groups responding to a given stimulus, accompanies by the absence of research. Routine results from memory, replication, habits, imitation and target for control (Nelson & Winter, 1982). Experiments have shown that both individuals and organizations have a habit of repeating previously successful practices or actions (Pentland & Rueter, 1994). In a firm, people may repeatedly exhibit a functionally similar pattern of behavior in a given stimulus situation without explicitly selecting out over alternative ways (Gersick & Hackman, 1990).

Routinized behavior defines a firm's action as well as knowledge/competence (Nelson & Winter, 1982). A firm's reliability depends on its competence to repeat similar functions in certain settings (Amburgey et al., 1993). Such repeated behavior is constrained by and reflect the firm's current knowledge (Hannan & Freeman, 1984). In other words, firms cannot easily change their routinized behavior. Therefore, when a revolutionary innovation emerges, many previously successful firms may not be able to change their routinized behavior to fit the innovation and consequently lose their dominance. The innovation can be a technological breakthrough or a different business practice. In the past decade, Sony in TV industry, RIM in cellphone industry and Sears in retail industry are examples of such routinized behavior. A firm's routinized behavior is its "genotype." Changing the "genotype" increases the risks of failure, independent of any changes in the risk brought about by the reorganization of the firm's attributes. Routinized behavior also defines a firm's external linkages with environments (Amburgey et al., 1993). Routinized behavior of a firm involves extensive direct and indirect interactions with other organizations. A modification in such routinized behavior will involve disruptive changes of ties and linkages between the firm and its immediate environments and the spillover effects of the changes will affect the ties and linkages between the firm and its distant environments. As such, Nelson & Winter (1982) conclude that changes in a firm's routinized behavior will threaten the legitimacy of the firm. Empirical studies confirm that changes in a firm's routinized behavior may lead to the disruption and even loss of the firm's competence (e.g., Amburgey et al., 1993).

However, a firm's routinized behavior may not fit a dynamic environment continuously. Routinized behaviors are not built to adapt to discontinuities. Routinized behaviors are tightly aligned with a particular environment and they are self-reinforcing (Gilbert, 2005). The original motivation for designing a routinized behavior will not fit the new environment any more. However, the logic of the original motivation may continue to pervade the thinking of the firm, often manifesting as deeply ingrained cognition. As a consequence, decision makers of the firm often rely on a learned pattern of response that is structurally and cognitively reinforced, instead of employing new search efforts (Gilbert, 2005).

Strategic alliances provide a solution for the firm to keep its routinized behavior and take advantage of partners' behavior to match the changed environments. In dynamic environments, a firm's routinized behavior can easily lose its alignment with the environments. More importantly, due to the genetic attributes of routinized behavior, a firm's routinized behavior results from the firm's past and, moreover, shape its future. The routinized behavior is based on the firm's internal knowledge/capabilities and administrative heritage, which is developed over a long period of time and cannot be changed easily by management decree (Kimberly & Bouchikhi, 1995). In other words, it is difficult, if not impossible, for the firm to modify such routinized behavior to fit environmental uncertainties. Outsourcing different routinized behavior externally turns out to be the only option for the firm to survive environmental dynamism. Due to the organizational inertia, changes in a firm's routinized behavior may result in failure. Consequently, the firm has to use partners' routinized behaviors to match the changed environments. As the "borrowed" routines are outside of the firm's boundary, they do not threaten the firm's existing knowledge, competence, and legitimacy. Therefore, we propose:

> **Proposition 1**: In dynamic environments, the more routinized behavior a firm has, the more likely that it will have strategic alliances with other firms.

Organizational Structure and Strategic Alliances

Organizational structure is the rule of an organization. It is manifested in various aspects, including role specialization, formalization, centralization, verticality, etc. (Miller & Chen, 1994). A firm's structure is based on its goals, core technology, authority structure and marketing strategies (Hannan & Freeman, 1984). Organizations need structure. Organizations with too little structure tend to be confused and lack efficiency (Davis et al., 2009). On the other hand, the structure hinders the development of competitive advantage. Organizations with too much structure tend to be constrained and lack flexibility (Davis et al., 2009). A well-structured firm can hardly survive in dynamic environments which require frequent adaption (Davis et al., 2009). Existing studies show that a low degree of organizational structure (e.g., decentralized decision making, broader and more fluid roles, and wider span of control) enables and promotes creativity, innovation, and fast response to market shifts (e.g., Brown & Eisenhardt, 1997). In dynamic environments like high-tech industries, such creativity and fast responses to market shifts determine a firm's success or failure (Porter, 1985).

However, a firm cannot change its organizational structure easily. Externally, a firm's structure is determined, to a great degree, by its linkages with external resource suppliers (Gilbert, 1985). A firm's linkages with external resource suppliers shape and constrain the firm's organizational structure in that these suppliers have great control on how the firm operates and responds to market shifts. Internally, inertia resulting from goals, core technologies, identities, roles, interests of individuals and interest-group politics as well as marketing strategies, make it difficult, if not impossible to re-organize a firm's existing structure (Hannan et al., 2003).

Obviously, a firm will be pressed to change its structure in order to match market changes in dynamic environments. However, due to structural inertia, such structural re-organization is impossible or difficult to achieve. A firm's structure is built on its history. Transformation cannot simply be mandated (Kimberly & Bouchikhi, 1995). Firms create organizational structures (e.g., hierarchies, rules, roles) to address market opportunities. These structures can hardly be changed overnight. Strategic alliances provide a solution for the dilemma. Through strategic alliances, a firm can access, or "borrow", different structures from firms that fit the changed environments better without disrupting its current organizational structures. When environments get highly dynamic, the firm can access multiple more flexible structures to cope with a fast, complex and unpredictable flow of opportunities. When environmental dynamism slows down, the firm can select certain alliances to maintain or buy up, others to exit, and can even shift to yet other partners to refocus on increasing efficiency. Existing studies show that firms that work with more and less structured partners were more effective than those who use one type of structure (e.g., Davis et al., 2009). Moreover, "borrowing" external rules and roles reduces the risks of internal conflicts. Keeping the existing organizational structure increases the firm's accountability and reliability and helps the firm to avoid internal "power wars." More importantly, a firm cannot make and maintain an optimal structure because such structure is often unstable and dissipative (Davis et al., 2009). The firm has to shift between different partners in order to keep its "borrowed" rules and roles optimal. Therefore, we propose:

> **Proposition 2**: In dynamic environments, the more structured a firm is, the more likely that it will have strategic alliances with other firms.

Firm Age and Strategic Alliances

Firm age is an explicit factor in organziational inertia theory. The basic assumption of the theory is that organizations must produce their products or services reliably and account for their decisions and actions rationally. To do so, they must be able to reproduce their strutcures smoothly (Hannan & Freeman, 1984). The reproducibility of structures increases monotonically with firm age (Barnett & Carroll, 1995). Accordingly, firms' reliability and accountability increase with their age (Peli, & Masuch, 1994). Therefore, structural inertia increases monotonically with age and organizational death rates decrease with age. Such arguments echo Stinchcombe's (1965) famous hypothesis about the liability of newness.

A firm's internal inertia and its age are positively associated. When firms get old, their internal roles and formal structures are more throughly established and their routines are more standardized (Hannan & Freeman, 1984). These estabished roles and standardized routines result in bureaucracy which delays firms' response to market changes. Changing these established roles and standardized routines will disrupt existing relations among internal elements and lead to failure (Amburgey et al., 1993). Externally, firm's linkages with external resources suppliers will be routinized with age. Internally, firms must unlearn routines before new routines can be learned, but unlearning established organizational practices becomes more difficult as firms get older (Autio, Sapienza & Almeida, 2000). History and experience of old firms add to their inertia. Firms survive because of their previous success and firms tend to repeat their previously successful pratices (Nelson & Winter, 1982). Existing studies also show that past performance success makes decision makers complacent and content with the status quo so that they resist change (Miller & Chen, 1994). Firm experience also influences how firms select alternative ways to respond to market changes. Existing studies show that managers tend to rely on their past experience to predict market shifts and to respond to competitors (e.g., Miller & Chen, 1994). In dynamic environments, however, environmental changes are unpredictable and past experiences hardly can be used to predict future directions (Davis et al., 2009). As such, when older firms exprience market shifts, their responses, in many cases, are slower and less efficient. Even if the decision makers of these firms want to make changes in their organizations to adape to environmental changes, the complexities and the rigidity of their established structures inhibit their doing so.

The positive association of a firm's structural inertia and its age has important implications for the firm's tendancy to use strategic alliances. With strong structural inertia, older firms have to "borrow" different roles and routines from partners to survive environmental turmoil rather than expecting to develop new roles and routines on their own to replace existing inappropriate roles and routines. In contrast, such tendencies to use strategic alliances to work around structural inertia is relatively weak among young firms. Young firms with more flexibility and fewer structural constraints are more likely to operate independently because they can change their existing roles and routines with relative ease. Therefore, we propose:

Proposition 3: In dynamic environments, the older a firm is, the more likely that it will have strategic alliances with other firms.

Firm Size and Strategic Alliances

Existing studies suggest that firm size is positively related to a firm's structural rigidity and consequently to its responsiveness to environmental changes (e.g., Haveman, 1993). Small firms have simple structure and simple rules because decision makers and decision implementers can maintain direct and straightforward communication and report mechanism. Such simple mechanism enhances small firms' flexibility and responsiveness to managing contingencies. Empirical studies demonstrate that simple organizational structures associated with smaller firm sizes lead to superior firm performance in dynamic environments because the flexibility allows firms to keep pace with environmental changes (e.g., Davis et al., 2009). Because small firms do not suffer much structural inertia, they do not have a strong need for strategic alliances to get access to external routines and structures to manage environmental dynamism.

When firms grow larger, their needs for strategic alliances increase. Large firm size leads to substantial specialization and corresponding differentiation within a firm, resulting in greater complexity (Havema, 1993). In order to manage this complexity, the firm has to formalize its structures in order to achieve and maintain efficiency as it grows (Davis et al., 2009). The formalized structure results in bureaucracy which is positively associated with rigidity, i.e., inflexibility and stability. Bureaucracy is necessary for large firms. Large firms need reliability and predictability of behaviors in the markets in order to sustain their business across different product lines. To do so, they have to standardize their operating procedures and formalize their actions by applying inflexible rules (Haveman, 1993). Such formalization increases the use of categorization as a decision-making technique and thus decreases the extent of search for alternatives (Haveman,1993). Increased bureaucracy inhibits the firms' response to environmental changes in three ways. First, the communication mechanisms in the firm are formalized and formalization delays the timely transfer of information between members of the firms. Second, bureaucracy needs a great extent of control and coordination to manage the functions of various units within a firm. Such control and coordination delays the implementation of decisions. Third, formalized authority structures associated with bureaucracy create interest groups within the firm, and the decision makers who benefit from the existing authority structure will try to protect the existing authority structure against changes (Hannan & Freeman, 1989).

In dynamic environments, firms have to act or respond to opportunities or threats quickly. However, internal and external constraints or inertia make it difficult for large firms to change their organizational structure in order to explore unknown markets and quit the hazardous ones before the market entry becomes jeopardous. As such, large firms have to resort to strategic alliances to take advantage of external routines, norms, processes and functions in order to survive environmental changes. The argument explains why large firms use strategic alliances extensively even though they do not suffer severe resource shortages. Therefore, we propose:

Proposition 4: In dynamic environments, the larger a firm is, the more likely it will have strategic alliances with other firms.

Structural Inertia and Forms of Strategic Alliances

Strategic alliances can be classified as equity-based and contract-based. Equity-based alliances include minority and majority equity joint ventures while contract-based alliances include licensing and R&D contracts. Equity alliances require significant resource commitment in a different location because they call for an actual investment to set up an independent operation (Pan & Tse, 2000). Such commitment leads to high transaction costs, such as asset specificity and switching costs, which reduce firms' flexibility (Williamson, 1985). In comparison, contractual alliances do not require significant transaction –specific resource commitments or the establishment of an independent organization. Accordingly, partner flexibility is not significantly reduced (Kogut, 1991). In short, equity alliances differ dramatically from contract alliances in resource commitment, risk, return, control and flexibility (Pan & Tse, 2000).

Equity alliances decrease a firm's structural inertia less than contractual alliances. The structural inertia perspective suggests that an important source of a firm's structural inertia results from failure to change its resource pattern associated with its stakeholders, such as suppliers, partners and customers (Gilbert, 2005). When a firm integrates its resources with those of its partners in an equity joint venture, the combination of the two firms' resources makes the focal firm's resource pattern more complicated and thus constrains the firm's strategic choices. Asset specificity and switching costs of the equity joint ventures increase the inflexibility and thus adds to the structural inertia. High environmental dynamism aggravates the risks of structural inertia because a firm's resource pattern is tightly aligned with one environment only (Sigglekow, 2001). Empirical studies show that a firm's resource pattern is self-reinforcing and not built to adapt to discontinuities (e.g., Gilbert, 2005). Taken the other way around, perception of the risks increases the structural inertia as well. Higher perceived risk reduces the number of alternatives that a firm's leader is willing to consider and reduce the level of experimentation in firm's response (Tripsas & Gavetti, 2000). On the other hand, resource commitment outside a firm expands the firm's boundary. Such boundary spanning behavior enhances task specialization and decentralizes managerial decision-making authority. Empirical studies show that the task specialization and authority decentralization increases bureaucracy (e.g., Haveman, 1993). As such, equity alliances do not reduce and may even intensify the firm's structural inertia.

In contrast, contractual alliances reduce the resource commitment outside the firm's boundary. They do not create an independent operation and a separate management team. Therefore, contractual alliances do not increase the focal firm's size and switching costs are kept low. In other words, contractual alliances do not aggravate the firm's structural inertia. As discussed earlier, firms in dynamic environments have to "borrow" roles and rules from different partners to adapt to frequent discontinuities. Due to lower switching costs, a firm can shift to different partners through contractual with relative ease to access different roles and rules. More importantly, in contractual alliances partners' boundaries remain relatively clearly cut and well defined. Consequently, their internal structures, including rules and roles, remain separate and different. Therefore, it makes sense for a focal firm to "borrow" such different rules and roles externally. With equity alliances, partners span their resources across different firms and thus blur the boundaries between them. Resource sharing makes their internal roles and rules similar. Such similarity erodes the necessity to "borrow" external roles and roles from partners. Therefore, we propose:

> **Proposition 5**: In dynamic environments, the higher structural inertia a firm experiences, the more likely that it will resort to contract alliances rather than equity alliances.

Discussion and Conclusion

This study proposes that an important rationale for creating strategic alliances is to get access to external routines, functions and organizational structures to match changing environments. By doing so, firms can keep their existing routines, structures and processes intact, while still adapting their activities to the environmental turmoil. When the cultures, norms, rules, and routines of firms become entrenched and inflexible, their fit or compatibility with their environment dwindles dramatically if that environment becomes more dynamic. Outsourcing external structures can be an effective means of achieving a fit with the new environment. By sourcing routines, functions, and processes externally, strategic alliances increase the lifespan of a firm. This means that old firms do not necessarily die and are not necessarily replaced by new firms. Altering a firm's internal core structure to fit environmental change can be a slow, difficult, and even destructive process, whereas outsourcing new structural elements through strategic alliances to subdue or prevent environmental change is faster, easier, and more effective.

This study contributes significantly to the existing literature. First, the argument proposed in this study extends structural inertia theory because the argument provides a solution for a long standing managerial dilemma. Firms face a critical dilemma when they encounter unexpected environmental changes. On the one hand, they must evolve to fit such changes, but, on the other hand, reorganizing is dangerous and firms face pressures to keep their existing core structure unchanged. This study proposes that strategic alliances, and particularly contractual alliances, provide an effective solution to this dilemma, as they do not disrupt a firm's existing core structures but can provide new routines, new functions and new processes externally to allow the firms to survive environmental jolts. Through strategic alliances, a firm can access new routines without disrupting its existing capabilities. As new functions, processes, norms and activities are implemented by the firm's partners, the focal firm's norm institutionalization and activity routinization remain intact, which allow it to maintain its reliability and accountability, but it gains the benefits of immediate access to different functions, processes, norms and routines. Should the environment stabilize in the future, the firm will face reduced uncertainty if it then chooses the option of internalizing some of these functions, processes, norms and routines. In other words, gradual adaptation may apply.

The organizational inertia perspective suggests that firms face powerful forces of inertia and reorganization attempts increase death rates (Hannan & Freeman, 1984). If firms adapt to environmental change, such reorganizations typically involve changes in core structure. Because a firm's core structure is largely inert due to the complexity and interdependence of the resources and capabilities of which it consists, such changes are dangerous. For example, factors such as sunk costs, political coalitions, and the hazard of losing legitimacy inhibit the flexibility and adaptation of firms when goals change (Peli et al., 1994). More importantly, environmental selection favors firms with highly reliable performance and high levels of accountability, both of which require a firm's organizational structure to be highly reproducible. However, high levels of structural reproducibility generate strong inertia. The process of attempting reorganization thus lowers performance reliability. In spite of its powerful argument, the organizational inertia theory does not explain why many firms survive discontinuous environmental dynamism. In other words, it does not explain the mechanism that firms use to manage structural inertia. This study has proposed a straight forward answer.

Second, this study proposes a new rationale for strategic alliances in dynamic environments; that is, strategic alliances are used to protect a firm's core structure by outsourcing external routines, functions, and processes. Based on the new rationale, this paper proposes that the possibilities of forming strategic alliances are related to firms' routinized behavior, organizational structure, age and size in dynamic environments. Moreover, it sheds light on the mechanism that firms use to select different forms of strategic alliances when they face environmental dynamism. Transaction cost theory suggests that partners suffer high transaction costs, such as partner opportunism, when environments become highly dynamic. However, transaction cost theory does not explain why strategic alliances are common in dynamic environments with such high transaction costs. Existing studies of strategic alliances use resource, cost and risk sharing to explain strategic alliances and thus conclude that firms that suffer severe resource limitations, such as small and young firms, are more likely to resort to strategic alliances. Based on the resource-based rationale, it is difficult to explain why large and well established firms, like Sony and Microsoft, have a variety of strategic alliances. Real option theory uses future growth and opportunities as the rationale for using more alliances in uncertain environments. However, this rationale has its limits in very dynamic situations because prediction about future is difficult, if not impossible. More importantly, to survive firms have to take care of their short-term problems before they can address long term issues when environments grow uncertain and hostile, and real option theory does not address short term problems. The rationale proposed in this study has provided a clearly defined answer for these questions; one that is clearly compatible with these existing economic models, but which provides superior insights in highly dynamic environments in which firms face high external uncertainty and in which environmental changes outpace the rate at which firms can make internal changes.

References

Adner, R., & Levinthal, D. (2004). What is not a real option: considering boundaries for the application of real options to business strategy. *Academy of Management Review, 29*, 74-85.

Amburgey, T.L., Kelly, D., & Barnett, W. (1993). Resetting the clock: The dynamics of organizational change and failure. *Administrative Science Quarterly, 38*, 51-73.

Autio, E., Sapienza, H., & Almeida, J. (2000). Effects of age at entry, knowledge intensity, and imitability on international growth. *Journal of Management, 43*, 905-924.

Barnett, P., & Carroll, G. (1995). Modeling internal organizational change. *Annual Review of Sociology, 21*, 217-236.

Baum, J., Calabrese, T., & Silverman, B. (2000). Don't go it alone: Alliance network composition and startup's performance in Canadian biotechnology. *Strategic Management Journal, 21*, 267-294.

Brown, S., & Eisenhardt, E. (1997). The art of continuous change: Linking complexity theory and time-paced evolution in relentlessly shifting organizations. *Administrative Science Quarterly, 42*, 1-34.

Cui, A., Calantone, R., & Griffith, D. (2011). Strategic change and termination of interfirm partnerships. *Strategic Management Journal, 32*, 402-423.

Davis, J., Eisenhardt, K., & Bingham, C. (2009). Optimal structure, market dynamism, and the strtategy of simple rules. *Administrative Science Quarterly, 54*, 413-452.

Dierickx, I. & Cool, K. (1989). Asset stock accumulation and sustainability of competitive advantage. *Management Science, 35*, 1504-1511.

Folta, T. (1998). Governance and uncertainty: The trade-off between administrative control and commitment. *Strategic Management Journal, 19*, 1007-1028.

Gersick, C., & Hackman, R. (1990). Habitual routines in task-performing groups. *Organizational Behavior and Human Decision Processes, 47*, 65-97.

Gilbert, C. (2005). Unbundling the structure of inertia: Resource versus routine rigidity. *Academy of Management Journal, 48*, 741-763.

Goerzen, A. (2007). Alliance networks and firm performance: The impact of repeated partnerships. *Strategic Management Journal, 28*, 487-509.

Gulati, R. (1998). Alliances and networks. *Strategic Management Journal*, *19*, 293-317.

—. (1995). Does familiarity breed trust? The implications of repeated ties for contractual choice in alliances. *Academy of Management Journal*, *38*, 85-112.

Hannan, M. T., & Freeman, J. (1984). Structural inertia and organizational change. *American Sociological Review*, *49*, 149-164.

Hannan, M. T., & Freeman, J. (1989). *Organizational ecology*. Cambridge: Harvard.

Hannan, M. T., Polos, L., & Carroll, G. (2003). Cascading organizational change. *Organization Science, 14*, 463-482.

Harrison, J. S., Hitt, M., Hoskisson, R., & Ireland, R. (2001). Resource complementarity in business combinations: Extending the logic to organizational alliances. *Journal of Management*, *27*, 679-690.

Haveman, H. A. (1993). Organziational size and change: Diversification in the savings and loan industry after deregulation. *Administrative Science Quarterly*, *38*, 20-50.

Joshi, A., & Nerkar, A. (2011). When do strategic alliances inhibit innovations by firms? Evidence from patent pools in the global optical disc industry. *Strategic Management Journal*, *32*, 1139-1160.

Kimberly, J., & Bouchikhi, H. (1995). The dynamics of organizational development and change: how the past shapes the present and constrains the future. *Organization Science, 6,* 9-18.

King, D. R., Covin, J. G., & Hegarty, H. (2003). Complementary resources and the exploitation of technological innovations. *Journal of Management*, *29*, 589-606.

Kogut, B. (1991). Joint ventures and the option to expand and acquire. *Management Science, 37*(1): 19-33.

Lin, Z., Yang, H., & Arya, B. (2009). Alliance partners and firm performance: Resource complementarity and status association. *Strategic Management Journal*, *30*, 921-940.

Luo, Y. (2007). Are joint venture partnerships more opportunistic in a more volatile environment? *Strategic Management Journal*, *28*, 39-60.

Madhok, A., & Tallman, S. (1998). Resources, transactions and rents: Managing value through interfirm collaborative relationships. *Organization Science*, 9, 326-339.

McGrath, R., Ferrier, W., & Mendelow, A. (2004). Real options as engines of choice and heterogeneity. *Academy of Management Review*, *29*, 86-101.

Miller, D., & Chen, M. (1994). Sources and consequences of competitive inertia: A study of the U.S Airline industry. *Administrative Science Quarterly, 39,* 1-23.

Nelson, R., & Winter, S. (1982). *An evolutionary theory of economic change.* Cambridge, MA: Harvard University Press.

Oliver, C. (1997). Sustaining competitive advantage: Combining institutional and resource-based view. *Strategic Management Journal, 18,* 697-713.

Pan, Y., & Tse, D. (2000). The hierarchical model of market entry modes. *Journal of International Business Studies, 31,* 535-554.

Park, S.H., & Ungson, G.R. (1997). The effect of national culture, organizational complementarity, and economic motivation on joint venture dissolution. *Academy of Management Journal, 40,* 297-307.

Peli, G., Bruggeman, J., Masuch, M., & Nuallain, B. 1994. A logical approach to formalizing organizational ecology. *American Sociological Review, 59,* 571-593.

Pentland, B., & Tueter, H. (1994). Organizational routines as grammar of action. *Administrative Science Quarterly, 39,* 484-510.

Phene, A., & Tallman, S. (2012). Complexity, context and governance in biotechnology alliances. *Journal of International Business Studies, 43,* 61-83.

Porter, M.E. (1985). *Competitive advantage.* New York: Free Press.

Qian, G., & Li, L. (2003). Profitability of small- and medium-sized enterprises in high-tech industries: The case of the biotechnology industry. *Strategic Management Journal, 24,* 881-887.

Sampson, R. (2007). R&D alliances and firm performance: The impact of technological diversity and alliance organization on innovation. *Academy of Management Journal, 50,* 364-386

Santoro, M.D., & McGill, J. (2005). The effect of uncertainty and asset co-specialization and governance in biotechnology alliances. *Strategic Management Journal, 26,* 1261-1269.

Sigglekow, N. (2001). Changes in the presence of fit: the rise, the fail, and the renaissance of Liz Claiborne. *Academy of Management Journal, 44,* 838-867.

Sirmon, D., Hitt, M., & Ireland, D. (2007). Managing firm resources in dynamic environments to create value: Looking inside the black box. *Academy of Management Review, 32,* 273-292.

Stinchcombe, L (1965). Social structure and organizations. In J.G. March (Ed.) *Handbook of Organizations.* Chicago, IL: Rand McNally.

Tripsas, M., & Gavetti, G. (2000). Capabilities, cognition, and inertia: Evidence from digital imaging. *Strategic Management Journal, 21,* 1147-1161.

Williamson, O.E. (1985). *The economic institutions of capitalism.* New York: Free Press.

Woodcock, A., & Davis, M. (1982). *Catastrophe theory.* New York: Penguin Books

Zahra, S.A., Neubaum, D.O., & Huse, M. (1997). The effect of the environment on export performance among telecommunications new ventures. *Entrepreneurship Theory and Practice, 22,* 25-46.

CHAPTER FOURTEEN

CULTIVATING POLITICAL WISDOM FOR BUSINESS DIPLOMACY IN CHINA AND BEYOND LIKE CONSIGLIERI

LEIGH ANNE LIU, KAREN D. LOCH AND DAVID C. BRUCE
GEORGIA STATE UNIVERSITY, USA

Abstract

A consigliere is an advisor to a mafia boss on political relationships. Even mob bosses recognize the importance of a consigliere and formally define this position within the mob hierarchy. The *Blue Ocean Strategy* (Kim & Mauborgne, 2005) describes consiglieri who counsel business leaders on navigating political relationships with all levels of governments. The central message is that managers need to develop political wisdom, like the mafia's consiglieri, to effectively navigate the complex maze of government/business relations in emerging markets such as China.

Representing the blending of wisdom and business diplomacy in practice, *political wisdom* entails three elements: *cognitive insights* on the complexity of business/government relationships, *behavioral astuteness* to execute sophisticated strategies to manage relationships with government on all levels, and sustained *motivation* for continuous learning and development to be masterfully savvy in managing business/government relations. The current institutional uncertainty in China, which simultaneously encompasses market liberalization and a tenuous rule of law, makes political wisdom an essential ingredient for success. It is political wisdom that builds bridges between business organizations and the institutional environments and may provide the elusive competitive edge. We further discuss political wisdom in the context of business diplomacy in the global business environments.

Keywords: political wisdom; business diplomacy; ethics; social networks; emerging markets

Introduction

Business's political connections have been controversial across the global marketplace (Faccio, 2006). On one hand, politically connected firms are more likely to receive government contracts, emergency bailouts, bank loans, more market share, and favorable IPO prices (Bunkanwanicha & Wiwattankakantang, 2008; Francis et al., 2009). On the other hand, being too close to government officials may carry financial and reputation liabilities for business, especially when a "sudden death" of a political connection happens (Boubakri et al., 2008; Faccio & Parsley, 2009), resulting in difficulty to weather political storms when having "wrong friends at the wrong time" (Segel, 2007, p.621).

Handling business government relationships in a sophisticated manner calls for strategies beyond the conventional wisdom of immersing one into the host culture's drinking parties or being carefully shrewd in gift giving. Ethical concerns and the Foreign Corrupt Practice Act (FCPA) add another layer of complexity in highly uncertain foreign markets. We propose that business leaders need to cultivate more sophisticated *political wisdom* in order to navigate such complexity and uncertainty.

Although political wisdom is relevant for business operations in all markets, we use China as a vantage point to illustrate the importance, intricacies, and critical components of political wisdom. The current institutional uncertainty in China, which simultaneously encompasses market liberalization and a lack of rule of law, makes political wisdom even more valuable to gain competitive edge. On a higher level, political wisdom also facilitates better integration with the business environment in China.

We conducted an extensive literature search and developed theoretical models for relationship management in the global marketplace, specifically for business government relationship in China. Empirically, we conducted an ethnographical field study with interviews and executive briefs from 71 MNCs and SMEs in various industries, NGOs, and government agencies in the U.S. and China during 2006-2011.

This idea builds on previous work about human relationships in psychology, sociology, and management. We adopt ideas from Fiske's

(1991) relational models, Goleman's work on emotional and social intelligence, research on the nature of wisdom and its attributes, and the benefits and liabilities of Guanxi and political connections in management.

Political Maze in the Chinese Business Environment

In the recent dispute between Alibaba and Yahoo over Alipay, *The Economist* (Schumpeter, 2011) reports:

> "Whether Yahoo! has any leverage at all in this dispute, however, is an open question. It may just have to be thankful for whatever Mr Ma cares to offer it." "... but China's politics are complex and either by law or procedure, it appears the payment business is yet another bit of the Chinese market that will be hard for a foreigner to crack."

This example illustrates the high level of uncertainty faced by foreign as well as domestic companies in China. A key feature of business government relationships in China is the expansive role of government and the dominance of state owned enterprises in the marketplace. The prevalence of state capitalism makes a comprehensive strategy in managing government relationships ever more critical for the survival and growth of foreign companies. The different priorities between central and provincial/local governments present additional challenges for foreign business operation.

Oversimplified strategies of dealing with government relations have proven to be costly for business, as reported by Tim Clissold in his book *Mr. China* and statistics shown by the U.S. Commercial Services that seven out of ten American businesses lose huge margins or fail in the first five years of entering the China market. Market purists disregard the importance of government relations with the potential significant loss of time and resources. In contrast, cultural enthusiasts place relationships with government officials to the extreme and disregard legitimate business practices such as contracts, making themselves susceptible to business calamities.

Senior managers develop political wisdom by cultivating knowledge on managing relations with governments, consciously learning and practicing skills to handle relationships with government officials, and being curious and motivated to learn and implement sophisticated strategies in managing political connections. Astutely executed political wisdom not only helps companies capture market opportunities and access to resources through political connections but can also prevent the liabilities of being too closely aligned with government officials.

Most firms need political wisdom. Large MNCs may have an advantage due to their widespread networks, readily available resources, and brand recognition. Political wisdom is critical for the survival of SMEs too. SMEs have smaller margins and limited social and financial resources to weather market fluctuations. They lack brand recognition or alternative networks to initiate meaningful relationships with government officials. Irrespective of size, business leaders in "preferred sectors," as defined by the government, may have an advantage in cultivating political wisdom. While situated in China for the purposes of the study, we argue that political wisdom is a critical core competency needed by managers to effectively operate around the world.

Configuring the Business-Government Relational Context in China

Guanxi networks in the Chinese society are interlocking and hierarchical (Chen, 2001). Figure 14-1, adopted from Chen (2001), illustrates the clear distinctions between insiders and outsiders in the network, which is also exclusive and closed, in comparison to the rather loose social networks in the west. In other words, the Guanxi network encompasses more communal relationship models while the social networks in western societies such as the U.S. is more exchange-based (Fiske, 1991).

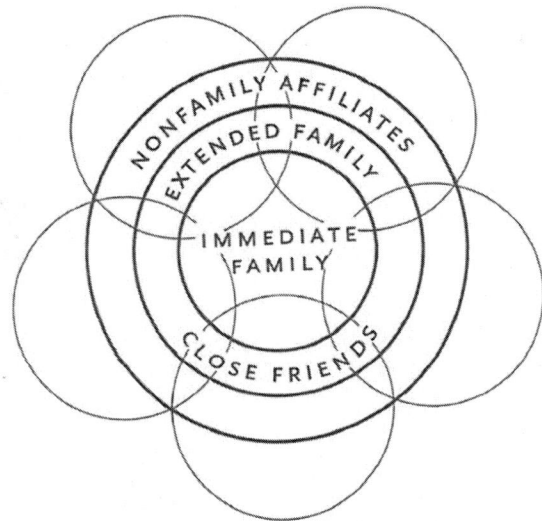

Figure 14-1. Interlocking Guanxi Networks adopted from Chen (2001, p.49).

Although business government relationship is also important for business' access to resources such as bailout help around the world (Faccio, 2006; Faccio & Parsley, 2009), the state capitalism in China and the market dominance by State Owned Enterprises make the business-government relationship in China even more complex (Bremmer, 2010).

In Guanxi networks, there is often a blurred boundary between personal and professional domains, therefore individual relationship often represent organizational relationship, and vice versa. After all, relationships between organizations were often operated at the individual level. These relations are relevant to governance institutions at home country, host country, or international organizations. At the individual level, there seem to be three ways to initiate relationship between business managers and government officials. Figure 14-2 shows three types of relationships between business leaders and government officials: purposeful, professional, and personal. The considerable overlapping space between and among the types of the relations suggests the initiation and maintenance of these relationships are dynamic and fluid.

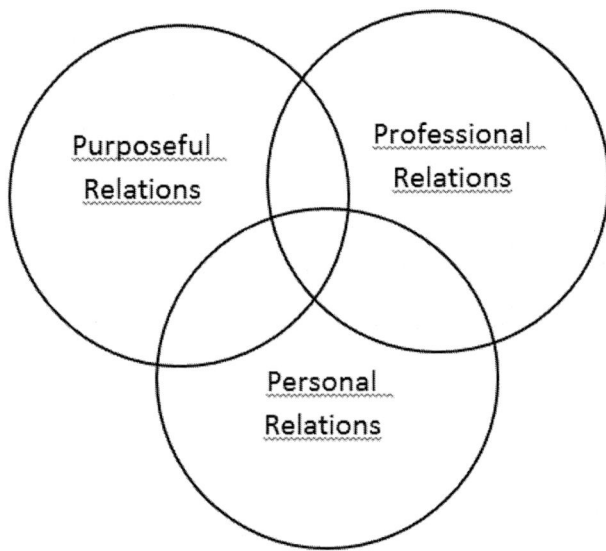

Figure 14-2. Types of Relationship between Business and Government Officials

After the initiation of a relationship with government officials, business leaders often expand and deepen their different types of relationship with government in their networks, including those with central and local government officials in both the home country and the host country. During the process of expansion and deepening, the overlapping spheres of purposeful, professional, and personal relationship often increase. Factors that stimulate or hinder the degree of overlapping may include common interests and shared needs in a sustained connection.

Political Wisdom and Consiglieri

Navigating the high degree of complexity and uncertainty of the business-government relationship in China requires sophisticated advice and strategies from a consigliere. The fictional character Tom Hagen in *The Godfather* serves as a voice of reason (Puzo, 1969). Kim and Mauborgne (2005) maintain that consiglieri can help business leaders manage relationships with all levels of government officials with a strategic advantage. We propose that in order to marshal optimal resources from the three types of relations in the context of business government relationship, consiglieres often develop political wisdom that includes three components:

1) *Cognitive insights* refer to knowledge to understand people, culture, and the complexity of the relational landscape with government officials at different levels.

2) *Behavioral astuteness* represents sophisticated skills to execute a comprehensive strategy for managing government relations.

3) *Sustained motivation* suggests continuous curiosity and attention to constant learning and monitoring both internal and external resources of one's own organization for social connections that are beneficial in managing government relations. Identifying key individuals to handle and connect in this complex social network with government provides opportunities for mature operation in the larger and sustainable strategic picture of a business.

Evidence from our interviews of business leaders operating in China supports these three critical elements in political wisdom. For *cognitive insights,* our interviewees described their understanding of the complexity in managing business-government relationships in China:

> "A U.S. government official advised business people coming to China to "find out who's really behind the scenes who has power."

A manager at a non-for-profit organization mentioned the importance of the "Invisible rules"—government wants them to give and this is enough and they give exact same number/amount, it is more the notion of meeting the obligation and doing the job. If the grassroots Non-Governmental Organizations are all registered then becoming visible, they would have more influence; but government will expect more involvement in their operations. Therefore their strategy is to stay involved with quite small network of those that are really causing impact and find projects that meet donor's interest, use in house assessment tool to find projects.

A manager at a large engineering multinational company mentioned the need to have a "local person with background—background and budget between the 2 communities." This person mentioned that in big bureaucracy 'everyone has the right to vote (a project) down but hard to know who has the authority to approve." Therefore it is important to know about leadership hierarchy that can simplify things.

A venture capitalist talked about being "mindful of laws and government need, local knowledge, as well as Karaoke and KTV—typical for building networks."

A journalist told us that it is also important to understand the Chinese leaderships' belief about slow social changes because there is no model that fits China and their steady steps. Chinese describe "its' like crossing the river" (feel the people would crouch so as not to trip).

An executive in the financial industry mentioned that "Lobbying on relationships is frequent but in a soft way in China. US group typically deal straight/hardball. Family and Guanxi are everything in China."

For *behavior astuteness*, we have found an array of strategies and tactics to execute sophisticated strategies in their management of the relationship with all levels of governments:

When trying to issue a credit card but the government policy would not allow at the time, a U.S. financial institution masterfully took advantage of the network with their joint venture to work around the issue indirectly.

A foreign journalist handled the tricky situation of interviewing government officials by pretending not being aware of some strict rules on application for permission to interview. At the same time, the journalist showed respect for the rules when granted permission without application.

A manager at a large multinational company (MNC) talked about combining the advantages of local workforce and international resources by hiring the "right" people, often are Chinese who were educated in western graduate schools.

Another MNC manager talked about using good projects, knowledge transfer, good salary, faster good environment to keep staff, especially those who have good connections.

For *sustained motivation*, our data show that foreign managers in China are constantly on the lookout for changes in policies, ideas, and personnel in their relationship with the Chinese governments. One MNC noted the importance of intentionally interacting regularly with all parties which fosters good working relationships and as a result, frequently heads up or insights into pending policy shifts and their potential implications. Participants of all industries mentioned about working with different sources partners, including competitors, to gather information about new movements in Chinese government policy. Their sources of learning include all levels of Chinese government agency, officials at the local, regional, and central governments, both mid-level and high level officials, as well as members of the U.S. commercial service in China, plus all levels of managers of their Chinese and foreign partners.

The consequences of deploying political wisdom can pay off handsomely for foreign companies in China. In one occasion, when it was difficult to open a branch in a second tier city, a U.S. MNC worked with their politically connected local partner, who in turn worked with provincial officials at the second tier city, then the government "suggested" that the MNC open a branch at their desired location, circumventing the barriers in the first place.

The "Golden Mean" and Ethical Concerns

Although it is important for foreign business leaders to cultivate good relationship with all levels of Chinese government, a converging message from our interviewees is to keep some degree of distance from the political connection: "Not too far, not too close." This strategy is another hallmark of shrewd operation of political wisdom because foreign business in China needs to be close enough to gain access to resources and information from government officials or their "Red Hat" or politically connected partners (Chen, 2007). At the same time, they also want to be far enough from the center of political volatility. Another wise strategy is to cultivate relationships with middle-level government officials or middle-level managers in politically connected firms, because compared to the top-level officials or executives, they often hold professional and expert operating knowledge, are less mobile, and can weather political storms better.

The Foreign Corrupt Practices Act (FCPA) of the United States and other comparable regulations for other countries do define parameters that need to be honored. In some cases, there may be less strict enforcement of these laws. While there is some suggestion that FCPA may be circumnavigated through the use of joint venture partners or outsourcing of activities, this **is** ill-advised. Rather the consigliere can assist the respective organization in the nuances and ensure not just adherence to the law but behaviors holding high ethical standards.

Business Diplomacy beyond China

Developing sophistication in political wisdom can provide social capital and allies for business in other transitional economies and in one's home country. Xin and Pearce (1996) show that where there is a lack of institutional support for market operation, Guanxi can substitute for such supportive and procedural infrastructure. Similar relationship mechanisms also work in other cultures where getting things done through connections and relationship networks represent the norm. For example, Wa in Japanese culture shows similar function of Guanxi in Keiretsu network and Inhwa in Korean Chaebol networks (Alston, 1989). Jeitinho in Brazilian cultures also involve similar functions (Duarte, 2006).

Domestically in the U.S., business investment in government relations has paid off handsomely in financial performance (Chen, Parsley, & Yang, 2008). In today's global marketplace, competent management of the business government relationship, or business diplomacy has become critical for improving the effectiveness of multinational companies (Saner, Yiu, & Sondergaard, 2000). We believe that political wisdom can be generalized from our discussion in China to other markets, as well as from the interpersonal level to organizational and country levels. In this section, we offer a mapping of the complex relationships involved in multinational business diplomacy and discuss the monitoring and evaluation of relationships in these complex relationships.

Organization and country can be personalized through leaders or key players. Their relationship schemas can set the tone for the whole organization/country, for example, U.S. business managers intentionally use communal schema when doing business in China, so would Chinese managers dealing with Africa. Organizations, especially countries provide the cultural context for relationship networks to evolve and develop. For example, due to a higher degree of cultural tightness in Japan, it will be hard to join a network, or it is hard to break in to a tightly knitted network because of close monitoring (Gelfand et al., 2006). Organizations in certain industries (like restaurants vs. banks vs. universities) and countries in certain organizations (such as G77 or G8) may have different norms and expectations on their relationship networks both inside and outside their own identified networks. Therefore, the relationship schemas held by individual players in those organizations or nations, would be represented at the higher level of interactions, thus influence the corresponding practices at the organization and country levels.

In today's world environment, countries are engaged in a variety of activities under the broad umbrella of "business diplomacy." In other words, they conduct diplomacy regarding commercial relations in the form of bilateral and multilateral negotiations and on-going involvement with inter-governmental organizations from regional economic integration institutions to the World Trade Organization (WTO). When a company is facing global competition, there is often a strong push within the enterprise to open new markets, expand foreign trade, and build international sales. All are understandably high priorities for the firm's executives. Yet, the relevant business decisions will be made in the context of the potential host government's political culture and economic realities. Add to each of these situations the vast array of local customs, cultures, policies, and regulations and it is quickly evident that in reality, business practices vary dramatically from market to market. Also, governments affect the environment of doing international business by creating bilateral and multilateral trade agreements with other governments. In this extended abstract, we first present an effort to map the relationships involved in business diplomacy. Then we prescribe a framework to manage, monitor, and evaluate those dynamic relationships. Finally we discuss theoretical and practical significance of managing the relationships in business diplomacy.

Business diplomacy involves managing and engaging in a wide array of relationships. From a relationship management perspective, these relationships can be grouped into three categories: interpersonal relationships, meso level relationships between business and government and other organizations, and macro level relationships that involve public diplomacy between business and the general public. In most cases, relationship building and maintenance occurs at the interpersonal level. At the same time, those individuals are representatives of business, government, or organizations. Also, there are both internally oriented relationships that involve relations inside the company and inside the domestic country border and externally oriented relationships that involve relations across the cultures and the national borders.

Figure 14-3 depicts four areas of relations that are involved in business diplomacy:

I.) Relationships for In-house and Outsourced Risk Assessment, Analysis, and Forecasting: These functions are often carried out by specialists in risk identification, assessment, analysis, and forecasting. These experts may be found within the company — in the headquarters or at the business unit level. Information may flow into the HQ unit from local in-country staff and/or from outside vendors. Beyond risk consulting firms, analysis may also come from banks, accounting firms, law firms, and insurance organizations. In each case, units may specialize in country analysis as a whole, or they may have primary responsibilities in disciplines such as risk assessment, accounting, law, and government affairs. Headquarters may receive the analysis from the in-house units or from local managers. In any case, to most effectively operate in-country, the local or line-of-business managers need to understand the issues addressed by the specialists and the methodologies they use in making assessments and forecasts.

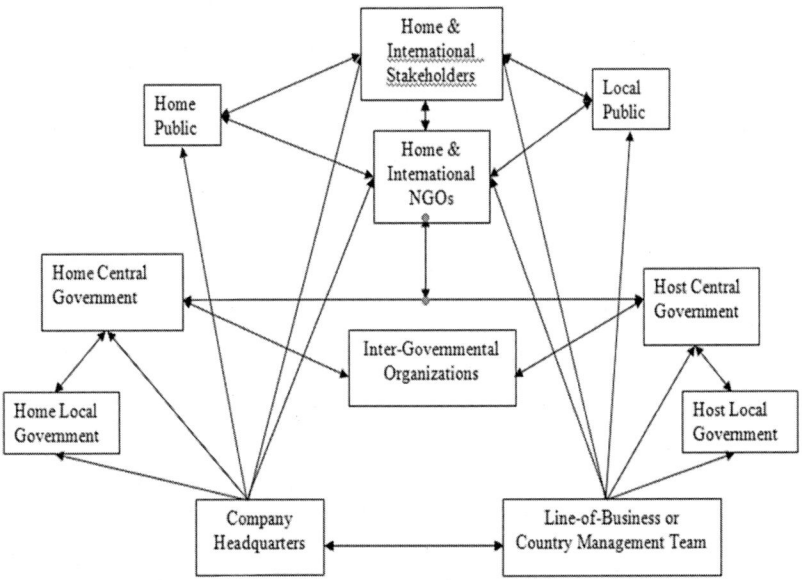

Figure 14-3. Business Diplomacy Relationships

II.) Headquarters Links with Stakeholders and the Broader Society: The company headquarters may maintain relationships with its own home government as well as other stakeholders including stockholders, employees, customers, and industry organizations, interest and advocacy groups-non-governmental organizations (NGOs), and the general public. This category of links includes the traditional areas of business-government relations and public affairs. Companies can relate to international trade and financial institutions, or inter-governmental organizations (IGOs), through their home governments but may also maintain IGO ties through their industry association or directly, especially when trade disputes are under adjudication.

III.) Relationships between Home and Host Governments and Trade Organizations: Trade regimes involve individual country policies and direct bilateral agreements between countries. In addition, multilateral agreements are carried out by IGOs. IGOs report to the governments of their respective member states. At the same time, the IGO bureaucracy has a degree of independence. Furthermore, companies must recognize the importance of relationships between their home government and the governments serving as their hosts whether as an export target or as sites for foreign investment. Such relations are going to be colored by the perspective of leaders in the target countries in reference to the role of trade and investment as part of overall strategies of development.

IV.) Relationships in Host Countries: From the business perspective of the country or line-of-business manager, the most central set of relationships in business diplomacy are between the country operation or the line-of-business and key groups within the target country. These relationships will contribute information to the assessment function and must be maintained for that purpose as well as for affecting the outcome of policy and the link between the company and its in-country external environment. Managers need skills for negotiation and for maintaining relationships with the local players; these include government officials — executive, legislative, and judicial -- opposition leaders, leaders of NGOs from industrial associations and chambers of commerce to labor unions and advocacy groups, and the general public.

Conclusion

We have proposed and provided evidence that managing business-government relationship can provide strategic competitiveness in China and other places in the global market. Cultivating political wisdom in cognitive insights, behavioral astuteness, and sustained learning motivation will facilitate better navigation of the political maze for business leaders. Finding partners and team members with such talent can also be the next challenge that offers a competitive edge. The increasing need for business leaders to be savvy networkers and learners of political wisdom suggests a new direction in global business that relational capital may transcend the dynamics of competition and create values.

References

Alston, J. P. (1989). Wa, guanxi, and inwha: managerial principles in Japan, China, and Korea. *Business Horizon, 32*, March-April, 26-31.

Boubakri, N., Cosset, J., & Saffar, W. (2008). Political connections of newly privatized firms. *Journal of Corporate Finance, 14*(5), 654-673.

Bremmer, I. (2010). *The End of the Free Market: Who Wins the War between States and Corporations.* New York: Portfolio.

Bunkanwanicha, P., & Wiwattankakantang, Y. (2008). Big business owners in politics. *Review of Financial Studies, 22*(6): 2133-2168.

Chen, H., Parsley, D. C., &Yang, Y-w. (2008). Corporate Lobbying and Financial Performance. Working paper. Available at SSRN: http://ssrn.com/abstract=1014264

Chen, M.J. (2001). *Inside chinese business: a guide for managers worldwide.* Boston, MA: Harvard Business School Press.

Chen, W. (2007). Does the color of the cat matter? the red hat strategy in China's private enterprises. *Management and Organization Review, 3*(1), 55-80.

Clark, M.S., & Mills, J. (1979). Interpersonal attraction in exchange and communal relationships. *Journal of Personality and Social Psychology, 37*, 12.24.

Clissold,T. (2004). *Mr.China: A memoir.* New York: HarperCollins

Duarte, F. (2006). Exploring the interpersonal transaction of the Brazilian Jeitinho in bureaucratic contexts. *Organization, 13*, 509-527.

Faccio, M. (2006). Politically connected firms. *American Economic Review, 96*(1), 369-386.

Faccio, M., & Parsley, D. C. (2009). Sudden death: Taking stock of geographic ties. *Journal of Financial and Quantitative Analysis, 44*(3), 683-718.

Fiske, A. P. (1991). *Structures of social life: the four elementary forms of human relations.* New York: Free Press.

Francis, B.B., Hasan, I., & Sun, X. (2009). Political connections and the process of going public: Evidence from China. *Journal of International Money and Finance, 28*(4): 696-719.

Gelfand, M. J., Nishii, L., & Raver, J. (2006). On the nature and importance of cultural tightness-looseness. *Journal of Applied Psychology, 91*, 1225-1244.

Kim, W. C., & Mauborgne, R. (2005). *Blue ocean strategy*. Cambridge, MA: Harvard Business School Press.

Puzo, M. (1969). *The godfather*. New York, NY: G.P. Putnam's Sons.

Saner, R., Yiu, L., & Sondergaard, M. (2000). Business diplomacy management: A core competency for global companies. Academy of Management Executives, *14*, 80-92.

Segel, J. (2007). Contingent political capital and international alliances: Evidence from South Korea. *Administrative Science Quarterly, 52*(4), 621-666.

Schumpeter, J. (2011). Yahoo! and Alibaba: What was ours is now mine. *The Economist*, May 13th http://www.economist.com/blogs/schumpeter/2011/05/yahoo_and_alib aba

Xin, K. R., & Pearce J. L. (1996). Guanxi: Connections as substitutes for formal institutional support. *Academy of Management Journal, 39*(6), 1641-1658.

CHAPTER FIFTEEN

IT'S A WORK-CENTRAL WORLD AND THEY'RE JUST VISITING: FAMILY-CENTRAL EMPLOYEES IN ORGANIZATIONS

MATTHEW B. PERRIGINO
PURDUE UNIVERSITY, USA

Abstract

Work-family centrality remains as one of the understudied constructs in the organizational behavior literature. In general terms, this construct refers to the value that an individual places on the work and family domains. Work-central individuals value work more highly, while family-central individuals value family more highly. Although empirical research has linked family-central individuals to lower levels of job satisfaction and higher levels of turnover, there is a lack of understanding about how the family-central individuals who do remain in the organization handle the complex balance of succeeding at work while maximizing family time. As a result, Family Centrality Theory (FCT) is proposed. This theory explains how the values of a family-central individual translate into action as these individuals navigate the daily challenges of work. Specifically, limiting the amount of time spent working and utilizing flexible work arrangements are the two proposed mechanisms through which these individuals can reduce their amounts of work-family conflict and maximize time spent with family. However, career stagnation (either voluntary or involuntary) is likely to be an eventual outcome. Reasons why family-central individuals enter the workforce are also discussed.

Keywords: work-family centrality, extrinsic and intrinsic rewards, prosocial motivation

Introduction

The work-family centrality construct has been established in a variety of ways. Edwards & Rothbard (1999) draw upon the work of Gecas & Seff (1990) to conceptualize *domain centrality* as "the degree to which work or family is considered important to the person's life as a whole" (p. 98). Bagger & Li (2012) cite Stryker's work (Stryker, 1980; Stryker, 1987, and Stryker & Serpe, 1982) and use identity theory to establish that "individuals organize the various identities that comprise the self into a hierarchy based on their importance" (p. 477). Specifically, *work centrality* "refers to the importance that is ascribed to the work role," while *family centrality* "refers to the importance ascribed to the family role" (Bagger & Li, 2012: 477).

Carlson & Kacmar (2000) conceptualize the construct in terms of centrality, priorities, and importance, incorporating the idea of values into the construct. Citing Rokeach (1973), the authors define *values* as "an individual's basic convictions that a specific mode of conduct or end-state of existence is personally or socially preferable" (Carlson & Kacmar, 2000: 1035). Carr, Boyar, & Gregory (2008) also draw upon this definition, noting that values "help to determine what is important to an individual" (p. 245).

Beyond these definitions and a handful of empirical findings, there remains limited knowledge of and a lack of theory surrounding the work-family centrality construct and, in particular, family-central individuals within organizations. As the title of the paper suggests, when family-central individuals are in organizations, they are not operating in their primary domain of choice. Accordingly, the overall purpose of this paper is to develop an original theoretical framework that explains how family-central individuals navigate the work domain on a daily basis. As a secondary concern, the reasons why these individuals enter the workforce will also be addressed. The proposed framework will be referred to as Family Centrality Theory (FCT).

The specific contributions of this paper are three-fold. First, theories of prosocial, extrinsic, and intrinsic motivation are utilized to explain how the values of family-central individuals translate into action, including why family-central individuals enter the workforce. Second, although family-central individuals have been found to have a higher propensity to exit the organization (Carr, et al., 2008), little is known about the behaviors of the family-central individuals who remain in the organization. Reducing the number of hours worked and utilizing flexible work arrangements are the two proposed tactics to help reduce the negative impact of work-family conflict. Third, little is known about the career paths of family-central individuals who don't voluntarily exit the organization. The ultimate outcome is likely career stagnation, which may be voluntary or involuntary. To begin to develop this model, the existing empirical findings and limitations of the work-family centrality literature are discussed.

Work-Family Centrality

Work-family centrality has been identified as a predictor of work-family conflict (Michel, Kotrba, Mitchelson, Clark, & Baltes, 2011), intention to retire (Post, Schneer, Reitman, & Ogilvie, 2013), and turnover behavior (Amah, 2009). Specifically, work-centrality was found to lead to intentions to work longer and lower turnover rates, while family-centrality was found to lead to higher turnover rates. Additionally, the construct has also been found to moderate various relationships involving work-family conflict. In their study of employees at a manufacturing and automotive plant, Carr, et al. (2008) found work-family centrality to moderate the relationships between work-family conflict and job satisfaction and work-family conflict and turnover, consistent with Amah's (2009) findings. Carson & Kacmar (2000) found moderating effects on the relationship between stress and job satisfaction in a study of government employees, while Boyar, Maertz, Mosley, & Carr (2008) found that there was a stronger relationship between work demands and work-family conflict for individuals higher in family centrality. Examining family-to-work conflict, Bagger & Li (2012) found moderating effects on the relationships between family-to-work conflict and job/family satisfaction for parents in Sweden.

   A better understanding of the construct comes from examining its operationalization. In their study, Carlson & Kacmar (2000) measured centrality, priorities, and importance separately. To measure centrality, respondents distributed 100 points across the domains of work, family, leisure, community, and religion; to measure importance, participants were asked about how important or significant work/family was in their lives. Bagger & Li (2012) assessed work centrality using 12 items from Hischfeld & Field's (2000) measure. They list one of the sample items as "Work should only be a small part of one's life (R)" (Bagger & Li, 2012: 482). They also measured family centrality by replacing the word "work" with "family" and created a 10-item scale. Carr, et al. (2008) developed five items for their study. Sample items were similar to those used in Bagger & Li's (2012) study, including "Work should be central to life rather than family" and "Overall, I consider work to be more central to my existence than family" (p. 259).

It's clear from all of these works and measures that importance and values play critical roles. For some, family is more important or more highly valued than work. For others, work may be considered to be more important than family or family and work may be of equal value. Furthermore, family centrality appears to have more negative consequences in organizations – more severe experiences of work-family conflict, lower levels of satisfaction, and so on – compared to work centrality. However, the construct lacks any theory behind its motivating nature. How do the values of family-central individuals translate into action? In particular, why do these individuals enter the workforce and what compels them to remain once they have entered?

Family-Central Individuals Entering The Organization

Prosocial Motivation and Behaviors

Prosocial motivation, defined as "the desire to protect and promote the well-being of others" (Grant & Berg, 2012: 28), has yet to be explicitly linked to work-family centrality. Batson (2012) uses the term altruism to describe this concept and gets at the idea of increasing the welfare of another person. Specific studies have examined prosocial motivation in the context of volunteerism (Van Lange, Schippers, & Balliet, 2011; Unger, 1991; Sobus, 1995) and donating blood (Goette, Stutzer, & Frey, 2010). A positive relation has also been found between empathy and prosocial behaviors (Eisenberg & Miller, 1987; Batson, Ahmad, & Lishner, 2009). Both Lee & Murnighan (2001) and Pavey, Greitemeyer, & Sparks (2012) also found empirical support for the hypothesis that empathy encourages prosocial behavior.

Prosocial motivation can either be extrinsic or intrinsic (Grant & Berry, 2011). Specifically, Grant (2008) conducted field studies involving firefighters and fundraising callers, finding that that persistence, performance, and productivity were most likely to be predicted by prosocial motivation when accompanied by intrinsic motivation. Intrinsic motivation "involves people doing an activity because they find it interesting and derive spontaneous satisfaction from the activity itself" (Gagné & Deci, 2005: 331). Intrinsic motivation may be the result of a situation where no stimulus exists, in which individuals seek an activity to derive satisfaction from it (Deci, 1975). An example of this type of intrinsic motivation in the context of the present discussion might be a couple who desires to start a family so that they can parent and raise children. Alternatively, intrinsic motivation may be the result of a situation where a stimulus does exist and individuals attempt to conquer it (Deci, 1975). Extending the previous example, a parent may already have children and strive to be as good of a mother or father as possible.

While prosocial motivation has not been linked to work-family centrality, it has been linked to a few family-related topics. A brief review of this literature may help to explain some of the motivational and behavioral tendencies of family-central individuals. Maner & Gailliot (2007) found that prosocial motivation was more pronounced in the context of kinship relationships than it was among strangers. Similarly, DeWall, Baumeister, Gailliot, & Maner (2008) found that when self-regulatory energy was depleted, helping behaviors toward strangers were reduced while helping behaviors toward family were not. Schoenrade, Batson, Brandt, & Loud (1986) found altruistic motivation to be the cause for helping others with whom the individual had a prior relationship, but egoistic motivation to be the cause for helping others with whom the individual had no prior relationship. Additionally, Chasiotis, Hofer, & Campos (2006) linked prosocial power motivation as a predictor variable and childbearing as a behavioral outcome variable. Based on this limited evidence, it appears likely that prosocial motivations directed toward family are also intrinsically motivated rather than extrinsically motivated. However, in their development of the Family Caregivers' Motives for Helping Scale, Smith, Kleinbeck, Boyle, Kochinda, & Parker (2001) found evidence for three of the theoretically derived motivations for helping others: reward seeking, altruism, and punishment-avoidance. Thus, exceptions to the intrinsic prosocial motivation combination towards family do exist.

Additionally, even though many of the examples in this paper will be based on traditional families (since many of the empirical studies have examined outcomes like spousal support and time with children), it's important to note that a family-central individual does not necessarily have to be a married parent. An unmarried person with no children may be family-central in that he or she places significant value on taking care of elderly parents.

Proposition 1: Family-central individuals will have high levels intrinsic prosocial motivation towards family.

Extrinsic Rewards of Work

If family-central individuals value family so highly, then why do they enter the work domain at the expense of additional time and enjoyment in the family domain? Lack of resources – proper food and clothing for children, medication for parental eldercare, and so on – creates a need. For example, raising a family can be a costly venture, as popular press articles estimate that it will cost parents in the United States at least $250,000 to raise one child (Wadsworth, 2012; Taha, 2012). The extrinsic (monetary) rewards that work has to offer satisfy this need. Thus, family-central individuals enter the workforce to acquire these monetary rewards that can be reinvested in the family.

> Extrinsic motivation "requires an instrumentality between the activity and some separable consequences such as tangible or verbal rewards, so satisfaction comes not from the activity itself but rather from the extrinsic consequences to which the activity leads" (Gagné & Deci, 2005: 331).

While rewards fuel extrinsic motivation, the effect of rewards on intrinsic motivation has been mixed (Deci, 1975). In a meta-analysis of 128 studies, Deci, Koestner, & Ryan (1999) found that tangible rewards generally decreased intrinsic motivation, while verbal positive feedback generally enhanced intrinsic motivation. These results were consistent with three previous meta-analyses (Rummel & Feinberg, 1988; Wiersma, 1992; Tang & Hall, 1995). Since family-central individuals seek these tangible rewards, the intrinsic rewards of work are likely to be unappealing. Work itself is likely somewhat unappealing, viewed simply as a means to an end.

Finally, these characteristics are not mutually exclusive. Individuals might consider both the family and work domains to be high in value. Thus, they might be high in intrinsic prosocial motivation towards family, high in extrinsic motivation towards work, and high in intrinsic motivation towards work. Work-central individuals, on the other hand, might be high in both extrinsic and intrinsic motivation towards work but lower in intrinsic prosocial motivation towards family. Given that the primary focus of this paper is on the family-central group, one avenue for future research could be to examine group differences in these types of motivation.

> **Proposition 2**: Family-central individuals will experience: (a) moderate to high levels of extrinsic motivation towards work, but (b) low levels of intrinsic motivation towards work.

Proposition 3: The extrinsic rewards of work will appeal to family-central individuals and will cause them to enter the workforce.

Family-Central Individuals in the Organization

Now that the reasons why family-central individuals enter organizations have been established, the discussion turns to how family-central individuals behave in the workplace and the consequences of these behaviors. In essence, the framework proposes that family-central individuals will attempt to maximize time spent with family while still reaping the extrinsic rewards that work has to offer, which may or may not come at the expense of completing work or the approval of supervisors. The complete framework of FCT is displayed in Figure 15-1.

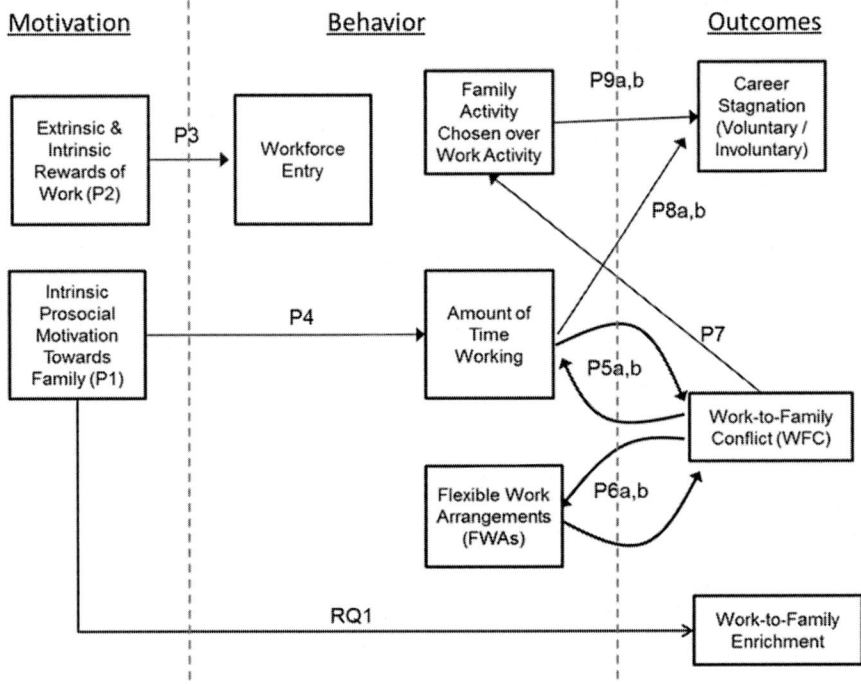

Figure 15-1. Family Centrality Theory Model

Time Spent Working

Sonnentag (2012) notes that time is a construct that has been neglected for decades in organizational theory. Family-central individuals will seek to achieve an optimum balance of time, such that they can minimize the amount of time worked and maximize the amount of time spent with the family while still being successful in both domains. Harter & Arora (2010) suggest that working between 35 and 44 hours per week leads to optimum well-being. Of course, achieving this optimum balance or limiting the amount of time worked is not easy.

People can't increase the amount of time they have (Barnes, Wagner, & Ghumman, 2012: 789). Indeed, time is a zero-sum entity. Many studies have noted the recent changing trends in organizations, which include a significant increase of demands placed on employees (Cartwright & Holmes, 2006), increases in the number of hours worked and nonstandard work schedules (Barnett, 2006; Feldman, 2002), more dual-earner couples and less traditional families in the workforce (Jacobs & Gerson, 2001; Schneer & Reitman, 1993), and the growing amount of work performed at the fringes of traditional regular working hours (Hamermesh, 1999). These trends can also potentially lead to work overload (Avery, Tonidandel, Volpone, & Raghuram, 2010). The concerns of Barnes, et al. (2012) were raised over a decade earlier with the idea of time famine, "a feeling of having too much to do and not enough time to do it" (Perlow, 1999: 57).

All of these trends indicate that more time will be spent working, which will leave less time for non-work activities. This includes less time for child care (Baydar, Greek, & Gritz, 1999), elder care (Doty, Jackson, & Crown, 1998), and sleeping (Barnes, et al., 2012; Knutson, Van Cauter, Rathouz, DeLeire, & Lauderdale, 2010). According to a survey from the Families and Work Institute, 75% of the employees reported not having enough time with their children (Breaugh & Farabee, 2012). Even part-time employees with the autonomy to reduce working hours have been found to work more hours than they prefer (van Echtelt, Glebbeek, & Lindenberg, 2006).

Family-central individuals will attempt to limit the amount of time spent in the work-domain. This behavior may manifest itself in a variety of ways. For example, family-central individuals might spend less time working at the fringes of traditional work hours (Hamermesh, 1999), perhaps leaving the office at 5:30pm when other colleagues normally do not leave before 6:00pm. The reason for leaving early may simply be due to going home for dinnertime, which has been found to reduce negative outcomes related to the amount of long hours worked and interference with family (Jacob, Allen, Hill, Mead, & Ferris, 2008). Work hours have even been linked as a barrier to healthy eating (Escoto, Laska, Larson, Neumark-Sztainer, & Hannan, 2012). Family-central individuals might also work through the lunch hour or spend less time on non-work activities at work (such as taking coffee breaks) so that they can either arrive later to work or leave work earlier. Time management techniques such as these have been found to have negative relationships with strain (Jex & Elacqua, 1999).

Additionally, family-central individuals might choose to stick to standard working hours or might choose part-time work. Both of these options have been found to have beneficial effects and can lead to more time spent with family. Part-time work resulted in 18 more free hours per week compared to full-time work (Buck, Lee, MacDermid, & Smith, 2000), while non-standard work hours have been linked to less time spent with children (Craig & Powell, 2011). In a study of Dutch employees, Jansen, Kant, Nijhuis, Swaen, and Kristensen (2004) found that shift-work led to the highest levels of work interfering with family, followed by day-work. Part-time work had the lowest level of association with work interfering with family. In a study of women professionals with small children, Hill, Martinson, & Ferris (2004) found that the additional time gained from part-time work was used to care for and nurture dependent children.

Proposition 4: Family-central individuals will spend less time in the work domain compared to work-central individuals.

Work-Family Conflict

Work-family conflict is defined as "a form of interrole conflict in which the role pressures from the work and family domains are mutually incompatible in some respect" (Greenhaus & Beutell, 1985: 77). The authors elaborate on this definition, noting that the conflict can occur in the work-to-family direction (WFC) or family-to-work direction (FWC). Additionally, there are three forms of each: time-based, strain-based, and behavior-based. This paper focuses on the work-to-family direction. Specifically, time-based WFC is focused on, defined as "time pressures associated with membership in one role"; these time pressures "may make it physically impossible to comply with expectations arising from another role" or might lead to preoccupation in one role while attempting to fulfill expectations in the other role (Greenhaus & Beutell, 1985: 78).

The part that time plays in exacerbating WFC has long been recognized (Carlson, Kacmar, & Stepina, 1995: 17). Voydanoff (2004; 2005a) found that time-based demands were strongly related to higher levels of work-family conflict. Major, Klein, & Ehrhart (2002), Steinmetz, Frese, & Schmidt (2008), Skinner & Pocock (2008), and Adkins & Premeaux (2012) all found that time spent working was positively related to WFC, while working overtime has also been linked to WFC (Simon, Kummerling, & Hasselhorn, 2004). In terms of marriage, irregular work schedules were linked to work-spouse conflict (Day & Chamberlain, 2006); nonstandard work schedules have been found to predict higher levels of separation and divorce (Presser, 2004); and work hours had a strong, negative association with marital satisfaction for both fathers and mothers (Hostetler, Desrochers, Kopko, & Moen, 2012). In a meta-analysis, Michel, Mitchelson, Pichler, & Cullen (2010) found a statistically significant effect size of .21 for the relationship between time demands and WFC. On the other hand, Voydanoff (2005b) found that time off from work to address family demands had a negative relation to WFC and Matthews, Swody, & Barnes-Farrell (2012) found that family involvement was negatively related to work hours and FWC.

Work time has been found to mediate the relationship between obsessive passion for work and work-family interference (Caudroit, Boiché, Stephan, Le Scanff, & Trouilloud, 2011). Joy in work has been identified as one such motive for working long hours (Burke & McAteer, 2007). In an investigation of managers who worked "extreme hours" (defined as 61 or more hours per week), Brett & Stroh (2003) determined that the financial and psychological rewards of work served as motivation. At a higher level, Feldman (2002) identified several individual, organizational, economic, and job factors as reasons for why managers work long hours. Bakker, Demerouti, Oerlemans, & Sonnentag (2013) examined workaholism in the context of daily recovery, recommending that organizations shouldn't encourage employees who score high on workaholism to do work during non-work hours; Geurts, Beckers, Taris, Kompier, and Smulders (2009) reached a similar conclusion that long working days should be prevented. Snir and Zohar (2007) found workaholics to prefer work over leisure activities. It's likely that these are all characteristics exhibited by work-central individuals. Family-central individuals are less likely to work extreme hours or be workaholics. Based on these findings, it also stands to reason that family-central individuals will attempt to maintain low levels of WFC by working fewer hours per week.

It should be noted that a handful of moderating variables have been identified for the relationships between time spent working and WFC. Job control is one moderator (Hughes & Parkes, 2007). Valcour (2007) found that when the amount of work hours rose, "workers with low control experienced a decline in work-family balance satisfaction, while workers with high control did not" (p. 1512). Grandey, Coredeiro, & Michael (2007) identify family-supportive work environments as a moderating variable between long hours worked and WFC. Additionally, role commitment was found to moderate the relationship between irregular work schedules and work-spouse conflict (Day & Chamberlain, 2006). These relationships likely apply to both family-central and work-central individuals. The purpose of this section is not to re-assert which variables might moderate the relationship, but rather is to address how family-central individuals deal with the relationship between the amount of time spent working and WFC once WFC arises.

It's clear that as the amount of time spent working increases, WFC increases. Does the relationship exist in the other direction? Reynolds (2005) found that WFC was cited as a reason by both men and women for wanting to decrease the number of hours worked. In a study of Singaporean workers, Ahmad and Skitmore (2003) found that most of the respondents were willing to trade some earnings for family time. As a result, a feedback loop is proposed, where family-central individuals will attempt to reduce or control the number of hours worked when WFC is at an undesirably high level.

Carver & Scheier's (1985) control-systems approach to self-regulation of action explains feedback loops in terms of humans having "an ongoing comparison of present behavior against salient behavioral standards, and the attempt to bring the one into correspondence with the other" (p. 238). Feedback loops have been applied to the goal setting literature, where "a goal is considered a referent or desired state to which performance is compared; any discrepancy (error) between goals and performance creates a corrective motivation" (Campion & Lord, 1982: 265). In the present case, the goal or desired state may be conceptualized as a lower level of WFC than the level which currently exists. According to the feedback loop, time spent working will be adjusted since this is the cause for the discrepancy.

Proposition 5a: By limiting the amount of time spent working, family-central individuals will maintain acceptably low levels of WFC.

Proposition 5b: When WFC for family-central individuals is high, they will attempt to reduce it by working fewer hours.

Flex Loops

Regulating the amount of time spent working is not the only mechanism for family-central individuals to reduce WFC. Drawing upon role boundary theory (Ashforth, Kreiner, & Fugate, 2000), flexible work arrangements (FWAs) are proposed as a second mechanism that family-central individuals might utilize. FWAs increase the spatial and temporal boundaries of work, coming in the form of flexplace arrangements – "where work is conducted" – or flextime arrangements – "when work is conducted" (Rau & Hyland, 2002: 112).

Although the use of FWAs is believed to be beneficial (Staines, 1985), findings have been mixed in various studies. A multitude of studies have found FWAs to be associated with lower levels of WFC (Raghuram & Wiesenfeld, 2004; Madsen, 2003; Madsen, 2006; Hornung, Rousseau, Glaser, Angerer, & Weigl, 2011; Hill, Yang, Hawkins, & Ferris, 2004; Hill, Erickson, Holmes, & Ferris, 2010; Hicks & Klimoski, 1981; Geurts, et al., 2009). Allen, Shockley, & Poteat (2008) found that flexplace usage was associated with less frequent fast food meals for children's dinner and Clark (2001) found work flexibility was associated with higher levels of family well-being. However, Hill, Ferris, & Martinson (2003), Voydanoff (2005b), Allard, Haas, & Hwang (2007), and Anderson, Coffey, & Byerly (2002) all found FWAs to be related to higher levels of WFC.

A recent meta-analysis by Allen, Johnson, Kiburz, & Shockley (2013) attempted to resolve these discrepancies. Overall, FWAs were found to have a statistically significant negative association with work interfering with family. At a more specific level, use of flexplace had a statistically significant negative relation to WFC, while the use of flextime – although negatively related to WFC – was not statistically significant.

The model proposed in Figure 15-1 incorporates both the negative and the positive sides of the FWA-WFC relationship. There is no direct causal link from family-central motives to the use of FWA's. This is due to the findings above where FWAs lead to higher levels of WFC, including the finding that flexible work hours were found to have weak independent relationships with mothers' and fathers' time with children (Baxter, 2011: 239). Because higher levels of work-life integration can have a positive relation to WFC (Kossek, Lautsch, & Eaton, 2006), FWAs will be used as a reactionary measure to deal with WFC rather than a preventive measure to avoid WFC. FWAs will not be used as a preventive measure because of the threat of boundary violations, or "behaviors, events, or episodes that either breach or neglect the desired work-home boundary" (Kreiner, Hollensbe, & Sheep, 2009: 704).

To capture the benefits that FWAs have, including reduced levels of WFC, a second feedback loop – the "flex loop" – is proposed in the model. The flex loop is stimulated by high levels of WFC. As a result, FWAs will be utilized. If FWAs help to reduce WFC, then the WFC will be reduced to a tolerable level. If FWAs add to the WFC or don't do anything to decrease it, then the loop will continue back through the amount of time spent working. In other words, if the FWA mechanism fails to reduce the WFC to the desirable level, the family-central individual will resort back to the first mechanism – amount of time spent working – to reduce the WFC. There is no proposed link between FWAs and the amount of time spent working. Theoretically FWAs should simply shift when and where work is conducted. As a result, FWAs shouldn't directly result in a significant increase or decrease in the amount of hours worked.

Proposition 6a: When WFC is high, FWAs will be utilized in order to reduce WFC.

Proposition 6b: When FWAs fail to reduce WFC, family-central individuals will attempt to reduce the amount of time spent working to reduce the WFC.

Family Activity Choice

There are some WFC events which are unavoidable, despite an individual's best efforts to manage the amount of time spent working and utilize FWAs. For example, a meeting with important clients who have travelled in from out of town may be scheduled at the same time as the Mother's Day breakfast at a child's school. As a result, the mother has to pick one activity over the other. Greenhaus & Powell (2003) found in such circumstances that both work (manager) and family (spouse) pressures affect activity choice, as did the salience of the work and family roles.

Powell & Greenhaus (2006) offer a decision-making perspective for managing these WFC incidents. Specifically, they suggest that internal cues (related to the priorities of the individual), role sender cues (the priorities and influence of other work and family members involved), and role activity cues (the nature of the situation, such as whether one activity can be rescheduled) will influence the decision. This paper suggests that family-central individuals will make decisions in a similar way, but that the different cues will be more heavily weighted towards family than they would be for work-central individuals. Internal cues include family salience and work salience. For family-central individuals, family salience will be higher than work salience. Similarly, role sender cues include family pressure and work pressure. The family-central individual will likely feel more family pressure (i.e., the family activity should be chosen) than work pressure. In the example above, even though a family-central mother may have celebrated Mother's Day with her family during the previous weekend, the desire (or obligation, even) to attend the breakfast at school may still take priority over the important work meeting.

> **Proposition 7**: When a WFC arises, family-central individuals will be more likely to choose the family activity over the work activity compared to work-central individuals.

Career Stagnation

In their description of work central individuals, Bagger & Li (2012) offer the example of how an individual may be willing to pass on a promotion so that he or she can spend more time with the family. This section provides a theoretical foundation for why such decisions might occur and why career stagnation (as opposed to career advancement) might be an attractive and viable option.

Fear of success theory, which is an extension of achievement motivation theory (Horner, 1978) partially helps to explain Bagger & Li's hypothetical example of career stagnation. The main premise of the theory is that there is "a tendency to avoid success among females in competitive-achievement-oriented situations, particularly those involving competition against males" (Horner, 1978: 42). The theory received much attention in the 1970's (e.g., Feather & Raphelson, 1974; Olsen & Willemsen, 1978; Janda, O'Grady, & Capps, 1978) and the 1980's (e.g., Gross & Gross, 1985; Popp & Muhs, 1982). Many of these studies focused on gender differences (e.g., Tresemer, 1976; Hoffman, 1977; Shapiro, 1979; Hoffman, 1974), but the results have been mixed. While Esposito (1977), Mulig (1985), and Fried-Buchalter (1997) found women to be higher in fear of success than men, Marshall & Karabenick (1977), Fleming (1982), Forbes & King (1983), Weinreich-Haste (1978), and Bremer & Wittig (1980) all did not find any significant effects for gender differences. These results have been not without controversy, as a measurement issues have been well documented. In a psychometric evaluation of four different measures of fear of success, Paludi (1984) suggested that "each had its own limitations and should not be employed until a replicable body of research exists" (p. 765).

Some studies have attempted to re-frame the theory. For example, although Wood & Greenfeld (1979) did not find any fear of success gender differences, they did find that managers in the private sector were likely to be higher in fear of success than were managers in the public sector. Recently, Ivers & Downes (2012) suggested that fear of success was not driven by gender but driven by social class, as success would "lead to alienation from their community, and the loss of identity and loss of overall sense of belonging within their culture" (p. 369). In this re-conceptualization sense, consistent with Bagger & Li's (2012) hypothetical example, family-central individuals may exhibit a fear of success tendency when it comes to ascending the corporate ladder. However, there are two crucial differences between this conceptualization and the previously referenced fear of success studies.

First, in all of the previous studies, "success" has a positive connotation and the consequence of "fearing success" resulted in some worse (performance) outcome. However, consider a family-central individual who has ascended to the managerial ranks but turns down an executive level promotion. It's difficult to argue that he or she has not built a successful career by reaching that managerial position. Second, unlike the conditions of the previous studies, there is an opportunity for success in a second domain – the family domain. In this context, to consider fear of success exclusively in the work domain would only tell half of the story and ignores the potential to consider a successful parent who has a great relationship with his or her children despite a mediocre career. Therefore, while the overall idea of "fearing success" from Horner's theory is applicable, it would be improper to consider the original fear of success conceptualization as the motivating force behind such career-related decisions. Horner's theory may be thought of as more of an analogy to explain this premise of FCT than it should be as a foundation for it.

Returning to the ideas in previous sections of the paper, some evidence links the amount of time worked to career advancement. For example, in their investigation of research productivity among faculty, Liddle, Westergren, & Duke (1997) found that "high producers" spent 7 more hours per week working, specifically working on research. Feldman (2002) suggested that some of the reasons that managers work long hours include job factors such as visibility of work, tangibility of results, and performance appraisal criteria; these factors might not apply to employees at lower levels of an organization. Lyon & Woodward (2004) cite the demand for long working hours in leading positions as a reason why leaders of organizations have significant temporal constraints (p. 205). Consistent with the propositions in Figure 15-1, it seems reasonable that family-centered individuals would be wary of these greater time commitments at work, which would result in more time spent away from family. This fearing of "success" (to again draw upon the analogy of Horner's theory) can result in voluntary career stagnation.

Career stagnation may be involuntary, as well. The choice of family activities over work activities and the limitation of hours worked could mean that some individuals get passed over for desired promotions. For example, as one might expect, Hall, Lee, Kossek, & Las Heras (2012) found that full-time workers received more promotions than part-time workers. Yet what about parents who "have developed strategies to maximize their time with children and with family" (Offer & Schneider, 2008: 179)? Although employees can either accept or resist the ways in which managers try to control the number of hours worked, "those who resist are penalized by the reward system, even when they devise creative ways to schedule and complete their work" (Perlow, 1998: 328).

Proposition 8: Over time, limiting the amount of time spent working will result in (a) voluntary career stagnation, or (b) involuntary career stagnation.

Proposition 9: Over time, a propensity to choose family activities over work activities when WFC exists will result in (a) voluntary career stagnation, or (b) involuntary career stagnation.

Future Directions

Work-Family Enrichment

Work-family enrichment has been defined as "the extent to which experiences in one role improve the quality of life in the other role" (Greenhaus & Powell, 2006: 73), where one role refers to family and the other role refers to work. According to the authors, there are two paths through which this may occur. The first path is the instrumental path, where resources from one role may be directly transferred to the other role, enhancing performance in the second role. These resources include flexibility, defined as "the discretion to determine the timing, pace, and location at which role requirements are met" (Greenhaus & Powell, 2006: 80) and psychological resources. The second path is an affective one, where these resources generate positive affect, which in turn leads to high performance and positive affect in the second role.

Similarly, work-family facilitation has been defined as "the extent to which an individual's engagement in one social system, such as work or family, contributes to growth in another social system" (Grzywacz, Carlson, Kacmar, & Wayne, 2007: 559). There are four types of work-family facilitation: energy-based, time-based, behavioral-based, and psychological-based (van Steenbergen, Ellemers, & Mooijaart, 2007).

Both constructs are similar in that there are suggested benefits of how one domain can help enhance experiences in the other domain. Consistent with the work-family conflict discussion earlier, this paper addresses the work-to-family enrichment/facilitation direction, although these constructs can also be bi-directional (Greenhaus & Powell, 2006). The empirical evidence has been consistent in determining that work-family enrichment leads to higher levels of satisfaction and commitment (McNall, Nicklin, & Masuda, 2010; Bhargava & Baral, 2009; Jaga & Bagraim, 2011; Michel & Clark, 2009). Similar results have occurred when work-family facilitation was examined (Wiese & Salmela-Aro, 2008). Additionally, work-family facilitation has also been linked to better health outcomes, less absenteeism, and better job performance (van Steenbergen & Ellemers, 2009)

Work-family centrality has yet to be linked to work-family enrichment. At first glance, it might seem that family-central individuals would experience lower levels of enrichment. If family-central workers have low levels of intrinsic motivation towards work or if some don't want to be at work at all, then it's difficult to assess how the work domain would be enriching for them. In their study of Chinese employees, Siu, Lu, Brough, Lu, Bakker, Kalliath, O'Driscoll, Phillips, Chen, Lo, Sit, & Shi (2010) found that work engagement was the most proximal predictor of work-family enrichment (p. 470), which lends support to this idea. Alternatively, since these individuals are extrinsically motivated, one might hypothesize that work will be enriching to the family domain to the extent that extrinsic rewards meet or exceed expectations.

An examination of some of the empirical works on work-family enrichment paints a slightly different picture. When examined as a mediating variable, work-family enrichment and work-family facilitation seem to enhance the positive effects of antecedents such as family supportive supervisor behaviors (FSSB's; Odle-Dusseau, Britt, & Greene-Shortridge, 2012), schedule control (Carlson, Ferguson, Kacmar, Grzywacz, & Whitten, 2011), informal emotional support (Wayne, Randel, & Stevens, 2006), supportive work-family culture (Peeters, Wattez,

Demerouti, & de Regt, 2009; Gordon, Whelan-Berry, & Hamilton, 2007), autonomy (Warner & Hausdorf, 2009) and flexible work arrangements (McNall, Masuda, & Nicklin, 2009) on similar outcomes listed earlier, most notably increased job satisfaction, lower turnover intentions, and family performance (Carlson, Grzywacz, & Kacmar, 2010). Since supportive work-family cultures, FSSB's, autonomy, emotional support, and flexible work arrangements are all likely to help family-central individuals navigate the daily challenges of work, it seems that enrichment could be experienced. Because both sides of the discussion have reasonable arguments and because a variety of variables might moderate the relationship, a research question is put forth instead of a formal proposition:

> **Research Question** 1: To what extent will family-central individuals experience work-family enrichment?

Limitations and Future Research

One limitation of the current propositions is that they are designed to apply specifically to family-central individuals. However, it's quite possible that certain aspects of the model would apply to a much broader range of employees. Although rare, there is limited evidence for cyclical models to exist in the work-family literature. For example, Steinmetz, Frese, & Schmidt (2008) found that job stressors led to depression, which led to work-home interference. In turn, work-home interference led back to job stressors. A longitudinal, empirical examination of flex loops might reveal a pattern that exists for both family-central and work-central individuals. A second area that warrants further examination is the idea of voluntary career stagnation, which also could apply to a broad range of employees. Both of these future research directions could help to enhance the work-family and organizational behavior literatures.

Propositions about job satisfaction and turnover are notably absent from this paper. There are two reasons for this. First, the core focus of the discussion was to better understand family-central individuals in the organization. Therefore, the left and middle pieces of the model – the entering and navigating of the workplace – received the primary focus. Job satisfaction and turnover have been shown to be more distal outcomes, often preceded by WFC (e.g., Carlson & Kacmar, 2000; Bagger & Li, 2012; Carr, et al. 2008). Second, unlike the discussion concerning FWAs where there were many conflicting findings, the findings concerning family-central individuals in terms of job satisfaction and turnover have been consistent. Specifically, family-central individuals have been lower in job satisfaction (Carlson & Kacmar, 2000; Bagger & Li, 2012) and have shown higher turnover rates (Carr, et al., 2008). However, also unlike the literature on FWAs, there are a limited amount of studies concerning work-family centrality. Future research would do well to replicate these findings. Other distal outcomes that have been examined in the work-family literature including spillover (e.g., Bass, Butler, Grzywacz, & Linney, 2009; Heller & Watson, 2005), positive and negative affect (e.g., Judge, Ilies, & Scott, 2006; Ilies, Schwind, Wagner, Johnson, DeRue, & Ilgen, 2007), and feelings of guilt (e.g., Offer & Schneider, 2008) might be examined in the context of work-family centrality, as well. Experience sampling method studies employing daily diary survey techniques may also be useful for capturing these distal outcomes and extending the literature on work-family centrality.

There are practical implications for understanding family-central individuals in the organizational context, too. First, organizations might tailor specific jobs to family-central individuals. These may be lower-exposure roles that are designed to have less of a time commitment. Of course, these roles might also have fewer extrinsic rewards (slower career advancement, a lower salary, etc.). Second, organizations might re-evaluate their parental leave policies. Misra, Budig, & Boeckmann (2011) found that leaves moderate in length can have positive effects, but that tradeoffs exist if the policies are too long. In addition to maternity leave, paternity leave may also be offered since Yeung, Sandberg, Davis-Kean, & Hofferth (2004) found that "fathers' involvement relative to that of mothers appears to be on the increase" (p. 136). Tanaka & Waldfogel (2007) also found that taking a leave of absence and working shorter hours led to fathers being more involved with their baby.

Organizations must be careful in terms of how generous these policies are and how these policies are implemented, as these policies may not be for everyone. Sometimes efforts to reduce the number of hours worked can be met with resistance (Lautsch & Scully, 2007; Barnett & Gareis, 2000). Additionally, Martin, Sinclair, Lelchook, Wittmer, & Charles (2012) have linked non-standard work schedules to higher turnover levels. If these policies are executed correctly, however, the low levels of job satisfaction may begin to rise and higher levels of turnover may begin to decrease for family-central individuals.

Conclusion

It's important to remember that "mastering time conflicts is an integrated part of doing the job" (Kamp, Lund, & Hvid, 2011: 229). If individuals can't do this – regardless of whether they are work-central or family-central – then they will either seek new roles or exit the organization. Nevertheless, work-central individuals are more "at home" in the organization compared to family-central individuals, who consider the organization to be their second domain of interest. As a result – and as this paper suggests – it's important to better understand the family-central individuals so that they can feel more at home in the organizational domain while their family domain remains as pleasant and as undisturbed as possible. Doing so would ultimately benefit both these individuals and the organization.

References

Adkins, C. L., & Premeaux, S. F. (2012). Spending time: The impact of hours worked on work–family conflict. *Journal of Vocational Behavior, 80*(2), 380-389.

Ahmad, S., & Skitmore, M. (2003). Work-family conflict: a survey of Singaporean workers. *Singapore Management Review, 25*(1), 35-52.

Allard, K., Haas, L., & Hwang, C. P. (2007). Exploring the paradox. *Community, Work and Family, 10*(4), 475-493.

Allen, T. D., Johnson, R. C., Kiburz, K. M., & Shockley, K. M. (2013). Work- family conflict and flexible work arrangements: Deconstructing flexibility. *Personnel Psychology, 66*, 345-376.

Allen, T. D., Shockley, K. M., & Poteat, L. F. (2008). Workplace factors associated with family dinner behaviors. *Journal of Vocational Behavior, 73*(2), 336-342.

Amah, O. E. (2009). Job satisfaction and turnover intention relationship: The moderating effect of job role centrality and life satisfaction. *Research and Practice in Human Resource Management, 17*(1), 24-35.

Anderson, S. E., Coffey, B. S., & Byerly, R. T. (2002). Formal organizational initiatives and informal workplace practices: Links to work-family conflict and job-related outcomes. *Journal of Management, 28*(6), 787-810.

Ashforth, B. E., Kreiner, G. E., & Fugate, M. (2000). All in a day's work: Boundaries and micro role transitions. *Academy of Management Review, 25*(3), 472-491.

Avery, D. R., Tonidandel, S., Volpone, S. D., & Raghuram, A. (2010). Overworked in America? How work hours, immigrant status, and interpersonal justice affect perceived work overload. *Journal of Managerial Psychology, 25*(2), 133-147.

Bagger, J., & Li, A. (2012). Being important matters: The impact of work and family centralities on the family-to-work conflict–satisfaction relationship. *Human Relations, 65*(4), 473-500.

Bakker, A. B., Demerouti, E., Oerlemans, W., & Sonnentag, S. (2013). Workaholism and daily recovery: A day reconstruction study of leisure activities. *Journal of Organizational Behavior, 34*(1), 87-107.

Barnes, C. M., Wagner, D. T., & Ghumman, S. (2012). Borrowing from sleep to pay work and family: Expanding time-based conflict to the broader nonwork domain. *Personnel Psychology, 65*(4), 789-819.

Barnett, R. (2006). Relationship of the number and distribution of work hours to health and quality-of-life (QOL) outcomes. In P. L. Perrewé, & D. C. Ganster (Eds.) , *Employee health, coping and methodologies (pp. 99-138).*

Barnett, R. C., & Gareis, K. C. (2000). Reduced-Hours Employment The Relationship Between Difficulty of Trade-Offs and Quality of Life. *Work and Occupations, 27*(2), 168-187.

Bass, B. L., Butler, A. B., Grzywacz, J. G., & Linney, K. D. (2009). Do job demands undermine parenting? A daily analysis of spillover and crossover effects. *Family Relations, 58*, 201–215.

Batson, C. (2012). A history of prosocial behavior research. In A. W. Kruglanski, W. Stroebe (Eds.) , *Handbook of the history of social psychology (pp. 243-264).* New York, NY US: Psychology Press.

Batson, C., Ahmad, N., & Lishner, D. A. (2009). Empathy and altruism. In S. J. Lopez, & C. R. Snyder (Eds.), *Oxford handbook of positive psychology* (2nd ed.) (pp. 417-426). New York, NY US: Oxford University Press.

Baxter, J. (2011). Flexible work hours and other job factors in parental time with children. *Social Indicators Research, 101*(2), 239-242.

Baydar, N., Greek, A., & Gritz, R. M. 1999. Young mothers' time spent at work and time spent caring for children. *Journal of Family and Economic Issues, 20*(1), 61-84.

Bhargava, S., & Baral, R. (2009). Antecedents and consequences of work-family enrichment among Indian managers. *Psychological Studies, 54*(3), 213-225.

Boyar, S. L., Maertz, C. R., Mosley, D.R., & Carr, J. C. 2008. The impact of work/family demand on work-family conflict. *Journal of Managerial Psychology, 23*(3), 215-235.

Breaugh, J. A., & Farabee, A. M. (2012). Telecommuting and flexible work hours: Alternative work arrangements that can improve the quality of work life. In N. P. Reilly, & M. Sirgy, C. Gorman (Eds.) , *Work and quality of life: Ethical practices in organizations (pp. 251-274)*. New York, NY US: Springer Science + Business Media.

Bremer, T. H., & Wittig, M. A. (1980). Fear of success: A personality trait or a response to occupational deviance and role overload? *Sex Roles, 6*(1), 27-46.

Brett, J. M., & Stroh, L. K. (2003). Working 61 plus hours a week: why do managers do it?. *Journal of Applied Psychology, 88*(1), 67-78.

Buck, M. L., Lee, M., MacDermid, S. M., & Smith, S. (2000). Reduced–load work and the experience of time among professionals and managers: Implications for personal and organizational life. In C. L. Cooper, D. M. Rousseau (Eds.), *Trends in organizational behavior, Vol. 7: Time in organizational behavior (pp. 13-35)*.

Burke, R. J., & McAteer, T. (2007). Work hours and work addiction: The price of all work and no play. In P. L. Perrewé, D. C. Ganster (Eds.) , *Exploring the work and non-work interface (pp. 239-273)*.

Campion, M. A., & Lord, R. G. (1982). A control systems conceptualization of the goal-setting and changing process. *Organizational Behavior and Human Performance, 30*(2), 265-287.

Carlson, D. S., Grzywacz, J. G., & Kacmar, K. (2010). The relationship of schedule flexibility and outcomes via the work-family interface. *Journal of Managerial Psychology, 25*(4), 330-355.

Carlson, D. S., Ferguson, M., Kacmar, K., Grzywacz, J. G., & Whitten, D. (2011). Pay it forward: The positive crossover effects of supervisor work—family enrichment. *Journal of Management, 37*(3), 770-789.

Carlson, D. S., & Kacmar, K. (2000). Work–family conflict in the organization: Do life role values make a difference?. *Journal of Management, 26*(5), 1031-1054.

Carlson, D. S., Kacmar, K. M., & Stepina, L. P. (1995). An examination of two aspects of work-family conflict: time and identity. *Women in Management Review, 10*(2), 17-25.

Carr, J. C., Boyar, S. L., & Gregory, B. T. (2008). The moderating effect of work-family centrality on work-family conflict, organizational attitudes, and turnover behavior. *Journal of Management, 34*(2), 244-262.

Cartwright, S., & Holmes, N. (2006). The meaning of work: The challenge of regaining employee engagement and reducing cynicism. *Human Resource Management Review, 16*(2), 199-208.

Carver, C. S., & Scheier, M. F. (1985). A control-systems approach to the self-regulation of action. In J. Kuhl and J. Beckmann (Eds.), *Action control: From cognition to behavior* (pp. 237-265). Berlin: Springer-Verlag.

Caudroit, J., Boiché, J., Stephan, Y., Le Scanff, C., & Trouilloud, D. (2011). Predictors of work/family interference and leisure-time physical activity among teachers: The role of passion towards work. *European Journal of Work and Organizational Psychology, 20*(3), 326-344.

Chasiotis, A., Hofer, J., & Campos, D. (2006). When does liking children lead to parenthood? Younger siblings, implicit prosocial power motivation, and explicit love for children predict parenthood across cultures. *Journal of Cultural and Evolutionary Psychology, 4*(2), 95-123.

Clark, S. C. (2001). Work cultures and work/family balance. *Journal of Vocational Behavior, 58*(3), 348-365.

Craig, L., & Powell, A. 2011. Non-standard work schedules, work-family balance and the gendered division of childcare. *Work, Employment and Society,* 25(2), 274-291.

Day, A. L., & Chamberlain, T. C. (2006). Committing to your work, spouse, and children: Implications for work–family conflict. *Journal of Vocational Behavior, 68*(1), 116-130.

Deci, E. L. (1975). Intrinsic motivation. New York: Plenum.

Deci, E. L., Koestner, R., & Ryan, R. M. (1999). A meta-Analytic review of experiments examining the effects of extrinsic rewards on intrinsic motivation. *Psychological Bulletin, 125,* 627-668.

DeWall, C., Baumeister, R. F., Gailliot, M. T., & Maner, J. K. (2008). Depletion makes the heart grow less helpful: Helping as a function of self-regulatory energy and genetic relatedness. *Personality and Social Psychology Bulletin, 34*(12), 1653-1662.

Doty, P., Jackson, M. E., & Crown, W. (1998). The impact of female caregivers' employment status on patterns of formal and informal eldercare. *The Gerontologist, 38*(3), 331-341.

Edwards, J. R., & Rothbard, N. P. (1999). Work and family stress and well-being: An examination of person–environment fit in the work and family domains. *Organizational Behavior and Human Decision Processes, 77*(2), 85-129.

Eisenberg, N., & Miller, P. A. (1987). The relation of empathy to prosocial and related behaviors. *Psychological Bulletin, 101*(1), 91.

Escoto, K., Laska, M., Larson, N., Neumark-Sztainer, D., & Hannan, P. J. (2012). Work hours perceived time barriers to healthful eating among young adults. *American Journal of Health Behavior*, *36*(6), 786-796.

Esposito, R. P. (1977). The relationship between the motive to avoid success and vocational choice. *Journal of Vocational Behavior*, *10*(3), 347-357.

Feather, N. T., & Raphelson, A. C. (1974). Fear of success in Australian and American student groups: Motive or sex-role stereotype?. *Journal of Personality*, *42*(2), 190-201.

Feldman, D. C. (2002). Managers' propensity to work longer hours: A multilevel analysis. *Human Resource Management Review*, *12*(3), 339-357.

Fleming, J. (1982). Fear of success in Black female and male graduate students: A pilot study. *Psychology of Women Quarterly*, *6*(3), 327-341

Forbes, G. B., & King, S. (1983). Fear of success and sex-role: There are reliable relationships. *Psychological Reports*, *53*(3), 735-738.

Fried-Buchalter, S. (1997). Fear of success, fear of failure, and the imposter phenomenon among male and female marketing managers. *Sex Roles*, *37*(11-12), 847-859.

Gagné, M., & Deci, E. L. (2005). Self-determination theory and work motivation. *Journal of Organizational Behavior*, *26*, 331-361

Gecas, V., & Seff, M. A. (1990). Social class and self-esteem: Psychological centrality, compensation, and the relative effects of work and home. *Social Psychology Quarterly*, *53*(2), 165-173.

Geurts, S. E., Beckers, D. J., Taris, T. W., Kompier, M. J., & Smulders, P. W. (2009). Worktime demands and work-family interference: Does worktime control buffer the adverse effects of high demands?. *Journal Of Business Ethics*, *84*(Suppl2), 229-241.

Goette, L., Stutzer, A., & Frey, B. M. (2010). Prosocial motivation and blood donations: a survey of the empirical literature. *Transfus Med Hemother*, *37*(3), 149-154.

Gordon, J. R., Whelan-Berry, K. S., & Hamilton, E. A. (2007). The relationship among work-family conflict and enhancement, organizational work-family culture, and work outcomes for older working women. *Journal of Occupational Health Psychology*, *12*(4), 350.

Grandey, A. A., Cordeiro, B. L., & Michael, J. H. (2007). Work-family supportiveness organizational perceptions: Important for the well-being of male blue-collar hourly workers?. *Journal of Vocational Behavior*, *71*(3), 460-478.

Grant, A. M. (2008). Does intrinsic motivation fuel the prosocial fire? Motivational synergy in predicting persistence, performance, and productivity. *Journal of Applied Psychology, 93*(1), 48.

Grant, A. M., & Berg, J. M. 2012. Prosocial motivation. In K. S. Cameron, G. M. Spreitzer (Eds.) , *The Oxford handbook of positive organizational scholarship (pp. 28-44).*

Grant, A. M., & Berry, J. W. (2011). The necessity of others is the mother of invention: Intrinsic and prosocial motivations, perspective taking, and creativity. *Academy of Management Journal, 54*(1), 73-96.

Greenhaus, J. H., & Beutell, N. J. (1985). Sources of conflict between work and family roles. *Academy of Management Review, 10*, 76-88.

Greenhaus, J. H., & Powell, G. N. (2006). When work and family are allies: A theory of work-family enrichment. *Academy of Management Review, 31*(1), 72-92.

Greenhaus, J. H., & Powell, G. N. (2003). When work and family collide: Deciding between competing role demands. *Organizational Behavior and Human Decision Processes, 90*(2), 291-303.

Gross, M., & Gross, E. (1985). Hypnoanalytic treatment of fear of success. *Medical Hypnoanalysis, 6*(1), 46-52.

Grzywacz, J. G., Carlson, D. S., Kacmar, K. M., & Wayne, J. H. (2007). A multi-level perspective on the synergies between work and family. *Journal of Occupational and Organizational Psychology, 80*(4), 559-574.

Hall, D. T., Lee, M., Kossek, E., & Las Heras, M. (2012). Pursuing career success while sustaining personal and family well-being: A study of reduced-load professionals over time. *Journal of Social Issues, 68*(4), 742-766.

Hamermesh, D. S. (1999). The timing of work over time. *The Economic Journal, 109*(452), 37-66.

Harter, J. K., & Arora, R. (2010). The impact of time spent working and job fit on well-being around the world. In E. Diener, J. F. Helliwell, D. Kahneman (Eds.) , International differences in well-being (pp. 398-435). New York, NY US: Oxford University Press.

Heller, D., & Watson, D. (2005). The dynamic spillover of satisfaction between work and marriage: The role of time and mood. *Journal of Applied Psychology, 90*(6), 1273-1279.

Hicks, W. D., & Klimoski, R. J. (1981). The Impact of Flextime on Employee Attitudes. *Academy of Management Journal, 24*(2), 333-341.

Hill, E., Erickson, J., Holmes, E. K., & Ferris, M. (2010). Workplace flexibility, work hours, and work-life conflict: Finding an extra day or two. *Journal of Family Psychology, 24*(3), 349-358.

Hill, J.E., Ferris, M., & Märtinson, V. (2003). Does it matter where you work? A comparison of how three work venues (traditional office, virtual office, and home office) influence aspects of work and personal/family life. *Journal of Vocational Behavior, 63*(2), 220-241.

Hill, J.E., Märtinson, V., & Ferris, M. (2004). New-Concept Part-Time Employment as a Work-Family Adaptive Strategy for Women Professionals with Small Children. Family Relations, *53*(3), 282-292.

Hill, J.E., Yang, C., Hawkins, A. J., & Ferris, M. (2004). A cross-cultural test of the work-family interface in 48 countries. *Journal of Marriage and Family, 66*(5), 1300-1316.

Hirschfeld, R. R., & Feild, H. S. (2000). Work centrality and work alienation: Distinct aspects of a general commitment to work. *Journal of Organizational Behavior, 21*(7), 789-800.

Hoffman, L. W. (1977). Fear of success in 1965 and 1974: A follow-up study. *Journal of Consulting and Clinical Psychology, 45*(2), 310-321.

—. (1974). Fear of success in males and females: 1965 and 971. *Journal of Consulting and Clinical Psychology, 42*(3), 353-358.

Horner, M. S. (1978). The measurement and behavioral implications of fear of success in women. In J. W. Atkinson & J. O. Raynor (Eds) *Personality, Motivation, and Achievement*. Hemisphere Publishing Corp, Washington, DC.

Hornung, S., Rousseau, D. M., Glaser, J., Angerer, P., & Weigl, M. (2011). Employee-oriented leadership and quality of working life: Mediating roles of idiosyncratic deals 1, 2. *Psychological Reports, 108*(1), 59-74.

Hostetler, A. J., Desrochers, S., Kopko, K., & Moen, P. (2012). Marital and family satisfaction as a function of work–family demands and community resources: Individual- and couple-level analyses. Journal of Family Issues, *33*(3), 316-340

Hughes, E. L., & Parkes, K. R. (2007). Work hours and well-being: The roles of work-time control and work-family interference. *Work & Stress, 21*(3), 264-278

Ilies, R., Wilson, K.M., Wagner, D.T., Johnson, M.D., DeRue, S.D., & Ilgen, D.R. (2007). When can employees have a family life? The effects of daily workload and affect on work-family conflict and social behaviors at home. *Journal of Applied Psychology, 92*(5), 1368-1379.

Ivers, J. H., & Downes, P. (2012). A phenomenological reinterpretation of Horner's fear of success in terms of social class. *European Journal of Psychology of education, 27*(3), 369-388.

Jacob, J. I., Allen, S., Hill, E., Mead, N. L., & Ferris, M. (2008). Work interference with dinnertime as a mediator and moderator between work hours and work and family outcomes. *Family and Consumer Sciences Research Journal, 36*(4), 310-327.

Jacobs, J. A., & Gerson, K. (2001). Overworked individuals or overworked families? Explaining trends in work, leisure, and family time. *Work and Occupations, 28*(1), 40-63.

Jaga, A., & Bagraim, J. (2011). The relationship between work-family enrichment and work-family satisfaction outcomes. *South African Journal of Psychology, 41*(1), 52-62.

Janda, L. H., O'Grady, K. E., & Capps, C. F. (1978). Fear of success in males and females in sex-linked occupations. *Sex Roles, 4*(1), 43-50.

Jansen, N. W., Kant, I., Nijhuis, F. J., Swaen, G. M., & Kristensen, T. S. (2004). Impact of worktime arrangements on work-home interference among Dutch employees. *Scandinavian journal of work, environment & health, 30*(2), 139-148.

Jex, S. M., & Elacqua, T. C. (1999). Time management as a moderator of relations between stressors and employee strain. *Work & Stress, 13*(2), 182-191.

Judge, T.A., Ilies, R., & Scott, B.A. (2006). Work-family conflict and emotions: Effects at work and at home. *Personnel Psychology, 59*(4), 779-814.

Kamp, A., Lund, H., & Hvid, H. (2011). Negotiating time, meaning and identity in boundaryless work. *Journal of Workplace Learning, 23*(4), 229-242.

Knutson, K. L., Van Cauter, E., Rathouz, P. J., DeLeire, T., & Lauderdale, D. S. (2010). Trends in the prevalence of short sleepers in the USA: 1975-2006. *Sleep: Journal of Sleep and Sleep Disorders Research, 33*(1), 37-45.

Kossek, E. E., Lautsch, B. A., & Eaton, S. C. (2006). Telecommuting, control, and boundary management: Correlates of policy use and practice, job control, and work–family effectiveness. *Journal of Vocational Behavior, 68*(2), 347-367.

Kreiner, G. E., Hollensbe, E. C., & Sheep, M. L. (2009). Balancing borders and bridges: Negotiating the work-home interface via boundary work tactics. *Academy of Management Journal, 52*(4), 704-730.

Lautsch, B. A., & Scully, M. A. (2007). Restructuring time: Implications of work-hours reductions for the working class. *Human Relations, 60*(5), 719-743.

Lee, J., & Murnighan, J. (2001). The empathy-prospect model and the choice to help. *Journal of Applied Social Psychology, 31*(4), 816-839.

Liddle, B. J., Westergren, A. J., & Duke, D. L. (1997). Time allocation
     and research productivity among counseling faculty. *Psychological
     Reports*, *80*(1), 339-344.
Lyon, D., & Woodward, A. E. (2004). Gender and Time at the Top
     Cultural Constructions of Time in High-Level Careers and Homes.
     European Journal of Women's Studies, *11*(2), 205-221.
Madsen, S. R. (2006). Work and family conflict: Can home-based
     teleworking make a difference?. *International Journal of Organizational
     Theory and Behavior*, *9*(3), 307-350.
—. (2003). The effects of home-based teleworking on work-family
     conflict. *Human Resource Development Quarterly*, *14*(1), 35-58.
Major, V. S., Klein, K. J., & Ehrhart, M. G. (2002). Work time, work
     interference with family, and psychological distress. *Journal of
     Applied Psychology*, *87*(3), 427.
Maner, J. K., & Gailliot, M. T. (2007). Altruism and egoism: Prosocial
     motivations for helping depend on relationship context. *European
     Journal of Social Psychology*, *37*(2), 347-358.
Marshall, J. M., & Karabenick, S. A. (1977). Validity of an empirically
     derived projective measure of fear of success. *Journal of Consulting
     and Clinical Psychology*, *45*(4), 564-574.
Martin, J. E., Sinclair, R. R., Lelchook, A. M., Wittmer, J. L., & Charles,
     K. E. (2012). Non-standard work schedules and retention in the entry-
     level hourly workforce. *Journal of Occupational and Organizational
     Psychology*, *85*(1), 1-22.
Matthews, R. A., Swody, C. A., & Barnes-Farrell, J. L. (2012). Work
     hours and work–family conflict: The double-edged sword of
     involvement in work and family. *Stress and Health: Journal of the
     International Society for the Investigation of Stress*, *28*(3), 234-247.
McNall, L. A., Masuda, A. D., & Nicklin, J. M. (2009). Flexible work
     arrangements, job satisfaction, and turnover intentions: the mediating
     role of work-to-family enrichment. *The Journal of Psychology*, *144*(1),
     61-81.
McNall, L. A., Nicklin, J. M., & Masuda, A. D. (2010). A meta-analytic
     review of the consequences associated with work–family enrichment.
     Journal of Business and Psychology, *25*(3), 381-396.
Michel, J. S., & Clark, M. A. (2009). Has it been affect all along? A test of
     work-to-family and family-to-work models of conflict, enrichment,
     and satisfaction. *Personality and Individual Differences*, *47*(3), 163-
     168.

Michel, J. S., Kotrba, L. M., Mitchelson, J. K., Clark, M. A., & Baltes, B. B. (2011). Antecedents of work–family conflict: A meta-analytic review. *Journal of Organizational Behavior*, *32*(5), 689-725.

Michel, J. S., Mitchelson, J. K., Pichler, S., & Cullen, K. L. (2010). Clarifying relationships among work and family social support, stressors, and work–family conflict. *Journal of Vocational Behavior*, *76*(1), 91-104.

Misra, J., Budig, M., & Boeckmann, I. (2011). Work-family policies and the effects of children on women's employment hours and wages. *Community, Work & Family*, *14*(2), 139-157.

Mulig, J. (1985). Relationships among fear of success, fear of failure, and androgyny. *Psychology of Women Quarterly*, *9*(2), 284-287.

Odle-Dusseau, H. N., Britt, T. W., & Greene-Shortridge, T. M. (2012). Organizational work–family resources as predictors of job performance and attitudes: The process of work–family conflict and enrichment. *Journal of Occupational Health Psychology*, *17*(1), 28-40.

Offer, S., & Schneider, B. (2008). The emotional dimension of family time and their implications for work-family balance. *Handbook of Work-family Integration. Research, Theory, and Best Practices, Elsevier, London, 177-90.*

Olsen, N. J., & Willemsen, E. W. (1978). Fear of success—fact or artifact? *Journal of Psychology: Interdisciplinary and Applied*, *98*(1), 65-70.

Paludi, M. A. (1984). Psychometric properties and underlying assumptions of four objective measures of fear of success. *Sex Roles*, *10*(9), 765-781

Pavey, L., Greitemeyer, T., & Sparks, P. 2012. "I help because I want to, not because you tell me to": Empathy increases autonomously motivated helping. *Personality and Social Psychology Bulletin*, 38(5), 681-689.

Peeters, M., Wattez, C., Demerouti, E., & de Regt, W. (2009). Work-family culture, work-family interference and well-being at work: Is it possible to distinguish between a positive and a negative process?. *The Career Development International*, *14*(7), 700-713.

Perlow, L. A. (1999). The time famine: Toward a sociology of work time. *Administrative Science Quarterly*, *44*(1), 57-81.

—. (1998). Boundary control: The social ordering of work and family time in a high-tech corporation. *Administrative Science Quarterly*, *43*, 328-357.

Popp, G. E., & Muhs, W. F. (1982). Fear of success and women employees. *Human Relations*, *35*(7), 511-519.

Post, C., Schneer, J., Reitman, F., & Ogilvie, D. (2013). Pathways to retirement: A career stage analysis of retirement age expectations. *Human Relations*, *66*(1), 87-112.

Powell, G. N., & Greenhaus, J. H. (2006). Managing incidents of work-family conflict: A decision-making perspective. *Human Relations*, *59*(9), 1179-1212.

Presser, H. B. (2004). Nonstandard work schedules and marital instability. *Journal of Marriage and Family*, *62*(1), 93-110.

Rau, B. L., & Hyland, M. M. (2006). Role conflict and flexible work arrangements: The effects on applicant attraction. *Personnel Psychology*, *55*(1), 111-136.

Raghuram, S., & Wiesenfeld, B. (2004). Work-nonwork conflict and job stress among virtual workers. *Human Resource Management*, *43*(2-3), 259-277.

Reynolds, J. (2005). In the face of conflict: Work-life conflict and desired work hour adjustments. *Journal of Marriage and Family*, *67*(5), 1313-1331.

Rokeach, M. (1973). *The nature of human values*. New York: Free Press.

Rummel, A., & Feinberg, R. (1988). Cognitive evaluation theory: A meta-analytic review of the literature. *Social Behavior and Personality*, *16*, 147-164.

Schneer, J. A., & Reitman, F. (1993). Effects of the alternate family structures on managerial career paths. *Academy of Management Journal*, *36*(4), 830-843.

Schoenrade, P. A., Batson, C. D., Brandt, J. R., & Loud, R. E. (1986). Attachment, accountability, and motivation to benefit another not in distress. *Journal of Personality and Social Psychology*, *51*(3), 557-563.

Shapiro, J. P. (1979). 'Fear of success' imagery as a reaction to sex-role inappropriate behavior. *Journal of Personality Assessment*, *43*(1), 33-38.

Simon, M., Kümmerling, A., & Hasselhorn, H. M. (2004). Work-home conflict in the European nursing profession. *International Journal of Occupational and Environmental Health*, *10*(4), 384-391.

Siu, O., Lu, J., Brough, P., Lu, C., Bakker, A. B., Kalliath, T., O'Driscoll, M., Phillips, D.R., Chen, W., Lo, D., Sit, C., & Shi, K. (2010). Role resources and work–family enrichment: The role of work engagement. *Journal of Vocational Behavior*, *77*(3), 470-480.

Skinner, N., & Pocock, B. (2008). Work-life conflict: Is work time or work overload more important? *Asia Pacific Journal of Human Resources*, *46*(3), 303-315.

Smith, C. E., Kleinbeck, S. V., Boyle, D., Kochinda, C., & Parker, S. (2001). Family Caregivers' Motives for Helping Scale derived from motivation-to-help theory. *Journal of Nursing Measurement, 9*(3), 239-257.

Snir, R., & Zohar, D. (2007). Workaholism as Discretionary Time Investment at Work: An Experience-Sampling Study. *Applied Psychology, 57*(1), 109-127.

Sobus, M. S. (1995). Mandating community service: Psychological implications of requiring prosocial behavior. *Law & Psychology Review, 19*, 153-182.

Sonnentag, S. (2012). Time in organizational research: Catching up on a long neglected topic in order to improve theory. *Organizational Psychology Review, 2*, 361-368.

Staines, G. L. (1985). Men's work schedules and family life. *Marriage & Family Review, 9*(3), 43-65.

Steinmetz, H., Frese, M., & Schmidt, P. (2008). A longitudinal panel study on antecedents and outcomes of work–home interference. *Journal of Vocational Behavior, 73*(2), 231-241.

Stryker, S. (1987). Identity theory: Development and extensions. In: K. Yardley, & T. Honess (Eds.), *Self and identity: Psychosocial perspective* (pp. 89-103). New York: Wiley.

Stryker, S. (1980). *Symbolic interactionism: A social structure version.* Palo Alto, CA: Benjamin/Cummings.

Stryker, S. & Serpe, R.T. (1982). Commitment, identity salience, and role behavior: Theory and research example. In W. Ickes, & E. S. Knowles (Eds.) *Personality, roles, and social behavior* (pp. 199-218). New York: Springer-Verlag.

Taha, N. (2012). The cost, in dollars, of raising a child. *The New York Times.* Retrieved March 17, 2013 from http://bucks.blogs.nytimes.com/2012/11/13/the-cost-in-dollars-of-raising-a-child/

Tanaka, S., & Waldfogel, J. (2007). Effects of parental leave and work hours on fathers' involvement with their babies: Evidence from the millennium cohort study. *Community, Work & Family, 10*(4), 409-426.

Tang, S., & Hall, V. (1995). The overjustification effect: A meta-analysis. *Applied Cognitive Psychology, 9*, 365-404.

Tresemer, D. (1976). Do women fear success? *Signs, 1*(4), 863-874.

Unger, L. S. (1991). Altruism as a motivation to volunteer. *Journal of Economic Psychology, 12*(1), 71-100.

Valcour, M. (2007). Work-based resources as moderators of the relationship between work hours and satisfaction with work-family balance. *Journal of Applied Psychology*, *92*(6), 1512-1523.

van Echtelt, P. E., Glebbeek, A. C., & Lindenberg, S. M. (2006). The new lumpiness of work: Explaining the mismatch between actual and preferred working hours. *Work, Employment and Society*, *20*(3), 493-512.

Van Lange, P. M., Schippers, M., & Balliet, D. (2011). Who volunteers in psychology experiments? An empirical review of prosocial motivation in volunteering. *Personality and Individual Differences*, *51*(3), 279-284.

van Steenbergen, E. F., & Ellemers, N. (2009). Is managing the work–family interface worthwhile? Benefits for employee health and performance. *Journal of Organizational Behavior*, *30*(5), 617-642.

van Steenbergen, E. F., Ellemers, N., & Mooijaart, A. (2007). How work and family can facilitate each other: Distinct types of work-family facilitation and outcomes for women and men. *Journal of Occupational Health Psychology*, *12*(3), 279.

Voydanoff, P. (2005a). Work Demands and Work-to-Family and Family-to-Work Conflict Direct and Indirect Relationships. *Journal of Family Issues*, *26*(6), 707-726.

—. (2005b). Consequences of boundary-spanning demands and resources for work-to-family conflict and perceived stress. Journal of Occupational Health Psychology; *Journal of Occupational Health Psychology*, *10*(4), 491-503.

—. (2004). The effects of work demands and resources on work-to-family conflict and facilitation. *Journal of Marriage and Family*, *66*(2), 398-412.

Wadsworth, C. (2012). The cost of raising a child. *USA Today*. Retrieved March 17, 2012 from http://www.usatoday.com/story/money/personalfinance/2012/12/23/cost-raising-kids/1788415/

Warner, M. A., & Hausdorf, P. A. (2009). The positive interaction of work and family roles: Using need theory to further understand the work-family interface. *Journal of Managerial Psychology*, *24*(4), 372-385.

Wayne, J., Randel, A. E., & Stevens, J. (2006). The role of identity and work-family support in work-family enrichment and its work-related consequences. *Journal of Vocational Behavior*, *69*(3), 445-461.

Weinreich-Haste, H. (1978). Sex differences in fear of success among British students. British *Journal of Social & Clinical Psychology*, *17*(1), 37-42.

Wiersma, U. J. (1992). The effects of extrinsic rewards in intrinsic motivation: A meta-analysis. Journal of Occupational and Organizational Psychology, *65*, 101-114.

Wiese, B. S., & Salmela-Aro, K. (2008). Goal conflict and facilitation as predictors of work–family satisfaction and engagement. *Journal of Vocational Behavior*, *73*(3), 490-497.

Wood, M. M., & Greenfeld, S. (1979). Fear of success in high achieving male and female managers in private industry vs. the public sector. *Journal of Psychology: Interdisciplinary and Applied*, *103*(2), 289-297.

Yeung, W. J., Sandberg, J. F., Davis-Kean, P. E., & Hofferth, S. L. (2004). Children's time with fathers in intact families. *Journal of Marriage and Family*, *63*(1), 136-154.

Chapter Sixteen

Dynamics of Cluster Firms' Identity Orientations and the Emergence of Cluster Macrocultures

Andaç T. Arikan
Florida Atlantic University, USA

Abstract

Cluster macrocultures are theorized to help firms safeguard and coordinate exchange relationships characterized by a high potential for opportunism and thus help facilitate the emergence of clustering as a specific form of industrial organization. Yet explanations as to their emergence remain limited to the highly contested functional instrumentality proposition. In this paper, I conceptualize cluster macrocultures as the manifestations of the extent to which identity orientations of the firms inside a cluster are convergent, and offer a conceptual model that outlines the process by which they emerge and transform. Specifically, I focus on the dyadic exchange relationships inside clusters as the nexus of cluster macrocultures, and outline the process by which cluster firms' identity orientations transform as cluster firms collect social proof as to the appropriate ways of approaching negotiation situations during relational practices. I explore the implications of these dynamics for the emergence and transformation of cluster macrocultures and discuss implications.

Keywords: cluster, macroculture, organizational identity orientation

Introduction

Since Piore and Sabel's (1984) seminal discussion of the flexible specialization model, clusters defined as "geographically proximate groups of interconnected companies and associated institutions in a particular field linked by commonalities and complementarities" (Porter, 2000: 16) have attracted increasing scholarly attention as a novel form of industrial organization. Early discussants (e.g., Brusco, 1982; Becattini, 1990) argued that increasingly customized demand and an increasing need for fast response times made vertically-integrated, mass producing firms of the Fordist era ill-matched with their new environments (Essletzbichler, 2003). The solution, they argued, is for firms to disintegrate, specialize in particular industry-value-chain activities and become embedded in local networks of similarly specialized firms (Lazerson, 1995). Comparable arguments were made also in more recent studies that view clusters as a form of industrial organization for the production of knowledge (Antonelli, 1999; Robertson & Langlois, 1995). These studies highlight the importance of interfirm knowledge exchange relationships within clusters in terms of improving firms' innovativeness (Arikan, 2009).

Both streams of literature suggest that geographical clustering is a solution to the governance problem that arises due to firms choosing to resort to inter-firm exchanges for transactions involving high levels of demand-related and/or technological uncertainty as well as possibly asset specificity; that is to say transactions that would typically be internalized by the firm due to a high hazard of opportunism (Williamson, 1991). Geographic proximity is proposed to alleviate the governance problem specifically by facilitating the emergence of a cluster macroculture, defined as idiosyncratic beliefs, assumptions and values that are collectively shared attributes of a cluster (Abrahamson & Fombrun, 1994; Bell, Tracey & Heide, 2009; Jones, Hesterly & Borgatti, 1997). It is suggested that these collectively shared attributes define appropriateness criteria inside the cluster and consequently help firms safeguard and coordinate exchange relationships characterized by a high potential for opportunism (Harrison, 1992; Iammarino, 2005; Tallman, Jenkins, Henry & Pinch, 2004).

Despite the large role theorists ascribe to cluster macrocultures in facilitating transactional governance inside clusters, explanations as to their emergence remain limited to the form of the highly contested classical functionalist instrumentality proposition (Abrahamson & Fombrun 1992; Opp, 2001; Thibaut, 1968). In particular, cluster macrocultures are proposed to emerge automatically in a way to efficiently solve transactional governance problems associated with increased specialization/ interdependence within clusters. This proposition is at odds with accounts that show the presence of different types of macrocultures in different clusters characterized by similar transaction characteristics

(Saxenian, 1994; Weiss & Dalbecq, 1987). Furthermore, not all clusters have favorable macrocultures that increase the effectiveness of transactional governance inside the cluster, and cluster macrocultures transform over time (Florida & Kenney, 1990; Mesquita, 2007). These developments suggest that there is more to the emergence of a cluster macroculture than the characteristics of the transactions inside the cluster, yet despite calls for research on the nature of cluster macrocultures (Bell, et al., 2009) a conceptual model that outlines the process by which they emerge/transform is still missing. It is this gap I intend to fill in the present study.

The model I build is based on a conceptualization of cluster macrocultures as the manifestations of the extent to which "identity orientations" (Brickson, 2005, 2007) of the firms inside a cluster are convergent. In an effort to outline how cluster macrocultures emerge/ transform, I concentrate on the micro-process by which cluster firms' experiences during exchange relationships inside the cluster shape their identity orientations over time.

The paper proceeds as follows. In the theoretical background section, I first conceptualize cluster macrocultures and then define and explain the key concepts (i.e., relational practice, logic of exchange, and a cluster firm's identity orientation) that I use throughout the paper. The next section is devoted to the model where I outline the dynamics of cluster firms' identity orientations during relational practices inside a cluster as the nexus of the emergence/ transformation of cluster macrocultures. The following section outlines how these dynamics shape the emergence/ transformation of cluster macrocultures. In the final section, I discuss contributions and implications.

Theoretical Background

Cluster Macrocultures

Clusters are places where firms tend to specialize in particular value chain activities or technologies, and rely on exchanges with other co-located firms for activities or technologies outside their area of expertise. Firms choose to do this because their environment is characterized by high levels of demand-related or technological uncertainty, and they need both specialized expertise and flexibility to be able to adjust to the changes in the market place (Piore & Sabel, 1984). This situation gives rise to intra-cluster transactions that are likely to be characterized by asset specificity and uncertainty, which according to transaction cost economics would increase the hazard of opportunism. Normally, these types of transactions would be handled through hierarchical control inside a firm (Williamson, 1991). When they are handled through interfirm exchanges inside a cluster, a firm may approach the governance of a particular transaction in a range of ways as defined by a continuum between two polar extremes (Faems, Janssens, Madhok & Van Looy, 2008; Hansen, Hoskisson & Barney, 2008): On one extreme, the firm may choose to direct its focus solely on the present transaction and reducing the associated threat of opportunism. On the other extreme, the firm may choose to direct its focus on the identity of the partner rather than the transaction and make building a long-term relationship with the partner the dominant imperative over reducing the opportunism threat in the context of the present transaction.

The presence of a cluster macroculture essentially implies that there is a high level of convergence among firms' approaches to transactions inside the cluster. This convergence can take place at any point on the continuum defined by the above polar extremes. If cluster firms converge on the first polar extreme, the cluster is said to have a hierarchical macroculture, and if they converge on the second polar extreme, the cluster is said to have a relational macroculture (Bell et al., 2009). Regardless of where the convergence takes place on the continuum, to the extent that it does takes place, cluster firms will have a shared understanding of what constitutes opportunistic behavior as well as the consequences of such behavior, which in turn helps prevent them (Wathne & Heide, 2000; Greve et al., 2010). Viewed from this lens, the question of how do cluster macrocultures emerge/ transform is a question about the process by which cluster firms' approaches to exchange relationships form and evolve. Before I start answering this question, I would like to introduce some terminology and discuss the building blocks of my model.

Relational Practice: Exchange Relationships as a Series of Negotiation Situations

Let me first clarify my unit of analysis. I follow the work of authors who argue that the foundations of macro-sociological concepts are micro level interactions among the constituents of the social collective (Collins, 1981; Abrahamson & Fombrun, 1992). Based on this idea, my overarching argument is that the genesis of cluster macrocultures is dyadic exchange relationships between cluster firms. In addition, I focus on entire exchange relationships between dyads of cluster firms rather than individual transactions. Finally, while I do not deny its importance and relevance, I shift my attention away from the fit between transaction characteristics and the form of governance used for individual transactions – namely the logic of economic instrumentality. Instead, I follow the authors who take a behavioral (e.g., March, 1995; Messick, 1999), process-based approach to inter-firm exchanges and focus on cluster firms' negotiation behaviors along with associated cognitions and situational perceptions during the different phases of an exchange relationship (Ballinger & Rockmann, 2010; Blois, 2002; Faems et al., 2008; Lui & Ngo, 2005; Macaulay, 1963; Ness, 2009). I follow Ness and use the term "relational practice" to refer to the totality of negotiations that take place in the context of an exchange relationship between two cluster firms. Relational practices between dyads of cluster firms and the constituent set of negotiations are the unit of analysis in this study.

Logic of Exchange and Cluster Firms' Identity Orientations

At the beginning of a relational practice between two cluster firms (i.e., when the firms start transacting for the first time), each firm experiences a high level of uncertainty as to how the other firm will approach a particular negotiation situation. This uncertainty exists because a "shared logic of exchange" (McGinn & Keros, 2002) which would constitute a common basis of action/interpretation for the parties does not yet exist (Bettenhausen & Murnighan, 1985). In the absence of a shared logic of exchange, each firm's actions in the context of a negotiation situation are largely determined by its own logic of exchange, which is shaped by the firm's preexisting action scripts and cognitive frames (Beech & Huxham, 2004; Gray, 2004; Pinkley & Northcraft, 1994). These preexisting cognitions not only determine each firm's own actions but they also shape its expectations about the other party's actions as well as interpretations of those actions (Messick, 1999).

A firm's action scripts and interpretive frames that shape its logic of exchange as well as its expectations about its partner's logic of exchange in the context of a relational practice are embedded in the firm's identity (Albert & Whetten, 1985), more specifically, in its identity orientation (March, 1995). The term organizational identity orientation is coined by Brickson (2005, 2007) and refers to "the nature of assumed relations between an organization and its stakeholders as perceived by members" (Brickson, 2007: 864). Brickson distinguishes between individualistic and relational identity orientations.[1] She defines the former as "an organizational

---

[1] In fact, Brickson (2005: 579) first distinguishes between the broad categories of "individualistic" and "socially focused" organizational identity orientations. Then she breaks the latter further down into two, finer grained categories and argues that relational and collectivistic identity orientations are meaningfully distinct. I agree

self-conception as a sole entity atomized and distinct from others" and the latter as "a self conception of the organization as a dyadic inter-entity relationship partner possessing particularized bonds with specific stakeholders" (Brickson, 2007: 865). In this paper, I conceptualize individualistic and relational identity orientations not as qualitatively different characteristics but as two polar ends of the same continuum. I take it as a central premise and starting point for my model that firms in a cluster are likely to be situated at different points on the identity orientation continuum, and accordingly have different logics of exchange (c.f., Flynn, 2005). These differences in turn are likely to cause firms to both act differently and interpret the other party's actions differently in the context of negotiation situations during relational practices inside a cluster.

Considering the presence of such differences among cluster firms, a relational practice and the associated set of negotiations between two cluster firms essentially constitute an arena where each firm enacts it own logic of exchange as shaped by its identity orientation, observes its partner's behaviors to compare its own logic of exchange with that of its partner (i.e., collect social proof (Rao, et al., 2001)), and engage in an interactive sensemaking/improvisation process with the partner in an effort to converge on a shared logic of exchange (Carson, Madhok, Varman & John, 2003; Greve, et al., 2010; McGinn & Keros, 2002; Van Kleef, De Dreau, 2002; Vlaar, Van den Bosch & Volberda, 2006). Such convergence may not take place, which may lead to the termination of the relational exchange. If it does take place, the shared logic of exchange on which firms eventually converge may be different from both firms' initial logics of exchange. Such differences have the potential to trigger incremental changes in the cluster firms' identity orientations. To put it differently, they may cause one or both firms to move along the identity orientation continuum leading firms to approach future relational practices differently. The emergence and transformation of a cluster macroculture thus concern the process by which cluster firms' experiences in the context of a series of relational practices inside the cluster shape their identity orientations. I now turn to the details of this process.

---

with Brickson's position in general. However for the purposes of the present paper and considering the dyadic negotiations framework I adopt, I use her broader categorization.

Dynamics of Cluster Firms' Identity Orientations during Relational Practices Inside a Cluster

In this section, I examine the process of a cluster firm's identity-orientation revision in three sequential stages. The first stage involves the firm's observing its partner's behaviors throughout the relational practice, making attributions for those behaviors, and eventually making a discrepancy assessment between its own and its partner's logics of exchange. If the firm perceives the presence of a discrepancy, the resulting disconfirmation of the firm's logic of exchange constitutes negative social proof and prompts the firm to evaluate its logic of exchange. The second stage involves the firm's making a judgment as to whose logic of exchange is more "appropriate" in the context of the cluster by way of referring to its experiences in a series of recent relational practices inside the cluster as well as its partner's characteristics. The third stage involves the firm's formulating its response to the disconfirmation of its logic of exchange in light of the appropriateness judgment made on the second step.

Discrepancy Assessment and the Disconfirmation of a Cluster Firm's Logic of Exchange

The trigger that is necessary to start the process of identity-orientation revision for a cluster firm is for the firm to face negative social proof, namely find evidence that calls the firm's logic of exchange into question as the appropriate logic of exchange inside the cluster. The firm faces negative social proof when its partner's behaviors in the context of the totality of the negotiation situations during the relational practice fail to conform to the firm's initial expectations. This situation reveals a discrepancy between the firm's and its partner's logics of exchange, which amounts to a disconfirmation of the firm's logic of exchange.

As mentioned previously, cluster firms' identity orientations vary along a continuum ranging from a highly individualistic orientation to a highly relational orientation (Brickson, 2005, 2007). A focal cluster firm's location on the identity orientation continuum is likely to have a heavy influence on how the firm approaches negotiations situations during a relational practice. The logic of exchange for a cluster firm that is located on the individualistic end of the identity orientation continuum is the logic of "economic exchange" (Shore, Tetrick, Lynch & Barksdale, 2006). The firm is likely to have a short term orientation and view each transaction as a separate, independent exchange with relative disregard to who the partner is or what the history of exchanges with the partner has been like. Given this orientation, the firm is less likely to consider the possibility of future transactions with the partner and/or regulate its behavior during the present transaction due to such considerations. It is more likely to frame conflicts that emerge during negotiations as task conflicts, concentrate on material aspects of the dispute, and downplay emotional elements (Pinkley, 1990). A heavily distributive approach to negotiations and a focus on "winning" causes the firm to pursue self interest vigorously. Expecting a similar stance from its partner, the firm views behavioral uncertainty (Krishnan, Martin & Noorderhaven, 2006) on behalf of the partner as a threat and makes it a goal to minimize it through increasing the formalization of the transaction through the design and application of increasingly complex, "prevention-framed" contracts (Weber & Mayer, 2011) focused primarily on avoiding negative behaviors by the partner (Argyres & Mayer, 2007; Faems, et al., 2008).

In contrast, the logic of exchange for a cluster firm that is located on the relational end of the identity orientation continuum is the logic of "social exchange" (Blau, 1964). The firm is likely to have a long term orientation and approach each transaction as milestones of a possible long-term relationship with the partner. Accordingly, the firm is more likely to be willing to make concessions in the context of the present transaction for the sake of building and maintaining the relationship. A heavy focus on building and maintaining a relationship causes the firm to be more likely to frame conflicts as relational conflicts and pay closer attention to the emotional aspects of negotiations (Pinkley, 1990). The firm approaches negotiations with an integrative frame of mind and pursues the dyad's interests even though doing so may be against the firm's own interests in the short run. The firm welcomes behavioral uncertainty and is more likely to be willing to accept vulnerability against the partner. Thus it prefers relational contracts based on trust and norms of reciprocity (MacNeil, 1980) over formal, complex contracts, and spends time and effort to understand/ read the partner during negotiations in an effort to find integrative solutions that would satisfy both parties (Carson, et al., 2003; Vlaar, et al., 2006).

A cluster firm's location on the identity orientation continuum, and the associated logic of exchange have a strong bearing on its behavior in some key negotiation situations. For example when the negotiation situation is characterized by asymmetric dependence, an individualistic firm is likely to leverage its bargaining position to force concessions on behalf of the partner whereas a relational firm is likely to consider disregarding its powerful position for collective gains or for the maintenance of the relationship. The firms are also likely to behave differently when environmental changes result in changes in bargaining position. An individualistic firm (due to a relative disregard for the relational aspects of the exchange) is likely to start negotiations and force concessions in an effort to increase its own gains as soon as such changes occur, versus a relational firm may avoid initiating negotiations frequently and show a tendency to stick with original contractual terms with the expectation that gains and concessions will even out in the long term. An individualistic firm is likely to share information only on a need basis thinking that sharing too much information may cause the partner to exploit the firm. In contrast, a relational firm may choose to take a more open approach and share information freely to explore collective gains (Huxham & Hibbert, 2008). When grievances emerge, an individualistic firm is likely to refer to the contract and interpret it in ways favorable to itself (Shavell, 2006). The firm is likely to be relatively intolerant of its partner and quick to resort to legal means. In contrast a relational firm may prefer to avoid legal means until all else fails.

What is important about such differences in logics of exchange and associated behaviors is that what the individualistic firm considers as fair and simple self-interest seeking behavior is likely to be perceived as opportunistic behavior by a relational partner. Similarly, an individualistic firm may view a relational firm's behaviors, requests and expectations as senseless and/or unjustified in the context of what it views to be a primarily economic exchange, and question the relational firm's motives. As Wathne and Heide (2000) and MacNeil (1980) argue, some behaviors (e.g., lying, cheating, stealing, etc.) are clearly against generally accepted norms but for most behaviors, classifying them as opportunistic requires an assessment of whether it was against the principles of the relationship in which it occurs. When exchange partners have different logics of exchange, they disagree on what these principles are for the current relationship. Consequently, each firm acts within the confines of what it considers "appropriate" behavior (Messick, 1999), but the differences in their logics of exchange and the resulting differences in fairness judgments (Molm, Takahashi & Peterson, 2003) cause firms to be (repeatedly) dissatisfied with the way the other party approaches negotiation situations. This in turn leads to one or both parties' logics of exchange to be disconfirmed.[2]

---

[2] I view disconfirmation of a cluster firm's logic of exchange as a perceptual outcome. So I accept the possibility that there may be relational practices where one party's logic of exchange is disconfirmed and the other's is not.

Proposition 1. The higher the distance between the identity orientations of a cluster firm and its exchange partner on the identity orientation continuum, the more likely it is that the relational practice will disconfirm the cluster firm's logic of exchange.

The distance between the exchange partners on the identity orientation continuum creates an inherent potential for the disconfirmation of the parties' logics of exchange during the course of a relational practice. However this potential may remain unrealized because some relational practices may be characterized by very few negotiation situations making it hard for firms to make attributions about their partners' behaviors. Each negotiation episode with a partner constitutes a data point for a focal cluster firm in terms of observing its partner's behaviors and making attributions for such behaviors (Moussavi & Evans, 1993). In the context of a given negotiation situation, when a cluster firm observes behaviors on behalf of its partner that seemingly disconfirm its logic of exchange, the firm can attribute these behaviors to various causes including the logic of exchange of its partner, the characteristics of the particular negotiation situation, or some other external factor. Attribution theory suggests that in the absence of multiple observations, it is hard for the cluster firm to decisively make one of these attributions because "the role of a given cause in producing a given effect is discounted if other plausible causes are also present" (Kelley, 1973: 113). If on the other hand the firm gets the opportunity to observe its partner's behavior in multiple, varying negotiation situations and environmental conditions and still observe similar behaviors, it is more likely to attribute the behaviors to the partner's logic of exchange (i.e., make a trait attribution) rather than other possible causes (Sjovall & Talk, 2004). A higher number of negotiation situations in a relational practice thus gives a cluster firm the opportunity to observe its partner's (seemingly disconfirming) behaviors under varying conditions (i.e., collect "consistency data" (Kelley, 1973)), eliminate alternative explanations for such behaviors, and decisively conclude that its partner's logic of exchange is different from its own (Ballinger & Rockmann, 2010).

Proposition 2. The higher the number of negotiation situations during a relational practice, the more likely it is that the relational practice will disconfirm a cluster firm's logic of exchange.

A relational practice may give rise to a high number of negotiation situations but the issue characteristics of those negotiations may prevent differences between logics of exchange to surface, making it less likely for firms' logics of exchange to be disconfirmed. O'Connor (1997) argues that negotiations may have a distributive, integrative, or common value character.

Distributive negotiations consist of issues where firms' interests in the majority of issues on the table collide so that one party's gains come at the expense of the other party's gains. During such negotiations, the short vs. long term orientations of individualistic and relational firms are likely to come into play. The relational firm may concede early on with the expectation that gains will even out in the long run. However when such gains fail to materialize in future negotiations (e.g., because the individualistic firm negotiates with disregard for past or possible future transactions), the relational firm may perceive that its logic of exchange is disconfirmed. Similarly, the individualistic firm is unlikely to attribute early concessions by a relational partner to a desire to establish a long term relationship, and even it does, it may view it as a risk that the relational firm is taking. So when such concessions create reciprocity expectations on behalf of the relational firm in future negotiations and eventually give rise to grievances, the individualistic firm may perceive that its logic of exchange is disconfirmed.

Integrative negotiations consist of issues where parties' interests may collide on some issues but they give different weights to different issues, therefore finding common ground is relatively easier. During such negotiations, the individualistic firm may concede on issues because they are not important to the firm (and not because of a concern for the relational firm's interests) which may give the relational firm the sense that its logic of exchange is confirmed.

Finally, common value negotiations are characterized largely by issues where parties' interests are aligned. So even though the firms may have different logics of exchange, those differences never come to the fore during the negotiations as firms find themselves rooting for the same options. Naturally, relational practices that consist largely of distributive negotiations are more likely to cause differences in exchange partners' logic of exchange to surface than relational practices that consist predominantly of integrative or common ground negotiations.

Proposition 3. The more negotiation situations during a relational practice are characterized by distributive issues, the more likely it is that the relational practice will disconfirm a cluster firm's logic of exchange.

Cluster Firm's Appropriateness Judgment

A disconfirming relational practice constitutes negative social proof for a cluster firm such that the firm's interactions with another cluster firm during a relational practice have exposed the firm to a set of different values, beliefs and assumptions (e.g., a competing logic of exchange) as to the appropriate way of approaching intra-cluster exchanges. In the presence of a competing logic of exchange, the firm(s) whose logic of exchange is disconfirmed is prompted to make a judgment as to which logic of exchange is more "appropriate" inside the cluster (Ballinger & Rockmann, 2010; Blau, 1964; Cropanzano & Mitchell, 2005). An appropriateness judgment involves evaluating a given stimuli (e.g., partner's conflicting logic of exchange) by comparing it with a referent standard (Boles & Messick, 1995). My arguments in this section concern the formation of that standard for a cluster firm.

Cluster firms can perceive a cluster macroculture primarily through their interactions with other cluster firms. In this regard, a series of recent relational practices with different exchange partners constitute occasions where cluster firms collect data (i.e., social proof) as to the appropriate way to approach exchange relationships inside the cluster (Davis & Greve, 1997). Thus the first requirement for a cluster firm to form perceptions of a cluster macroculture is for the firm to experience a sufficient number of relational practices inside the cluster so that it can collect enough data to be able to observe patterns of prevalent practices. The second requirement concerns the temporal order of the confirming and disconfirming relational practices in a given number of its recent relational practices. Several studies show that the order by which pieces of data are presented to an observer influences the observer's perceptions, judgments and behaviors (Boles & Messick, 1995; Messick, 1999). A cluster firm's recent relational practice experience may exhibit three temporal patterns.

First, the firm's latest relational-practices could have all been of the same type (i.e., all confirming (C) or all disconfirming (D) – e.g., a (D, D, D, D, D, D, D) pattern). This means that the firm has not experienced an "alternation" (i.e., a switch from a confirming to a disconfirming or vice versa) in the temporal order of its recent relational practices. In this case, the message that the firm receives from the cluster environment essentially suggests that all cluster firms are acting consistently (Kelley, 1973), and there is a lot of commonality across cluster firms in terms of the values, assumptions and beliefs they hold as to how intra-cluster exchanges are to be approached. Accordingly, the firm is likely to perceive a strong cluster macroculture.

Second, the firm may have experienced only a few alternations (e.g., a

(C, C, C, C, D, D, D) pattern showing only one alternation or a (C, C, C, D, C, C, C) showing two alternations). In this case, the firm once again receives a consistent message from the environment albeit perhaps not as strong as the previous one. Such patterns may lead the firm to perceive a changing macroculture (e.g., because of a (C, C, C, C, D, D, D) pattern), or that there is a strong macroculture and some of the firm's exchange partners a simply outliers (e.g., because of a (C, C, C, D, C, C, C) pattern with the partner in the disconfirming relational practice perceived to be an outlier). Regardless, the firm is still likely to perceive a relatively strong cluster macroculture.

Finally, the firm may have experienced a high number of alternations (e.g., a (C, C, D, C, D, D, C) pattern showing four alternations). This pattern is similar to the above mentioned (C, C, C, C, D, D, D) pattern in terms of the numbers of confirming and disconfirming relational practices. Yet the lack of temporal consistency (i.e., the higher number of alternations) in the former prevents the firm from getting a consistent read from the environment. To put it differently, the firm's previous experience signals an essentially random pattern and does not help the firm develop an appropriateness standard. Under these circumstances, the firm is unlikely to perceive a strong cluster macroculture.[3]

Proposition 4. The lower the number of alternations between confirming and disconfirming relational practices a cluster firm experiences in the temporal order of its recent relational practices, the stronger the firm will perceive the cluster macroculture to be.

A cluster firm's perception as to the strength of the cluster macroculture is highly important because a cluster macroculture constitutes a standard against which the firm can compare its own and its partner's logics of exchange while making an appropriateness judgment (Boles & Messick, 1995). A disconfirming relational practice can be viewed as a form of "failure" for a cluster firm in that different logics of exchange on behalf of the partners have made the relational practice difficult for the firm. To illustrate, research on alliance success shows that

---

[3] I expect that cluster firms would vary on the number of recent relational practices they consider while making judgments about a cluster macroculture. Firms would also vary on the number of a particular type of relational practice they need to see before they would perceive a change in the cluster macroculture (e.g., last 2, 3, 4...). I leave the examination of these differences to others and limit my argumentation to the effect of alternations on the firm's perception of a cluster macroculture.

partnership attributes of commitment, coordination and trust, which are likely to be functions of the difference/similarity of the partners' logics of exchange, are highly important determinants of partnership success (Mohr & Spekman, 1994). A well-established finding on causal attribution is that typically, successes are attributed to reasons related to the self whereas failures are attributed to external reasons (Bettman & Weitz, 1983; Harvey & Weary, 1984). When a cluster firm faces a negative outcome in the form of a disconfirming relational practice, and when it does not perceive a strong macroculture (and thus lack a clear standard by which to evaluate its partner's logic of exchange), it is more likely to fall prey to self-serving biases and attribute the failure to the inappropriateness of the partner's logic of exchange rather than its own.

> **Proposition 5**. The weaker a cluster firm perceives the cluster macroculture to be, the more likely it is to question the appropriateness of its partner's logic of exchange when faced with a disconfirming relational practice.

In contrast, when the firm perceives a strong cluster macroculture, it now has a benchmark against which to evaluate its own as well as its partner's logics of exchange, therefore it is less likely to fall prey to the above self-serving bias. The stronger a cluster macroculture the firm perceives, the more the firm's appropriateness judgment in the face of a disconfirming relational practice is likely to be based on the level of perceived fit between its logic of exchange and the cluster macroculture. If the firm perceives a cluster macroculture that is closer to its own logic of exchange, then it is more likely to find the partner's logic of exchange inappropriate. If on the other hand, it perceives the cluster macroculture to be closer to the partner's logic of exchange, then it is more likely to find its own logic of exchange inappropriate.

> **Proposition 6**. The higher (lower) the perceived fit between a cluster firm's logic of exchange and the perceived cluster macroculture, the more likely that the firm will question the appropriateness of its partner's (own) logic of exchange when faced with a disconfirming relational practice.

Propositions 3 to 6 are based on the idea that a cluster firm's appropriateness standard against which the firm compares its own and its partner's logics of exchange is formed using consistency data from multiple recent relational practices. Implicit in this idea is that each of the recent partners has an equal influence in shaping the firm's appropriateness standard. In reality, firms may place more weight on some referents than others while setting their appropriateness standard (Davis & Greve, 1997; Still & Strang, 2009). In particular, partners that are centrally located in the cluster's exchange network are likely to have disproportionately higher influence.

When a cluster firm is centrally located in the cluster's exchange network, the firm is perceived as a high-status firm because its network position constitutes evidence that the firm engages in successful exchanges with many other firms in the cluster without its logic of exchange creating any problems (Dollinger, Golden & Saxton, 1997; Shrum & Wuthnow, 1988; Stuart, Hoang & Hybels, 1999). Thus when a relational practice disconfirms a focal cluster firm's logic of exchange and the partner happens to be centrally located in the cluster's exchange network, the focal firm essentially faces a situation where its logic of exchange conflicts with the logic of exchange of a firm that does not seem to have this type of conflict with a large majority of others inside the cluster. This situation bestows a higher level of legitimacy upon the partner's logic of exchange, making it more likely for the focal firm to question the appropriateness of its own logic of exchange regardless of the pattern of its recent relational-practice experience.

Proposition 7: The more a cluster firm perceives its partner to be centrally located in the cluster's exchange network, the more likely it is to question the appropriateness of its own logic of exchange when faced with a disconfirming relational practice.

Cluster Firm's Capability Investments in Response to a Disconfirming Relational Practice and Changes in its Identity Orientation

Extant research shows that over time and with repeated experience, firms specialize in particular governance capabilities (Aggarwal & Hsu, 2009; Villalonga & McGahan 2005). A cluster firm's identity orientation and the associated logic of exchange determine the governance capability the firm finds strategically important (Glynn, 2000) and is likely to have specialized in over time (Livengood & Reger, 2010). Thus, when a relational practice disconfirms the firm's logic of exchange, the firm faces the possibility that it is out of fit with the cluster environment in relation to not only its logic of exchange but also its governance capabilities. This situation prompts the firm to make capability investments to correct possible deficiencies in its governance capabilities (Gavetti, 2005; Laamanen & Wallin, 2009; Maritan, 2001), which in turn lead to possible changes in the firm's identity orientation.

An individualistic firm's primary focus during a relational practice is to reduce the threat of opportunism in the context of a given transaction through designing complex, hierarchical contracts. This type of focus makes *contract design capability* the strategically important governance capability for the firm (Argyres & Mayer 2007; Reuer & Arino, 2007; Weber & Mayer, 2011). In contrast, a relational firm's primary focus is to build a long term relationship by working collaboratively with the partner and maximizing synergistic value creation. This type of focus makes *partner reading capability* the strategically important governance capability for the firm (Carson, et al., 2003; Schoorman, Mayer & Davis, 2007; Vlaar et al., 2006). Finally, in addition to these identity-orientation-driven governance capabilities, a cluster firm may choose to develop a third governance capability, namely a *partner selection capability* to be able identify potential partners that have a similar logic of exchange to the firm's (Bierly III & Gallagher, 2007).

A disconfirming relational practice calls into question not only a cluster firm's logic of exchange as the appropriate logic of exchange inside the cluster, but also the governance capability associated with that logic of exchange as the strategically important governance capability inside the cluster as perceived by the firm. Consequently, it reveals a perceived deficiency in the firm's governance capabilities and prompts the firm to initiate new capability investments (Gavetti, 2005; Laamanen & Wallin, 2009; Maritan, 2001).

A cluster firm is likely to invest in different governance capabilities based on whose logic of exchange it questions in the face of a disconfirming relational practice. In particular, if the firm questions its partner's logic of exchange when faced with a disconfirming relational practice, it is likely to make investments in its partner selection capability. If on the other hand, the firm questions its own logic of exchange when faced with a disconfirming relational practice, it is likely to make investments in the capability that is consistent with the partner's logic of exchange (i.e., an individualist firm is likely to make investments in partner reading capability and a relational firm is likely to make investments in contract design capability).

As already mentioned, the logic of exchange a cluster firm initially brings into a relational practice is likely to change during the relational practice due to interactions between the partners. However, such changes are largely contextual, partner-specific, and situated in the particular relational practice; therefore they do not necessarily transfer to the firm's future relational practices.[4] On the other hand, when they lead to investments in a new governance capability, the more stable and enduring characteristic of the firm - its identity orientation - is likely to change, due to the new organizational roles, routines and structures that come with the new capability and the behaviors of people associated with these roles, routines and structures. This situation amounts to an individualistic (or relational) cluster firm moving towards the relational (or individualistic) end of the identity orientation continuum.

Emergence and Transformation of Cluster Macrocultures

Cluster macrocultures are conceptualized here as the extent to which cluster firms' identity orientations are convergent. Based on this definition, three types of cluster macrocultures can be envisioned: (1) A *weak cluster macroculture* where cluster firms do not converge on any point along the identity orientation continuum, (2) a *strong, uni-modal cluster macroculture* where cluster firms converge on a single point along the identity orientation continuum (e..g, the type of macroculture theorized to facilitate the emergence of clustering as a novel form of industrial organization), and (3) a *hybrid, multi-modal cluster macroculture* where groups of cluster firms converge on different points along the identity orientation continuum. The identity orientation dynamics outlined above imply a highly path-dependent process of cluster macroculture emergence/ transformation driven primarily by cluster firms' experiences during exchange relationships inside the cluster. While it is hard to anticipate how these dynamics will unfold in a particular cluster, a few tentative predictions can be made.

The more uniformly cluster firms are initially distributed on the identity orientation continuum, the less likely that a strong cluster macroculture will emerge. A uniform distribution makes it highly likely that the cluster firms will have a lot of alternations between confirming and disconfirming relational practices. This situation makes it unlikely for many cluster firms to perceive a strong macroculture, which in turn makes it unlikely that they will question the appropriateness of their own logic of

---

[4] For example an individualistic firm may develop trust against a particular partner over time and through repeated interactions (Vlaar, Van den Bosch & Volberda, 2007). This may cause the firm to start acting more like a relational firm in the advanced stages of that particular relationship. However, these behaviors do not necessarily transfer to the firm's next relational practice with a different partner since the firm remains to be an individualistic firm.

exchange when faced with disconfirming relational practices. These factors would prevent identity orientation revisions, causing the initial uniform distribution on the identity orientation continuum to remain largely intact over time. In some cases, it may be possible for a hybrid cluster macroculture to emerge in such clusters if firms develop a partner selection capability as a result of repeatedly questioning the appropriateness of their partner's logic of exchange. As cluster firms become adept at finding partners whose logics of exchange are close to theirs, groups of cluster firms may converge locally on different points on the identity orientation continuum, avoid partnering with distant firms, and form cliques of firms with different logics of exchange transacting largely among themselves.

Another prediction concerns the transformation of cluster macrocultures. The identity orientation dynamics outlined above imply that cluster macrocultures are in fact ever evolving qualities of clusters. However, assuming that they may have evolved at a given point in time to a stable state, a transformation may be triggered in three ways. First, changes in environmental conditions may cause latent differences between partnering cluster firms' logics of exchange to surface. For example the cluster's environment may become more dynamic increasing the number of negotiation situations, or less munificent causing the negotiation situation during relational practices to become largely distributive. These types of environmental changes increase the chances that relational practices will be of the disconfirming type, and eventually lead to identity orientation revisions (see Florida & Kenney (1990) for illustrations of such changes in Silicon Valley and Route 128). Second, cluster firms that are centrally located in the cluster's exchange network may change their behaviors during relational practices. Changes by such firms create rippling effects as less central firms start questioning the appropriateness of their own logics of exchange, leading to identity orientation revisions. Dyer and Nobeoka's (2000) account of how Toyota's policies in the Toyota City cluster influence its suppliers' actions and interpretations is illustrative. Finally, the cluster may go through a technological or otherwise paradigm shift causing existing firms to die and new firms to be founded. To the extent that new firms have a different identity orientation than the older firms, they may trigger identity orientation revisions by older firms through disconfirming relational practices. These triggers may destabilize existing cluster macrocultures as they give rise to changes in the strategically important governance capability inside the cluster prompting firms to make investments in new governance capabilities.

Also worthy of note is the importance of the essentially random order with which cluster firms partner with each other over time. Cluster firms' perceptions of a cluster macroculture and relatedly their appropriateness judgments in the face of disconfirming relational practices are largely a function of the temporal consistency in intra-cluster partnering patterns. Different temporal orderings of partnering patterns thus lead firms to make different types of capability investments which in turn may influence the emergence/ transformation speed of a cluster macroculture as well as the type of cluster macroculture that eventually emerges.

Discussion

The primary contribution of this study is thus a conceptual model that sheds light into the micro-level processes through which cluster macrocultures emerge/ transform. A unique aspect of the model is its focus on exchange relationships as series of negotiation situations during which firms make appropriateness judgments as to their logics of exchange by observing their partners' behaviors. A focus on behavioral aspects of exchange relationships rather than transaction characteristics (and the logic of economic instrumentality) allows for the possibility of different clusters with similar transaction characteristics ending up with different cluster macrocultures. The latter has been observed empirically but until now has not been accounted for theoretically.

The study's second contribution is a conception of opportunistic behavior that is different from that found in transaction cost economics, which in turn implies a different governance benefit associated with clustering. In transaction costs economics, opportunistic behavior is clearly defined (i.e., self-interest seeking with guile (Williamson, 1991)), and the governance problem relates primarily to its prevention. In this scheme of thought, clustering creates a governance benefit primarily by making it easy to monitor partners for opportunistic behavior, and by creating a local reputation system which in turn creates a disincentive for opportunistic behavior (Maskell, 2001). In contrast, in this study, the primary governance problem is not necessarily the prevention of clearly defined opportunistic behaviors but rather firms' reaching an agreement on what constitutes opportunistic behavior in the first place.

The study's third contribution is to the emergent literature on organizational identity orientation. First, the study makes a contribution by explaining in detail how a firm's identity orientation shapes its logic of exchange and its behaviors in the context of negotiations associated with exchange relationships. Second, the study offers the first conceptual model that outlines the dynamics of organizational identity orientation. Researchers have already offered conceptual models of organizational identity dynamics as driven by the interactions between organizational identity, image and culture (Gioia, et al., 2000; Hatch & Schultz, 2002). In contrast, organizational identity orientation is a relatively new concept and the process by which firms' identity orientations evolve has not yet been explored. The model offered in this paper focuses on firms' experiences during relational practices, their appropriateness judgments as to their logics of exchange, and resulting governance-capability investments as the primary drivers of organizational identity orientation dynamics.

The most important research implication of the study relates to the conclusion that the emergence of favorable cluster macrocultures is not automatic as theorized by the many scholars who view clustering as a novel form of industrial organization. Instead, macrocultures emerge/ transform through a highly path dependent process, the outcomes of which are largely influenced by a number of factors including the initial distribution of cluster firms on the identity orientation continuum and the temporal order with which cluster firms engage in exchange relationships with each other. The flexible specialization model comes largely out of research on early Italian clusters where predominantly family-owned small firms are linked to each other through family/ friendship ties, and more importantly a common history and heritage (Lazerson, 1995). These commonalities make it highly likely that the firms in these clusters were relatively close to each other on the identity orientation continuum form the onset, which creates a situation germane to the emergence of strong cluster macrocultures. Such commonalities may be the real reason why these clusters were highly successful as a way to organize economic activity. In the absence of such commonalities (e.g., as in "made clusters" such as industrial and science parks (Arikan & Schilling, 2011), the emergence of governance-related benefits of clustering may take a long time or never materialize. Overall, the arguments in this paper suggest that researchers should not take cluster macrocultures (and their governance benefits) for granted, and treat them as variable qualities of clusters that may give rise to performance differentials across clusters.

References

Abrahamson, E., & Fombrun, C. J. (1992). Forging the Iron Cage: Interorganizational networks and the production of macro-culture. *The Journal of Management Studies, 29*, 175-194.

Abrahamson, E., & Fombrun, C. J. (1994). Macrocultures: Determinants and consequences. *Academy of Management Review, 19*, 728-755.

Aggarwal, V. A., & Hsu, D. H. (2009). Modes of cooperative R&D commercialization by start-ups. *Strategic Management Journal, 30*, 835-864.

Albert, S., & Whetten, D. (1985). Organizational identity. In B. M. Staw & L. L. Cummings (Eds.), *Research in Organizational Behavior, 7* (pp. 263-295). Greenwich, CT: JAI Press.

Antonelli, C. (1999). The evolution of industrial organization of the production of knowledge. *Cambridge Journal of Economics, 23*, 243-260.

Argyres, N., & Mayer, K. J. (2007). Contract design as a firm capability: An integration of learning and transaction cost perspectives. *Academy of Management Review, 32*, 1060-1077.

Arikan, A. T. 2009. Interfirm knowledge exchanges and the knowledge creation capability of clusters. *Academy of Management Review, 34*, 658-676.

Arikan, A. T., & Schilling, M. A. (2011). Structure and governance in industrial districts: Implications for competitive advantage. *Journal of Management Studies, 48*,772-803.

Ballinger, G. A., & Rockmann, K. W. (2010). Chutes versus ladders: Anchoring events and a punctuated-equilibrium perspective on social exchange relationships. *Academy of Management Review, 35*, 373-391.

Baptista, R., & Swann, P. (1998). Do firms in clusters innovate more? *Research Policy, 27*, 525-540.

Becattini, G. (1990). The Marshallian industrial districts as a socio-economic notion. In F. Pyke, G. Becattini & W. Sengerberger (Eds.), *Industrial districts and inter-firm cooperation in Italy* (pp. 37–51). Geneva: International Institute for Labour Studies.

Beech, N., & Huxham, C. (2003). Cycles of identity formation in interorganizational collaborations. *International Studies of Management & Organization, 33*, 28-52.

Bell, S. J., Tracey, P., & Heide, J. B. (2009). The organization of regional clusters. *Academy of Management Review, 34*, 623-642.

Bettenhausen, K. & Murnighan, J. K. (1985). The emergence of norms in competitive decision making groups. *Administrative Science Quarterly, 30*: 350-372.

Bettman, J. R., & Weitz, B. A. (1983). Attributions in the board room: Causal reasoning in corporate annual reports. *Administrative Science Quarterly, 28*, 165-183.

Bierly III, P. E., & Gallagher, S. (2007). Explaining alliance partner selection: Fit, trust and strategic expediency. *Long Range Planning, 40*, 134-153.

Blau, P. M. (1964). *Exchange and power in social life*. New York: Wiley.

Blois, K. (2002). Business to business exchanges: A rich descriptive apparatus derived from Macneil's and Menger's analyses. *Journal of Management Studies, 39*, 523-551.

Boles, T. L., & Messick, D. M. (1995). A reverse outcome bias: The influence of multiple reference points on the evaluation of outcomes and decisions. *Organizational Behavior and Human Decision Processes, 61*, 262-275.

Brickson, S. L. (2005). Organizational identity orientation: Forging a link between organizational identity and organizations' relations with stakeholders. *Administrative Science Quarterly, 50*, 576-609.

—. (2007). Organizational identity orientation: The genesis of the role of the firm and distinct forms of social value. *Academy of Management Review, 32*, 864-888.

Brusco, S. (1982). The Modena model: Productive decentralization and social integration. *Cambridge Journal of Econoomics, 6*, 167-184.

Carson, S. J., Madhok, A., Varman, R., John, G. (2003). Information processing moderators of the effectiveness of trust-based governance in interfirm R&D collaboration. *Organization Science, 14*, 45-56.

Collins, R. (1981). On the microfoundations of macrosociology. *American Journal of Sociology, 86*, 984-1014.

Cropanzano, R., & Mitchell, M. S. (2005). Social Exchange Theory: An Interdisciplinary Review. *Journal of Management, 31*, 874-900.

Davis, G. F., & Greve, H. R. (1997). Corporate elite networks and governance changes in the 1980s. *American Journal of Sociology, 103*, 1-37.

Dollinger, M. J., Golden, P. A., & Saxton, T. (1997). The effect of reputation on the decision to joint venture. *Strategic Management Journal, 18*, 127-140.

Dyer, J. H., & Nobeoka, K. (2000). Creating and managing a high performance sharing network: the Toyota Case. *Strategic Management Journal, 21*, 345-367.

Essletzbichler, J. (2003). From mass production to flexible specialization: The sectoral and geographical extent of contract work in US manufacturing, 1963-1997. *Regional Studies, 3,* 753-771.

Faems, D., Janssens, M., Madhok, A., & Van Looy, B. (2008). Toward an integrative perspective on alliance governance: Connecting contract design, trust dynamics, and contract application. *Academy of Management Journal, 51*,1053-1078.

Florida, R., & Kenney, M. (1990). Silicon Valley and Route 128 won't save us. *California Management Review, 33*, 68-88.

Flynn, F. J. (2005). Identity orientations and forms of social exchange in organizations. *Academy of Management Review, 30*, 737-750.

Gavetti, G. (2005). Cognition and hierarchy: Rethinking the microfoundations of capabilites' development. *Organization Science, 16*, 599-617.

Gioia, D. A., Schultz, M., & Corley, K. G. (2000). Organizational identity, image, and adaptive instability. *Academy of Management Review, 25*, 63-81.

Glynn, M. A. (2000). When cymbals become symbols: Conflict over organizational identity within a symphony orchestra. *Organization Science, 11*, 285-298.

Gray, B. (2004). Strong opposition: Frame-based resistance to collaboration. *Journal of Community & Applied Social Psychology, 14*, 166-176.

Greve, H. R., Palmer, D., & Pozner, J. (2010). Organizations gone wild: The causes, processes, and consequences of organizational misconduct. *The Academy of Management Annals, 4*, 53-107.

Hansen, M. H., Hoskisson, R. E., & Barney, J. B. (2008). Competitive advantage in alliance governance: Resolving the opportunism minimization-gain maximization paradox. *Managerial and Decision Economics, 29*, 191-208.

Harrison, B. 1992. Industrial districts: Old wine in new bottles? *Regional Studies*, 26: 469-483.

Harvey, J. H., & Weary, G. (1984). Current research in attribution theory and research. *Annual Review of Pscyhology, 35*, 427-459.

Hatch, M. J., & Schultz, M. (2002). The dynamics of organizational identity. *Human Relations, 55*, 989-1018.

Helfat, C. E., & Peteraf, M. A. (2003). The dynamic resource-based view: Capability lifecycles. *Strategic Management Journal, 24*, 997-1010.

Huxham, C., & Hibbert, P. (2008). Manifested attitudes: Intricacies of inter-partner learning in collaboration. *Journal of Management Studies, 45*, 502-529.

Iammarino, S. (2005). An evolutionary integrated view of Regional Systems of Innovation: Concepts, measures and historical perspectives. *European Planning Studies, 13*, 497-519.

Jones, C., Hesterly, W. S., & Borgatti, S. P. (1997). A general theory of network governance: Exchange conditions and social mechanisms. *Academy of Management Review, 22*, 911-945.

Kelley, H. H. (1973). The processes of causal attribution. *American Psychologist, 28*, 107-128.

Krishnan, R., Martin, X., & Noorderhaven, N. (2006). When does trust matter to alliance performance? *Academy of Management Journal, 49*, 894-917.

Laamanen, T., & Wallin, J. (2009). Cognitive dynamics of capability development paths. *Journal of Management Studies, 46*, 950-981.

Lazerson, M. (1995). A new Phoenix? Modern putting-out in the Modena knitwear industry. *Administrative Science Quarterly, 40*, 34-59.

Livengood, R. S., & Reger, R. K. 2010. That's our turf! Identity domains and competitive dynamics. *Academy of Management Review, 35*: 48-66.

Lui, H. Y.,, & Ngo, S. S. (2005). An action pattern model of inter-firm cooperation. *Journal of Management Studies, 42*, 1123-1153.

Macaulay, S. (1963). Non-contractual relationships in business: A preliminary study. *American Journal of Sociology, 28*, 55-67.

Macneil, I. R. (1980). *The new social contract.* New Haven, CT: Yale University Press.

March, J. G. (1995). *A primer on decision making.* New York: Free Press.

Maritan, C. A. (2001). Capital investment as investing in organizational capabilities: An empirically grounded process model. *Academy of Management Journal, 44*, 513-531.

Maskell, P. (2001). Towards a knowledge based theory of the geographical cluster. *Industrial and Corporate Change, 10*, 921-943.

McGinn, K. L., & Keros, A. T. (2002). Improvisation and the logic of exchange in socially embedded transactions. *Administrative Science Quarterly, 47*, 442-473.

Mesquita, L. F. (2007). Starting over when the bickering never ends: Rebuilding aggregate trust among clustered firms through trust facilitators. *Academy of Management Review, 32*, 72-91.

Messick, D. M. (1999). Alternative logics for decision making in social settings. *Journal of Economic Behavior & Organization, 39*, 11-28.

Mohr, J., & Spekman, R. (1994). Characteristics of partnership success: Partnership attributes, communication behavior, and conflict resolution techniques. *Strategic Management Journal, 15*, 135-152.

Molm, L. D., Takahashi, N., & Peterson, G. (2003). In the eye of the beholder: Procedural justice in social exchange. *American Sociological Review, 68*, 128-152.

Moussavi, F., & Evans, D. A. (1993). Emergence of organizational attributions: The role of a shared cognitive schema. *Journal of Management, 19*, 79-95.

Ness, H. (2009). Governance, negotiations, and alliance dynamics: Explaining the evolution of relational practice. *Journal of Management Studies, 46*, 451-480.

O'Connor, K. M. (1997). Motives and theoretical cognitions in negotiation: A theoretical integration and empirical test. *The International Journal of Conflict Management, 8*, 114-131.

Opp, K. D. (2001). How do norms emerge? An outline of a theory. *Mind & Society, 2*, 101-128.

Phillips, N., Lawrence, T. B., Hardy, C. (2004). Discourse and institutions. *Academy of Management Review, 29*, 635-652.

Pinkley, R. L. (1990). Dimensions of conflict frame: Disputant interpretations of conflict. *Journal of Applied Psychology, 75*, 117-126.

Pinkley, R. L., Northcraft, G. B. (1994). Conflict frames of reference: Implications for dispute processes and outcomes. *Academy of Management Journal, 37*, 193-205.

Piore, M. J., & Sabel, C. F. (1984). *The second industrial divide: Possibilities for prosperity.* New York, NY: Basic Books.

Porter, M. E. (2000). Location, competition, and economic development: Local clusters in a global economy. *Economic Development Quarterly, 14*, 15-34.

Rao, H., Greve, H. R., & Davis, G. F. (2001). Fool's gold: Social proof in the initiation and abandonment of coverage by Wall Street analysts. *Administrative Science Quarterly, 46*, 502-526.

Reuer, J. J., & Arino, A. (2007). Strategic alliance contracts: Dimensions and determinants of contractual complexity. *Strategic Management Journal, 28*, 313-330.

Robertson, P. L., & Langlois, R. N. (1995). Innovation, networks and vertical integration. *Research Policy, 24*, 543-562.

Saxenian, A. (1994). *Regional advantage: Culture and competition in Silicon Valley and Route 128.* Cambridge, MA: Harvard University Press.

Schoorman, F. D., Mayer, R. C., & Davis, J. H. (2007). An integrative model of organizational trust: Past, present, and future. *Academy of Management Review, 32*, 344-354.

Shavell, S. (2006). On the writing and interpretation of contracts. *The Journal of Law, Economics, & Organization, 22*, 289-314.

Shore, L. M., Tetrick, L. E., Lynch, P., & Barksdale, K. (2006). Social and economic exchange: Construct development and validation. *Journal of Applied Social Psychology, 36*, 837-867.

Shrum, W., & Wuthnow, R. (1988). Reputational status of organizations in technical systems. *American Journal of Sociology, 93*, 882-912.

Sjovall, A. M., & Talk, A. C. (2004). From actions to impressions: Cognitive attribution theory and the formation of corporate reputation. *Corporate Reputation Review, 7*(3),269-281.

Still, M. C., & Strang, D. (2009). Who does an elite organization emulate? *Administrative Science Quarterly, 54*, 58-89.

Stuart, T. E., Hoang, H., & Hybels, R. C. (1999). Interorganizational endorsements and the performance of entrepreneurial ventures. *Administrative Science Quarterly, 44*, 315-349.

Tallman, S., Jenkins, M., Henry, N., & Pinch, S. (2004). Knowledge, clusters and competitive advantage. *Academy of Management Review, 29*, 258-271.

Thibaut, J. (1968). The development of contractual norms in bargaining: Replication and variation. *Journal of Conflict Resolution, 12*, 102-112.

Van Kleef, G. A., & De Dreu, C. K. W. (2002). Social value orientation and impression formation: A test of two competing hypothesis about information search in negotiation. *The International Journal of Conflict Management, 13*, 59-77.

Vlaar, P. W. L., Van den Bosch, F. A. J., & Volberda, H. W. (2006). Coping with problems of understanding in interorganizational relationships: Using formalization as a way to make sense. *Organization Studies, 27*, 1617-1638.

Vlaar, P. W. L., Van den Bosch, F. A. J., & Volberda, H. W. (2007). On the evolution of trust, distrust, and formal coordination and control in interorganizational relationships. *Group and Organization Management, 32*, 407-429.

Villalonga, B., McGahan, A. M. (2005). The choice among acquisitions, alliances, and divestitures. *Strategic Management Journal, 26*, 1183-1208.

Wathne, K. H., & Heide, J. B. (2000). Opportunism in interfirm relationships: Forms, outcomes and solutions. *Journal of Marketing, 64*, 36-51.

Weber, L., & Mayer, K. J. (2011). Designing effective contracts: Exploring the influence of framing and expectations. *Academy of Management Review, 36*, 53-75.

Weiss, J., & Dalbecq, A. High technology cultures and management. *Group & Organization Studies, 12*: 39-54.

Williamson, O. E. (1991). Comparative economic organization: The analysis of discrete structural alternatives. *Administrative Science Quarterly, 36*, 269-296.

CHAPTER SEVENTEEN

MANAGERIAL ACTION TO PROMOTE
CONTROL, TRUST, AND FAIRNESS
IN ORGANIZATIONS:
THE EFFECT OF CONFLICT

CHRIS P. LONG,
GEORGETOWN UNIVERSITY, USA
SIM B. SITKIN
DUKE UNIVERSITY, USA
AND LAURA B. CARDINAL
UNIVERSITY OF HOUSTON, USA

Abstract

This paper develops a theory to explain the drivers of managerial efforts to promote trust, fairness, and control. We specifically theorize about how the presence of superior-subordinate conflicts stimulate managers' concerns about managerial legitimacy and subordinate dependability in performing tasks. We then hypothesize about how managers attempt to address these concerns using trustworthiness-promotion, fairness-promotion, and control activities. The paper concludes with a discussion about how our theory refines and extends organizational trust, fairness, and control research.

Keywords: control, trust, fairness, authority, power

Introduction

Over more than a quarter century, researchers have argued that when managers promote organizational trust and fairness, they enhance the quality of their subordinates' contributions and their capacity to achieve organizational objectives (Colquitt, 2001; Lind & Tyler, 1988; Thibaut & Walker, 1975). While research connecting subordinate trust and fairness perceptions to positive organizational outcomes is extensive, research on factors that influence managers to promote trust and fairness has been limited in two ways (Folger & Skarlicki, 2001; Whitener, Brodt, Korsgaard, & Werner, 1998). First, because trust and fairness research has primarily examined subordinates' evaluations of managerial actions, "there is a dearth of research on the perspective adopted by managers" (Folger & Skarlicki, 2001: p. 98). This has led scholars such as Bies (2003) to request that more effort be put forth to examine "not just the victim and the provocation but also the 'provoker' or the perpetrator" (i.e., of fairness or unfairness) (p. 4) to develop a clearer understanding of the reasons why managers promote (or do not promote) fairness. Similar observations related to the trust literature have been made by Whitener, Brodt, Korsgaard, and Werner (1998) and Long and Sitkin (2006).

Second, we contend that managers' efforts to promote trust and fairness do not exist in a vacuum but often occur concurrently with their efforts to exert organizational controls. While scholars have acknowledged that managers may not select their actions in isolation, most research to date has examined the determinants of trust, fairness, and control actions as though they were independent phenomena. As a result, scholars currently maintain an incomplete understanding of how managers balance their efforts to promote trust, fairness and control in organizational contexts (Das & Teng, 1998; Long & Sitkin, 2006). McEvily, Perrone, & Zaheer (2003), for example, contend that there currently exists "a somewhat fragmented view of the role of trust in an organizational context as a whole" (p. 91) and, as a result, scholars are uncertain how managers balance their attempts to promote both trust and control in organizations. Taylor, Masterson, Renard and Tracy (1998) generally concur with this assessment and argue that while both fairness and control comprise important managerial activities, research findings are inconclusive regarding how managers view choices between their efforts to promote fairness and their efforts to exert organizational control.

In this paper, we attempt to clarify these dynamics by presenting a descriptive (i.e., not normative) theory that outlines how superior-subordinate conflicts influence managers' efforts to implement trust, fairness, and control in organizations. Specifically, we propose that superior-subordinate conflicts lead managers to question their own authority and, thus, to examine two components of that authority: managerial legitimacy and subordinate dependability. We hypothesize that, to the extent that managerial concerns about these elements are activated, managers will attempt to address them by varying the efforts they make to promote their trustworthiness, promote fairness, and apply controls. Building from the general model we propose, we further argue that managers respond to these concerns with particular configurations of trustworthiness-promotion, fairness-promotion, and control activities.

Trustworthiness-Promotion, Fairness-Promotion, and Organizational Control Activities

We begin our discussion by describing the concepts of *trustworthiness-promotion*, *fairness-promotion* and *control* as we use them in this paper. Although previous research on trust, fairness, and control has tended smooth the distinctions between them, we contend that trustworthiness-promotion, fairness-promotion, and control activities differ from each other in terms of the actions that managers take to promote each activity and in terms of the specific outcomes that managers anticipate achieving through the implementation of each activity.

Trustworthiness-Promotion Activities

Managers' trustworthiness-promotion activities reflect their efforts to create conditions where individual subordinates are willing to be vulnerable because they are confident that their manager will reliably act in their best interest (Mayer, Davis & Schoorman, 1995; Rousseau, Sitkin, Burt, & Camerer, 1998). Through trustworthiness-promotion activities, managers attempt to increase their subordinates' confidence that, through them, they can achieve their personal goals. To achieve these objectives, managers demonstrate their trustworthiness along three key dimensions (Mayer et al., 1995): managerial reliability, competence, and concern for their subordinates' personal welfare.

Managers interested in promoting their trustworthiness will *demonstrate reliability* and display a willingness to make their actions correspond with their words (Mayer et al., 1995; Simons, 2002). Reliability describes the extent to which employees perceive that their managers behave consistently over time, honor their commitments and fulfill both the implicit and explicit promises they make to them (Mishra, 1996).

Managers try to demonstrate reliability by aligning their actions with their subordinates' expectations in ways that give those subordinates increased confidence that their managers will honor their obligations to them.

Second, managers interested in promoting their trustworthiness will try to *demonstrate managerial competence* by displaying their managerial capabilities in ways that provide their subordinates with confidence that "they know what they are doing" (Mayer et al., 1995; Mishra, 1996; Sitkin & Roth, 1993). In an effort to demonstrate their competence managers may, for example, communicate an extensive knowledge of organizational procedures or display a developed ability to understand and perform subordinates' task activities.

Third, managers will attempt to increase their perceived trustworthiness by putting forth efforts to *demonstrate concern* for their subordinates (Mayer et al., 1995). Consistent with Whitener et al. (1998) and Mishra (1996), we argue that managers' efforts to demonstrate concern for their subordinates consists of displaying an active interest in the personal welfare of individual subordinates under their discretion. Managers may do this in various ways. For example, by informing subordinates that they share common experiences and values, managers attempt to provide those subordinates with increased confidence that they understand and will accommodate their subordinates' interests when they make decisions. By advocating for employees' interests with their own superiors, managers attempt to provide their subordinates with the confidence that their personal interests will be furthered.

Fairness-Promotion Activities

Fairness-promotion activities describe the efforts managers make to promote impartiality, representation, and civility in managing their subordinates' activities. Our conceptualization of fairness-promotion concurs with observations made by Kim and Mauborgne (1997), who suggest that when managers are asked what it means to be fair they "will describe how they give people the authority they deserve, or the resources they need, or the rewards they deserve" (p. 140). Consistent with these observations, we argue that, through their efforts to promote *distributive* (Deutsch, 1975), *procedural* (Thibaut & Walker, 1975), and *interactional* fairness (Bies & Moag, 1986) managers attempt to communicate to their subordinates that they will protect the general interest that they have in being treated fairly. In addressing these concerns, we contend that managers focus on responding positively to the social comparison processes that they assume their subordinates engage.

Distributive Fairness-Promotion. Managers' efforts to *promote distributive fairness* describe the actions they take to positively influence subordinates' assessments of reward and resource allocations (Deutsch, 1975). While organizational context dictates primary allocation rules (Meindl, 1989), managers attempting to promote distributive fairness align their allocations of organizational rewards and resources with accepted allocation norms. In most cases, managers focus their efforts here ensuring that they distribute rewards and resources to similar subordinates according to normative allocation standards (Leventhal, 1976). However, we hypothesize that distributive fairness-promotion activities also describe the efforts of managers to ensure that the resources and rewards their subordinates receive compare favorably with those that they themselves receive.

Procedural Fairness-Promotion. Managers' *procedural fairness-promotion* activities describe a slightly different set of social comparison processes. Here, managers attempt to apply organizational procedures in ways that standardize the treatment that subordinates receive and decrease the differences in power that they and their employees hold over decision-making activities.

Consistent with the work of Gilliland and Paddock (2005), we argue that three categories of activities encapsulate the ways managers attempt to promote procedural fairness: promoting accuracy, promoting consistency, and promoting voice. When applying organizational procedures, managers use these activities to positively influence subordinates' evaluations of how rules and procedures are implemented and developed. By *promoting accuracy*, managers work to ensure that their decisions and evaluations are based on accurate, objective, and non-biased information. When promoting accuracy, managers place a premium on accurately evaluating the work of their employees and on using objective, non-biased information in their decision-making. By *promoting consistency*, managers work to ensure that procedures are consistently applied to all subordinates that those procedures affect.

Through the *promotion of voice,* managers focus on a slightly different set of subordinate social comparisons. To promote voice, managers invite subordinates to become part of their decision-making processes and thereby to affect both the processes of decision-making and the implementation of decisions and procedures. By promoting employee voice, managers attempt to positively impact subordinates' assessments of decision-making discretion by increasing the relative control that their subordinates have over decision-making responsibilities (Thibaut & Walker, 1975).

Interactional Fairness-Promotion. Managers' efforts to *promote interactional fairness* reflect their attempts to respond positively to an alternative set of social comparison processes they assume their subordinates engage. Here, managers assume that subordinates will compare the interpersonal treatment they *do* receive with the interpersonal treatment they believe that they *should* receive from their manager. As such, managers' interactional fairness-promotion efforts specifically reflect their attempts to acknowledge the dignity and status of their subordinates by interacting with them in ways that they would perceive as respectful and in ways which communicate esteem (Bies & Moag, 1986; Cronin & Weingart, 2007).

We focus on two mechanisms managers use to communicate that they respect and hold their subordinates in esteem. Managers' efforts to engage in *respectful communication* represent their responses to subordinates' particular sensitivities about the way in which information should be communicated. Specifically, managers who engage in respectful communication activities work actively to ensure that they use polite, non-offensive language when communicating with their subordinates. Managers' efforts to provide *timely and truthful accounts* describe their attempts to provide legitimate and verifiable justifications of their actions. Here, managers deliver the candid social accounts that they assume their subordinates expect and prefer to receive (Sitkin & Bies, 1993).

Organizational Control Activities

Organizational controls describe the *formal* (e.g., written contracts and rules, monetary incentives) and *informal* (i.e., values, norms, and beliefs) mechanisms that managers use to direct and motivate the completion of organizational tasks by their subordinates (e.g., Cardinal, 2001; Ouchi, 1979). Organizational control activities differ from trustworthiness-promotion and fairness-promotion activities in that they reflect managers' efforts to prepare, direct, and motivate their subordinates to achieve particular production standards. For example, managers may use behavior-based rules to ensure that subordinates perform tasks according to pre-specified operating procedures. They may also use output targets and incentives to ensure that their subordinates provide them with outputs of a particular quality or quantity.

Scholars have classified various types of controls based on the portion of the production process to which they are applied (Cardinal, Sitkin, & Long, 2004; Merchant, 1985; Snell, 1992). Managers select *input controls* to guide the selection and preparation of human and material production resources. Here, managers develop training and socialization to regulate employees' skills and abilities or implement screening mechanisms to obtain a specific quality and quantity of material production inputs (Cardinal et al., 2004; Van Maanen & Schein, 1979). Managers also use *process controls* while employees perform tasks to ensure that they use appropriate task production methods in those efforts (Merchant, 1985). Finally, managers use *output controls* to ensure that employees achieve desired performance standards by measuring the outputs they produce against metrics such as production targets or profit goals (Ouchi, 1979).

In Table 17-1, we summarize our discussion above by outlining the characteristics of each of these three categories of managerial activities. We describe the primary mechanisms managers use and the intended outcomes they attempt to achieve through their attention to these activities.

A Focus on Managerial Action

While they represent distinct categories of activities, researchers do acknowledge that managers often concurrently pursue their efforts to promote trustworthiness, fairness, and control. Despite this, researchers have devoted relatively little effort towards identifying and examining factors that affect managers' independent and joint implementation of these activities. In the section that follows, we attempt to address this gap in the literature by outlining a general process by which managers choose to promote their trustworthiness, promote fairness, and exert control over their subordinates' activities.

The core premise of our arguments is that the superior-subordinate conflicts that managers encounter stimulate them to evaluate the stability and strength of their managerial authority by identifying ways in which their authority might be compromised. Drawing from the assumption that managerial authority is a fundamental attribute that managers generally seek to protect (Barnard, 1938, Pfeffer, 1981b), we argue that managers will utilize particular trustworthiness-promotion, fairness-promotion, and control efforts to secure and bolster the elements of their authority they believe are compromised.

Figure 17-1 outlines the relationships we develop in this section. This figure graphically depicts the factors that impact the trustworthiness-promotion, fairness-promotion, and control activities that managers implement.

Table 17-1. Managerial Applications Of Trustworthiness-Promotion And Fairness-Promotion, And Control Activities

	Trustworthiness-Promotion Activities	Fairness-Promotion Activities	Control Activities
Intended Outcomes	Foster positive assessments of a manager's trustworthiness	Produce assessments that treatment is fair.	Align subordinate inputs, behaviors, and outputs with demands of organizational tasks
Primary Mechanisms	1. Demonstrate a Manager's: a. Reliability b. Competence c. Concern for their Subordinates' Welfare	1. Distributive Fairness-Promotion a. Fair Distribution of Resources and Rewards 2. Procedural Fairness-Promotion a. Promote Consistency b. Promote Accuracy c. Promote Voice 3. Interactional Fairness-Promotion a. Respectful Communication b. Provide Timely and Truthful Accounts	1. Input Controls a. Selection b. Training 2. Process Controls a. Rules b. Monitoring 3. Output Controls a. Performance Targets b. Incentives

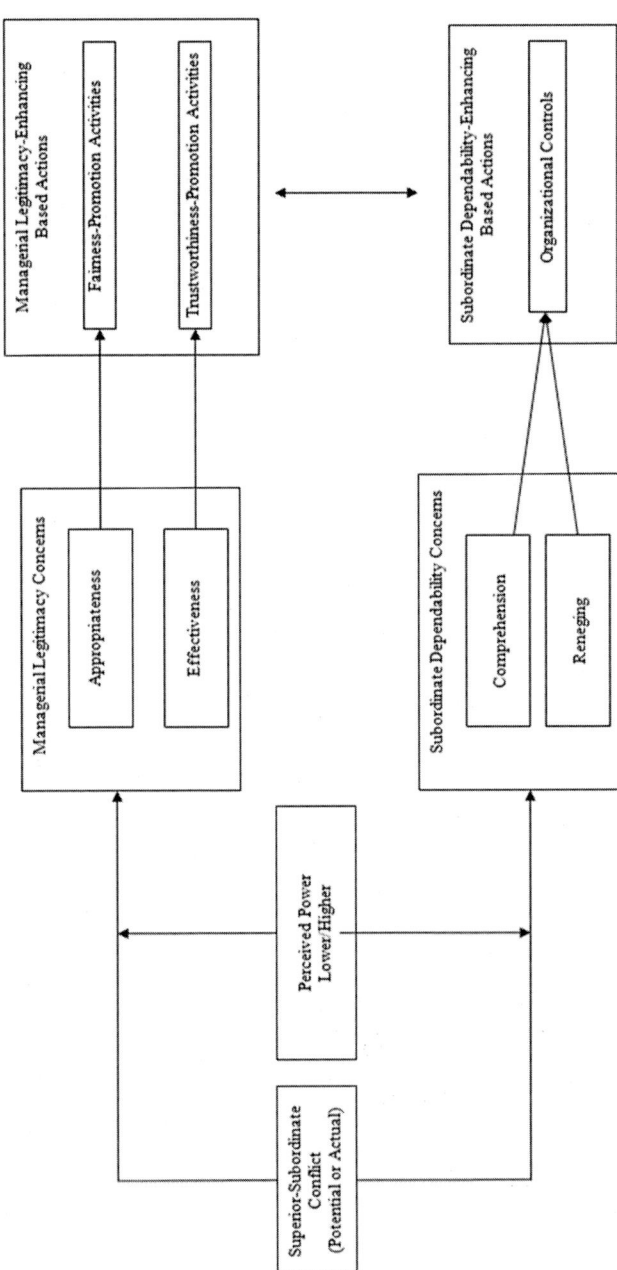

Figure 17-1. Process Model of How Superior-Subordinate Conflicts Influence Managerial Fairness-Promotion, Trustworthiness-Promotion, and Control Activities

Superior-Subordinate Conflicts as Challenges to Managerial Authority

We begin by identifying that a manager's recognition of superior-subordinate conflicts (i.e., real or potential) constitute important events that affect the efforts of managers to promote trustworthiness, promote fairness, and exert control. Our arguments are consistent with managerial action accounts (e.g., Kim & Mauborgne, 1997; Rosenblatt, Rogers, & Nord, 1993) that chronicle how managers adjust their efforts to promote what we have classified as trustworthiness-promotion, fairness-promotion, and control in order to respond to the superior-subordinate conflicts they encounter. In addition, our arguments generally concur with the theoretical work of Bies (1987) and Greenberg (1990), who argue that managers respond to their subordinates' "moral outrage" with efforts to promote fairness, and with control researchers who suggest that persistent superior-subordinate conflicts motivate managers to implement organizational controls (Ouchi, 1979).

Despite previous acknowledgements that conflicts can stimulate managerial trustworthiness-promotion, fairness promotion, and control actions, scholars have yet to fully specify the underlying processes by which these decisions occur (Folger & Cropanzano, 2001; Long & Sitkin 2006). In our effort to increase our understanding of these dynamics, we begin by recognizing that the presence or potential presence of superior-subordinate conflicts is an important factor in this process because it stimulates managers to evaluate the composition and strength of their managerial authority. We contend that managers conduct these evaluations because their authority constitutes their perceived capacity to direct, influence, and control the actions of others (Barnard, 1938; Karniol & Miller, 1981; Pfeffer, 1981a). As such, managerial authority serves as arguably the fundamental mechanism by which managers can ensure that their subordinates willingly follow and commit to the implementation of their directives (Dornbusch & Scott, 1975).

While a manager's authority is generally stable, Pfeffer (1981b) and others (e.g., Zelditch & Walker, 1984) have argued that superior-subordinate conflicts signal to managers ways in which their authority is unstable. For example, Dornbusch and Scott (1975: p. 17), observe that "the greater the discrepancy (i.e., conflict) between preferred and actual work arrangements as perceived by performers, the greater would be the instability of their authority systems."

We argue that, for managers, this perceived instability can manifest within two general categories of concerns related to the composition and exercise of managerial authority: concerns about their managerial legitimacy and concerns about subordinate dependability. Regarding the composition of their authority, superior-subordinate conflicts may signal to managers that their authority is unstable because their *managerial legitimacy* is being questioned or challenged. Here, managers may believe that conflicts arise from subordinates' beliefs that managerial power is inappropriately distributed or utilized (Scott, 2003). Regarding concerns about the exercise of their authority, superior-subordinate conflicts may signal that subordinates will be unreliable in their efforts to perform tasks. Issues related to *subordinate dependability* constitute a category of concerns that are related to but distinct from managerial legitimacy concerns. This is because, while subordinates may view their manager as legitimate, those subordinates may still compromise that manager's authority by simply being unable or unwilling to follow their directives (Zelditch & Walker, 1984).

Below, we describe how managers' efforts to address the specific managerial legitimacy and subordinate-dependability concerns that arise in the face of superior-subordinate conflicts motivate them to undertake trustworthiness-promotion, fairness-promotion, and control activities.

Concerns about Managerial Legitimacy

From the work of Barnard (1938) to the present, managerial legitimacy has been identified as a key condition for the effective exercise of one's authority. Managerial legitimacy is defined as "a generalized perception or assumption that the actions of an entity (manager) are desirable, proper, or appropriate within some socially constructed system of norms, values, beliefs, and definitions (Suchman, 1995: p. 574). Tyler and Lind (1992) suggest that being viewed as legitimate "nearly always facilitates and is often crucial for the effective exercise of authority […and], once established, functions to enhance acceptance of decisions (p. 118)."

By acknowledging that subordinates maintain the divergent ideas and objectives that comprise superior-subordinate conflicts, managers concede that they or their directives may not be viewed as legitimate by those subordinates (Bies, 1987; Pfeffer, 1981b). Within superior-subordinate conflicts, managerial legitimacy concerns tend to arise around the primary components of legitimacy: *appropriateness* and *effectiveness* (Dornbusch & Scott, 1975, March & Olsen, 1995; Zelditch & Walker, 1985). "Appropriateness" describes how actions are consistent with subordinates' normative views of desirable behaviors. "Effectiveness" describes how a manager and his or her actions tend to reliably produce beneficial results for them.

We build from our proposition that managers will take actions to protect their authority by addressing the elements of their legitimacy they believe are compromised. As we argue below, to the extent that managers are concerned about their perceived appropriateness, they will tend to increase their fairness-promotion efforts. We also posit that to the extent that managers are concerned about their perceived effectiveness, they will tend to increase their trustworthiness-promotion efforts.

Appropriateness Concerns

When superior-subordinate conflicts raise managerial appropriateness concerns, managers display an awareness that their subordinates may not view their actions as being "proper" and in alignment with standards of conduct that subordinates view as acceptable (Dornbusch & Scott, 1975). Circumstances where subordinates view their managers as "acting inappropriately" are problematic because subordinates may not be able to relate to and identify with that manager. As Tyler (1999), van Knippenberg and Hogg (2003) and Lord and Brown (2004) argue, when an individual's capacity to identify with an authority weakens, their willingness to accede to that authority lessens because an association with that manager does not positively influence their self-identity.

As managers respond to their appropriateness concerns, they will seek out ways to align their actions with standards of conduct that their subordinates view as appropriate. Here, managers tend to increase fairness-promotion efforts because fairness norms constitute arguably the most recognizable and generally applicable collection of appropriateness standards present in organizations (Lerner, 1977). Because managers understand that these principles are acceptable to their subordinates (Cropanzano, Goldman, & Folger, 2003), we argue that managers seeking to be viewed as appropriate will tend to increase their fairness-promotion activities.

By communicating that they are "fair managers" who uphold standards that subordinates respect, managers attempt to increase subordinates' tendencies to identify with them. Lerner (1981) argues that one reason managers promote fairness is to decrease the perceived dissimilarities between themselves and their subordinates. As the descriptions of Leventhal (1976), Bies (1987) and Greenberg (1990) suggest, these efforts can encompass a range of activities, from distributing rewards and resources to developing procedures to altering the ways in which one interpersonally interacts.

We argue that the potential to decrease subordinate distrust is often a related objective of managers' fairness-promotion efforts. Sitkin and Roth (1993), who describe these dynamics, suggest that managers rely on fairness-promotion to signal to their subordinates that they are working to protect their rights and general interests. In other words, managers understand that, through their fairness-promotion activities, they can decrease the tendency of subordinates to distrust their manager's intentions and behaviors and, thereby, preserve and protect their legitimacy and authority.

> **Proposition 1a**: To the extent that superior-subordinate conflicts increase managerial appropriateness concerns, managers will increase their fairness-promotion efforts.

Effectiveness Concerns

When superior-subordinate conflicts raise managerial effectiveness concerns, managers question whether they are seen as "effective" in that their subordinates believe their actions facilitate the attainment of expected and desirable outcomes. While previous research has identified several, more objective forms of effectiveness (Cameron et al., 1983), our research defines effectiveness more subjectively in the context of the superior-subordinate dynamics we describe. We argue that managers' effectiveness concerns arise out of fears that their subordinates view them as incapable of "getting the job done" and of producing results that subordinates both expect and value.

We propose that effectiveness concerns increase the salience of managerial trustworthiness issues. Specifically, when managers identify that subordinates question their effectiveness, they are acknowledging that their subordinates do not "trust" that their manager can reliably deliver expected outcomes. Tyler (1999), who juxtaposes these social exchange dynamics to the identity-based dynamics described above, suggests that when subordinates do not have confidence in their manager's capacity to deliver desired resources, they will be less likely to accede to that authority and cooperate with their directives.

To preserve and protect their authority when effectiveness is a salient concern, we argue that managers will focus on promoting their trustworthiness by taking actions that bolster their subordinates' confidence in their willingness and ability to deliver the outcomes they predict. By enhancing their perceived trustworthiness, managers aim to decrease subordinates' perceptions of their own vulnerability and to

increase the chances that subordinates will accede to their authority
because they "trust" that they will reliably provide them with predicted
and desired outcomes.

March and Olsen (1995) display this by describing how leaders attempt
to enhance their perceived effectiveness through visible and public efforts
towards achieving ends that their constituents desire. Leaders in their
research assume that constituents will view positive outcomes as evidence
that they are a "good bet" and, as a result, should be rewarded with
constituent support. In addition, Whitener et al. (1998) and Spreitzer and
Mishra (1999) both argue that a keen interest in being seen as effective at
achieving organizational goals and in gaining subordinate support can
stimulate managers to engage in actions that promote their perceived
trustworthiness.

> **Proposition 1b**: To the extent that superior-subordinate conflicts
> increase managerial effectiveness concerns, managers will increase
> their trustworthiness-promotion efforts.

Concerns about Subordinate Dependability

Legitimacy provides managers with confidence to exert their authority, but
for managers to exercise that authority effectively, subordinates must also
be willing and able to execute their directives. Issues related to subordinate
dependability then constitute a second category of authority-based
concerns that can arise in the context of superior-subordinate conflicts.
Conflict management and control researchers have observed that managers
who acknowledge superior-subordinate conflicts, in part, are recognizing
the potential for subordinates to hold goals, desired ways of doing work,
and values that differ significantly from their own (Ouchi, 1980). For
managers then, superior-subordinate conflicts can signal that their
subordinates may lack the interest or capacity to fulfill the specifications
outlined in established written and psychological contracts (Ouchi, 1979;
Snell, 1992).

According to control theorists, superior-subordinate conflicts increase
the salience of potential opportunistic threats and, as a result, signal to
managers that subordinates have reason to misrepresent their abilities (i.e.,
information asymmetry) or work efforts (i.e., moral hazard) (Levinthal,
1988, Williamson, 1975). When subordinates act in these ways, they may
fail to reliably perform organizational tasks or may impede both the
efficient completion of those tasks and the ultimate achievement of
organizational goals (Barney & Hesterly, 1996, Levinthal, 1988).

Consistent with Morrison and Robinson's (1997) work on contract violations and Sitkin and Roth's (1993) work, we outline two general categories of subordinate dependability concerns that can arise from superior-subordinate conflicts: *comprehension concerns* and *reneging concerns*. Comprehension concerns describe managers' fears that subordinates may deviate from contact specifications because their understanding of those specifications differs from their manager's understanding. Here, subordinates may be willing to fulfill their obligations, but may deviate because their understanding of their obligations is incongruent with their manager's understanding of their obligations (Morrison and Robinson 1997). Reneging, on the other hand, describes how subordinates may knowingly deviate from established and mutually understood employee obligations. In other words, managers exhibit concerns about subordinate reneging when they believe that subordinates understand what is expected of them but anticipate that subordinates will operate opportunistically and refuse (either explicitly or implicitly) to follow their managerial directives.

While different factors stimulate managerial comprehension and reneging concerns, we contend that managers will use controls in the presence of either concern to prevent potential contract violations from occurring (Merchant, 1985; Ouchi, 1979). Here, managers will attempt to motivate desirable subordinate production behaviors by increasing training and socialization mechanisms, by implementing behaviorally-focused rules and norms, and by clarifying outputs and incentives. By increasing the quality of training subordinates receive, by outlining specific standard operating procedures (SOPs) for completing organizational tasks, or by increasing their attempts to measure key output variables, managers attempt to increase the ability and willingness of their subordinates to perform tasks according to desired specifications (Sitkin & Roth, 1993).

Proposition 1c: To the extent that superior-subordinate conflicts increase managerial concerns about subordinate comprehension or subordinate reneging, managers will increase their efforts to exert organizational controls.

The Moderating Effect of Managerial Power

Although the conflicts that managers encounter with their subordinates can potentially stimulate concerns about both their own legitimacy and subordinate dependability, we contend that the amount of power that a manager perceives affects the extent to which a category of concern is actually activated. We build our understanding of these dynamics on the precepts of power-approach theory (Keltner, Gruenfeld, & Anderson, 2003), which examines how perceived power affects individual cognition and behavior.

This research reports that individuals who possess low power tend to exhibit a greater overall sensitivity to social threats, to manifest a high level of controlled cognition, and to maintain a tendency to work towards the ends that others desire (Galinsky et al., 2006). This research also suggests a contrasting effect, in that individuals who possess high power tend to exhibit lower levels of perspective-taking and a proclivity towards making self-serving attributions. More powerful individuals also tend to focus on how they may use others to achieve their objectives, and they behave more aggressively (Keltner et al., 2003).

The findings of this research identify important factors that affect how managers respond to the conflicts they encounter. Specifically, we interpret it as suggesting that managers' perceptions of their own power affect whether conflicts with their subordinates will focus their attention towards managerial legitimacy-based issues or to subordinate dependability-based issues. The focus of a manager's attention here is important because it directs the ways in which that manager evaluates his or her authority and, as a result, affects the types of action-based responses that he or she will tend to implement.

Consistent with the findings of power-approach theory, we argue that managers who perceive themselves to be less powerful will tend to direct their attention to managerial legitimacy concerns when they encounter conflicts with their subordinates. These self-perceived less powerful managers will exhibit both an increased sensitivity to the ways that others view them and a high level of awareness of their role in creating and maintaining a particular conflict. In many cases, these less powerful managers will tend to assume more responsibility for these conflicts and will devote more attention to evaluating both how their subordinates think and how they may align their behaviors with their subordinates' expectations.

Proposition 2a: A manager's perceived level of power moderates the relationship between superior-subordinate conflict and managerial legitimacy concerns such that the lower a manager's perceived power, the more likely it is that increases in superior-subordinate conflicts will increase that manager's concerns about their managerial legitimacy.

We also use the basic precepts of power-approach theory to argue that when managers who perceive themselves to be more powerful encounter conflicts with subordinates, those conflicts tend to raise concerns about subordinate dependability. More powerful managers will tend to evaluate such conflicts with a decreased level of perspective-taking and an increased tendency to make self-serving attributions. In other words, because more powerful managers focus their attention on how they may use others to achieve their desired ends, these managers will often assign more blame for the conflicts they encounter on the inability or unwillingness of their subordinates to reliably follow their directives and reliably perform tasks.

Proposition 2b: A manager's perceived power moderates the relationship between superior-subordinate conflict and subordinate dependability concerns such that the higher a manager's perceived power, the more superior-subordinate conflicts will tend to increase managers' concerns about the dependability of their subordinates.

Multiple Concerns Elicit Multiple Responses

While organizational control, trustworthiness-promotion, and fairness-promotion represent distinct activities, a key part of our argument is that because they address related concerns, managers do not consider or pursue the implementation of these activities in isolation. To the contrary, because the issues associated with control, trust, and fairness are interrelated, we argue that managers will tend to integrate and balance their organizational control, trustworthiness-promotion, and fairness-promotion efforts.

We contend that managers do this because organizational control, trustworthiness-promotion, and fairness-promotion represent "complementary" activities. Our conception of these three managerial actions fits Bendersky's (2003: p. 644) definition of complementarity as involving "the interplay among the components (i.e., activities) which enables each type of component to influence individuals' attitudes and behaviors more significantly than it could without reinforcement from the others." We theorize that managers build on complementarities between organizational control, trustworthiness-promotion and fairness-promotion activities to formulate responses to the dependability-based and legitimacy-based threats they identify.

We argue, however, that managers will build from comparative strengths and compensate for comparative weaknesses by integrating their organizational control, trustworthiness-promotion, and fairness-promotion activities. Organizational controls, for example, present managers with ways to inform, direct, and motivate subordinates to complete their task objectives. Organizational controls that are applied without attention to fairness concerns, however, may stimulate conflicts by compromising subordinates' perceptions that responsibilities and rewards are fairly allocated (Deutsch, 1975), that they can exert voice over decision processes (Lind & Tyler, 1988; Thibaut & Walker, 1975), and that organizational authorities are treating them with respect (Bies & Moag, 1986). If managers do not take these issues into consideration when applying controls, subordinates may come to believe that their managers are willing to unduly assert their authority in ways that are untrustworthy because they neglect their personal needs and interests (Ghoshal & Moran, 1996; Sitkin & Stickel, 1995).

Alternatively, through trustworthiness-promotion activities managers are able to effectively build and deepen relationships with their subordinates by addressing their individuals concerns, needs, and interests (Mayer,et al., 1995). However, Leader-Member Exchange (LMX) researchers (e.g., Scandura, Graen, & Novak, 1986; Schriesheim, Neider & Scandura, 1998) highlight how managers often deepen relationships with only particular, individual subordinates within their span of control. Thus, trustworthiness-promotion initiatives that are pursued without regard to how multiple subordinates might be affected can lead to compromised fairness perceptions. In these situations, managers may stimulate conflicts by concentrating too much on deepening relationships with certain, individual subordinates while neglecting the interests of other subordinates under their authority (Deutsch, 1975). Regarding controls, because trustworthiness-promotion initiatives may require managers to spend too much time attending to their relationships with subordinates, they may comprise their inherent desires to maintain levels of control that are sufficient to achieve organizational objectives (Spreitzer & Mishra, 1999).

Lastly, we argue that managers can utilize fairness-promotion initiatives in an effort to promote a sense among subordinates in their unit that they are equally respected, empowered, and compensated (Tyler & Lind, 1992). However, if managers focus too much of their time and energy on fairness-promotion, they may neglect developing appropriate levels of trust by attending to the subordinates more particularized concerns. In these situations, a manager's sense that they are able to maintain control may also be compromised. This is because managers who focus too much time concentrating on treating employees equitably and respectfully may begin to feel they have ceded too much decision-making discretion and authority to their subordinates.

The overarching general proposition underpinning the foregoing discussion is that managers react to the interdependencies among organizational controls, trustworthiness-promotion activities and fairness-promotion activities and that our theories need to reflect this explicitly rather than assume it away. Proposition 3 builds from the discussion above and outlines our argument that organizational control, trustworthiness-promotion, and fairness-promotion constitute complementary activities.

Proposition 3: Complementary relationships exist between organizational control, trustworthiness-promotion, and fairness-promotion activities.

Balancing between Control, Trust, and Fairness

While managers attempt to respond to superior-subordinate conflicts in a balanced way, we argue that they will work to align how they allocate the attention they pay to organizational control, trustworthiness-promotion, and fairness-promotion activities in ways that allow them to effectively address situational demands. Cardinal and colleagues (2004) suggest that, in attempting to achieve this balance managers will work to apply a "harmonious" combination of organizational control, trustworthiness-promotion, and fairness-promotion activities that allow them to achieve their performance objectives, while they attend to the institutional, social, and relational demands that they perceive.

Because organizations differ significantly in their definitions of what would be viewed as legitimate and dependable, the particular balance a manager achieves and the particular emphasis they place on organizational controls, trustworthiness-promotion initiatives, and fairness-promotion initiatives will differ depending on the context within which a particular manager operates (Cardinal et al., 2004). This may lead managers in highly formal organizational contexts, where managerial authority is rarely questioned, to put most of their effort into developing and implementing elaborate formal control systems and spend significantly less time informally interacting with subordinates and promoting relational elements of fairness (Tyler & Lind, 1992). Alternatively, in contexts where interpersonal interaction is highly valued and where subordinates routinely challenge managerial authority, managers may focus primarily on facilitating high quality superior-subordinate interactions through relational trustworthiness-promotion and interactional fairness-promotion activities and on using informal organizational controls.

Proposition 4 encapsulates this discussion and our argument that, because they constitute complementary activities, managers will attempt to integrate and balance their organizational control, trustworthiness-promotion, and fairness-promotion efforts.

> **Proposition 4**: Because organizational control, trustworthiness-promotion and fairness-promotion activities are complementary, managers will attempt to integrate and balance their organizational control, trustworthiness-promotion, and fairness-promotion efforts according to situational conditions.

Different Conflicts, Different Activities

While contextual (i.e., personal, relational, and organizational) factors will significantly influence the relative emphasis managers place on organizational controls, on trustworthiness-promotion, and on fairness-promotion activities, we contend that the desire to address potential or actual conflicts remains a primary motivation for undertaking these managerial activities. Building from this premise, we argue here that the particular types of activities managers engage in will be significantly influenced by the types of conflicts managers encounter. As conflict researchers have shown, individuals do differentiate between forms of conflict (Pinkley, 1990; Pinkley & Northcraft, 1994) and those interpretations differentially affect their subsequent actions (Jehn, 1995, 1997). Studies on influence and impression management, for example, suggest that managers choose how they influence subordinates based, in large measure, on the forms of resistance employees exhibit (Yukl, Falbe, & Youn, 1993; Yukl, Guinan, & Sottolano, 1995). As Sullivan, Albrecht, and Taylor (1990) note, "the nature and amount of resistance that a manager expects from a subordinate are the major determinants" of how managers attempt to secure compliance with organizational directives (p. 336).

Drawing upon these literatures to extend our theory, we reason that goal, task, and personal conflicts focus managers on addressing different types of dependability-based and legitimacy-based concerns. These different concerns then lead managers to promote different organizational control, trustworthiness-promotion, and fairness-promotion activities. Managers do this in order to efficiently and effectively address the key concerns a particular conflict raises by leveraging particular complementarities between specific types of activities.

While focusing on applications of organizational controls, control theorists have presented evidence consistent with this perspective. They have shown how managers choose to apply various controls based on the forms of conflicts managers encounter with their subordinates. Ouchi

(1980), for example, argues that the level of goal incongruence (i.e., goal conflict) managers experience with subordinates should influence their choices between market, bureaucratic, or clan-based controls. Some support for Ouchi's ideas can be found in Sitkin and Roth (1993), who explore how task and personal conflicts with subordinates lead managers to choose highly formal (i.e., legalistic) control mechanisms, and Cardinal et al. (2004) who observe that the adoption of specific mixes of organizational controls can be stimulated by various types of conflicts between managers and subordinates.

Our perspective is also consistent with Wicks et al.'s (1999) theory of "Optimal Trust" and the general notion that managers promote levels of trust consistent with the goals they seek to achieve and the situational constraints they face (Barney & Hansen, 1994). Building from this work, we argue that managers act as though "trust is good-but a conditional good" (Wicks et al., 1999: p. 99) and tend to produce levels of trust that are consistent with relational contingencies. Drawing upon this idea, we argue that managers will respond to the concerns highlighted by specific superior-subordinate conflicts with activities designed to build the levels of trust necessary to both manage those conflicts and produce desirable organizational outcomes.

In addition, our perspective refines and extends the work of fairness researchers who have argued that managers will generally attempt to produce fairness in order to decrease feelings of resentment and deprivation among their subordinates and establish an environment beneficial to the pursuit of specific organizational goals (Lerner, 1977; Leventhal, Karuza, & Fry, 1980). Extending the work of both conflict management and control researchers, that managers maintain a goal of effectively managing conflict (Leventhal, 1988; Ouchi, 1980; Sitkin & Bies, 1993), Proposition 5 summarizes our argument that managers attempt to respond to the specific, dependability-based and legitimacy-based concerns raised by a particular form of conflict with particular combinations of organizational control, trustworthiness-promotion, and fairness-promotion activities.

Proposition 5: Managers respond to the specific dependability-based and legitimacy-based concerns raised by particular types of conflict with specific combinations of organizational control, trustworthiness-promotion, and fairness-promotion activities

Discussion

This paper presents a new theoretical direction for research on trust, fairness, and control. As such, we contend that our theory makes three primary contributions to organizational research. First, our perspective highlights important relationships between managerial authority and managerial actions. Specifically, we identify how conflicts may stimulate four types of managerial authority concerns. Building from this, we describe how managers apply their trustworthiness-promotion, fairness-promotion, and control activities in ways that preserve, protect, and promote their authority.

Second, building from the extensive research on organizational trust, fairness, and control, we describe the conditions under which each of these issues is more salient for managers, thus outlining circumstances where managers are more likely to engage in trustworthiness-promotion, fairness-promotion, and control activities. We also describe factors impacting managers' choices between their independent and joint efforts to promote trustworthiness, promote fairness, and exert control.

Third, we suggest that managers attempt to achieve an appropriate balance of activities by working to apply complementary activities. In addition, we hypothesize about how managers use various combinations of trustworthiness-promotion, fairness-promotion, and control activities to respond to the specific dependability-based and legitimacy-based concerns conflicts raise.

A Focus on Authority and Legitimacy

The descriptive theory that we propose here builds from our contention that managers concern themselves, in part, with how others perceive their authority, and that managers promote trustworthiness, fairness, and control to preserve, protect, and enhance that authority. These ideas build directly from previously posited relationships between subordinates' trust and fairness perceptions and managerial authority (e.g., Tyler & Lind, 1992) as well as relationships between authority and control (e.g., Zelditch & Walker, 1984).

While we contend that conflicts often stimulate managers' concerns about their own legitimacy, we acknowledge the possibility that many managers may possess overly optimistic ideas about their own power (Keltner et al., 2003). Building from our theory, we recognize that one important reason that managers may often respond to conflicts by focusing primarily on dependability-based concerns which, in turn, lead the manager to rely on organizational controls. This is a potentially important observation because it may explain how superior-subordinate relationships often develop into "pathological spiraling relationships" where "surveillants come to distrust their targets (i.e., employees) as a result of their own surveillance, and targets, in fact, become unmotivated and untrustworthy" (Enzle & Anderson, 1993, p. 263).

While we acknowledge that managers may often exhibit imbalanced responses to the conflicts they encounter, we contend that managers who balance their attention to authority-based and dependability-based threats over time are more likely to build positive working relationships with their subordinates. When this happens, managers can gain production efficiencies and enable themselves to more easily obtain valuable employee insights that can be incorporated into their future decision-making and planning activities.

Future research is necessary to more clearly examine the factors that lead managers to focus more on legitimacy-based concerns or on dependability-based concerns. These investigations, for example, should examine a range of organizational, relational, and individual factors that researchers are beginning to identify as influencing managerial intentions and actions (Gilliland & Paddock, 2005; Sitkin, 1995; Whitener et al., 1998).

Distinguishing between Trustworthiness-Promotion, Fairness-Promotion, and Control

By specifying theoretical distinctions between trustworthiness-promotion, fairness-promotion and control activities, we are able to describe these activities more clearly. Contrary to work that has portrayed trust and fairness initiatives as merely "a class of more general control mechanisms" (Bradach & Eccles, 1989, p. 104) or as a substitute for control (Long & Sitkin, 2006), we conceptualize trustworthiness-promotion, fairness-promotion, and control activities as distinguishable but potentially complementary categories of managerial actions. Thus, our theory illuminates important relationships between trust, fairness, and control that previous research has considered but has yet to fully develop.

An important issue to consider here is the distinction we draw between managers' responses to appropriateness concerns and their responses to effectiveness concerns. We believe and clearly state here that appropriateness concerns and effectiveness concerns are neither mutually exclusive nor necessarily conjunctive. We argue instead that these terms describe distinct but related managerial legitimacy concerns. Consistent with this general proposition, March and Olsen (1995) suggest that leaders recognize that appropriateness and effectiveness constitute separate but related spheres of accountability. They argue that leaders distinguish the actions they take to ensure that they are in alignment with accepted rules, norms, and customs from the actions they take to produce desirable outcomes. Similarly, we argue that it is important to differentiate managers' concerns about these issues—because this separation can help to illuminate different categories of managerial motivations.

Under some circumstances, managers' responses to their concerns about appropriateness and effectiveness are closely related and lead managers to synergistically integrate their efforts to promote trust and fairness. For example, Bradach and Eccles (1989) observe that managers often integrate their efforts to effectively achieve organizational goals with their efforts to act appropriately and in concert with accepted social norms. Whitener et al. (1998) describe a similar dynamic and argue that managers who are directed to promote procedural justice norms in employee appraisal procedures also tend to take actions that promote their managerial trustworthiness.

Under other circumstances, however, managers' appropriateness and effectiveness concerns may cause tension. For example, Blader (2005) describes how managers' efforts to promote fairness by consistently implementing organizational rules may compromise their capacity to be viewed as effective because a manager's efforts to be fair to all employees can compromise subordinates' assessments that decisions accommodate their own individual interests. Conversely, managers interested in being effective may compromise their tendency to promote fairness. As Tsui and Barry (1986) observe, managers who maintain close, trusting relationships with their subordinates often fail to provide impartial, unbiased performance evaluations of those individuals.

Although we have suggested why managers' concerns about appropriateness and effectiveness might stimulate them to act in predictable ways, we also propose that future research should more closely examine how specific concerns develop and how managers initiate specific fairness-promotion and trustworthiness-promotion actions. For example, we might examine how managers negotiate through matrices of different allocation norms or how their particular goals may affect their tendencies to initiate various fairness-promotion behaviors (Karniol & Miller, 1981; Levinthal, 1976). Additionally, we may explore how various forms of interdependencies affect the types of trustworthiness-promotion efforts in which managers engage (Wicks, Berman, & Jones, 1999).

Refining our Understanding of Control Applications

We contend that our research also makes several significant contributions to research on managerial control. By outlining different subordinate dependability concerns, our arguments increase our understanding of how superior-subordinate conflicts stimulate managers to apply organizational controls (Ouchi, 1980). In contrast to previous research, which has largely tended to emphasize the impact of managers' reneging concerns, our theory tends to temper that perspective somewhat. While we contend that issues related to subordinate opportunism are important, we argue that this is but one of four managerial concerns that drive managerial actions.

Using our framework, we can explain how managers simultaneously produce high levels of control and trust (Sitkin, 1995; Long & Sitkin, 2006). As a result, our work helps to explain how managers who use high levels of informal or "clan" control also tend to promote high levels of superior-subordinate trust. We suggest that, in such cases, potential threats to authority that arise in control systems that rely heavily on interpersonal associations lead managers to promote informal controls while they attempt to enhance perceptions of their benevolent intentions and interactional fairness.

Our perspective can also be used to explain how managers effectively combine their applications of formal controls (i.e., bureaucratic or legalistic) with appropriate levels of trustworthiness-promotion and fairness-promotion. It explains how managers respond to these real and potential threats with strict but legitimate combinations of formal controls, trustworthiness-promotion, and fairness-promotion initiatives. By implementing these initiatives, managers direct task efforts while simultaneously communicating that they recognize subordinate achievement and the need to provide subordinates with increased control over their task efforts (Sitkin, 1995; Whitener et al., 1998).

Trustworthiness-Promotion and Fairness-Promotion as Conflict Leadership

The focus we place on multiple forms of superior-subordinate conflict also refines and extends the arguments presented in traditional Leader-Member Exchange (LMX) research that disagreements between managers and employees generally lower the quality of their exchange relationships and lead managers both to delegate responsibilities to subordinates less actively and to be less willing to involve subordinates in their decision-making (Schriesheim, Neider, & Scandura, 1998). Because LMX researchers tend to focus primarily on the effects of superior-subordinate goal conflicts within management-employee exchanges (and have largely ignored other kinds of conflict), this research really has examined how conflicts affect managerial efforts regarding distributional issues and outcome-based issues. In contrast, we acknowledge the presence of multiple forms of superior-subordinate conflicts (i.e., goal, task, personal). This allows us to predict instances where conflicts stimulate managers to improve their exchange-based relationships with subordinates.

Lastly, because we acknowledge that different forms of conflicts may motivate different managerial actions, our theory also holds the potential to contribute to conflict management research. Specifically, managerial responses to conflict in the conflict management literature are primarily represented as influence strategies (e.g., Van de Vliert & Kabanoff, 1990) or impression management tactics (e.g., Yukl, et al., 1993). While we contend that trustworthiness-promotion, fairness-promotion, and control activities can be used in these ways to address the immediate effects of conflicts on superior-subordinate relationships, we also suggest that conflicts can lead managers to craft longer-term and more systematic, institution-based solutions to organizational problems. For example, in organizational environments where managers encounter persistent superior-subordinate task conflicts, they may institutionalize procedural fairness principles. In organizations where superior-subordinate personal conflicts persist, managers may formalize input control mechanisms to more effectively screen organizational entrants before they select them into their organization.

Conclusion

The relationships between control, trust, and fairness described in this paper encompass fundamental, essential features of managerial life. As a result, we contend that it is not enough for scholars to simply recognize that organizational trust, organizational fairness, and organizational control are important ingredients of positive organizational outcomes. Instead, we argue that scholars must seek to understand how and why managers decide to promote or not promote organizational trust, fairness and control. The theory we present in this paper is a building block in that larger effort.

References

Barnard, C. I. (1938). *The functions of the executive.* Cambridge, MA: Harvard University Press.

Barney, J. B., & Hansen, M. (1994). Trustworthiness as a source of competitive advantage. *Strategic Management Journal*, 15, 175-190.

Barney, J. B., & Hesterly, W. (1996). Organizational economics: Understanding the relationship between organizations and economic analysis. In S. R. Clegg, C. Hardy, & W. R. Nord (Eds.), *Handbook of organization studies* (pp. 115-147). Thousand Oaks, CA: Sage Publications.

Bendersky, C. (2003). Organizational dispute resolution systems: A complementarities perspective. *Academy of Management Journal*, 28, 643-656.

Bies, R. J. (1987). The predicament of injustice: The management of moral outrage. In L. L. Cummings, & B. M. Staw (Eds.), *Research in organizational behavior* (pp. 189-320). Greenwich, CT: JAI Press.

Bies, R. (2003). The Question of Injustice: Why Do Good People Do Bad Things? Presentation at the *Sixty-third Annual Meeting of the Academy of Management*, Seattle, WA.

Bies, R., & Moag, J. (1986). Interactional justice: Communication criteria of fairness. In R. J. Lewicki, B. H. Sheppard, & M. H. Bazerman (Eds.), *Research on negotiations in organizations* (pp. 43-55). Greenwich, CT: JAI Press.

Blader, S. (2005). The Compassionate Side of Unfairness: Empathy and Unjust Managerial Decisions. Presentation at the *Sixty-fifth Annual Meeting of the Academy of Management*, Honolulu, HI.

Bradach, J. L., & Eccles, R. G. (1989). Price, authority and trust: From ideal types to plural forms. *Annual Review of Sociology, 15*, 97-118.

Cameron, K., & Associates. (1983). *Organizational effectiveness.* New York, NY: Academic Press.

Cardinal, L. B. (2001). Technological innovation in the pharmaceutical industry: Managing research and development using input, behavior, and output controls. *Organization Science, 12,* 19-36.

Cardinal, L. B., Sitkin, S. B. & Long, C. P. (2010). A configurational theory of control. In S. B. Sitkin, L. B. Cardinal, & K. Bijlsma-Frankema (Eds.), *Organizational control.* Cambridge, UK: Cambridge University Press.

Cardinal, L. B., Sitkin, S. B., & Long, C. P. (2004). Balancing and rebalancing in the creation and evolution of organizational control. *Organization Science, 15,* 411-431.

Colquitt, J. A. (2001). On the dimensionality of organizational justice: A construct validation of a measure. *Journal of Applied Psychology, 86,* 386-400.

Cronin, M. A., & Weingart, L. R. (2007). The differential effects of trust and respect on team conflict. In L. Thompson, & K. J. Behfar (Eds.), *Conflict in teams.* Evanston, IL: NU Press.

Cropanzano, R., Goldman, B. M., & Folger, R. (2003). Deontic justice: The role of moral principles in workplace fairness. *Journal of Organizational Behavior, 24,* 1019-1024.

Das, T. K. & Teng, B. (1998) Between trust and control: Developing confidence in partner cooperation in alliances. *Academy of Management Review, 23,* 491-512

Deutsch, M. (1975). Justice in the "crunch." In M. J. Lerner, & S. C. Lerner (Eds.), *The justice motive in social behavior.* New York, NY: Plenum Press.

Dornbusch, S. M., & Scott, W. R. (1975). *Evaluation and the exercise of authority.* San Francisco, CA: Jossey-Bass Publishers.

Enzle, M. E., & Anderson, S. C. (1993). Surveillant intentions and intrinsic motivation. *Journal of Personality and Social Psychology, 64,* 257-266.

Folger, R., & Cropanzano, R. (2001). Fairness theory: Justice as accountability. In J. Greenberg, & R. Cropanzano (Eds.), *Advances in organizational justice* (pp. 1-55). Stanford, CA: Stanford University Press.

Folger, R., & Skarlicki, D. (2001). Fairness as a dependent variable: Why tough times can lead to bad management. In R. Cropanzano (Ed.), *Justice in the workplace: From theory to practice* (pp. 97-118). Mahwah, NJ: Lawrence Erlbaum Associates.

Galinsky, A. D., Magee, J. C., Inesi, M. E., & Gruenfeld, D. H. (2005). Power and perspectives not taken. *Psychological Science, 17,* 1-7.

Ghoshal, S., & Moran, P. (1996). Bad for practice: A critique of the transaction cost theory. *Academy of Management Review,* 1, 13-47.

Gilliland, S. W., & Paddock, L. (2005). Organizational justice across human resources management decisions. In G. P. Hodgkinson, & J. K. Ford (Eds.), *International review of industrial and organizational psychology, 20* (pp. 149-175). Chichester, England: Wiley and Sons.

Greenberg, J. (1990). Looking fair vs. being fair: Managing impressions of organizational justice. In B. M. Staw, & L. L. Cummings (Eds.), *Research in organizational behavior* (pp. 111-157). Greenwich, CT: JAI Press.

Jehn, K. A. (1995). A multi-method examination of the benefits and detriments of intragroup conflict. *Administrative Science Quarterly, 40,* 256-282.

—. (1997). Affective and cognitive conflict in work groups: Increasing performance through value-based intragroup conflict. In C. K. W. de Dreu, & E. Van de Vliert (Eds.), *Using conflicts in organizations* (pp. 87-100). Thousand Oaks, CA: Sage Publications.

Karniol, R., & Miller, D. T. (1981). Morality and the development of conceptions of justice. In M. J. Lerner, & S. C. Lerner (Eds.), *The justice motive in social behavior* (pp. 73-96). New York, NY: Plenum Press.

Keltner, D., Gruenfeld, D. H., & Anderson, C. (2003). Power, approach, and inhibition. *Psychological Review, 110,* 265-284.

Kim, W. C., & Mauborgne, R. A. (1997). Fair process: Managing in the knowledge economy. *Harvard Business Review, 38,* 65-75.

Lerner, M. J. (1977). The justice motive in social behavior: Some hypotheses as to its origins and forms. *Journal of Personality, 45,* 1-52.

Leventhal, G. S. (1976). The distribution of rewards and resources in groups and organizations. In L. Berkowitz, & E. Walster (Eds.), *Advances in Experimental Social Psychology, 9* (pp. 91-131). New York, NY: Academic Press.

Leventhal, G. S., Karuza, J., & Fry, W. R. (1980). Beyond fairness: A theory of allocation preferences. In G. Mikula (Eds.), *Justice and social interaction (pp.*167-218). New York: Springer-Verlag.

Levinthal, D. 1988. A survey of agency models of organizations. *Journal of Economic Behavior and Organization, 9,* 153-185.

Lind, E. A., & Tyler, T. R. (1988). *The social psychology of procedural justice.* New York, NY: Plenum Press.

Long, C. P. (2010). Control to cooperation: Examining the role of managerial authority in portfolios of managerial action. In S. B. Sitkin, L. B. Cardinal, & K. Bijlsma-Frankema (Eds.), *Organizational control* (pp. 365-395). Cambridge, UK: Cambridge University Press.

Long, C. P., & Carroll, T. N. (2012). How managers' trust and control activities influence subordinates' perceptions. *Proceedings of the Seventy-Second Annual Meeting of the Academy of Management* (CD), ISSN 1543-8643.

Long, C. P., Bendersky, C., & Morrill, C. (2011). Fairness monitoring: Linking managerial controls and fairness judgments in organizations. *Academy of Management Journal, 5,* 1045-1068.

Long, C. P., & Sitkin, S. B. (2006). Trust in the balance: How managers integrate trust-building and control. In R. Bachmann, & A. Zaheer (Eds.), *Handbook of trust research* (pp. 87-106). Cheltenham, UK: Edward Elgar.

Lord, R. G., & Brown, D. J. (2004). *Leadership processes and follower self-identity*. Mahwah, NJ: Lawrence Erlbaum Associates.

March, J., & Olsen, J. P. (1995). *Democratic governance.* New York, NY: Free Press.

Mayer, R. C., Davis, J. H., & Schoorman, D. (1995). An integrative model of organizational trust. *Academy of Management Review, 20,* 709-734.

McEvily, B., Perrone, V., & Zaheer, A. (2003). Trust as an organizing principle. *Organization Science, 14,* 91-103.

Merchant, K. A. (1985). *Control in business organizations.* Marshfield, MA: Pitman Publishing.

Meindl, J. (1989). Managing to be fair: An exploration of values, motives, and leadership. *Administrative Science Quarterly, 34,* 252-276.

Mishra, A. K. (1996). Organizational responses to crises: The centrality of trust. In R. M. Kramer, & T. R. Tyler (Eds.), *Trust in organizations: Frontiers in theory and research* (pp. 261-287). Thousand Oaks, CA: Sage Publications.

Morrison, E. W., & Robinson, S. L. (1997). When employees feel betrayed: A model of how psychological contract violation develops. *Academy of Management Review, 22,* 226-256.

Ouchi, W. G. (1979). A conceptual framework for the design of organizational control mechanisms. *Management Science, 25,* 833-848.

—. (1980). Markets, bureaucracies, and clans. *Administrative Science Quarterly, 25,* 129-141.

Pfeffer, J. (1981a). Management as symbolic action: The creation and maintenance of organizational paradigms. In L. L. Cummings, & B. M. Staw (Eds.), *Research in organizational behavior, 3* (pp. 1-52). Greenwich, CT: JAI Press.

Pfeffer, J. (1981b). *Power in organizations.* Marshfield, MA: Pitman Publishing, Inc.

Pinkley, R. L. (1990). Dimensions of conflict frame: Disputant interpretations of conflict. *Journal of Applied Psychology, 75,* 117-126.

Pinkley, R. L., & Northcraft, G. B. (1994). Conflict frames of reference: Implications for dispute processes and outcomes. *Academy of Management Journal, 37,* 193-205.

Rousseau, D. M., Sitkin, S. B., Burt, R. S., & Camerer, C. (1998). Not so different after all: A cross-discipline view of trust. *Academy of Management Review, 23,* 393-404.

Rosenblatt, Z., Rogers, K. S. & Nord, W. R. (1993). Toward a political framework for flexible management of decline. *Organization Science, 4*: 76-91.

Scandura, T. A., Graen, G. B, & Novak, M. A. (1986). When managers decide not to decide autocratically: An investigation of leader-member exchange and decision influence. *Journal of Applied Psychology,* 71, 579-584.

Schriesheim, C. A., Neider, L. L., & Scandura, T. A. (1998). A within-and between-groups analysis of leader-member exchange as a correlate of delegation and as a moderator of delegation relationships with performance and satisfaction. *Academy of Management Journal, 41,* 298-318.

Scott, W. R. (2003). *Organizations: Rational, natural, and open systems.* Upper Saddle River, NJ: Prentice-Hall.

Simons, T. R. (2002). Behavioral integrity: The perceived alignment between managers' words and deeds as a research focus. *Organization Science, 13,* 18-35.

Sitkin, S. B. (1995). On the positive effect of legalization on trust. In R. J. Bies, R. J. Lewicki, & B. H. Sheppard (Eds.), *Research on negotiations in organizations* (pp. 185-217). Greenwich, CT: JAI Press.

Sitkin, S. B., & Bies, R. J. (1993). Social accounts in conflict situations: Using explanations to manage conflict. *Human Relations, 46,* 349-370.

Sitkin, S. B., & Roth, N. L. (1993). Explaining the limited effectiveness of legalistic remedies for trust/distrust. *Organization Science, 4,* 367-392.

Sitkin, S. B. & Stickel, D. 1996. The road to hell: The dynamics of distrust in an era of quality. In R. M. Kramer & T. R. Tyler (Eds.), *Trust in organizations. Frontiers in theory and research.* (pp. 196-215). Thousand Oaks, CA: Sage Publications.

Snell, S. A. (1992). Control theory in strategic human resource management: The mediating effect of administrative information. *Academy of Management Journal, 35,* 292-327.

Spreitzer, G. M., & Mishra, A. K. (1999). Giving up control without losing control: Trust and its substitutes' effects on managers' involving employees in decision making. *Group and Organization Management, 24,* 155-187.

Suchman, M. A. (1995). Managing legitimacy: Strategic and institutional approaches. *Academy of Management Review, 20,* 571-610.

Sullivan, J. J., Albrecht, T. L., & Taylor, S. (1990). Process, organizational, relational, and personal determinants of managerial compliance-gaining communication strategies. *The Journal of Business Communication, 27,* 331-355.

Taylor, S, Masterson, S., Renard, M. K., & Tracy, K. B. (1998). Managers' reactions to procedurally just performance management systems. *Academy of Management Journal, 41,* 568-579.

Thibaut, J., & Walker, L. (1975). *Procedural justice: A psychological analysis.* Hillsdale, NJ: Lawrence Erlbaum Associates.

Tsui, A. S., & Barry, B. (1986). Interpersonal affect and ratings errors. *The Academy of Management Journal, 29,* 586-599.

Tyler, T. R. (1999). Why do people help organizations?: Social identity and pro-organizational behavior. In B. M. Staw, & R. L. Sutton (Eds.), *Research on organizational behavior, 21* (pp. 201-246). Greenwich, CT: JAI Press.

Tyler, T. R., & Lind, E. A. (1992). A relational model of authority in groups. In M. P. Zanna (Ed.), *Advances in experimental social psychology* (pp. 151-191). New York, NY: Academic Press.

Van de Vliert, E. & Kabanoff, B. (1990). Toward theory-based measures of conflict management. *Academy of Management Journal, 33,* 199-209.

van Knippenberg, D., & Hogg, M. A (Eds.). (2003). *Leadership and power: Identity processes in groups and organizations.* London: Sage Publications.

Van Maanen, J., & Schein, E. H. (1979). Toward a theory of organizational socialization. In B. W. Staw, & L. L. Cummings (Eds.), *Research in organizational behavior* (pp. 209-264). Greenwich, CT: JAI Press.

Whitener, E. M., Brodt, S. E., Korsgaard, M. A., & Werner, J. M. (1998). Managers as initiators of trust: An exchange relationship framework for understanding managerial trustworthy behavior. *Academy of Management Review, 23,* 513-530.

Wicks, A. C., Berman, S. L., & Jones, T. M. (1999). The structure of optimal trust: Moral and strategic implications. *Academy of Management Review, 24,* 99-116.

Williamson, O. E. (1975). Markets and hierarchies. New York, NY: Free Press.

Yukl, G., Falbe, C. M., & Youn, Y. J. (1993). Patterns of influence behavior for managers. *Group and Organization Management, 18,* 5-28.

Yukl, G., Guinan, P. J., & Sottolano, D. (1995). Influence tactics used for different objectives with subordinates, peers, and superiors. *Group & Organization Management, 20,* 272-296.

Zelditch, M., Jr., & Walker, H. A. (1984). Legitimacy and the stability of authority. *Advances in Group Processes: Theory and Research, 1,* 1-25.

Chapter Eighteen

Indigenous Management Theory: Why Management Theory is Under Attack (And What We Can Do To Fix It)

Roy Suddaby
University of Alberta, Canada

Management theory is under attack. The attack is occurring on several fronts. Scholars complain about the growing gap between management theory and practice and argue that theory needs to become managerially relevant (Rynes, Bartunek, & Daft, 2007). Some bemoan the fact that precious little theory ever gets empirically tested (Davis & Marquis, 2005). Many suggest that we should place a moratorium on theory and devote our time to accumulating empirical "evidence," as our colleagues in medicine do (Rousseau, 2006; Pfeffer & Sutton, 1999).

The common element of the attack is simply that there is too much theory (Hambrick, 2007; Pfeffer, this volume). Our devotion to theory is attributed as the cause of several serious ills in our profession, including the lack of progress in accumulating knowledge (Davis, 2010), incoherence in teaching management principles to students (Pfeffer, this volume), bad writing (Hambrick, 2007) and academic cheating (Pfeffer, this volume).

While the causal connection between theory and most of these outcomes is not obvious – academic cheating and bad writing are clearly not caused by theory – it *is* clear that theory has become a magnet for the increasing complaints and critiques within the profession. There appears to be a growing consensus that management research has serious ills that could be resolved if we were only to get back to the task of "hard" empirical data collection and the accumulation of managerial knowledge.

I disagree. Theory is not the real demon here. *Bad* theory perhaps is a problem and I suppose the critics are confusing the two. But while there has always been bad theory floating about (and not just in management

scholarship), I don't really understand why theory has become the
scapegoat for a range of, often unrelated, issues that currently plague our
discipline. Why is there such a concerted effort to denigrate theory in our
profession? Why is theory such an easy scapegoat? More importantly,
what can we do to correct it?

I explore these questions in this essay. I argue that, rather than being
disaffected with theory, the critics are largely taking issue with "fetishistic
theory" or theory that has become ritualized and rationalized, largely in
response to the increasing career pressures to publish. I begin by outlining
what makes theory fetishistic. I then identify three key ways in which we,
as an academic discipline, can avoid the problems of fetishism in theory, a
framework that I describe as "indigenous" management theory. Finally, I
discuss the implications of a return to "dustbowl" empiricism.

Fetishistic Theory

By fetishistic theory I mean theory that has become divorced from
phenomena, theory that has become ritualized, mechanical and artificial,
or theory that has, largely, been drawn from parsing texts rather than
experience. Fetishistic theory has three defining features (see Birkenshaw,
Healy, Suddaby, & Weber, 2014 for an early description of the construct);
it is overly rational, scientistic, and lacks reflexivity. I elaborate each of
these elements in this section.

Rationalism: Philosophers identify two counterbalancing sources of
knowledge, rationalism, and empiricism (Kenny, 1986). Rationalism
argues that new knowledge comes from reason or logic (Aune, 1970).
Empiricists deny this and claim, instead, that new knowledge comes from
sensory experience (Adams, 1975). Rationalists counter that, without
theoretically derived categories, humans would be unable to organize
sensory experience (Quine, 1951). Empiricists reply that theoretical
categories are not innate and that humans need sensory experience to
construct them (Casullo, 2003).

Pragmatists recognize the need to balance both rationalism and
empiricism to construct true knowledge. Peirce (1958) observed that
knowledge is created through *abduction*, an iterative process of rational
deduction followed by empirical induction. Research, however, both at the
level of the individual researcher and the collective paradigm, tend to
cycle from phases that privilege one mode of knowledge construction over
another. For several decades, for example, American psychology rejected
theoretical induction and emphasized the collection of data, with
considerable effort devoted to refining measurement scales and perfecting

methodologies, a period now referred to as "dustbowl empiricism" and identified as a clear reaction against the proliferation of inductive theories generated by prominent European theorists including Freud and Jung (Landy, 1997; Latham, 2012).

Fetishistic theory is inherently rational. That is, it clearly privileges deduction over induction. New theory tends to be derived, not from trying to explain phenomena in the sensory world, but rather by exploring and exploiting ever-narrowing gaps in existing theoretical categories. Fetishistic theory tends to emphasize the status and elitism of past writers thus producing elaborate literature reviews peppered with honorific citations. Theorists become like priests engaging in the microscopic examination and interpretation of "ancient" texts. Rather than trying to explain the phenomenal world, fetishistic theorists engage in the elaborate and often formulaic exegesis of texts.

The problem with emphasizing rationalism over empiricism is that management theory becomes increasingly detached from the phenomenal world. The ability of "past-masters" to exercise a gate-keeping function over theoretical domains increases. And it requires theorists to identify increasingly narrow gaps in existing theory. Ultimately, management theory becomes increasingly insular and distant from practice.

Scientism: As theories become more fetishistic, they also become more "scientistic." That is, they adopt the appearance – the form, language and presentation of science – without the functional contribution of new knowledge. Scientism, thus, applies the formal language of theory and method to explain the obvious or to re-characterize existing knowledge – a process colloquially described as "putting old wine in new bottles." The reproduction of the form and appearance of scientific theorizing, i.e., applying a more sophisticated method or an embellished theoretical framing to solve an old issue, becomes more important than the production of new knowledge or a fresh insight.

That contemporary management theory is becoming increasingly scientistic is perhaps most evident by the number of theoretical papers that draw on an increasingly narrow and often outdated set of empirical studies. As Pfeffer (this volume) and others (Davis, 2010) observe, our discipline is inundated with studies drawn from convenient data sets – i.e., newspapers and wineries – while studies of industries with consequence, such as fast food empires, the political power of the large corporation, or the role of social media, go begging.

Perhaps the biggest problem with scientism, however, is the un-reflexive, and often inappropriate, application of scientific thinking and methods. In management theory, this means adopting the erroneous assumption that the subject of our studies – management, organizations – is somehow immune or independent of the knowledge that we produce. Unlike physics or chemistry, our subjects of inquiry actually change in response to our research and teaching. MBA-trained executives understand and apply Porter's (1985) model of competitive advantage. Financial instruments created and produced in academia have had a profound influence on global markets.

Donald McKenzie (2006), for example, traces the recent financial collapse to academic theory. Financial theorists not only created derivates, they also served to legitimate and diffuse them globally. These theories are not "cameras" that objectively describe reality, McKenzie observes, they are "engines" that shape reality, often in destructive ways.

The notion that our theories actually shape reality is not new (Farraro, Pfeffer, & Sutton, 2005). But in spite of that understanding, we continue to embrace a scientistic fantasy of objective independence between researcher and research subject. We also embrace the myth of progress in objective knowledge based, in large part, on envying the "progress" of our foundational disciplines of economics, psychology and sociology, ignoring loud internal critiques of their own fetishistic tendencies (McClosky, 1994; Guthrie, 2004, Bannister, 2004).

Scientism also tends to arbitrarily exclude other sources or forms of knowledge production. In management, the most obvious exclusion is the marginalization of knowledge drawn from arts and the humanities. As the scientific method has grown in popularity in management research, the role of the arts in generating insight and understanding has diminished. Business history, for example, has become largely irrelevant in management scholarship (Rowlinson, Hassard, & Decker, 2014; Keiser, 1994). The notion that we might gain additional and perhaps more nuanced insight from the application of methods of scholarship and critique from the arts has largely vanished in business and organizational studies (Gagliardi & Czarniawski, 2006).

Arts and the humanities have been marginalized in management research and education despite decanal critiques of the narrowness and irrelevance fostered by the inappropriate application of scientific methodology to living, breathing and self-reflexive subjects (Gordon & Howell, 1959; Pierson, 1959; Mulligan, 1987; Bennis & O'Toole, 2005). Bennis & O'Toole (2005: 9-10) describe why our understanding of leadership has suffered because of the marginalization of humanities in business school research:

> Traditionally, business schools have lacked offerings in the humanities. That is a serious shortcoming. As teachers of leadership, we doubt that our

topic can be understood properly without solid grounding in the humanities. When the hard-nosed behavioral scientist James March taught his famous course at Stanford using War and Peace and other novels as texts, he emphatically was not teaching a literature course. He was drawing on works of imaginative literature to exemplify and explain the behavior of people in business organizations in a way that was richer and more realistic than any journal article or textbook. Similarly, when executives are given excerpts from the classics of political economy and philosophy in seminars at the Aspen Institute, the intent is not to turn them into experts on Plato and Locke but to illuminate the profound recesses of leadership that scientifically oriented texts either overlook or oversimplify.

The authors conclude that it is not the narrowness of scientific method, in itself, that diminishes our knowledge of management, but rather it is the fact that management scholars have allowed scientism to exclude other sources of knowledge. Scientism, thus, contributes to fetishistic theory by narrowing both the sources and methods of new knowledge discovery.

Self-Reflexivity: A third component of fetishistic theory derives from a growing ignorance of our own intellectual history. That is, in its pursuit of the scientific ideal of universal knowledge, we tend to assume that current knowledge builds inexorably on past knowledge. We "stand on the shoulders of giants" and our review of literature, in a theoretical or empirical article, reflects objective progress toward truth.

There are several problems with this assumption, however. Foremost, literature reviews are not actually objective summaries of the intellectual history of a subject area. Rather, they are literary constructions or rhetorical devices designed to persuade the reader of the legitimacy of, and motivation for, a specific theoretical argument. They tend to focus quite narrowly on the somewhat mechanical task of parsing texts in order to rhetorically constructing a "gap" in existing theory. Indeed, there is a lively thread of publications devoted to how this process should be performed (i.e., Locke & Golden-Biddle, 1997; Alvesson & Sandberg, 2011).

A second problem with this assumption is that it underestimates our scholarly appetite for novelty. Most reviewers will be dismissive of literature reviews that emphasize studies more than twenty years old over more recent studies. Because we erroneously assume that current knowledge builds on old knowledge, we tend to privilege new over old. As a result, the field is subject to recurring fads and fashions in which management thought becomes recycled over generations (Abrahamson, 1996) a process that is enabled by a rhetorical strategy of rationalistically parsing texts (Kieser, 1997).

That we are relatively unreflective about our own intellectual history can be easily demonstrated by how we train and socialize incoming members of our profession. Newly minted Ph.D. students are well trained in the most recent research methods and substantive subject areas, but few programs offer courses on the history of management thought. And most Ph.D. syllabi, like the literature reviews in our published work, tend to privilege more recent research over older, classical studies.

Moreover, simply studying the classic papers in a subject area is quite different from studying our intellectual history. There should be space in our PhD curricula, and in our journals, for more normative debates about the role and purpose of management knowledge. While much of this debate has occurred within the confines of Critical Management Studies (Alvesson & Willmott, 1992), this type of intellectual conversation has become rather marginalized in North American Ph.D. training and in Academy journals.

The absence of self-reflexivity, thus, contributes substantially to fetishistic theory.

Dustbowl Empiricism

So far I have outlined the dangers of over emphasizing rationalism in theory building. These dangers are, largely, consistent with the critiques leveled against management theory. There is much to agree with in these critiques of theory. However, I do not agree with the emerging solution, a moratorium on the management theory morass (Pfeffer, this volume) and a return to "dustbowl empiricism" (Hambrick, 2007; Davis & Marquis, 2010). Just as there are dangers in overemphasizing deductive theory, so too are there serious dangers in swinging the pendulum too far in the direction of unbridled empiricism.

Perhaps the best indicia of this direction within the Academy, is the promulgation of a proposed new "facts based" electronic journal, the *Academy of Management Discoveries*. The journal is touted as publishing "important" or "interesting and useful" facts accumulated rigorously but without the need to contribute to theory. Inspired by Hambrick's (2007) critique of theory, the creation of the journal represents a retrenchment against theory and a return to unfettered empiricism.

Alfred North Whitehead coined the term "dustbowl empiricism" to describe the arid accumulation of facts without logic or meaning (Nisbet, 1962). He pointed out that the random accumulation of data often promotes the dangerous tendency to elevate spurious relationships to the status of knowledge. Spurious relationships can be dangerous. Theory, he argued, offers a useful self-corrective mechanism that requires the accumulation of facts into larger causal frameworks.

In fact, the random accumulation of data has been rejected throughout history by scientists, including empiricists, beginning with Mill and Bacon who argued that knowledge can never be based on raw data. Rather, they observe, it is the integration of facts (empiricism) and concepts (rationalism) that provides the foundation of true knowledge. This is the balance of abduction that Peirce identified over a hundred years ago.

To emphasize one element of this balance at the expense of the other, presents unique dangers. Bacon, famously described pure empiricists as "ants" who randomly and furiously stumble over each other in the futile accumulation of facts (Fulton, 1931). He also described pure theorists as "spiders" who "spin webs out of themselves." Rejecting both of these options, Bacon suggested that we should aspire to become "bees" that diligently gather nectar from flowers (i.e., facts) and creatively digest them to produce something (theory) bigger, better and ultimately more useful.

Solutions: Indigenous Management Theory

Based on the discussion above, the solution to fetishistic theory is clearly not to declare a fatwa on new theory. Rather, the answer is simply to improve the institutional context within which management theory is generated. We need to become more "beelike" and avoid the pendulum swings between "spiders" and "ants." We can accomplish this in several ways. Foremost, we need to develop an indigenous approach to management theory.

Indigenous management theory would avoid the pitfalls of fetishism by being more attentive to the phenomenon of management. It would balance rationalism and empiricism with a clear methodological mandate toward abduction. Both qualitative and quantitative techniques would be given equal space in our doctoral training and our journals. It would avoid scientism by discouraging practices of text-parsing and incremental gap construction in order to motivate papers. It would police honorific citation and the beatification of past masters. It would embrace a broad range of disciplines, including arts and humanities, as foundational sources for knowledge production.

Most importantly, indigenous management theory would create space and legitimacy within our profession for a higher degree of self-reflexivity. That is, it would become less careerist in our efforts to publish and more engaged in the professional project of building knowledge about management and organizations. There is no question that considerable theory is "unintelligible, banal, or pointless" (Craib, 1984: 3). However, there is considerable management theory that is accessible, coherent, and useful. It serves the core purpose of any theory – to systematically organize experience in a logically coherent way.

To theorize is an inherently human activity. Despite our best efforts to de-legitimate it, theory is here to stay and will always be a defining element of human knowledge. Moreover, elegant theory will always occupy an elite status in any project of scholarship. As a scholarly community, we need to develop a more discriminate taste for what constitutes good (and bad) theory.

References

Abrahamson, E. (1996). Management fashion. *Academy of Management Review*, *21*(1), 2564-285.

Adams, R. (1975). Where do our ideas come from? Descartes vs Locke, reprinted in Stitch S. (ed.) *Innate ideas*, Berkeley, CA: California University Press.

Alvesson, M., & Willmott, H. (1992). *Critical management studies*. London: Sage.

Alvesson, M., & Sandberg, J. (2011). Generating research questions through problematization. *Academy of Management Review*, *36*(2), pp.247-271.

Aune, B. (1970). *Rationalism, empiricism and pragmatism: An introduction*, New York: Random House.

Bannister, R. C. (1991). *Sociology and scientism: The American quest for objectivity*, 1880–1940, The University of North Carolina Press.

Bennis, W. G., & O'Toole, J. 2005. How Business Schools Lost Their Way. *Harvard Business Review*, May, 83(5):96-104.

Birkenshaw, J., Healy, M., Suddaby, R., & Weber, K. (2014). Debating the future of management research. *Journal of Management Studies*, Forthcoming.

Casullo, A. (2003). *A priori knowledge and justification*. New York: Oxford University Press.

Craib, I. (1984). What's wrong with theory and why we still need it. In I. Craib, *Modern social theory from Parsons to Habermas* (pp. 3-13). New York: St. Martin's Press.

Davis, G. F. (2010). Do theories of organization progress? *Organizational Research Methods, 13*(4), 690-709.

Davis, G. F., & Marquis, C. (2010). Prospects for organization theory in the early twenty-first century: Institutional fields and mechanisms. *Organization Science, 16*(4), 332-343.

Ferraro, F., Pfeffer, J., & Sutton, R. I. (2005). Economics theories and language: How theories can become self-fulfilling. *Academy of Management Review, 30*(1), 8-24.

Fulton, J.F. (1931). The rise of the experimental method: Bacon and the royal society of London. *Yale Journal of Biology and Medicine, 3*(4), 299–320.

Gagliardi, P., & Czarniawksi, B. (2006). *Management education and the humanities.* Cheltenham, UK: Edward Elgar Publishing.

Gordon, R.A., & Howel, J. E. (1959). *Higher education for business.* New York: Columbia University Press.

Guthrie, R. V. (2004). *Even the rat was white: A historical view of psychology* (2nd ed.). Upper Saddle River, NJ: Pearson Education.

Hambrick, D. (2007). The field of management's devotion to theory: Too much of a good thing? *Academy of Management Journal*, 50(6): 1346-1352.

Kenny, A. (1986). *Rationalism, empiricism and idealism*, Oxford: Oxford University Press.

Kieser, A. (1997). Rhetoric and myth in management fashion. *Organization, 4*(1), 49-74.

Landy, F.J. (1997). Early influences on the development of industrial-organizational psychology. *Journal of Applied Psychology*, 82(4),467-477.

Latham, G. 2012. *Work motivation: History, theory and practice* (2nd edition), London: Sage.

Locke, K., & Golden-Biddle, K. (1997). Constructing opportunities for contribution: Structuring intertextual coherence and "problematizing" in organizational studies. *Academy of Management Journal, 40*(5), 1023-1062.

McCloskey, D. N. (1994). *The rhetoric of economics.* Madison, WI: University of Wisconsin Press.

McKenzie, D. (2006). *An engine, not a camera.* Cambridge, MA: MIT Press.

Mulligan, T. M. (1987). Two cultures in business education. *Academy of Management Review, 12*(4), 593-599.

Nisbet, R. A. (1962). *The quest for community.* Oxford: Oxford University Press.

Peirce, C. S. (1958). *Collected Papers of Charles Saunders Pierce.* Vols. 7-8 Ed. A.W. Burks. Cambridge: Harvard University Press.

Pfeffer, J. (2014). The management theory morass: Some modest proposals. This volume.

Pfeffer, J., & Sutton, R. I (1999). Hard facts, dangerous half-truths and total nonsense: Profiting from evidence based management. Boston: Harvard Business School Press.

Pierson, F. C. (1959). *The education of American businessmen.* New York: McGraw-Hill Book Company.

Porter, M. E. (1985). *Competitive Advantage: Creating and sustaining superior performance.* New York: Free Press.

Quine, W. V. O. (1951). "Two Dogmas of Empiricism," in *W.V.O. Quine, From a logical point of view*, Cambridge, MA: Harvard University Press, 1951.

Rowlinson, M., Hassard, J., & Decker, S. (2014). Strategies for organizational history: A dialogue between historical theory and organization theory. *Academy of Management Review,* Forthcoming.

Rousseau, D. (2006). Is there such a thing as "evidence based management?" *Academy of Management Review, 31*(2), 56-269.

Rynes, S., Bartunek, J. M., & Daft, R. L. (2001). Across the Great Divide: Knowledge creation and transfer between practitioners and academics. *Academy of Management Journal, 44*, 340–356.

CHAPTER NINETEEN

THE MANAGEMENT THEORY MORASS: SOME MODEST PROPOSALS

JEFFREY PFEFFER
STANFORD UNIVERSITY, USA

I am somewhat surprised to be doing a paper for a management theory conference and book. When I got an invitation to participate, I e-mailed Jeffrey Miles, the organizer, and told him I thought the last thing the world needed was more emphasis on management theory and more venues, including conferences and books, that would encourage even more management theory development.

That view comes from my having seen the landscape of management theory close up. It is, in my view, not a pretty sight. First of all, management theory constitutes a sprawling, vast, sometimes redundant, set of ideas. As such, management theory stands in stark contrast to the logical parsimony of economics with its relatively small set of fundamental assumptions and a logical deductive apparatus to derive theoretical and empirical insights from first principles. Moreover, as might be expected for a field that has borrowed from several diverse social sciences as well as creating its own theory, management theory offers a theoretical landscape that differs in its scope and complexity even from related social sciences such as social psychology and sociology, themselves not necessarily paragons to be emulated.

Management publication is more concerned with theory and particularly with the articulation of new theory than other business school-based disciplines. As Hambrick has (2007) noted, the field of management is more theory-obsessed, at least in terms of using the word "theory" in published papers, than marketing, accounting, or finance, for example. At the same time, management theory's level of paradigm development lags many if not most of the adjacent social sciences.

Operations research and management science often publish the development of models and the empirical results that come from such models that help shed light on important and practical problems such as how to make better decisions and methods for optimization. While there are clearly methodological papers published in management, including the development of scales to assess important constructs, an emphasis on methodology, measurement, and models rather than theory seems clearly less prominent in management theory scholarship than it is in social psychology, where there is more emphasis on scale construction, or in management sciences with its emphasis on building the modeling technology that permits understanding complex technical and social systems.

The emphasis on theory over measurement and particularly the emphasis on new theory has resulted in the articulation of numerous theoretical ideas. As many of you know, Sage recently published the Encyclopedia of Management Theory, edited by Eric Kessler of Pace University. I had the privilege of serving on the board of advisors for this venture and actually writing some chapters. To be clear, Kessler did a stunning job as editor, ensuring that this enormous undertaking concluded expeditiously and also doing his best to make sure the volumes reflected the major constructs of management theory. The Encyclopedia consists of 1,056 pages, sells for $350, and has more than 280 signed entries. It is, in a word, massive. So is The Encyclopedia of Strategic Management published by Palgrave Macmillan, which has some 700 entries, 1.2 million words, and is about 2,000 pages long.

And how could such efforts not be humungous if they attempt to cover the theory in these fields, which continues to proliferate in profusion? The profusion comes from the following fact: In the management and organization studies world, virtually every journal—not just the major ones, but all of them—evaluate contributions by, among other things, whether they contribute to the development of new theory (e.g., Hambrick, 2007). Schmidt (2009: 95) has commented, "Within the social sciences, only the discovery of a new fact is credited" (emphasis added), a statement that certainly applies to management and organization studies. No big surprise, then, that since the field asks for, and in fact demands, new theory, we have new theory and new concepts in abundance. Whether this is good for either theory or practice is, of course, quite another matter.

This emphasis on the new and unique (e.g., Mone &McKinley, 1993) as important for publication, rather than on rewarding the testing and replication of already existing theoretical ideas, and the emphasis on theory over the presentation of interesting data, has had some negative effects, many of which are predictable and some of which may at first glance seem surprising. One predictable consequence has been the proliferation of "theories" and also writing that is filled with theoretical pretense rather than insight. Hambrick (2007: 1349) noted, "Our insistence on theory in every article has caused a lot of bad writing." Management scholarship persists in worsening the problem of a theoretical overgrowth that needs tending and pruning, something I bemoaned decades ago (Pfeffer, 1993).

The elevation of theory over all else has actually harmed our ability to generate insight. For instance, Hambrick (2007) argued that the insistence on theory in every article possibly retarded the development of understanding. One reason that we don't understand more is that the field largely eschews the task of testing theory. For instance, Davis and Marquis (2005: 334) documented that at least for the journal Administrative Science Quarterly from 1991 through 2001, only 11 percent of the published papers "followed a theory testing model in which the research question flowed directly from the logic of a particular theory." Without testing theory against data, there is little prospect for figuring out what is true and what is not and also little hope for refining our understanding to improve theoretical ideas.

Nosek, Spies, and Motyl (2012: 616) have convincingly articulated the conflict between the pressures for publication, which at least in management has an emphasis on the new and the seemingly interesting, and the quest to understand what is true:

> The real problem is that the incentives for publishable results can be at odds with the incentives for accurate results. This produces a conflict of interest. The conflict may increase the likelihood of design, analysis and reporting decisions that inflate the proportion of false results in the published literature. The solution requires making incentives for getting it right competitive with the incentives for getting it published.

The emphasis on theory over understanding fundamental social institutions and social processes also leads to studies of epiphenomena and institutions of little social power or importance, while neglecting possibly messier but more substantively important concerns. For instance, with network methods and a ready data base, there are numerous studies of patent citation patterns (e.g., Gittelman &Kogut, 2003; Podolny & Stuart, 1995). With data on stock analysts and the firms they cover, there are studies of the portability of analyst performance as they move to new firms (Groysberg &Nanda, 2008) and studies of the determinants and consequences of analyst coverage of companies (e.g., Zuckerman, 1999;

Zuckerman, 2000). This observation is not meant to imply that there is not useful information in patent citations or in understanding analysts and their effects on the securities markets. But the stock market is not the real economy—witness the recent stock market highs while incomes stagnate, inequality in wealth, income, and health and lifespans increase, and millions of people remain unemployed—and not all important parts of the economy are highly dependent on innovations and particularly the kinds of innovations that get patented. There are numerous other examples of studying either old and no longer existing or relatively unimportant organizations, such as microbreweries and old newspapers, not because such studies necessarily produce insight into important contemporary issues, but because the data and analytical methods are available and publication of results is possible.

Meanwhile, as Gerald Davis has noted, one would need to look very hard in the management journals to find much written about America's largest employer, Wal-Mart (for an exception, see Cascio, 2006). One would also not find much published about the causes and consequences of the rise of finance as an ever-growing fraction of the economy and as the dominant logic inside corporations (for an exception, see Fligstein, 1990, or Davis, 2009), or about the profound changes in labor markets and the employment relationship (but see Cappelli, 1999), or the changing size distribution of organizations (Granovetter, 1984) and what social forces have caused such changes, or, with few exceptions, the rising degree of income, wealth, and health inequality (but see Davis and Cobb, 2010)

Another predictable consequence of the emphasis on theory, and particularly new theory, rather than testing and refining ideas, has been the absence of demonstrable progress in knowledge development in the organization sciences (e.g., Davis, 2010). With no emphasis on or reward for replication, and with little encouragement of theoretical elaboration or refutation in contrast to new theory development, people are always starting new theoretical structures rather than completing and refining the finish work of the ones already under construction. Little wonder that ideas get recycled and there is scant evidence of development of the field.

A third predictable outcome of this emphasis on new theory and from the Academy of Management's publishing a journal of theory is the articulation of ideas that may, or may not, be testable. Yes, many theoretical statements have hypotheses. But as any empirical researcher knows, operationalizing and successfully testing hypotheses is quite different from simply laying out some interesting ideas and predictions. The emphasis on new theory and on attaching one's name to a theory results in, to use James March's (1991) apt phrasing, a great deal of new exploration but precious little exploitation of what is already present. The absence of testing or possibly even a concern with testability results in developing theories that may not be very useful in either a practical or a scientific sense. And a related but distinct problem is the virtually omnipresent tendency to avoid testing theories against each other or against alternative explanations for the same empirical results.

The theoretical profusion in management makes the task of teaching management to either students or executives more difficult. That is because students are confronted with too many disconnected terms and concepts, which because of their lack of fundamental connections, become more difficult to remember and understand. And such profusion also makes it more difficult for practitioners, even if they so desired, to access the literature to obtain actionable advice. Providing practitioners multi-thousand page handbooks summarizing the field of management seems almost guaranteed to have them throw up their hands in despair. And a field filled with inadequately tested ideas offers little to a practitioner audience that needs to know what really works—what is true—and not just what is interesting or novel.

Calls for evidence-based management (Pfeffer & Sutton, 1999; Rousseau, 2006) seek to bridge the science-practice gap by encouraging thoughtful practitioners to use research results at least to some degree in their decision-making. There are undoubtedly many reasons why there is less evidence-based practice in management than in medicine. But certainly one such reason is the difference in the scientific literatures of the two fields. Medicine is concerned with rigorous findings about disease processes and treatment outcomes. Replication is encouraged. Management publications discourage replication and mostly want new, clever ideas, regardless of their applicability, substantive importance, or even their ability to cumulatively advance understanding.

One possibly unanticipated, surprising but important consequence of the current state of encouragement for theory development instead of testing and replication has been the proliferation of various degrees and forms of scientific misconduct. The worst cases of misconduct entail actually making up data, as the case of social psychologist Diederik Stapel illustrated (e.g., Bhattacharjee, 2013). But to be clear, the reason that people can successfully make up data that demonstrate phenomena that don't actually exist is because once the data and idea behind the empirical work get published, there is absolutely no point in someone else who is seeking publication in a high-prestige outlet revisiting the issue in anything remotely like the same way. Thus, there is little likelihood that the false results will be uncovered.

Although this particular instance in social psychology was extreme, in that a successful person continued to not just selectively discard or analyze data but to literally create false data sets long after he obtained tenure and earned wide recognition and many powerful editorial positions, less severe issues abound and are much more widespread and common. Those issues include selectively discarding data, running studies until one obtains an effect and not reporting the number of failed attempts to find that effect, and collecting multiple measures of constructs and only reporting the ones that worked. Such practices can be successful because of the absence of testing and replication created by the emphasis on (new) theory. As Nosek, et al. (2012: 617), noted, "direct replication of another's study procedures to confirm the results is uncommon in the social sciences." This absence of replication inflates the prevalence of false effects in published research. "Publishing a result does not make it true" (Nosek, et al., 2012: 617). There is hearsay evidence that these problems bedevil the published work on psychological priming, but the practices are apparently pervasive.

Although much discussed in social psychology, these problems are scarcely unique to that discipline and must certainly affect the organization sciences as well. And this conduct, which makes developing let alone refining theory problematic, even affects the harder sciences. For instance, a recent critique of clinical trials in medicine noted the incentive to run phase 3 clinical trials to evaluate drugs, even when there is little hope, based on earlier stage clinical trials, of the drug achieving the desired therapeutic outcome. With a 5% random chance of achieving a .05 level of statistical significance, and with a large enough economic payoff for successfully navigating the drug approval process, the effort is worth the risk of clinical trial failure. So drug makers roll the dice, "not on the prospect that the therapy will suddenly work, but on the chance that a trial will suggest that it does" (Leaf, 2013). At least in the case of medicine, follow-up studies often discover that apparently successful drugs do not work or that their effects are far less than first reported. In the behavioral and social sciences, with little attention to testing the full range of theoretical implications of ideas and with even less reward for replication, specious results can—and do—live on, as they are unlikely to be uncovered. How could they be, when there are no incentives and many disincentives for efforts to find the truth—as contrasted with simply getting something published.

Fixing the State of Theory and Theory Development

We are where we are for a host of reasons that have been long discussed (e.g., Hambrick, 2007; Pfeffer, 1993; 2007; Sutton & Staw, 1995; Nosek, et al., 2012). The fact that not much has changed, even though the problems are well-recognized, does not inspire much optimism. A reasonable rule of thumb for predicting behavior or for that matter the economy is that the past predicts the future—not perfectly for sure, but better than other prediction logics. Nonetheless, there are things to be done, and at least some evidence that fundamental change might occur.

Recognizing the oft-bemoaned overemphasis on theory and novelty, the Academy of Management is launching a new journal, Academy of Management Discoveries. Its mission is "to promote the creation and dissemination of new empirical evidence that strengthens our understanding of substantively important yet poorly understood phenomena....AMD welcomes phenomenon-driven research." In the slide deck sent to people associated with the journal (which includes me), one page speaks to the sort of studies appropriate for publication: "timely evidence about phenomena that have or may have implications for public policy or managerial practice; important and interesting replications/extensions of prior findings that significantly change our understanding of an issue or its boundary conditions; evidence that informs major scholarly debates in the field of management and organizations; new evidence-based assessments of managerial and organizational interventions." The journal has yet to publish, but its creation by a leading management scholarly association speaks to an acknowledgement that we need publications of a different sort and particularly those that provide data on important issues and address replication and scientific controversies and maybe even misunderstandings. AMD's goals are largely consistent with the recommendation by Pfeffer (2009), who noted how many of the important, policy-relevant articles published in the health-related journal, Health Affairs, would almost certainly never see the light of day in management because the papers did not develop and test new theory but rather offered important information about facts concerning the health care domain.

Nosek and Bar-Anan (2012) offered a complementary but slightly different prescription for the problems besetting the social sciences: completely open scientific communication. One model is PLOS-1 that has been implemented in the physical sciences, particularly biology. Their argument is that with the development and evolution of the internet and the related phenomena of crowd sourcing and on-line recommendations and evaluations, the idea of having articles reviewed by two or three people selected by some editor makes little sense. Nor is it necessary to treat publication as a scarce commodity. The physical pages of traditional journals, that need to be printed and mailed, obviously are scarce as such a publication model consumes significant resources. But online publication does not. And Nosek and Bar-Anan argued that having reviewers anonymously make comments that may or may not be accurate but in any case have no consequences for the reviewer is also nonsensical. Their model is open publication, which includes open, unlimited, free access to the scientific literature—with the scientific community potentially providing reviews and commentary, and with such commentary being identified with specific individuals so that the quality of the comments can themselves be rated.

Furthermore, and this is something that is advocated and with increasing frequency being actually required by journals as a condition for publication, Nosek and Bar-Anan also recommended having data submitted so that it can potentially be re-analyzed and supplemented by other scholars, to truly make research cumulative. In addition, they advocated encouraging people to submit all the data they gather with some degree of rigor, even for those ideas that don't turn out to be supported. This recommendation overcomes the so-called file-drawer problem (Rosenthal, 1979), in which, because of the bias to publish only positive results, even meta-analyses work from incomplete and possibly inaccurate information about effects. This last recommendation, to make all data, not just positive results, more available, is now increasingly required for drug trials, although enforcement is at the moment somewhat problematic. The requirement in the case of drugs comes from the fact that much of the evaluation of new drugs is sponsored by pharmaceutical companies and there is evidence that unfavorable trials that show a lack of efficacy are never published. This practice of suppressing unfavorable outcomes results in difficulty obtaining accurate, unbiased assessments of the actual efficacy of new drugs.

Nosek and Bar-Anan (2012) have argued that open publication norms will in the end prevail, because these practices overcome many of the problems inherent in the current scientific review and publication process, including the long delays in getting results eventually in print. Using as an example papers from Nosek's own lab, they reported an average time between original submission of articles and their eventual publication in print of some 721 days, when articles published in digital only form were excluded (Nosek & Bar-Anan, 2012: 219).

In some sense, Nosek and Bar-Anan's recommendations for a much more open and transparent publishing regime would be a logical extension of the Social Science Research Network (SSRN), begun by Michael Jensen in 1994. Jensen, an economist who very much believes in the power and efficiency of markets, particularly financial markets, thought that if markets were useful for goods and services and financial transactions, why not build an efficient marketplace for ideas, also? Thus, anyone can submit a working paper to SSRN which is then automatically posted and freely available for download. It has become common practice in economics and law and somewhat less common in other social sciences to post papers to SSRN and get comments on them before they are published in refereed journals. Both papers and authors on the SSRN website are ranked by the number of times their work is downloaded. But it would also be possible to rank papers by their citations by other work, and to encourage open commentary on papers by members of the academic community (not just comments offered privately to the author) and also promote the evaluation of the quality of such commentary according to its insight and usefulness.

One barrier to the open publishing model is the belief that scientists' careers would be adversely affected by not having the gatekeeping function of journals. But such concerns are probably misplaced. In the first place, as is well-known, the review process is unreliable, with typically tiny relationships among evaluators (Pfeffer, 2007). This unreliability leads to good work getting rejected. Second, only about 12 to 18 percent of an article's citation impact is predicted by the journal in which it appears (Nosek & Bar-Anan, 2012: 219). And third, according to an analysis by Google Scholar reported by Nosek and Bar-Anan (2012: 231), three repositories, including SSRN, were ranked among the top ten journals in terms of scientific impact as measured by the h-index. This last result shows that non-refereed repositories of research can successfully compete with even the most elite journals—and this holds for physics as well as the social sciences.

Conclusion

Many of the problems that beset management scholarship—the presumed lack of relevance and application (e.g., Hambrick, 2004), the absence of demonstrable scientific progress, and even the growing plague of scientific misconduct, all derive at least in part from a common cause—the particular emphasis in management publishing on new theory. As noted here, this emphasis on theory is not something found, at least to the same degree, in other social sciences, business disciplines, or other writings of scientific professions such as medicine.

The solutions to these problems require some fundamental changes in how we evaluate and review colleagues and practice science. Some positive trends are discernible—the launching of a new journal on discoveries, the growing use and even status of open publishing platforms, and increasing attention, particularly in social psychology, to the profound dysfunctions our current scholarly predilections are creating. It will not take too many more Stapel-magnitude scandals to erode scientific credibility and, as a reaction, produce mandated changes such as those discussed by Brian Nosek and his colleagues.

In the meantime, we as management academics have the capability to be either the problem or the solution. In what we cite, in our own scholarly activities, in the reviews of manuscripts, in our evaluations of colleagues—in these and scores of everyday interactions, we either reproduce the current problems or disrupt the status quo. We need to be more self-reflective in all of these decision arenas and much more aware of the downsides of our preoccupation with management theory.

References

Cappelli, P. (1999). *The new deal at work*: *Managing the market-driven Workforce*. Boston: Harvard Business School Press.

Cascio, W. F. (2006). Decency means more than "always low prices": A comparison of Costco to Wal-Mart's Sam's Club. *Academy of Management Perspectives, 20*(3), 26-37.

Davis, G. F. (2009). *Managed by the markets: How finance re-shaped America*, New York: Oxford University Press.

—. (2010). Do theories of organizations progress? *Organizational Research Methods, 13* (4), 690-709.

Davis, G. F., & Cobb, J. A. (2010). Corporations and economic inequality around the world: The paradox of hierarchy. *Research in Organizational Behavior, 30*, 35-53.

Davis, G. F., & Marquis, C. (2005). Prospects for organization theory in the early twenty-first century: Institutional fields and mechanisms. *Organization Science, 16*(4), 332-343.

Fligstein, N. 1990. *The transformation of corporate control*. Cambridge, MA: Harvard University Press.

Gittelman, M., & Kogut, B. (2003). Does good science lead to valuable knowledge? Biotechnology firms and the evolutionary logic of citation patterns. *Management Science, 49*(4), 366-382.

Granovetter, M. (1984). Small is bountiful: Labor markets and establishment size. *American Sociological Review, 49*, 323-334.

Groysberg, B., & Nanda, A. (2008). Can they take it with them? The portability of star knowledge workers' performance. *Management Science, 54*(7), 1213-1230.

Hambrick, D. C. (2004). What if the Academy actually mattered? *Academy of Management Review, 19*(1), 11-16.

—. (2007). The field of management's devotion to theory: Too much of a good thing? *Academy of Management Journal, 50*(6), 1346-1352.

Leaf, C. (2013). Do clinical trials work? *The New York Times,* July 13, 2013.

March, J. G. (1991). Exploration and exploitation in organizational Learning. *Organization Science, 2*(1), 71-87.

Mone, M. A., & McKinley, W. (1993). The uniqueness value and its consequences for organization studies. *Journal of Management Inquiry, 2,* 284-296.

Nosek, B. A., & Bar-Anan, Y. (2012). Scientific utopia I: Opening Scientific communication. *Psychological Inquiry, 23,* 217-243.

Nosek, B. A., Spies, J. R., & Motyl, M. (2012). Scientific utopia II: Restructuring incentives and practices to promote truth over Publishability. *Perspectives inPsychological Science, 7*(6), 615-631.

Pfeffer, J. (1993). Barriers to the advance of organizational science: Paradigm development as a dependent variable. *Academy of Management Review,18,* 599-620.

—. (2007). A modest proposal: How we might change the process and product of managerial research. *Academy of Management Journal, 50,* 1334-1345.

—. (2009). Renaissance and renewal in management studies: Relevance regained. *European Management Review, 6,* 141-148.

Pfeffer, J., & Sutton, R. I. (1999). *Hard facts, dangerous half-truths, and total nonsense: Profiting from evidence-based management.* Boston: Harvard Business School Press.

Podolny, J. M., & Stuart, T. E. (1995). A role-based ecology of technological change. *American Journal of Sociology, 100* (5), 1224-1260.

Rosenthal, R. (1979). The file drawer problem and tolerance for null results. *Psychological Bulletin, 86,* 638-641.

Rousseau, D. M. (2006). Is there such a thing as "evidence-based management?" *Academy of Management Review, 31* (2), 256-269.

Schmidt, S. (2009). Shall we really do it again? The powerful concept of Replication is neglected in the social sciences. *Review of General Psychology, 13,* 90-100.

Sutton, R. I, & Staw, B. M. (1995). What theory is not. *Administrative Science Quarterly, 40* (3), 371-384.

Zuckerman, E. W. (1999). The categorical imperative: Securities analysts and the illegitimacy discount. *American Journal of Sociology, 104*(5), 1398-1438.

—. (2000). Focusing the corporate product: Securities analysts and de-diversification. *Administrative Science Quarterly, 45* (3), 591-619.

INDEX